JAMES D. G. DUNN

JESUS AND THE SPIRIT

new
Test
ament
lib
Rary

JAMES D. G. DUNN

JESUS
AND THE SPIRIT

A Study of the Religious and
Charismatic Experience of Jesus
and the First Christians
as Reflected in the New Testament

SCM PRESS LTD
BLOOMSBURY STREET LONDON

TO META

my love

334 00785 2
FIRST PUBLISHED 1975
© SCM PRESS LTD 1975
PRINTED IN GREAT BRITAIN BY
W & J MACKAY LIMITED
CHATHAM

CONTENTS

PART TWO

THE RELIGIOUS EXPERIENCE OF THE EARLIEST
CHRISTIAN COMMUNITIES

PART THREE

THE RELIGIOUS EXPERIENCE OF PAUL AND
OF THE PAULINE CHURCHES

VIII THE CHARISMATIC SPIRIT – THE CONSCIOUSNESS OF GRACE

PREFACE

The subject of this book is as old as man himself. It is written out of the conviction that religious experience is a vitally important dimension of man's experience of reality – that this dimension of his experience is integral to his manhood, what finally marks him off as a man from the rest of this planet's life – that only when he recognizes this dimension and orients his living in appropriate relation to it can he begin to achieve personal wholeness and fulfilment in his relationships. The preparatory study for what follows has greatly strengthened that conviction.

The expressions of and claims to religious experience can be studied from many angles, and many such investigations have been attempted in the past. But knowledge increases, new tools of research are developed, new generations testify to their own unique experience of reality and ask new questions. As a theologian and New Testament specialist I can only join the forward-moving line of searchers at the point where I can contribute most, little though that be. There are sufficient grounds for hoping that the area of Christian origins will yield its share of clues to the mystery of man's religious experience.

Even within this narrow field the literature is enormous. I have however attempted to read or at least refer to all the major twentieth-century works relevant to this study. That I have not entirely succeeded in this aim is in no way the failure of the excellent Inter-Library Loans service which has served me so well here at Nottingham. Such a study as this overlaps with many other areas of specialist concern and I am more than a little conscious of my shortcomings in many of them and of the articles and monographs I have neglected. May I excuse myself simply by saying that at some point or other in a project like this one has to turn his back on the new doors which continually open up and shut one's ears to the new questions which continually spring up, otherwise nothing would be written. I only hope that the area chosen for study is sufficiently self-contained to justify the attempt to answer at least some of the questions, and that not too many loose ends have been left dangling.

In order to make the book accessible to as wide a readership as possible I have transliterated or translated such Greek terms as I found it necessary to use. For the sake of such wider readership I have also made it a habit to refer to English translations of German and French literature where possible.

Finally it is my pleasure to thank all those who have commented on various drafts of the material – particularly my colleagues here at Nottingham, Dr D. R. Catchpole of Lancaster, Dr G. N. Stanton of King's College, London, and Professor C. F. D. Moule of Cambridge. The hospitality of John and Margaret Bowker made my researching at Cambridge more than ordinarily pleasant. Above all, my wife's patience and considerateness during the whole period of gestation and production is beyond praise.

University of Nottingham   JAMES D. G. DUNN
March 1975

ABBREVIATIONS

Arndt-Gingrich	W. F. Arndt and F. W. Gingrich, *A Greek–English Lexicon of the New Testament*, ET 1957
AV	Authorized (King James) Version
BZ	*Biblische Zeitschrift*
Blass-Debrunner-Funk	F. Blass and A. Debrunner, *A Greek Grammar of the New Testament and Other Early Christian Literature*, ET and ed. R. W. Funk, 1961
BJRL	*Bulletin of the John Rylands Library*
CBQ	*Catholic Biblical Quarterly*
CSNT	*Christ and Spirit in the New Testament: Studies in Honour of C. F. D. Moule*, ed. B. Lindars and S. S. Smalley, Cambridge 1973
DBS	*Dictionnaire de la Bible*, Supplément
EB	Etudes Bibliques
ed.	Editor
ENTT	E. Käsemann, *Essays on New Testament Themes*, ET SCM Press 1964
ET	English translation
EvTh	*Evangelische Theologie*
ExpT	*Expository Times*
Hennecke, *Apocrypha*	E. Hennecke, *New Testament Apocrypha*, ed. W. Schneemelcher, ET ed. R. McL. Wilson, SCM Press, Vol. I 1973, Vol. II 1974
HNT	Handbuch zum Neuen Testament
HTR	*Harvard Theological Review*
ICC	The International Critical Commentary
JB	The Jerusalem Bible
JBL	*Journal of Biblical Literature*
JSS	*Journal of Semitic Studies*
JTS	*Journal of Theological Studies*

KEK	Kritisch-exegetischer Kommentar über das Neue Testament
KuD	*Kerygma und Dogma*
LXX	Septuagint
Moffatt	The Moffatt New Testament Commentary
Moulton-Milligan	J. H. Moulton and G. Milligan, *The Vocabulary of the Greek Testament*, 1930
NEB	The New English Bible
NF	*Neue Folge*
NovTest	*Novum Testamentum*
NovTestSuppl	Supplements to *Novum Testamentum*
NTD	Das Neue Testament Deutsch
NS	New Series
NTQT	E. Käsemann, *New Testament Questions of Today*, ET SCM Press 1969
NTS	*New Testament Studies*
par.	parallel
RB	*Revue Biblique*
RGG[3]	*Die Religion in Geschichte und Gegenwart*, [3]1957ff.
RHPR	*Revue d'Histoire et de Philosophie religieuses*
RSV	Revised Standard Version
SEA	*Svensk Exegetisk Årsbok*
SJT	*Scottish Journal of Theology*
Strack-Billerbeck	H. L. Strack and P. Billerbeck, *Kommentar zum Neuen Testament aus Talmud und Midrasch*, 1920ff.
StTh	*Studia Theologica*
TDNT	*Theological Dictionary of the New Testament*, ET of *Theologisches Wörterbuch zum Neuen Testament*, ed. G. Kittel and G. Friedrich, 1933ff.
THNT	Theologischer Handkommentar zum Neuen Testament
ThStud	*Theological Studies*
TZ	*Theologische Zeitschrift*
TheolEx	Theologische Existenz heute, München
TLZ	*Theologische Literaturzeitung*
ZNW	*Zeitschrift für die neutestamentliche Wissenschaft*
ZThK	*Zeitschrift für Theologie und Kirche*

I

INTRODUCTION

§1. THE SCOPE AND AIMS OF THIS STUDY

1.1 The core of religion is religious experience.[1]

If a man must say that he cannot find God in the reality of his own present life, and if he would compensate for this by the thought that God is nevertheless the final cause of all that happens, then his belief in God will be a theoretical speculation or a dogma; and however great the force with which he clings to this belief, it will not be true faith, for *faith can be only the recognition of the activity of God in his own life*.[2]

These two quotations provide the starting point for the present study. Granted that religious experience is the core of religion, the questions have to be asked, What is religious experience? and What religious experience? Granted that faith, or at least an important aspect of faith, is 'the recognition of the activity of God' in one's life, the questions have to be asked, What do we mean by 'the activity of God' in our lives? How do we distinguish 'activity of God' from the merely physiological or sociological, or indeed from the more sinister forces and pressures active in any society?

Such questions as these are particularly relevant to a student of the NT, or to anyone who is interested in the history of Christian origins, for Christianity is one of the most important religious movements in human history – no one would dispute that. It must be important therefore to inquire closely into the religious experience which launched this new religion: what were those recognitions of God's activity which constituted a new faith of such dynamic and durable vitality? The task we set ourselves in the following pages is to attempt to answer this and similar questions. In particular, no one doubts that Jesus was a 'religious genius' of towering stature, at the very least. What was the religious experience out of which he lived and which enabled him to minister and die as he did and to make such a lasting impact on his disciples? Again, few students of Christian origins would deny that Christianity proper goes back to certain deeply significant experiences of the first disciples – experiences in which they saw Jesus 'risen from the dead', experiences of Spirit understood by them as the Spirit of the end-time. What were those 'resurrection appearances'? What happened at 'Pentecost'? What were the experiences of Spirit which transformed a Jewish sect into an independent religion of international significance? Again, few would deny that the most important single influence within first-generation Christianity in that transformation was Paul, and that it was in and through the churches established by Paul that Christianity attained its independence and maturity over against Judaism. What was the religious experience which made Paul so sure of himself and so influential? What were the religious experiences which shaped Pauline Christianity and the religious life of his communities? Finally, we will have to bear in mind the overarching question, How do these experiences relate to one another? In particular, how did Jesus' own experiences relate to those of his followers? Was Jesus' experience of God unique or exemplary? Does early Christian experience merely repeat Jesus' experience or somehow derive from it? Is Jesus simply the first Christian or somehow the source of post-Easter Christian experience?

Such questions could be asked of any period of Christianity, but clearly they become of central significance for the founding era, for first-generation Christianity. It is upon this area that we focus our attention. I had initially hoped that I would be able to take in the whole of the NT period, that is, the first 70 to 100 years of Christianity. For the transition from the first generation to the second and third generations in any movement of spiritual or emotional vitality is always a fascinating one. But to analyse even the material relating to first-generation Christianity in sufficient detail made the study extensive enough, so that I have had to confine myself to the first 30 years of Christianity and only allow a brief glance forward to the end of the first century in the concluding chapter.

1.2   It should be made clear at the outset that our task is a hazardous one – some would say that it is impossible to reach any worthwhile conclusions. This is for two principal reasons. First, our sources are too few, too one-sided; they illuminate too little of the whole. That is true, but nevertheless they do afford some light. And it is my hope that by studying a few key areas and periods in depth we will be able to understand better the experiences and the faith which gave Christianity its distinctive character. The problem here however is a real one, and we shall have to concern ourselves with it at each stage, often at some length. Second, it is impossible to enter into someone else's experience, particularly when the historical and cultural gap between the thought world of first-century eastern Mediterranean countries and that of twentieth-century Europe is so wide. That also has a large degree of truth in it. Nevertheless, our own experience and the knowledge which we have of human experience in general does enable us to enter at least some way into the experience of others and even to appreciate sympathetically something of experiences otherwise strange to us.[3] Moreover, as we now realize more clearly, any attempt to understand religious phenomena must take into account the explanations which others offer for their own experience. A sympathetic study of the language with which Jesus and the first Christians articulated their religious experience should therefore enable us to gain some insight into their self-understanding and evaluation of their religious experience. Of course, religious experience is notoriously ambiguous, as we shall have occasion to note later. But if we can detect what it was in the experience of first-generation Christians which caused them to refer it to God or the Spirit or Jesus, then our own evaluation of their experience will become that much more feasible.

We must also beware of tendencies to narrow our investigation in ways which would artificially restrict or bias our evaluation. First we must beware of prejudging *the range of religious experience* which is 'proper' or of religious value. Christian theology has often attempted to reduce Christian experience in effect to a rather bare 'feeling of dependence', or to the moral earnestness of the categorical imperative, and has withdrawn in ill-concealed horror from more extravagant manifestations of religious feeling. I think, for example, of Luther's reaction to the radical reformers,[4] of Kant's attack on Swedenborg as the typical visionary,[5] of W. Bousset's readiness to attribute such manifestations in early Christianity to the influence of 'the decadent religion of Hellenism',[6] and of R. A. Knox's classic treatment of 'enthusiasm'.[7] Few have had the experience or the urge to share Jonathan Edwards' task of analysing 'the religious affections'.[8] Most have been content to write off these wider expressions of religious zeal as fringe fanaticism, youthful excess or in terms of what William James called 'medical materialism'.[9] I am, of course, not advocating an uncritical approach to the subject. But it will soon become apparent that some of the more extravagant manifestations of religious experience played a not unimportant role in earliest Christianity (not least, resurrection appearances as visionary experiences;

Pentecost as an ecstatic experience). We must be prepared to examine these with special care, lest modern predispositions prejudice our judgment. It is principally for this reason that I have included 'charismatic (experience)' in the title, although 'religious experience' as the more comprehensive term would have sufficed – not, I hasten to add, because 'charismatic' is synonymous with 'ecstatic', but precisely because 'charismatic' denotes a broader range of religious experience which includes 'enthusiasm' but cannot be confined to it. The sense in which 'charismatic' can be used of Jesus and the early Christians will become apparent as the study proceeds.

Second, we must beware of discounting *the creative force of religious experience*. I have in mind here a comment made by Johannes Weiss:

An 'origin' in the sense of an entirely new creation never occurs . . . the 'new' is always in the broad sense a re-grouping of older elements according to a new principle, based upon stronger forces and unique experience of actuality.[10]

Using Weiss's terms, the danger is that the 'new' of Christianity will be regarded *solely* in terms of 'a regrouping of older elements' without due regard to the 'unique experience of actuality'. The point can be easily illustrated from Pauline studies. Where in the earliest decades of this century study after study of Paul's life and faith focussed to greater or lesser degree on his conversion experience as the great explanatory key to unlock the whole, today the great quest is for literary parallels, the 'older elements' which can be adjudged to explain his language and theology – to such an extent indeed that one might be tempted to conclude that Paul's theology is simply the end product of a process of literary natural selection. Such a conclusion is patently absurd. We may not be able to write a biography of Paul, the value of Acts as a historical source remains in dispute, and I readily acknowledge Paul's debt to both Jew and Greek for the great bulk of his language and concepts. But his own writings bear eloquent and passionate testimony to the creative power of his own religious experience – a furnace which melted many concepts in its fires and poured them forth into new moulds (notably, as we shall see, his language of grace). Nothing should be allowed to obscure that fact. As Hermann Gunkel asserted by way of protest against similar emphases in the research of his own day, 'The theology of the great apostle is an expression of his experience, not of his reading . . . Paul believes in the divine Spirit, because he has experienced it/him'.[11] It is out of such *experience(s)* that new religions are born and old faiths are born again (witness, for example, Mohammed, Luther, George Fox, John Wesley). This is why our attempt to uncover the religious experience of Jesus and of the first Christians is important as part of a wider investigation of religion and of religious phenomena.[12]

Third, we must beware of assuming that early Christian experience is something unique or that it was a peculiarly first-century phenomenon. The history of religions approach to NT documents has been very fruitful on the first count: we now recognize that there were many competitors of earlier Christianity, often making similar or the same claims, particularly in terms of religious experience. But too often a narrowly conceived history of religions approach can give the impression that the phenomena of first-century Christianity, particularly the manifestations of charismatic experience, belonged only to the ancient world of pre-scientific superstition. A larger phenomenology of religion approach begins from the recognition that similar 'charismatic' or 'supernatural' phenomena have been reported throughout the history of religion, no less in the popular religion of today than in the popular religion of yesterday. As the early history of religions approach shed great light on the world of the NT and on the NT itself, so I believe more light can be shed by the wider comparison I have suggested.[13] I claim no expertise in this wider field, none whatsoever, apart from a fairly close acquaintance with and interest in Pentecostalism and the modern 'charismatic movement'. But an attempt at some wider reading has thrown up some interesting and often striking parallels to the 'charismatic' phenomena reported in the NT. Without a thorough investigation of both sides of the comparison one cannot of course draw out any very extensive conclusions. Nor would I for a moment want to minimize the manifest legend-mongering of popular religion. But the very fact that such phenomena have often been claimed throughout the history of religion, that, for example, present-day reports of NT-type 'miracles' can be shown in many cases to go back to eyewitnesses, means that we should hesitate before dismissing similar claims within early Christianity as merely legendary accretion or apologetic constructions. There is much work that could be done in this area, but perhaps it requires an interdisciplinary competence (in theology, psychology, sociology and anthropology for a start) that too few possess.

1.3 The subject matter of our present task has often been worked over, and I make no claim to entering upon an unploughed field. I think, for example, of earlier works like D. A. Frövig, *Das Sendungsbewusstsein Jesu und der Geist*, Gütersloh 1924, P. G. S. Hopwood, *The*

Religious Experience of the Primitive Church, T. & T. Clark 1936, P. Gardner, *The Religious Experience of St Paul*, Williams & Norgate 1911 – all of them dated and of limited value – and particularly of the classic monograph of H. Gunkel already cited (above n.11). Among more recent works I would mention particularly J. Lindblom, *Gesichte und Offenbarungen*, Lund 1968, and G. Hasenhüttl, *Charisma: Ordnungsprinzip der Kirche*, Herder 1969. But all of these are more limited in scope and do not ask the same questions that urge us forward.

I should perhaps also mention that this volume serves as something of a sequel to my earlier study, *Baptism in the Holy Spirit*, SCM Press 1970. There I examined the NT writers' conception of conversion-initiation and came to the conclusion that for them all, with differing degrees of emphasis, the 'gift of the Spirit' is the one essential element and focal point in the event of 'becoming a Christian'. In the final paragraph I posed some questions which seemed to follow hard upon that conclusion:

Accepting that the gift of the Spirit is what makes a man a Christian, how do he and others know if and when he has received the Spirit? In what ways does the Spirit manifest his coming and his presence? What indications are there that the Spirit is active in a congregation or in a situation?[14]

The research which led to the following chapters began as an attempt to answer these questions at a NT level. It quickly broadened out however, into an investigation of religious experience as such, since to think only in terms of 'experience of Spirit' could impose an artificial restriction on subsequent matter and method; besides which 'experience of Spirit' like 'charismatic experience' can only be understood as part or as an aspect of the broader term 'religious experience'. Our task in this book can therefore be summed up as an attempt to answer the following questions: What were the religious experiences of Jesus and of first-generation Christianity? What was the range of experiences enjoyed and valued by Jesus and by first-generation Christianity? How did first-generation Christianity recognize experiences of God or of his Spirit to be such? Was there any distinctive element, or elements, in that range of experience which could be said to mark it out as *Christian* experience, or to constitute the key characteristic and hallmark of Christian experience? If the following chapters provide an answer to these questions I shall be well satisfied. Whether they are the right answers and whether they are of continuing value I leave to the judgment of the reader.

One final word by way of introduction. As is proper in a study of the NT, my aim at all times has been *to take nothing from the text except that which the text demands when expounded in its historical context.* Inevitably this has involved a good deal of careful exegesis at several points, with only a few cautious results at the end of it all. Some will no doubt conclude that the exegesis is too brief, the conclusions too bold; others that the exegesis is too lengthy,[15] the conclusions too sceptical. Criticism from both sides I welcome. I have lived with this research intensively for two years and have set it out on the following pages as definitively as I can at this stage. I submit it now to a wider readership in the hope not only that errors of exegesis can be corrected and mistaken judgments reconsidered, but also that its conclusions where sound may provide the basis for an evaluation of contemporary claims and movements, traditional and new, and a stimulus for further thought about the essence and form of Christianity in its individual and corporate expression.

PART ONE

THE RELIGIOUS EXPERIENCE
OF JESUS

III

JESUS' EXPERIENCE OF GOD – SONSHIP

§2. INTRODUCTION

2.1 *What was Jesus' experience of God?* It should be noted at once that I am not asking, What was Jesus' *concept* of God, his teaching about God? The two questions are of course closely bound up: Jesus' personal experience, if accessible at all, is accessible only as conceptualized experience. Nevertheless, the distinction between teaching about God and experience of God remains viable and valid. The more public teaching of Jesus about God is easier to track down and has frequently been treated in modern studies of Jesus' life and ministry.[1] But it is the subject of Jesus' more private experience of God on which I wish to focus attention, and that is a much more difficult, less tangible question, for obvious reasons.

Our question can be posed thus: What was it in Jesus' own experience which he referred to God? Assuming that Jesus believed himself to be inspired by God, what does the phrase 'inspired by God' mean in Jesus' case for Jesus himself? What were the evidences, the signs which convinced Jesus that the Supreme Being of the universe was working in and through him? Or to pose the issue at the same time more broadly and more precisely, *What was the correlate in Jesus' experience of his belief in God?*

2.2 *But is this a legitimate quest?* This response may come from two sides. First, traditional, classic Christianity strongly affirms the deity of Jesus – that Jesus of Nazareth was God become man. In what sense can we speak of the God-man's experience of God? In fact, however, traditional Christianity would not wish to press this question too far; for the classic creeds have always seen the need to affirm the humanness of Jesus as strongly as his divinity – as an adequate doctrine of incarnation requires. Thus traditional Christianity has recognized, however inadequately, that whatever else he is, Jesus is (a?) man before God. It could hardly do otherwise in view of the tradition present in all four gospels, not to mention Hebrews, that on several occasions at least Jesus took himself off into solitude to *pray* to God – as we shall see (§3). He who *prays* to God, whoever or whatever else he is, is *man*. And the experience of prayer is part of the experience of God we must attempt to examine.

Even if the question of Jesus' experience of God is posed in classical terms of Jesus' humanity, Logos Christology (Jesus = the Word, Logos, become flesh) and the doctrine of Jesus' two natures (divine and human) may appear to make it rather absurd. But this only happens if we forget that traditional Christology, including the two natures doctrine, had to wrestle with much the same question, though in its own terms: viz., not just, What was Jesus' relation to God?, but also, What was Jesus' own experience, consciousness of the divine in him?[2] Furthermore, Chalcedonian Christology would presumably claim to be an abstraction from the NT material. Our own investigation of the synoptic evidence will therefore have the secondary effect of providing a check on traditional formulations.

The second criticism as to the legitimacy of pursuing these questions comes from this century. F. D. E. Schleiermacher, the 'father of modern theology', had argued that while Jesus was 'like all men in virtue of the identity of human nature', he was unique precisely because of the quality of his experience of God, his unique God-consciousness: 'like all men . . . but distinguished from them all by the constant potency of His God-consciousness, which was a veritable existence of God in Him'.[3] Following Schleiermacher, Liberal Protestantism's 'quest of the historical Jesus' often involved reconstructions and evaluations of Jesus' messianic- and self-consciousness – an aspect of the nineteenth-century quest which brought it into greatest disrepute when the advance of gospel criticism showed the impossibility of such reconstructions and when A. Schweitzer's well known critique of the quest pointed out that it revealed more of the psychology of nineteenth-century Christians than of Jesus.[4]

Since then it has become almost commonplace to deny the possibility of writing a biographical study of Jesus or of saying anything about his self-consciousness or 'inner life'.[5] Unfortunately these two things are often linked together, the denial of the former being taken as a denial of the latter. But while a biography of Jesus is indeed impossible, particularly a biography in the modern sense which traces out the hero's growth in self-awareness and in understanding of himself and his world, that does not mean that we can say nothing at all about Jesus' self-consciousness and spiritual experience at *some* points in his ministry. On the contrary, it is my contention that we are in a position to see fairly deeply into Jesus' experience of God at certain points, and so may begin to understand how he conceived of his relation to God. Indeed, we may well be able to apprehend something of the heart of that experience – in so far as any man can apprehend the experience of another. By this I do not mean that we can trace the *development* in his experience and self-consciousness. I mean simply that *we can see something of the experiential basis of Jesus' faith in God*.

2.3 *The importance of this investigation* need hardly be stressed. For a strong tradition of Christian thought Jesus' supreme role has been as exemplar for faith. In modern theology this was particularly strong in Liberal Protestantism, and, apart from its widespread popular appeal, has reappeared in the revived Liberalism of, for example, G. Ebeling (Jesus 'the witness of faith')[6] and increasingly in so-called 'secular Christianity'.[7] It should also be noted that it is possible to argue for a clear strand of *imitatio Christi* in the NT itself.[8] For this whole tradition the question of Jesus' own experience of God becomes important – important for *our* faith in God, perhaps even for the possibility of faith in God. Given that Jesus was a 'religious genius' at the very least – that is, his consciousness was open and attuned to wider dimensions of reality than the great bulk of other men, that he had insights into the human condition and relationships which come to few – given this, then Jesus' understanding of his experience of these wider dimensions, as well as his response to his neighbour, may become paradigmatic and determinative for my faith and world-view.

Our quest is important also for those who reject exemplarist Christology and hold rather to a kerygmatic Christology – that is, they deny that Jesus' chief significance is as example of faith, and stress that Christianity centres on Jesus who died and rose again; they affirm that Christian faith is not merely repeating the faith *of* Jesus, the man of Nazareth, but is essentially faith *in* Jesus, the Lord of glory. It is important because kerygmatic theology cannot simply ignore Jesus of Nazareth as the forerunner of the kerygma, the John the Baptist of the church. Theology must always attempt to clarify afresh the relation between the gospel *of* Jesus and the gospel *about* Jesus – that is widely recognized. But so too should be the fact that the *experience* of the early believers was at the *heart* of their gospel: their gospel was in large measure the expression of their experience.[9] More fundamental therefore is the question of the relation between Jesus' experience of God and the experience of the early believers after Jesus' death. Does Jesus' own experience of God provide a blue-print for later Christian experience? How does Paul's experience of Jesus as exalted relate to Jesus' experience of God? Unless some sort of correlation can be established between the two, and unless Jesus' experience can be shown to be not only archetypal but in some way *determinative* of the experience of Paul, then the old charge that Paul and not Jesus is the founder of Christianity will revive with renewed force.

2.4   *How shall we pursue our quest?* Two avenues immediately com-mend themselves. The first may be called the nineteenth-century way of Liberal Protestantism – to which we have already alluded above; the second, the twentieth-century way of eschatology. The first focusses on Jesus' consciousness of sonship; the second on his con-sciousness of Spirit. In chapters II and III we will explore these avenues, and, particularly in chapter II, probe the strengths and weaknesses of earlier conclusions. In chapter IV we will broaden the inquiry into an investigation of the question, Was Jesus a charismatic?

The Liberal Protestant quest after the religious consciousness of Jesus achieved what is probably its classic expression in Adolf von Harnack's famous Berlin lectures, *What is Christianity?* Earlier treat-ments, including especially those of Schleiermacher and Ritschl, had been too heavily dependent on John's gospel. But Harnack en-deavoured to make his case on the basis primarily of the historically more defensible synoptic tradition. Moving out from Matt. 11.27 Harnack maintained:

It is 'knowledge of God' that makes the sphere of the Divine Sonship. It is in this knowledge that he came to know the sacred Being who rules heaven and earth as Father, as *his* Father. The consciousness which he possessed of being *the Son of God* is, therefore, nothing but the practical consequence of knowing God as the Father and as his Father. Rightly understood, the name of Son means nothing but the knowledge of God. Here, however, two observations are to be made: Jesus is convinced that he knows God in a way in which no one ever knew Him before, and he knows that it is his vocation to communicate this knowledge of God to others by word and deed – and with it the knowledge that men are God's children. In this consciousness he knows himself to be the Son and instituted of God, to be *the* Son of God, and hence he can say: *My* God and *my* Father, and into this invocation he puts something which belongs to no one but himself.[10]

Two points are worthy of attention here: first, the focus on sonship in terms of consciousness, as an *experienced* relationship; second, Harn-ack's emphasis on the uniqueness of this consciousness – '*the* Son of God'. If these points remain valid for us today, then an important first answer to our opening question has already been given. But

much water has flowed under the bridge since Harnack delivered
these opinions, and Liberal Protestantism is regarded by most
modern theologians as *passé*. We must therefore review the synoptic
evidence which provides the strongest support for Harnack's conclusions and see whether it still bears the weight Harnack put upon it.

Where do we start? The way of Liberal Protestantism often
started as, or quickly became, the path leading to Jesus' 'messianic
self-consciousness'. The problem for us is that this path soon disappears in a tangle of theological thicket and dogmatic undergrowth.
The chief difficulty is that no one is quite sure what 'Messiah' here
signifies: how much of its meaning derives from pre-Christian Judaism,
how much from Jesus, and how much from developing Christian
thought. The same problem and liability to frustration attends any
attempt to approach Jesus from the angle of christological titles,
since in fact it is highly questionable whether Jesus thought of himself
in terms of titles at all.[11]

A more promising way is indicated by A. Deissmann in his 1923
Selly Oak lectures.[12] Too little known in all the talk about old and
new quests of the historical Jesus, they can be regarded as one of the
last attempts of Liberal Protestantism to uncover the 'inner life of
Jesus'.[13] Moreover, they commend themselves to us by virtue of the
fact that their aim and scope comes closer to that of the present study
than any other work of that era – though at a much more popular
level and without the concern for charismatic experience. Above all,
perhaps, they provide us with the starting point for our investigation;
for before examining 'the communion of Jesus with God the Father
. . .', Deissmann looks first at 'the prayer-life of Jesus as the reflex
of his communion with God'. This too is where we begin before
moving on to the central issue of Jesus' consciousness, particularly in
prayer, of God as Father.

§3. THE PRAYER LIFE OF JESUS

It has been well said that a religious man is most truly himself in his
private prayers.[14] What part did prayer play in Jesus' life? And can
we somehow 'listen in' on Jesus' praying and so gain an immediate
insight into what Jesus experienced in his prayers? The answer to the
first question is clear enough; the answer to the second less certain.

3.1   *The importance of prayer for Jesus* becomes apparent both from his
teaching on prayer and from the tradition of his own praying. The

value Jesus placed upon prayer is stressed in all four strata of the synoptic tradition. Mark 11.17 pars. – the Temple is valued precisely as a house of prayer (quoting Isa. 56.7) – a logion whose authenticity is indicated by the presence of the distinctive note of Jesus' eschatology.[15] Mark 11.24 – the disciples are encouraged to an astonishing boldness in prayer: 'Whatever you ask in prayer, believe that you receive it, and you will'![16] From Q comes the well-known exhortation to ask, seek and knock with the confidence of children before their Father (Matt. 7.7–11/Luke 11.9–13).[17] The two versions of the 'Lord's Prayer' possibly derive from Q, but more likely belong to divergent traditions (Matt. 6.9–13; Luke 11.2–4).[18] Also from Matthew's special material comes the strong denunciation of the abuse of prayer (Matt. 6.5–8; cf. Mark 12.40/Luke 20.47). And to Luke's pen we owe the preservation of the parable of the friend at midnight, the challenge to 'unashamed prayer' (Luke 11.5–8), as perhaps also the parable of the unjust judge (Luke 18.1–5).[19] Although some of these sayings stand in a developed tradition *it can hardly be doubted that Jesus regarded prayer as of first importance.*

Since Jesus encouraged his disciples so emphatically to avail themselves of prayer, it can hardly be doubted that prayer was at the basis of his own relationship with God as Jesus understood and experienced it.[20] But here the problems start to come thick and fast, for as soon as we begin to probe into Jesus' own practice of prayer the question marks begin to gather round the relevant material.

3.2   *The lack of strong evidence.* We know next to nothing about Jesus' appreciation and experience of corporate worship. We are told that he attended the synagogue and may assume that this was his regular practice – although according to our evidence his primary purpose in doing so was to teach and proclaim his message (Mark 1.21ff. par.; 1.39 pars.; 3.1 pars.; 6.2 par.; Matt. 9.35; Luke 4.15f.; 13.10). His zeal for the functioning of the Temple as a place of prayer is on record (Mark 11.17 pars. – see above §3.1). But that is the extent of our knowledge. As to personal prayer, J. Jeremias concludes from various allusions within the gospel material that

with all probability no day in the life of Jesus passed without the three times of prayer: the morning prayer at sunrise, the afternoon prayer at the time when the afternoon sacrifice was offered in the Temple, the evening prayer at night before going to sleep.[21]

But this deduction is by no means certain, and is put in question by the fact that so much of Jesus' teaching was critical of traditional Jewish worship.[22]

Even the synoptic testimony that Jesus maintained a discipline of private prayer is not so strong as it at first appears. There are nine references to Jesus praying in Luke, that is true – 3.21; 5.16; 6.12; 9.18, 28f.; 11.1; 22.41–5; 23.34, 46. But a straight literary comparison with Luke's Markan source would seem to indicate that seven of these references have all been added by Luke.[23] In Q there are no references, except the unique Matt. 11.25f./Luke 10.21, to which we shall return.

In Mark, apart from the Gethsemane tradition (see below §3.3), the only references to Jesus praying are 1.35 and 6.46. But 1.35 stands in what appears to be an editorial section (1.35–9).[24] Matthew does not reproduce it. Even more striking is the fact that Luke omits the reference to prayer in his parallel (Luke 4.42); and since, as we have seen, Luke likes to include references to Jesus at prayer, it is just possible that Mark's 'and he prayed' is a later addition not present in Luke's copy of Mark.[25] Mark 6.46 is less controversial on literary grounds, but it occurs in the context of two of the miracles most difficult for modern man (the feeding of the 5,000 and the walking on the water). Matthew simply reproduces the whole passage more or less. But again Luke leaves us somewhat puzzled, since he follows the feeding of the 5,000 with the episode of Peter's confession at Caesarea Philippi, but begins it with one of his non-Markan descriptions of Jesus at prayer: 'One day when he was praying alone in the presence of his disciples, he asked them . . .' (Luke 9.18). Why does Luke omit the second Markan reference to Jesus' praying, or was this fourth Lukan reference to Jesus praying prompted by Mark 6.46?[26] At any rate, the evidence of Jesus' prayer habits is not the soundest.

3.3 *The Gethsemane tradition* – Mark 14.32–42 pars. When so much else is uncertain the account of Gethsemane assumes considerable importance as the strongest synoptic testimony of Jesus' dependence on prayer – and also as the only explicit testimony that Jesus addressed God as 'Abba' (see below and §4). We must therefore subject it to some scrutiny, since without it we are too much dependent on inference and secondary tradition.

Many doubts have in fact been cast on the historicity of the Gethsemane scene. For Bultmann it has 'a thorough-going legendary character'.[27] M. Dibelius argues that the scene presents Jesus as the ideal martyr whose sufferings correspond to those spoken of by the psalmist and so constitute proof of his messiahship.[28] And the difficulty of resting a claim to historicity on eyewitnesses who were asleep! has often been noted.[29]

On the other hand, a number of considerations weigh heavily in favour of the substantial historicity of the episode at the point which concerns us, viz., the prayer of Jesus:

(v.35) [Jesus] prayed that, if it were possible, the hour might pass from him. (v.36) And he said, 'Abba, Father, all things are possible to you; take this cup away from me. Yet, not what I want but what you want'.

(a) The number of independent sources which testify to it. It is probable that Mark (or his source) has drawn v. 35 and v. 36 from independent traditions, or, more likely, drawn in v. 36 from an independent tradition when taking up the (fuller) tradition containing v. 35.[30] Verse 36 is not simply a development of v. 35, as the quite different metaphors 'hour' and 'cup' show;[31] the 'hour' is thematic for the construction of the whole (vv. 35, 37, 41), but there has been no attempt to integrate the cup metaphor in a similar way (contrast Mark 10.38f.). Moreover, it is precisely the two versions of Jesus' prayer which give least evidence of Markan redaction;[32] and the appearance of *abba* in v. 36 suggests both independence from v. 35 and age (see below). Matthew follows Mark in a straightforward fashion, except that he runs the two versions of Jesus' prayer together. But Luke very likely has access to a third independent source.[33] In addition we must note Heb. 5.7, which probably refers to this period of Jesus' life and which again appears to be almost entirely independent.

Finally there is John 12.27: 'Now is my soul in turmoil. And what shall I say? "Father, save me from this hour"? No, for this purpose have I come to this hour'. This is probably not independent since John seems to be denying here a possible (even likely) interpretation of the Mark 14.35 tradition – 'Jesus prayed that, if it were possible, the hour might pass from him' – viz., that Jesus asked to be relieved from his messianic task.[34] Two important points emerge however: first, that John preserved the tradition of Jesus' praying, even though he was all too conscious of its inconsistency within his overall portrayal of Jesus (cf. 11.41f.); second, that the tradition of Jesus' prayer for deliverance from 'the hour' was well established in Christian circles. Both points confirm that the episode in Gethsemane was too well rooted in Christian tradition for John to ignore it.

(b) There is certainly a degree of editorial stylizing in Mark's treatment of his source(s) and particularly in his portrayal of Jesus' prayer thrice repeated.[35] But the whole account can hardly be said to have originated from the martyr tradition. Verse 35 sounds more like a request for escape from martyrdom; only in the second version, v. 36, do we find the martyr-like submission – 'but it's not what I want that matters, only what you want'. Both Matthew and Luke seem to recognize the weakness of the v. 35 tradition – Matthew by conflating it with the v. 36 tradition, and Luke by ignoring it. John, as we noted above, seems deliberately to deny the unmartyr-like interpretation of v. 35.

Nor can it be demonstrated that the account derives its central elements from the Psalms. Certainly v. 34 echoes Pss. 42.5, 11; 43.5 – 'Why are you cast down, O my soul' – but the echo might as well have been in the mind of Jesus as in the reflection of the early church. More decisive is the fact that the actual prayer itself, unlike Mark 15.34, is not framed in words from the Psalms.[36] At its central point the origin of the Gethsemane tradition lies elsewhere.

Equally significant is the strength of Mark's language in v. 33 – particularly ἐκθαμβεῖσθαι, a word which seems to denote shuddering horror. 'The Greek words (ἐκθαμβεῖσθαι καὶ ἀδημονεῖν) portray the uttermost degree of boundless terror and suffering'.[37] This language is too strong even for the psalmist,[38] and the martyr parallel is here marked more by contrast than by agreement.[39] Again Matthew is all too conscious of the seeming discredit to Jesus and softens Mark's horrifying picture by substituting the lighter λυπεῖσθαι ('to be sad, distressed, grave') for ἐκθαμβεῖσθαι. For myself I find it difficult to attribute the origin of this record to any other source than the all too vivid scene brutally etched on the memory of even the dullard disciples. The presentation of Jesus in such emotional straits, so utterly drained of his usual strength of character and purpose, is not the sort of creation which would occur to any but the consummate artist and most skilful novelist, and Mark certainly does not deserve such acclaim.[40]

(c) There is no denying that there is some tension between the report that the disciples slept while Jesus prayed and a claim that the disciples overheard Jesus' prayer. If it were simply a matter of treating Mark as a straightforward historical narrative there would be little problem: one could readily speculate that the closest disciples, only separated by a little (μικρόν) according to Mark, heard something of Jesus' praying before they fell asleep, or even were occasionally disturbed by his praying ('loud cries' – Heb. 5.7).[41] But if one grants that theological motifs also shaped the narrative, then this too strengthens the case for the historicity of Jesus' Gethsemane prayer – for the strongest evidence of theological redaction is not the praying of Jesus (see above p. 18), but the sleep of the disciples: it is of a piece with the motif of the so-called 'messianic secret' which contrasts the clarity of Jesus' perception of his task with the dullness of the disciples (cf. Mark 9.5f.).[42] Alternatively, the report that the disciples slept could simply be a mistaken inference from the use of γρηγορεῖτε ('Keep awake').[43] Whatever the correct solution, it is evident that the objection of Goguel lacks penetration.

(d) Finally there is the use of ἀββά (abba) in Mark 14.36. Principally as a result of the painstaking researches of Jeremias, to whose conclusions we shall refer more fully below (§4), it is now generally accepted that with abba we reach back to the very speech and language of Jesus himself. Few would dissent from the statement of F. Hahn, that 'the Aramaic form of address abba can be regarded with certainty as a mark of Jesus' manner of speech'.[44] The presence of abba in Mark 14.36, its only occurrence as such in the gospel traditions, must weigh strongly, though in itself not decisively, in favour of the age and authenticity of the prayer which contains it.

Thus the historicity of Jesus' prayer in Gethsemane stands on solid ground. It follows that, despite the literary difficulties present in many of the other passages in Mark and Luke, a tradition of Jesus' private prayer which includes Gethsemane cannot be lightly dismissed or ignored. When taken in conjunction with the strong presumption concerning Jesus' own practice of prayer which follows from his teaching on prayer, we can be confident that Jesus' turning to prayer in Gethsemane was an action born of habit as much as anything. It was not the despairing cry for help of a man unaccustomed to prayer reduced to clutching at any straw. It was rather the action of one who had always found strength in prayer now desperately searching for that same strength through the usual channel.

3.4 *Conclusion.* Despite the difficulties then in the other Markan and Lukan references to Jesus' praying they probably give a fair representation of Jesus' habit.[45] We may therefore call upon their testimony, even though with some reserve. Particularly noteworthy is the consistent emphasis in both Mark and Luke that Jesus liked to get away, to be alone (Matt. 14.23; Luke 9.18; cf. Luke 9.28f. with Mark 9.2) in his prayer, either in the desert (Mark 1.35; Luke 5.16), or on a mountain (Mark 6.46; Luke 6.12; 9.28) away from the crowds (Mark 1.35; 6.46; Luke 5.16), sometimes going off very early in the morning (Mark 1.35), sometimes spending much or the whole of the night in lonely prayer (Mark 6.46; 14.32–42; Luke 6.12). Noteworthy also is the fact that each of the three occasions recorded by Mark seems to have been a time of stress and crisis;[46] while Luke portrays Jesus consistently resorting to prayer on occasions of great moment and decision (Luke 3.21; 6.12; 9.18, 28f.; 22.41–5). It is therefore more than probable that *prayer was Jesus' regular response to situations of crisis and decision.*

§4. JESUS' SENSE OF SONSHIP – ABBA

Having established the importance of prayer for Jesus the next question to be answered is obviously, Why? Why was prayer so important to Jesus? What was his experience in prayer which made it so valuable? What was the source of Jesus' strength in his aloneness? On what power and assurance did he fall back in times of crisis? At first sight these might seem to pose a hopeless quest. Jesus has left us no writings, no personal diaries. How can we begin to approach him in his aloneness, in his inner strength? Fortunately, however, the tradition does enable us to 'listen in' and to gain an insight into Jesus' experience in prayer. And fortunately we have the benefit of what must rank as one of the more important advances in the quest of the historical Jesus in the past few decades. I refer to Jeremias's researches into the use of the word *abba*.

4.1   *The use of* abba *in Jesus' prayers.* Jeremias notes that all five strata in the gospel tradition agree that in prayer Jesus addressed God as 'Father' – in Jesus' speech, 'Abba', as preserved in Mark 14.36. Their testimony is also unanimous that Jesus used this address in *all* his prayers.[47] It must be said at once that the evidence is not substantial in quantity: Mark 14.36: Q – Matt. 6.9/Luke 11.2; Matt. 11.25f./ Luke 10.21; Luke 23.34, 46; Matt. 26.42; John 11.41; 12.27f.; 17.1, 5, 11, 21, 24f. Yet, although some of the material is suspect as to whether it preserves the actual words of Jesus, particularly John of course, the fact remains that it appears in every one of the gospel traditions and that there is no contrary testimony. The one passage where Jesus does not preface his prayer with 'Abba' is the cry on the cross – 'My God, my God, why have you forsaken me?' (Mark 15.34/ Matt. 27.46). But here, as Jeremias has reminded us, Jesus has expressed his feelings in the words of Ps. 22.1 (see further below p. 23). Thus where Jesus prayed in his own words the testimony remains unshaken that his emotions and faith found clearest expression in the word 'Abba'.[48] When we 'listen in' on Jesus' prayers *the distinctive word we hear is 'Abba'.*

Since the *abba*-prayer was evidently in currency in the early churches (Rom. 8.15; Gal. 4.6), it could be argued that it stemmed originally from the Aramaic speaking communities – like 'Maranatha'

(I Cor. 16.22) – and that Mark 14.36 etc. is a reading back of the churches' later practice into the Jesus-tradition. But, as we shall see below, to address God as 'Abba' was very unusual in Judaism, since 'abba' was the language of family intimacy. And if Jesus did not take the step of addressing God so intimately, which of his followers would? Moreover, it is clearly implied in Rom. 8.15 and Gal. 4.6 that *the early Christians' experience of sonship was understood as an echo and reproduction of Jesus' own experience*; it is precisely *the Spirit of the Son* who cries 'Abba' (see below pp. 319f.). This reinforces the testimony of the gospel traditions that the *abba*-prayer was the distinctive characteristic of Jesus' own prayer; the alternative of postulating an unknown fountainhead of devotional influence in the early churches hardly carries as much weight.[49]

The significance of this address to God is clear. The OT has made us familiar with the Hebrew concept of fatherhood as implying a relationship of care and authority on the one side and of love and obedience on the other (Deut. 1.31; 8.5; 14.1; Isa. 1.2; Jer. 3.19; Mal. 1.6).[50] 'Father' for the Hebrew denoted 'absolute authority and tenderness'.[51] Significantly, both of these aspects find clear expression in the Gethsemane prayer. This, together with his more negative attitude to traditional Jewish worship, strongly suggests that Jesus' calling on God as 'Father' was *the language of experience rather than a formal address*. It was his experience of God which found expression in the *abba*-prayer. It was because he found God in the experience of a love and authority which constrained him as from beyond that he addressed God as 'Father'.[52]

But can we say more than that? Was Jesus' experience of God as Father distinctive within contemporary Judaism? Was it indeed something unique – denoting a unique relationship between Jesus and God? These questions are posed by Jeremias's study, and we must pursue them closely since important corollaries obviously hang upon their answer.

4.2 *Was Jesus' use of abba distinctive within contemporary Judaism?* Jeremias's thorough investigations have highlighted two points of immediate relevance.[53] First, *abba* was in common currency at the time of Jesus as a family word – a word which children, including tiny children, used to address their fathers. It was thus an address of courtesy and respect; but much more, it was the expression of warm intimacy and trust. Second, nowhere in Judaism is *abba* used by an individual in prayer to God:

In the literature of Palestinian Judaism *no evidence has yet been found* of 'my Father' being used by an individual as an address to God . . . there is no instance of the use of *'Abbā* as an address to God in all the extensive prayer-literature of Judaism, whether in liturgical or in private prayers.

Jeremias sums up this 'fact of fundamental importance':

We do not have a single example of God being addressed as *'Abbā* in Judaism, but Jesus *always* addressed God in this way in his prayers.[54]

If Jeremias is right then we have to conclude that Jesus' *abba*-prayer expressed an unusual and unprecedented sense of intimacy with God.

This conclusion, however, does have to be qualified at two points. First, it is not in fact true that we have no examples of a Jew saying 'my Father' to God. I am thinking here particularly of Ecclus. (Ben Sira) 23.1, 4: that the Greek πάτερ is like the πάτερ of Jesus' prayers (except Mark 14.36) and denotes a sense of intimate trust, is strongly suggested by Ecclus. (Ben Sira) 51.10.[55] We cannot therefore maintain that Jesus' use of *abba* was *unprecedented*. Of course, 'Abba' was not simply an occasional usage by Jesus, rather, so far as we can tell, his *regular* way of speaking to God in prayer. All we can say then is that when we compare the literature available to us, Jesus' regular approach to God as 'Abba' appears to be *unusual* for his day.

Second, H. Conzelmann points out that *abba* 'need not have had a connotation of familiarity'.[56] This is quite true. Jeremias does note that *abba* was used in the pre-Christian period as a respectful address to old men. But this usage is clearly an extension of the family usage.[57] The more regular and typical use of *abba* at the time of Jesus was within the family and did express family intimacy. Obviously it was precisely because of this note of intimacy that *abba* was so little used by Jesus' contemporaries in addressing God.[58] More important, this is the note which is present in the uses of *abba* in the NT (Mark 14.36; Rom.8.15; Gal.4.6), as in Matt.11.25ff.; Luke 23.46. In all these cases 'Abba/Father' expresses more than respect – viz., child-like confidence and obedience. It is significant that the only occasion we know of where Jesus did not use *abba* in prayer to God was in his cry of dereliction on the cross (Mark 15.34) – in his awful experience of *abandonment* by God he could not cry 'Abba'.[59] It is difficult therefore to escape the conclusion that Jesus said 'Abba' to God for precisely the same reason that (most of) his contemporaries refrained from its use in prayer – viz., because it expressed his attitude to God as Father, his experience of God as one of unusual intimacy.[60]

It would appear then that Jeremias has pressed his argument too far. But nevertheless much of value remains from his researches. In particular, we are not being over bold if we conclude that Jesus' use of *abba* enables us to see into the heart of his relationship with God as he understood it. The divine reality he experienced in those moments of naked aloneness was God as Father. This experience was so vital and creative that it had to find expression in an address to God which would have sounded shockingly familiar to the great majority of his contemporaries. We may presume that this language alone could express the unusual intimacy he found in prayer – the intimacy, trust and obedience of a child with his father.

4.3   *Does Jesus' use of 'Abba' imply a unique sense of sonship?* Did Jesus think of his sense of sonship as something all might enjoy? Did he think of the relationship with God which it implied as one already shared by all men, if only they realized it? The testimony of the gospel tradition is fairly clear cut at this point. Jesus certainly taught his disciples to pray in the same way (Luke 11.2), but *it was precisely his disciples that he so taught*. The passages in question[61] all seem to be addressed to his followers; they all speak in one way or another of the trust and obedience of disciples; that is, they are addressed to those who have already begun to recognize, to trust and obey God as Father.[62] This conclusion cannot be regarded as certain, for the simple reason that the relevant material has come to us through the early churches, a process which may have filtered out more universalistic teaching, or which may have set more generalized statements (Matt. 5.45?) within a context of particular teaching to disciples. Consequently, some have argued that Jesus said 'your Father' to *all* his hearers.[63] On the other hand, the dominance of the eschatological note in Jesus' preaching (see below ch. III) and what Bultmann calls the 'either-or' of his challenge,[64] does imply that Jesus envisaged something new in God's relations with men and that the eschatological relationship into which he called men can not be separated from their response of repentance and commitment (cf. e.g. Matt. 3.7–12/Luke 3.7–9, 16f.; Mark 10.23b, 25; Matt. 7.13f.; Luke 9.60a, 62; 14.26).[65] And since Jesus' teaching on divine fatherhood can hardly be isolated from this 'either-or',[66] we should hesitate before blunting the latter's sharpness by defining the former in terms of a generalized concept of divine benevolence. The association of 'fatherhood' with 'discipleship' implied in the passages cited above in n. 61 therefore probably belongs to the original teaching of Jesus.[67]

The question then becomes one of the relation between Jesus and his disciples. Granted that Jesus encouraged his disciples to address God as 'Abba', did he think that they might enjoy precisely the same relationship with God as he did himself, or did he regard his own relationship as something unique? Bornkamm argues for the latter alternative:

Although we find numerous passages where Jesus says 'My Father (in heaven)' and 'thy Father' or 'your Father', there is nowhere a passage where he himself joins with his disciples in an 'Our Father'. We have no reason to doubt that this usage was truly characteristic for Jesus himself, and certainly as an expression of his mission.[68]

On the other hand, we know from Rom. 8.15 and Gal. 4.6 that Jesus did not keep the 'Abba' form of address to himself, but rather encouraged his disciples to use it (Luke 11.2).[69] Consequently we must ask, Did Jesus never join with his disciples in corporate prayer, using an 'Abba' form like the 'Lord's prayer'? It is a question which our sources do not permit us to answer. But certain considerations counsel against giving it too much weight, whatever the answer.

(1) If it was only his disciples that Jesus encouraged to pray 'Abba', then the implication is that their use of *abba* was somehow *dependent* on their relationship with Jesus, that their 'Abba' was *derivative* from Jesus' 'Abba'.

(2) We should not assume too quickly that 'the basic difference between "my Father" and "your Father" is a matter of the Christological style of the community' (Conzelmann). For the community was quite able to retain the christological distance between Jesus and his followers without removing any element in the tradition which set Jesus and his disciples on the same level. Thus, in particular, the tradition in which the earthly Jesus calls disciples 'brother' (Mark 3.34f. pars.) caused them no difficulty or embarrassment, even though elsewhere it is only the exalted one who so speaks (Matt. 25.40; 28.10; John 20.17). So too Rom. 8.15 and Gal. 4.6 both heighten *and reduce* the christological distance between Jesus and Christians in a striking way. On the one hand, there is a recognition that their sonship depends on and derives from Jesus' sonship (the Spirit of the Son); yet, at the same time, the Spirit who cries 'Abba' makes the believer not just a son (at one remove from Jesus as it were) but a *fellow-heir with Christ* (Rom. 8.17; Gal. 4.7). In fact, deliberate christological distancing at this point only really becomes evident in John's gospel with the fourth evangelist's reservation of υἱός (son) for Jesus alone: there are many 'children of God' (τέκνα Θεοῦ – John 1.12; I John 3.1f., 10; 5.2), but only one 'Son of God' (υἱός Θεοῦ).

(3) If we accept the tradition that Jesus chose an inner circle of twelve disciples during his ministry, as seems most probable,[70] then the significance lies in the fact that he chose *twelve* and not just eleven.

Jesus himself was not the twelfth; the circle was complete without him. That is to say, the Israel of the end-time (cf. Matt. 19.28b) was represented not by himself plus eleven others, but by the twelve as such. Jesus' own role was something else and distinctive.

There are grounds therefore for holding that Jesus was conscious of some degree of distinctiveness in his relation with God over against that of his disciples, and that the 'my Father', 'your Father' distinction is a reflection of that consciousness as it came to expression in Jesus' teaching, rather than something later imposed on the Jesus-tradition. Here is a conclusion of great importance, even though the uncertainties of the synoptic tradition mean that it can only be put forward tentatively.

4.4   *Conclusion.* In short, we can say with some confidence that *Jesus experienced an intimate relation of sonship in prayer*: he found God characteristically to be 'Father'; and this sense of God was so real, so loving, so compelling, that whenever he turned to God it was the cry 'Abba' that came most naturally to his lips. We can also say, though with less confidence, that Jesus himself thought or *sensed this relationship with God to be something distinctive* – not unique, but distinctive:[71] he encouraged his disciples to pray in the same way, but even then he seems to have thought of their relationship as somehow *dependent* on his own, as somehow a *consequence* of his own. Whether this last conclusion has any stronger backing in the synoptic traditions is the next question to be investigated.

§5. JESUS' SENSE OF SONSHIP – MATT. 11.27(?) et al.

A first answer appears to be emerging to our initial question: What was it in Jesus' experience that he referred to God? What was the correlate in his experience of his belief in God? The answer can be simply expressed – *a sense of sonship* – the sense that God cared for him as an individual with a fatherly care, the sense that he had a filial duty to God which no personal wishes could set aside (Mark 14.36), the sense of something distinctive in this relationship. There is other relevant evidence which, while it would not stand on its own, may possibly serve to buttress this conclusion – the synoptic testimony that Jesus spoke of himself as God's son (or should we say God's Son?).

5.1   *The view of the evangelists.* It is quite clear that for the writers of the gospels Jesus' sense of sonship was unclouded and unique: he knew himself to be the Son (of God) and his assurance of sonship was fundamental to his mission. This comes out most explicitly in the narratives of Jesus' experience at Jordan (Mark 1.9–11 pars.) and in the Q account of Jesus' temptations (Matt. 4.1–11/Luke 4.1–13). It is still widely accepted that there is a deliberate allusion to Ps. 2.7 in the Markan report of the voice from heaven (Mark 1.11);[72] and it is quite possible that the original Lukan text quoted only Ps. 2.7; 'You are my son; today I have begotten you'.[73] The Synoptics are thus in no doubt that Jesus was hailed as God's Son at Jordan. Was it the strength of divine approval and commissioning which sent Jesus forth to his ministry? This is certainly one of the intended implications of the temptation narrative, since two of the tests focus primarily on Jesus' conviction of sonship – 'If you are God's son . . .' (Matt. 4.3, 6/Luke 4.3, 9).[74] The evangelists therefore intend their readers to understand that Jesus' consciousness of divine sonship was a fundamental factor in his decision to move out into the public eye.

In addition we may recall the Lukan account of Jesus' boyhood visit to the Temple (Luke 2.41–51),[75] and the transfiguration episode (Mark 9.2–8 pars.). In the former we are clearly intended to understand that Jesus' sense of sonship was already deep-rooted and mature prior to Jordan. And in the latter, Jesus is again hailed as 'my beloved Son' (Mark 9.7 pars.).[76] As for the Fourth Gospel we need refer only to John 5.19–26; 8.35f.; 10.36; 14.13; 17.1, where Jesus speaks of himself openly and without reserve as 'the Son'.

The question inevitably arises: How justified historically are these reports? Did Jesus think of himself as *the* Son? Was this consciousness fundamental to his sense of mission? Did he *speak* of himself as 'the Son'? The best way to answer these questions is to scrutinize the synoptic *logia* in which Jesus speaks of himself as God's son.[77] If they give an affirmative answer we need look no further. If they give a negative answer we are thrust back upon the *abba* material and must be content with the conclusions already drawn. The passages in question are Matt. 11.25–7/Luke 10.21–2; Mark 13.32; Mark 12.6; Luke 22.29.

5.2   *Matt.11.27* is a verse of particular importance. It was the passage out of which Harnack drew the exposition cited above (p. 14), and has regularly offered itself as the corner stone for other attempts to penetrate back to Jesus' self-consciousness. Others have found it to be more a stumbling block!

Everything is entrusted (παρεδόθη) to me by my Father;
and no one knows (ἐπιγινώσκει) the Son except the Father,

and no one knows (ἐπιγινώσκει) the Father except the Son
and those to whom the Son chooses to reveal him (ἀποκαλύψαι) (NEB).[78]

Is this an authentic word of Jesus, and if so does it give us an insight into Jesus' self-awareness in his standing towards God?

It must be said at once that the weight of opinion among the front-runners in NT studies over the past sixty years or more has come down against finding here the *ipsissima verba* of Jesus.[79] The three principal reasons are as follows.

(*a*) The whole saying is untypical of the synoptic material and has a distinctively Johannine ring; it therefore shares the presumption of post-Easter theological development which inevitably attaches to the Johannine discourses.[80] In particular,

(*b*) the idea of mutual knowledge of the Father and the Son together with the ἀποκαλύψαι marks v. 27 as a 'Hellenistic Revelation saying'.[81]

'The function of the Son as the Revealer rests clearly on the fact that the Father recognizes him and that he therefore knows the Father. But that is an idea of Hellenistic mysticism quite foreign to Judaism'.[82]

In v. 27 'Jesus speaks as a gnostic redeemer'.[83]

(*c*) The absoluteness and exclusiveness of the relation here postulated between God and Jesus is unprecedented in the Synoptic Gospels and smacks of later christological development.

Here indeed a Christological narrowing has obviously taken place. Originally every one could say 'Father', now access to the Father is tied to Jesus.[84]

Similarly the claim to 'unrestricted authority' in v. 27a, when compared with Mark 13.32 and Matt. 28.18, must belong to a relatively late layer of tradition.[85]

(*a*) The comparison with John is a two-edged argument. For it is most unlikely that a Q logion derives from Johannine theology, which, in the only (written) form we know, is at least thirty years later than Q. If there is any influence between the two, direct or indirect, and the 'Johannine' nature of the saying makes this very likely, then the direction of influence is almost certainly from the Q saying to John. That is to say, the Johannine Father–Son theology is probably developed from a small block of early sayings tradition which Q has preserved in part at least.[86] And this is wholly to be expected; unless John's portrayal of Jesus is to be regarded as *totally* the creation of an early prophet and theologian, without any regard to actual words and deeds of the man from Nazareth – and the 'Johannine school' itself repudiates the suggestion (John 1.14; 19.35; I John 1.1–3) – then it is surely most natural to explain much at least of the Fourth Gospel's discourses as the end product of lengthy reflection on original sayings of Jesus. The problem of why only two sayings are preserved (in Q and Mark 13.32) is thus open to other solutions than that of late origin.

(b) The question of formal and verbal parallels is disputed. Long ago G. Dalman noted that the two clauses referring to the mutual knowledge of the Father and the Son 'really constitute a detailed Oriental mode of expressing the reciprocity of intimate understanding'.[87] More recently the doyen of Aramaic specialists among NT scholars has repeated Dalman's opinion: the chiastic parallelism of the two lines 'is simply an oriental periphrasis for a mutual relationship: only father and son really know each other'.[88] As to the actual terminology, knowledge of God is a common theme in the OT,[89] and W. D. Davies has drawn particular attention to passages in the Dead Sea Scrolls where 'insight into the *eschaton* and intimate "knowledge" of God are conjoined' in a manner parallel to Matt. 11.25ff. and distinct from Hellenistic gnosis.[90] The parallels Davies cites, however, are not very close.[91] More convincing are those in Jewish Wisdom literature, most recently noted by F. Christ and M. J. Suggs,[92] particularly Wisd. 2.10–20, where it is said of the righteous man:

He claims to have knowledge of God,
and calls himself a son of the Lord.
. . . . .
and boasts of having God for his father (cf. Ecclus. 4.10; 51.10).

The most striking feature of v. 27 in this context is the emphasis on the *unknowability* of the Son in line 2. This lacks any real parallel in gnostic literature and indeed is offensive to gnostic thought, which would stress rather *knowledge* of the Son.[93] The closest parallels are again to be found in Wisdom literature (Job 28.1–28; Ecclus. 1.6, 8; Bar. 3.15–32; cf. I Cor. 2.11),[94] but without the conciseness of v. 27. Indeed, the conciseness of the saying, like those preserved in the Sermon on the Mount as compared with Wisdom and rabbinic parallels, could perhaps be regarded as a mark of Jesus' own style.

In addition, the more firmly Matt. 11.27 belongs to its context the stronger the Wisdom associations become. In particular, the parallel between Matt. 11.25–30 and Ecclus. (Ben Sira) 51 has been familiar since Norden's work.[95] Verses 28–30 certainly have all the marks of a Wisdom saying[96] and translate easily into Aramaic.[97] But the absence of these verses from the Lukan parallel and their reappearance as an isolated saying in the Gospel of Thomas (logion 90) puts the original unity of vv. 25–30 in doubt, and so reduces the support which forward context might afford to the view that Wisdom provides the background of v. 27.[98] The link is firmer between v. 27 and vv. 25f., where again the Wisdom background[99] and Aramaic origin[100] are clear enough. Indeed, it would be difficult to argue for the independence in origin of vv. 25f. and v. 27,[101] since subject matter is so closely connected,[102] and structure is precisely parallel – four lines in both cases, each with the two middle lines in antithetic parallelism contrasting hiddenness with revelation, and each with an emphatic last line.[103] There are good grounds therefore for Jeremias's judgment that 'language, style and structure thus clearly assign the saying to a Semitic-speaking milieu'.[104]

The arguments from *religionsgeschichtliche* parallels are therefore indecisive. The later parallels in Hermetic and gnostic writings provide no proof for the lateness of 11.27's formulation. Nor do the pre-Christian parallels in Wisdom literature serve to establish its early date. Wisdom speculation appears to have provided a borderland between Judaism and other near Eastern and Hellenistic cultures from the first, where hellenizing and gnosticizing influences were most active.[105] In such a situation it is almost impossible to determine by means of form-criticism the point of origin of such a passage as Matt. 11.27 – as indeed 11.25–30 itself most clearly demonstrates, with its closest links both with pre-Christian Jewish Wisdom literature on the one side and with the Gospel of Thomas on the other.[106]

Granted then that here we have a saying which emerges from Jewish Wisdom speculation, the question becomes, Could *Jesus* have been influenced by such reflection? Was Jesus familiar with that borderland of Jewish thought where Hellenistic influences were most rife? The strongest considerations in favour of an affirmative answer are these: (1) v. 27 hangs together with v. 25 which can be assigned to Jesus with greater assurance (*abba*-prayer, straightforward Jewish character, positive use of νήπιος (babe, infant), lack of christological claim).[107] (2) Jesus was certainly influenced by the more popular type of Jewish wisdom,[108] and was probably not unaware of its more Hellenistically developed variations. Thus, in particular, we can detect the influence of Ecclus. (Ben Sira) in at least one other undisputed passage where Jesus teaches his disciples in intimate fashion – Matt. 6.12 (Ecclus. 28.2); also Matt. 6.13 (Ecclus. 23.1; 33.1). (3) Perhaps also, as already suggested, the conciseness of the saying could be regarded as a mark of Jesus' own style.[109] Whether these considerations are strong enough to allow us to make a firm claim for the authenticity of the saying as a word of Jesus is another question. The *religionsgeschichtliche* and formal criteria simply show that it is by no means impossible for Jesus to have so spoken; but it must be recognized that, in the absence of better parallels within the Jesus-tradition, the balance of probability tips only in favour of the *possibility* of authenticity and leaves the issue open.[110]

(c) The third reason for denying Matt. 11.27's authenticity as a word of Jesus has probably been the most decisive in the history of the debate. A claim to 'unrestricted authority' (v. 27a) and to unique sonship (*the* Son) is more readily recognizable in the faith of post-Easter Christianity than on the lips of the pre-Easter Jesus. But this antithesis can be posed much too sharply.

In the first place, v. 27a does not constitute a claim to 'unrestricted authority'. The 'all things' (πάντα) which the Father has delivered to Jesus can be nothing other than 'these things' (ταῦτα) which the Father has hidden from the learned and wise (v. 25 – the 'twin' stanza). That is, 'all things' must refer to knowledge, not to power and authority. This is implied also by the παραδιδόναι (a technical term for the transmission of doctrine, knowledge, holy lore) and the talk of ἐπιγινώσκειν and ἀποκαλύψαι in the rest of v. 27.[111] The 'all things' delivered to Jesus are therefore the 'mystery of revelation',[112] and the closer parallel is the 'all things' of Mark 4.11 rather than the 'all authority' of Matt. 28.18. In short, according to Matt. 11.27a, Jesus claims to have received a divinely given understanding of God, which is the basis of his whole understanding of his mission.

Secondly, we should take note of Suggs's observation that in Matt. 11.25–7 Jesus presents himself as 'the mediator of revelation', the envoy of Wisdom, not as Wisdom itself (cf. Matt. 11.19/Luke 7.34f.; Luke 11.49ff.). Only with the addition of vv. 28–30 is Jesus actually identified with Wisdom.[113] While it is reasonable to assume that the identification of Jesus with Wisdom was first made by the post-Easter community (by Paul at Corinth and Matthew in Syria?),[114] there are no substantial grounds for denying that Jesus saw himself in the former role. The charge that Matt. 11.27 represents Jesus as making a claim to 'unrestricted authority' is therefore unfounded. The relatively more modest claim to being a recipient of divine revelation, specially appointed as a channel of divine Wisdom, is certainly consistent with what we know of the historical Jesus in his proclamation of God's rule and in his teaching on the law (see below §§7, 8, 13).

Thirdly, Hahn's characterization of Matt. 11.27 as a 'Christological narrowing' has also to be questioned. Once it is recognized that Jesus addressed God as 'Abba', the expression of an unusual personal intimacy with the God above all gods, then it follows as an almost inevitable consequence that Jesus thought of himself as son, God's son.[115] R. H. Fuller's criticism of Hahn is therefore justified: 'Matt. 11.27 is not a "christological contraction", but an explicit expression of the implicit Christology of Jesus' own use of Abba'.[116]

However, even with these qualifications, the key question still remains: whether Jesus actually spoke of himself as *'the* Son' in such an absolute and exclusive manner. Jeremias has attempted to soften the sharpness of this question by elaborating a further suggestion of Dalman:[117] he argues that the definite articles with 'son' and 'father' have to be understood semitically in a generic sense. The middle couplet he thinks should be translated:

> Only a father knows his son
> and only a son knows his father.

Thus for Jeremias, what we have originally is 'a quite general statement about human experience: only a father and a son really know each other'.[118] But can one so readily abstract the middle couplet from v.27 and argue for its authenticity independently of the other two lines? The whole verse obviously follows from vv.25f. and cannot be so easily dissected. Furthermore, the saying which Jeremias claims to uncover is hardly memorable and is only of doubtful truth as a general proverb. No! v.27 almost certainly stands or falls as a whole. And if Jesus or the early church did incorporate such a proverb in the saying of v.27, then the first and last of the four lines make it quite plain that the middle couplet applies the proverb to Jesus' own relationship with the Father; that is, the verse as a whole speaks only of Jesus' sonship. The exclusiveness and absoluteness of the claim remains!

The question of the authenticity of Matt. 11.27 thus reduces itself finally to the key question: Could Jesus have spoken of his relationship with God in such an absolute and exclusive manner? The answer cannot be a clear cut 'Yes', since the saying is itself unique among synoptic logia and has its closest parallels in post-Easter Christology. But neither can it be an unequivocal 'No'. For we have already noted the sense of distinctiveness which seems to have characterized Jesus' *abba*-prayer. The presence of the *abba*-prayer in vv.25f. and the 'by my Father' in v.27a could quite well indicate that the language of v.27 arises directly out of Jesus' experience of God as Father, and that the father-son references in the middle couplet carry the same note of distinctiveness which Jesus felt marked out his relationship with God. This in turn makes it more plausible that the absoluteness of the claim made in the opening clause of v.27

and the exclusiveness of the claim made in the final clause of v. 27 is an authentic echo of Jesus' teaching. But great uncertainty remains, and I can do no more than leave the reader to decide for himself. The alternatives may be posed thus: In these words do we hear Jesus himself boldly elaborating his sense of distinctive intimacy with the Father and his consciousness of commission in a moment of high spiritual exaltation (cf. Luke 10.18, 21)? Or is the elaboration the work of the post-Easter churches in reflective, or inspired or more dogmatic mood?

(d) Finally, I should perhaps make two brief comments on the thesis that the saying first originated in a post-Easter community and demonstrates the merging of Wisdom and apocalyptic motifs in their identification of Jesus as the Son of Man.[119]

First, the title 'Son' in v. 27 is not the content of the revelation, but rather its presupposition. It is the Son who reveals the Father, who reveals, if Hoffmann is right, the Son's dignity as Son of Man. This implies that the thought of Jesus' sonship arises immediately as a corollary to Jesus' addressing God as 'Abba' (vv. 25f.); or that Jesus' sonship is already taken for granted by the earliest community. But the Father-Son motif did not have much currency in the early church's tradition of Jesus' sayings – hence the uniqueness of Matt. 11.27 within the synoptic tradition; the great elaboration of the Father-Son motif only appears at a later date.[120] This suggests that it did not have the force of new revelation or dominant category of thought in the earliest community, unlike 'the Son of Man' and 'Messiah'. The other possibility therefore re-emerges that Jesus' sonship was an aspect of Jesus' *own* teaching, which lay fallow for quite some time in the early Christian communities.

Second, the thesis of post-Easter origin fails to explain why line 2 should feature as part of the interpretation of vv. 25f. – 'No one knows the Son except the Father'. This stresses the *unknowability* of the Son, not a revelation about him. Whereas the earliest communities were surely more conscious of their special election as recipients of new revelation about Jesus – his Messiahship, perhaps already his Lordship (cf. I Cor. 16.22), and his Son of Man dignity (Hoffmann).[121] The fact that v. 27 speaks more of revelation concerning the Father than revelation concerning the Son, again suggests a pre-Easter rather more than a post-Easter origin for the saying.[122]

To sum up: can we use Matt. 11.27 as evidence of Jesus' self-understanding? Some will dismiss it at once as post-Easter speculation. Others will feel that the distance between the self-consciousness of Jesus' *abba*-prayer and that of Matt. 11.27 does not extend to the other side of Easter. For myself I confess that I remain undecided. It is certainly not impossible that Jesus should have said these words, but the evidence is such that we are left only with the possibility. Their testimony therefore should not be wholly ignored, but it would be foolish to build anything of importance upon it. We may summarize that testimony by comparing it with our earlier findings.

(1) Jesus prayed to God as Father. Here he claims to *know* God. In the Hebrew tradition knowledge in the context of personal relationship 'does not denote the contemplative knowledge of the wise, but a perceiving which at the same time always includes an interior relation to the one known'. In particular, in the God-man relationship it describes 'the *responsive love and trustful surrender* awakened by the unmerited love of God'.[123] Here then is the same I-Thou relationship which is also denoted by *abba*. Jesus knows God with the warmth and intimacy of a son with his father. For Jesus, to know God is to know him as Father.

(2) Jesus may well have felt his relationship with God to be something distinctive. In Matt. 11.27 the note of distinctiveness becomes the note of uniqueness (contrast n. 71 above): Jesus claims to have been so specially set apart by God that he can speak of 'all things' having been handed over to him by God; he has been made a unique recipient of divine revelation and channel of divine Wisdom. Even more striking, his knowledge of God is unique: he knows God as no man ever has; the mutual relation he experiences with God is without parallel. At the same time, that unique knowledge of God can be shared by others – 'anyone to whom the Son chooses to reveal him' (11.27d) – just as others (his disciples) can address God as 'Abba'.

(3) In saying 'Abba' Jesus did not seek to escape reality but rather expressed his willingness to undergo a reality all too horrible (Mark 14.36). So in Matt. 11.27, knowledge of God expresses not mystical piety but acceptance of mission (11.27d) – a mission which contained the note of judgment as well as of gospel (11.25f.).

5.3 *Mark 13.32; 12.6; Luke 22.29f.* Nothing can compensate for the loss of Matt. 11.27 from among the front rank witnesses to Jesus' experience of God. These three passages are the only others which come into serious reckoning as potential witnesses to Jesus' self-consciousness of sonship and deserve some attention.

(*a*) Mark 13.32 is the nearest parallel to Matt. 11.27 – 'Of that day or that hour no one knows, not even the angels in heaven, nor the Son, but only the Father'. Although an isolated saying, it belongs clearly to an apocalyptic context and must derive either from Jesus' ministry or from the early church. The difficulty with the latter alternative is this: the earlier we postulate its origin the less need was there to attribute ignorance to Jesus, since Jesus' generation did not die out for some decades (cf. Mark 13.30); but the later we postulate its origin, to explain the delay of the parousia, the more exalted Jesus had become in the thought of the Christian communities and the less likely that the ascription of ignorance to Jesus would be permitted (as I Cor. 12.3 and Luke's [perhaps also Matthew's] omission of the whole verse make plain). On the other hand, as C. K. Barrett points out, this sort of consideration

> can defend at most the substance, and in no way the formulation of the verse. Even if the substance of the verse is genuine . . . the description of Jesus by the most honorific title available would be precisely the sort of compensation that tradition would introduce.[124]

In other words, the verse at most expresses Jesus' confidence in God as Father for the future, but beyond that may confess more to ignorance of God's designs than to possession of special revelation.[125]

(b) Mark 12.6. There is a widespread hesitation about accepting Mark 12.1–9 as a parable of Jesus – justifiably, because of its plainly allegorical character.[126] Yet in its synoptic form it is not like the later church allegories, since the allegory does not extend to all the details; and to deny that Jesus told parables containing allegorical elements is to force through a dogmatic definition of parable in the face of strong evidence to the contrary (particularly Mark 4.3–8).[127] After all, Isaiah's vineyard (Isa. 5), the most likely source of inspiration for the Mark 12 parable, is itself an allegory.[128] Likewise the threat of forfeiture and judgment is simply a variant form of Jesus' warnings against rejecting his message (cf. Matt. 12.41f./Luke 11.31f.; Luke 13.6–9) and cannot be used as an argument to deny the parable to Jesus.[129] The chief problem lies in the reference to the 'beloved son' (υἱὸν ἀγαπητόν – Mark 12.6) and his death, since the whole reads so much like the early church's representation of salvation-history. However, the simpler version of the parable in the Gospel of Thomas (logion 65) and the absence of ἀγαπητόν in the variant version of Matthew (21.37) strongly suggest that an original parable of Jesus has been elaborated to some extent by the early church.[130] Moreover, there is good evidence both that Jesus saw himself standing in the prophetic line and that he expected a violent death.[131] It thus becomes quite likely that Jesus told this parable referring to his own mission under the allegorical figure of the owner's son.[132] In which case Mark 12.6 testifies to *the unforced way in which Jesus thought of himself as God's son.* On the other hand, the passage says nothing about

Jesus' 'messianic self-consciousness', and nothing can be made of the distinction between servants (prophets) and son, since the contrast can be fully explained from the dramatic climax of the parable.[133]

(c) Luke 22.29f. – 'As my Father appointed a kingdom for me, so do I appoint for you that you may eat and drink at my table in my kingdom, and sit on thrones judging the twelve tribes of Israel.' These may very well be the closing words of Q (/Matt. 19.28) – the collection of sayings being rounded off with Jesus' testamentary disposition of his inheritance.[134] That Matt. 19.28a is an embellished form of the saying is indicated by the repetition of the Matthean catchword 'follow' (ἀκολουθεῖν),[135] the Hellenistic word 'regeneration' (παλιγγενεσία) and perhaps 'the Son of Man' formulation instead of Luke's 'kingdom'.[136] It is probable therefore that Luke does preserve the earlier Q form. It is also quite likely that Q has preserved here an authentic word of Jesus. The archaic character of the saying has often been noted;[137] and the idea of kingdom expressed in vv. 29f. coheres very closely with the 'vow of abstinence' of Mark 14.25, a text whose claim to be regarded as the very words of Jesus must be highly ranked.[138] Since Jesus taught his disciples to share in some sense in his 'abba-relationship' with God, sent them forth to participate in his mission of proclaiming the kingdom to Israel (see below ch. IV, n.55), and regarded his table fellowship as a foretaste of the life of the kingdom, the sentiments of Luke 22.29f. become readily comprehensible within the context of the closing period of Jesus' ministry. The explicit association of sonship ('my Father') and kingdom is unparalleled in the Synoptics, but in the context of a testamentary disposition is quite natural; nor can it be attributed to the early communities, since there the motif of sonship-inheritance-kingdom assumes a standard pattern which is close to but not quite the same as the thought here (Rom. 8.17; I Cor. 6.9f.; Gal. 4.7; 5.21). We may also note that Mark 10.35ff. provides a very plausible situation within the life of Jesus. Indeed it is quite probable that the request of James and John was prompted by some such saying as Luke 22.29f. If this is so, then Luke 22.29f. provides some confirmation that Jesus thought and occasionally spoke of God as his Father. Once again the thought is of a distinctive (though not necessarily unique) relation between God and Jesus (the 'inheritance' of the kingdom), but also of a relation which Jesus could 'pass on' to his disciples.

There are other passages where Jesus speaks of God as his Father, but they cannot be quoted with much confidence since there has been a clear tendency to introduce the title 'Father' into the sayings of

Jesus.[139] Possibly Matt. 16.17; 18.35; 25.34 deserve consideration.[140] Mark 8.38 is also a possible claimant, but Luke 12.8f. is probably the more original formulation,[141] and there is no talk of 'Father' in the latter. Any conclusion therefore must rest upon the passages examined above in so far as they supplement the *abba* material treated earlier.

§6. CONCLUSIONS

6.1　We began our study of Jesus' experience of God by quoting Harnack's exposition of Matt. 11.27. It is now clear that so far as firm conclusions are concerned we are both better off than Harnack and worse off at the same time. We are better off, because our knowledge of Jesus' prayer-life and our appreciation of his *abba*-prayer shows us more clearly than Harnack saw that Jesus' sonship was a *consciousness* of sonship, an experienced relationship. We are worse off, as Christian theologians, because the evidence no longer enables us to assert the uniqueness of Jesus' sense of sonship with any certainty.[142] In addition, Harnack seemed to use 'Son of God' in a more titular sense than is justified by the synoptic evidence – even including Matt. 11.27. And in summarizing Jesus' teaching as 'God is the Father of all men', he failed to appreciate the close link which Jesus seems to have maintained between sonship and discipleship (cf. Rom. 8.14).

Nevertheless, even when all that is said, it must be acknowledged that Harnack's presentation of Jesus was more soundly based and of more lasting worth than is frequently recognized. The reaction against Liberal Protestantism which has so marked twentieth-century theology has let slip one of its most valuable insights. The element in Jesus' teaching, that God is Father, has of course been retained,[143] but at too rational, too cerebral a level. The existential dimension has been largely lost sight of, and with it the warmth and intimacy of Jesus' own devotion and obedience. Not the least importance of Jeremias's work has been to confirm this insight of Liberal Protestantism into the character of Jesus and to establish its foundations at a far deeper level. For the sake of clarity I will elaborate the most important points.

6.2　For Jesus prayer was something of first importance. It was the well from which he drew his strength and conviction. This was primarily because in prayer he was most conscious of God's care and authority, of God as Father – his Father. He occasionally gave expression to this consciousness of sonship. But only to his disciples was it expressed in any explicit way. With others, in the one case in point (Mark 12.6), the self expression was veiled, in parable form.

6.3 This fatherly love and authority Jesus believed was focussed upon him in a particular way, for Jesus seems to have thought of himself as God's son in a distinctive sense. Though he taught his disciples also to address God as 'Abba', he probably saw their sonship as somehow dependent on his own: the distinctive nature of the 'my Father' was retained even when he encouraged others to say 'our Father'. This *sense of a distinctiveness in his relation to God, in which nevertheless his disciples could participate*, comes to expression also in Luke 22.29, and most (too?) strongly in Matt. 11.27.

6.4 Jesus' sense of being God's son was an *existential conviction*, not merely an intellectual belief.[144] He *experienced* a relation of sonship – felt such an intimacy with God, such an approval by God, dependence on God, responsibility to God, that the only words adequate to express it were 'Father' and 'son'. The crystallization of this awareness quite possibly goes back to his experience at Jordan, if not before (see further below §10), although the evidence certainly does not permit us to trace a psychological development in Jesus.[145] The point to be underlined is that 'son' here expresses an experienced relationship, an existential relationship, not a metaphysical relationship as such. Although it is of course possible to postulate a metaphysical relationship lying behind Jesus' consciousness of sonship, the evidence permits us to speak only of Jesus' consciousness of an intimate relationship with God, not of awareness of metaphysical sonship, nor of a 'divine consciousness',[146] (far less consciousness of being 'second Person of the Trinity'!).[147] Even to speak of a consciousness of 'divine sonship' is misleading. And certainly to speak of an awareness of pre-existence goes far beyond the evidence.[148] After all, the whole concept of Israel's sonship was one of adoption rather than of creation.[149] And the king in Israel could be hailed as God's son (Ps. 2.7), but the son is never thought of as having a divine nature, and the prophets who often criticized the kings never seem to have accused them of claiming divinity,[150] whereas they roundly attacked the kings of neighbouring nations on this score (Isa. 14.12ff.; Ezek. 28.1–10).[151] Similarly, the righteous man of Wisd. 2, quoted above (p. 29), would not be accused of claiming 'divine sonship'. Of course, the title 'Son of God' and ultimately the dogma of a sonship of essence and substance, 'begotten from the Father before the ages', developed out of

Jesus' understanding of himself as God's son.[152] And the process has already begun within the NT documents with the addition of the full title of divinity in several of the gospel narratives,[153] and particularly in the Johannine presentation of Jesus. Moreover, and most important, as we have seen, Jesus did believe his sonship to be something distinctive (even unique if Matt. 11.27 could be accepted as an authentic word of Jesus). Yet how much we can read into that sense of distinctiveness is by no means clear, and we shall have to return to the subject in the light of our fuller investigation. At all events, the point can bear reiteration, that for Jesus himself, his sonship was primarily an existential conviction and relationship, not a merely intellectual belief nor something fully metaphysical.

6.5   Out of this confidence that he stood in a specially intimate relation with God arose Jesus' sense of mission. 'Sonship means to Jesus not a dignity to be claimed, but a responsibility to be fulfilled'.[154] As son he had been commissioned by God. As son, according to Matt. 11.27, he was conscious of 'being in a singular way the recipient and mediator of knowledge of God'.[155] In the same way and for the same reason, 'Abba' became the expression of the complete surrender of Jesus as son to the Father's will (Mark 14.36). In other words, *Jesus' consciousness of sonship was probably a fundamental element in his self-consciousness out of which his other basic convictions about himself and his mission arose.* To put it another way, this experience of intimacy in prayer gave Jesus his deep insight into both the character and the will of God. These insights probably lie at the heart of his unique claim to authority (see further below ch. III and §13).

6.6   If we may speculate a little further, it probably also follows that Jesus' existential consciousness of sonship was the primary datum of Jesus' self-awareness which enabled him to apply the various categories and passages from the OT to himself and round which he gathered the inspiration and ideas of these passages. Contrary to a still frequently used but undeclared assumption, the primary concept for Jesus does not appear to have been messiahship. He did not first regard himself as Messiah and conclude from this that he was God's son.[156] On the contrary, the evidence is that Jesus refused the title 'Messiah', or at least was far from happy with it.[157] On the other hand, it may well be that for Jesus the idea of being God's son had something of a representative significance – Jesus as an individual in some way representing the collective sonship of God's people.[158] This would be confirmed if the 'son of man' concept of Dan. 7 or the

Servant passages of Second Isaiah influenced Jesus' concept of his mission, as I believe was the case, but cannot stop here to demonstrate.[159] The point is that basic to Jesus' self-consciousness and consciousness of mission was not any particular messianic title or OT concept to which he then added the concept 'Son of God'. The evidence indicates rather that Jesus' sense of sonship was primary, and that it was this catalyst and key which led him to see that certain other passages of the OT were related to and descriptive of his mission.[160]

I am suggesting therefore that Jesus' self-consciousness was a lot less clear cut and structured than is frequently supposed. The concepts he used when speaking of himself were more fluid, more inchoate, than talk of 'titles' would suggest. So far as his relation to God was concerned, the concept of 'son' to God as Father was basic and most appropriate; just as in his relation to men his chosen self-reference seems to have been *bar nasa* (the son of man = 'I as a man', 'one' – see particularly Mark 2.27f; Matt. 11.18f./Luke 7.33f.; probably also Mark 2.10; Matt. 8.20/Luke 9.58).[161] With Jesus, in short, we see the freshness of an original mind, a new spirit, taking up old categories and concepts, remoulding them, creating them afresh, using them in a wholly new way in the light of his basic experience of God caring and commanding him and of being bound to God by the closest ties of love and obedience.

III

JESUS' EXPERIENCE OF GOD – SPIRIT

§7. INTRODUCTION

Our initial answer to the questions: What was it in Jesus' experience that he referred to God? What was the correlate in his experience of his belief in God? can be summed up in terms of the word 'sonship'. The reality which Jesus experienced in his moments of aloneness was God as Father, caring but commanding (Mark 14.36). The basis of his self-assurance in his ministry was his confidence that he knew God in this intimate way; and out of this intimacy sprang the compulsion to bring others into the same living relationship with God as Father (Luke 11.2; 'your Father'; Luke 22.29; cf. Matt. 11.27).

7.1 *The deficiency of Liberal Protestantism.* So far we have followed the way of nineteenth-century Liberal Protestantism, and that path has taken us some way into the religious experience of Jesus. But now we must turn from that path and head in a different direction, for Liberal Protestantism's presentation of Jesus was seriously defective. In an excess of optimism, moralism and this worldliness, it almost wholly discounted the *eschatological* dimension of Jesus' message and experience. This deficiency was ruthlessly exposed at the turn of the century by the studies of J. Weiss and A. Schweitzer, which demonstrated conclusively that eschatology is an integral part of Jesus' message, that his outlook was inescapably eschatological.[1] Harnack's attempt to minimize the link between Jesus' teaching and Judaism and to dismiss apocalypticism as 'a religion of miserabilism', the Jewish husk which should not be allowed to obscure the quite different kernel of his message,[2] was a quite inadequate counter to Weiss. As is generally recognized, there is no going back behind Weiss and Schweitzer, inadequate and lopsided though their treatments were. We may not ignore the eschatological and apocalyptic[3] dimension of Jesus' ministry and self-understanding.

7.2   *The twentieth-century way of eschatology.* Without treading the well-worn path of the debate about Jesus and eschatology/apocalyptic, we may simply note that the element of eschatology in Jesus' teaching which is relevant to our study has more recently and more adequately been expressed in two ways. The first is in terms of Jesus' proclamation of the presence of the future kingdom – his claim that the new age of apocalyptic hope was in some sense already present. Thus, for example, Bornkamm, commenting on this note as that which distinguished Jesus from John the Baptist states:

Between these two and their preaching there is a difference like that between the eleventh and the twelfth hours. For Jesus calls: The shift in the aeons is here, the kingdom of God is already dawning.[4]

There is now a considerable consensus in favour of the view that Jesus proclaimed the presence in some sense of what had thitherto been regarded as the 'still future kingdom'.[5] E. Käsemann would go so far as wholly to exclude the apocalyptic note of futurity from Jesus' preaching, as inconsistent with his proclamation of 'the immediacy of the God who was near at hand';[6] but to set a non-apocalyptic Jesus between an apocalyptic John the Baptist on the one hand and an apocalyptic primitive Christian community on the other, is to strain the 'criterion of dissimilarity' beyond breaking point.[7] However, without denying the apocalyptic note in Jesus' preaching, the emphasis most relevant to our study is that of realized eschatology.

The second eschatological aspect of Jesus' preaching goes with the first – viz., the high authority implicitly claimed by Jesus. Referring particularly to the ἐγὼ δὲ λέγω ('But I say') sayings of Jesus (Matt. 5), Käsemann launched the 'new quest of the historical Jesus' by calling attention to this claim to authority as 'the distinctive element in the mission of Jesus':

Jesus felt himself in a position to override with an unparalleled and sovereign freedom, the words of the Torah and the authority of Moses.[8]

The antitheses of Matt. 5 have since proved a less certain *entrée* to the historical Jesus: Bultmann had already distinguished three of the antitheses as primary (Matt. 5.21f., 27f., 33–7) from the others which he considered to be Matthean formulations on the basis of these three.[9] But the distinction has recently been questioned and the suggestion made that all the antitheses are Matthean formulations,[10] although the possibly implied antithesis of Luke 6.27 may still offer support for the view that some of the antitheses are pre-Matthean.[11] Be that as it may, the note of authority present in Jesus' ministry is too widespread and well-grounded in the tradition to be dismissed – not simply in what Jeremias calls 'the emphatic ἐγώ ('I'),[12] but also in Jesus' use of ἀμήν (*amēn*), which even on the strictest criteria must be counted as a characteristic feature of Jesus' speech, since it lacks parallel elsewhere in Jewish literature and the rest of the NT.[13] It is also implicit in the sovereign freedom of his conduct with respect to sabbath and ceremonial law and in the openness of his table fellowship to taxcollectors and prostitutes;[14] and is most explicit, as we shall see shortly, in his exorcisms.

7.3 *Jesus' eschatological consciousness*. A second answer to our basic questions is obviously beginning to emerge. Was Jesus' proclamation of the kingdom's presence merely a logical deduction from certain apocalyptic texts? This is not likely. It is more probable that his message was rooted in his own *sense* that something new and final was happening in him and through him. So too with the note of authority in Jesus' mission: what we are in fact talking about is Jesus' *consciousness* of authority. Only a compelling consciousness of the authority of his words, a powerful certainty that his inspiration or insights were right, could explain the magisterial 'But I say' and the imperious 'Amen'.

So much emerges by way of deduction. Can we substantiate these deductions? And if so, can we thereby investigate this sense of eschatological newness, this consciousness of authority more fully? Can we ask whence it arose with any hope of reaching an answer? Clearly Jesus' own answer would be of first importance and would give us deeper insight into his self-consciousness. As we were able to 'listen in' to Jesus at prayer, can we overhear the historical Jesus speaking on this subject, laying bare the springs of his eschatological convictions and authority?

The answer to these questions fortunately is, Yes. We have a number of sayings of Jesus which throw considerable light on his self-consciousness at this point, above all on *his consciousness of eschatological power, of God's Spirit upon him and working through him*. I refer first to those passages where Jesus speaks about his work as an exorcist, and secondly to those passages where he reveals his conviction that the prophecy of Isa.61.1ff., was being fulfilled in and through him. Finally we shall look more closely at the accounts of Jesus' experience at Jordan to see whether anything more can be gleaned from them in answer to our questions.

§8. JESUS' CONSCIOUSNESS OF SPIRIT – THE POWER OF EXORCISM

8.1 *Jesus' exorcisms*. That Jesus healed mentally deranged and/or 'demon-possessed' people belongs to the base-rock historicity of the gospels. Exorcisms were the one group of miracles to which D. F. Strauss, in his epochal work on the mythical nature of the miracle stories in the gospels, attached a high degree of historical probability.[15] And no developments in gospel criticism since then have given any reason to question his judgment. On the contrary, they have reinforced the essential historicity of Jesus' work as an exorcist.[16]

There are at least two passages where Jesus refers directly to his cure of demoniacs, and in both he seems to give some explanation for his success as an exorcist – Matt. 12.27f./Luke 11.19f. and Mark 3.28f. pars. The tradition at this point is somewhat confused; but a quick comparison of the Synoptics is enough to reveal that four and probably five different sayings have been grouped together by Q and the evangelists: (1) the Beelzebul charge and Jesus' reply – Mark 3.22–6 and its Q parallel, Matt. 12.24–6/Luke 11.15–8; (2) the Spirit/ finger of God saying, which only Q preserves – Matt. 12.27f./ Luke 11.19f.; (3) the strong man saying – Mark 3.27/Matt. 12.29; Luke probably preserves the Q version (Luke 11.21f.), to which was already attached a further probably independent saying, Matt. 12.30/Luke 11.23; (4) the blasphemy saying, Mark 3.28f./Matt. 12.31, 32b, with its Q parallel which Luke preserves in a quite different context – Luke 12.10/Matt. 12.32.[17] How independent they originally were is not clear, but even if they do derive from distinct life-settings there is a wide measure of agreement that these settings in the life of Jesus are very similar or closely parallel – viz., a situation of controversy arising out of Jesus' work as an exorcist.

8.2 *Matt. 12.28/Luke 11.20* There is little dispute about the authenticity of this saying[18] – and rightly so, since it expresses one of the most distinctive and characteristic emphases of Jesus' teaching (the 'present' aspect of the kingdom). Indeed, if we cannot be sure that the Q saying preserved in Matt. 12.28/Luke 11.20 is a genuine saying of Jesus, we might as well give up all hope of rediscovering the historical Jesus, the man or his message.

There is, however, one small problem which confronts us before we can draw out the significance of the logion – viz., the original wording.

If it is {by the Spirit of God ἐν πνεύματι Θεοῦ – Matthew)
by the finger of God (ἐν δακτύλῳ Θεοῦ – Luke)

that I cast out demons,

then has come upon you (ἔφθασεν ἐφ᾽ ὑμᾶς) the kingdom of God.

The question is, did Jesus speak of casting out demons by the *Spirit* of God (Matthew) or by the *finger* of God (Luke)? The principal argument in favour of the Lukan wording is the relative prominence of Spirit in Luke's gospel; he has evidently introduced the or a particular notion of the Spirit on several occasions when his source was less specific (Luke 4.1a, 14; 10.21; 11.13). Thus, had his source read 'Spirit of God' he is hardly likely to have altered the 'Spirit' to 'finger'. There is no denying the cogency of this argument, and most scholars accept the priority of Luke's version.

On the other hand, a number of considerations strengthen the case for the originality of 'Spirit'.

(*a*) The Matthean version speaks simply of 'the kingdom of God'. But Matthew's favourite expression is 'kingdom of *heaven*'. He uses it thirty-three times, but 'kingdom of *God*' only four times. More important, his regular practice on finding 'kingdom of God' in his source is to alter it to 'kingdom of heaven' (Matt. 5.3; 8.11; 10.7; 11.11f.; 13.11, 31, 33; 19.14, 23; perhaps also 4.17). On only one other occasion does he leave his source's 'kingdom of God' unaltered (19.24). This suggests that Matthew has hurried over the Q version of Matt. 12.28 without stopping to modify it as he would normally have done.

(*b*) That Matthew has been influenced to a marked extent by Moses typology in his presentation of Jesus' life and words has been widely recognized, although the thesis of Matthew's Jesus as the new Moses and the Sermon on the Mount as the 'new law' can be pressed too hard.[19] If 'finger of God' had stood in Q, the allusion to Ex. 8.19 (Heb./LXX – 8.15) would have been unmistakable, as it is in Luke 11.20.[20] It must be judged unlikely that Matthew would sacrifice such an unforced allusion to Moses when it would so obviously (and unobjectionably) further his careful parallel between Jesus and Moses. The counter suggestion that Matthew has replaced 'finger' with 'Spirit' is hardly as cogent since the motif of the Spirit is less prominent in Matthew; indeed his opposition to the enthusiasts who over-valued their charismatic powers (Matt. 7.22f.)[21] makes it most improbable that Matthew would go out of his way to heighten the parallel between Jesus and the enthusiasts.[22]

(*c*) If it is hardly likely that Matthew would change 'finger' to 'Spirit' it is quite possible that Luke altered Q's 'Spirit' to 'finger', despite his liking for 'Spirit' references, for although Luke does not have the same marked Moses typology as Matthew, he does have a clear and distinctive Exodus typology.[23] It may well be, therefore, that Luke sacrifices an original Q reference to the Spirit (as he does in Luke 20.42 and perhaps also 21.15) in order to bring out a parallel between the miracles which brought Israel out of bondage (Ex. 7.4f.; 8.19; 9.3, 15) and the mighty works by which the 'stronger man' of the new exodus despoiled Satan of his captives (Luke 11.19–22). Similarly he uses the almost identical metaphor, 'hand of the Lord' (see below), in several passages in Acts where 'Spirit' might have been as or more appropriate (Acts 4.28ff.; 11.21; 13.11).

(d) A more speculative point arises from Luke's three-period view of salvation history. I have suggested elsewhere[24] that Luke believed that at this second stage, the period of Jesus' ministry, Jesus was the uniquely anointed Man of the Spirit, but not yet Lord of the Spirit (an authority which came only with exaltation and Pentecost – Acts 2.33). Luke may therefore have hesitated to use a phrase which could be misunderstood to mean that the Spirit was already, before Pentecost, subordinate to Jesus, that the Spirit, even during his ministry on earth, was merely the instrument of Jesus' will.[25]

I must confess that I find it difficult to reach a final opinion on whether 'Spirit' or 'finger' was original in Q, although the considerations adduced above certainly seem to tip the scales in favour of 'Spirit'.[26] However, the point may be largely academic, since in fact the two concepts are synonymous. 'Spirit' and 'hand of the Lord' (= finger of God; cf. Ex. 3.20; 8.19)[27] are used as equivalent concepts on a number of occasions in the OT (Ezek. 3.14; 8.1–3; 37.1; cf. Ps. 8.3 with 33.6, I Kings 18.12 with II Kings 2.16, I Chron. 28.12 with 28.19; Isa. 8.11).[28] This is natural, since both are ways of describing the powerful action of God. The equation, finger of God = power of God = Spirit of God, is one which arises directly out of the Hebrew understanding of God's action (see below n. 31), and one which was obvious to either Matthew or Luke when he altered the Q original. Thus, whatever the precise language of Q at this point, its meaning is quite clear: Jesus claimed that his exorcisms were performed by the power of God.

8.3   *The significance of Matt. 12.28/ Luke 11.20.* I need not elaborate on the meaning of the individual elements of the logion – demons, kingdom of God, and Spirit/finger of God. Anyone who is familiar with NT or biblical studies will be able to understand and enter sympathetically (to some extent) into the thought world of the ancient near East. For any less familiar with this thought world I will simply mention the key points. Belief in demons was widespread throughout the ancient world, in particular the belief that evil spirits could enter, possess and control a human person using him as the instrument of superhuman knowledge or power.[29] 'Kingdom of God' was one, though only one, of Judaism's ways of speaking about the hoped for new age, the eschatological age, when God's rule would be fully realized, his people (Israel) vindicated, and his enemies judged; in apocalyptic thought the distinction between the present age and the age to come became much deeper and sharper, though apocalyptists did not use the phrase 'kingdom of God' very much.[30] 'Spirit of God' in Judaism denoted the power of God which could take hold of a man and inspire him to act as God's prophet in word or deed; the outpouring of the prophetic Spirit in plentiful supply upon Israel was commonly regarded as one of the chief blessings and hallmarks of the new age.[31]

The important points for our present study are as follows:

(a) Jesus believed that he cast out demons by the power of God. Here coming to clear expression is *Jesus' consciousness of spiritual power, the visible evidence of the power of God flowing through him to overcome other superhuman power, evil power, to restore and make whole*. We should not attempt to discount this sense of divine power, to 'demythologize' it, as though we now in the twentieth century are somehow in a better position to determine the facts. This was no mere expertise of technique, a 'way' with people; nor was it basically a sense of possessing a power of his own, a 'strong personality'. It was an *awareness* of *otherly* power working through him, together with the *conviction* that this power was *God's* power. In his action God acted. When he spoke or stretched out his hand *something happened* – the sufferer was relieved, the prisoner freed, the evil departed; this could only be the power of God. Here, we may already conclude, is the source of Jesus' authority – the sense that God's Spirit was ready to act through him, the knowledge that God would use him to heal, to overcome demons when they confronted him.

(b) There was something wholly distinctive, indeed *unique* about this consciousness of power. So far as Jesus was concerned, the exercise of this power was *evidence that the longed-for kingdom of God had already come upon his hearers*; his exorcisms demonstrated that the last days were already present.[32] We should not permit our familiarity with this aspect of Jesus' preaching to dull the edge of his assertion. For this was an astonishing and audacious claim. The *eschatological* kingdom was *already present*![33] The apocalyptic precursors and accompaniments were nowhere visible: the old age had not yet been brought to an end, there were no cosmic convulsions or nationalistic triumphs, the messianic woes had not been experienced, the Gentiles were neither being destroyed nor brought in. Jesus certainly believed that (some of) these features of the Eschaton would *soon* be fulfilled.[34] Yet something had happened which enabled him to distinguish the *power* of the End kingdom from the consummation of the End itself. This could only be his consciousness of effective spiritual power – such power as he believed belonged only to the end-time. The power he was so vitally aware of was that power which the prophets had looked for and longed for – the power (the Spirit) they thought was reserved for the messianic age, the kingdom of God. But Jesus experienced such a fulness of this divine power in him and through him that he could only conclude that the kingdom had already come.

The distinctiveness of Jesus' sense of divine power is further under-lined when we consider Matt. 12.27 in conjunction with v. 28 – assuming that the two sentences belonged together from the first.[35] When Jesus compared his work with that of contemporary Jewish exorcists he was simply using an *ad hominen* argument. He did *not* imply that the Jewish exorcisms likewise demonstrated the presentness of the kingdom. On the contrary, he distinguished himself from them;[36] *his* exorcisms were performed by the *Spirit/finger of God*.[37] This is so too in the following saying about the binding of the strong man (Matt. 12.29/Mark 3.27/Luke 11.21f.).[38] Jesus saw his exorcisms not merely as the healing of demented people, not merely as the casting out of demons, not merely as a victory over Satan, but as that binding of the powers of evil which was looked for at the end of the age.[39] The final battle was already joined and Satan was already being routed (cf. Luke 10.18).[40] These claims imply *a clear sense of the eschatological distinctiveness of his power:* Jesus' mighty acts were in his own eyes as epochal as the miracles of the Exodus and likewise heralded a new age. This distinctiveness of Jesus' consciousness of the eschatological Spirit is in these two sayings more clearly delineated than the dis-tinctiveness of his consciousness of sonship.

(c) It is important to grasp precisely what it was that led Jesus to the conclusion that the eschatological rule of God was already operative. It was *not* present because *he* was present; 'where Jesus is, there is the kingdom', is more or less how it is usually expressed. This gives Jesus a uniqueness he did not claim. *The eschatological kingdom was present for Jesus only because the eschatological Spirit was present in and through him:*

'Since it is by the *Spirit of God* that I cast out the demons,
then has come upon you the *kingdom of God*'.

In other words, it was not so much a case of 'Where *I* am there is the kingdom', as, 'Where the *Spirit* is there is the kingdom'. It was the manifestation of the power of God, which was the sign of the kingdom of God.[41] Similarly in Mark 3.27 pars. it was no doubt Jesus' conviction that it was only by virtue of the eschatological Spirit acting through him that he was able to bind the strong man (Satan). Of course, later christological deduction emphasized that it was not merely the unique empowering of the Spirit that made the difference, but the unique empowering of *the unique man Jesus*.[42] But there is little to indicate that the second half of this christological corollary was already present in Jesus' mind. All we can say so far with firm confidence is that Jesus saw in his experience of power to cast out demons a manifestation of God, and of God acting through him in a decisively new and final way.

8.4   *Mark 3.28f./Matt. 12.31f./Luke 12.10.* This is the most disputed of the four 'exorcism sayings' collected by Q and Mark.

Matthew 12.31f.	*Mark 3.28f.*	*Luke 12.10*
Therefore I tell you, every sin and blasphemy will be forgiven men, but the blasphemy against the Spirit will not be forgiven. And whoever says a word against the Son of Man will be forgiven; but whoever speaks against the Holy Spirit will not be forgiven; either in this age or in the age to come.	Truly, I say to you, all sins will be forgiven the sons of men, and whatever blasphemies they utter; but whoever blasphemes against the Holy Spirit never has forgiveness, but is guilty of an eternal sin.	And every one who speaks a word against the Son of Man will be forgiven; but he who blasphemes against the Holy Spirit will not be forgiven.

The synopsis makes it quite clear that the same saying has been preserved in two forms by Mark and Q;[43] Luke has preserved the Q form, but in a different context; Matthew has run Mark and Q together to form a composite logion. The most striking difference between Mark and Q is that Q reads 'the Son of Man' while Mark reads 'the sons of men'.

(*a*) Which of the forms, Mark or Q, is original? The most probable answer is, Neither. Both forms of the logion probably stem from an original Aramaic saying which could be taken either way. That is to say, behind 'the sons of men' and 'the Son of Man' probably stands the generic singular, *bar nasa* – 'the son of man' = 'man' in Aramaic idiom – which could be taken in effect either as subject or as object of the verb 'speak against/blaspheme'. Thus, on one plausible reconstruction of the Aramaic original, the sentence could be read either as, 'All (= everything) that (the son of) man blasphemes will be forgiven him . . .', or as, 'All (= everyone) who speaks against the son of man will be forgiven . . .'.[44]

H. E. Tödt has argued strongly against Wellhausen that Q preserves the more primitive form of the saying.[45] But apart from the plausibility of the case just presented, there are several other considerations which militate against Tödt's view. (1) The ἀμὴν λέγω ὑμῖν ('Truly, I say to you') of Mark 3.28 is a sign of the primitiveness of the form, an indication of the immediacy of inspiration, whether of Jesus or of an early Christian prophet. It is less likely that the phrase was introduced at the stage of literary redaction.[46] (2) The unusual 'the sons of men', although a well-known semitism, is without parallel in the sayings attributed to Jesus,[47] and is unlikely to have been introduced once the more familiar phrase, 'the son of man' had become established. (3) Matt.|12.31a appears to be a tidying up of Mark 3.28, and Luke 12.10b seems to unite elements from Matt. 12.31b (Q) and Mark 3.29;[48] it is less likely that Mark's clumsy form was a development from the Q tradition. It is true, on the other hand, that Q's 'whoever speaks against the Holy Spirit' almost certainly preserves the Aramaic more literally than Mark's βλασφημήσῃ ('blasphemes').[49] But this does not mean that Mark's form originated in Greek,[50] or that the underlying Aramaic version of Mark 3.28f. is later than the Aramaic of Q, since βλασφημεῖν is a quite appropriate translation of the Aramaic 'speak against' (cf. Dan. 3.29).[51]

In short, so far as literary analysis takes us, the most cogent reconstruction of the tradition history of this saying is that it originated in Aramaic in a form of words which could be understood in the two ways preserved for us by Mark and Q.

(*b*) Where did the saying originate? It has frequently been urged that the saying, especially in its Q form, first emerged in the mission or controversies of the primitive Palestinian community, perhaps as a 'sentence of holy law'.[52] In this form it would contrast hostility towards the earthly Jesus, either during his ministry or thereafter, as forgivable, with hostility towards the Holy Spirit, manifested in the mission and utterances of the community, as *un*forgivable; and so would testify to the very strong consciousness within the early community of its own inspiration. Others have urged that the saying has a 'Pentecostal content', that the unforgivable sin only became possible after the full manifestation of the Spirit at Pentecost.[53]

Plausible though this seems, we must however ask whether it is likely that a contrast between Jesus as Son of Man and Spirit-possessing believers would have been drawn so sharply and so acceptably within the early churches. (1) Would 'the Son of Man' have been used on the 'wrong' side of such an antithesis? Accepting for the moment that 'the Son of Man' was a popular title for Jesus in the primitive community (see further below pp. 159f.), and that it was coming to be used for Jesus in his pre-Easter humility, as Tödt argues, would they so neatly have pigeon-holed and distinguished different types of 'Son of Man' sayings (in twentieth-century style!), so that blasphemy against the Son of Man was acceptable?[54] (2) Even if we accept this possibility, is it so likely that early prophets would have set their own inspiration above the inspiration of the albeit earthly Son of Man? To blaspheme the earthly Jesus, though anointed with the Spirit, was acceptable; to reject the prophet's message inspired by the same Spirit was unforgivable! There is no doubt that the tradition of the saying developed in the direction of heightening the contrast between blasphemy against the Son (of man) and blasphemy against the Spirit – the Gospel of Thomas, (logion 44) makes that clear enough.[55] But that says nothing as to the saying's origin. (3) The thesis of a post-Easter saying ignores the fact that in the early communities prophetic oracles were not accepted without question as words of the exalted Lord. The danger of false prophecy would be familiar to all Jewish Christians, and the necessity of *testing* prophetic utterances would be little disputed in Christian communities (see further below pp. 173f. and §41.3). The same considerations apply if 'the Son of Man' form of the saying was an interpretation of a less precise Aramaic prophecy. To interpret a word of the earthly Jesus in the Q way was one thing. To interpret a word of prophecy spoken in an early Christian assembly in the same way was another. That such a word could have been uttered in the *hubris* of inspiration is of course quite possible (cf. I Cor. 12.3); that it would be accepted by the primitive community and become a prized part of the Jesus-tradition is most unlikely – or are we to assume that Matt. 10.32f./Luke 12.8f. and I Cor. 12.3 were directed against the primitive Jewish Christian community?! In particular, Matthew would be hardly likely to incorporate such a logion (see Matt. 7.22f.) were it not a saying firmly rooted in the tradition of Jesus' words spoken during his ministry, rather than some more contentious oracle of the exalted Lord as claimed by an enthusiastic prophet.[56]

Above all, in attempting to gain a proper appreciation of the sense of prophetic inspiration among the early Christian churches, we should not forget that the first to experience and claim this inspiration in such measure was Jesus himself. We have already seen this in the case of his exorcisms (Matt. 12.28/Luke 11.20 – see above §8.3), and it will become even clearer as we proceed (see below §9). Jesus has more claim to be considered as an eschatological prophet, in terms of his powerful consciousness of the inspiration of the end-time, than any of the unknown prophets of the primitive Palestinian churches.

I can only conclude that the most probable origin of the saying in its more ambiguous Aramaic form is the controversy stirred up within the historical ministry of Jesus by his exorcisms.[57] Mark's setting is unquestionably appropriate, whereas Luke's can hardly be intended to be original.[58] The context of the logion and the logic of Jesus' reasoning is itself sufficient explanation of how the saying could be interpreted in the two different ways. I would suggest that the most plausible life-setting is as follows. The number and variety of sayings preserved here by Mark and Q indicate that Jesus' ministry of exorcism brought forth charges and criticisms against Jesus on more than one occasion. In one case he responded to the criticisms levelled against him by warning his critics of the seriousness of their charge. His power to cast out demons was the Spirit of God. Therefore criticism of his exorcisms was a speaking against God's Spirit. Now for all sorts of slanders and other sins there was every chance of forgiveness, but to slander and reject the manifest power of God in overcoming illness and evil was to commit the unpardonable sin. This is more or less the form in which Mark has preserved the saying. But the Q tradition, also conscious of the original setting of the saying, sharpened its antithetical form by interpreting the forgivable slander in terms of the criticism which called the saying forth. Jesus must be referring to this criticism in both parts of the logion.[59] If the critic had failed to recognize the source of Jesus' power and was criticizing only Jesus, *bar nasa*, his sin was forgivable. But if he was wilfully ignoring the plain evidence of his eyes, that the power was God's Spirit, then he was putting himself in a position where forgiveness could not reach him.

8.5 *The significance of Mark 3.28f. pars.* This logion also throws important light on Jesus' experience of God.

(a) Again *his consciousness of spiritual power* is evident. His sensation of power was no mere light-headedness, no wishful thinking; when he spoke the demon obeyed, the demoniac was liberated. This could only be the Spirit of God at work through him. Here we have expressed again the consciousness of such power as could only be understood in terms of the promised end-time Spirit. Jesus was convinced that his exorcisms constituted clear evidence that the 'drought' of the Spirit had ended.[60] He was experiencing here and now 'the powers of the age to come' (Heb. 6.5).

(b) *The source of his power was self-evident to Jesus.* His critics could not deny his power; the charge of Satan possession indicates their recognition that Jesus was a man possessed by powerful spiritual forces, though they tried to explain it away as evil spiritual power. But the beneficial effects made it abundantly plain to Jesus that it was a power for good. Indeed he seems to have treated their attack with some scorn. It was so obvious to him that the power he experienced and demonstrated was of God that he was rather short with those who refused to recognize what was so unambiguous. What Jesus in effect said to his critics is: 'You may think you are criticizing only me, but surely you must realize that you are in fact blaspheming the Spirit'.[61]

(c) *The uniqueness of Jesus' consciousness of eschatological empowering* comes through very strongly in this logion – in the seriousness with which he regarded the criticisms of his exorcistic activity. To reject or deny the power he displayed was to put the critic beyond forgiveness! *All* other sins and blasphemies could be forgiven – including presumably curses directed against heavenly beings, even against the name of God itself (despite Lev. 24.11ff.)![62] For the rabbis 'to speak against the Holy Spirit' would mean 'to speak against the Torah'.[63] Jesus put his own inspiration above that of the Torah! Here indeed is a consciousness of Spirit without real parallel at the time. Here we see coming to clear expression Jesus' sense of the awfulness, the numinous quality, the eschatological finality of the power which possessed him.[64] In him, in his action, God was present and active in a decisive and final way – to reject his ministry was to reject God and so to reject forgiveness.

§9. JESUS' CONSCIOUSNESS OF SPIRIT – THE ANOINTED ONE OF ISA. 61.1

In Jesus' understanding of his exorcisms we have begun to see into the

heart of his authority and of his eschatological convictions. His consciousness of a spiritual power so real, so effective, so new, so final,
was the well-spring of both his proclamation of the presentness of the
future kingdom and his authority in deed and word. This consciousness is summed up in the word 'Spirit'. His awareness of being
uniquely possessed and used by divine Spirit was the mainspring of
his mission and the key to its effectiveness. This conclusion gains
strength when we weave it into another strand of synoptic material
which we can trace back into a situation in the life of Jesus with
confidence. I refer to the sayings which draw on Isa.61.1 – Luke
4.18f.(?), Luke 6.20f./Matt.5.3–6 and Matt.11.2–6/Luke 7.18–23.

9.1   *Luke 4.18f.* is the only formal quotation of Isa.61.1f.; Jesus in
the synagogue at Nazareth makes explicit claim to fulfil the Isaianic
prophecy – he has been anointed with the Spirit of the Lord. If this
were an authentic tradition it would afford an invaluable insight into
Jesus' consciousness of Spirit. However, the whole passage is almost
certainly a Lukan construction on the basis of Mark or a variant
tradition similar to Mark, as most commentators recognize.[65] The
unprompted and open claim to messianic significance at the *beginning* of
Jesus' ministry is too far removed from what we know of the historical
Jesus from the Synoptics themselves, and too similar to the un-
historical roll-call of christological titles in the first chapter of John's
gospel to permit a contrary judgment. To be sure, some scholars have
suggested that Luke 4.16–30 belongs to Q, and H. Schürmann has
recently argued the case with care and some persuasion.[66] But his
argument does not take us much further since he is of the opinion
that though Luke 4.17–21, 25–27 belong to Q, they are nevertheless
secondary expansions of the original narrative by Christian apologists.[67] In any case, Schürmann's attempt to attach the Lukan
Nazareth pericope to Q does not carry conviction. It is questionable
whether the Q material had already reached such an advanced stage
in its literary development, and we know that Luke was influenced
by Isa.61.1 independently of Q (Acts 10.38). Moreover, why
Matthew should ignore such a Q tradition with its emphasis on Jesus'
fulfilment of scripture is not at all clear.[68] It remains more probable
therefore that Luke himself is responsible for setting the words from
Isa.61.1f. on the lips of Jesus; this opening announcement proclaims
the character of Jesus' ministry; his subsequent words and deeds
must be seen as the fulfilment of this text.[69]

In short, it is clear that Luke himself was influenced by Isa.61.1
in his understanding and presentation of Jesus' ministry. The only

question therefore which arises for us from Luke 4.18f. is whether Luke's presentation of Jesus was inspired by authentic Jesus-tradition to the same effect? Does his Christology have historical justification?

9.2   This brings us to the second allusion to Isa.61.1 – *Luke 6.20bf./ Matt.5.3–6*. There are certainly redactional elements present in both passages, as the characteristic Matthean phrase 'the kingdom of heaven' and reference to 'righteousness' make clear;[70] and Luke has probably altered the order and wording to make for a closer parallel with the equivalent, albeit secondary 'Woes' (Luke 6.24f.).[71] But the correspondence between Luke 6.20f. and Matt.5.3–6 is sufficiently close to assure us that we are directly in touch with Q material. Moreover, it is almost certain that this Q passage has preserved authentic words of Jesus, as most scholars agree – the *eschatological* μακάριος ('Blessed') is almost as distinctive of Jesus' speech as 'Abba' and 'amen'.

The significant fact for our study is that these Beatitudes have been determinatively influenced by Isa.61.1ff.; 'the poor' and 'those who weep/mourn' clearly describe a group identical with those envisaged by the prophet.[72] This means that Isa.61.1 played an important role in Jesus' own thinking. He believed that those who heard him, probably his own disciples, were the 'poor' of whom Isa.61.1 spoke – that is, the chosen ones of God who were now experiencing the sufferings of the end-time, but who would shortly enjoy the healing and liberty of God's kingdom.[73] Furthermore, the implication is that since Jesus is the one who speaks these words, he is the one who fulfils the role of the Spirit-anointed figure of Isa.61.1: the beatitudes themselves are a proclamation of the good news to the poor. The probability is therefore that in uttering these words Jesus gave expression to a basic conviction: viz., that he had been anointed by the Spirit of God, commissioned to proclaim the good news of the end-time kingdom. Moreover, we should not ignore the manifest strength of this conviction, for the beatitudes can hardly be understood as constituting a *claim* to eschatological significance. Rather by their very style and content they seem to express an *already established*, deeply held and firm assurance of Jesus that the Isaianic prophecy was being fulfilled in himself and in his ministry.

9.3   Even more explicit is our third passage – *Matt.11.2–6/Luke 7.18–23*, particularly the words of Jesus:

Go and tell John what you have seen and heard:
the blind receive their sight,

(and) the lame walk,
lepers are cleansed,
and the deaf hear,
(and) the dead are raised to life,
(and) the poor hear the good news.
And blessed is he who takes no offence at me.

The pericope as a whole has been under suspicion since Strauss pointed out how improbable it was that the Baptist could transmit and receive messages while in prison, whereas there was an obvious apologetic motive in fabricating an episode which demonstrated that the Baptist recognized Jesus as Messiah in some way before his death.[74] Even more decisive has been the consideration that the herald of an apocalyptic figure of fiery judgment could hardly have thought of identifying the Coming One with Jesus.

There is for John no possible meeting-ground between the wonder-working preacher of the Kingdom and the transcendent 'man-like one' who destroys the wicked in unquenchable fire, save on the assumption of a break with his fundamental convictions, for which there is no adequate justification.[75]

We may add that Matthew's 'the deeds of Christ' (11.2) and Luke's description of Jesus as 'the Lord' (7.19) – as perhaps also the phrases 'lepers are cleansed', and 'the dead are raised to life' (Matt. 11.5/Luke 7.22) – show clearly that the episode is regarded from a post-resurrection viewpoint.

W. G. Kümmel attempts to defend the narrative's essential historicity, but the attempt falls short of proof, particularly since he fails to take adequate account of the pericope's context in Q. It is true that ὁ ἐρχόμενος ('the coming one') 'was by no means a customary designation in the early church nor a current Jewish one',[76] but it was familiar to the Q community (Matt. 23.39/Luke 13.35), and the question could have arisen from the (Q?) tradition of the Baptist's preaching.[77] Similarly the argument that 'legend would not have allowed the Baptist, whom it portrayed as Jesus' herald, to give evidence of half-faith by his answers'[78] hardly applies to Q. Of a Baptist testimony to Jesus at Jordan there is no trace in Q. Indeed such testimony only really appears in the distinctively and late Matthean and Johannine accounts of the episode at Jordan. Strauss's thesis concerning the development in the traditions about relations between the Baptist and Jesus is by no means without foundation.[79] Of greater weight is the observation that the story fails to narrate the Baptist's reaction to Jesus' message, for if the tradition was inspired by a growing apologetic desire to present John as a witness to Jesus' messiahship, then one would expect the climax of the account to be some expression of John's submissive faith (cf. Matt. 3.14f.). On the other hand, the absence of such reaction may simply be due to the tradition being formulated as an apophthegm or pronouncement-story: the saying of Jesus is the climax.[80] The most weighty of Kümmel's considerations is the veiled nature of Jesus' response;[81] for though it could just possibly be explained by a Q form of the 'messianic secret', its similarity to other probably authentic words of Jesus (Luke 10.23f./Matt. 13.16f.) tells strongly in favour of the authenticity of Matt. 11.5–6 as genuine words of Jesus.

This last fact has led many scholars to the judgment that the pericope as a whole is a composite production, and that the last two verses originally had an independent existence. They probably go back to Jesus, but the framework is secondary, the work of a Christian (probably Q) community. An influential form of this thesis is the view that the roots of the tradition in its present form are to be found in an argument between the early Christian community and continuing followers of the Baptist about the significance of Jesus.[82] Others think the episode has its origin among those who had been influenced by the Baptist's teaching, possibly disciples of John, and who now sought to reconcile this with their faith in Jesus.[83]

The pericope can be recognized as a literary reflex of the transfer of the Baptist's proclamation to the prophet Jesus of Nazareth which the (Q) group had itself brought about.[84]

The difficulty with both these suggestions is that they do not really resolve the central problem: viz., How, and in what sense, does Matt. 11.4ff. answer the Baptist's question? Fridrichsen's original suggestion took the question of the Baptist's disciples as equivalent to 'Are you the Messiah?'; the continuing disciples of the Baptist disputed the messianic character of Jesus' acts (cf. 'the deeds of the Christ' – Matt. 11.2).[85] But for one thing the equation 'Coming One = Messiah' derives more from the Matthean editing than from the Q tradition of the Baptist's preaching[86] and for another, in Judaism Messiah was not expected to be a worker of wonders.[87] So neither question nor answer appear to be particularly appropriate.

P. Stuhlmacher reshapes Fridrichsen's thesis in terms of the eschatological Prophet. The one eschatological figure of whom signs were expected in Judaism was the Prophet.[88] Moreover, 11QMelch. is proof that already in Judaism the figure of Isa. 61.1 had been identified with the eschatological Prophet.[89] He therefore suggests that the dispute between the Baptist group and the early Christians was over whether John or Jesus was the expected Prophet. The miracles and the fulfilment of Isa. 61.1 would constitute decisive proof of the Christians' claim.[90] But this thesis is little better than the last. For one thing, the evidence that the eschatological Prophet would be a wonder worker is very slight: the only concrete references are from Josephus, and there the miracles (expected but not actually performed) are *wonders*, of a quite different character from those claimed in Matt. 11.5 – usually re-enactments of the wilderness and conquest miracles.[91] And for another, if the dispute was about who was the Prophet, John or Jesus, where does the question 'Are you the Coming One?' derive from, and what function does it fulfil in the pericope?[92] *No thesis can be regarded as satisfactory which fails to explain the relation of John's question to Jesus' answer.*

The same problem proves to be the weak link in Hoffmann's hypothesis. If the question of Matt. 11.3 is prompted by the Baptist's proclamation of the Coming One as a fire-dispensing figure of final judgment, then vv. 4–6 are hardly an appropriate answer for the Christian community to give. For those who have already identified the exalted Jesus with the coming Son of Man (the Q community),[93] the sort of answer which one would expect is, 'I am; and you will see the Son of Man sitting at the right hand of power, and coming (ἐρχόμενον) with the clouds of heaven' (Mark 14.62). Matt. 11.4–6 is scarcely credible as the answer of a Christian (Q) community to the question, 'Is Jesus the Coming One?' for the answer appears to be, No! not the Coming One, but the Prophet (Isa. 61.1). To argue in reply that Matt. 11.5 really means: Jesus is *now* the Coming One soon to return as fiery judge because in his life on earth he was *already* the eschatological Prophet and forerunner of God,[94] is to pack a wealth of interpretation into 11.5 (particularly on the relation of Prophet to Coming One) that the verse hardly contains. In short, if the Baptist's question is inappropriate in Stuhlmacher's hypothesis, the same holds true of Jesus' answer in Hoffmann's.

The central problem thus remains: to relate Jesus' answer to the Baptist's question in a satisfactory manner. Several points call for comment.

(*a*) Verse 5, whether an authentic word of Jesus or not, cannot be understood except as a reference to actual events in Jesus' ministry. The parallel of Luke 10.23f./Matt. 13.16f. falls short precisely at this point. Q is not simply taking colours from Second Isaiah and painting a picture of final blessedness without relating the particular statements to particular events for which Jesus was responsible.[95] Unless Jesus actually did bring sight to the blind, cause the lame to walk, etc., at least by repute, then the saying is meaningless. In other words, the context (vv. 4, 6) only brings to sharper expression what is implicit in v. 5 – viz., that it is the manifest power of Jesus which is the sign that the end-time prophecies are fulfilled.

(b) Verse 6 could conceivably have existed as an independent saying of Jesus.[96] But were that the case it would probably have been applied to more than one situation and tradition by the early community, as, for example, with Mark 10.31 = Matt. 19.30; Matt. 20.16; Luke 13.30, the 'He that has ears (to hear) let him hear' saying (preserved in five different contexts), and the 'there shall be weeping and grinding of teeth' saying (six times in Matthew). It is more likely that vv. 5 and 6 were joined from the first.[97] For one thing, v. 5 could only have point if it referred to the works and words of Jesus – the 'in me' of v. 6 only brings this point to sharper expression. And for another, Isa. 61.1 seems to be a source of inspiration common to Jesus' eschatological $\mu\alpha\kappa\dot\alpha\rho\iota\sigma$[98] and to v. 5, and so ties v. 5 and v. 6 together – not at the literary level, be it noted, but at the level of prophetic inspiration.

(c) As vv. 5–6 hang together, so do vv. 4b and 5. The association in v. 4b of 'hearing' and 'seeing' is unusual in the context of Jewish end-time expectation and may well have been characteristic of Jesus in reference to the words and deeds of his ministry – as again Luke 10.23f./Matt. 13.16f. in conjunction with Matt. 11.4/Luke 7.22 implies.[99] If this is the case, then v. 4b can hardly stand by itself without v. 5, and both must be regarded as in all probability authentic words of Jesus.

(d) v. 4b carries with it the reference to John and raises the possibility that the question, 'Are you the Coming One?' was indeed put to Jesus during his life by disciples of the Baptist. This possibility gains strength from two considerations. First, we must ask, When would the question of Matt. 11.3 arise? The most obvious answer is, *As soon as the note of imminence characteristic of John's preaching was supplanted or at least supplemented by the note of fulfilment characteristic of Jesus' preaching.* As soon as the presence of the kingdom was proclaimed, the Baptist's camp would inevitably ask, Where is the judgment proclaimed by the Baptist as the chief mark of the end-time? This question could be expressed in the form 'Are you the Coming One, or should we look for another?', for the Coming One was to bring in the end-time, and Jesus' proclamation clearly implies that *his* works, particularly of exorcism, prove the presence of the end-time. The question of Matt. 11.3, whether posed in terms of enquiring bewilderment or polemical sarcasm, slots very naturally therefore into a situation in the life of Jesus.

Second, the words of Jesus in vv. 4–6 speak directly to the question as explicated above. For, as Jeremias has observed, each of the three Isaiah passages alluded to by Jesus (Isa. 35.5f., 29.18f., 61.1) contains an equal promise or warning of judgment: Isa. 35.4 - 'Behold, your God comes with vengeance'; Isa. 29.20 - 'The ruthless shall come to nought'; Isa. 61.2 - 'the day of vengeance of our God'.[100] By alluding to these passages Jesus acknowledges the point of the Baptist's question and speaks to it. He says in effect: 'Despite the absence of judgment, the blessings promised for the end-time prove that it is already here. The day of God's vengeance is not yet; the year of the Lord's favour is now' (cf. Luke 4.19). 'Blessed is he who does not find me a stumbling block' (v. 6) matches this precisely: the stumbling block is Jesus' proclamation of the presence of God's eschatological grace and the 'not just yet' of his final judgment; the ones who might stumble are those who have believed the warnings of the Baptist.

The conclusion seems obvious: question and answer fit so neatly within the life-situation of Jesus and lack coherence if either or both were first prompted by a post-Easter situation, that the substance at least of the account must be regarded as historical. Jesus' words in vv. 4-6 only really make sense as an answer to such a question posed by disciples of the Baptist.

9.4 *The significance of the Isa. 61.1 passages* for our present study can be briefly stated.

(*a*) Jesus regarded his deeds and words as indications of the end-time, proof that the end-time prophecies had been fulfilled. As Bultmann noted, *'the immediacy of eschatological consciousness'* is given emphatic expression in Matt. 11.5f./Luke 7.22f., as in Luke 10.23f./Matt. 13.16f.[101] This confirms and extends the conclusions drawn from Matt. 12.28/Luke 11.20 and Mark 3.28f. pars.; that Jesus saw in the wide range of healings (not just exorcisms) which resulted from his ministry signs of the kingdom's presence. Whatever the 'facts' were, Jesus evidently believed that he had cured cases of blindness, lameness and deafness - indeed there is no reason to doubt that he believed lepers had been cured under his ministry and dead restored to life (see further below §12.3). And these were 'signs of God', signs for him of the End - manifestations of salvation, it should be noted, rather than of judgment, as the Baptist expected.

What is most striking at this point, however, is that the climax of Matt. 11.5 is not the miracle of resurrection, but the fact that 'the poor have the gospel preached to them'.[102] More important as an indication of the eschatological Now is the proclamation of the good news to the oppressed. As the beatitudes confirm, the blessedness of the end-time is most clearly expressed in Jesus' gospel for the poor. (The 'gospel' here for Jesus would be his announcement that the poor share in God's kingdom [Luke 6.20], that God's forgiveness and acceptance was for them and was already expressed in the openness of his table-fellowship to 'tax-collectors and sinners'.)[103] This is an important development from the conclusion reached when considering the exorcism passages: *not merely in his exorcisms and healings, but chiefly in his preaching, is God's eschatological reign visible and present.*

(b) As Bultmann also notes, in not altogether characteristic vein, in Matt. 11.5f. we also see Jesus' self-consciousness coming to expression.[104] *Jesus believed himself to be the one in whom Isa. 61.1 found fulfilment; his sense of being inspired was such that he could believe himself to be the end-time prophet of Isa. 61.1*: he had been anointed with the Spirit of the Lord. Luke is quite justified therefore when he depicts Jesus as opening his public ministry in the full conviction and inspiration of the Spirit upon him. The power which he experienced in himself, the power which became evident in his healings (in his exorcisms in particular) and especially in his proclamation of the good news to the poor, was in Jesus' view the eschatological Spirit operating in and through him – the power which brought God's forgiveness and acceptance effectively to his hearers. This power was the rule of God; to experience it in the ministry of Jesus was already to share in the kingdom of God (Luke 6.20).[105]

We should also point out the significance of the fact that Jesus' ministry differed so markedly in character from that expected of the Coming One by the Baptist. Why should Jesus so fully ignore the prophetic expectation of one so obviously inspired (cf. Mark 11.30)? Why did Jesus not see his ministry in terms of judgment? How came he to be so selective in his use of OT prophecy? The most obvious answer is that he had found God in his own experience to be a God of grace more than of judgment. The power which he experienced working through his ministry was a power to heal not to destroy. The message given him to proclaim was the message of God's favour not of God's vengeance. *His own experience of God, of divine power and inspiration, made clear to him what parts of OT prophecy were applicable to and descriptive of his ministry, and what were not.*

We will not do justice to Matt. 11.2–6 unless we draw attention finally to *the strength of Jesus' conviction regarding himself.* This is explicit in v. 6 – he himself, not just his preaching, was the stumbling block. It is also implicit in the question put to Jesus: Jesus had clearly not simply proclaimed the presence of the end-time kingdom, he had proclaimed its presence in himself, or, more precisely, in *his own* ministry. Hence the question was not the impersonal one, 'How can the end-time be present when judgment has not begun?', but, 'Are you the Coming One?', that is, 'Is it *you* who is to bring in the End (as you claim)?' This strength of Jesus' consciousness of inspiration and eschatological significance comes through even more clearly in vv. 5f. for, as we have seen, in Jewish expectation the miracles of v. 5 would not necessarily be regarded as proof of the eschatological significance of the individual who performed them (hence Mark 8.11f. pars.). It is Jesus' overpowering *conviction* that *his* deeds and words are signs of God's end-time rule which meets us in these words. Likewise the blessing of v. 6 is really a very weak response to the Baptist's question, except as the expression of an overwhelming conviction that *he* himself *is* the one anointed by the end-time Spirit, the focus of eschatological significance and so a potential stumbling block for that reason.

§10. SONSHIP AND SPIRIT

It must be clear now that quite basic to Jesus' experience of God, to his self-consciousness and to his understanding of his mission, was his sense of *sonship* and his consciousness of *Spirit*. Before we move on to the next chapter we should make some attempt to examine the relationship of these two facets of Jesus' religious experience. The link between Jesus' sonship and the Spirit is certainly well established in the developed christological reflection of the early church (e.g. John 3.34f., 20.21f.; Acts 2.33; Rom. 1.3f.; Gal. 4.4–6). But within the Synoptics only one passage directly associates 'Son' and 'Spirit' in the case of Jesus – Jesus' experience at Jordan when he had been baptized by John (Mark 1.9–11 pars.).

10.1 *Jesus' experience at Jordan.* As Jeremias points out, the two statements on which all accounts of this episode are agreed are that the Spirit of God descended upon Jesus, and that the descent of the Spirit was followed by a proclamation.[106] We can be more precise: all accounts agree that in the proclamation Jesus was hailed as son.[107]

The question of course has to be asked: is this association of Spirit and son historically justified? Are the accounts rooted in history at this point? There is no doubt that Jesus was actually baptized by John: the difficulty and embarrassment which the *repentance* baptism of *Jesus by John* caused the early churches, particularly in their dealings with disciples of the Baptist or those influenced by the Baptist's message, is already evident in Matt. 3.14f., and perhaps also Acts 19.1–7. Clearly the episode was retained because it had a more than ordinary significance for the life and mission of Jesus. But how much more than the baptism itself remains after critical scrutiny?

On the one hand, there is evident a clear tendency to give the tradition greater objectivity as it was passed on: the personal word, 'You are my son . . .' of Mark 1.11 becomes the open proclamation, '*This* is my son . . .' in Matt. 3.17. In Luke the descent of the Spirit as a dove becomes '*in bodily form* as a dove' (3.22). In the Fourth Gospel the whole event becomes the Baptist's testimony (1.32ff.). In Justin *fire* is kindled in the Jordan (*Dial.* 88.3). And in Epiphanius '*a great light*' shines around the place (*Adv. Haer.* 30.13.7–8). Inevitably we must ask how far this tendency had already shaped the tradition *before* Mark wrote it down.

Secondly, Dibelius points out that if the tradition is historical it would have stemmed from Jesus, in which case it would have taken the form of a saying of Jesus (cf. Acts 7.56).[108]

Thirdly, the Synoptics present this encounter between John and Jesus as tangential in both their careers: with this baptism John's ministry effectively ceases (Mark 1.14; Luke 3.19f.);[109] with this proclamation Jesus is more or less launched in his mission. Whereas the rather odd traditions preserved in John 3.22ff.; 4.1 indicate that there was a considerable degree of overlap between the ministries of John and Jesus. This further suggests that there was a longer and deeper association between John and Jesus, and that Jesus originally underwent baptism at the hands of John in order to associate himself with John in his message and ministry, perhaps initially as John's disciple. This in turn suggests that Jesus' experience at Jordan at his baptism was not so decisive or explicit as the Synoptics portray it.

On the other hand, it is certain that Jesus believed himself to be empowered by the Spirit and thought of himself as God's son. These convictions must have crystallized at some point in his life. Why should the traditions unanimously fasten on this episode in Jesus' life if they had no reason for making the link and many reasons against it? As yet within the NT there is no evidence of the later tendency to portray Jesus' baptism as a prototype of Christian baptism,[110] and to associate Jesus' anointing with his baptism by John played into the hands of Baptist sect apologetic. The most probable reason therefore is that Jesus underwent a significant experience – significant in terms of his consciousness of sonship and Spirit – on the occasion of his baptism by John.[111]

Secondly, although it is likely that there was a longer period of

overlap between John and Jesus, the more weighty evidence implies
that it cannot have been very long, and that the break between John
and Jesus must have come quite quickly. After all, the central
emphasis of their respective proclamations was quite different: John
believed that the end-time was at hand; Jesus believed that the shift
in the aeons had already taken place. And the decisive indication
that the kingdom was present for Jesus was the presence of the *Spirit*
working in and through him. The break between John and Jesus must
therefore have been occasioned by Jesus' awareness of the Spirit: the
eschatological Spirit was already upon him – therefore John's
message and ministry was already superseded. How quickly Jesus
saw these corollaries and applied them is not clear (the retreat to the
wilderness is the obvious period of rethinking), but we should certainly hesitate to read too much into the Fourth Gospel's traditions
about the overlap: they imply only a period of 'competition' between
John and Jesus, not a period when Jesus was John's disciple.

Thirdly, Jesus' answer to the challenge about his authority (Mark
11.27–33 pars.) may well indicate that he himself attached considerable significance to the occasion of his baptism by John.

His counter-question, whether the baptism of John was or was not from God (v. 30)
is hardly an evasion, a move by which Jesus seeks to avoid a direct answer. Now
if his counter-question is meant seriously, it means: 'My authority rests on John's
baptism', and that again will mean in concrete terms: 'My authority rests on what
happened when I was baptized by John'.[112]

Jeremias certainly presses his case over-confidently here. But nevertheless the saying may permit some such inference: that the authority
of the Baptist's ministry had been ratified existentially for Jesus by
God, that is, by Jesus' experience of God when baptized by John.[113]

The objection by Dibelius is a weighty one. But since Strauss it has
not been uncommon to argue that certain sayings of Jesus have been
elaborated into narratives – as for example, the stilling of the storm
(Mark 4.35–41, pars.), the miraculous catch of fishes (Luke 5.1–11),
and perhaps the cursing of the fig tree (Mark 11.12–14 par.).[114]
If this is a real possibility, how much more likely is it that the
(Markan) account of Jesus' experience at Jordan was an elaboration
of some indications given by Jesus to his disciples such as we have just
noted? Moreover, we know from religious history that it was quite
common for a prophetic figure to relate his call to his disciples – so,
for example, Isaiah, Jeremiah and Ezekiel (all visions and audi-
tions);[115] as one instance outside Judaeo-Christianity we might
mention Mohammed.[116] By comparison Jesus seems to have been
much more reserved about describing his experience of God to his

disciples; this is why we have had to depend to such a large extent on inferences and implications of key sayings. The only real parallel to the self testimony of the prophets' religious experiences is Jesus' exultant cry in Luke 10.18: 'I saw Satan fall like lightning from heaven' (see below p.85). We can of course only speculate; but it remains quite probable that Jesus never spoke directly of what happened at Jordan, but made some allusions which have provided the basis of the earliest account. In addition, the fact that the earliest Christian communities seem to have practised baptism from the first is probably best explained by the suggestion that Jesus gave his disciples some indication of how important the occasion of his own baptism was for him.

The case is hardly proved, but we may say with some confidence that Mark's narrative is a quite justifiable interpretation of the event at Jordan, and that historical criticism can speak quite properly of Jesus' experience at his baptism, even though Mark himself is not concerned to present the episode as a piece of biography.[117] *Jesus' baptism by John was probably the occasion for an experience of God which had epochal significance for Jesus*, even though that significance may only have been fully grasped after some reflection by Jesus. The most striking elements of this experience were *Spirit and sonship*. He experienced an insurge of spiritual power and became aware that he was being anointed with the eschatological Spirit of God. The 'like a dove' may have referred originally to a vision, or it may simply have been an interpretative metaphor drawn in when the narrative was first formulated, either to contrast Jesus' experience of Spirit with the fiery purgative experience of Spirit anticipated by the Baptist,[118] or by way of allusion to the epochal role ascribed to the Spirit in creation and to the dove after the flood.[119] As to the heavenly voice, in view of the religious history parallels and the further material reviewed below in ch. IV, it is quite likely that Jesus was convinced that at his baptism he had heard God's voice addressing him as son and setting him apart for a special task (as he had the Baptist).[120]

10.2 *Relationship of Spirit and sonship.* We must note the way in which descent of Spirit is associated with word of sonship in this episode. In the accounts as we have them the words of the proclamation are obviously intended to *explain* the descent of the Spirit: the Spirit anoints Jesus as Son. The allusion to, if not complete citation of Ps. 2.7 (Luke 3.22 D),[121] suggests that *the gift of the Spirit was understood to be Jesus' adoption as Son* – 'You are my son, this day I became your father'.[122] However, it is most doubtful whether we should or are

able to attempt any further analysis of Jesus' consciousness of Spirit
and sonship on the basis of this narrative. The tradition is far from
adequate to feed any speculation as to whether this experience of
Jesus was the climax or decisive 'clincher' of a growing experience of
God, or whether it was something abruptly new and totally unexpected. After all, Q preserves the saying of Jesus where he likens
prayer to a son's request: 'If you, who are evil, know how to give good
gifts to your children, how much more will your Father in heaven
give good things (Luke – 'Holy Spirit') to those who ask him' (Matt.
7.11/Luke 11.13). And we cannot exclude the possibility that this
confidence of Jesus was based partly at least on his own experience at
Jordan; he may have come to the Baptist already with some awareness of God's fatherly care and calling; his baptism may have
expressed his willingness to respond to that call and his request for
the good things necessary to obey it.[123] At any rate we would do
better to treat consciousness of sonship and consciousness of Spirit as
two sides of the one coin. We cannot say that the one gave birth to
the other, and to build dogmatic conclusions on the priority of one or
other is to build on sand, without foundation. The most we can say
on the basis of the Jordan pericope is that from the very beginning
(more or less) of Jesus' ministry he was conscious of God as Father
and of the power of God.

Likewise we cannot assess priority to one or other aspect of his
experience of God in respect to Jesus' mission. The son obeys the
Father's will. The Spirit drives him forth. The two statements
describe the same inward compulsion which could not be denied,
which had to find expression in word and deed. It is not surprising
then that in the account of Jesus' temptations in the wilderness ('The
Spirit drove him into the wilderness' – Mark 1.12 pars.), the two
temptations which are explicitly aimed at his consciousness of sonship ('*If* you are the son of God . . .') are temptations to prove his
sonship by means of miraculous power ('. . . command these stones
to become bread') and through the wonder working of ecstasy
('. . . throw yourself down' from the parapet of the temple).[124]
Likewise, it is precisely the demoniacs who are represented as
recognizing Jesus' *exorcistic power* as that of God's *Son* (Mark 3.11,
5.7).[125] Again, it is perhaps significant that the *authority* of his preaching can be said to derive from his sense of being Spirit-inspired (see
above §9), but also from his sense of sonship (Matt. 11.27). 'Father' as
much as 'Spirit' spells 'authority'. So too is authority present in the
realized eschatology note so distinctive of Jesus' ministry. It expressed
his consciousness of that power of God reserved for the end-time and

manifested particularly in his exorcisms. But it expressed also his consciousness of God as Father, he who had drawn near in forgiveness and healing to deliver the poor. In short, Spirit and sonship, sonship and Spirit, are but two aspects of the one experience of God out of which Jesus lived and ministered.

10.3 *Conclusion.* So far then we have investigated Jesus' religious experience from two sides – his sense of sonship and his consciousness of eschatological Spirit. In both cases the amount of material we have been able to use has been very limited – but that may be due to several reasons, including a reticence on Jesus' part to speak often or openly about his experience of God or about the authority for his actions and words. More important, the paucity of material does not disturb the conclusions we draw from it. The passages we have used (particularly in §§4, 8 and 9) have been of demonstrable authenticity as words of the historical Jesus and however few such sayings are, their resilience in the face of critical scrutiny enables us to draw conclusions from them with confidence. In addition, the material in question has come from key points in Jesus' life – from sayings which reflect his own experience of prayer, and from situations where Jesus' authority was questioned or challenged. The religious experience which is clearly reflected in these sayings cannot be dismissed as peripheral or secondary; on the contrary, the experience on which he draws in such situations is thereby demonstrated to be the source of his spiritual dynamic, the basis of his authority. In short, our contention at the beginning of chapter II (§2.2), that it is possible to see fairly deeply into Jesus' experience of God, at least to the extent that we can begin sympathetically to understand how he conceived of his relation to God, has been vindicated. *Jesus thought of himself as God's son and as anointed by the eschatological Spirit, because in prayer he experienced God as Father and in ministry he experienced a power to heal which he could only understand as the power of the end-time and an inspiration to proclaim a message which he could only understand as the gospel of the end-time.*

We will not elaborate these conclusions in more detail just yet, for our investigations in the present chapter open up another way through the synoptic material and we must explore it before attempting to draw together the threads of our understanding of Jesus' religious experience. I refer to the evidence which marks out Jesus as a charismatic.

IV

WAS JESUS A CHARISMATIC?

§11. INTRODUCTION

Thus far we can say with some assurance that Jesus' understanding of his religious experience in ministry was of a supernatural power (the Spirit of God) inspiring his words to effect forgiveness and his actions to achieve healing. As soon as we recognize Jesus as a man inspired, it becomes appropriate to describe him as a *charismatic* figure. But 'charismatic' in the context of Jesus' time could describe anything from the ecstatic frenzy of the early prophets (e.g. I Sam. 19.20–24; Hos. 9.7) to the majestic utterances of Second Isaiah. The question therefore arises, In what sense can Jesus properly be described as a charismatic figure? The issue was frequently aired in the first half of this century,[1] and the growth of a more charismatic type of Christianity in the past few decades, particularly in Africa and Latin America, and now increasingly within the older traditions in America and Europe,[2] gives it added weight.

Nor is the question as peripheral to our primary concern as it might at first appear, since, in the first place, it has obvious relevance to the larger question of Jesus' credibility and may well afford us further insights into his self-understanding; and, in the second place, it bears directly on the issue of continuity-discontinuity between Jesus and the early church, with the obvious christological corollaries: viz., the more Jesus conforms to 'the charismatic type' (Otto) the greater the continuity between Jesus and the charismatics of the early church; but on the other hand, the greater the continuity, the less distinctive, the less unique is Jesus.

We will look first at Jesus as a *miracle-worker*[3] and attempt to determine the character and range of his 'mighty works'. Then we shall examine the nature of Jesus' *authority* and consider to what extent Jesus can rightly be described as a *prophet*. Finally, we shall have to ask whether or to what extent *ecstatic* experience was part or constitutive of his experience of God.

§12. JESUS AS A MIRACLE-WORKER

12.1 *Jesus as a 'divine man'*? One of the liveliest debates in current NT scholarship is the question of 'divine-man Christology' – the issue being whether and to what extent Jesus was regarded chiefly or solely as a miracle-worker in some early Christian circles. Since it can be argued that performance of miracles was regarded within the sphere of Hellenistic influence as one of the ways by which an individual's 'divine' status could be authenticated, the question naturally arises, Did Christian apologists present Jesus as a 'divine man', authenticated by his miracles?[4] It has been strongly argued that Paul's opponents in II Corinthians regarded themselves as 'divine men' and maintained a 'divine man Christology'.[5] Less decisive but almost as persuasive is the thesis that Mark was written from the Pauline standpoint of a Christology of the cross (*theologia crucis*) to counter a similar 'divine man Christology' (*theologia gloriae*)[6] – a positive advance on the view of early form critics that Mark simply took over earlier miracle tales and presented Jesus as Son of God = 'divine man' = a miracle-worker who excelled all others.[7]

In point of fact, it is very questionable how legitimate the use of 'divine man' talk is within this context: the phrase itself occurs only seldom in Hellenistic writings, and it has been used with far too much imprecision.[8] Obviously we cannot pursue these questions here, fascinating though they are for our knowledge of the early churches and of early Christian apologetic (see further below §52), but the debate does bear on our present task in two ways. First, the fact that it was possible to present Jesus as a (divine?) man authenticated by his 'mighty works', demonstrates how strongly rooted was Jesus' reputation as a miracle-worker. It is noticeable that Mark does not counter this defective Christology by denying Jesus' miracles; rather he concedes the basis of their case by incorporating miracle tales in the first half of his gospel before applying the corrective of his suffering Son of Man Christology in the second half. Second, comparison of the miracle stories of the Synoptics with those within the literature of Hellenism and Hellenistic Judaism highlights the *reticence* of the evangelists.[9] This contrast also holds good between the miracles attributed to the mature Jesus in the Synoptics and those attributed to the child Jesus in the apocryphal gospels, and strongly suggests that where there were eyewitness accounts of the 'mighty works' of Jesus' ministry, they served as a moderating influence on the elaboration of the tradition and provided something of a check on the full-scale development of a 'divine man' apologetic.[10]

12.2   *Jesus as a charismatic miracle-worker.* The chief point which we must note is that *Jesus' reputation as a miracle-worker comes to us in explicitly charismatic terms and is clearly present in our earliest sources.* The key word here is δυνάμεις (*dunameis* – mighty works). In Hellenistic circles at least the working of *dunameis* belonged to the charismata, a manifestation of the Spirit (I Cor. 12.10, 28f.) which authenticated the miracle-worker as a man of the Spirit (Gal. 3.5; II Cor. 12.12).[11] Jesus was recognized as a charismatic figure in that *dunameis* were a feature of his ministry. Acts 2.22 – Jesus is described as 'a man attested . . . by mighty works', and the (Palestinian) audience are themselves cited as witnesses ('as you yourselves know'); Jesus' *dunameis* are well known and can be confidently appealed to as God's attestation of Jesus (cf. Acts 10.37f.). *Dunameis* is also used of Jesus' acts in three Markan passages (Mark 6.2, 5, 14) and one Q passage (Matt. 11.21, 23/Luke 10.13) – never in John! The congregation at Nazareth are represented as expressing surprise at Jesus' *dunameis* (Mark 6.2); likewise the popular report which reached Herod's ears (Mark 6.14).

That all these passages rest on good tradition is indicated by their typical Jewish outlook, where God is regarded as the true author of the miracle: Acts 2.22 – God performed the *dunameis* through Jesus;[12] Mark 6.2 – the *dunameis* were said to have 'happened through his hands'; Mark 6.14 – the *dunameis* were said to have 'been at work *in him*'. Mark 6.5 is certainly good tradition: 'Jesus could do no mighty work there (Nazareth)' because of their lack of faith.

The offence, which the addition of v. 5b and the rephrasing in Matt. 13.58 attempts to mitigate, guarantees the trustworthiness of the account, which presupposes that *dunameis* were the norm for Jesus.[13]

Especially interesting is the one Q passage, Matt. 11.21 (23)/Luke 10.13, since it is the only place where the tradition shows Jesus himself describing his ministry in terms of 'mighty works'. Despite Bultmann, it is not easy to dismiss the saying as 'a community formulation'.[14] The tradition of Jesus' miraculous activity in the area of the Sea of Galilee is too firmly established in the traditions, and the apocalyptic tone of Matt. 11.23/Luke 10.15 is hardly inconsistent with Jesus' other apocalyptic utterances. Nor do we possess any other evidence of an early Christian mission to Chorazin, Bethsaida (and Capernaum) which relied exclusively on the *dunameis* performed there for its success.[15] This is the singular feature of the logion, that it makes no mention whatsoever of any preaching, whether Christian or pre-Christian. The judgment on Chorazin and Bethsaida is determined solely by their response to the 'mighty works' done in their midst. This feature is without real parallel in the Jewish (Palestinian) mission of the early church, and though Jesus regarded proclamation of the good news to the poor as his chief work (Matt. 11.5), nevertheless we have already examined the clear evidence that Jesus himself regarded his exorcisms as manifest proof of the Spirit (Mark 3.28f.). Our present Q saying is of a piece with that.

The evidence just reviewed shows how deeply this reputation of Jesus as a charismatic miracle-worker is rooted in the earliest traditions of Jesus.[16] Taken together with the considerations marshalled above (ch. III nn. 16, 17, 57), there can be no doubt that Jesus justified this reputation. Above all, the sayings of Jesus examined in detail prove that Jesus saw himself as a Spirit-inspired exorcist and healer and if the words of Matt. 11.21 go back to Jesus, as seems most probable, they confirm that *Jesus saw himself as a charismatic, a worker of miracles*. As we noted above (p.60), whatever the 'facts', Jesus clearly believed that power had gone forth from him to heal a variety of diseases and to work (other?) miracles.

12.3 *The range of Jesus' miracles.* Unfortunately, these authentic words of Jesus do not enable us to determine the full range of his 'mighty works'. Just how extraordinary his healings were by the standards of modern medical knowledge is not clear. No doubt Jesus was responsible for curing mental illness, blindness, lameness and deafness; but these could all be hysterical disorders. Even the healing of leprosy and raising of the dead, which Jesus probably claimed (Matt. 11.5),[17] may not take us beyond the range of psycho-somatic illnesses: in the one case a nervously conditioned disease which gave the appearance of leprosy and which was described as a form of leprosy,[18] and in the other some form of coma or catalepsy. What is rather striking is that no instances of healing purely physical injuries or mending broken limbs are attributed to Jesus in the earliest stratum of tradition[19] – that is to say, there is no instance of a healing miracle which falls clearly outside the general category of psycho-somatic illnesses.[20]

There is no end to the number of good parallels to this sort of healing in the history of religions.[21] With such parallels available to us, including first hand claims and eyewitness reports even today, we must beware of confining the discussion of Jesus' miracles to the *literary* search for the 'divine man' type. At the very least we must say, I think, that Jesus was that type of charismatic (what Robert Graves might call the 'psychic 5%')[22] who could draw on sources of energy within himself of which the ordinary man is only rarely aware, or who was so in tune with wider reality that he could act as a sort of receiver and transmitter from a richer source of energy outside himself.

If Jesus' mighty works of healing can be established as facts on the basis of his own words, the same does not hold for the so-called 'nature miracles' – particularly calming the storm, walking on the water, feeding the five thousand (or four thousand) in the desert, and cursing the fig tree.[23] The *dunameis* of Matt. 11.21 could be held to include such miracles, especially since Paul seems to distinguish 'gifts of healing' from 'working of *dunameis*' in I Cor. 12.9f., but unfortunately the mighty works described by *dunameis* are never defined in the NT. Furthermore, none of the nature miracles ascribed to Jesus could be said to have been performed *in* Chorazin and Bethsaida. It is true that probably authentic sayings of Jesus have been given a reference to two of the nature miracles: 'Beware of the leaven of the Pharisees and of the leaven of Herod' (Mark 8.15) has been elaborated by allusion to the feeding miracles; and an exhortation to faith in God (Mark 11.22f.) has been attached to the cursing of the fig tree. However, neither passage can be referred back to Jesus in its present form with any confidence, since the artificiality of the connection in both cases demonstrates the work of a Christian editor – as even more conservative commentators recognize.[24]

On the other hand, we cannot ignore Mark 11.23f., even if the variant forms of the saying (Matt. 17.20, Luke 17.6) demonstrate that it had no certain life-setting in the narrative traditions of Jesus.[25]

I tell you this (ἀμήν): if anyone says to this mountain, 'Be lifted up from your place and hurled into the sea', and has no inward doubts, but believes that what he says is happening (γίνεται), it will be done for him. I tell you, then, whatever you ask for in prayer, believe that you have received it (ἐλάβετε) and it will be yours (NEB).

These words could indicate a conviction on Jesus' part that the spiritual powers at work in him and through him could affect and alter the course of nature (though see below p. 75). A complete spiritualization of the text has not yet been justified (cf. Luke 10.19).

Moreover, it is possible that the origin of the nature miracle reports is best explained in charismatic terms. Otto, in particular, has drawn attention to 'the power of the charismatic to satisfy the hunger of the recipients by a small gift which he has blessed', and cites parallels including Francis of Assisi.[26] The walking on the water may likewise be explained. Levitation could be cited as a possibly comparable phenomenon, for which there are several well-attested examples.[27] Otto, however, thinks the better parallel is the well-known psychical phenomenon of spiritual *operatio in distans*, particularly

where one person intends to affect another; this is perceived by the latter, possibly in a hallucinative visual way as a vision of the distant person. Circumstances, such as the moment of death or times of great affliction, are most prominent in this respect.[28]

He also notes that John's simpler, probably more original version of the episode does not speak of Jesus coming aboard the boat, only of an 'appearance' of Jesus which brought comfort and help. That is, John's account does not really go beyond an apparition or vision (John 6.21). This more original tradition may well explain the strange words of Mark: 'He meant to pass by them' (Mark 6.48). The suggestion then is that Jesus saw the disciples in distress on the lake (Mark 6.48) and his concern and thought for them was projected in a vision of him which (at length) brought them the comfort of his presence. A striking parallel from within the NT itself is I Cor. 5.3–5, where Paul believes he can be with the Corinthian church 'in spirit' – that is, not just in his thoughts and prayers: 'In all reality and without hesitation he believed that he was capable of operating spiritually at a distance'.[29] Another possible parallel is Matt. 18.20 – 'Where two or three have met together in my name, I am there among them' – although this should more probably be recognized as a word of the exalted Jesus spoken through prophecy (see below §31.2).

The power of a charismatic personality, the force of a charismatic presence may therefore underlie some at least of the so-called 'nature miracles'. As presented to us by the evangelists, of course, they are much more difficult to correlate with the reality of the world which we have learned so much about in recent centuries. Unless we are to see the records of such miracles as the feeding of the five thousand and the stilling of the storm as elaborations of much simpler events (or sayings – see above p. 64), we may simply have to accept that they are theological constructions of the earliest communities.[30] I hesitate only because I half suspect that reality is much more complex than those of us brought up in this scientific age generally realize. We have after all only recently become aware that matter and energy are in dynamic relation to each other, and that there are depths in the human psyche which we have hardly begun to plumb. It is so unscientific to ask whether there are energies and fields or lines of force

of which we are not generally aware, because hitherto only a few
(the 'psychic 5%'?) have been attuned to them?

Such speculation certainly goes beyond the scope of this study, but
perhaps it does underline the point that danger lies in both extremes
of interpretation – that is, both in literalistic fundamentalism and in
medical and scientific materialism. On the one hand, no one should
attempt to use such speculation as a lever to reinstate the miracles
as proof of Jesus' divinity. History of religions parallels (see also below
§52.1) show that similar miracles have been attributed to many
others beside Jesus; are all of them 'divine men'? The dilemma of
(popular) Christian apologetic is that the more credible it shows the
miracles of Jesus to be by virtue of such parallels, the less significance
can be attributed to Jesus' miracles as 'proofs' of his uniqueness. But
then Jesus himself never used them in this way.[31] On the other hand,
we must beware of confining discussion of the charismatic features of
the gospel miracles to purely literary and theological analysis. Otto
in particular has reminded us that a history of religions, or better,
history of religious phenomena approach may point to other conclusions than those of form criticism. Until we know more from research into telepathy and psychical phenomena the prudent scholar
would do well to keep an open mind on many features of Jesus'
charismatic 'mighty works'.[32]

12.4   *Miracles and faith.* One other point must be highlighted before
we move on: that is the role that Jesus attributed to *faith.* A striking
feature about the synoptic use of πιστεύειν (believe) and its cognates
is that nearly two-thirds of the references to faith occur in relation
to miracles.[33] Faith here must be understood as a trusting in God's
power, an openness and receptivity to the power of God to perform
a mighty work. Moreover, almost all of these references to faith occur
in sayings of Jesus – sayings which either encourage faith (Mark 5.36;
9.23f.; 11.22ff.; Matt.9.28; Luke 17.6) or commend faith ('Your
faith has made you whole' – Mark 5.34; 10.52; Matt.8.10/Luke 7.9;
Matt.8.13; 15.28; Luke 7.50; 17.19) or rebuke lack of faith (Mark
4.40; 9.19; Matt.6.30; 14.31; 16.8; 17.20). Not all of these sayings
can be traced back to Jesus with confidence, but the strong orientation to miracles on the one hand,[34] and the almost total absence of the
post-Easter demand for faith in Jesus in response to the kerygma on
the other (Mark 1.15, cf. 11.31 pars.) make it quite clear that we have
reflected here a typical attitude of Jesus.[35]

It was characteristic of Jesus therefore that he looked for faith in
those to whom he ministered. Faith was the necessary complement

to the exercise of God's power through him, hence his inability to perform any mighty work in Nazareth because of their lack of faith (ἀπιστία – Mark 6.6/Matt. 13.58). Faith in the recipient as it were completed the circuit so that the power could flow. In other words, there was nothing automatic, nothing magical in the power of Jesus, either in its exercise or in his consciousness of it. It was not something he could use or display at will, nor did he want to (Mark 8.11f. pars.; cf. Matt. 4.5–7 par.). It is this *dependence* on winning a response, on winning people to faith, which distinguishes Jesus' *dunameis* from the possible parallels in Jewish or Hellenistic circles, where faith plays no part.[36] It is this *consciousness of supernatural power which is yet not solely at his own disposal* which marks Jesus out as a charismatic rather than a magician (contrast Acts 8.19).[37]

Finally we must notice that none of these passages speaks of the faith *of* Jesus. It is always the faith of others in response to God's power, of which Jesus speaks, never of his own faith. The one possible exception is Mark 11.23 quoted above (p.72): if these are Jesus' words he could have included himself in the 'whoever/anyone'. The Markan context, where the saying follows the cursing of the fig tree, suggests that Mark at least saw Jesus' mighty act as an expression of Jesus' *own* faith. However, as we have already noted, the Markan context is most probably secondary. More important, comparison with the independent Matthean and Lukan versions of the saying (Matt. 17.20; Luke 17.6) strongly suggests that Mark 11.23 is itself a secondary form developed out of these earlier versions.[38] If then Matthew and Luke are closer to the actual words of Jesus, as seems probable, we must note that they both call the disciples to faith and do not speak at all of Jesus' own faith. If the idea of Jesus as the model of the miracle working man of faith is present in Mark it is there by virtue of Markan redaction.[39]

The testimony of the Synoptics is clear therefore that Jesus called others to faith but did not set himself forward as an example of faith. This is the critical exegetical weakness of Ebeling's exposition of Jesus as 'the witness of faith': 'it was as a witness of faith that he healed the sick'.[40] On the contrary, Jesus called *others* to faith – faith in the power of God at work in him and through him. It was not a matter of Jesus being open to the power of God for himself. He always saw himself as the vehicle of God's power to others – anointed to proclaim, to heal. If we may put it epigrammatically: Jesus is the witness of *grace* not the witness of *faith*. Here again then we must qualify our picture of Jesus the charismatic by the sense of distinctiveness evident in Jesus' consciousness of power. He did not set himself

in the midst of his disciples and speak of 'our faith'; in his own understanding of the matter he stood somehow over against his disciples,
conscious of the power (*dunamis*) of God in him to work miracles
(*dunameis*) and calling *others* to the appropriate response of faith. It
was not yet faith in him, of course (that was a post-Easter development), but it was faith in the power/Spirit of God uniquely present
in him and working through him.[41]

§13. THE AUTHORITY OF JESUS

We next turn to examine briefly the ἐξουσία (*exousia*) of Jesus – the
authority expressed and claimed by Jesus. We have already drawn
attention to the note of authority implicit in Jesus' style of preaching,
in his attitude to the law and in his exorcisms. What I wish to highlight now is *the charismatic nature of Jesus' authority*.

13.1 *The impact of Jesus' words and presence*. It is natural to turn from
a study of Jesus' *dunameis* to a study of his *exousia* since the two are
closely linked in the synoptic tradition. Jesus had a reputation not
only as a worker of *dunameis* but also as a teacher: his teaching had
the same otherly authority as his exorcisms – 'What is this? A new
kind of teaching – with authority! When he gives orders even the un-
clean spirits submit' (Mark 1.27/Luke 4.36 – ἐν ἐξουσίᾳ καὶ δυνάμει);
'Where does he get this wisdom from, and these mighty works?' Matt.
13.54/Mark 6.2). In the synoptic traditions *astonishment* is the response
to the *exousia* of his teaching as much as to the *dunamis* of his miracles.[42]

More striking is the fact that in the tradition this sort of reaction
is drawn out of people not simply by his teaching and actions, but
apparently by his very presence. Important men kneel at his feet
(Mark 5.22; 10.17); disciples follow without question at his call
(Mark 1.17–20; 2.14); demoniacs are represented as recognizing his
authority before he speaks (Mark 1.24; 3.11; 5.7; 9.20).[43] Most
striking of all is Mark 10.32:

They were on the road, going up to Jerusalem, and Jesus was walking ahead of
them; and they were filled with awe, while those who followed behind were afraid.

In its context of the most detailed passion prediction, v. 32 could be
an artistic variation of the 'messianic secret' theme.[44] On the other
hand, it is a variation without parallel in the 'messianic secret' motif,
and this sentence with its awkward phrasing is probably better understood as an authentic reminiscence of one who followed Jesus to Jeru-

salem. It certainly seems to take us behind the more stereotyped expressions of astonishment already noted, and it testifies to some intensely numinous quality about Jesus and his singleness of purpose.

How much weight we can rest upon this evidence is not clear: much of it has been shaped by the missionary preaching of the early church, and when we contrast Mark with Q, talk of Jesus' authority and of astonishment at his teaching seems to be noticeably lacking in the latter. Yet there is probably sufficient evidence in Jesus' own words and in the earliest tradition explicitly on the subject of Jesus' authority to strengthen the conclusion that the reactions of astonishment at his teaching and presence are not simply a literary or apologetic device of the Christian mission.

13.2 *Sayings relating to Jesus' authority.* In the first place, there are two passages with a good claim to authenticity which show that Jesus' *exousia* was common knowledge among his contemporaries. Matt. 8.9/Luke 7.8 – the precise verbal agreement extends to the words of the centurion as well as to those of Jesus, and probably indicates Q material. This basic core (Matt. 8.9f./Luke 7.8f.) has been considerably elaborated in the course of transmission, differently by Matthew and Luke, but the Aramaic character of the centurion's words,[45] the unusual ascription of amazement to Jesus, and the apophthegmatic nature of the dialogue (in the context of a miracle story),[46] all point to a setting in the life of Jesus. The Syriac versions suggest that in the Aramaic original the centurion said, 'I also am a man *having authority*. . . .'[47] In which case the recognition of Jesus' authority was even more explicit.[48]

Almost certainly an authentic episode from the life of Jesus (though not necessarily in the Markan context) is the question posed by the representatives of the religious authorities: 'By what *exousia* do you act in this way? (Mark 11.28 pars.).[49] The aim of the question was to expose Jesus' *lack* of authority;[50] but the very fact that it was put demonstrates a recognition on the part of Jesus' opponents that his words and actions embodied and expressed a claim to high authority – only it was an authority they could not recognize, without rabbinic or priestly sanction. In his reply Jesus showed that he took the point by setting in sharp antithesis authority 'from heaven' and authority 'from men'. The implication is clear: Jesus was conscious of a direct and unmediated authority – a transcendent authority which set him above party and (at times) even the law – a *charismatic* authority whose compulsion had to be obeyed whatever men might say (cf. Gal. 1.1, 11f.).

This brings us to the second point – to two other passages where Jesus explicitly claims *exousia* in so many words. Mark 2.10 – 'so that you might know that the son of man has authority on earth to forgive sins . . .'. In view of the dispute about Son of Man sayings this cannot be counted among the strongest evidence. Yet it can hardly be doubted either that Jesus regarded forgiveness of sins as a chief part of the good news he came to bring,[51] or that the early communities' own otherwise unprecedented claim to forgive sins (Matt. 16.19; 18.18) was rooted in and a reflection of a similar claim made by Jesus.[52] Moreover, Mark 2.10 is one of the clearest examples of a 'Son of Man' title being read out of the more ambivalent *bar nasa* = 'one' or 'I as a man' (cf. Mark 2.27f; Matt. 11.18f./Luke 7.33f.; Matt. 12.32 – see above p.40 and §8.4).[53] Whatever its original form, the saying seems to express a belief held by Jesus himself that he was agent and mediator of God's forgiveness – in other words, a consciousness that he had a (unique?) authority to exercise the prerogative of God.

Luke 10.19 is the other explicit claim by Jesus in reference to authority: 'Behold, I have given you authority to tread upon serpents (Ps.91.13) and scorpions, and over all the power of the enemy; and nothing shall hurt you'. This can certainly be regarded as a saying of the exalted Lord[54] – it is clearly an exultant expression of prophetic vision and inspiration. But for that very reason it can equally well be attributed to the earth bound Jesus. The apocalyptic enthusiasm of the early community was simply a mirror of his own. And the other reports of Jesus passing on his *exousia* to his disciples during his life (Mark 3.15; 6.7 pars.) and sending them out to proclaim the same message (requiring some delegation of authority) are too well grounded in the tradition to be removed (Mark 6.7–11 par.; Luke 10.2–12; Matt. 9.37f.; 10.5–16)[55] – factors which strengthen the case for regarding Luke 10.19 as an authentic logion of Jesus. The sense of authority which must lie behind such a delegation of authority hardly needs any comment; it is the statement of one who not merely trusts implicitly in God, but who also knows himself to be distinguished by divine authority as the agent of the end-time rule of God (cf. Matt. 12.28/Luke 11.20).

13.3 *The charismatic nature of Jesus' authority.* The picture which emerges from all this is of a *charismatic* authority. The one who already in his own lifetime provoked such respect and even awe in his presence is one who had divine charisma.[56] Here we have a sense of charisma which is nearer to the modern use of the word – that is, charisma as the mysterious 'ability' to inspire fear and awe, confidence and trust. The charisma of Jesus is evident as much in the hostility of his opponents as in the faith of those he made whole (by healing and forgiveness). It was evidently impossible to be neutral towards Jesus once one had encountered him. The authority of his very presence and words posed a challenge and a claim which could not be ignored and which had to be either welcomed or rejected, with no third alternative possible.[57]

His authority was charismatic also in the sense that it was immediately received from God, or rather *was the immediate authority of God*. This is the clear implication of Jesus' 'emphatic ἐγώ' and 'Amen' – a style of speaking expressing a consciousness of transcendent authority (see above §7.2, 3). And the same conviction emerges from the episode in which Jesus' authority is questioned (Mark 11.28 pars.). This was not the self-confidence of massive erudition deriving from rabbinic schooling or of proper status deriving from ceremony and ritual, but a powerful certainty of a direct and unmediated kind – a charismatic insight in particular situations into the will of God. He did not appeal to other authoritative teachers for precedent and confirmation. His well-spring of authority was not the law, the fathers and the traditions, but his own certainty that he knew God's will – a certainty which compelled him to set aside even the authority of Moses when the two were not compatible (Matt. 5.33–42; Mark 10.5ff.). Mark 1.22/Luke 4.32 and Matt. 7.28f. seem therefore to catch a genuine echo of the astonishment which must have greeted the manner and content of Jesus' teaching: 'They were astonished at the way he taught, for he taught them like a teacher who needed no authority other than his own, and not like the experts in the Law' (Barclay).[58]

Most striking of all, there is a self-consciousness and self reference about Jesus' teaching. When others in the tradition in which Jesus stood expressed the immediacy of their authority, they prefaced their words with 'Thus says the Lord'. But Jesus said, 'Amen, *I* say to you' and, 'But *I* say to you'.[59] Where the prophet said, The beauty of the earth will fade, 'but the word of our *God* will stand for ever' (Isa. 40.6ff.), Jesus said, 'Heaven and earth will pass away, but *my* words will not pass away' (Mark 13.31 pars.).[60] His words were the foundation for life and basis of final judgment (Matt. 7.24–7/Luke 6.47–9; Mark 8.38/Luke 9.26). It is this charismatic nature of Jesus' authority, the immediacy of his sense of authority together with *the conscious self reference* of so much of his teaching, which seems to set Jesus apart from other men of comparable significance in the history of religions.[61]

13.4 *Jesus and discipleship*. Finally we should note the character of the movement at the centre of which Jesus stood, since Jesus' concept of discipleship may illuminate still further his authority and self-understanding.[62] Moreover, Jesus' concept of discipleship is obviously relevant to the discussion in later chapters where we examine early Christian experience in its corporate expression (chs. VII and IX), since later Christians described themselves as 'disciples' (see particularly Acts), and as those who 'followed' Jesus (Matt. 8.18-27).[63] As to the basic facts there is little dispute. There can be no doubt that Jesus was known among his contemporaries as a teacher[64] (that is, one who had disciples), and that he called men to follow him.[65] Without going into the several historical and exegetical problems involved we need only single out a few key characteristics.

First, the distinctiveness of Jesus' call to discipleship has recently been clearly demonstrated by M. Hengel in his *Nachfolge und Charisma*. Outwardly like other contemporary teacher–pupil,[66] or leader-follower relationships, the relationship between Jesus and his disciples was distinctive by reason of its 'charismatic–eschatological' nature. Where the rabbis sought to establish the oral tradition on the authority of earlier teachers, Jesus proclaimed a radical obedience in face of the inbreaking kingdom on the authority of his own immediate understanding of God's will. Where rabbinic discipleship was a matter of 'learning Torah', discipleship for the disciples of Jesus was a matter of 'following' Jesus in his eschatological mission.[67] Unlike the zealot bands which could be described as 'charismatic-eschatological', the only weapon Jesus used was the spoken word,[68] and his message was not directed against any earthly kingdom as such (Rome), but proclaimed the eschatological kingdom, and to that extent was hostile to all human power structures. The Qumran community could also to some extent be described as 'charismatic-eschatological', but that was a highly organized and closed community with strict entry qualifications (see particularly IQS 2.3–9; 4QD6), whereas the circle round Jesus was characterized precisely by its *openness*. Jesus' proclamation was for the *poor* (that is the downtrodden and oppressed – Matt. 5.3/Luke 6.20; Matt. 11.5/Luke 7.22; see also Luke 14.13, 21); he was known disparagingly as the friend of tax-collectors and sinners because he welcomed them to his table (Matt. 11.19/Luke 7.34; see also Mark 2.16f. pars.; Luke 7.37, 39; 15.1f.; 19.7). Discipleship for Jesus was marked by the openness of grace.[69] This brings us to our second point.

It is not at all certain whether we should speak of Jesus' disciples as a 'community'. There is no clear dividing line between those who literally followed Jesus and the wider circle of discipleship which must have included those who responded to his message though remaining at home – 'Whoever does the will of God is my brother, and sister, and mother' (Mark 3.35 pars.).[70] If Jesus or his disciples started by baptizing converts (John 3.22, 26; 4.1f.) they soon abandoned the practice – presumably because they did not want any cultic or ritual acts which might become a hurdle or barrier to be surmounted. Certainly his table-fellowship was in no sense a ritual or ceremony from which non-disciples were excluded. So too 'the "Lord's Prayer" is not the prayer of a closed ecclesiastical community, but the prayer of all those whose sole desire is that the kingdom of God may come and that they themselves may be ready for it'.[71] To be sure, a group of twelve were singled out and seem to have had closer relationships with Jesus in terms of teaching and mission;[72] but the immediate circle of those who followed Jesus was certainly wider than 'the twelve' and included women (Mark 15.40f. par.; Luke 8.1–3; cf. Luke 10.38–42). The twelve's primary function as 'the twelve' was to symbolize the eschatological people of God in its totality; even if an important role is promised to them (in a symbolic way?) in the age to come (Matt. 19.28b/Luke 22.30), there is no evidence that they were regarded or acted as functionaries constituting a community gathered round Jesus in Palestine (cf. Matt. 23.8 – 'You are not to be called rabbi, for you have one teacher, and you are all brothers'). Furthermore, although they themselves probably experienced charismatic power, as is suggested by Mark 3.14f.; 6.7 pars.; Luke 10.17ff., these charismata were not given for the service and upbuilding of community, but to enable them to share in Jesus' mission. In short, the circles round Jesus are better described as a movement than a community.[73]

Thirdly, the vitality and continuance of this movement depended solely on Jesus. Discipleship was precisely a matter of 'following' Jesus, and following Jesus had to take precedence over every other human relationship and responsibility (Mark 1.17–20 par.; 10.21 pars.; 10.28f.; Matt. 8.19–22/Luke 9.57–62; cf. Matt. 13.44f.; Luke 14.25–33).[74] So too the call to discipleship was a call to mission, that is, to share in his mission (Mark 1.17 par.;[75] 3.14ff.; 6.7ff. pars.; Matt. 10.5ff.)[76] – and in its likely end (Mark 8.34 pars.; Matt. 10.38/ Luke 14.27; cf. Matt. 5.11/Luke 6.22; Matt. 10.16–31).[77] 'Discipleship means to be totally bound to Jesus' person and his mission.'[78] *It was only as they shared in his mission that his disciples shared in his authority and charismatic power* (Mark 3.14f.; 6.7 pars.; Luke 10.19). In short, as Jesus did not live for himself but for the kingdom and for others, so it had to be with his disciples. Here again emerges the strength of Jesus' eschatological consciousness in regard both to his mission and to himself as having the distinctive and urgent task of proclaiming the kingdom both in its presence and its imminence. Those who gathered round him did so to share in that task, to follow him in his mission, and for no other reason.

§14. JESUS AS PROPHET

The charisma which Paul prized most highly was the gift of *prophecy* (I Cor. 14.1–5, 39 – see below §41.2). It is important to notice therefore that Jesus was known as a prophet and that apart from parables most of Jesus' sayings fall into the prophetic and apocalyptic category.[79] The relevant evidence has been reviewed on several occasions[80] and we need not cover the ground again. Suffice it to underline a few points of relevance to our study.

First, Jesus had the reputation of a prophet even during his life (Mark 6.15 par.; 8.28 pars.; 14.65 par.; cf. Matt. 21.11, 46; Luke 7.16, 39; 24.19) – the inevitable conclusion to be drawn from his manifest inspiration and authority. This is a sufficiently striking fact in itself. The gift of prophecy was commonly thought to have ceased after the early post-exilic period; neither charismatic prophets nor cult professionals were recognized as exercising the prophetic charisma (cf. Ps. 74.9; Zech. 13.2–6; II Baruch 85.1–3).[81] But now after 'the drought of the Spirit' lasting several centuries two men had appeared whose prophetic inspiration could not be gainsaid. Whether Jesus (or John) was regarded as the eschatological prophet by their contemporaries[82] is not clear, but whether known as *a* prophet or as *the* prophet, the recognition that the gift of prophecy had reappeared in Jesus is significant in itself.[83]

Second, it is clear that Jesus regarded himself as a prophet. He was certainly vividly aware of his anointing and empowering by God's Spirit as we have seen, and within Judaism 'to possess the Spirit of God was to be a prophet'.[84] His exorcisms and definitive apprehension of God's will were evidence enough of his prophetic charisma, but the reaction and hostility to him by his own townsfolk and the religious authorities confirmed that he stood fully within the prophetic tradition: 'A prophet is not without honour, except in his home town, and among his relatives and family' (Mark 6.4 pars.); 'I must go on my way today and tomorrow and the day following; for it cannot be that a prophet should perish away from Jerusalem'

(Luke 13.33; see also Matt. 23.31–6/Luke 11.47–51; Matt. 23.37ff./ Luke 13.34f.).[85] Also expressive of his consciousness of prophetic vocation is Jesus' occasional talk of himself as one who had been 'sent' by God (Matt. 10.40/Luke 10.16; Matt. 15.24; see also Mark 9.37/ Luke 9.48; Luke 4.43/(Mark 1.38); cf. Matt. 23.34, 37).[86] In addition, Jesus may have consciously set himself within the prophetic tradition by performing symbolic actions: the entry into Jerusalem, the purge of the temple,[87] and above all the last supper (perhaps also the more obscure meal in the desert – 'feeding the five thousand' – and the puzzling 'cursing of the fig tree') come to mind here.[88] It is possible that Jesus thought of himself as the eschatological prophet, in view of his application of Isa. 61.1 to himself, but it would be more accurate to say that he saw his ministry as the fulfilment of several eschatological prophecies.[89]

Third, Jesus' mission can certainly be described as prophetic in its proclamation,[90] in its reaction against the formalism of contemporary Judaism,[91] and in its ministry to 'the poor'.[92] But two other features highlight the charismatic nature of his prophetic role more clearly. I refer first to the gift of *prophetic insight* into the inmost thoughts and motives of those in his company. This 'ability' to lay bare 'the secrets of the heart' was regarded by Paul as the distinctive charisma which marked out the gift of prophecy (I Cor. 14.24f. – see below p. 232), and it appears to have been regarded as the mark of the prophet by Jesus' contemporaries in the same way, if Luke 7.39 is any guide. It is not surprising then that this manifestation of inspiration is attributed quite frequently to Jesus. Indeed, the tradition is so well established in the gospel material that it would be difficult to deny its presence in the historical ministry of Jesus.[93] Undoubtedly Jesus possessed that uncanny insight into men's thoughts which marks the otherness, the givenness of charismatic authority.

The other more distinctively charismatic feature of Jesus the prophet was his conviction that in certain instances he had been given foreknowledge of the future – *prophetic foresight*. We must be careful not to claim too much here. Jesus certainly foresaw his death, and probably vindication too,[94] even though his predictions have almost certainly been given greater precision in the light of events.[95] But this particular expectation seems to have been part of his wider apocalyptic expectation – that the consummation of the kingdom was at hand, and so also the 'messianic woes' involving himself and his disciples (e.g. Mark 8.31; 9.1; 14.22ff., 27; Matt. 23.37–9; Luke 13.33; 22.35–8).[96] There are, however, other prophecies of Jesus which have more the character of momentary disclosures of the future – Mark

10.39 par.; 13.2 pars.; 14.8 par.; 14.25 par.; 14.30 pars.; cf. Mark 5.36, 39 pars.[97] In these cases we see not logical corollaries drawn from wider expectations but the partly detailed partly obscure premonitions in respect to particular individuals or places which are the mark of the charismatic and inspired prophet.[98]

A final word must be said again on the distinctiveness of Jesus' prophetic consciousness. As we have mentioned above, he was not the only prophet to appear after the centuries of silence, and so was not the only herald of the end-time. Moreover, if Mark 6.14 is good tradition – the belief attributed to Herod that Jesus was John the Baptist risen from the dead – then, as G. Friedrich notes, 'there must have been a sense that John was unique'.[99] Yet the decisive distinction remains between John and Jesus: that John always looked away from himself to a greater who was to come (and despite the veneration in which his disciples held the Baptist, we have no traditions to the contrary); whereas Jesus consistently centred the final revelation in himself and his ministry and nowhere else (see above pp. 47f., 53). The same point emerges from his sense of mission. He expressed this not only in the ἀπεστάλην (I was sent) sayings, but also in the more direct ἦλθον (I came – Mark 2.17 pars.; Matt. 11.19/Luke 7.34; Luke 12.49; see also Mark 1.38 par.; 10.45 par.; Matt. 5.17; 10.34ff.). As C. H. Dodd suggests, 'We may perhaps trace here the same transition from the prophetic to the more-than-prophetic which is marked by the difference between "Thus saith the Lord" and "I say unto you"'.[100] In short, *there is a clear sense in which Jesus the prophet was unique* – because in his ministry alone the final revelation, the end-time had come (Matt. 13.16f./Luke 10.23f.; Matt. 12.41f.) – *and* it was a uniqueness of which Jesus was conscious.

§15. WAS JESUS AN ECSTATIC?

15.1.   *Was Jesus more than a charismatic figure?* Can he also be described as an *ecstatic* – one whose inspiration came from experiences of ecstasy? By 'ecstasy' I mean here an unusually exalted state of feeling, a condition of such total absorption or concentration that the individual becomes oblivious to all attendant circumstances and other stimuli, an experience of intense rapture or a trance-like state in which normal faculties are suspended for a shorter or longer period and the subject sees visions or experiences 'automatic speech', as in some forms of glossolalia. Paul had some such experiences, this we know (II Cor. 12.1ff.; cf. I Cor. 14.14, 18 – see below §§40.3, 41.7); did Jesus?

The question was posed most sharply at the turn of the century as part of the impact of history of religions researches upon the then current quest after Jesus' messianic self-consciousness. If Jesus' message and ministry was so dominated by apocalyptic expectation as Weiss argued, did it not follow that Jesus was also an ecstatic? Could he even be presented as the forerunner of the Reformation *Schwärmer* (enthusiasts)? O. Holtzmann attempted to answer the question, Was Jesus an ecstatic? in 1903. But his definition of ecstasy was too loose, and most of the material he examined can be better described as apocalyptic (the imminence of God's reign), or charismatic (e.g. Mark 11.22f., which he unjustifiably compared with I Cor. 13.2), or prophetic (e.g. Matt. 23.29–36/Luke 11.47–51).[101]

The relevant evidence which remains is minimal. Jesus certainly seems to have had one or two visionary experiences. Luke 10.18 – 'I saw Satan fall like lighting from heaven'[102] suggests this and it is quite likely that his experience at Jordan when baptized by John was visionary,[103] though it can be called 'ecstatic' only when we use 'ecstasy' imprecisely.[104] It is possible that the narrative of Jesus' temptation in the wilderness (Matt. 4.1–11/Luke 4.1–13) is likewise rooted in visionary experiences of Jesus.[105] The episode of the 'transfiguration' (Mark 9.1–8 pars.), if visionary, describes visions experienced by the *disciples* not Jesus,[106] and Matt. 11.23/Luke 10.15, though apparently of exalted or visionary character, is simply an application of Isa. 14.13ff. to Capernaum.

Apart from that there is no evidence that Jesus sought to attain inspiration by artificial stimulation of ecstasy. There is nothing of a group frenzy such as we find in the early prophets, the dervishes and shamanism, no rituals, techniques or drugs, such as we find elsewhere.[107] Apart from the tradition of the temptations in the wilderness Jesus seems to have shunned fasting; indeed his reputation was quite the opposite from that of the introspective ascetic who tries to induce mystical ecstasy by means of fasting (Mark 2.18f.; Matt. 11.19/Luke 7.34). Certainly he seems to have spent lengthy periods in solitary prayer (see above §3), but there is no evidence of ecstatic behaviour resulting from these times of prayer, and they are better explained in terms of an intensity of devotion and dedication which is certainly unusual but not necessarily abnormal.

There are, however, some sayings of Jesus which could justly be said to come from an unusually exalted state of mind. I think particularly of Matt. 11.25ff./Luke 10.21f., examined above in ch. II, which Luke prefaces with the words, 'At that moment Jesus exulted in the Holy Spirit and said . . .'[108] also of Mark 14.25 par. – 'Truly I say to you, I shall not drink again of the fruit of the vine until that day when I drink it new in the kingdom of God'. Again, the promise of the Spirit to prompt testimony in time of trial (Mark 13.11 pars.) has a recognizable life-setting within the context of Jesus' expectation of imminent end-time persecution for his disciples (cf. Mark 14.38 – Spirit).[109] In which case it is probable that Jesus' assurance was based on similar experiences of inspiration at critical moments in his ministry.[110] The talk of words being 'given', 'for it is not you that speak but the Holy Spirit', could be described as ecstatic speech, although it is more precisely understood in terms of the otherly givenness of prophetic inspiration, which in turn has close parallels in artistic and literary inspiration.

15.2 *Did Jesus speak in tongues?* It has been suggested to me that the use of (ἀνα)στενάζω (sigh deeply) in Mark 7.34, 8.12 could be interpreted of glossalalic speech in view of Rom. 8.26 (στεναγμοῖς ἀλαλήτοις – 'inarticulate groans').[111] The fact that Mark 7.34 occurs in the context of a healing (cf. ἐμβριμάομαι 'warn sternly' – Mark 1.43; John 11.33, 38)[112] may be significant since in contemporary parallels the miracle working word is frequently spoken in strange, incomprehensible sounds, or in some foreign language.[113] The argument that Jesus spoke in tongues in these cases, however, falls a good way short of proof. Στενάζω and ἐμβριμάομαι indicate deep feeling, but not necessarily ecstasy. Although Rom. 8.26 can be understood in terms of glossolalia with some justification (see below p.241), this is because the groans are described as 'unutterable, inarticulate, too deep for words' and ascribed to the Spirit; the use of στενάζειν by itself does not suggest glossolalia. And the religious history parallels break down, since in Mark 7.34 Jesus' word of healing was spoken in Aramaic, his native tongue.

15.3 One last question cannot be ignored: *Was Jesus mad?* It was a question which also came to the fore at the turn of the century, prompted, perhaps inevitably, by Weiss and Schweitzer's bold presentation of Jesus in starkly apocalyptic garb, as also by the fourth evangelist's presentation of Jesus: did Jesus suffer from paranoia, megalomania, or some other form of insanity? The question was answered forcefully in the negative by Schweitzer himself in his Doctor of Medicine thesis.[114] But the fact remains that the synoptic tradition preserves an opinion concerning Jesus to the effect that he was mad (Mark 3.21 – 'people were saying that he was out of his mind (ἐξέστη)' – NEB; cf. John 8.48).[115] Presumably the opinion was based on unusual if not abnormal behaviour or expressions of Jesus. Mark sets it immediately before the accusation by the scribes that Jesus was possessed by Beelzebul, so probably we are meant to understand the charge of madness and devil possession as both prompted by Jesus' exorcisms and by the power and authority he expressed on such occasions.

The question of madness has to be raised also in the light of the *distinctiveness*, even uniqueness Jesus sensed in his relation to God and to his kingdom, in his exercise of power and authority and in his role as a prophet – a feature of his self-expression to which we have had continually to draw attention. Certainly we can hardly deny that Jesus was abnormal in some sense; but it is an abnormality which cannot really be explained in terms of insanity. Madness is a possible interpretation of a few sayings and actions of Jesus, but it hardly belongs to the fuller picture of Jesus with which we are familiar from the Synoptics and from modern Life of Jesus research. Perhaps after all we are dealing not just with an abnormal person but with a unique abnormality which has no real parallel either in the history of religions or in the case history of modern psychiatry. And if insanity will not serve as an adequate interpretation of the distinctive otherness which Jesus sensed about himself and his mission, then it may well be that the way lies open to that other line of interpretation which led eventually to the Christian dogma of Jesus' divinity (see further below § 16.6).

15.4   *Conclusion.* Was Jesus an ecstatic? The answer appears to be No!; although he did have one or two experiences which could be called ecstatic, whether visionary or moments of high exultation. But he did not attempt to stimulate ecstasy or work up inspiration. It is the *givenness* of these experiences which is characteristic of Jesus. The key marks of ecstatic religion are completely lacking in his case.

Was Jesus charismatic (Pneumatiker)? The answer is, Yes! And the sense in which he may be called 'charismatic' can be fairly clearly defined. He was charismatic in the sense that he manifested a *power* and *authority* which was not his own, which he had neither achieved nor conjured up, but which was given him, his by virtue of the Spirit/ power of God upon him. The *power* did not possess him and control him so that he was its instrument willing or unwilling. But neither was he the author of it; nor was he able to dispose of it or ignore it at will. It was a compulsion which filled him, a power which he could exercise in response to faith or which faith could draw through him from its source beyond him. The *authority* was not his by academic merit or social standing; he had not earned it as a right. And yet it set aside all other authority however sacrosanct, and claimed a hearing before all others, for it came directly from his relation to God, immediately from his insight into God's will. It was not merely self-confidence or strength of conviction. There was an otherly givenness about his words so that they were fully his own and yet with an authority which called forth far more than ordinary respect, and even awe and wonder. *It is in terms of this consciousness of power and authority his own and yet not his own, this inspiration immediate and direct from beyond, that Jesus can be called a charismatic.*

§16. CONCLUSIONS

16.1   There is clear evidence in the Synoptics that *Jesus' consciousness of the Spirit of God empowering him, inspiring him was basic to his mission.* The evidence is not extensive, but it cannot be dismissed.[116] We have Jesus' own understanding of his exorcisms as manifestations of this power, and of his ministry to the poor as the fulfilment of Isa.61.1. And the unequivocal testimony of these passages is confirmed by the evidence that Jesus was a charismatic, and probably by the account of Jesus' experience at Jordan. The evidence in fact is more extensive than is often recognized.[117] Indeed it may be, as Windisch postulated, that there was a much stronger pneumatic element in the earlier traditions of Jesus, an element which our present synoptic tradition has suppressed to some extent.[118] Certainly there is no evidence of a counter tendency in the earliest traditions: pneumatic experiences of the early communities do not appear to have been read back into the life of Jesus, and Jesus is not portrayed simply as the first charismatic.[119] The evidence therefore points clearly to the conclusion that the pneumatic features of the synoptic tradition are authentic – *Jesus' experience of God was of a supernatural power compelling him to speak and to act.*

16.2   *The manifestations of the Spirit for Jesus were the manifestations of power* – of *effective* power: the demons obeyed, the blind saw, the lepers were cleansed; the poor and the sinner experienced forgiveness and acceptance; or in a word, power to bring *wholeness*, of mind, of body and of relationships. The other charismatic traits of his ministry were presumably also understood by Jesus as manifestations of the Spirit. But these two, healing and proclamation of the good news to the poor, are the only charismata that Jesus specifically attributed to the Spirit, so far as we know. There is certainly never any suggestion that Jesus thought God could be known only in experiences of ecstasy; he does not seem to have spurned such experiences when they were given to him, but he never sought or cultivated them. On the contrary, of the two charismata, healing and proclamation, it was the latter, the less sensational, the more rational, that he regarded most highly (Matt. 11.5). Yet having said that, the fact remains that *Jesus' experience of God embraced non-rational as well as rational elements – dunamis to heal as well as exousia to proclaim*[120] *– and he regarded both as valid and important manifestations of God's Spirit.*

16.3   Jesus' consciousness of Spirit in large measure explains what has so often puzzled commentators – the tension between his understanding of kingdom as present and his proclamation of the kingdom as imminent-future. The proclamation of the end-time's imminence was nothing new; it was the proclamation of its presence which was so astonishing. What on earth could make Jesus think the kingdom was already present, when the claim was contradicted on every side? The answer lies in the presence of one element, a key characteristic of the end-time – the plenitude of the Spirit's power. Jesus' sense of power was so overwhelming in his consciousness, so manifest in his ministry, that he could reach no other conclusion than that the end-time prophecies were already being fulfilled in his ministry, the kingdom was already present. Moreover, his conviction of the *imminence* of the End sprang as much from this source as any other; for if the end-time was already present, the End could not long be delayed – certainly not beyond his own generation's life-time (Mark 13.28f. pars.; cf. 9.1; 13.30; Matt. 10.23).[121] *The already-not yet tension in Jesus' proclamation stems immediately from his consciousness of Spirit.*

16.4   This recognition of Jesus' consciousness of Spirit fills out the Liberal portrayal of Jesus where it was completely lacking. If we spell out Jesus' own religious experience, his experience of God, solely in terms of sonship, we misunderstand Jesus almost totally. Jesus' experience was also of God as Spirit. And by 'Spirit' I do not mean the Zeitgeist of Liberal idealism, but 'Spirit' as Gunkel rediscovered it – Spirit as power, the same primitive power that fell upon Samson and inspired Ezekiel – charismatic Spirit that inspired Jesus' ministry, apocalptyic Spirit that filled Jesus with consciousness of the End.

Jesus' consciousness of Spirit is the eschatological dimension to Jesus' ministry which Liberalism missed.

16.5   It is important that we do not repeat Liberalism's mistake in the other direction – that is, by ignoring Jesus' consciousness of sonship and overemphasizing his consciousness of Spirit. This was the mistake made in the Quest of the Charismatic Jesus. We must hold closely together these two sides of Jesus' self-understanding. *As he found God in prayer as Father, so he found God in mission as power* – these are but two sides of the one character, of the one experience of God. *In this two-fold experience of Jesus we see closely interwoven both the ethical and the charismatic, both the obedience of the Son and the liberty of the prophet.* Jesus can be presented neither simply as a moralist nor simply as an ecstatic. *It is the interaction of sonship and Spirit that gives Jesus' ministry its distinctive character.*

16.6   At every stage with remarkable consistency the evidence has forced us to recognize an element of distinctiveness, at times even uniqueness, in Jesus' experience of God. His habit of addressing God as 'Abba' was as unusual for his day as it was characteristic of his own prayer; and though he taught his disciples to pray likewise, he never seems to have united his voice with theirs but rather to have retained the distinctiveness of his own *abba*-relationship. He regarded himself as God's son, and may possibly have seen his mission in terms of sharing his (unique?) knowledge of God with his disciples (Matt. 11.27?). His exorcisms were for him something unique – as distinctive manifestations of the Spirit they demonstrated the eschatological kingdom's presence (Mark 3.28f.; Matt. 12.28/Luke 11.20). In his ministry the prophecy of Isa. 61.1f. was fulfilled – he himself was the focus of eschatological significance (Matt. 11.5f.). He looked for faith in others, but seems to have regarded himself more as a 'manifestation of grace' than as a 'witness of faith'. His sense of authority and inspiration set him in the tradition of Moses and the prophets, but its immediacy and numinous quality transcended all that went before and set him apart as someone without close parallel. And though he may have been able to share something of that authority and charismatic power with his disciples (Luke 10.19), just as he sought to share something of his relationship with the Father (Luke 22.29 and above), our sources are unanimous that it was precisely *his* authority and power, precisely *his* relationship that they shared. In short, *Jesus himself seems clearly to have recognized a distinctive and even unique element in his own experience of God.*

As soon as we acknowledge this the dogmatic questions of wider Christology come crowding in upon us – in particular: Was the uniqueness of his experience qualitative or quantitative – the experience of one other than man, more than man, or just authentic man, perfect man? Is the relationship underlying this consciousness merely existential or also metaphysical? Is this ultimately what Christian dogma is referring to when it speaks of the divinity of Jesus?

So far as our evidence goes, it is certainly possible to interpret some of it in terms of a qualitative distinction: Matt. 12.28 – his exorcisms are without comparison in their eschatological significance; Mark 1.22 – he taught with authority, that is, not simply better than the scribes, but not at all like the scribes; the unparalleled 'Amen, I say to you'; and, of course, above all, Matt. 11.27 – nobody knows the Father except himself; he alone can reveal the Father. But such an interpretation would not go unchallenged; the evidence could be alternatively interpreted in terms of an unusually high degree of inspiration – does 'divinity' then become merely inspiration to the nth degree? The problem is that the story is only half told, the evidence incomplete. Christological reflection cannot confine itself solely to Jesus' experience of God, or his claims, or his ministry. It must include, perhaps begin with, the Easter proclamation and faith – particularly, as W. Pannenberg following U. Wilckens has so rightly argued, Jesus' claims also contain a proleptic element – Jesus himself looked for a future confirmation and verification.[122] The fact is that we cannot analyse the content of Jesus' self-consciousness in any detail. We cannot answer with any precision the question, Who did Jesus think he was? As we have already pointed out, his self-consciousness was much less structured, more inchoate than is often recognized (see above §6.6). Whatever titles and concepts he took over from the OT did not shape his experience of God, but were as much, if not more, much more, shaped and interpreted by it. All we can say is that he lived out of a consciousness of sonship and power, of commissioning and authority, which seems to have transcended the ordinary prophetic experience of inspiration. By how much it transcended ordinary human experience we cannot say – qualitatively or quantitatively, metaphysically or existentially, we cannot say. These questions can only be answered in the light of the first Easter – and even then the answers will only be a little less tentative.

What we can and must say is that without this element of uniqueness in Jesus' experience of God the gap between the historical Jesus and the Christ of faith would become a yawning, unbridgable abyss. It may be true, as P. Althaus says, that 'Jesus was what he is before he knew about it'.[123] But *unless there is some correlation between Christian claims for Jesus and Jesus' own self-awareness, these claims lose touch with reality.*[124] *It is the transcendent otherness of Jesus' experience of God which roots the claims of Christology in history.* If Christology must be pursued 'from below', as I believe, it is only this transcendent otherness of Jesus' consciousness of God which enables it to link up with Christologies 'from above', which, if we may put it thus, allows the approach 'from below' to be called 'Christology'. Certainly it is quite clear that if we can indeed properly speak of the 'divinity' of the *historical* Jesus, we can only do so in terms of his experience of God: *his 'divinity' means his relationship with the Father as son and the Spirit of God in him.*[125]

16.7   The other side of this issue is the question of the continuity-discontinuity between Jesus and the early church; the problem being, as we noted above (§11), the greater the continuity the less weight we must give to Jesus' consciousness of the distinctiveness and uniqueness of his experience of God. We cannot answer the question till we have examined the spiritual experience of the early Christians. But we must note that a considerable degree of continuity has already come to light: as Jesus addressed God as 'Abba', so he encouraged his disciples to speak to God in the same way; as his Father had appointed a kingdom for him, so he appointed for his disciples (Luke 22.29); (as he knew God in intimate manner, so he saw it as his mission to bring others into the same knowledge – Matt. 11.27?). In addition, as we shall see in due course, as he was charismatic, so were many, if not all of the earliest believers (see below ch. VII); as Jesus' ministry was characterized by an already-not yet tension, particularly in his experience of the Spirit, so Paul's theology is similarly characterized (see below §53); as there was a balance in Jesus' ministry between the ethical and the charismatic, so there was in Paul (see below §§49.2, 54, 55). As we proceed therefore we will have to bear in mind the question: Was Jesus' experience of God the prototype of Christian experience; and if so, was Jesus simply the first Christian? Or does the distinctiveness which set Jesus' experience of God apart from that of his contemporaries also set it apart from the experience of the first Christians?

PART TWO

THE RELIGIOUS EXPERIENCE OF THE EARLIEST CHRISTIAN COMMUNITIES

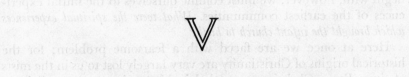

V

RESURRECTION APPEARANCES

§17. INTRODUCTION

17.1   When we turn from our study of Jesus' religious experience to that of the earliest Christian believers and communities we become aware at once of a significant difference. Where Jesus was the *subject* of religious experience, he now features as the *object* of religious experience. The religious experience of the historical Jesus can be described and characterized in terms of experience of God in a relatively straightforward manner. But in the religious experience of the early church a distinctive new element becomes obvious: the early believers claim to experience not simply God, but *Jesus as well*. For example, in Luke's Acts Jesus encounters Paul at various times in visions (18.9; 22.17f., etc.); Paul speaks of Christ living *in him* (Gal. 2.20); likewise the Johannine Christ promises to dwell in his disciples after his glorification (John 14.18–23). There are also experiences which are attributed directly to the Spirit (e.g. the glossolalia of Acts, the charismata of I Cor. 12–14, and the experience of new vitality in John 3.5; 4.14; 7.38f.) – experiences of Spirit more like those of Jesus examined above in chapter IV. But here too the picture becomes confused – for the Spirit can be described by Luke and Paul as the Spirit *of Jesus* (Acts 16.7; Phil. 1.19), and by John as the 'other Paraclete', that is, as Jesus' successor (John 14.16).

Clearly the problem of continuity and discontinuity is posed here in a striking way. In what sense is the religious experience of the earliest Christians the same as that of Jesus? In what sense are they different? How are they related? In what sense was Jesus the object of their experience? Or was talk of experiencing the 'Spirit of Jesus' simply their way of saying that the spiritual influence of Jesus lives on?[1] To pose the problem in more general terms: What was it that the early Christians were experiencing? What were the charismatic features of their experience? How distinctive was their experience within the religious milieu of their time? These are some of the questions we must bear in mind in this and subsequent chapters. To begin with, however, we must confine ourselves to the initial experiences of the earliest communities. *What were the spiritual experiences which brought the infant church to birth?*

Here at once we are faced with a fearsome problem; for the historical origins of Christianity are very largely lost to us in the mists of time. For a Christian no period in history is more tantalizingly obscure than the mysterious thirty years between the death of Jesus and the publication of the earliest gospel. To be sure Paul's letters illuminate the darkness in part, but only from one side. So too the work of form critics, despite most strenuous efforts, has really only succeeded in letting in a few more shafts of light at particular points. Acts of course purports to portray this period in some detail; but the observant student soon becomes aware of what we may call for the moment a certain stylizing of both material and history and of large gaps spanned in a word or two or not at all, so that again and again the mystery of the first few years is rather heightened than reduced by the narrative of Acts.

17.2   At first sight the historical knot which confronts our particular study seems to unravel itself into two clear strands – *resurrection appearances* and *experiences of Spirit*. Anyone familiar with the Bible knows well that the book of Acts begins its history of Christianity with a block of resurrection appearances over a forty day period, followed by a quite different experience of the Spirit (Pentecost) with a clear-cut ten day break separating and distinguishing the one from the other. But closer analysis of all the relevant material at once raises the question, Were there at the beginning of Christianity two such separate and distinct categories of religious experience? Can we (and did they) distinguish resurrection appearances and experiences of Spirit quite so clearly as Luke suggests? The question is forced on us for the very good reason that *only Luke makes this sharp dichotomy*. In Paul's discussion of resurrection in I Cor. 15 he seems at first to agree with Luke in treating the resurrection appearances as something unique; but then he confuses the issue by describing the risen Jesus as 'the life-giving Spirit' (I Cor. 15.45). And John depicts the Spirit as being given by the risen Jesus during his first appearance to the disciples; resurrection appearance and Pentecostal experience of Spirit are run together (John 20.22). Inevitably therefore we must ask: Is the separation and distinction of resurrection appearances and Pentecost the work of Luke, part of his stylizing? Could it be that

'resurrection appearance' and 'Pentecost' are simply variant interpretative ways of describing the birth of Christianity? – that 'resurrection appearance' and 'gift of Spirit' are simply variant ways of
classifying certain important conversion experiences at the beginning?
This is an issue we must take up at once when we examine Paul on
this point; but we will not be able to resolve it fully until we examine
the Pentecost tradition in chapter VI.

This first major issue brings into sharper focus a second and more
fundamental problem. What were the 'resurrection appearances'?
No one doubts that Christianity began with 'resurrection appearances' – that fundamental to the Christian gospel and church was the
claim that Jesus had appeared to various individuals and groups after
his death. But what was it they actually experienced? Did they
actually *see* something? Was the 'seeing' a perception of mind or of
eye? We will be treating this question as exclusively as possible in
terms of religious experience. But we cannot ignore the fact that it is
precisely at this point that the critical questions bite most deeply:
since D. F. Strauss the 'subjective vision' hypothesis has been upheld
in one form or another as the best explanation of the resurrection
appearances by a sequence of prominent scholars, including Harnack,
Bousset, Goguel and Bultmann.[2]

Our task in the next three chapters thus becomes clear. First we
will examine Paul's understanding of the resurrection appearance to
himself, asking in particular the question, *Was this experience different
from his subsequent experiences of 'life-giving Spirit'? And if so, in what way?*
Second, we will examine the records of the earlier resurrection
appearances in Paul and the gospels, asking the question, *Were the
experiences underlying these accounts different from the resurrection appearance
to Paul?* In the following chapters we will examine more closely the
tradition of Pentecost and attempt to uncover other expressions of the
spiritual vitality of the earliest communities.

§18. THE RESURRECTION APPEARANCE TO PAUL

18.1   *Introduction.* We must start with Paul for two obvious reasons.
First, his documentation of resurrection appearances in I Cor. 15
takes us right back to the beginning of the mysterious thirty year
period. As is generally recognized, in I Cor. 15.3ff. Paul passes on
primitive tradition(s) which he must have received at the time of his
conversion in Damascus or no more than three years later in his first
visit to Jerusalem (Gal. 1.17f.).[3] Moreover, though his testimony is

almost all hearsay evidence, it has not come to us through innumerable intermediaries. On the contrary, much of it is only second hand. Paul had met and spoken with Peter and James on his first visit to Jerusalem (Gal. 1.18f.); he was on terms of close intimacy with several at least of 'the apostles' (Andronicus and Junias – Rom. 16.7;[4] Barnabas–Gal. 2.9; I Cor. 9.5f.; probably Silvanus–I Thess. 2.6f.; and probably Apollos – I Cor. 4.9);[5] and he must have known not a few of the 'more than 500 brethren' (I Cor. 15.6), since it is probably Paul himself who has added the phrase, 'most of whom are still alive . . .'. There is some dispute as to how many of the clauses in vv. 3–8 were initially received by Paul as authoritative tradition,[6] and how many were gathered together or added by him personally.[7] But in either case, assuming Paul's conversion took place within two or three years of Jesus' death (see below ch. VI n.16), I Cor. 15.3–8 affords us an unparalleled glimpse into these earliest days of the primitive community. More to the point, in either case *we are but one remove from the resurrection appearances which began and constituted the earliest gospel of Christianity.*

The second reason why we start with Paul is because *only with him do we have a first hand account of a resurrection appearance.* No matter how ancient the sources underlying the final chapters of the gospels, we can have no certainty that they consist of eyewitness records. Only in the case of Paul do we have immediate access to such a witness. 'Last of all . . . he appeared also to me' (I Cor. 15.8). Moreover, in addition to I Cor. 15 there are other allusions and references which throw fuller light on his experience at conversion. The relevant passages for our study then are Gal. 1.12, 15f.; I Cor. 9.1f.; 15.8ff.; II Cor. 4.6 (cf. Eph. 3.2f.; Phil. 3.7).

18.2 *Did Paul regard his conversion experience as something unique in his own experience?* What was distinctive about the resurrection appearance to Paul for Paul himself? Was it different from his other experiences of Spirit? and if so, how?

At first sight the answer to these questions is straightforward. Paul claimed to have seen Jesus alive from the dead (I Cor. 9.1 – 'Have I not seen Jesus our Lord?'). And with this appearance came his commission to the Gentiles (Gal. 1.16 – God 'was pleased to reveal his Son in me, in order that I might preach him among the Gentiles'). At first glance the distinctive features of Paul's initiating experience were that Jesus appeared to him in visible form and commissioned him as missionary to the Gentiles (cf. Acts 26.13–18).

But it is not quite so simple. Apart from I Cor. 15.45, with its suggestion that experience of Spirit and experience of risen Jesus were not very different, there are two further considerations.

(a) First, there is more than a hint of suspicion rising from Paul's letters themselves that Paul is pleading a special case. The observant reader will notice that in each of the passages referred to above Paul associates his apostleship directly with the resurrection appearance of Jesus. Not only so, but on each occasion the claim to a resurrection appearance constitutes something of a defence of Paul's assertion of apostolic authority (Gal. 1.12; I Cor. 9.1 – 'Am I not an apostle? Have I not seen the Lord?'; I Cor. 15.8f. – 'Last of all', 'untimely born', 'least of the apostles'; II Cor. 3.1ff.). These passages, along with others, strongly suggest that Paul's claim to apostolic authority was widely disputed (cf. Gal. 1.1; II Cor. 11.5; 12.11f.; I Thess. 2.3–6).[8] It is possible therefore that the associated claim (to a resurrection appearance) was also contested. Is Paul then indulging in special pleading? – interpreting a less distinctive religious experience as a resurrection appearance in order to boost his claim to apostolic authority?

The same question is posed by the old problem of how to relate to each other the rather different descriptions of Paul's conversion and call in Gal. 1.15f. and I Cor. 15.8f. Thus W. Marxsen points out that in his earlier reference to his Damascus road experience Paul does not speak of *seeing* Jesus; he speaks rather of God's having *revealed* his Son to him (Gal. 1.15f.). That is to say, Paul's first description of his experience was more in terms of a truth being uncovered than of a person being seen. Only in the later letter of I Corinthians does he go on to define this revelation as a seeing – a step taken by assimilating his own self-chosen description to what had probably become the accepted way of speaking of the resurrection appearances. 'God revealed his Son in me' thus became, 'he appeared also to me'.[9] The question naturally arises: *Has Paul expressed his conversion experience in the language of a resurrection appearance for apologetic purposes without other justification?*

(b) Second, Luke seems to contest Paul's description of his Damascus road experience as a resurrection appearance in his account of the primitive church. He equates 'the apostles' with 'the twelve', and cites as definition of an apostle, one who was not only a 'witness to Jesus' resurrection' but who had also accompanied Jesus during the length of his ministry (Acts 1.21–6). In the same spirit, resurrection appearances are restricted to a well-defined forty-day period, and brought to a clear-cut conclusion by the 'ascension' (Acts 1.9ff.). Consequently Paul's experience outside Damascus can be characterized simply as a 'vision' (ὀπτασία – Acts 26.19) – similar, presumably, to the visions of which Paul himself speaks in II Cor. 12.1 and which Luke describes elsewhere in Acts (18.9; 22.17; 23.11 cf. *Clem. Hom.* XVII. 19). And Paul presumably cannot be ranked as an apostle in the full sense, only in the weakened sense of 'delegate' or 'missionary' (Acts 14.4, 14) – a usage with which Paul is also familiar (II Cor. 8.23; Phil. 2.25).[10] The issue is clear: Was Paul's conversion experience a resurrection appearance? Was it distinct from his subsequent experiences of Spirit or his other ecstatic visions?

This question too has been more sharply posed in J. Lindblom's recent study. He points out that the Acts accounts of Paul's conversion have all the hallmarks of an 'ecstatic vision' – light and sound phenomena, the subsequent state of shock, and the suddenness and unexpectedness of the event. Its visionary character is of a piece with the other visions mentioned in Acts (esp. 7.55f.; 10.9ff.), including the other visions of Christ experienced by Paul (22.17f., and implied in 26.16). And Paul's description of his experience in terms of revelation (Gal. 1.12, 16) and of seeing (I Cor. 9.1; 15.8; II Cor. 4.6) is consistent with this understanding. The only difference, Lindblom suggests between Paul's conversion experience and the ecstatic visions of II Cor. 5.13; 12.1 lay in the former's conclusiveness (Beweiskraft); the latter did not carry the same conviction and assurance (concerning Jesus and his own commission) as the Damascus experience.

The meaning of the Damascus appearance lay in the fact that it was the first and fundamental for the life of the apostle. Therein lay also its Beweiskraft for the Corinthian readers.[11]

Was Paul's conversion experience something distinctive and different from his subsequent 'visions and revelations' (II Cor. 12.1)? Ought it to be described as a 'resurrection appearance'? These questions cannot be avoided. They are posed by the NT itself.

18.3 *The distinctiveness of Paul's conversion experience for Paul himself.* The first point which can be established with some certainty is that *Paul himself makes a clear distinction between his conversion experience and subsequent spiritual experiences.* Rightly or wrongly, justified or not, Paul is of the definite opinion that the appearance of Jesus to him was something unique in his own experience.

(*a*) I Cor. 15.8 – 'last of all'. It can hardly be disputed that Paul here ranks his own conversion experience of the risen Christ with that of earlier witnesses.

He appeared to Cephas, *then* to the twelve.
Then he appeared to more than 500 brethren at one time . . .
Then he appeared to James, *then* to all the apostles.
Last of all . . . he appeared also to me.

Paul clearly ranks his experience as one of the resurrection appearances which form the basis and substance of the Christian proclamation. More to the point, he regards his own experience as the *last* of these resurrection appearances. He knows of no further resurrection appearances either to himself or to others since then. His was the last resurrection appearance; he is the last of the apostles.[12] The point is sometimes weakened by those who argue that the εἶτα, ἔπειτα, ἔπειτα, εἶτα ('then', 'then') sequence does not signify a chronological order but merely simple association.[13] But whatever source(s) Paul drew his information from, the εἶτα, ἔπειτα, ἔπειτα, εἶτα sequence is surely best explained as Paul's attempt to set out the traditions he had received in chronological order – especially as the sequence is itself framed by clear-cut time notes (v. 4 – 'on the third day'; v. 8 – 'last of all').[14] And even if the chronological character of the first part of the list in I Cor. 15.5–8 is more open to question, it can hardly be disputed that with v. 8, 'last of all', Paul draws the list of resurrection appearances to a firm and final conclusion.[15]

(*b*) I Cor. 15.8 – ἔκτρωμα (*ektrōma* – 'abortion'). The debate on the significance of this word is of long standing.[16] (i) One would expect from the context that it should denote a late birth: Paul who had not known Jesus before his death nevertheless belongs to the apostolic family – a late arrival, but an apostle nevertheless.[17] But *ektrōma*, if it has temporal significance, denotes *early*, not late arrival – premature birth.[18] (ii) An alternative and venerable explanation is that *ektrōma* denotes the suddenness and violence of Paul's conversion – like Macduff in Shakespeare's *Macbeth*, 'from his mother's womb untimely ripped'.[19] But *ektrōma* signifies the *result* of premature birth, not its manner; as J. Munck has demonstrated, the word generally denotes a prematurely born child, usually but not necessarily stillborn.[20] (iii) Another ancient view is that the word was used to underline Paul's unworthiness of apostolic office. The popular tendency to associate premature birth with deformity suggests, moreover, that the sense intended was 'freak' or 'monstrosity' – perhaps a term of abuse taken up by Paul from his opponents ('last of all as to "the monstrosity"') – perhaps even with reference to his physical appearance.[21] This is a very plausible explanation, but it does ignore the time element almost entirely – and in the context of I Cor. 15.3–8 the time element cannot be unimportant.[22] (iv) A further possibility is to retain the time element but more in relation to Paul's Jewish past before Damascus. *Ektrōma* here is taken to mean an unformed foetus, 'something embryonic, that needs to be formed'. In which case it could describe Paul's attitude as he looked back to his state before he encountered Christ – formed under the law, but not yet formed by Christ.[23] But *ektrōma*, as Munck himself has shown, indicates the outcome of premature birth, not simply the unborn foetus; so in the context of I Cor. 15 it must denote Paul's state *as a result of* his encounter with Christ. (v) The best sense seems to be given by retaining the time element, but with reference to Paul's claim to be the last of the apostles, not with reference to his Jewish past. As the Greek shows, *ektrōma* is linked primarily with the 'last of all . . . he appeared also to me', not with his talk of persecuting the church.[24] Taken this way Paul's claim to be a 'witness to Jesus' resurrection' justifies the jibe 'the abortion' precisely because his conversion and call was a *premature* birth not a late birth. Instead of becoming a Christian by gradual development, after the due period of gestation, his coming to faith in Jesus was unexpectedly premature, when he was hardly ready for it.[25] The point of the metaphor for us, and the reason why Paul accepted it, was because without his premature birth his coming to faith would have been too late even for the last of the resurrection appearances.[26] If we are right the implication is clear: the resurrection appearances took place over a limited period and after a time ceased, and only those who experienced one could justify their claim to apostleship. Paul accepts this and afirms it for himself. He was privileged with a resurrection appearance and so can be counted an apostle only because his birth into faith in Christ was unnaturally hastened before he was ready. '*All* the apostles' had already seen Jesus and been commissioned by him (I Cor. 15.7); *only by premature birth was Paul enabled to join the apostolic circle before it finally closed.*[27]

It is of course quite possible that Paul uses the word casually and imprecisely, in which case either senses (ii) or (iii) above would be intended. But if he uses *ektrōma* in its proper sense, then it strengthens the view that Paul saw his Damascus experience as something unique and distinctive among the rest of his experiences. It had to be unique for him to justify his claim to be an apostle of the risen Jesus.

(c) I Cor. 15.9 – 'the least of the apostles'. This too seems to have been prompted by Paul's consciousness that he was 'last of all' the apostles. The stab of conscience over his persecuting past causes him to reduce his self-estimation even lower in a parenthetical aside ('unfit to be called an apostle, because I persecuted the church of

God'). But the humbling of himself to the lowest rank in the company of the apostles may well carry forward the previous thought – that he only just scraped home into that position before it was too late. He was the least of the apostles because he came last, brought forcibly into their number when he was unprepared, unformed. Here too the implication suggests itself that so far as Paul was concerned there had been no other resurrection appearances in the interval between his conversion and the time of writing to Corinth – some twenty years. There could be no other claimants to the title of 'last and least of the apostles'.

(d) I Cor. 9.1 – ἑώρακα ('I saw'). The choice of tense here is no doubt deliberate. The perfect tense denotes an event which took place in the past and whose effect is still operative – an event which made possible and constituted Paul's existence as an apostle.[28] Paul did not think of his apostleship as something re-established by every fresh experience of the risen Jesus. *His initial experience determined his apostleship for the rest of his life.* His initial experience in other words was something distinctive – different from all his subsequent experiences.

(e) It may be also, as several have suggested, that Paul himself deliberately refrains from using the word 'vision' to describe his Damascus experience – thereby carefully setting it apart from the kind of ecstatic experiences to which he refers in II Cor. 12.1ff.[29] Despite the fact that he describes both as 'revelation' (Gal. 1.12, 16; II Cor. 12.1), this suggestion gains in plausibility when we recall the point of dispute between Paul and his Corinthian opponents – viz., as to whether resurrection involved the body or not (I Cor. 15.12 – see below n.43). His opponents answered in the negative. Their experience of Christ therefore was of the pneumatic Christ, Christ the life-giving Spirit. Paul answered in the affirmative, and thus clearly marked off the appearance of the risen Lord from heaven (in spiritual body) from such 'visions and revelations' and experiences prompted by the Spirit from within (with which he was also familiar).[30]

It is clear then that Paul himself made a firm distinction between his conversion experience and his subsequent spiritual experiences. *His Damascus road experience was not simply the first of several or many experiences of the same kind; for Paul it was the last of a number of experiences of a unique kind.*

§19. THE DISTINCTIVENESS OF PAUL'S CONVERSION EXPERIENCE – AN APPEARANCE OF JESUS

Wherein lay the distinctiveness of Paul's conversion experience? Part of the answer must lie in the element of *seeing* and in *what was seen*. This is explicit in I Cor. 9.1, 'Have I not *seen* Jesus our Lord?', and implicit in the ὤφθη of I Cor. 15.8 – 'he *appeared* also to me'. But these passages only pose the further questions: What was the mode of seeing? and, What was it that was actually seen? – *How* seen? and, *What* seen? And the answer to both these questions is by no means clear.

19.1   *What kind of 'seeing'?* The immediate problem is that the verb 'see' has a fairly extensive range of meaning.[31]

(*a*) At one end it can denote *mental perception* – the intellectual apprehension of some truth or insight by means of logic or intuition (or revelation). (*b*) At the other end of its semantic range it denotes *physical perception* – the seeing of a three-dimensional object present to the subject in time and space with the physical eyes. (*c*) Between (or beyond) these two ends of the spectrum comes *visionary perception*, where an actual seeing is involved, but where the status of what is seen is disputed: does the seeing takes place in the mind, wholly internally, as in a dream? Is the seeing the projection of mental images, as in some forms of vision? Or is there an external reality present to the visionary which others are unable to see for some reason?

(*a*) *Mental perception.* W. Marxsen, as we have already noted, argues from the analogous use of ἀποκαλύπτειν (reveal) in Gal. 1.16 that Paul in talking of his conversion experience is thinking rather of the uncovering of a truth than the seeing of a person – mental perception rather than visual perception.

Earlier, W. Michaelis in his study of the resurrection appearances and his Kittel Wörterbuch article on ὁράω (see) attempted to cut the knot by denying that ὁράω said anything at all about the mode of seeing. In his view ὀφθῆναι (to be seen) signifies the *presence of revelation*, not sensual perception; it does not express the *visual* quality of the experience.

When ὤφθη is used as a technical term to denote the resurrection appearances there is no primary emphasis on seeing as sensual or mental perception. . . . ὤφθη Κηφᾷ etc. means . . . they experienced his presence. . . . This presence is in non-visionary reality.³²

However, against both Michaelis and Marxsen, it must be emphasized that in the passages before us ὀφθῆναι can hardly have any other sense than *visual perception*. In biblical Greek ὀφθῆναι always denotes seeing with the eyes.³³ This applies equally to seeing physical objects, theophanies, visions and dreams – the one who sees really sees.³⁴ This is not of course to deny the revelatory character of the resurrection appearance to Paul, but simply to affirm that in I Cor. 15.8 as in I Cor. 9.1 Paul claims actually to have seen something.³⁵

(b) *Physical perception*. Does Paul's ὀφθῆναι fall within the category of physical perception or visionary perception? K. H. Rengstorf rejects not only Michaelis's mental perception interpretation of ὤφθη but also the visionary hypothesis, both the 'subjective vision' thesis of Strauss and the 'objective vision' thesis more recently championed by H. Grass. He suggests indeed that

in the ὤφθη of I Cor. 15.5ff. (cf. Acts 13.31, 9.17, 26.16) we have the earliest available protest of a Christianity still on the soil of the early Palestinian community against the attempt to strip the Easter event of its objective character and to transform it thereby from an affair (Sache) of God into an affair of the disciples.³⁶

It is certainly true that most of the resurrection appearances in the gospels, particularly in Luke, seem to be intended to convey the impression that a straightforward physical perception was involved (see below §21.1). And it would be possible to argue that Paul by describing *all* the resurrection appearances in I Cor. 15.5–8 with the same word (ὤφθη) intends to give his own experience the same objectivity as the resurrection appearances related in the gospels.³⁷ However, in Paul's case it would be difficult to deny the subjectivity of the experience.

For one thing, Paul describes his conversion as to some extent at least an internal experience: Gal. 1.16 – 'God chose to reveal his Son in me (ἐν ἐμοί) . . .' The ἐν ἐμοί could stand simply for the dative – 'to me' – and it is frequently taken in this way.³⁸ But when Paul wants to use a dative with ἀποκαλύπτειν he does so; indeed this is his normal usage (I Cor. 2.10; 14.30; Eph. 3.5; Phil. 3.15). Presumably then the ἐν ἐμοί is chosen deliberately; and the obvious reason is to heighten the subjectivity of the revelation in the moment of encounter and in its impact on his inner life.³⁹ To be sure, Paul is not talking here about the visionary side of his conversion experience as such – ἀποκάλυψις (Gal. 1.12) does not mean 'vision'⁴⁰ (though II Cor. 4.6 probably warns us not to press the distinction too far). But he *is* describing his conversion experience; and he describes it as a personal subjective experience. To this extent Marxsen is correct: in denying that the ὤφθη of Paul's conversion can be reduced to mental perception we must not deny that subjective mental perception was also integral to that experience.

Furthermore, the Acts accounts of Paul's conversion cannot be understood otherwise than in visionary and subjective terms. Not only is the experience specifically described as a 'heavenly vision' (by Paul himself! – Acts 26.19); but in addition, whereas all his companions were said to have seen the 'great light from heaven' (22.6, 9), only Paul was blinded and only Paul heard the voice from heaven (22.9–11). That is to say, only Paul experienced a personal encounter (cf. 9.7); only Paul understood what he saw as a Christophany. As Pannenberg notes, 'An event of this sort must be designated as a vision. If someone sees something that others present are not able to see, then it involves a vision'.[41] Now of course the Acts presentation of Paul's conversion may owe this particular characteristic to Luke's editing (see above §18.2). But that Luke is in fact drawing on good tradition at this point is suggested by II Cor. 4.6. This verse almost certainly alludes to Paul's conversion[42] and describes it in terms of a heavenly light (= the glory of God – II Cor. 3.18; 4.4, 6). Here too the subjectivity of the experience is underlined, for 'God caused his light to shine *within us* (ἐν ταῖς καρδίαις ἡμῶν), to give the light of revelation – the revelation of the glory of God in the face of Jesus Christ' (NEB).

It seems impossible therefore to deny the subjectivity of the resurrection appearance to Paul. His seeing Jesus on the road to Damascus cannot be described as physical perception.

(c) This leaves us with the third alternative – *visionary perception*. There can be little doubt that Paul saw something; but was the seeing internal, 'all in the mind', or was there something there to be seen, something external to him? The problem here is, as noted above, the status of that which was seen.

What was it Paul actually saw? The only answer that Paul allows us to give is 'Jesus'. And having said that we can say little more, for Paul nowhere describes what he saw – nor even attempts to do so. When answering the question, What is the resurrection body like?' (I Cor. 15.35), he does not reply, 'Like the resurrection body of Jesus'. Instead he uses analogies and verbal contrasts which in the end of the day do not really clarify very much. To opponents who accepted that Jesus rose again but who apparently denied the idea of a resurrection *body*,[43] he does not avail himself of what would appear to be his most powerful response, 'I know that the body is raised after death, because when I saw the risen Jesus he appeared to me as a spiritual body'.

Does this imply that there was something indescribable in Jesus' mode of existence as Paul perceived it, or that there was no definition or detail in what he saw?

So too when defending himself against those who questioned his apostleship he does not elaborate the event of his call. He lays claim to it, but he does not describe it (Gal. 1.1, 11f., 15f.). Instead he appeals to his integrity and to the change effected by his conversion (Gal. 1.10, 13ff.) – and in I Cor. 9.2 to the impact of his ministry on the Corinthians themselves. Would a more detailed account of his conversion and call not have made as powerful an argument as these others (as in Acts 26.12–19)? Why did Paul not elaborate on his Damascus road experience? Was it because he would not, or because he could not? Likewise when discussing the 'signs of an apostle' in II Cor. 10–13 he does not speak at all of his resurrection appearance. When forced to trade experiences with 'these superlative apostles' (II Cor. 12.11) he can boast of 'visions and revelations' (12.1) and goes on to attempt some description of one such event (12.2ff.), but no description of his conversion experience is ever attempted. This suggests that his conversion and call was of a different character – that Paul himself could go no further than the description, 'I saw Jesus our Lord'.[44]

The only passage which sheds a little more light is II Cor. 4.6 (see above n. 42). What Paul saw was a blinding light which he identified with the risen Jesus – 'the light of the knowledge of the glory of God in the face of Jesus Christ'.[45] This light was for Paul the visible manifestation of God (II Cor. 3.18; 4.4); it was all that could be seen by the human eye of the risen Jesus in his new mode of existence, his new embodiment, 'his body of glory' (Phil. 3.21).

19.2 *The reality of the appearance for Paul.* What then was the status of what Paul saw? Was Jesus 'out there', alive and making himself known to Paul? Or did the Damascus experience simply mark 'the moment when the unconscious complex of Christianity broke through into consciousness'?[46] Crucial though this question is it is impossible to demonstrate either answer. Religious phenomena are notoriously ambiguous and it is no different here. Those who opt for the former view cannot exclude the possibility that they are wrong, that Paul's experience was after all, all 'in the mind'. But those who opt for the latter view cannot exclude the possibility they are wrong, that the psychological explanation only casts light on the subject's mental mechanism and does not provide a full or exhaustive explanation of all that took place on that Damascus road.[47]

What we can say with more certainty is that Paul himself was convinced that what he saw was external to him – was Jesus alive from the dead, alive in a new mode of existence (spiritual body). This is apparent in Paul's use of ὤφθη – the passive indicating that the initiative in the seeing lay not with the see-er but with the one seen – he appeared, showed himself to (dative), not he was seen by (ὑπό).

It is 'the one who appears' who acts, the person who receives the appearance is passive, he experiences the appearance. In this sense, such an experience means seeing something which is given to the seer to see.[48]

Likewise the phrase 'the revelation of Jesus Christ' in Gal. 1.12 clearly means not 'the revelation given by Jesus Christ', but 'the revelation which is Jesus Christ himself'; for when Paul takes up the thought again in 1.15f. he explains that 'the revelation of Jesus Christ' was given to him in order that he might preach *Jesus Christ* among the Gentiles. Christ himself is the gospel. That which was revealed to him was the gospel, that is, Jesus Christ, that is, Jesus alive from the dead, Jesus as Son, as agent of eschatological salvation, and all the consequences that flowed therefrom.[49]

Paul then was convinced that Jesus had appeared to him alive from the dead. He is unable to affirm more than the bare *that* of the experience – 'I saw Jesus' – but *that* he is able to affirm in all good conscience. To revert to our opening question, herein must lie part of our answer. *The distinctiveness of Paul's conversion experience consisted in part at least in his seeing Jesus – a seeing which was visionary in mode but nevertheless for Paul was a real perception of and encounter with Jesus, albeit in a sphere of existence which cannot be brought within the limitations of visual description.*[50]

This claim of Paul's cannot be dismissed as special pleading, because it seems to have been accepted without serious dispute by the 'pillar apostles' (Gal. 2.9);[51] and certainly Paul can rank his ὀφθῆναι with the others without having to argue the point or indulge in polemics in the key passage (I Cor. 15.5–8). The appearance was a 'revelatory act' to be sure; but that which was 'revealed' was Jesus Christ himself (Gal. 1.12, 15f.).

Nor can the affirmation of a distinctive seeing element in his conversion experience be dismissed as typical of the arbitrary elitist claim of the ecstatic. Paul was familiar with spiritual experiences initiated by the proclamation of the gospel and inspired speech (I Cor. 2.4f.; 14.24f.; Gal. 3.2–5; I Thess. 1.5f.). He was familiar with 'visions and revelations' (II Cor. 12.1) and could match the claims of the Corinthian ecstatic apostles at every stage. He was no stranger to the experience of Christ as a power within him (Gal. 2.20; Rom. 8.10);

it is his own formulation which defines the experience of life-giving Spirit as experience of the last Adam (I Cor. 15.45). In all this he readily agrees with his gnostic opponents; he was as familiar as they were with the pneumatic Christ, the power within. But at Damascus he not only experienced power within but more than that, he perceived a person without – not only the gift of grace (I Cor. 15.10) but the appearance of the risen Jesus (15.8). His claim that his seeing of Jesus was something distinctive therefore was not lightly made and cannot be lightly dismissed.

One passage which might have provided something of a check on this conclusion is Col. 2.18 – the only other passage in which Paul uses ὁράω for a visionary seeing. Unfortunately, it is not altogether clear what Paul means: 'Let no one disqualify you, taking pleasure (θέλων) in self-mortification and angel worship, what he saw in his initiation (ἃ ἑόρακεν ἐμβατεύων), inflating himself to a false importance by his worldly attitude . . .'. The problem of what the middle phrase, ἃ ἑόρακεν ἐμβατεύων, means has never wholly been solved; difficulties remain for every hypothesis.[52] The most probable clue to a solution lies in the recognition that ἐμβατεύω was a technical term in the mystery religions for the act of initiation into the mysteries.[53] It looks as though Paul has picked up the phrase from his Colossian adversaries,[54] and half quoted it in exclamatory fashion, linking it only loosely to the context.[55] Here then is a likely parallel to Paul's own initiatory vision. Why should Paul, who built so much on his own ὀφθῆναι, speak so slightingly of the initiatory visions of his Colossian protagonists? The answer may lie in the direction of the distinctiveness we have already charted. Paul's ὀφθῆναι was a seeing of Jesus, with all the eschatological and salvation-history (Col. 2.17), as well as cosmological (Col. 1.15–20) and corporate (Col. 2.19) implications which that had for Paul, not simply a vision of angels[56] or of cosmic relationships.[57] And it was a seeing which thrust him out in mission, did not lead merely to a round of ascetic practice which pandered to individualistic pride and a more subtle form of self-indulgence (2.18, 23). But here we are anticipating (§20).

In short, Paul was convinced that Jesus was alive and had appeared to him. With the blinding light which he saw outside Damascus was borne in upon him the unquenchable conviction that this was Jesus whom he was seeing – 'the glory of God in the face of Jesus Christ'. *He could describe it no further; but he could describe it thus far.* This experience was without comparison in his subsequent life; nor did he recognize its like in the experience of others. The only comparable experiences were the resurrection appearances to the earlier apostles.

§20. THE DISTINCTIVENESS OF PAUL'S CONVERSION EXPERIENCE – APOSTOLIC COMMISSIONING

The other significant aspect of the Damascus experience for Paul was his commissioning. It is important to re-emphasize the point made earlier (§18.2) that when Paul mentions his experience at Damascus it is always in the context of talk of his kerygma and his apostleship. He never speaks of his conversion as such; the resurrection appearance is never cited as the beginning of his Christian faith and life.[58] He never speaks of the appearance of Jesus to him as something of significance in its own right. The emphasis lies on the commissioning. Gal. 1.16 – God 'was pleased to reveal his Son in me *in order that I might preach him among the Gentiles*'. I Cor. 9.1 – 'Am I not an apostle? Have I not seen Jesus our Lord'? – and in what follows it is his apostleship which is the central concern, not the seeing. I Cor. 15.8ff. – 'he appeared also to me . . . and his grace to me was not in vain. On the contrary I worked harder than any of them . . .' II Cor. 4.6 – 'the revelation of the glory of God in the face of Jesus Christ' is the gospel with which he had been commissioned (4.4f.). The Damascus experience for Paul meant primarily his commissioning to proclaim Jesus (as Son of God and Lord) to the Gentiles.[59]

20.1   *The source of his gospel.* It is of first importance for Paul that the commissioning came in the experience at Damascus – the point he makes so emphatically in his letter to the Galatians: 'not from men nor through man, but through Jesus Christ' (Gal. 1.1). His concept of the gospel and his compulsion to take it to the Gentiles did not stem from any memory he had of Jesus; almost certainly he never met Jesus during Jesus' ministry. Nor was it inspired by the tradition of Jesus' own message and style of life; otherwise it would have left a more substantial mark in Paul's letters. Nor was Paul's gospel derived from the kerygma of the primitive communities; that he denies vehemently and emphatically, and there is no reason to doubt his word (Gal. 1.1, 11f., 20).[60] In other words, Paul claims that his basic and characteristic understanding of Christ and of Christ's significance for men came to him direct from God 'through a revelation of Jesus Christ'.

This tells us something about the nature of the experience for Paul – viz., its *givenness* from without. It was because of the givenness of this wholly new understanding, because it came to him with the force of *revelation*, that Paul could insist so fiercely on the authoritativeness and normativeness of his gospel (Gal. 1.8f.). To be sure it had been accepted and confirmed by the 'pillar apostles' in Jerusalem (Gal. 2.6–9), and so he could assert its authority over others on the basis of more than personal conviction. But so far as Paul was concerned, that authority came in the first place from his direct encounter with the risen Jesus, and in the last analysis from no other source (see further below §47.2).

How this sense of commissioning achieved verbal expression in Paul's mind is something we need not determine. It may have been the breaking through into conscious expression of a growing conviction long repressed (cf. Jung in n. 46 above), although the talk of 'revelation' implies that for Paul at least the information content and its theological corollaries came to him as something totally new and unexpected. Or it may have come in some auditive element in the vision ('voice from heaven' – cf. above ch. III, n. 120) – as Luke would have us believe[61] – although Paul himself never speaks of hearing words in his Damascus experience. And of course it is not necessary to hold that the great Pauline distinctives sprang immediately into his mind in full flower in the moment of that encounter; his understanding of Jesus as the eschatological Lord to be proclaimed to all nations no doubt took some time to reach mature expression (cf. Acts 9.9, 17f. – 'three days without sight' before he was 'filled with the Holy Spirit' and baptized;[62] Gal. 1.17 – the time in 'Arabia'). But however Paul achieved the conscious expression of his gospel, the point for us to note is that in Paul's mind the gospel was already contained within that appearance outside Damascus; his gospel was simply an 'unpacking' of 'the revelation of Jesus Christ' (see above p. 108).[63]

20.2 *Eschatological apostleship.* If it is hard for us today to recapture the eschatological significance of Jesus' proclamation of the kingdom (Matt. 12.28 – already upon you!), it is even harder to recapture the eschatological significance of the appearance of Jesus to Paul. Jesus was not merely alive after death; he was risen from the dead! Incredible though it was, the resurrection of Jesus meant that the eschatological resurrection had already begun (Rom. 1.4). The risen Jesus was the ἀπαρχή (first-fruits) of the general resurrection at the end of time (I Cor. 15.20, 23). The End had begun! The harvest of resurrected humanity was already in process of reaping. This was no idle play on words or the talk of an enthusiastic visionary too heavenly minded for earthly realities. So far as Paul was concerned it was an existential truth verifiable in his own experience. The glory which Paul had seen on the Damascus road (II Cor. 4.6) was for him the glory of the age to come.[64] And that glory which was already Christ's (Phil. 3.21), was having a continuing and growing effect on Paul himself in transforming him into the same image (II Cor. 3.18; cf. I Cor. 15.20, 23, 49; II Cor. 4.17; Col. 1.27). Paul really felt himself to be standing inside this climactic process of eschatological transformation and perceived its outworkings in his own life. We will explore this theme more fully in chapter X. Here we must concern ourselves only with the eschatological impact of the commission which the risen Jesus laid upon Paul.

It was O. Cullmann and A. Fridrichsen who first drew attention to the eschatological nature of Paul's apostleship.[65] Cullmann interpreted II Thess. 2.7 as a self reference. Paul shared the belief that the gospel must first be preached to the Gentiles before the End could come (Mark 13.10). That which restrains (τὸ κατέχον – neuter) the appearance of the 'man of lawlessness' (II Thess. 2.6) is therefore the preaching of the gospel to the Gentiles. And since this preaching was his own special commission, he who restrains (ὁ κατέχων – masculine) the mystery of lawlessness (II Thess. 2.7) was the apostle to the Gentiles, Paul himself.[66] Fridrichsen in turn hailed Paul inelegantly as 'an eschatologic person'. The sense of being called to play an essential role in the drama of the final days was fundamental to his apostolic self-consciousness. That role was his apostleship to the Gentiles.

Cullmann's interpretation of II Thess. 2.7 cannot stand, if only because Paul did not at this stage envisage his 'disappearance from the scene' before the parousia (I Thess. 4.15ff.; I Cor. 15.51ff.).[67] Nor can Fridrichsen's thesis escape criticism in the form in which he presented it.[68] But it is not possible to deny that Paul saw himself fulfilling an important and essential role in the last act of the history of salvation. This is sufficiently clear from Rom. 11.13ff.; 15.15ff.; Gal. 2.7–9; Eph. 3.1–10. His ministry is to the Gentiles – to the Gentiles as a whole. This is why he hastens to take the gospel to the bounds of the known world (Spain – Rom. 15.28). He wants to 'complete the preaching of the gospel of Christ' to the Gentiles so that he may 'offer the Gentiles to him as an acceptable sacrifice' (Rom. 15.16, 20). The completion of this task is of crucial eschatological significance, for only when 'the full number of the Gentiles has come in' will Israel be saved and the resurrection harvest be successfully concluded (Rom. 11.15, 25f.); see also below pp. 273f.[69]

The same sense of playing a decisive part in the climax of history is clearly evident in another striking aspect of Paul's understanding of his missionary vocation. I refer to his conviction that in his ministry he was fulfilling the role of the servant of Second Isaiah;[70] the same conviction has impressed itself upon the related Acts material.[71] When we recall that the thought of Jesus as the Isaianic Servant plays a less dominant role in Paul's writings than later apologetic would lead us to think,[72] an interesting conclusion follows: viz., that Paul has almost as much claim to the title 'Servant of Yahweh' as Jesus.[73] Or to be more precise, Paul completes the role of the Servant which Jesus left incomplete. This is obviously true of the Servant's mission to the Gentiles. But it is true too of the Servant's suffering; for in bold language Paul does not hesitate to claim that his own sufferings fill up what is lacking in Christ's (Col. 1.24); in other words, his hope is that his own suffering will complete the messianic affliction which must be endured before the End comes.[74] *Jesus and Paul together fulfil the eschatological role of the Servant.*

It is surely this overpowering sense of something epochally new, of being recipient of a revelation which supersedes all earlier revelations in priority and authority, of eschatological urgency and responsibility, which explains how Paul the Pharisee could turn his back so fully on his chief heritage – the law – and become apostle to the Gentiles. The revelation of Jesus Christ had superseded the revelation of the law.[75] Now before the End, and as precursor of the End, the Gentiles must be offered the gospel as speedily and as freely as possible. Here clearly is a key feature which distinguished the Damascus 'revelation of Jesus Christ' from his other and subsequent particular experiences; none other of his revelations had this epochal and eschatological significance for Paul. That one experience determined the rest of his life; from it everything else flowed.[76]

In short, the distinctiveness of Paul's conversion experience as commissioning lay in the fact that the *'revelation of Jesus Christ' was the first source and final authority both for his new faith in its distinctive expression and for the eschatological compulsion which moulded his whole life to be its apostle and mouthpiece.*

20.3 *Conclusion. The distinctive feature of Paul's Damascus experience lies both in its nature as appearance and in its character as commissioning.* It was not simply a commissioning, the verbal expression of a given conviction. It was an *appearance*: 'I saw Jesus our Lord'. He did not need to express his experience in terms of seeing (Marxsen). But he could do so, and when it was necessary did so without dishonesty. For it was this element of seeing, of Jesus manifesting himself to Paul in visual encounter, which marked off Paul's experience from gnostic experiences of the pneumatic Christ – which enabled Paul to include his own experience within that select and closed list of 'witnesses of Jesus' resurrection': 'last of all he appeared also to me'. But neither was it simply a seeing – an appearance. The 'more than 500 brethren' also saw Jesus, but presumably not all of them were regarded by Paul as apostles.[77] In other words, there was something more than a visionary perception of the exalted Jesus in the case of 'all the apostles' and of Paul. In their case a *call to mission* came with the appearance.

Thus it becomes clear that *it was not the seeing itself nor the commissioning itself which was distinctive for Paul but the appearance as call, the encounter as commission.* The commissioning did not come alongside, apart from the seeing. *The appearance itself was the commissioning. The revelation was itself the gospel.* With the appearance of the divine glory came the overwhelming conviction that this was Jesus raised from the dead, that here was God's eschatological gospel for both Jew and Gentile, that henceforth his whole life must be dedicated to its proclamation, cost what it might. The perception of the risen Lord without became for Paul, when he yielded to it, an experience of compulsion and grace within (I Cor. 15.10; Eph. 3.7). It was in the *Ineinander* (in-each-other-ness) of appearance and commission, of revelation and grace, that the distinctive and unsurpassable nature of the experience lay for Paul.

§21. THE EARLIER RESURRECTION APPEARANCES

The question we ask here is whether the other resurrection appearances differed from the appearance to Paul. As we have seen, there were two important features of Paul's experience: it was a visionary experience, though Paul had no doubt that he saw a Jesus who was there, an external and present reality; and so far as Paul was concerned, his call to eschatological mission sprang immediately from this experience and had no other foundation. It was the combination of these two factors which led Paul to the conclusion that his experiences belonged to a distinctive group of experiences in the past – commissioning appearances; and the fact that this combination was not repeated in future experiences of himself or of others, led him to the further conclusion that his conversion had completed and brought to an end the sequence of apostle-making experiences. If then we are to compare the earlier resurrection appearances with the appearance to Paul we must examine them at the two points of visual element and commissioning element.

21.1　*The differences between the appearance to Paul and the earlier appearances.* The most marked difference between the resurrection appearance to Paul and the appearances narrated in the gospels lies in the seeing element. Paul's seeing was visionary in character; what he saw was non-physical, non-material – strictly speaking, non-objective in that it could not be examined as an object by an observer. And what he saw probably appeared to him from heaven, as though in the sky (cf. Acts 26.19 – 'heavenly vision'). Furthermore, Paul's concept of the resurrection body (I Cor. 15.42–50) and the fact that he describes the resurrection appearances in I Cor. 15.5–8 in precisely the same way,[78] suggests that Paul regarded them all as appearances of the same sort – visionary, 'from heaven'. Yet when we turn to the gospel accounts the picture is quite different – particularly in Luke. Jesus walks and talks like any wayfaring companion (Luke 24.15ff.); he blesses and breaks the bread (24.30); he invites the troubled disciples to touch him as proof that he is no ghost but has 'flesh and bones' (24.39); he eats a piece of cooked fish 'in front of them' (24.42f.); he is often in their company ($\sigma\upsilon\nu\alpha\lambda\iota\zeta\acute{o}\mu\epsilon\nu o\varsigma$)[79] and shows that he is alive 'by many proofs' (Acts 1.3f.); and finally he is objectively removed from their sight in a final act of physical separation (Acts 1.9). It is true that in his appearances prior to his 'ascension' his coming and going was most mysterious (Luke 24.31, 36), but the 'massive realism' (Grass) of the appearances themselves can only be described as visionary with great difficulty – and Luke would certainly reject the description as inappropriate (cf. Acts 12.9).

Likewise in the Fourth Gospel the risen Jesus can be touched by Mary (John 20.17); he shows the disciples his hands and feet and breathes on them (John 20.20, 22); he invites Thomas to put his finger in Jesus' hands and his hand in Jesus' side (20.27); and in the appendix Jesus has apparently lit a charcoal fire, he cooks breakfast and proceeds to distribute bread and fish to the disciples (21.9–13). Again there is something mysterious about him, particularly as he suddenly appears 'behind closed doors' (20.19, 26), but again the appearances are quite different from that experienced by Paul.

The same applies to Matthew to lesser extent. The final appearance on 'the mountain' in Galilee could well be understood as a 'heavenly vision' (Matt. 28.16–20); but earlier, in the curious little account of an appearance to the women on the way from the tomb, Matthew records that 'they came up and took hold of his feet' (28.9). So the three gospels which record appearances are unanimous in asserting the objective, physical nature of the appearances – and this seems to put them at odds with Paul.

What is the explanation for this striking difference between Paul's ὀφθῆναι and the gospel accounts of the other resurrection appearances? The one apparently so intangible, the others so manifestly tangible – why the difference? Were the experiences different in kind, or all ultimately the same? Three answers have been proposed.

(a) First, the tradition of resurrection appearances has developed in the direction of reducing detail, that is, presumably, from the more material, physical appearances to the more visionary, spiritual appearances. So Käsemann, believes,

There can remain scarcely any other hypothesis for the historian than that more detailed narratives which were available were suppressed on dogmatic grounds, because they had ceased to correspond to the views of the second and third generations of Christians.[80]

On this view the restraint of Paul's references to the resurrection appearances is due to his respect for Hellenistic repugnance at the thought of the physical body being raised. The grosser materialistic accounts of the gospels stem from the earlier understanding of the risen Jesus' mode of existence.

(b) Second, much more highly favoured by scholars is the view that the tradition has developed in precisely the opposite direction – that the visionary appearances belong to the earliest stratum and that the gospel accounts represent a progressive and legendary materialization of the appearance tradition[81] – a development of appearance *narratives* 'by borrowing the traits of the earthly Jesus'.[82]

(c) A third possibility is to take a mediating position – to argue that there were different kinds of appearances. Thus Lindblom distinguishes appearances on earth (what he calls 'Christepiphanies') from appearances from heaven ('Christophanies'). The former he suggests took place before Pentecost (to Peter and 'the twelve'), the latter after Pentecost (to the more than 500, James, the apostles and Paul).[83] Alternatively, the different types of appearances could conceivably be traced back to different sources – Jerusalem tradition represented by Acts 1.3ff. and Galilee tradition represented by I Cor. 15.3ff.[84]

The basic problem here is that we seem to have two conflicting tendencies within the appearance traditions: a tendency *away* from the physical (*a*), and a reverse tendency *towards* the physical (*b*). On the face of it there is much more evidence for the latter. If we set out the relevant documents in the chronological order of their dates of writing it is difficult to deny a tendency to elaborate the appearances. Paul lists only appearances; Mark records no appearance, but gives promise of appearances to Peter and presumably the twelve without further detail;[85] the first narrative proper of a resurrection appearance is to be found in Matthew's so brief account of the women's encounter with the risen Jesus; both narrative and materializing tendency only come to full expression in the records of Luke and John; the tendency continues into the second century in Ignatius, *Smyrneans* 3.2f., in *The Gospel of the Hebrews* 7, in the *Gospel of Peter* 35–45, and especially in *Epistula Apostolorum* 1off.[86]

But in fact the other tendency is also in evidence, and this I will attempt to demonstrate at the risk of digressing somewhat from our central theme. In particular, there are some indications that a more physical understanding of Jesus' resurrection was current in the earliest Jerusalem community – in which case Paul's treatment of the resurrection body has to be regarded as something of a hellenizing refinement, a demythologizing (see below §21.3).

21.2   *The earliest conceptualization of Jesus' resurrection.* We know that the concept of an eschatological resurrection was developing in the apocalyptic literature of the intertestamental period. Its roots[87] may be traced back to the late addition to the book of Isaiah – chs. 24–27 (fourth or third century BC) and to Dan. 12.2 (*c.* 165 BC).

Isa. 26.19 – But thy dead live, their bodies will rise again.
          They that sleep in the earth will awake and shout for joy . . .[88]

Dan. 12.2 – (Many of) those who sleep in the dust of the earth shall awake,
          some to everlasting life and some to everlasting contempt.

Initially the mode of resurrection does not seem to have been very clearly defined – a straightforward physical resurrection is neither explicit nor excluded (cf. Isa. 26.19c; Dan. 12.3). In some later apocalyptic writings a more spiritualized concept gains the upper hand – see e.g. II Esd. 2.39, 45 ('immortal clothing'); I Enoch 62.15 ('garments of glory'); 108.11ff.[89] But belief in the resurrection of the physical body also developed throughout the course of Jewish apocalyptic and came to unequivocal expression in other writings of the period – no doubt partly at least by way of reaction to the competing influence of the Hellenistic body-soul dualism.[90] Thus, in particular, the Maccabean martyrs look for a restoration of life and physical organs (II Macc. 7.11, 23; 14.46);[91] in the Sibylline Oracles IV the hope is expressed that 'God himself shall fashion again the bones and ashes of men, and shall raise up mortals once more as they were before' (181f.) so that 'all who are godly shall live again on the earth' (187);[92] and in II Baruch 50.2 we read:

For the earth shall then assuredly restore the dead,
......
It shall make no change in their form,
But as it has received, so shall it restore them,
And as I delivered them unto it, so shall it raise them.[93]

In Baruch at least the transformation into a more glorious form of existence takes place *after* the resurrection from the dead and not simultaneously with it (II Bar. 49–51).[94]

It is probable that it was this cruder, less sophisticated, more straightforward concept of resurrection which was taken up by the first disciples when they attempted to conceptualize their apprehension of Jesus alive after death. Traces of such a primitive view are probably to be found in Matt. 27.52f., John 5.28f. and Acts 2.26f., 31, 13.35ff.

Matt. 27.52f.: 'The tombs also were opened, and many bodies of the saints who had fallen asleep were raised (ἠγέρθησαν), and coming out of the tombs after his resurrection they went into the holy city and appeared to many' (RSV). This is obviously an ancient tradition, which Matthew has felt it necessary to retain without integrating it very well into his narrative; and it may well reflect in one form or another the primitive Christian view that Jesus' resurrection was the beginning (ἀπαρχή – I Cor. 15.20, 23) of the general resurrection at the end of time.[95] At any rate, the point for us to observe is that resurrection here is conceived in terms of the bodies of the dead coming out of the tombs in which they were laid.

John 5.28f.: 'All those in the tombs will hear his voice and will come forth'. The concept of resurrection is again simple and straightforward – like the tradition in Matt. 27.52f., wholly of a piece with the important strand of Jewish apocalyptic at which we have just looked. It is almost certainly therefore a snatch of early Christian apocalyptic which the evangelist has incorporated to act as a counterweight to his more sophisticated and manifestly much later realized eschatology.[96] We should also notice that the evangelist himself recognizes the concept of resurrection contained in 5.28f. as implying a very close one to one correlation between the physical body and the resurrection mode of existence – more or less a resuscitation or restoration of the corpse understanding of resurrection; indeed he seems to highlight the crudeness of the concept by drawing deliberate parallels between 5.28f. and the raising of Lazarus, who literally heard Jesus' *voice* while *in the tomb* and *came forth* (11.17, 43),[97] and between the raising of Lazarus and the resurrection of Jesus.[98]

Acts 2.26f., 31; 13.35ff. Both Peter's sermon on the day of Pentecost and Paul's in the synagogue at Antioch quote Ps. 16.8–11 as a prophecy fulfilled by Jesus' resurrection.

Acts 2.26f. – . . . my flesh will dwell in hope.
    Thou wilt not abandon my soul to Hades, nor let thy holy one see corruption.
2.31 – [David] foresaw and spoke of the resurrection of the Christ, that he was not abandoned to Hades, nor did his flesh see corruption.

Similarly 13.35ff. Whatever the date of composition of the speeches,[99] it is likely that Luke or his source is here taking up an ancient testimonium or proof text used by the first Christians to justify their belief that God had raised Jesus from the dead – one of the scriptures in fact to which I Cor. 15.4 refers. It is true that the text is taken from the LXX and not the Hebrew,[100] not unnaturally since the LXX permits a resurrection interpretation more readily than the Hebrew, but this does not necessarily imply that the text was first taken up as a testimonium in a Greek speaking church. The rabbis also interpreted Ps. 16.9 (in its *Hebrew* form) as a reference to resurrection in terms of preservation of the flesh *beyond* death;[101] and since they are unlikely to have taken the interpretation from the Christians, their resurrection interpretation presumably antedates the Christian interpretation – one of the proof texts by which the Pharisees sought to gain greater authority for their belief in resurrection against the Sadducees. This suggests that the line of argument developed from Ps. 16.8–11 was a piece of primitive Christian apologetic.[102] In which case we must again note the crudely physical concept of resurrection which it defends: the resurrection of Jesus was achieved by preventing and reversing the usual processes of corruption of the physical body.[103]

That the first believers took up the straightforward resuscitation of the corpse view of Jesus' resurrection is also suggested by the tradition of the empty tomb. The debate on the age and historicity of this tradition is long and detailed, and we cannot enter it here. It must suffice to say that literary analysis of the gospel traditions has proved decisive neither for nor against its primitiveness.[104] Perhaps the two most persuasive considerations in favour of its essential historicity are these: first, in view of the then current thought about resurrection outlined above it is questionable whether *without an empty tomb* either the disciples would have interpreted their 'resurrection appearance' experience in terms of resurrection, or many would have believed them when they proclaimed, 'God has raised Jesus from the dead' – that is, as a past event, *before* the general resurrection. Second, there is the remarkable absence of any tomb veneration. In the history of religions (not least Judaism – Matt. 23.29/Luke 11.47) the sacredness of a dead prophet's tomb or burial place is a regular feature.[105] But we find absolutely no trace of any interest in the place of Jesus' burial within earliest Christianity[106] – a surprising fact if Jesus' tomb remained undisturbed or if his body had been removed and buried elsewhere, but not if the tomb was found to be empty.

It is likely therefore that the first disciples believed that there was a very close one to one correlation between the body of Jesus dead and buried and the body of his new life – that his flesh had not been permitted to decompose and putrefy – that his body had indeed quite literally been raised from the dead.

Thus there is evidence both for a development within the NT documents themselves from a more spiritual to a more physical interpretation of the resurrection appearances, and yet also for an earlier more physical interpretation of Jesus' resurrection. This suggests that there has been a more complex development in the history of the resurrection traditions than is generally allowed.

21.3 *The development in early Christian conceptualization of Jesus' resurrection* was probably something as follows. The first stage we have already outlined above. The resurrection appearances to Peter and 'the twelve' (and the women?), taken in conjunction with the discovery that Jesus' tomb was empty, led the first believers to the conclusion that God had raised up Jesus' body from the grave – raised Jesus, that is, to heaven, for, as most scholars agree, there was originally no material distinction in the early Christian mind between resurrection, ascension and exaltation.[107] There is no reason to suppose that this physical understanding of Jesus' resurrection was ever abandoned by the Jerusalem centred believers.

The second stage would be occasioned by the spread of the gospel into areas more dominated by Hellenistic thought. Hellenistic distaste for the material would make the idea of a resurrection of the physical body a subject of scorn (cf. Acts 17.32; I Cor. 15.12, 35 – see above p.106). The second stage then was marked by a move away from the idea that the flesh was restored in resurrection, and by a redefining of the concept of resurrection body. So far as we can tell it was Paul himself who took this step. He rejected the belief in a straightforward physical resurrection – for 'flesh and blood cannot inherit the kingdom of God' (I Cor. 15.50).[108] To this extent he was influenced by Greek thought – but no further: he did not fall into a body/spirit dualism or affirm an 'immortality of the soul' hope.[109] The *flesh* would not be resurrected, but the *body* would. This distinction between flesh and body was a bold and venturesome stroke, for in the general usage of the time σῶμα (*sōma* – body) and σάρξ (*sarx* – flesh) were more or less synonymous – both referring to the physical body. Hebrew thought had no word for 'body', and in LXX and the apocryphal books both *sōma* and *sarx* are used for the Hebrew *basar*, which means essentially 'flesh'.[110] So too in more gnostically influenced thought, although the basic anthropology was very different, *sōma* stood together with *sarx* (and ψυχή – soul) in disparaging contrast to *pneuma* (spirit).[111] Paul, faced with the problem of how to present resurrection faith in a Hellenistic context, resolved it by driving a wedge between *sarx* and *sōma*; he diverted Hellenistic aversion to the material wholly on to the 'flesh', and successfully neutralized the concept 'body', so that 'body' could be used on both sides of the antithesis between 'spirit' and 'flesh' or 'spirit' and 'soul'. So resurrection, including the resurrection of Jesus, could be presented not as a restoration of the physical, but as a transformation, a quite new mode of existence – as *spiritual body* (σῶμα πνευματικόν) in contrast to *natural body* (σῶμα ψυχικόν). By thus developing this neat distinction between 'flesh' and 'body' Paul was able to go some way in making the concept of resurrection more intelligible to more sophisticated Greek readership while at the same time retaining the important Hebrew understanding of resurrection as resurrection of the whole man.[112]

If the second stage in the development of Christian understanding of the resurrection was an abandonment of the idea of physical resurrection,[113] the third stage was marked by a very definite swing of the pendulum in the other direction – a reassertion of the earlier physical view as against Paul's spiritualizing compromise. This is most clearly seen in the Lukan accounts of the resurrection appearances (see above §21.1). Yet Luke's resurrection narratives cannot be regarded simply as a reversion to the primitive conceptualization of Jesus' resurrection state. Rather are they to be understood as a heightening and deliberate underscoring of the physical tangibility of Jesus' resurrection body (see particularly Luke 24.39–43; Acts 1.9–11).[114] As even a more conservative scholar like J. Denney recognized: '(Since) Luke everywhere betrays a tendency to materialize the supernatural, it is not too much to suppose that this tendency has left traces on his resurrection narratives too'.[115] It is not difficult to demonstrate this tendency. We know from other parts of Luke's writings that he liked to emphasize the objectivity of spiritual experiences – to make them more manifest as wonders: observe his addition of σωματικῷ ('in bodily form') to the narrative of Jesus' experience at Jordan (Luke 3.22); the Lukan addition to the account of the transfiguration denying that the disciples dreamed it all (Luke 9.32);[116] and Acts 2.3 – 'tongues like fire', not 'like tongues of fire' (see below ch. VI n. 55). In particular in this connection we should note Luke's special interest in the direct intervention of angels into events on earth,[117] and his rather crude concept of Spirit as almost identical with glossolalic and prophetic inspiration (Acts 2.4, 33; 8.17f.; 10.44ff.; 19.6 – see below §34). The materializing tendency of Luke's resurrection narratives is all of a piece with this special Lukan trait. His stress on the firm objectivity of Jesus' resurrection body may be due to an antidocetic motive,[118] or it may simply be a characteristic expression of Luke's own conceptualizing of spiritual experience.

Perhaps a further development can be traced in the Fourth Gospel's treatment of the resurrection appearances. There is certainly clear emphasis on the tangibility of Jesus' resurrection body; but (in chapter 20) Jesus does nothing so physical as eating, and Mary is firmly discouraged from touching him (20.17). To be sure Thomas is invited to touch and feel, but John does not say that he did so. Indeed the implication is that Thomas was so overcome by the mere appearance that he at once confessed his faith and dispensed with physical proof; and the blessing of v. 29 is specifically for 'those who have *not* seen and *yet* believe'.[119] So perhaps John 20 is to be seen as a slight retreat from Luke's bold attempt to produce tangible proof of the reality of Jesus' resurrection body.

Here then is a first and probable answer to our question, Why are there such striking differences between the narratives of the resurrection appearances in the gospels and the resurrection appearance to Paul? *The earliest believers understood their resurrection appearance experiences in much more physical terms, whereas Paul understood his encounter with the risen Jesus in much more spiritual terms* – a bodily resurrection to be sure, but a *spiritual* body. Luke for one reason or another retained and heavily underlined the original view, and John concurred perhaps with some reserve.

§22. WHAT DID THE FIRST WITNESSES SEE AND HEAR?

22.1   *The ambiguity of the earlier appearances.* If the above outline is a fair assessment of the evidence, what does it tell us about the resurrection appearances which preceded the appearance to Paul? We have concluded that Paul's ὀφθῆναι was a visionary seeing, which he could not elaborate. How was it that the earlier appearances could be understood in such physical terms and lend themselves to such elaboration as we find in Luke and John? What did the earliest disciples actually see?

One possible answer is that there were different kinds of appearances – appearances on earth as well as appearances from heaven. There is no *a priori* reason why a resurrected Jesus should not have appeared as present in the company of some disciples or even have moved about and spoken.[120] No doubt some such experiences underlie some at least of the OT theophanies and Lukan angel-epiphanies.

But perhaps a more plausible suggestion is that there was *a certain ambiguity* in the appearances, a lack of distinctiveness and clarity of detail, which left undisturbed the overmastering impression of the one central fact ('Jesus is risen'), but also gave scope for a degree of variety in the interpretation of the reality which had been witnessed.[121] The strong materializing tendency of Luke and John makes it difficult to get back to the original experiences, but there are some indications which seem to favour this hypothesis.

(a) Matt. 28.17 – *some of the original eleven doubted.* It was C. H. Dodd who drew particular attention to this note of doubt in the earlier stratum of the tradition. His form critical study of the resurrection narratives in the gospels distinguished three 'concise' narratives (Matt. 28.8–10, 16–20; John 20.19–21) whose form, as against that of the 'circumstantial' narratives, suggested that they were 'drawn directly from the oral tradition handed down by the corporate memory of the Church'. 'In all three *pericopae*', he noted, 'there is at least a hint of an element of doubt or fear' (Matt. 28.10, 17; John 20.20). He went on,

It is, perhaps, legitimate to say that this type of resurrection narrative carries within it, as an integral element, a suggestion that the appearance of the Lord does not bring full or immediate conviction to the beholders.

(These narratives emphasize) the recognition of the Lord by his disciples, almost always with the implication that such recognition was neither immediate nor inevitable.[122]

The doubt motif is of course taken up by Luke and John and elaborated, since it provides such excellent apologetic material. The doubt and disbelief are emphasized in order that the physical demonstration of proof might be seen to be all the more convincing (Luke 24.36–43; John 20.24–9).[123] But in Matt. 28.17 ('but some doubted') the doubt is not treated apologetically; Jesus neither addresses himself to it nor removes it. The words which follow (28.18–20) cannot be shown to serve any other function than that of commissioning – seeing and commissioning, as we shall see, being the two most characteristic and primitive features of the resurrection appearances generally. The bare mention of doubt in Matt. 28.17 is best seen therefore as a genuine historical echo.[124] And to that extent Dodd's conclusion seems to be justified; in the appearance recorded in Matt. 28.16ff. there was an element of ambiguity about what was seen.

Two other considerations strengthen this conclusion. First, it is not at all clear whether Matt. 28.16–20 relates a Christophany or Christ-epiphany (to use Lindblom's distinction – above p. 116); it is the one resurrection narrative in the gospels which cannot be firmly assigned to one category or the other. Does this indicate an early stage in reflection about the appearance? – a stage before the attempt to describe it more fully either as an appearance on earth or an appearance from heaven? It looks very much as though elaborating tendencies have concentrated on the commissioning element (the Trinitarian baptismal formula, etc.) and left the seeing element untouched. If so, then we may infer that *the perception of Jesus' presence in this appearance was sufficiently ambiguous that it could be understood either as a Christophany or as a Christepiphany.*

Second, this appearance, in its essence at least of a seeing and commissioning in Galilee, has the best claim of all the gospel appearances to be equated with the appearance to 'the twelve' listed by Paul (I Cor. 15.5; see also Mark 16.7, and cf. John 21). This in turn suggests a reason for the ambiguity of the appearance – viz., that, like Paul's, the ὀφθῆναι of the twelve was a visionary seeing and so was to some extent conditioned (though not wholly determined) by subjective factors; *the visionary mode of seeing meant that there were different degrees of perception of the reality before them.* Some at once saw with clarity of vision that it was Jesus alive from the dead; for others their vision was to some extent obscured and unclear. For some the appearance was so real and tangible that their report of it could be readily elaborated in physical terms; for others the fact that it was Jesus before them did not become clear at first sight, or was not made clear by sight alone – the vision had to be defined and confirmed by the conviction of commission which accompanied it, and perhaps by the testimony of Peter and the rest for whom sight alone had been sufficient.

In short, we seem now to be in a position to say something more definite about the resurrection appearance experience of 'the twelve'. All were convinced that they had seen Jesus alive from the dead (I Cor. 15.5, 11). But for some the conviction came immediately in the experience, whereas for others the conviction was less immediate, though in the event no less certain. This was so presumably because for the former the appearance of Jesus was sufficiently clear and tangible to sight alone, whereas for the latter the appearance of Jesus to sight alone was not clear or convincing enough but had to be complemented by revelation to ear and mind.

(b) *The appearance to Peter.* One of the most striking features of the resurrection narratives is the complete absence of any account of the appearance to Peter. We know that the primitive kerygma regarded the appearance to Peter as the first of the appearances, the decisive encounter for the faith of the earliest communities, and beginning of the gospel as gospel. This is clearly indicated by I Cor. 15.5 ('and that he appeared to Cephas', by Mark 16.7 ('Go and tell his disciples and Peter that he is going before you to Galilee; there you will see him'), and by Luke 24.34 ('The Lord has risen indeed, and has appeared to Simon').[125] This primacy of Peter as witness to the risen Jesus is confirmed by the primacy which tradition attributes to him – particularly his initial leadership of the Jerusalem community (Gal. 1.18; Acts 1–5) – and it may perhaps be reflected also in his authority as Cephas the 'rock' and possessor of 'the keys of the kingdom of heaven' (Matt. 16.18f.).[126] Given then the supreme importance of the appearance to Peter, it is astonishing that we possess no record of it whatsoever.[127] One would have thought that Luke in particular would have seized the opportunity of presenting a convincing account of the appearance to the key witness. This strongly suggests that no such account was available to him, even in rudimentary form, which suggests in turn that Peter himself made no attempt to elaborate his experience, either in visionary or in materialistic terms. The conclusion seems to follow that Peter's experience was similar to Paul's: Peter had no doubt whatsoever that Jesus had appeared to him, but could describe this appearance no further. Presumably there was a seeing element, as the ὤφθη of I Cor. 15.5 implies, and with the ὀφθῆναι came the assurance that he was forgiven and commissioned by Jesus (as John 21.15ff.; Luke 22.32 and perhaps Matt. 16.18f. imply). But in the end of the day the appearance was probably something so intensely personal that its full character and significance could not be conveyed in words and would only be lost in the telling. He could only say, 'Jesus is risen; he has appeared to me'. To say any more was to say less. His manner and conduct must say the rest.[128]

It is interesting to note, perhaps as confirmation, that the resurrection appearances which are most elaborated are those to more than one individual at a time. We have no account of the appearances to Peter, to James, to Paul (as a resurrection appearance), or to any of the apostles (see below ch. VI n.36), whereas there are several narratives which presumably owe their origin ultimately to the appearance to 'the twelve' – Matt. 28, Luke 24, John 20, 21. Perhaps a partial explanation can be offered in the following terms: the same subjective, visionary, intensely personal quality which made the individual draw back from any attempt to describe his experience, made also for a diversity in conceptualizing the experience when more than one was involved; the variety of individual and personal perception and response within a corporate experience gave to the preacher and teacher the scope which he lacked in the case of Peter, James and the other individuals.

(c) *The appearance(s) to the women* (Matt. 28.8ff.; John 20.14–18). The historical status of these narratives is a notorious problem. The very possibility that there was any appearance which preceded the appearance to Peter seems to be excluded by Paul, Mark and Luke (I Cor. 15.5; Mark 16.6–8; Luke 24.22ff.). Mark and Luke speak only of the women seeing angel(s) (Mark 16.5ff.; Luke 24.4ff.) – Luke specifying the experience as an angelophany ('a vision of angels' – Luke 24.23). Consequently the appearances to the women are frequently dismissed as legendary developments, whose purpose was to establish a connection between the tradition of the empty grave and the tradition of the resurrection appearances.[129] A plausible suggestion on this thesis is that the empty tomb Christophanies have been developed out of the earlier angelophanies.[130] But the thesis itself lacks plausibility. Since women were not qualified to give testimony,[131] it is most unlikely that the first testimony to the risen Jesus would be attributed to women without good cause.[132] And the desire to link empty tomb and appearance traditions does not provide sufficient cause, for according to the earlier (angelophany) tradition some of the disciples (Peter and John) had also seen the empty tomb (Luke 24.24; John 20.3–10). The link between empty tomb and resurrection appearances could be established much more convincingly by setting the appearance to Peter rather than that to Mary in the vicinity of the empty tomb.

Perhaps our hypothesis of a degree of ambiguity in the appearances and of the very personal nature of the experience for the individuals involved may point to a more adequate solution. If we once grant that the women discovered the tomb of Jesus empty (see above pp. 119f.), then we must also allow the possibility, even probability that they had one (or more?) visionary experiences at or near the tomb.[133] It will simply not do to dismiss the claim that the women saw angels as legendary. The *status* of what they saw may of course be disputed on psychological grounds. That is one thing. But the *claim* to have seen an angel or had a vision can hardly be disputed on historical grounds simply because post-Enlightenment man no longer believes in angels! Visionary experiences are too common in the history of religions for the account here to be dismissed on that score.[134]

If then the likelihood be granted that the women who discovered the empty tomb had a visionary experience there or thereabouts, we must go on to ask, What was it that they saw? And here the element of ambiguity becomes strongly marked. Mark speaks of one young man in the tomb wearing a white robe (Mark 16.5); Luke speaks of 'two men in dazzling garments', and later of 'a vision of angels' (Luke 24.4, 23); Matthew speaks of 'an angel of the Lord' whose 'appearance was like lightning, and his raiment white as snow' who sat on the stone, outside the tomb (Matt. 28.2f.), and goes on to report briefly the women's encounter with Jesus on their way back from the tomb (28.8ff.); and John speaks of two angels in white inside the tomb whom only Mary saw, and then of the resurrection appearance to Mary alone (John 20.12, 14ff.). As for the appearance itself, Matthew reports that the women 'took hold of his feet'; while John tells of a Jesus who was tangible, but who did not welcome Mary's touching (John 20.17).

Two other important strands of evidence must be drawn in here. First, the evidently numinous quality of the women's experience is a good example of what Otto calls the *mysterium tremendum et fascinans*.[135] The women were 'beside themselves with terror', 'afraid' (Mark 16.8); they left the tomb in a muddled state of fear and joy, and fear was their response to the appearance of Jesus (Matt. 28.8, 10); and perhaps John 20.17 also echoes an experience of the taboo of the *tremendum*.[136] Second, the recurring note either that the women did not say anything (Mark 16.8) or that their testimony was not believed (Luke 24.11; Mark 16.11).

Out of all this emerges a plausible and coherent picture: the women who visited the tomb had a visionary experience in which they themselves were not at first certain of whom and what they saw. They came to recognize the vision as an appearance of Jesus (perhaps on the basis of Peter's experience), but their account of it was so confused and confusing that it was not taken seriously by the other disciples. Some ignored it, since the testimony of women did not count anyway; some interpreted it as 'a vision of angels'; some accepted it as a genuine appearance of the risen Lord.[137] In the latter two cases the traditions which resulted underwent the various elaborations which left them as we now have them.

In short, the evidence available to us of the appearances to the women, to Peter and to 'the twelve', all points towards *a sequence of visionary experiences which were intensely personal and ambiguous*, particularly in their visual element, but such that when all was said and done *those involved could do no other than affirm, 'I have seen Jesus, risen from the dead'.*

22.2 *The earliest appearances as commissioning.* In comparing the appearance to Paul with the earlier appearances the second feature we must look at is the element of commissioning. Paul experienced the risen Jesus as one who sent him forth in the last days of the old age with the message of the new age burning in his heart. Was it so with the earliest witnesses?

At first sight the answer is a firm affirmative. It is a characteristic feature of the resurrection appearances in the gospels that they are commissioning experiences. Commission is the hallmark of the account in Matt. 28.16–20 – '. . . Go therefore and make disciples . . .'. Even the strange little episode of the appearance to the women is characterized by the command to 'go and tell' (Matt. 28.8ff. – so too the angelophany, Mark 16.6f.; Matt. 28.5ff.). The climax of the resurrection narratives in Luke's gospel is likewise the commission to preach repentance and forgiveness to all nations in Christ's name (Luke 24.46f.). So too in Acts the final appearance is essentially a commissioning: '. . . you shall be my witnesses . . .' (Acts 1.7f.). Finally in the Fourth Gospel the risen Lord's commissioning marks three of the four appearances, including that of the appendix: to Mary (20.17 – 'Go . . . tell'), to 'the disciples' (20.21 – 'As the Father has sent me, even so I send you'), and to Peter (21.15ff. – 'Feed my sheep').

But further reflection demands a less certain note.

(*a*) The desire, particularly of Luke, to make the visual element of the appearances more tangible is hardly likely to have left unaffected any auditory element.[138] Thus the universal nature of the commission in Matt. 28.18ff.; Luke 24.46f.; Acts 1.8, must be the expression of later reflection or revelation, since the conviction that the gospel was to be taken to the world at large only emerged in a forceful form with the Hellenistic Jews (Acts 7; 8.4;11.19f.; Eph. 3.3–6 – see further below §27.1). Note also the developed theology of Matt. 28.19 (Trinitarian formula) and of the commissionings in John 20 (Jesus speaks in the language of Johannine theology).

(b) It is not even clear whether the initial appearances contained an effective commission to preach Jesus to the Jews. The to-ing and fro-ing from Galilee leaves the point obscure (but see further below §§25, 27). Luke suggests that the resurrection appearances in themselves resulted in no proclamation; only with Pentecost did mission start (Acts 1–2). And it is noteworthy that the earliest announcements of the appearance to Peter contain no word of commission – simply that the risen Jesus had appeared to him (Luke 24.34; I Cor. 15.5).

(c) Above all, the eschatological note so characteristic of Paul's understanding of his commission is almost wholly absent. It appears not at all in Luke, Acts or John, unless we count Acts 1.11 and John 21.22f.; but they hardly constitute a real equivalent to Paul's expectation (see further below §29). It has been argued that Mark 16.7 refers to the parousia – 'he is going before you to Galilee';[139] but a reference to resurrection appearances in Galilee still appears more plausible, in the light of the traditions in Matt. 28 and John 21 of appearances located in Galilee.[140] The only passage which brings us anywhere near Paul's eschatological evaluation of the resurrection of Jesus is the primitive tradition in Matt. 27.52f. already referred to above (p. 118), which gives expression in its own way to the belief that Jesus' resurrection was the beginning of the general resurrection of the end of the age. But that tradition is in no way linked with any of the commands to the disciples to bear witness (though cf. 27.54).

Yet despite all this, it would be difficult to deny the element of commissioning to the earliest appearances, even though in less developed form. (1) Some word of command seems to be integral to the most primitive of the resurrection narratives.[141] (2) Paul's claim to apostleship is based on the assumption that earlier appearances, to 'all the apostles' at least, were commissioning appearances. It is obvious that *he would insist that his commissioning was an appearance only if earlier appearances were widely and reliably understood as commissionings*.[142] (3) The appearance to Peter is proclaimed in a kerygmatic formula (see above p. 125). The impulse to use it as kerygma must stem to some extent from Peter himself, and would no doubt be traced back by Peter in part at least to the appearance itself. (4) It is also relevant to remember that those who were acknowledged as leaders within early Christianity undoubtedly owed their leadership to the fact that the risen Jesus had appeared to them (Peter, 'the twelve', James, the apostles, Paul). Commission to leadership, that is, to initiative-taking and spokesmanship, must have been accepted as an integral part of these appearances from the first. (5) However confused our present picture of the location of the various resurrection appearances is, it is fairly certain that there were appearances in Galilee,[143] subsequent to which those who had experienced them returned to Jerusalem. Presumably this decision to return to Jerusalem was occasioned by the Galilean appearances, understood as a command to proclaim Jesus' victory and to await his imminent triumph.[144] That is to say, the movement from Galilee to Jerusalem was probably the result and expression of the same sort of eschatological excitement which motivated Paul in his mission to the Gentiles (see further below pp. 138f., 141f. and §29).

We cannot complete the discussion of this issue until we have examined the Pentecost tradition (Acts 2). But we can sum up thus far by saying that in many cases *the experience of seeing Jesus risen from the dead was also the beginning of a compulsion to make the fact of his resurrection known*. Not all the experiences had this effect, at least in the same measure: the 'more than 500 brethren' (I Cor. 15.6) could be appealed to as witnesses, but were not all preachers or apostles; so presumably part of the ambiguity of the first experiences was that some could not keep their experience to themselves, believing that Jesus wanted them to proclaim his resurrection as the sign of the end, while others responded in a quieter, less outgoing manner, perhaps believing that the purpose of Jesus' appearances was simply to assure his disciples that he had conquered death (cf. Luke 24.13-43; John 20.26-9). But those who emerged as leaders of the infant sect were convinced that the risen Jesus had commissioned them personally, and their conviction was accepted by the rest. Whether the conviction came initially through an auditory element in their initial experience, or through an inward conviction, we can no longer clearly decide – they knew it as the voice of the exalted Jesus in either case. That the initial conviction was elaborated in the light of the fuller inspiration and revelation of later days is fairly certain (see further below §27.1). But it is also probable that whatever impulse to mission there was among the earliest witnesses, it was integrally rooted for them, as for Paul, in the appearances themselves.

22.3 *The characteristics of the earliest appearances*. The question we posed
at the beginning of this section was whether the earlier appearances
differed from the appearance to Paul. The answer which the evidence
demands is that *they were the same and yet different – the same in that it
was the same reality which encountered them, Jesus alive from the dead;
different in that his appearance made a very different impact on the different
individuals whom he encountered*. Some were so overcome with fear and
terror at the unexpectedness and numinous quality of the experience
that at first they did not know quite what to make of it, and their
attempt to conceptualize it caused only confusion and incredulity.
Some spoke not at all about their experience except to affirm that they
had seen Jesus – perhaps because the attempt to put their experience
into words was one they could not or would not make. In the case of
Peter in particular we must presume that the strength of his conviction and the manifest change in his bearing and life was such as to
give his testimony compelling power by itself.

But the faith of the other disciples was not dependent on Peter's
testimony alone.[145] Others in turn saw Jesus, some with such a vivid-
ness of recognition that seeing Jesus alone was enough, others with a
conviction cemented both by the voice of revelation in their inward
ear and perhaps by the testimony of earlier witnesses, particularly
Peter's, as the interpretative key.

There were differences too in that in some cases the appearance
was that and no more – God opening the eyes of disciples to recognize
Jesus as present in their midst. But in other cases, of which Paul's is
the best available example, the overpowering impression made by
the appearance was not simply of seeing Jesus but of a charge thereby
being laid on them to make him known as risen and exalted, Messiah,
Son of God and soon-coming Lord.

In short, *the three most primitive characteristics of the resurrection
appearances prior to Paul are a visionary seeing, an element of doubt and fear,
and a sense of obligation to make the vision known*. Not all three characteristics are present, by any means, in all resurrection appearances,
and they occur in different combinations. But in every case on record
the consequent conviction is firm and sure: 'Jesus is risen; he appeared
to me/us'.

Having drawn attention to the ambiguity of the appearances for
some at least of the first disciples, it is perhaps necessary to say one
word more. As in the case of Paul it is possible that subjective and
psychological factors played an even larger role than I have allowed
– that the appearances were indeed 'all in the mind' from start to
finish. The ambiguity suggested by the records is part of the wider

ambiguity of religious experience to which we referred earlier – so that the possibility of self-delusion and mass hallucination cannot be ruled out. Nevertheless, I must confess that the weight of probability seems to me to tilt the scales in the other direction. Quite apart from such other matters as the empty tomb, the degree of independence of several at least of the appearance experiences (Peter, James and Paul), and the divine significance so quickly attributed by monotheistic Jews to one of their fellows,[146] it remains an indisputable fact that the earliest believers (including the initial doubters), no less than Paul, were absolutely convinced that they had seen Jesus risen from the dead. And yet why should they assume that what they saw was *Jesus*? – why not an angel? And why did they conclude that it was Jesus *risen from the dead*? – why not simply a vision of the dead man? – why not visions 'fleshed out' with the apparatus of apocalyptic expectation, coming on clouds of glory and the like (cf. Mark 8.38–9.8; 14.62; Matt. 28.2–4; Acts 1.9–11; 7.55f.)? Why draw the astonishing conclusion that the *eschatological* resurrection had *already* taken place in the case of a *single individual* quite separate from and prior to the general resurrection?[147] There must have been something very compelling about the appearances for such an extravagant, not to say ridiculous and outrageous conclusion to be drawn. For myself the most satisfactory explanation is that it *was* Jesus whom they saw – Jesus alive from the dead, making himself known to them in a mode of existence which transcended the limitations of time and space.

§23. CONCLUSIONS

23.1   In this chapter we have begun to look at the question, What were the spiritual experiences which gave birth to Christianity? Our first answer has been in terms of resurrection appearances, and could not be otherwise. *At the beginning of Christianity we find a number of experiences in which those involved believed Jesus had appeared to them.* We should not allow our familiarity with Christian belief in the resurrection of Jesus to dull or muffle the extraordinary boldness of this claim. To be sure 'resurrection of Jesus' was a *metaphor* (Pannenberg), a way of *interpreting* their experience (Marxsen).[148] But the interpretation tells us something about the experience interpreted; and an experience which led first-century Jews to the conclusion that a single individual had already anticipated the general resurrection of the dead, by however brief an interval, must have been a very compelling experience – an experience which pointed very forcibly to that interpretation.

The visionary and subjective element of their experience does of course leave their interpretation, their faith, open to some question. The possibility that these were solely subjective visions cannot be ruled out. But it is also possible that Jesus did live again beyond death in a dimension and mode of reality which can only be disclosed to some form of visionary perception. Certainly it is significant that the earliest strata of tradition bear testimony to the difficulty of conceptualizing the appearances (ambiguity, 'spiritual body' – what is that?). Yet *the fact remains that the conclusion to which they came was that it was Jesus himself who had encountered them.* The ὤφθη of I Cor. 15.5–8 need not specify a uniform mode of appearance, but it does imply that, despite all ambiguities and differences of conceptualization, all those listed were convinced that it was the same reality which they all had experienced – an encounter with one over against them – and that one the same Jesus crucified, dead and buried some days or weeks previously.

23.2   In many of the experiences the most compelling part of the appearance was not the visionary element, but the *call* which came with the vision. On most occasions the appearance contained a demand to tell others. As so many of the great prophets experienced a visionary call which determined their whole life thereafter, so it was with Peter, 'the twelve', and 'all the apostles', including Paul. Only here, in a special way, *the Jesus who appeared was himself the good news to be proclaimed.* The experience of Jesus as risen was of such compelling power that henceforth he and it became the driving force in their lives, the touchstone of their hermeneutic, the norm for their gospel.

It was the combination of these two elements in his conversion (seeing and commissioning) which led Paul to the conclusion that the appearance to him was of the same order as the earlier appearances to all the apostles. And subsequently, failure of these elements to recur in his own experience or in the experience of others led him to the conclusion that his encounter with the risen Jesus outside Damascus was something distinctive in his own experience and brought to an end the (unrepeatable) sequence of resurrection appearances.

23.3   Two final comments arise out of the last paragraph. First, the fact that Paul so clearly distinguished his conversion experience from all his later experiences, not excluding visions, charismatic manifestations and the experience of 'Christ in me', has an important corollary for modern discussion about the resurrection of Jesus. Paul would not have accepted that his experience was simply a 'subjective vision' (Strauss, etc.), or that 'Jesus is risen' could be adequately re-expressed as 'Jesus has risen into the kerygma' (Bultmann), or as 'Still he comes today' (Marxsen).[149] Paul was no stranger to the experiences suggested by these formulae. He knew well enough the impact of visions, of the kerygma, of the Spirit, and so on. Yet for him it was important to stress that the resurrection appearances were something different again – Jesus choosing to make himself known in a particularly distinctive and once-for-all way. Paul's distinctions may be rejected, but they cannot be ignored in this discussion. We are in no position to evaluate them at this distance in time, but the fact that Paul could and did distinguish his first experience of Jesus from all subsequent experiences cannot be unimportant.

Secondly, can resurrection appearances still happen? What would we make of someone who insisted that he had seen Jesus as clearly (or unclearly) as Paul and had been commissioned like him to proclaim the good news of Jesus risen from the dead with the same eschatological urgency? Presumably Christianity is not averse to Paul's claim that the resurrection appearances were something unique and determinative for the whole of Christianity. But are we who accept that Jesus is risen to deny him the possibility of manifesting himself again as decisively to a twentieth century believer as he did to first-century Paul?[150] Obviously we need rather more criteria than a dogmatic *a priori* to evaluate claims made on the basis of religious experience. This question of how to evaluate religious experience will become of pressing importance as our investigation proceeds.

VI

PENTECOST

§24. INTRODUCTION

So far we have confined our examination of the earliest experiences of
the first believers to the resurrection appearances – in particular the
appearance to Paul, and more tentatively, the appearances to Peter,
to 'the twelve' and to the women. We will touch on the other appearances listed by Paul in I Cor. 15 below, and may compare the (other)
visions of Jesus described by Luke in Acts (see below §32.1). These
were all experiences of Jesus – where Jesus himself was in one way or
another part of the experience, that which was perceived and recognized and encountered. But there are other experiences claimed for
the primitive Christian community – experiences in which Jesus was
not thought to be involved in such an immediate and direct manner
– experiences of divine power, but less personally conceived – experiences of Spirit, more like those enjoyed by Jesus himself which we
examined in chapter IV. Our task in the next two chapters then is to
discover what other (non-resurrection-appearance) experiences
brought Christianity to birth and characterized its infancy.

The first and most important claim upon us is obviously the
narrative in Acts 2, in which Luke depicts the outpouring of the
Spirit upon the disciples in Jerusalem on the day of Pentecost following the first Easter. The theological significance of the event for Luke
himself is epochal – the beginning of the final stage of salvation
history, the birthday of the church, etc. I have already discussed
Luke's understanding of Pentecost in *Baptism in the Holy Spirit*
chapter IV, and there is no call to cover the same ground here. What
we must now inquire after is the historical reality underlying Acts 2.
What was the religious experience (or experiences) highlighted by
Luke in Acts 2? Undoubtedly there were enthusiastic and ecstatic
experiences within earliest Palestinian Christianity: the contrast
between a non-pneumatic Palestinian Christianity and a pneumatic

Hellenistic Christianity is no more soundly based than the contrast between a non-apocalyptic Jesus and an apocalyptic primitive Christianity.[1] The question is, Where and how soon did such experiences begin? Was the first such experience particularly memorable?

Unfortunately, the obscurity enveloping these early years leaves many questions unanswered and many possibilities open. And unfortunately too, we are almost wholly at the mercy of Luke for the answers. The range of scholarly options stretches from the more traditional view at one end, that Acts 2 is a more or less accurate account of what happened on the first Christian Pentecost, to the more radical thesis maintained most forcefully by E. Haenchen at the other, that Acts 2 is wholly the construct of Luke's theological expertise.[2] It is not enough therefore to pose the simple question, What happened at Pentecost? We must first ask whether we can in fact speak of 'the initial outpouring of the Spirit at Jerusalem' at all. Is the placing of the event in Jerusalem and the dating of it to Pentecost theologically motivated or historically sound? Is the present form of Acts 2 due more to Luke's reconstruction than to any traditions he had available to him? Only when we have seen that there are reasonable grounds for talking about 'the outpouring of the Spirit at Pentecost' can we go on to ask, What happened at Pentecost?

§25. HISTORICAL EVENT OR THEOLOGICAL CREATION?

25.1   One 'Pentecost' or many? The first question which must be asked is whether there were many 'Pentecosts' or just one. Luke's account of the early church's growth is so set out as to give the impression that the stream of spiritual vitality all came from the one source; that the life and power of the early church all derived ultimately from that one event in Jerusalem on the day of Pentecost. But were there not other centres of growth than Jerusalem? – centres whose springs of life and power were independent of Jerusalem and its 'Pentecost'? The tendency of religious folklore to oversimplify a more complex historical process is well known.[3] Has Luke, wittingly or unwittingly, oversimplified the earliest experiences of the Spirit among disciples of Jesus? There are three factors which give weight to this question.

First, the possibility, expressed most forcefully by E. Lohmeyer, that Jerusalem alone was not the earliest church, but that there were *two* 'earliest churches', a Galilee community as well as the one in Jerusalem.[4] Clearly there is a considerable degree of plausibility in the argument that in the area where Jesus had been most popular during his ministry various individuals continued to call themselves his disciples and to meet in table fellowship.[5] Did these groups catch fire independently of events in Jerusalem – by spiritual spontaneous combustion, as it were? There were resurrection appearances in Galilee according to sufficiently reliable tradition (Mark 16.7; Matt. 28.16ff.; John 21 – see above ch. V nn. 140, 143). Did these not result in some experience of community, some compulsion to mission? Was there a Galilean 'Pentecost'?

Second, a more powerful piece of evidence is the fact that Luke deliberately concentrates the beginning events of Christianity in Jerusalem – and does so in such a way as to exclude any other contender. This is evident from his treatment of Mark 16.7.[6] Where Mark reads, 'Go, tell his disciples and Peter that he is going before you *to Galilee*; there you will see him, as he told you'; Luke has instead, 'Remember how he told you *while he was still in Galilee* . . .' (Luke 24.6). He also completely omits Mark's earlier reference to resurrection appearances in Galilee (Mark 14.28). Likewise the command (given on Easter Sunday!), that the disciples should stay in Jerusalem 'until clothed with power from on high' seems to rule out the possibility, so far as Luke is concerned, of resurrection appearances in Galilee (Luke 24.49; so too Acts 1.4).[7] If Luke has so treated the resurrection appearance traditions, may he not have treated the Pentecost tradition similarly? To ignore all other traditions of parallel 'Pentecosts', and concentrate all attention on Jerusalem, would be quite in accord with the version of Christian origins which Luke wanted to propagate.

Third, it is fairly clear from Acts that Luke likes to bring out by his narrative the central role of Jerusalem in the Christian mission (especially 8.14ff.; 9.26ff.; 11.1ff., 22ff.; 15.6ff.). And yet on at least two occasions of great significance there is no attempt to establish a link with Jerusalem. The community at Damascus was evidently as charismatic as that at Jerusalem – Paul was 'filled with the Holy Spirit' (cf. 2.4) at the hands of Ananias (9.17) – but Luke does not even suggest that it derived its spirituality from Jerusalem. Did Damascus Christianity develop independently of Jerusalem (stemming perhaps from a Galilean 'Pentecost')?[8] Equally significant is Luke's description of Apollos on his first appearance. Quite clearly his Christian experience had not come from the Jerusalem source; he 'knew only the baptism of John', and his knowledge of 'the way of God' was defective (18.25f.). Yet 'he had been instructed in the way of the Lord' and was not lacking in his experience of the Spirit

(18.25; 'aglow with the Spirit').[9] What was Apollos's 'Pentecost'? When and where did it take place? In addition, we should not forget Mark 9.38–40 (cf. Matt. 7.15–23) as evidence of the existence of other charismatic groups who named the name of Jesus, but who were independent of the main stream(s) of Christianity represented by Mark (and Matthew).[10]

The impression therefore gains strength that the beginnings of Christianity were not quite so straightforward and clear-cut as Luke suggests; in particular that Jerusalem was not the only well-spring of Pentecostal enthusiasm – that there were other 'Pentecosts' elsewhere.

On the other hand, it would be quite unjustified to present the origins of Christianity as a scatter of diverse and unconnected mini-Pentecosts. Two considerations in particular indicate that Luke's presentation of a determinative Jerusalem Pentecost is not without historical foundation.

First, there is Paul's attitude to Jerusalem. It is quite evident from Gal. 1–2 that for Paul only one centre of Christianity could lay claim to primacy; only one centre could hope to justify its claim to determine the gospel – and that is Jerusalem. However much he derived his gospel from his own experience of Jesus (see above §20.1) and from the believers at Damascus or Antioch, it was still important to him that the Jerusalem apostles approved his gospel; no other centre or district even comes into consideration when he discusses the determinative shape of the Christian faith;[11] even for Paul the Jerusalem church retains its peculiarly representative role as 'the saints' (I Cor. 16.1 – not 'the saints *in Jerusalem*' as in Rom. 15.26).[12] If we find no hint in Paul that there was any other claimant to the title of Christianity's birthplace, then it is most unlikely that there was such a claimant. If Jerusalem could exercise its authority over so wide an area without serious challenge from any except such as Paul, then it follows that the Jerusalem Pentecost must have been *the* 'Pentecost' for most of the young church; *the uprush of new life which first animated infant Christianity must have centred on Jerusalem.*

Second, there is the significant fact that all the chief leaders of the earliest Jerusalem community were Galileans – James, Peter and John, the 'pillar' apostles. A Galilean leadership implies that the bulk of the first disciples in Jerusalem were also Galileans (cf. Acts 1.11; 2.7). If Galilee had provided a spiritual impetus of equal magnitude to a Jerusalem Pentecost why do we find so many Galileans in Jerusalem? If there were independent 'Pentecosts' in Jerusalem and Galilee, how did the Galileans gain the leadership in Jerusalem?

Again, if there were to some extent rival communities, how did James the brother of Jesus come to identify himself with the Jerusalem community, since his conversion was probably subsequent to the Jerusalem Pentecost (see below §25.3 and n.38), and presumably, on this hypothesis, influenced to some extent at least by the continuing Galilee community? These problems are somewhat eased by recognizing the apocalyptic significance of Jerusalem, which would explain a movement of disciples from Galilee to Jerusalem (see below pp. 141f.); but the problems are not thereby solved. The likelihood remains that the most important initial experiences of the Spirit happened in Jerusalem.

It looks therefore as though there were several individuals and groups whose experience of Spirit and faith in Jesus was initially at least independent of Jerusalem. At the same time it is difficult to avoid the conclusion that Jerusalem was the main growing point in the first instance – that the main impulse to the growth of a community rejoicing in rich experiences of Spirit and centring faith in Jesus as Messiah and Son of Man stemmed from Jerusalem. If the first years of Christianity may be likened to a bush fire, then we may illustrate the situation by envisaging the major outbreak (Jerusalem) spreading slowly to link up with and engulf much smaller outbreaks which had started independently or by chance sparks. If then Acts 2 represents the birth of the Christian community as such in Jerusalem, we may conclude that the Jerusalem Pentecost was determinative for the growth of Christianity as a whole.

25.2 *When?* If we have resolved the question, 'Where?', the next question to pose itself is obviously 'When?' When did the events underlying Acts 2.1–13 take place? Did the uprush of charismatic enthusiasm first overflow in the experience of the Jerusalem disciples on the very day of Pentecost? – or earlier, as a more immediate corollary to the first resurrection appearances (cf. John 20.19–23)? – or later, after the disciples had already begun to live as a community and to expand? Luke certainly intends us to believe that Pentecost was when it all began (Acts 2.1).[13] But then Luke is using the sequence of events recorded in Acts 1–2 to make a heavy theological point – in particular, to draw a sharp distinction between the before and after of the dawning of the age of the Spirit.[14] It is possible therefore that his dating of the event described in Acts 2 to the day of Pentecost is also the result of his theological design – viz., to present the new epoch of salvation-history, the age of the Spirit, as beginning on the anniversary of the law-giving at Sinai.[15]

The relative clarity of such theological insights makes the historical obscurity surrounding Christian beginnings at this point appear all the darker. Nevertheless, certain observations can be made with varying degrees of confidence. The first is on the unlikelihood of any great interval of time elapsing between the first resurrection appearances and the emergence of the distinctively enthusiastic Jesus sect in Jerusalem. (1) Given the usual dating of Paul's conversion, only two or at most three years after the death of Jesus,[16] sufficient interval must be granted for the growth of the sect (Acts 2–5), its initial tensions culminating in the Hebrew/Hellenist 'schism', the activity and martyrdom of Stephen, and the persecution of the Hellenists (Acts 6–8) in which Paul emerged as a leading figure (Gal. 1.13; Phil. 3.6; Acts 9) – all before his conversion. (2) It is wholly probable that the impetus of the initial resurrection appearances (the conviction of commission) began to gather the momentum depicted in Acts 2 quite soon after the appearances.

The main problem indeed is not the earliness of the Pentecost dating for the first great communal experience of Spirit, but the lateness (cf. again John 20.19–23; also Acts 2.33). Was there really such a lengthy gap between the first appearances and 'Pentecost'? In fact, the answer is quite probably, Yes. Indeed, it is quite possible, even likely, that the events of Acts 2.1–13 did fall on the day of Pentecost.

(a) As already noted, the main issue is whether Luke's theological presuppositions have determined the dating of the Acts 2 narrative. Several points tell in favour of Haenchen's view. It is likely that the feast of Pentecost, already in the time of Jesus, was coming to be regarded as the festival commemorating the lawgiving at Sinai.[17] We know also of Jewish traditions relating to the lawgiving at Sinai which have some striking resemblances to the Acts 2 account,[18] and a clear motif in Luke's presentation is that of fulfilment, Pentecost as the beginning of a new epoch of salvation history.[19] Haenchen therefore has some grounds for his conclusion: 'Insofar as he adopts the feast of Pentecost as the date of his episode, Luke is beholden to the Jewish heritage'.[20]

Nevertheless, the weight of probability seems to fall on the other side. For there is no evidence in Acts 2 (beyond the date itself, the issue in dispute) that Luke was aware of or determined by 'the Jewish heritage'.[21] The fulfilment theme is drawn out in relation to 'the promise of the Father' (Acts 1.4) – that is, presumably the promises of the prophets (Joel particularly – Acts 2.16ff., 33) and of Jesus (Luke 24.49; Acts 1.4f., 8) – not in any relation to Sinai or the law.

As for the Jewish legends about Sinai, the earlier they are the greater the differences from Acts 2,[22] while the closer they are to Acts 2 the later they have to be dated (from the middle of the second century AD on). Even then the legend is in terms of *God's* voice divided into *seventy* languages. The postulated tradition on which Luke is supposed to have drawn is one of those fabricated syncretistic legends of whose actual existence at the time in question we have grown suspicious – as in the equivalent searches for the Gnostic Redeemer myth and the Hellenistic 'divine man'. The evidence then of a determinative stimulus from Jewish tradition is lacking.[23] On internal grounds therefore it is quite as probable that Luke dated the events of Acts 2 to Pentecost because that was the date given to him in the earliest accounts of the outpouring of the Spirit – prosaic as such a solution may seem.

It is somewhat surprising that both Haenchen and Conzelmann also take up Bauernfeind's suggestion that the choice of Pentecost was determined by the presumably already established tradition of the forty days of resurrection appearances.[24] On the contrary, it is probable that the choice of the forty days was determined by the already established tradition of the outpouring of the Spirit on the day of Pentecost.[25] The most obvious reason for the choice of forty days is that it is the nearest round and 'sacred' number less than fifty which also allowed Luke to highlight the *Zwischenzeit* or interval between ascension and Pentecost.

Finally, on the point of theological presuppositions, it will simply not do to cite John 20.19–23 against Luke's dating of the outpouring of the Spirit. John's presentation of the gift of the Spirit is almost wholly inspired by theological considerations – in particular his desire to bring out the theological unity of the climactic salvation events of Jesus' ministry.[26] Luke's dating must be judged to have the superior claim to historicity.[27]

(*b*) In so far as a historical reconstruction of the first days of Christianity is possible, the plausibility of the Pentecost dating gains in strength, for if we may assume that the earliest appearances, to Peter and the twelve, took place in Galilee, as seems most likely, then the timing and occasion of the return to Jerusalem becomes a relevant issue. The reason for the return to Jerusalem was presumably the eschatological significance of Jerusalem, the city of God, the expected focus of God's final acts (see below §29). The most obvious occasion to return would be in time for the next great pilgrim festival (Pentecost);[28] and since Pentecost seems already to have become regarded as the feast of covenant renewal (see above n. 17), the disciples may have expected the decisive eschatological intervention of God on that date. This is all the more likely in view of the fact that Pentecost marked the end of the festival which began with the Passover; it was regarded as the closing feast of the Passover.[29] It would be very natural if the disciples cherished some hope that the sequence of events which had begun on the Passover would end on the day of Pentecost – that the last day of the feast which had been marked by the death and resurrection of Jesus would itself be the last great day of the Lord. The gathering together of the disciples in the sort of numbers mentioned in Acts 1-2 and the increasing anticipation and psychological preparedness which presumably led up to the experience of Spirit and glossolalia certainly makes it more than plausible that the climax was reached on the day of the festival itself, the hopes of the last age beginning to be fulfilled in the outpouring of the Spirit.

(c) Two other small considerations, of little weight in themselves, should perhaps just be mentioned. First, Acts 20.16 – a 'we' section reporting Paul's desire to reach Jerusalem in time for Pentecost if at all possible. This suggests that Paul wanted to celebrate the feast with the Christian community in Jerusalem,[30] which may in turn suggest that Pentecost had a particular significance for the Jerusalem Christians. Second, the Christian communities seem to have been charismatic from the first (cf. n.1 above). Certainly Paul takes it wholly for granted that possession of the Spirit is the hallmark of the Christian (Rom.8.9). It would be wholly in accord with our knowledge of charismatic movements in general if the language used by those first caught up in the experience of the Spirit became a sort of technical terminology for those involved at a later stage.[31] It is not surprising therefore that we can recognize distinctive Pentecost language in the NT. ἐκχέω (pour out) appears with the Spirit predominantly in the context of the Pentecost narrative (Acts 2.17, 18, 33), but the Pentecost usage is reflected also in Titus 3.6 and by the use of the Hellenistic Greek form ἐκχύννομαι in Acts 10.45 and Rom. 5.5. This suggests that Luke has been able to avail himself of traditional primitive Christian terminology in his Acts 2 account. Quite possibly therefore he had to hand a deeply rooted common tradition of the early communities which traced the first 'outpouring' of the Spirit to the time and place indicated by Luke.[32]

In short, it is by no means certain, but not at all unlikely that the historical events underlying Acts 2.1-13 took place on the first Pentecost after Jesus' death.[33]

25.3   *Was 'Pentecost' really a resurrection appearance?* We have now almost cleared the ground for what is our central concern: What actually happened at Pentecost? In the light of our earlier discussion the most appropriate way to approach the question is to ask first, What was the relation of the Pentecost experience to the resurrection appearances? Were they distinct experiences? And if so wherein did the distinction lie?

Once again Luke's portrayal of these first few months prevents the unsuspecting reader from recognizing the full force of the question. For, as we have already pointed out, Luke implies that Pentecost was something quite separate from and subsequent to the sequence of resurrection appearances; the resurrection appearances proper, that is the apostle-authenticating appearances, were confined to the forty days after Easter; the Spirit was not poured out until a clear ten days later. But Luke's presentation at this point cannot be accepted as it stands; it is of a piece with his materializing concept of resurrection appearances and ascension and is theologically determined.[34] The resurrection appearance to Paul certainly took place long after the forty days were past. If there had been an 'ascension' which brought the resurrection appearances to a decisive end, or if there had been some other full stop to the resurrection appearances which was recognized by the primitive community as closing the circle of apostles, then Paul would never have been accepted as an apostle. It is Paul himself who seems to be the first to write *finis* under the list of resurrection appearances ('last of all'). The real dispute over his own claim was not as to whether he really had experienced a commissioning appearance of the Lord, but whether he had understood his commission aright – to the Gentiles![35] The obvious implication is that *the sequence of resurrection appearances listed in I Cor. 15 ran far beyond Luke's forty days, and that Paul's own ὀφθῆναι was recognized, initially at least, as just another link in the chain.*

Where then does Pentecost come in the sequence of appearances listed by Paul? It is probable that the first two, to Peter and to 'the twelve', took place in Galilee, and so preceded the events of Pentecost. Of the others, the appearance(s) to 'all the apostles' most likely took place after Pentecost. The apostles were almost certainly a much wider group of missionaries than 'the twelve',[36] and their ὀφθῆναι most probably belongs to the period when the Jerusalem community began to move outwards in some strength – something which did not happen, so far as we can tell, much if at all before the persecution of the Hellenists (Acts 6–8).[37] Likewise the appearance to James is probably to be dated to the beginning of the young sect's initial growth within Jerusalem – his ὀφθῆναι is mentioned since he was the most significant of the early recruits to the young church.[38]

This leaves us with the appearance to the more than 500 'at one time' (I Cor. 15.6); on its relation to Pentecost we must pause for fuller reflection. One of the more intriguing hypotheses in NT scholarship is that usually linked with the name of E. von Dobschütz: that the appearance to the more than 500 and the account of Pentecost are variant traditions of one and the same event; that the event underlying the record of the outpouring of the Spirit is in fact the Christophany to the more than 500.[39] The relevance of this hypothesis to our study is obvious, and its continuing popularity[40] leaves us no choice but to examine it more closely.

Dobschütz builds his thesis on two main supports. First, the identification which we find so frequently in the NT between Christ and the Spirit. In Paul he cites Rom. 8.9f. and (mistakenly) II Cor. 3.17 (see below ch. X nn. 88, 103); we might add I Cor. 15.45 (see below pp. 322f.). The seer of Revelation attributes the letters to the seven churches equally to the dictation of the glorified Jesus and to the voice of the Spirit: 'He who has an ear, let him hear what the Spirit says to the churches' (Rev. 2–3). And in the Fourth Gospel Jesus' promise not to abandon his disciples is fulfilled in the sending of the Paraclete. Even in Acts itself Paul and Barnabas are appointed apostles (missionaries from Antioch – Acts 14.4, 14) by the Spirit (13.1–4), just as the twelve had been appointed by the risen Lord (Acts 1).[41]

Second, Pentecost and the appearance to the more than 500 have equal claims to be regarded as the birthday of the church.

We call Pentecost the birthday of the Christian church. And rightly so. But was the Christian church not born when 500 disciples reached the firm conviction through their personal experience that the Lord really lives and invests them with power to proclaim him as the coming Messiah to all men? . . . The appearance of the Lord before 500 is the birthday of the Christian mission, the Christian church.[42]

The community can have been established only once: either at Pentecost or on this occasion (I Cor. 15.6).[43]

It is difficult to evaluate such a thesis as this, dependent as it is on the assumption of a very diverse development of two versions of the same scene. We have already commented on the ambiguity inherent in several of the resurrection appearances, and this would presumably apply all the more forcibly when more than 500 were involved as witnesses. Nor is it beyond Luke to have stripped the Pentecost narrative of all appearance features in order to highlight Pentecost's distinctiveness. And yet in the end of the day von Dobschütz's thesis fails to carry sufficient conviction.

Firstly, the two passages, I Cor. 15.6 and Acts 2, really have no point of contact beyond the fact that they involve a large number of disciples in a single gathering.[44] The central feature of each is totally lacking in the other – the appearance of Jesus in the case of the 500, and the gift of the Spirit accompanied by glossolalia in the case of Pentecost.[45] Luke would not necessarily have been averse to including a visionary seeing of Jesus, even after the forty days, had that been part of the tradition of Pentecost (cf. Acts 22.17; 26.19).

Secondly, it does not follow from Dobschütz's first argument that Paul and John confused resurrection appearances with experiences of the charismatic Spirit. We have yet to examine why it is that Paul can describe his experience of the Spirit in terms of 'Christ in me' (see below ch. X). But it has already been demonstrated that Paul distinguished very clearly between his ὀφθῆναι on the one hand and his later visions and other charismatic experiences on the other. Paul would certainly not recognize Acts 2 as any sort of version of I Cor. 15.6.

Thirdly, von Dobschütz describes the appearance to the 500 too glibly in terms of mission. It is unlikely that the appearance to the 500 was understood as a commissioning, otherwise they would be recognized as apostles, not just as 'brethren'. Likewise there is no thought of the 500 as a community, as the founder church of Christianity. Consciousness of community is not associated with these resurrection appearances;[46] those involved are presented more as individuals and groups of individual witnesses to the resurrection. In the case of the 500 in particular Paul does not appeal to them as a community, but as individual witnesses ('most of whom are still alive'). Consciousness of community on the other hand is always associated with the Spirit – it was the communal experience of enthusiastic worship of κοινωνία, participation in the one Spirit, that made the first disciples a community, a distinct sect, a church. This is the testimony of Paul and John (I Cor. 12; Phil. 3.3; John 4.24) as much as of Luke (Acts 2.42). To be sure, it could be argued that the election of Matthias in Acts 1 to complete the twelve implies a consciousness of being the eschatological Israel. But this is an utterly astonishing episode – where an apostle is commissioned neither directly by the risen Lord (contrast I Cor. 9.1; 15.5–8) nor immediately by inspiration of the Spirit (contrast Acts 13.1ff.; Eph. 4.11)! This is not the spontaneous expression of community but appears rather as a misguided striving after community at an artificial and superficial level (cf. Acts 1.6). If this is historical, as is quite likely, it is an episode which Luke seems to condemn by contrast with the spontaneous and unforced flowering of community in the subsequent chapters – through the impact and inspiration of the Spirit.[47]

All in all then, von Dobschütz's thesis does not improve with age, and we shall have to judge it as probable that I Cor. 15.6 and Acts 2 are dealing with two different episodes. It is more likely that the appearance to the more than 500 took place *after* Pentecost – that is, after the sect had begun to grow and function as a community; how else can we explain the gathering together of more than 500 in one place at one time? *Pentecost therefore probably took place between the appearance to 'the twelve' and that to the 'more than 500'.*

The not unimportant corollary follows that *the gift of the Spirit was not something quite so distinct and separate from the resurrection appearances as Luke implies.* Although Pentecost does not itself seem to have involved a resurrection appearance or even a vision of Jesus, it would seem that after the initial resurrection appearances, charismatic and ecstatic phenomena became a not uncommon feature of the communal gatherings of the young church together with occasional visionary appearances of Jesus, on one occasion at least to the whole company. In other words, we can only go so far in distinguishing experiences of Spirit from resurrection appearances in the earliest Christian community. The problem of how the exalted Jesus and the Spirit of God were related in the religious experience of the early churches is by no means solved. We shall have to return to it in subsequent chapters.

§26. WHAT HAPPENED AT PENTECOST?

With the ground cleared we can now take up the central historical question: What actually happened at Pentecost? What was this experience which Luke describes as the outpouring of the Spirit? J. Kremer has recently subjected the passage (Acts 2.1–13) to close exegetical scrutiny;[48] we need only concern ourselves with particular points of interest.

26.1 *Dramatis personae and scene*. Who was involved? If our earlier observations are sound the obvious answer is, Those of Jesus' original disciples who had returned to Jerusalem from Galilee following the initial resurrection appearances (see above pp. 141f.). The figure of 120 (Acts 1.15) has a somewhat artificial ring, but Luke does add ὡσεί (*about* 120), and it is quite probable that this is a fair estimate of the numbers present on the day of Pentecost.[49]

Where did it happen? If the disciples had returned to Jerusalem because of the apocalyptic expectations centred on the temple (see below §29), then the temple itself would be the obvious gathering point for such a crowd (cf. especially Luke 24.53; Acts 5.12, 42). If speculation is appropriate, one can readily imagine the Galileans coming together in the temple on the day of Pentecost and their earnest hope and prayer for the decisive eschatological intervention by God, stimulated both by the day and by the place, being met by 'the promise of the Father'. Luke himself probably thought the gathering was in a private house (οἶκος – 2.2).[50] This is certainly not impossible: it is conceivable that the disciples met at a suitable house before going *en masse* (for safety?) to the temple.[51] The issue is of little importance.

What happened? The answer demanded by the narrative and made plausible by the circumstances is a communal ecstatic experience. The chief features of this experience were two-fold – visionary and auditory elements, and ecstatic speech, that is glossolalia.

26.2   *A communal vision*. Visions are common in the history of religions, frequently with an auditory element – particularly visions incorporating light phenomena (cf. e.g. Ezek. 1.4ff.; Mark 9.2f. pars.; II Cor. 4.6).[52] Collective visions are also well attested,[53] and such a vision would be not unnatural in the state of excitement which must have gripped the crowd of disciples at this time. The degree of vagueness (2.2–3: '*like* a rushing mighty wind'; '*as of* fire') is not un-characteristic of visions;[54] and though Luke says 'tongues like fire', not 'like tongues of fire' – which may be an example of his tendency to stress the objectivity of the experience[55] – his actual description does not go beyond a visionary experience (ὤφθησαν). The auditory phenomena do not include the hearing of words, as in the individual visions of the OT prophets and elsewhere in Luke's writings (Luke 3.22; 9.35; Acts 9.4ff., 10ff.; 10.13ff., etc.). But a more diffuse sound is only to be expected in a collective vision, and we need not assume that Luke has replaced divinely uttered words with the disciples' glossolalia. There is no reason then on history of religion grounds to doubt that Luke is following good tradition here.

It could, however, be argued that Luke has constructed the vision out of symbolical elements appropriate to the occasion. Both wind and fire were typical of theophanies within the Jewish tradition;[56] in particular, 'wind' was a familiar analogy to the divine *pneuma*,[57] and fire is prominent in the traditions regarding Sinai;[58] alternatively, the tradition of the Baptist's threat of a coming baptism in *pneuma* and

fire (Luke 3.16) could have suggested the elements of the vision to
Luke.[59] But, as we have already seen, indications are lacking that
Luke was influenced by the Sinai tradition; the ὥσπερ and ὡσεί (*like*
a wind, *like* fire) tell against it; and the form of the vision (particularly
the tongues 'dispersed among them . . .') is without any real parallel
in the Philo passages to which Haenchen alludes (see above n. 18).
So too it must be judged unlikely that the elements of the vision were
determined by the Baptist prophecy, for so far as Luke was concerned, Jesus had already radically reinterpreted that prophecy
(Luke 12.49f.; Acts 1.5).[60]

It is of course psychologically natural that an experience of Holy
Spirit should be accompanied by a vision whose content was appropriate to the experience. This indeed may well tell us something
about the divine givenness of the experience itself. For if our reconstruction of the disciples' mood of expectancy prior to the experience is correct, and if their excited state was itself alone the cause of
the vision (a mass hallucination), then we would have expected a
vision more in terms of 'the Son of Man coming in clouds of glory'
(cf. Mark 9.1 pars.; 13.26 pars.; 14.62 pars.; Acts 7.56). But a vision
in terms of wind and tongues of fire rather suggests the *unexpectedness*
of the experience. What came to them came not from the depths of
their subconscious, individual or collective, but from beyond themselves, outside themselves. *It was the experience of divine power unexpected
in its givenness and in its accompanying features which probably determined the
elements of the vision.*[61]

26.3   *Ecstatic glossolalia.* The other chief element in their experience
was the glossolalia – clearly here an ecstatic phenomenon (2.4ff., 13;
cf. 2.33).[62] Glossolalia is also well known to us from religious history
(see below §§41.7, 52.3). In psychological terms it is to be understood
simply as the resigning or abandoning of conscious control of the
speech organs to the subconscious, or 'superconscious' as some would
have it. The chief points of dispute about the phenomenon are, first,
whether the ultimate stimulus is divine or not; second, whether the
effect is one of integration or disintegration for the personality
involved; and third, whether the sounds uttered have the structure
of a language or are mere gibberish. We will comment further on all
three questions as appropriate in a later chapter (§41.7). For the
moment it is the third question alone which demands our attention.
Did the glossolalia of Pentecost take the form of language, of one
language or many languages, or of no language whatsoever?
Traditionally the debate has been on the issue of whether we have

here a miracle of speech or a miracle of hearing.[63] The dominant view favoured the former alternative, and it continues to win support.[64] Luke certainly believes that the 'tongues' were foreign languages (v. 4 – 'other tongues'; so vv. 8, 11). The problem with this view has always been the ribald comment of the 'others' in the crowd: 'They are filled with new wine!' (v. 13). If only some heard their own languages while others heard drunken-like babbling, it would presumably mean that any miracle lies in the hearing rather than the speaking. In which case Luke may have misinterpreted the accounts which came to him and inserted the ἑτέραις (other) in v. 4 on his own initiative.[65] But these straightforward alternatives by no means exhaust the debate.

One neat attempt to resolve the dilemma was that of J. G. Herder (1794), who sought to show that 'to speak with other tongues' means in Hebrew idiom no more than 'to speak with excitement, enthusiastically, vigorously and with feeling'. The 'new tongues' then means 'new ways of interpreting the old prophets'.[66] But this hardly meets the case. The interpretation is strained and without any foundation in the text. In particular the suggestion of C. S. Mann that we have here not 'wild and uncontrolled utterance, but an ordered recitation of appointed passages' hardly fits with 'a scene of wild enthusiasm'.[67]

Another possibility which has retained favour in this century should be mentioned for the sake of completeness. It starts from the justified observation that since Greek or Aramaic would be the *lingua franca* of all the hearers, who after all according to Luke were resident in Jerusalem (v. 5 – ἦσαν . . . κατοικοῦντες), no multiplication of languages need be assumed. The suggestion then follows that Luke's account deals with a diversity of *dialect*, not of *language*. The 'native language' (v. 8) of the hearers would be Greek or Aramaic; their surprise would be at understanding the speakers despite their Galilean accent, or perhaps at the fact that the disciples had been 'suddenly delivered from the peculiarities of their Galilean speech'.[68] This suggestion must also be judged deficient: it puts too much strain on the straightforward language of Luke, and leaves v. 13 as an awkward appendage.

In nineteenth-century exegesis the boldest contribution was made by E. Zeller. While almost all scholars attempted to explain the Acts 2 narrative on the assumption that it was basically historical,[69] Zeller tackled it as Strauss had tackled the gospel narratives – with equivalent results.[70] His conclusion was that the narrative was a dogmatic creation, constructed from three elements of which only the first was historical: the common experience among the early Christians of glossolalia, the language of the Spirit;[71] the parallel with and the legends concerning the giving of the law at Sinai (see above n. 18); and the universalism of Luke. The correlation of these elements made it natural and easy for Luke to assume that the first and most abundant bestowal of the gift was in fact a reversal of the curse of Babel, the restoration of the universal language of Paradise – what Trocmé has since called 'supernatural Esperanto'.[72] However, an adequate foundation in the text seems again to be quite lacking (see above pp. 140f.). Luke certainly thought in terms of more than one language (2.4, 8, 11), and if modern glossolalia is any guide, the historical reality was a good deal more complex.

In the present century three alternatives have dominated the critical discussion – with explanations being sought for the Acts account in terms of *myth*, by means of *source analysis*, and through *psychological analysis* of parallel phenomena. Since Zeller, the thesis that Acts 2 is a mythical narrative to explain the unknown origin of the church has gained ground, finding its most thoroughgoing expression in A. Loisy[73] and now Haenchen: all rationalizing expedients are to be eschewed; the 'miracle of tongues' was a literary construction built up out of reports of glossolalia as in Corinth and the rabbinic legends of the law-giving at Sinai. This 'wholly myth' thesis constitutes no real advance on the view of Zeller and we have already dismissed it as lacking sufficient foothold in the text.[74]

Source analysis thrived for a few decades at the turn of the century without advancing the discussion of our question. The attempt to demonstrate the presence of sources in Acts 2, most notably by F. Spitta (1891), broke on the grammatical and stylistic unity of the text.[75] More plausible have been the attempts to combine the strengths of these two approaches, the suggestions of a mythical elaboration of an original simpler narrative: Luke (or his source) took over an account of an experience of ecstatic glossolalia from the primitive church and transformed it into a miracle of speaking foreign languages under the influence of the Babel legend, the traditions concerning Sinai, or simply his own theological aim to present the birthday of the church in terms symbolizing the universal embrace of Christianity.[76]

The psychological explanations were prompted by the reappearance of glossolalia on a wider scale in the emerging Pentecostal movement, and in particular by the studies of E. Lombard and E. Mosiman.[77] The importance of such manifestations in religious history for our understanding of the event of Pentecost was rightly stressed by K. L. Schmidt.[78] The most plausible suggestions to emerge on this front are well represented by C. A. A. Scott and C. S. C. Williams. Thus Scott writes:

What they heard need not have been coherent or even intelligible speech, but such utterances as quickened in their minds a sympathetic response. Their own stored-up recollections of the 'wonderful works of God' were set loose by the ecstatic, though it may have been unintelligible, utterances of men with whom they were to some extent *en rapport*.

He goes on to cite the case where at a world-wide conference of the Salvation Army 'each time the theme (the saving love of God in Christ) was touched upon, it brought forth from the pent-up feelings of the vast assembly a sort of half-sigh of appreciation' – even though many in the cosmopolitan audience knew no English.[79] The parallel may however break down: whereas we can assume that the audience in the Salvation Army case was *en rapport* with the speaker, we cannot make the same assumption in the case of Pentecost.[80] Williams comments:

Anyone who has been present when others have been subject to strong emotional and spiritual or even alcoholic (cf. 2.15) pressure or stimulus may have observed that words of complete gibberish together with words suggesting a foreign tongue are mixed up when the 'censors' of the psyche are removed.[81]

A more elaborate parallel is given by the known phenomenon of cryptomnesia;[82] but this can hardly apply in the case of communal ecstasy.

Perhaps the most striking feature of glossolalia in Pentecostalism for the present discussion is the number of claims of an 'unknown tongue' which was actually a foreign language unknown to the speaker.[83] It is not necessary that any instance be proved authentic;[84] it is enough that the speaker or hearer thought that the glossolalist was speaking in a foreign language. If such claims can be made with such conviction in the twentieth century, it is more readily conceivable that they were made at the time of the first Christian Pentecost. If modern parallels tell us anything then we must judge it to be *quite probable that on the occasion itself (Pentecost), there were those who thought they recognized and understood words and phrases spoken by the disciples in their ecstasy*. This presumably would be the story Luke heard from the lips of the oldest surviving converts in the Jerusalem church.[85] Probably the *ultimate* explanation lies along the lines suggested by Scott and Williams – an identification of some of the sounds uttered by the disciples with the languages of their home land, together with the powerful spiritual impact of the disciples' evident rapture and ecstasy of praise. Others would hear only gibberish and be unmoved.

Quite likely too Luke has given the episode greater precision by clarifying the glossolalia into foreign languages proper and by introducing the note of universalism in v.5 (cf. vv.9–11). The introduction of other factors is not required by the text or by the probabilities of the situation.

In short, *there is no reason to doubt that the disciples experienced ecstatic speech on the day of Pentecost.*[86] And there is good reason, both from the text itself and from religious history parallels, to believe that *the glossolalia and the disciples' behaviour was such that many present thought they recognized words of praise to God in other languages.* More we cannot say. We can get no nearer to the actuality of the events of Pentecost than we can to the parallel events of early Pentecostalism.

26.4   *The gift of the Spirit.* One other point must be stressed before we move on from the question, What happened at Pentecost? Historical investigations naturally fasten on to the more striking features of the event – the vision and the glossolalia. But recognition of the psychological nature of these phenomena does not close the discussion. The source of the stimulus to ecstasy remains an open question. We must therefore not ignore the interpretation which those who experienced these phenomena put on them – viz., that these were the manifestations of the Spirit of God coming upon the disciples and taking possession of them. The key phrase in Acts 2 is v.4a, 'they were all filled with the Holy Spirit', not v.4b, 'and they began to speak in other tongues'.[87] Nor may this be understood as only Luke's interpretation read back into the earlier event. The eschatological consciousness of the earliest community of believers can only be understood in terms of their consciousness of divine power, uplifting, transforming, uniting them. This is clearly reflected in Paul's talk of the Spirit as ἀπαρχή (first fruits) and ἀρραβών (first instalment), as also in the sermon in Acts 2 – where Pentecost is presented as the fulfilment of Joel's prophecy (Joel 2.28ff.) of a general outpouring of the Spirit on all flesh manifested in prophecy, visions and dreams (Acts 2.17f., see further below §29). We need not doubt then that *Pentecost was for the disciples an experience of such inspiration and worship, of such liberation and power, of such givenness and numinous quality, that from the first they were sure that this was the Spirit of God.*

§27. PENTECOST AND MISSION

27.1   The last problem which the Acts 1–2 narrative raises for us is the relation of Pentecost and mission. This brings us once again to the difficulty of distinguishing resurrection appearances from outpouring of Spirit. On the one hand the appearance of the risen Lord in itself constituted Paul's call to mission, as we have seen (§20); so too in Matt. 28 the 'great commission' is set within the resurrection appearance to 'the twelve' (eleven); and we have noted that some form of commissioning seems to have been integral to the earlier resurrection appearances (§22.2). On the other hand, according to Luke's account, Pentecost provided an indispensable impulse to mission, and the commission of the resurrection appearances lay dormant until activated and energized by the outpouring of the Spirit (Luke 24.47ff.; Acts 1.8). Likewise in the rest of Acts it is the gift of the Spirit which determines and regulates the expansion of the church's mission (see especially 8.14ff.; 10.44ff.; so also 6.10; 8.39; 10.19f.; 13.1ff.; 15.28; 16.6f.; 19.1–7), and it is evident that one of Luke's aims in Acts is to demonstrate that the gift of the Spirit is the crucial factor in conversion and initiation.[88] Does the conclusion follow that the link between Pentecost and mission is another piece of Lukan theology?

Three factors perhaps point the way to an answer.

(a) The recognition that the resurrection appearances of I Cor. 15.5–7 extended over a lengthy period certainly goes some way towards easing the problem. The only member of that list which demands an association between appearance and commissioning is the appearance to 'all the apostles' – and, as we have seen, this appearance (or appearances) probably took place *after* Pentecost, and much nearer in time to Paul's conversion – to the time, that is, when the Jerusalem community, at least in the persons of the Hellenists, were beginning to move out in mission (see above pp. 141f., 143f.). The implication, borne out by Acts itself, is that the concept of a commission to the Gentiles did not take firm hold of the early church for some time (and then not all of them! – cf. p. 145 above). The picture which begins to emerge is of a growing sense of commission, in which resurrection appearances and Pentecost had a determinative, though not final part. Certainly Matthew's association of 'the great commission' with the appearance to the eleven must be regarded as a compression of a sequence of revelatory events spanning several years.[89]

(b) The resurrection appearances constitute an integral part of the missionary and evangelistic proclamation, whereas the outpouring of the Spirit does not seem to have been preached in the same way. This is true of both Luke and Paul (Acts 2.32; 4.2, 33; 10.40ff.;

13.30ff.; 17.18; I Cor. 15.3–8, 11; cf. Rom. 1.3–4; II Tim. 2.8). It was not Pentecost that was proclaimed but the risen Christ. This confirms that for the early church at large the obligation to mission was rooted in the appearances of the risen Jesus.

(c) At the same time we must also note that evangelism itself was regarded as a gift of the Spirit; without the inspiration and empowering of the Spirit the words of mission would have no impact on the hearers. On this point too Luke and Paul are one (Acts 4.8, 31; 6.10; 16.6; 18.25; I Cor. 2.4f.; 14.24f.; I Thess. 1.5; Eph. 4.11).[90] We may say therefore that Pentecost was widely recognized as the presupposition of mission no less than resurrection appearances.

Taking all these factors into account, together with our earlier discussion, it looks very much as though both the resurrection appearances (the complete sequence) and Pentecost (with further ecstatic experiences) played a determinative role in establishing and developing a sense of mission in the young church. The initial sense of obligation to 'make the vision known' in the Galilee appearances may have been satisfied, for the time being at least, by telling the rest of the disciples (120?). It would then probably be swallowed up, if our reconstruction of events is correct, in the eschatological excitement which led to the whole group returning to Jerusalem to await the return of Jesus as Christ and Son of Man (see below §29). With the eschatological anticipation fulfilled, in part at any rate, by the gift of the Spirit, the impulse to tell others probably re-emerged with fresh power. The history of religions reveals many examples of spiritual awakenings where high spiritual excitement creates a communal enthusiasm and boldness which is infectious and attractive to the devout seeker.[91] We need not doubt then that Pentecost brought a new sense of community (the eschatological Israel), established their faith with a fuller certainty, and stimulated their sense of commission, so that they could not keep their good news to themselves. The assurance of divine inspiration has always been the most potent factor in the boldness of prophetic proclamation (cf. below pp. 211f.). So it was in the reappearance of the prophetic Spirit at Pentecost.

We may add briefly that there is also no reason to doubt that Luke is essentially correct when he records that it was the manifestation of Spirit at various critical points which confirmed the broadening out of mission to an uncertain leadership. In particular, it is difficult to believe that Luke is responsible for the construction of the episode in 8.14ff. and 10.44ff. *ex nihilo*. In the former incident the otherwise astonishing separation of the gift of the Spirit from belief and baptism

(8.12f.) is hardly a step which would be taken without historical precedent.[92] A more coherent reconstruction of the origin of the narrative is that it was indeed ecstatic manifestations which re-assured Peter and John that the Spirit had been given to the Samaritans and therefore that God had welcomed them. Likewise in the case of the conversion of Cornelius in Acts 10 when again the decisive point in the episode is the gift of the Spirit, this time prior to baptism, the sign of God's acceptance making necessary the sign of the community's acceptance. It is clear that Luke with the benefit of hindsight draws out a significance in the conversion story which was probably not recognized at the time. However, it seems impossible to deny the historicity of this kernel of the account; if Luke, writing at a time of growing self-consciousness in the church, was so free with his material as to create from nothing an incident where Spirit preceded baptism, then it must be considered doubtful whether his account would have been acceptable to his fellow churchmen.[93] But if the original tradition told of the Spirit coming upon uncircumcised Gentiles with the result that they were accepted into the local Christian community, then Luke is justified in seeing here once again and in a decisive way the initiative of the Spirit in the widening mission of early Christianity.[94]

In short, the resolution of the problem set out at the beginning of this section is now evident. *The resurrection appearances were for some, though not all, a growing point of conviction which when energized by some charismatic and ecstatic experiences became a powerful evangelistic motive force.* From the resurrection appearances stemmed the sense of *obligation* to mission; but only the experiences of Spirit brought the inner *compulsion* to mission and *confirmation* of its widening outreach.

27.2 *Conclusion.* If any one experience can be said to have launched Christianity it is the experience of a largish group of Jesus' disciples on the day of Pentecost following Jesus' death. When gathered together in Jerusalem, presumably to await the consummation already begun in the resurrection of Jesus, they were caught up in a communal experience of ecstatic worship which manifested itself particularly in vision and glossolalia. This experience they recognized as the impact of the Spirit of God, and therein they saw the hand of the risen Jesus drawing them together into living community and giving them both impulse and urgency to testify for him.

This analysis leaves us with some key questions unresolved concerning the first Christians' understanding of their experience: in particular the question of how they related the risen Jesus to the

Spirit as the source (or sources?) of their experience. We shall have to bear this question in mind while we look at the enthusiastic beginnings of the Jerusalem community following Pentecost. As we shall see, Luke is only of marginal help, and for a theologically adequate answer we shall have to await the profounder treatments of Paul and of John (chs. X and XI).

VII

ENTHUSIASTIC BEGINNINGS IN LUKAN RETROSPECT

§28. INTRODUCTION

The enthusiast is an unpopular figure in Christian history and theology. He believes he has been specially favoured by God, that the Spirit of God has been given to him in a fuller way than to other believers. He claims to experience God more directly and in more evident manner than others. He knows God's will and acts as his agent, accountable only and directly to him. The world is for him an arena where supernatural forces are at work often with visible and powerful effect. His enthusiasm usually includes an overwhelming conviction that the return of Jesus is imminent, and sometimes bursts forth in ecstatic speech and action, particularly in the context of communal worship. So sure is he of the rightness of his beliefs and actions that he will not hesitate to break even with the most sanctified and respected tradition, and schism often begets schism.

This 'identikit picture' of the enthusiast, drawn from our knowledge of enthusiasm as a historical phenomenon,[1] would appear to 'fit' many of the earliest Christians with amazing precision – *Christianity began as an enthusiastic sect within first-century Judaism!* Such a claim may be distasteful to some, but it is one with which we will have to reckon with increasing seriousness as the present chapter progresses.

Our task then in the following paragraphs is to examine the characteristic features of the religious experience of the earliest Christian communities following Pentecost and prior to Paul. How did the upsurge of spiritual vitality at Pentecost manifest itself in the succeeding months? The possibility of gaining an accurate picture is of course always in question; we have already seen that Luke by no means always provides us with straightforward historical information. A further question therefore arises: Has Luke distorted his account of Christian beginnings in the matter of religious experience? Is it the early church's experience of Spirit or Luke's concept of Spirit that we find in the early chapters of Acts? Finally, in so far as we can answer these questions, the issue of distinctiveness posed at the end of chapter IV re-emerges: Was the spiritual experience of the early Christians distinctive when compared with the charismatic experience of Jesus and when compared with similar manifestations outside Christianity?

§29. ESCHATOLOGICAL ENTHUSIASM

The first feature of the spiritual experience of the earliest Jerusalem community which calls for comment was its eschatological enthusiasm. I have already indicated my conviction that it was belief in the imminence of Jesus' parousia and in the eschatological centrality of Jerusalem which led the disciples to return to Jerusalem after the initial resurrection appearances (p. 141). I must now justify that thesis. And justification is necessary, for it seems to lack all foundation in Luke's account of affairs. Here we meet one of Luke's significant silences; apart from one or two brief notes there is nothing to indicate that the enthusiasm of the earliest community was apocalyptic in character. However, it is almost certain that Luke has ignored or suppressed this feature. As probably the majority of scholars agree, the delay of the parousia has caused Luke to omit almost all expectation of an imminent parousia from Acts.[2] With the parousia delayed so long, he presumably thought it unnecessary or unwise to depict the earliest believers as living in daily expectation of the end of this age. And yet such apocalyptic excitement almost certainly was a prominent feature of the Jerusalem community.

(a) It is clear from the Synoptics that Jesus himself had a firm expectation of the imminence of the end of this present world's history, as had the Baptist before him (see above ch. III n. 34 and §16.3). It is obvious too that the same apocalyptic expectation featured strongly in Paul's early theology, as the Thessalonian epistles confirm. It is almost impossible to believe that a similar excitement and expectation did not grip the earliest believers, many of whom after all were direct disciples of Jesus and direct precursors of Paul.[3] Two striking indications of the way in which the enthusiastic faith of the earliest church continued to influence later Christian worship and thought are the Aramaic phrase *Maranatha* (I Cor.

16.22; Rev. 22.20) and the word ἀπαρχή (Rom. 8.23; I Cor. 15.20, 23). The former, 'Our Lord, come', certainly stems from 'the most ancient primitive tradition' and may well take us to the very beginnings of Christian worship. The fact that an Aramaic formula was carried over into the Greek speaking churches confirms that it must have been an important and regular feature of the primitive community's common life. It is significant then that the invocation is best understood as the community's yearning for the speedy return of Jesus as Lord. This is certainly the mood of Rev. 22.20 and it must have been a dominant mood in the earliest church.[4]

The same conclusion follows from Paul's use of ἀπαρχή (first fruits). The metaphor denotes the beginning of the harvest, more or less the first swing of the sickle. No interval is envisaged between the first fruits and the rest of the harvest. With the first fruits dedicated the harvest proceeds. The application of this metaphor to the resurrection of Jesus and the gift of the Spirit expresses the belief that with these events the eschatological harvest has begun; the resurrection of the dead has started, the end-time Spirit has been poured out. This anticipation of the consummation cannot have found its first expression in Paul, already separated by some years from Jesus' resurrection and from Pentecost. It too must go back to the earliest community, as the early formula in Rom. 1.3f. (ἐξ ἀναστάσεως νεκρῶν) confirms.[5] It was doubtless the earliest Jerusalem believers who saw the resurrection of Jesus and the outpouring of the Spirit as the beginning of the end, which means, of course, that the resurrection appearances of Jesus were initially understood not so much as an epilogue to Jesus' first parousia, but rather as a prologue to his second.

(b) Recent scholarship has highlighted the apocalyptic character of the Q material in the Synoptics.[6] Without going into too much detail or venturing into the Son of Man 'minefield', it is nevertheless clear enough that Son of Man sayings must have had a lively circulation in the early Jerusalem community – as the tradition-history of these sayings, and perhaps also Acts 7.56, confirm. Prominent among these were almost certainly the apocalyptic sayings about the expected coming of the Son of Man.[7] Many scholars indeed believe that these sayings belong to the earliest stratum of Son of Man sayings, and that the earliest community either formulated them themselves,[8] or identified the risen Jesus with the coming Son of Man expected by Jesus.[9] But even if we accept that 'the son of man' was a self-reference of Jesus himself in the first instance, which at several points gives a more coherent picture of the overall development of the tradition, the conclusion still cannot be refuted that expectation of the parousia of Jesus as the soon returning Son of Man was characteristic of the earliest communities.

(c) The eschatological fervency of the first believers in Jerusalem is directly reflected in two passages in Acts – 2.17f. and 3.19ff. In 2.17 the significant phrase is 'in these last days', which is *inserted* into the Joel prophecy. Since it is not Luke's policy to emphasize the eschatological character of the epoch of the church, this insertion can hardly be his work and must derive from his source. That this source goes back to the primitive community is suggested by the eschatological significance of the phrase itself.[10] In 3.19ff. we find embedded within Peter's speech what appears to be a very primitive expression of faith, viz., the apocalyptic expectation of 'times of refreshing' and of the coming of the Christ. To be sure Luke has integrated it into his own presentation, so that it can be understood without reference to an imminent parousia, but the apocalyptic hope still shines through, and almost certainly reflects the mood which characterized the first days of Christianity.[11]

(d) Two other indications of the eschatological enthusiasm of the earliest community emerge from a little reflection on the facts recorded by Luke. First, it is clear from Acts that the disciples stuck fast in Jerusalem and that their worship was centred on the temple; Jerusalem and the temple were obviously seen as the centre of the new community (2.46; 3.1ff.; 5.12, 20f., 25, 42). Why did the disciples return from Galilee to Jerusalem? Why did the men of Galilee abandon so completely that area of Palestine where Jesus had been so successful and popular? Why did they stay so exclusively in Jerusalem? The most obvious answer is that they expected the other prophecies concerning 'the last days' to be fulfilled – particularly Isa. 2.2f. and Micah 4.1f., which speak of the nations of the world streaming to Mount Zion for salvation in the last days before the end (cf. Matt.8.11/Luke 13.29). Similarly their continued loyalty to the temple is to be explained partly at least by their expectation that the temple would be the focus for the final total renewal of worship and the end-time consummation (Isa.56.7; Mal.3.1) – a hope which presumably they had to some extent inherited from Jesus (Mark 11.17; 14.58).[12] This is confirmed by the clear indications that the earliest community regarded themselves as the climax of Judaism, the eschatological Israel – 'the twelve' with their anticipated eschatological role as judges of Israel (Matt.19.28b/Luke 22.30b),[13] the 'last supper' seen as the institution of the new covenant (Mark 14.22–5 pars.; I Cor.11.23ff.),[14] the use of ἐκκλησία (people of God),[15] the Israel oriented attitude expressed in Acts 1.6, 21f.; 3.25, and the continued restriction of mission to the Jews only in view of the imminence of the Son of Man's coming (Matt. 10.5b–6, 23; 15.24).[16]

(e) Finally we may draw attention to the so-called 'community of goods' described by Luke in Acts 2.44f.; 4.32–7. In fact what Luke describes is a common (poor) fund which was established and maintained over a period of time by members of the community selling off possessions and handing over part or all of the money realized.[17] We need not doubt the essential historicity of this feature of Luke's account; the discontent and division implied in Acts 6.1 was hardly an invention of Luke; and Barnabas (4.36f.) may be singled out for mention *not* 'because it was something out of the ordinary',[18] but simply because he was the first notable convert, or even because he was a great landowner whose gift was the largest single contribution to the common coffer.[19] Besides, we know of a somewhat analogous 'community of goods' at Qumran (see below pp. 162f.). We may also mention that Luke's record does not imply that everyone contributed; many of those who had abandoned their source of livelihood in Galilee must have been nearly penniless; this was why the common fund was necessary in the first place. But presumably most contributed something, otherwise Ananias would not have felt the need to conform (5.1–11 – see further below p. 166).[20] The point we must underline here is that the 'community of goods' is best explained as a natural expression of the first disciples' spiritual enthusiasm as they waited for the imminent consummation. To that extent it also expresses a sense of community – but not a desire to establish a permanent 'communist' society or anything of the sort. The essence of communism is the common ownership of the means of production. But these first Christians were not at all concerned with 'means of production' – they *sold* their capital goods! The 'community of goods' in other words was probably not intended as a long term measure, but only as a temporary expedient to tide them over the period of waiting for the Son of Man's return. In these circumstances it was an impressive expression of love and mutual concern, although Luke's silence on the main motivation behind it (the eschatological enthusiasm) makes the community of goods seem a rather more careless and thoughtless venture than it actually was.

These various considerations make quite clear both the fact and the character of the eschatological enthusiasm which gripped the earliest Jerusalem community. This enthusiasm was a direct expression of their experience of Spirit. The link between enthusiasm and expectation of an imminent parousia is a recurring feature of the history of Christianity, from Montanism, or rather from Pentecost to Pentecostalism (see above ch. V n. 150). The immediate impression of divine power, the awareness of God's immanent presence has regularly gone hand in hand with a certainty of Christ's imminent return. It was so at Pentecost. Their experience was such – the experience, if we may fill out our understanding of it from the history of enthusiasm (cf. p. 157 above), of being lifted out of themselves, of self-transcendence, of inspiration, of well-being in time of praise ('maintaining the glow'), of fellowship in community, of being personally addressed by God when members of the community prophesied or took up and passed on sayings of Jesus, of confidence in God's Christ and certainty regarding the future – this experience they could only attribute to a divine power moving upon them and in them, to God's Spirit – indeed to God's Spirit of the end-time. In short, *their experience of the Spirit was such that they could not doubt that they were in the last days, that the salvation history of God was reaching its climax and consummation.*

Here at once we see *a very close parallel between the experience of Jesus and the experience of the first Christians.* As Jesus' experience of Spirit convinced him that the eschatological rule of God was already operating, so the first Christians' experience of Spirit convinced them that they were living in the last days. And as Jesus' experience of Spirit thus led him to the conclusion that God's kingdom was about to come, so the first Christians' experience of Spirit led them to the conclusion that God's Christ was about to return. To that extent Jesus' experience is archetypal of the first Christian's experience – although Luke's reticence on the subject of early Christian apocalyptic obscures the parallel. But there is one probable difference. Jesus' experience was such that he formulated his hope in terms of *self-reference* – either of 'the Son of Man' (someone else) who would confirm his words, or of himself as the Son of Man (Mark 8.38; Luke 12.8f.). *The experience of the first Christians however led them to base their hope not in themselves, but in the exalted Jesus.* It would appear then as though the first disciples' encounter with Jesus alive from the dead began very quickly to influence their interpretation of their experience of the Spirit; their experience *of* Jesus began to reflect on their experiences which were most like those enjoyed by Jesus himself.

The closest parallel to the experience of the first Christians and its expression in communal life is the community at Qumran (IQS 1.11–13; 5.2f.; 6.18–23; CD 16). They too seem to have thought that they were in the last days [21] with the End imminent;[22] they may even have believed that the Teacher of Righteousness would return.[23] But

there is a very striking difference. The eschatological enthusiasm of
the first Christians found spontaneous expression in community life
and the sharing of resources; the community at Qumran was more
contrived and organized – more like the striving after community of
Acts 1 than the charismatic community of Acts 2ff.[24]

§30. 'WONDERS AND SIGNS'

It is quite clear that Luke intends us to see the early community as
living in an atmosphere of the miraculous. The τέρατα and σημεῖα
('wonders and signs') prophesied by Joel (Acts 2.19)[25] characterize
the life of the Jerusalem community and the subsequent missionary
outreach (2.43; 4.30; 5.12; 6.8; 14.3; 15.12; σημεῖα – 4.16, 22; 8.6;
σημεῖα καὶ δυνάμεις – 8.13). By using the phrase so frequently Luke
underlines and probably reflects the early community's feeling that
they were living in 'the new Mosaic age of eschatological redemption',
characterized by the same kind of 'signs and wonders' that characterized the redemption of Israel from Egypt (7.36f.).[26]

30.1   *A review of the evidence.* For the sake of analysis we may divide
the Acts miracles into five groups. (*a*) Luke describes a number of
more 'ordinary' healings – of the lame man at the 'Beautiful Gate'
of the temple (3.1–10), of Paul's blindness during his conversion
(9.18), of Aeneas' paralysis (9.33f.), of a cripple in Lystra (14.8–10) –
as well as mentioning the various exorcisms and healings (paralysis
and lameness) of Philip in Samaria (8.7) and the healings (fever and
diseases) by Paul in Malta (28.8f.). (*b*) More striking are the restora-
tions from death of Tabitha by Peter (9.36–41) and of Eutychus by
Paul (20.9–12). (*c*) More striking still are healings brought about by
Peter's shadow (5.15f.) and by handkerchiefs or scarves touched by
Paul (19.11f.). (*d*) Most striking of all are the miracles of judgment –
the death of Ananias and Sapphira (5.1–11) and the blindness of
Elymas (13.8–11)[27] – and (*e*) the miracles of liberation – of Peter from
prison by angelic intervention (5.19–24, 12.6–11), of Paul also from
prison, this time by the good offices of an earthquake (16.26), and
Paul's escape from a viper (28.3–6).[28]

We need not doubt that it is a sound historical fact that many
healings of a miraculous sort did occur in the early days of the first
Christian communities and of the early Christian mission. This is
attested at first hand by Paul (Rom. 15.19; I Cor. 12.10, 28f.; II Cor.
12.12; Gal. 3.5), and also by the writer to the Hebrews (Heb. 2.4).

Periods of religious excitement have always produced healers and a crop of healings hailed as miraculous by those present at the time – as the history of Christianity testifies, from Jesus on through such figures as Gregory Thaumaturgos, Edward the Confessor, Louis VI of France[29] and St Vincent Ferrar, to the healing evangelists of twentieth-century Pentecostalism, George Jeffreys, Smith Wigglesworth, William Branham, T. L. Osborn and Oral Roberts.[30] Investigations in this field should certainly not be confined to literary parallels and the hunt for the 'divine man' type (see above §12.1). The history of Christian enthusiasm provides as many if not more pertinent and illuminating parallels.[31]

(a) In terms of strict historical judgment the 'ordinary' healings listed first above are such as we would expect – the psychological impact of a charismatic figure like Peter, Philip or Paul, often in the context of an excited crowd, would have a powerful effect where mental or nervous or spiritual factors were the chief cause of illness or lameness. We can still recognize the two most important factors in these healings. First, the use of Jesus' name, the significance of which is emphasized repeatedly in the first healing and its immediate aftermath (3.6, 16; 4.7, 10, 12, 30; also 16.18; cf. 19.13). The 'name' in ancient thought was much more closely associated with its bearer than is usual today; it represented him, expressed his nature, made his influence present.[32] We can understand this to some extent, since we know well enough the emotive power of certain names (e.g. Hitler, Churchill, Che Guevara). It was the same, only much more so in the ancient world.[33] So to speak the name of Jesus was to invoke his presence and his power, to act as his representative trusting in the effectiveness of his commission and authority.[34] When the earliest believers spoke the name of Jesus over someone who was sick they believed that Jesus himself effected the healing through them.[35]

Here is a rather striking difference between the healing ministry of Jesus and that of the first Christians. Where Jesus healed in his own right, by the immediate power and authority of God (cf. Acts 2.22; 10.38, and see above §12.4), his disciples healed in the name of Jesus. It would appear that from the first they recognized that their power to heal was somehow dependent on Jesus and derivative from him (cf. Luke 10.17). *Whereas he had been the direct representative of God in his healing ministry, they saw themselves primarily as representatives of Jesus.* They healed by the same power, but that power was now linked with the name of Jesus.

The second means to effect healing was the use of the healer's hand(s) – 5.12; 9.12, 17; 14.3; 19.11; 28.8; cf. 3.7; 9.41. The use of

the hand in such circumstances is very natural, but it was also probably seen as an act of prophetic symbolism – the hand of the healer
representing the hand of the Lord (= God) – the real power behind
the healing (4.30; cf. 13.11; 11.21 = II Sam. 3.12 LXX). No doubt
a flow of energy from healer to healed was actually experienced in
many cases through the physical contact (cf. Mark 5.28f. pars.),[36]
though whether the energy was thereby simply released from the
latent resources of one or other, or channelled through the man of
faith to the sick person from sources outside of himself (God/risen
Jesus) we cannot at this distance even begin to judge. It is perhaps
sufficient to note that so far as we can tell, the first believers did not ✓
consider the act of healing, or the naming of Jesus' name, as a mere
technique, or something that lay within the power of the healer, that
he could use at will, far less a piece of magic ritual or formula. The
power was God's, the name of Jesus could be invoked only by those
who already stood in a relation of discipleship to him (19.13ff.).

(b) If the first group of healings are probably based on authentic
tradition, a similar judgment may be passed, though less confidently,
on the raisings from the dead. In the case of Tabitha the parallels
with the similar miracles of Elijah and Elisha (I Kings 17.17–24;
II Kings 4.32–7) and of Jesus (Luke 8.49–56) do not really extend
beyond the natural and insignificant,[37] and certainly cannot be taken
to indicate the origin of the story. It is quite likely that the tradition
goes back to a genuine episode in the ministry of Peter,[38] in which perhaps he recognized with charismatic insight that Tabitha was in a
coma(?). This is even more probable in the case of Eutychus. The
account is particularly interesting since it comes to us first hand (a
'we' passage). Luke presumably intends the story to be understood
as a miracle of raising from the dead: when Eutychus fell down from
the window he was 'picked up dead' (20.9 – ἤρθη νεκρός). But v. 10 is
ambiguous: Paul went down, threw himself (ἐπέπεσεν) on the boy and
embraced him. Was this done to ascertain whether life was still
present, or in spontaneous emulation of Elisha (II Kings 4.34)? Paul's
reported comment leaves the issue in doubt. 'Do not be alarmed; his
life is in him'. Does that mean, '*still* alive', or 'alive *again*'? Verse 12
simply says, 'They took the boy away alive', but the insertion of v. 11
seems to imply that the boy was left to recover during the rest of the
night – without prayer or any further ministry from Paul.[39]

(c) The third group of miracles listed above, healings by shadow
and handkerchief, are more easily dismissed as legendary glorifica-
tions of the heroes of Luke's history.[40] But here too we must pause,
for what we have here is not simply literary aggrandizement, but

primitive superstition. Has the role of sacred shrines and relics in religious history not taught us that a charismatic figure takes on an aura of miracle-working power in the popular imagination – and that the expectation of a cure from objects pertaining to the 'saint' is often realized (perhaps as much by the expectation itself as by anything else)?[41] To be sure Luke takes up these stories in simple faith, and probably believes that Paul (and Peter) encouraged such faith; but that is not to deny that there were such cures or that Luke is drawing on good tradition.

(d) Even with the fourth group of miracles – the judgment on Ananias and Sapphira and on Elymas – we may not have moved out of the realm of the charismatic community. Paul certainly seems to believe in a divine authority and power whose exercise is a death sentence on the offender at Corinth (I Cor. 5.3–5).[42] And we know from more primitive religions the power of a curse – we need look no further than the voodoo practised in present day Haiti. In Acts 5.1–11 we probably see reflected the numinous power, *mysterium tremendum*, which gathered round the primitive Jerusalem community for the new convert (cf. 2.43; 5.5, 11; 9.31; 19.17). To offend against the Spirit of this community was for the superstitious a fearful and terrifying thing. In the case of Ananias and Sapphira the shock of terror at realizing their sin ('lied to the Holy Spirit', 'put the Spirit of the Lord to the test') may well have been sufficient to drop them dead in their tracks. Here again parallels among history of religions phenomena could well prove to be more weighty than the suggestion that the account was contrived on the basis of the Achan story (Josh 7).

In the case of Elymas (Acts 13.8–11) there is no substantial evidence that Luke has invented or greatly elaborated a much lesser tale. There is no description of competitive thaumaturgy, and it does not end with the conversion and cure of the opponent, as so often in such tales.[43] On the contrary, it has more the ring of a rather isolated reminiscence – the highlight of an early mission whose attendant events were only vaguely recalled. So perhaps the case is similar to that of Ananias and Sapphira: the recognition by one who prized magical powers that he stood before one possessed of greater powers could well be sufficient to ensure the effectiveness of Paul's curse (cf. 8.18–24).

(e) It is much less easy to deny the hand of legend a role in shaping the miracles of liberation (5.19–24; 12.6–11; 16.26; 28.3–6). The stories were probably in a developed state when they reached Luke, having gained somewhat in the telling. It is no longer possible to tell with any confidence what their foundation was in history.[44] What is more certain is that they probably appealed to Luke; he accepted them as they were at face value. This would be quite in character with his tendency to make the phenomena of spiritual experience more tangible and material.[45] A striking example of this *Tendenz* is his explicit insistence in 12.9 that 'the angel's intervention was real' (ἀληθές) and not simply a vision (ὅραμα). Evidently in his desire to draw out the parallel between the ministries of Peter and of Paul, Luke has had to draw on a wider range of material and had to use a grosser concept of miracle than perhaps would otherwise have been necessary.

30.2 *Luke's attitude to miracles*. An interesting issue arises here with a number of important corollaries for our understanding of Luke and for our evaluation of his work. Was Luke's treatment of miracles naive and lacking in discrimination?

(*a*) Two points would seem to favour an affirmative answer. First, Luke uses the phrase 'wonders and signs' uncritically. For Luke 'wonders and signs' appear to be something to boast of – this is why he uses the phrase so much. And even where he uses the less spectacular *dunameis*, only twice in reference to the miracles of the young church, he speaks of '*great dunameis*' (8.13) and '*extraordinary dunameis*' (19.11). His attitude seems to be: the more eye-catching the miracle the greater the propaganda value. All this is in notable contrast to the value placed on 'signs and wonders' elsewhere in the NT. Not only does Luke use the phrase far more frequently than other authors;[46] but elsewhere 'signs and wonders' are almost always something to be suspicious of – the sort of spectacular thaumaturgy that is more the stock in trade of charlatans and false prophets/apostles than of the servant of God (Mark 13.22/Matt. 24.24; John 4.48; II Cor. 12.12; II Thess. 2.9; cf. Rev. 13.13f.).[47] Only in Rom. 15.19 and Heb. 2.4 is the phrase used without negative connotation, and there the 'signs and wonders' are specifically associated with the Spirit – an association which surprisingly Luke does not wish to emphasize, despite Acts 2.19 (though presumably it is implied in 2.43; 4.30f. and 6.8).[48] In contrast to the caution of the other NT writers, not to mention Jesus and some OT writings,[49] Luke's uncritical parading of 'wonders and signs' as an advertisement for the early church seems to pander more to pagan superstitious veneration of omens and portents.[50]

Second, and equally significant, is Luke's portrayal of the relation between miracles and faith. We saw in chapter IV (§12.4) how important faith was for Jesus in the exercise of his power to heal –

the attitude of trust which drew forth from him the saving energy of
the Spirit. It was precisely this feature of Jesus' healing ministry
which set him apart from the miracle-working heroes of Judaism and
Hellenistic literature. Contrast Luke's Acts. In all this string of
wonders, signs and striking miracles, only *twice* is faith mentioned,
interestingly enough in the parallel (Peter/Paul) healings of cripples
– 3.16; 14.9. But in the actual account of the first healing the only
faith mentioned is the lame man's expectation of receiving alms (3.5),
and in the latter episode the faith is primarily faith in the message
just proclaimed.[51] On the other hand, on a number of occasions Luke
makes clear the faith-producing effect of miracles (5.14; 9.42; 13.13;
19.18). This is the aspect of the miracle/faith relation which apparently interests Luke – the publicity, propagandist value of miracle –
that which elsewhere in the NT is disparaged (Mark 8.11f.; Matt.
12.38f./Luke 11.16, 29; John 2.23; 4.48; 20.29; II Cor. 13.3f.).

This evidence suggests that Luke did not see any great need to
demonstrate the distinctiveness of the power active in early Christianity to heal and make whole. On the contrary he presents the early
church as another, but more powerful wonder worker than its competitors. He does not appear to recognize that there is a problem here
– the problem of distinguishing the power of God from its counter-
feits, the problem of weaning faith away from a diet of the miraculous.
The problem is recognized and tackled by the other leading NT
authors (Q – Matt. 4.1–11/Luke 4.1–13; Mark 9.38ff.; Matt. 7.22ff.;
John 2.23ff.; 4.48; II Cor. 12.5–10). But in presenting his account of
the early church Luke hardly seems aware of it.

(*b*) On the other hand, we must not judge Luke unfairly at this
point; he only appears in such a poor light because he has to stand
comparison with other NT writers who saw the problem in all its
sharpness and could not ignore it. When he is compared with later
literary efforts he appears in a much better light. Thus in Acts there
are no miracles merely for miracles sake or for entertainment value –
for example, no bed-bugs receive their marching orders as in the
Acts of John 60f. (third or fourth century)! In the Acts of Luke the
miraculous is subordinated to the theological purpose of demonstrat-
ing the wonderful progress of the 'Word of God'.[52] So too in Acts
8.18ff. Simon Magus is denounced for regarding the Spirit as a kind
of magical power whose secret or technique one could buy; in 13.8–11
Christianity is represented 'in very sharp contrast with *magia*';[53] in
14.8–18 Luke strongly resists and rejects any temptation to portray
Paul and Barnabas as 'divine men';[54] and in 19.13–16 he underlines
the fact that the name of Jesus is no mere exorcistic formula capable

of being used by any one who learns it, but can be used only by those who call upon that name (cf. 2.21; 9.14, 21; 15.17; 22.16).

More important, the charge of naivity levelled at Luke may be misdirected. His uncritical attitude to miraculous power may simply be a faithful reflection of the undiscriminating attitude of the early Christian mission. He may simply be content for the most part to reproduce stories handed on to him without comment. Thus, for example, as we noted above, he has not attempted to elaborate the encounter between Paul and Elymas into a narrative of contest and conversion, but has been content to leave a brief and rather bare tale unadorned (13.8–12). Likewise the encounter between Peter and Simon Magus ends on the rather anticlimactic note, 'Simon answered, "Pray for me to the Lord, that nothing of what you have said may come upon me"' (8.24).[55] At the same time, both here and in 19.11–20 Luke has done what he can to make it clear that the Spirit of God and 'the word of God' are not simply powers of a kind similar to magic but precisely 'the gift of God' and power of God to and through those who believe in the name of Jesus. It could be argued then that Luke found it impractical within a historical narrative to engage in anything more ambitious in the way of a critique of the evidential value of miracles.

In short, it is difficult to tell where Luke's role as a recorder of traditions ends and where his own attitude emerges. We have already seen reason to conclude that he himself thought of spiritual phenomena in very concrete and physical terms (pp. 121f.), and there is no reason to doubt that the same attitude is visible in his description of 'wonders and signs' in Acts. Perhaps the fairest way to evaluate Luke's treatment at this point is to recognize him as one who, on looking back from the comparative calmness and sophistication of later years, was enamoured and thrilled by the enthusiasm and power of the early mission as he heard of it from older witnesses and reports.[56] If so, it is quite likely that he wrote his account of Christian beginnings with the aim of conveying something of the same impact and impression to his readers; many of these past and present would testify to his success.[57]

30.3 To *sum up* then, we can recognize quite clearly from Luke's account the charismatic nature of the early Christian communities and the early Christian mission. There was a power to heal present in these first communities, and a numinous power too which seems to have caused as much fear as it did popularity. But such power was by no means without parallel at that time, and to mark out the

distinctive features of 'the powers of the age to come' was of considerable importance. Unfortunately, Luke is either unable or unwilling
to address himself to that task. We can, it is true, trace out a distinctiveness on one side – that is, in relation to Jesus; for though it is the same
eschatological power which was evident in their exorcisms and healings, the early churches linked this power with the name of Jesus –
its exercise was dependent on Jesus and on discipleship of Jesus. Jesus
was not simply the archetypal exorcist now dead whose example
lived on to inspire, but he himself was thought to be still ministering
to the sick through his followers. Yet while Luke is obviously aware
of the importance of these points (cf. 4.12; 19.13ff.) he does not clarify
them in any systematic way; 'wonders and signs' are attributed
variously to the Spirit of God, the name of Jesus and the hand of the
Lord, without any attempt being made to explain the relationship of
these concepts of power. More frustrating is Luke's failure to clarify
the relationship between the miracles of the early church and the
parallel miracles in Jewish and Hellenistic religion. 'Spirit of God',
'name of Jesus' and 'hand of the Lord' are obviously part of the
answer here too. But Luke only gives one or two indications that these
are *distinctive* means, rather than merely *superior* means (that is merely
power to effect more striking miracles, 'wonders and signs'). In short,
if we look in Acts for a profound treatment of the *distinctiveness* of the
eschatological power of the first Christians, we look in vain.

§31. THE SPIRIT OF PROPHECY

31.1 *Prophecy and prophets.* Also foretold by Joel was the widespread
experience of the gift of prophecy; in the new age of the Spirit the
ancient hope of Moses would be fulfilled – 'Would that all the Lord's
people were prophets, that the Lord would put his spirit upon them!'
(Num. 11.29). Luke and/or his source certainly regards Pentecost as
that fulfilment, and gives it special emphasis by repeating the 'and
they shall prophesy' at the end of v. 18.[58] His belief that all converts
were given the gift of prophecy seems to be reflected in 2.17f., 38;[59]
4.31; 10.46; 19.6. Here too we probably see a reflection of the
eschatological enthusiasm of the first community and the early
mission – *their consciousness of Spirit was in large part an awareness of
inspiration, of direct contact with God,* and the fullness of that inspiration
together with its widespread distribution evident in the communal
gatherings, all confirmed the first Christians' conviction that they
were in the end-time and were experiencing the outpouring of the

prophetic Spirit.[60] The experience of inspiration is clearly reflected in the talk of disciples being 'filled' with the Spirit on particular occasions (2.4; 4.8, 31; 9.17; 13.9; cf. Luke 1.41, 67); and the confidence of inspiration is clearly reflected in the references to the boldness (παρρησία) of the disciples' testimony to their new faith (2.29; 4.13, 29, 31; also 28.31; cf. Mark 13.11 pars.).

Although it was assumed that all had received the prophetic Spirit and could be inspired to prophesy (cf. I Cor. 14.1, 5, 24), it appears that, as would be natural, some emerged as having the gift of prophecy in greater measure; these were called 'prophets' – not because the gift of prophesying was confined to them, but presumably because their inspiration was more regular and more frequent.[61] Perhaps the description of various individuals as 'full' (πλήρης) of the Holy Spirit, which Luke evidently derives from a special and primitive source (6.3, 5, 8; 7.55; also 11.24), was the earliest attempt to express the realization that inspiration was not just an occasional thing which all might experience for a particular occasion (cf. 'filled' above), but that in addition some seemed to have a sureness of insight and conviction of speech which betokened a more sustained and lasting inspiration ('full').

These prophets appear at first as wandering prophets – prophets without a settled community to which they belonged and in and for which they exercised their gift – rather like some of the early Israelite prophets (e.g. Elijah and Amos). Thus Acts 11.27f. and 15.32 – prophets moving between Jerusalem and Antioch; in particular, on the two occasions we meet Agabus he has just come from Jerusalem to Antioch (11.27f.) and from Judea to Caesarea (21.10f.). But in two other passages it is probable that the prophets in question were more settled, attached to a single community where they were recognized as prophets because they prophesied frequently in the community's meetings for worship (13.1f.; 21.9 – four women prophets!).[62] The picture which emerges is of a diversity and freedom in the role of prophets.[63] The fact of inspiration was at this stage regarded as authority in itself; they were not subject to any higher authority who regulated their movements except the Spirit (cf. 8.39). We should perhaps note in passing here that Paul was not thought of as a prophet, at least so far as Luke was concerned – neither apostle in the full sense (see above pp. 99f.) nor prophet! According to Luke he was primarily a teacher (13.1) – as the distinction between 'prophets' (τε – Barnabas, Symeon and Lucius) and 'teachers' (τε – Manaen and Saul) seems to indicate.[64] This may be confirmed by the fact that Luke never describes Paul as 'prophesying', whereas διδάσκειν (teach)

is regularly used for his ministry within Christian communities
(11.26; 15.35; 18.11; 20.20; 28.31). Barnabas, on the other hand,
was obviously highly regarded as a prophet (13.1 – first named), and
evidently played a very important role in the life and developing
mission of the earliest churches (Acts 9.27; 11.22ff., 25f., 30; 12.25;
13.1–15.39; I Cor. 9.6; Gal. 2).[65]

31.2   The *functions* accorded to early Christian prophecy by Luke
are wholly within the scope of prophecy as we know it from the OT
and other parallels in religious history.[66] Prophets were given occasional premonitions and insights into the future (11.27f.; 21.4, 10f. –
the warning expressed by means of symbolic action; cf. 20.23);[67]
they were the mouthpieces of the Spirit in giving guidance for mission (13.1f., and perhaps 15.28;[68] 16.6f.);[69] and theirs was the more
humdrum task of exhorting and encouraging the brethren (11.23,
15.32).[70]

In addition it is probable that the early Christian prophets played
a significant role in developing and shaping the authoritative tradition on which the earliest communities drew for teaching and guidance. Their influence may be detected in two directions. First, they
helped to interpret the prophecies of the OT and the sayings of Jesus
in the light of what had happened (death and resurrection of Jesus,
and outpouring of the Spirit), and in relation to their own (changing)
situations. In so doing they were no doubt acting out of a consciousness of continuity of inspiration with these OT prophets and Jesus –
it was the same Spirit, the Spirit of Christ who inspired them all. This
consciousness seems to be reflected in I Peter 1.10–12.[71] Thus, as
Jesus himself had interpreted the OT in the freedom of prophetic
inspiration (Matt. 5.21–48), and as early Christian writers used the
OT with a liberty of interpretation which is often not appreciated (see
e.g. Matt. 2.23; 27.9f.; Acts 1.20; 4.11; Rom. 12.19; I Cor. 15.54ff.;
Eph. 4.8), so too it is to be expected that sayings of Jesus would be
taken up, interpreted in the light of Easter and Pentecost and applied
to the local community. A plausible example of this process is Mark
8.35–7 pars.,[72] which could well be an inspired meditation on the
original word of Jesus preserved in v. 34. Likewise Luke 21.20–4 may
be a prophecy taking up traditional words of Jesus (21.21a, 23a) and
delivered at a time nearer the Jewish rebellion (AD 66–70).[73] And in
the light of our discussion in chapter II, Matt. 11.28–30 may well
have to be recognized as a prophetic peshering of Matt. 11.25–7.
Perhaps also the exclamation, 'He who has ears (to hear) let him
hear', was a prophetic mannerism (inherited from Jesus?), as its

frequency in synoptic tradition (Mark 4.9, 23; 7.16(?); Matt. 11.15; 13.9, 43; Luke 8.8b; 14.35) and its use in Rev. 2–3 and 13.9 may suggest.[74]

The second way in which early Christian prophets probably influenced the tradition of the sayings of Jesus is through prophecies delivered not merely in the name of Jesus but as the very words of Jesus. Religious history shows us quite clearly how strong a characteristic of prophecy it is that the inspired prophet often speaks in the person of the god who inspires him.[75] Certainly many of the OT prophetic oracles given under the inspiration of the Spirit of Yahweh were given out as the words of Yahweh – the sense of divine compulsion being so strong that the prophet could only express his message as though Yahweh himself was speaking through him. We find this happening too in Christian prophecy: the seer of Revelation sends letters to the seven churches dictated through inspiration of the Spirit by the exalted Jesus (Rev. 2–3);[76] Paul's prophecy in I Thess. 4.15 is passed on as 'a word of the Lord' (see below p. 230), and the comforting word of II Cor. 12.9 ('My grace is sufficient for you . . .') quite possibly came to Paul through prophecy. So too a similar experience of inspired utterance is probably reflected in Acts 16.7 ('Spirit of Jesus').[77] Prophetic oracles in the first person which may have become counted among sayings of Jesus include Matt. 10.5 (possibly);[78] 18.20 (almost certainly)[79] and Luke 11.49–51 (probably).[80] Most likely the original form of Matt. 28.18–20 was a prophetic utterance in the first person in an early Hellenistic Jewish Christian community; the implication of the passage (see above §27.1) and the probabilities of the situation are that the impulse to breach the barricades surrounding Judaism and take the gospel to the Gentiles without restriction originated in a word of the risen Lord given through prophecy (cf. Acts 13.1f.). So too the famous 'I am's of John's gospel may be a combination of these two types of prophetic oracle – meditation on original sayings and parables of Jesus leading to an inspired oracle of a new and summary kind.

We are here touching the fringes of a very large field of discussion – the extent to which and the manner in which the early Christian communities transmitted traditions of Jesus' sayings and developed these traditions for their own uses. I can hardly enter further upon it in this study, and must confine myself to three comments. (1) A form-critical approach alone will scarcely prove decisive since Jesus was also a prophet; attempts made so far to isolate formal criteria for recognizing words of the exalted Jesus within the synoptic tradition have not been notably successful.[81] We must rely mostly on indications of life-setting and content at this point. (2) Insufficient attention has been paid to the manner in which NT authors handle OT prophecies; as I suggested above, the prophetic handling of authoritative tradition is not likely to be different as between OT prophecies and sayings of Jesus. But in the former case it is easier for the present day scholar to examine the extent and limitations of prophetic peshering. Further study on this question may well provide guidelines and controls which would enable us to determine more accurately the extent to which early Christian prophetic peshering has influenced and moulded the traditions of Jesus' sayings.[82] (3) We should not overestimate the early churches' readiness to add prophetic 'I'-words to the traditions of Jesus' sayings. I Cor. 7.10, 25, 40 imply that Paul at least maintained a clear distinction between traditional sayings of the earthly Jesus as such which carried authority by virtue of that fact, and inspired opinions and prophetic oracles which were of more questionable value and whose authority had to be proved (I Cor. 12.10; 14.29; I Thess. 5.20f. – see further below §§41.3, 49.2). The assumption so frequently made today,[83] that the tradition of Jesus' sayings was wholly fluid and lacked any boundaries and that it was frequently and regularly expanded by the addition of prophetic oracles with no questions asked, has therefore to be seriously challenged.[84]

31.3 *Luke's attitude to prophecy.* A final question which must be asked under the heading of early Christian prophecy is whether and to what extent it was ecstatic or merely charismatic (in terms of the distinction drawn above in §15). Here once again we are faced with the difficulty of trying to answer a question which Luke apparently never asked. Consequently it is difficult to gain a clear view on the matter. On the one hand he runs prophecy and glossolalia together in 19.6 and explicitly identifies the two in Acts 2: the *glossolalia* of Pentecost fulfils Joel's expectation of the outpouring of the Spirit in *prophecy* (2.16ff.). But the glossolalia mentioned in Acts, whatever we think of Paul's account of the gift (see below §41.7), cannot be described except in terms of ecstasy (see below §34). Luke therefore presumably thinks of prophecy in 2.16ff.; 19.6, and probably 4.31 ('spoke the word of God with boldness') and 10.46 ('speaking in tongues and extolling God') as ecstatic prophecy – more like that of the primitive prophets in ancient Israel (cf. I Sam. 10.5f.; 19.20–4) than the inspired utterances of the writing prophets. Moreover, much of the individual guidance narrated in the Acts account of the early church comes through (ecstatic) vision (ὅραμα – 9.10, 12; 10.3, 17, 19; 11.5;

16.9f.; 18.9; ὀπτασία – 26.19), and even, explicitly, when the recipient is in a trance (ἔκστασις – 10.10; 11.5; 22.17; see below pp. 177f.). Yet, on the other hand, there does seem to be something of a distinction between prophet and prophesying evident within the Acts material, and the utterances of the various prophets mentioned by Luke were evidently in rational speech. We may assume therefore that both ecstatic and charismatic prophecy were much in evidence in the earliest Christian communities, and we should take care neither to oversimplify the picture, nor to assume that from the first one was thought of more highly than the other. Paul certainly has strong views on the subject (see below §§41.2, 7); but the role and importance of ecstatic inspiration in the primitive churches and mission should not be ignored – nor undervalued. After all, many of the classical prophets had visionary experiences;[85] so perhaps did Jesus (see above § 15); and so certainly did Paul himself (II Cor. 12.1ff.).

The problem for us at this distance in time is that Luke's narrative does not enable us to clarify these issues – what the relation was between occasional prophesying and the more regular prophets or between glossolalia and prophecy, and to what extent primitive Christian prophecy was ecstatic and to what extent charismatic. No doubt the narrative's obscurity reflects a lack of clear thought on such subjects in the early communities,[86] and quite possibly Luke decided to let his account express this lack of clarity rather than to make it a didactic tool for resolving all issues of concern and dispute in the churches of his own day. Yet it would have been valuable to have more information on how the early communities tackled problems which must have troubled them from an early date. In particular, the problem of false prophecy, and of how to evaluate prophecy to determine whether it was of God or not, must soon have demanded attention. After all it was a problem which OT prophets had wrestled with for centuries without ever resolving it satisfactorily.[87] And it was certainly a burning issue in the early Hellenistic Jewish and Pauline communities (Matt. 7.15–23; I Cor. 12.1ff.; II Thess. 2.1ff.; see also I John 4.1ff.). But Luke seems to share the first flush of enthusiasm at the reappearance of prophecy; he shows us communities which seem to have regarded all inspiration within their meetings as coming from the Spirit, whether ecstatic or charismatic. The question of false prophecy was apparently never raised; even in the encounter with inspiration outside the communities it is only hinted at (13.6). That it could be a problem *within* a Christian community is hardly envisaged.[88] The fact that Paul ignored what seem to have been regarded as clear directions of the Spirit through prophecy (21.4; cf.

21.10–4) is recorded without comment; no attempt is made to give guidance on what should be done when two inspired utterances, *both* from the Spirit (20.22; 21.4), not merely differ but contradict each other!

In short, once again we can see clearly something at least of the charismatic, and ecstatic, nature of early Christian experience. But once again Luke's treatment of the subject leaves many important questions unanswered, or to be more precise, unasked.

§32. CHARISMATIC AUTHORITY

We turn now to the subject of authority in the earliest communities. Three questions in particular present themselves for discussion: (*a*) to what extent was the authority for a believer's speech and action individual and charismatic? (*b*) to the extent that authority in the earliest churches was charismatic, how does it compare with the charismatic nature of Jesus' authority? (*c*) how soon did charismatic authority begin to give way to a more institutionalized concept of authority?

32.1   *To what extent was the authority for faith and its expression direct and immediate for the believer in the earliest communities?* An examination of the material in Acts reveals three or four sources or expressions of authority which must be recognized as charismatic.

√   (*a*) The principal source of authority was evidently understood to be the *Spirit*. The Spirit was thought to be the source of the ecstacy which heralded the dawn of the last days at Pentecost (2.4); likewise similar manifestations were understood as divine confirmations of an individual's right to membership of the community, and so as confirmation of the extension of mission (8.14ff.; 10.44ff.; 11.15ff. – see above §27.1). So too the boldness of spontaneous inspiration in moments of test and exultation was attributed to the Spirit (4.8, 31; 13.9); the Spirit was the authority behind their testimony (5.32). The authority of leadership, of evangelism, of counselling, of teaching, was the charismatic authority of the Spirit (6.3, 5, 10; 7.55; 11.24; 18.25). The Spirit seems to have been regarded as the directing force within the community (5.3, 9; 9.31; cf. 7.51), and was certainly understood as the inspiration and guiding hand in mission (8.29, 39; 10.19; 11.12; 13.2, 4; 16.6f.; 19.21; 20.22). Not all these are cases of individual inspiration;[89] in many instances the directives of the Spirit came through the community, whether by an individual pro-

phetic utterance (11.28; 13.2; 20.23; 21.4, 11), or in conjunction
with discussion and mutual exhortation (15.28). How much Luke's
hand has determined his choice of material and shaped it on this
issue we cannot say with any certainty. Here again he gives no
guidance on how the authority of individual inspiration was or
should have been integrated with the authority of the communal
mind (cf. again 20.22; 21.4). Nevertheless, the picture is clear
enough, and it would be hard to dispute on historical grounds that
the authority of the Spirit was understood in predominantly charismatic terms in the primitive church.

(b) A second expression of the early communities' sense of authority is the phrase '*in the name of Jesus*', 'the name of the Lord', etc.
We have already seen how important a factor this phrase was in some
at least of the healings effected at that time (see above §30.1). It
expressed the believer's sense of authority and power to act as he did,
and its impact on the sufferer testifies to the authority which the
bearer of that name had for the sufferer, at least in that instance. So
too 'the name' expressed the early evangelist's authority in preaching
(5.28, 40; 9.15, 27ff.; cf. 8.12); they baptized 'in the name' (2.38;
8.16; 10.48; 19.5); they suffered gladly 'for the name' (5.41; 9.16;
15.26; 21.13). We have no reason to doubt the substantial accuracy
of Luke's record at this point. Here clearly then we see different
occasions when individual believers, and individuals presumably on
behalf of their communities, acted out of a consciousness that through
them the exalted Jesus was acting. This sense of authority, in most if
not all of the occasions listed here, was evidently direct and unmediated – in other words, charismatic authority.

(c) A third source of authority for individual action and assurance
in Acts are *visions*. And at once we must draw attention to the diversity of these visions. There are visions of *angels*: 'An angel of the Lord
said to Philip . . .' (8.26) – that is, presumably in a vision;[90] an
angel of the Lord directs Cornelius to send for Peter (10.7, 22; 11.13),
appearing to him in a vision (ὅραμα – 10.3); an angel stands by Paul
in the night (in a vision? – cf. 12.9) and assures him of the ship's
safety (27.23). There are visions of *Jesus*: Stephen sees the heavens
opened and the Son of Man standing at the right hand of God
(7.55f.); Paul sees and hears the exalted Jesus outside Damascus in a
vision (ὀπτασία – 26.19) and is apparently promised future visions
(26.16); Ananias hears the Lord in a vision (ὅραμα – 9.10); when he
returns to Jerusalem Paul sees and hears Jesus when in a trance (ἐν
ἐκστάσει – 22.17f.);[91] at Corinth he hears the Lord in a vision in the
night (18.9); and in Jerusalem 'the Lord stood by Paul' in the night

and encouraged him – that is, in a vision or dream (23.11). Other visions are more varied: Peter sees a symbolical scene and hears a voice (unspecified – 10.10–16; 11.5–10) when in a trance (ἐνέκα τάσει – 10.10, 17, 19; 11.5); at Damascus Paul sees Ananias in a vision (9.12); and at Troas he sees and hears 'a man of Macedonia' in a vision in the night (16.9f.).

Now, we have already observed that Luke has a hand in at least one of these visions – the appearance of Jesus to Paul outside Damascus.[92] But for the most part the visions and angelic directions are hardly to be dismissed as Lukan fabrications or later legend-mongering. It is entirely probable that the earliest believers did see visions and hear heavenly voices (cf. II Cor.5.13, 12.1, and perhaps Gal. 2.2). This is only to be expected in communities characterized by spiritual enthusiasm, as religious history clearly shows.[93] What reality lay behind and found expression in all these different visions we are no longer in a position to determine. We must rest as contentedly as we may with the recipients' own convictions that these were divine revelations, 'fleshed out' and clothed in their understanding with the apparatus of their own cosmology, as we would expect.

Two points call for comment. First, when one compares the various experiences particularly of Spirit, and of angelic and visionary intervention and direction, it is a picture of almost unending and apparently arbitrary variation which emerges. Why it should be an angel which first directs Philip (8.26) and then the Spirit (8.29) is not at all clear. This is so too with the visions generally: why sometimes only 'a voice', sometimes an angel, sometimes a man, sometimes the Lord (almost always to Paul!)? There is no pattern in all this, certainly not one imposed by Luke (cf. ch.V n.137 above). We must rather conclude that we see reflected here the diversity of spiritual experience in the early communities – so rich in its variety that it could not be interpreted and expressed by the first Christians in any standard form or formula. What we can and must say is that within this rich diversity of experience of first generation enthusiastic Christianity the authority for proclamation, for evangelism, for healing, for individual word and action, for mission, was presumably *the authority of immediate inspiration and personal conviction, of vision* – in a word, *charismatic authority*.

Secondly, Luke seems to have a high regard for ecstatic visions: their determinative role at decisive points in the early history of the church is noticeable (9; 10; 11; 16.9f.; 22.17–21; 26.19f.); the personalities in his account regard visions as sufficient legitimation of their actions.[94] Clearly Luke is doing his best to demonstrate how completely the Joel prophecy was fulfilled within the charismatic life of the early community (2.17), though we need not doubt for that reason that his picture is well founded: as there were visions in the early communities, so they would be regarded as authoritative in greater or lesser degree (cf. Gal. 2.2). Where again Luke is perhaps open to criticism is in his failure to take up the problem of an authority rooted in visionary experiences – which he could presumably have done by citing appropriate examples – in particular the problem that an authority based only on visions can be grossly abused. We know that the problem arose in an acute form at least twice within the time span of Luke's history – for II Cor. 12.1ff. and Col. 2.18 show that this was a key element in the problems facing Paul at both Corinth and Colossae (see above pp. 107ff. and below §46.1) – hence Paul's reticence in II Cor. 12.1ff. and *his* unwillingness to root his authority solely even in his 'seeing' in I Cor. 9.1ff. (cf. below pp. 276f.). And, of course, the prophets were aware of the same problem long before (Jer. 23.25–32).[95] But Luke is content to report the early church's reliance on visions, as on prophetic utterances, without comment.

32.2　We can answer the question about *the relation between the charismatic authority of the early churches and that of Jesus* without difficulty. There is one point of similarity and two points of dissimilarity. They are similar in that in several instances they are both referred back to the Spirit; the same confidence of inspiration, the same certainty of knowledge of the truth and of the true meaning of events, characterizes both Jesus and the early Christians in their ministries. They are different, first, in that Jesus' sense of authority did not depend to any extent, if at all, on visionary experiences; whereas, as we have just noted, visions and angelophanies were a not uncharacteristic feature of early Christianity. The second and most important difference lies in the *immediacy* with which the sense of authority was expressed. In the case of Jesus we drew attention to the self-consciousness and self-reference of Jesus' authoritative teaching – the *amēn* of the characteristic 'Truly I say to you', and the emphatic ἐγώ of 'But I say' logia (see above § 13.3) – similarly the distinctiveness of his prophetic consciousness (see above § 14). Nowhere in the early church do we find a prophet or teacher speaking in this way or with reference to himself. What we do find is a speaking 'in the name of Jesus', and a prophesying, as we may suppose, in the person of Jesus (see above § 31.2). Jesus is not seen as an archetypal prophet or teacher whose mannerisms can be simply taken over and copied. On the contrary, *the authority which Jesus seemed to see as centred in himself remains centred in Jesus.* The first Christians do not minister in their own right, but only as somehow representing Jesus, making *his* authority still effective in the world. In short, their authority differs from that of Jesus in that in the last analysis it is understood as derived from Jesus.

How *this sense of dependency upon the exalted Jesus* was to be related to the inspiration of the Spirit and to the directions of angels and other visionary voices is something which the early church does not seem to have seen as a problem. Certainly Luke gives us no help on the question. Acts 16.6f. probably provides the nearest thing to an answer; in the latter verse guidance is given by 'the Spirit of Jesus'. But it is not clear whether we should simply identify 'the Spirit of Jesus' with 'the Holy Spirit' (16.6), whether the Spirit and Jesus are being equated in some way (cf. 2.33),[96] or whether the reference is to an individual impulse and conviction (cf. 8.29; 20.22),[97] a prophetic oracle (cf. 13.2 and above p. 173), or, less likely, a heavenly voice in a vision.[98] The picture given by Acts is so confused on this point anyway (multiplicity of heavenly voices) that we can neither integrate 16.7 into the whole or use the whole to clarify 16.7 with any certainty. On this issue, as on so many other related issues we must await Paul's treatment.

32.3   *Does a more institutionalized authority appear at the same time as the more immediate spontaneous authority?* Does the authority of office and ceremony co-exist from the first with charismatic authority?[99] If we were to take Luke's account of the early church at its face value on this point we would have to answer in the affirmative. Such an assessment might run as follows. The twelve were instituted as apostles by the risen Jesus (Matthias by casting lots), and as apostles they constituted the leadership of the Jerusalem community and retained oversight of the Christian mission (2.42f.; 4.33, 35ff.; 5.2, 12, 18, 29, 40; 6.6; 8.1, 14; 9.27; 11.1; 15.2, 4, 6, 22f.; 16.4). At an early stage their office was supplemented by the appointment of seven others to a secondary office to take some of the administrative weight from the shoulders of the apostles (Acts 6.1–6) – just as Moses had appointed seventy elders to share his burden (Num. 11.16–25) and Jesus had appointed seventy to assist him in his mission (Luke 10.1ff.).[100] Unfortunately this neat reconstruction breaks down at the first test. For as we have already pointed out, Luke's identification of 'the apostles' with 'the twelve' runs directly counter to the concept of apostleship which we found in Paul (see above particularly ch. V n.4, 5, ch. VI n.36); 'the apostles' in I Cor. 15.7 are undoubtedly a much wider group than 'the twelve', and their apostleship consists primarily in mission, not in 'directing affairs' at Jerusalem.

A more accurate picture of the leadership of the early church would be as follows. In the eschatological enthusiasm of the early days 'the twelve' would almost certainly provide the focal point of community – naturally so by virtue of their role as primary witnesses to the risen Jesus and as representatives of eschatological Israel (cf. I Cor. 15.5; Matt. 19.28b; Acts 1.6, 21f.).[101] But for one reason or another their role at the centre of things diminished and seems to have more or less disappeared – presumably due in part at least to the fading of the first flush of eschatological enthusiasm as the parousia failed to materialize.[102] At all events Peter (and probably the brothers James and John) emerged as the recognized leaders. This was no doubt partly due to their being the inner circle of Jesus' disciples during his life (as it would appear – Mark 5.37; 9.2ff.; 10.35ff.; 14.33);[103] but in Peter's case more significant factors would be his primacy as witness to the resurrection (I Cor. 15.5; cf. Matt. 16.17ff.), and the charismatic effectiveness of his ministry (cf. Acts 4.8, 31; 5.3, 9; 8.14–24; 10.9ff.). The divisions within the early community, between Hebrews and Hellenists, the depth of which Luke tries to camouflage, resulted in the emergence of the seven, presumably the leading figures among the Hellenists (Acts 6).[104] Their election, be it noted, was a recognition of their charismatic authority more than institution to an office: their fullness of Spirit was neither lacking before the laying on of hands nor bestowed by it (6.3, 5, 8, 10). Besides, according to the more natural sense of the Greek it was the crowd of disciples and not 'the apostles' who laid their hands on the seven.[105] And their authority was certainly not confined, if at all, to 'serving tables'; as the sequel indicates, their charismatic authority was much more important and expressed itself in evangelism and mission (6.8ff; 8.4ff.), as that of their fellow Hellenists generally (11.19ff.).[106]

It was after the (almost) total withdrawal of the Hellenists from Jerusalem (cf. 21.16) that institutionalizing tendencies began to feature prominently within the Jerusalem church itself. James, the brother of Jesus, emerged among the Jerusalem leadership, and before long appears as the most prominent of the three 'pillar apostles' (Gal. 2.9).[107] But already Peter had begun to fade from the scene, being more concerned with 'the mission to the circumcised' (Gal. 2.8; cf. Acts 12.17); John anyway had never made much impact in his own right, at least at that stage, so far as we can tell;

consequently James attained a position of complete dominance (Acts 15.13ff.; 21.18; Gal. 2.12) – no doubt partly owing to his more conservative attitude to the law, and partly owing to his accepted claim to have experienced a resurrection appearance, but also probably because he was the brother of Jesus.[108] Round James there developed a circle of elders (11.30; 15.2, 4, 6, 22f.; 16.4; 21.18; cf. James 5.14) – a pattern of administration presumably taken over from Jewish synagogal government[109] – though on important issues the whole congregation was apparently still consulted (Gal. 2.2–5; Acts 11.1, 18; 15.22; cf. I. Clem. 44.3; 54.2). Henceforth Jerusalem became the strong-point of the conservative forces within the early church opposed to the free-er gospel and structures of the Gentile mission (Gal. 2.2–5, 11ff.; II Cor. 10–13; cf. Acts 21.20ff.).[110] To be sure, Luke suggests that Paul followed the Jerusalem pattern by appointing elders in his churches (14.23; 20.17); but we have absolutely no confirmation of this from Paul himself. It would appear that we must attribute this feature also to Luke's attempt to present as unified and standardized a picture of early Christianity as he can.[111] For Paul's rather different treatment of ecclesiastical authority we must await chapter IX (§§47–49).

The above outline is the merest sketch, and to fill it out would require a much more extensive discussion than is appropriate here. But perhaps enough has been said to substantiate the claim that *authority in the primitive church was primarily charismatic in nature*. In the earliest days different forms of leadership emerged without making any lasting institutional impact ('the twelve', the leadership of Peter, James and John, the seven, the pillar apostles).[112] This *flexibility and lack of clear form* is precisely what we would expect in a first generation charismatic community slowly developing in self-consciousness.[113] A set pattern only begins to appear after the expulsion of the Hellenists, when authority began to be structured and institutionalized in the church of Jerusalem under James's leadership.[114] But by then the living and growing heart of Christianity was to be found elsewhere.

§33. THE SENSE OF COMMUNITY AND THE WORSHIP OF THE EARLIEST CHURCH

We have touched on these subjects several times in the earlier sections of this chapter; but in view of their importance in their own right for our study we must draw the threads together to see what pattern appears.

33.1   To trace *the emerging self-consciousness of the earliest Christian community* with any certainty is as impossible as the composition of a biography of Jesus. But Acts is not so useless at this point as some scholars would argue, and a few features relevant to our study can be sketched in with some confidence. So far as we can tell, a clear consciousness of community seems to have developed from the experience of the Spirit at Pentecost (see above pp. 145f., 160f.). This is only what we might expect – communal enthusiasm and group ecstasy naturally tend to give the participants a sense of identity, of distinctiveness, of belonging together.[115] It is surely not by accident or artifice that the first occurrence of the word κοινωνία in the NT comes immediately after Luke's account of Pentecost (Acts 2.42); for in Paul this word expresses the believers' awareness that they participated in the one Spirit (II Cor. 13.13/14; Phil. 2.1 – see below §45.1); though whether this is what Luke understands by it in Acts 2.42 (the only time he uses it) is not quite so clear.[116]

We can define this sense of community more precisely. It was not merely the warm fellow feeling of a shared experience, but the consciousness of being the eschatological community of Israel. The Spirit they were filled with was the end-time Spirit of prophecy; as we noted above, the role of 'the twelve', the clinging to the temple, the community of goods, all testify to the enthusiasm with which they lived out their conviction that they constituted the Israel of the end-time (§29).

Two other aspects of this initial sense of community ought to be mentioned – baptism and the breaking of bread. To the best of our knowledge *baptism* was a feature of the earliest church from the beginning.[117] It is logical to assume that the adoption of baptism by the earliest believers was a further and immediate expression of their sense of eschatological community. Since the rite was taken over from John the Baptist, it probably served initially as an expression of repentance – preparation for the imminent consummation[118] (an emphasis we are not surprised to find lacking in Luke's account). But very quickly it became established as the rite of entry into the community of the end-time and expression of the initiate's commitment to that community and its Lord (Acts 10.48).[119]

The fact that baptism seems to have been performed '*in the name of Jesus*' from the beginning should not escape notice (Acts 2.38; 8.16; 10.48; 19.5; cf. I Cor. 1.13). It clearly denotes that the risen Jesus was seen as the head of the community: not only did he commission the central figures and apostles personally in resurrection appearances and direct its expansion through visions and other heavenly intermediaries (see above §32.1); but to join the community the initiate had to acknowledge his headship (Acts 2.21; 9.14, 21; 22.16; cf. Rom. 10.12ff.; I Cor. 1.12f.) and the rite of admission was performed in his authority and power (cf. above p. 164).

I need hardly add that at this stage the 'administration' of baptism was hardly understood as a 'charism' or 'office', such as only one duly recognized individual (apostle, prophet or whatever) could perform. It was rather a charismatic ceremony, in the sense that whenever an inquirer came to the point of conversion he was baptized by whichever believer was to hand – probably usually the one who was instrumental in his conversion, but not necessarily so (Acts 8.12f., 38; 9.18; 10.48; 16.33; 18.8; cf. I Cor. 1.14–17).[120]

As for the *common meal*: initially this too would be a natural expression of eschatological community. In so far as it harked back to the fellowship meals of Jesus' ministry, particularly the last, it would almost certainly carry the same note of eschatological expectation (Luke 22.18 – 'from now on I shall not drink of the fruit of the vine until the kingdom of God comes').[121] The Pauline interpretation of the formula passed on to him (I Cor. 11.26 – '. . . until he comes'), as perhaps also the 'Maranatha' (I Cor. 16.22),[122] no doubt reflects the eschatological enthusiasm into which Paul was introduced when he first sat at 'the Lord's table'. This note is again missing from Luke's description of the earliest church; but at least he seems to have preserved the atmosphere of fellowship and community which must have found expression in these common meals: Acts 2.46 – various gatherings of the first believers round the meal table in different homes in Jerusalem.

To what extent these meals were thought to have sacramental significance is very difficult to determine. Certainly Jeremias presents a convincing case for the substantial historicity of the last supper and the so-called 'words of institution': 'This is my body'; 'this cup is the covenant in my blood'.[123] In which case the words which Paul received in tradition (I Cor. 11.24f.) must have been passed down through the earliest community and must have been recalled or used at some if not all of their common meals.[124] But what their significance was at these early meals is by no means clear. They may have been used simply to recall that last meal with Jesus before his death (cf. I Cor. 11.24f. – 'in remembrance of me'), with the same sense of expectation of imminent consummation in the

messianic banquet (see above p. 160). They may have been repeated
(by a prophet? – cf. *Didache* 10.7) as the words of Jesus understood
as present at and presiding over the communal gatherings of the
community of the new covenant (cf. Luke 24.30; Matt. 18.20).[125] Certainly they are a testimony to the community's continuing consciousness that their new covenant status depended on Jesus both for its
inauguration and for its continuance. Beyond that it is difficult to go
with any confidence. In the traditions used by Acts we find no corporate significance attached to Jesus, such as features strongly in
Paul (last Adam, body of Christ, 'in Christ'); Jesus is still thought of
as an individual person, exalted to heaven, though present with his
community in resurrection appearances and visions.[126] So too no
soteriological significance is attached to Jesus' death: it is simply the
act of hostile Jews, though willed by God, which results in Jesus' vindication and exaltation to a position of heavenly authority and power
(Acts 2.23f., 33–6; 3.14ff.; 4.10ff.; etc.).[127] Perhaps most striking of
all, Luke makes no attempt to portray the 'breaking of bread' as a
liturgical act; it appears simply as the *sharing of food* – a simple but
important expression of fellowship (Acts 20.7, 11; 27.35).[128] In
short, we need not go all the way with H. Lietzmann and W. Marxsen[129] to recognize that the breaking of bread in Acts is *at most* only
an *embryonic* sacrament.[130]

33.2   *The worship of the earliest community* centred largely on the temple
(Acts 2.46; 3.1; 5.12; cf. Matt. 5.23f.) – not unnaturally in view of
their eschatological expectation (see above §29). But at the same time,
and probably from the beginning, other forms of worship began to
develop in spontaneous fashion in *ad hoc* gatherings in private homes
(κατ' οἶκον – Acts 2.46; 5.42). The Hellenists seem to have been much
more synagogue worshippers than temple worshippers – if Stephen's
speech is anything to go by (6.9, 13f.; 7); and as relations worsened
within the synagogues (6.9) they may have given more emphasis to the
house gatherings.

These latter appear to have been largely unstructured. We can
however discern various regular elements. There would be *teaching*
(2.42; 5.42; 11.26; 13.1; etc.). The earliest believers were familiar
with the important role of the scribe in the religious life of Judaism;[131]
they not unnaturally copied the practice (cf. James 3.1).[132] So we
may assume that some part of the house gatherings were given over
both to the recollection and discussion of Jesus' sayings and example
and to the interpretation of the OT (cf. Luke 24.25ff., 44ff.; Acts
8.32ff.; 17.2f., 11; 18.24, 28; I Cor. 15.3f.).[133] The concern of these

early believers would be to apply both the scriptures and the words and examples of Jesus to themselves and to their new situations. To what extent the twelve took the lead in this we cannot say with much confidence, despite 2.42; 6.2, 4 (for note also 6.10; 7.2–53; 8.35).[134] Nor can we assess the extent to which teaching was either formal or charismatic.[135] The epistle of James is probably a good example of the sort of paraenetic material which emerged, marked as it is both by its distinctly Jewish character and its various echoes of sayings of Jesus (e.g. 1.5, 6, 17, 22; 4.12; 5.12).[136] But the best example of a charismatic interpretation of a saying of Jesus, and its consequent reinterpretation of OT tradition, is Stephen's handling of the mysterious but doubtless authentic saying of Jesus about the destruction of the temple and its restoration (Mark 13.2 pars.; 14.58 par.; 15.29b par.; John 2.19)[137] – an exegesis (Acts 6.14) which led directly to the Hellenists' breach with Judaism and the development of Hellenistic Christianity away from the Christian (or perhaps better, messianic) Judaism of the earliest Palestinian communities (Acts 6.8–8.4; 11.19ff.). We should also recall that during this time the sayings of Jesus would be repeated and stories about Jesus would begin to assume a more regular and established form, especially the passion narrative.[138]

About the role of *prophecy* we need add nothing to what we have said above (§31). But two brief comments may be appropriate on the relation between prophecy and teaching. First, we should beware of distinguishing prophecy and teaching too sharply. Once we recognize that teaching includes interpretation, the dividing line between the two virtually disappears.[139] This was why it was possible (as well as more convenient) to speak earlier of *prophetic interpretation* of the OT and sayings of Jesus (§31.2). If it is necessary to maintain a distinction even here, we could reserve 'teaching' for that interpretation which does not create new sayings but presents itself explicitly as interpretation of an original saying,[140] and 'prophecy' for that interpretation which creates new sayings on the basis or as an extension of original sayings. A distinction should not be drawn in terms of interpretation given under inspiration (prophecy) and more formal interpretation (teaching), since, as we have seen above, there could be charismatic teaching as well (see further below §41.4). But second, although prophecy and teaching merge into each other in the middle, their roles otherwise can be readily distinguished: teaching – to pass on the tradition (written or oral) of the past; prophecy – to bring new revelation. It is important to notice that *from the beginning* we find both a *conserving* function (teaching) and a *creating* function (prophecy) within the early church. We shall see how important both are for Paul in due course and the significance of the fact that he regards prophecy more highly than teaching (I Cor. 12.28; Eph. 4.11).[141]

Prayer is the other important feature which Luke mentions (2.42; 6.4, 6; 12.5, 12; 13.3; etc.), including both observance of the Jewish times of prayer (3.1, probably 2.42) and prayer meetings among themselves (6.4; 12.5, 12). It would appear that in the house gatherings more regular and more spontaneous prayers both had a place, particularly no doubt prayers of thanksgiving and praise.[142] The 'Lord's Prayer' was obviously used frequently, thereby developing its divergent forms (Matt. 6.9–13/Luke 11.2–4). Apart from that we know only of single ejaculations – 'Abba' (Rom. 8.15; Gal. 4.6), 'Maranatha' (I Cor. 16.22), 'Amen' (I Cor. 14.16); perhaps also 'Allelouia' (Rev. 19.1, 3, 4, 6) and 'Hosanna' (Mark 11.9f. pars.). The first three must have had a regular place in the earliest worship since they are already fixed in Aramaic by the time they come to us through Paul. Otherwise we must assume that prayer was offered in more spontaneous fashion – as Acts 4.24–30; 12.5, 12; 13.3 implies. We should also include Matt. 18.19 here (see also n. 79 above).

A point worth drawing attention to is the influence and role of Jesus in the early community's prayers. On the one hand the use of 'Abba' is obviously an echo and adoption of Jesus' own personal style of prayer (see above §4): 'The prayer of primitive Christianity finds its starting-point and centre in the prayer of Jesus'.[143] On the other hand, Jesus begins to feature *in* the prayers themselves. By this I do not mean that prayer was made *to* Jesus – such a conclusion would go beyond the evidence. But it certainly seems that he was *appealed* to (ἐπικαλεῖσθαι – Acts 7.59; 9.14, 21; 22.16; also I Cor. 16.22) and *exhorted* or *implored* (παρεκάλεσα – II Cor. 12.8) as a figure of heavenly significance and power.[144] Here we observe an interesting interaction of influence – of the historical Jesus as example for the early church's religious experience, and of the exalted Jesus as object of the early church's religious experience. *As with the continuation of the common meal, so in prayer, the first Christians were not merely doing as Jesus did, but doing it in conscious reference to and continuing dependence on Jesus.*

Luke does not mention *singing*, apart from Acts 16.25 (cf. 2.47). But doubtless OT psalms were used. The canticles which Luke uses in Luke 1 and 2 he almost certainly would have drawn from the worship of the Palestinian community – their Jewish-not-yet-Christian character testifying to their age.[145] Whether there were any 'spiritual songs' (Col. 3.16), that is glossolalic singing, we cannot tell. It is quite possible.

All these elements stood in some sort of relation to the common meals, but whether there was a firm relationship or a regular relationship, or whether these different elements were ordered in a regular pattern, we cannot say. Jeremias's suggestion that in Acts 2.42 we have 'the sequence of an early Christian service'[146] is attractive, but certainly goes beyond the evidence.[147] The developments within the Pauline churches (I Cor. 14.26) suggest that no single clear pattern emerged from the earliest churches.[148] It is quite possible that the Hebrews in Jerusalem retained a more structured form, while the gatherings of the Hellenists were marked by greater flexibility.

Two other striking features of the community life and worship of the first Christians must be mentioned. One is their exuberance and joy (ἀγαλλίασις – 2.46; cf. Matt. 5.12; I Peter 1.6, 8; 4.13).[149] They *enjoyed* their worship and gatherings (cf. Acts 5.41; 8.39; 11.23; 13.48; 15.31). The second is their sense of the *numinous*. These were not simply social get-togethers marked by cheerful camaraderie. They were conscious of the eschatological Spirit, the power of God in their midst (see above p. 166). Perhaps no passage in Acts catches the atmosphere of these early days better than Acts 4.29–31 – the assurance and confidence in God, the almost physical presence of God's power,[150] and the enthusiastic ecstatic speaking.

It thus becomes clear that the earliest worship of the Christian church was largely dependent on the immediate inspiration of the Spirit – particularly prophecy, spontaneous prayer, including, indeed preeminently the 'Abba' cry (Rom. 8.15; Gal. 4.6), spiritual songs(?), and perhaps above all the enthusiasm and joy (cf. Luke 10.21 – ἠγαλλιάσατο) and the sense of the numinous (Acts 4.31).

33.3   We may note then by way of *summary*, that the early church's sense of community stemmed basically not from the first resurrection appearances but from Pentecost; not from an established hierarchy, not from an established tradition, not from an established liturgical or sacramental practice – all these were only at the very beginning of their development – but *from the common experience of the eschatological Spirit and the communal enthusiasm engendered thereby*. All these other features of the religious experience of the first Christians were the expression rather than the source of their sense of community. So too in the earliest churches' worship. In the house gatherings, where the distinctive style of Christian worship began to develop, the style which emerged combined both regular and spontaneous elements, conserving as well as creating, but was primarily charismatic and enthusiastic rather than institutional and structured.

§34. VISIBLE PROOFS?

Before we draw together our conclusions on this section of our study there is one further question we must attempt to answer. Were any of the physical or psychical manifestations regarded as a particular sign of the Spirit, a *necessary proof* of the Spirit's presence? – glossolalia, prophecy, healings, visions, or more generally, eschatological enthusiasm, inspired worship, charismatic authority? The question is one which has troubled Christianity more or less from the first. It arises from the human striving for certainty and assurance, the yearning for the divine to become tangible, for God to reveal himself by indisputable signs, the longing to rise above the ordinary believer's doubts and questions, to be *sure* of God. Successive generations of Christians sought the answer in martyrdom, asceticism, monasticism and mysticism.[151] In this century the question has re-emerged in sharpest form within Pentecostalism. Their answer was simple and to the point: *glossolalia* is the particular sign of the Spirit's entrance into a life in power.

In apostolic times, the speaking in tongues was considered to be the initial physical evidence of a person's having received the baptism in the Holy Spirit . . . It was this decision which has made the Pentecostal Movement of the Twentieth Century.[152]

It is the Pentecostal answer which provokes our question.

In favour of the Pentecostalist thesis it must be said at once that their answer is more soundly rooted within the NT than is often recognized. It is certainly true that Luke regarded the glossolalia of Pentecost as an external sign of the Spirit's outpouring.[153] In Acts 10.45f. 'speaking in tongues and extolling God' is depicted as proof positive and sufficient to convince Peter's Jewish companions that 'the gift of the Holy Spirit had been poured out even on Gentiles'. The Ephesian 'believers' speak in tongues and prophesy when the Holy Spirit comes upon them (19.6). The only other passage in which an initial giving of the Spirit is actually described is 8.17ff.,[154] and it is obvious that Luke has in mind here an eye-catching display of ecstasy – something more than sufficient to arouse the envy of an accomplished magician. It is a fair assumption that for Luke the Samaritan 'Pentecost', like the first Christian Pentecost, was marked by ecstatic glossolalia. If so, then the fact is that *in every case* where Luke describes the giving of the Spirit it is accompanied and 'evidenced' by glossolalia. The corollary is then not without force that

Luke *intended* to portray 'speaking in tongues' as 'the initial physical evidence' of the outpouring of the Spirit. It would also be possible to argue that Luke is a faithful historian at this point, at least to the extent that conversions in the early mission were frequently marked by charismatic manifestations (I Cor. 1.5, 7; Gal. 3.5; Heb. 2.4; 6.5).[155]

Two points must however be made. First, Luke's conception of the Spirit, or better of experience of Spirit, as of religious experience generally, can only be described as fairly crude. He shares the enthusiasts' desire for tangibility in spiritual experience. We have already noted this, particularly in his presentation of Jesus' experience at Jordan and of the resurrection appearances (see above pp. 121f.). The same desire is particularly evident in his treatment of charismatic experience. The Spirit is most clearly seen in extraordinary and supernatural phenomena, and in Acts is hardly visible anywhere else.[156] This is why he uses such vigorous, dramatic language to describe the giving of the Spirit – 'baptized into' (1.5; 11.16), 'come upon' (1.8; 19.6), 'poured out' (2.17f., 33; 10.45), 'fell upon' (8.16; 10.44; 11.15).[157] This is why in Peter's speech 'the promise of the Holy Spirit' can be further described as 'this which you see and hear' (2.33): the ecstatic behaviour and speech of the disciples is *identified* with the outpoured Spirit! As J. H. E. Hull rightly notes: for Luke 'seeing was believing; what he saw he could not disbelieve'.[158]

Second, the Pentecostalist thesis answers the question, What is the distinctive manifestation of the Spirit, or of the Spirit's outpouring? *Luke was not asking this question; nor was he attempting to answer it.* We have had to call attention several times to the deficiency of Luke's account on this sort of issue. He displays the 'signs and wonders' of the early community with too little discrimination; he is oblivious to the problem of false prophecy; an authority rooted solely in visionary experiences causes him no qualms. So it is with glossolalia and the gift of the Spirit. He seems to be unaware that there is a problem of distinctiveness here. Just as there was nothing distinctively Christian about miracles, prophetic utterance and visions, so there was nothing particularly indicative of the Spirit in ecstatic speech – glossolalia had several parallels in contemporary religious cults (see below §52.3) – as does its modern equivalent in Pentecostalism.[159] Luke here of course no doubt accurately reflects the unquestioning enthusiasm of the earliest days of the Jerusalem community before the questions and problems arose.[160] But the problems quickly came to the surface in the Gentile mission, and Paul was already confronting them and attempting to answer them *within the period covered by Luke's narrative*. We may justifiably ask therefore whether Luke was wise to have ignored both problems and answers so completely.

It follows from these two points that Luke's treatment of religious experience in the early community is inevitably lop-sided. He does not ask or answer the question of whether and to what extent there were less ecstatic manifestations of the Spirit in the earliest church. He sees only the grosser, more physical and tangible expressions of spiritual power. Nowhere is this lop-sidedness more evident than in *his complete disregard for the experience of sonship*. We have seen how important this was for Jesus. We will see how basic it was to the faith and religion of Paul (§54). And the fact that the Pauline and Gentile churches retain the *abba*-prayer in its Aramaic form shows how important it must have been in the earliest Palestinian communities. Yet one would never guess this from Luke's account. He ignores completely the concept and experience of sonship; God is never addressed as 'Father' in Acts; and on the only occasions in which he is spoken of as 'the Father' it is always in immediate relation to Jesus (1.4, 7; 2.33).

In consequence, certain comments are called for on the Pentecostal thesis about tongues from the standpoint of NT interpretation. First, Luke certainly believes that the glossolalia was *a* manifestation of the Spirit's coming, along with praise of God in 10.45 and prophecy in 19.6 (not to mention bold speech in 4.8ff., 31, and powerful speech in 13.9ff.). But it is equally certain that he has no intention of presenting glossolalia as *the* manifestation of the Spirit – otherwise he would have mentioned glossolalia in Acts 8 and made the point with greater force elsewhere.

Second, because Luke's presentation is lop-sided, we simply do not have sufficient data to enable us to answer the question posed by the Pentecostals. There may have been other, less eye-catching manifestations of the Spirit's coming than glossolalia; almost certainly there were. But Luke has no eye for these. To draw theological conclusions from a lop-sided historical account is to saddle oneself with a lop-sided theology. We do no justice to Luke if we foist on him answers to questions he never asked.

But thirdly, if anyone continues to insist on taking Luke's account of the outpouring of the Spirit as normative for the experience of the Spirit today, baptism in the Spirit or whatever, he must go all the way with Luke. The speaking in tongues which manifests the coming of the Spirit in Acts is ecstatic speech, a veritable torrent of utterance. It will not do to trim down the 'necessary physical sign' to a few words in an unknown language forming in the mind or on the tongue – to such casuistry has Pentecostal doctrine too often descended in *practice*.[161] Luke does not admit even that diversity. Pentecostals therefore must surely cut their doctrinal coat according to the Lukan cloth, or else make use of a greater diversity of materials than those provided by Luke alone.

The fact is that ecstatic and physical phenomena have been a regular concomitant of religious awakenings and revival movements within the history of Christianity.[162] I think, for example, of the 'faintings' which attended so much of Wesley's open-air evangelism,[163] of the physical prostrations which characterized the Ulster Revival of 1859,[164] or of the singing and dancing which has been a feature of the East African Revival in this century.[165] Not for nothing were the 'Quakers' and 'Shakers' so nicknamed. Pentecostals themselves laboured for long enough under the disparaging nickname 'Holy Rollers'. Such is the nature of the human psyche that as soon as a pattern of experience or of behaviour is thought to have significance it tends to reproduce that pattern under the appropriate stimulus.[166] Thus under the stimulus of religious excitement or the power of the Spirit, particular patterns of religious experience and of physical reaction tend to become established and repeat – different patterns in different revivals and cultures. We are not surprised then that Wesley should find his doctrine of instant sanctification confirmed by the experience of his converts,[167] or that early Pentecostals should find their belief in the significance of glossolalia confirmed by its regular manifestation in their converts.[168] To say this is *not* to disparage such experiences and manifestations, far less their source; it is simply to point out the inevitably large (subconscious) human element in them. Certainly anyone who is familiar with the history of enthusiastic Christianity would recognize the danger of placing too much significance on any particular type of experience or physical manifestation. One might as well try to draw a general pattern from the convulsions of the Camisards and the Jansenists,[169] or from the 'bodily agitations' of the eighteenth-century revivals in Britain,[170] or from the *hwyl* which characterized the Welsh Revival at the beginning of this century, or from the stereotyped dreams which have been regarded so highly in the crisis of conversion within the mission churches in South Africa.[171] The fact that conversions in the early days of the church were often accompanied by glossolalia does not make these other manifestations any less appropriate or glossolalia any more normative for later centuries.

Judged from the standpoint of the history of Christian enthusiasm therefore, it is more than likely that Luke gives us a reasonably accurate portrayal of the early churches' mission – that glossolalia and other expressions of religious excitement and ecstasy often attended the work of evangelism. But these were uncritical days, when the wave of religious enthusiasm swept all before it. Luke's own uncritical attitude on this issue[172] well reflects their lack of questioning on such matters. The questioning and the more penetrating treatment comes with Paul. In short, *we can hardly doubt that glossolalia was recognized as a manifestation of the Spirit in the earliest days of the church; but that the early believers gave it the significance which modern Pentecostals attach to it is not a conclusion we can justly draw from Luke's account; far less can we conclude that God intended it to have such significance.*

§35. CONCLUSIONS

35.1   If any event can be described as the birthday of Christianity it is the event which probably took place on the first Pentecost following Jesus' death and initial resurrection appearances. On that day a gathering of Jesus' disciples, in a state, it would appear, of some eschatological excitement, enjoyed an experience of such spiritual power that they could only conclude that the Spirit of God had been bestowed upon them in eschatological measure. The experience should neither be reduced to nor seen solely in terms of its phenomena, ecstatic vision and glossolalia. For those involved, so far as we can tell, these latter were only the concomitant circumstances of the invasion of divine power from without – a natural human expression of and reaction to the encounter with the divine. This initial experience of being filled with power from God was repeated not infrequently at individual or group level (Acts 4.8, 31; 8.17f.; 9.17; 10.44ff.; 13.9; 19.6; cf. Eph.5.18).

35.2   The enthusiasm which resulted from these experiences was a powerful force binding those involved in close fellowship. Since the outpourings of the Spirit, like the resurrection appearances, were seen as signs of 'the last days', this enthusiasm was primarily eschatological in character – a character clearly stamped on the community's worship and common meals, and on its initial attempts at some organization ('the twelve', baptism, community of goods). The eschatological enthusiasm also found expression in evangelism. This together with the aura of the numinous which gathered round the community made the new sect both awe-ful and attractive and resulted in quite rapid expansion.

The sensation of spiritual power and direct inspiration by God also manifested itself in miraculous healings, visions, prophecy and glossolalia. From the first, and for a considerable time thereafter, the community depended primarily on such immediate experiences of God (through Jesus, Spirit, angels or heavenly voices) for their worship and direction. Authority lay not in any office or status. Those who had been appointed by the risen Jesus in a resurrection appearance were recognized as having authority to act 'in his name', and for the first two years or so such appearances resulted in various individuals being recognized as 'apostles'. At the same time, any believer might see a vision, or prophesy, or be used in healing or evangelism. In other words, *the earliest Christian community was essentially charismatic and enthusiastic in nature, in every aspect of its common life and worship, its development and mission.*

35.3   In what relation do these charismatic experiences of the earliest church stand to the charismatic experience of Jesus? At first sight it may appear that Jesus was simply the charismatic exemplar – the same sense of eschatological realization and imminence arising out of the experiences of Spirit, the same sort of miracle-working power, the same Spirit of prophecy, the same charismatic authority, the same *abba*-prayer and exultation (ἀγαλλίασις) in worship, though many more ecstatic phenomena are apparent in the case of the earliest community. But at second glance we see that, as with the resurrection appearances, *Jesus began to feature more or less from the beginning as a source and object of the first Christians' religious experience.* According to Acts 2.33 the Pentecostal outpouring of the Spirit was attributed to the risen Jesus from the first – an attribution which is quite likely to be historical, since Pentecost would very quickly be seen as the fulfilment of the Baptist's prediction regarding the Coming One (Matt. 3.11/Luke 3.16).[173] Likewise the apocalyptic hope which the coming of the eschatological Spirit brought to a new pitch of expectation was not expressed in terms of self-fulfilment (vindicated Son of Man) as in the case of Jesus, but in terms of *Jesus'* return (Acts 3.19ff.; I Cor. 16.22). So too, visions *of Jesus* played an important role in directing the mission. Perhaps most striking of all is the authority and power attributed to *the name of Jesus* in the earliest church. The name of Jesus was used in the same way as the name of God or of a heavenly being. Miracles were performed 'in the name of Jesus', teaching was 'in the name of Jesus', converts were baptized 'in the name of Jesus'. Where

Jesus acted in his own right and authority, the community acted in his name. *The authority which Jesus claimed and acted out remained centred in him, and in its exercise in the primitive church was understood as derived immediately from him.* Even if the early prophets took up the formula of Jesus, 'Amen, I say to you', the 'I' was not the 'I' of the prophet, but the 'I' of the exalted Jesus speaking through the prophet – so perhaps similarly in the use in the common meals of Jesus' words at the last supper. How this authority of Jesus is to be related to visions of angels and experiences of Spirit is not an issue with which the earliest community wrestled – although perhaps in Acts 16.7 ('Spirit of Jesus') we see the beginning of an assimilation of these two at least. So the question of how Jesus and the Spirit are to be related in Christian experience and thought remains untackled and awaits the more sophisticated theologizing of Paul and John. Nevertheless it is important to note that *even at this early stage Jesus was understood not merely as a sort of archetypal Christian charismatic, but religious experiences of the earliest community, including experiences like those enjoyed by Jesus himself, were seen as dependent on him and derivative from him.*

35·4   *Luke is a valuable but undiscriminating guide when it comes to asking questions about the religious experience of the earliest Christian communities.* Through his account we can gain a fair impression of the range of spiritual experience in these first days. But he gives no attention to the question of the *distinctiveness* of the experience of the first Christians. Whether this is because his material or chosen form did not permit the handling of such issues, or simply because he did not see them as problems, is not clear. To be sure, he attempts to distance Christianity from magic with some effect, but his uncritical portrayal of 'wonders and signs' to advertise the gospel, proclaim its success and stimulate faith, testifies to a concept of miracle which stands too close to the miracles of popular paganism for his attempt to be wholly successful. Likewise in the case of prophecy: he lumps it indiscriminately with glossolalia and ignores the problem of false prophecy. He seems unaware that all these phenomena ('signs and wonders', prophecy, visions) are open to the greatest abuse, and he gives no real guidance on how to discern and check such abuses. So too his treatment of spiritual experience in general is rather crude and lop-sided – giving full attention to the ecstatic and eye-catching manifestations of the Spirit, and too little attention to others. If Luke had acted thus because he wanted to give a strictly impartial account of the religious experience of the earliest communities we would simply recognize the reflection of the young church's immaturity at this point and say no more. But his history covers a time when the problems of distinctiveness and abuse had already been highlighted in all their difficulty. And in Acts he dealt with the other large problem of the delay of the parousia very effectively (by omitting the eschatological dimension of the earliest community's enthusiasm).[174] So we are not altogether unjustified in expecting from Luke more help on the subject of religious experience than we find in Acts.

We turn our backs then on Luke's account of primitive Christianity both excited and frustrated. He has painted a vivid picture of Christianity's enthusiastic beginnings; but he has also raised important questions without beginning to answer them. As we move on to Paul then, we must bear in mind these questions in particular: Is there anything distinctive about early Christianity's experience of Spirit? How are we to evaluate such charismatic and ecstatic experiences as attract Luke's attention so exclusively within the wider context of religious experience? Granted that charismatic experience and authority is open to abuse by the charlatan and self-deceived, is it possible to discern and check the abuse of spiritual experience, to test whether an alleged experience of the risen Jesus or of the Spirit (vision, prophecy, glossolalia or whatever) is genuine or not?

PART THREE

THE RELIGIOUS EXPERIENCE OF PAUL
AND OF THE PAULINE CHURCHES

VIII

THE CHARISMATIC SPIRIT –
THE CONSCIOUSNESS OF GRACE

§36. INTRODUCTION

No figure in early Christianity stands out in sharper relief than Paul.
When we inquired after the religious experience of Jesus and of the
earliest communities we were always conscious of our distance from
the crucial events. We stood some way down the line of history and
the words and deeds which reflected the experiences came to us at
second or third hand, often in the language and accents of the intermediaries. But here we have Paul's own words, the letters which he
himself sent. And precisely because they are letters, and not poems
or manuals of discipline, or philosophical treatises, we gain an insight
into the mind and experience of the author such as no other literature
of the time affords. For in his reactions towards the very human
situations which arose in his various churches he speaks frankly of his
own religious experiences and of theirs, and expounds its significance,
its promise and danger, with words of counsel, encouragement and
caution that are of lasting value. Paul lived in no ivory tower, nor was
it his style to write dispassionate lectures on hypothetical problems or
interesting theological questions. His style is vigorous, impassioned,
always expressing the vitality of his experience of God and the reality
of his concern for his readers.

This does not mean, of course, that we have the material for
a full biographical study of Paul. The letters come from a comparatively short period of his life: how valuable it would be to possess
some of his correspondence from the first fifteen or so years after his
conversion! Nor will we be able to pursue here the interesting
question of how far detectable developments in his theology are due
to further significant experiences of Paul, or merely to the different
circumstances of his correspondents.[1] It is enough that we have a
selection of his correspondence written during his mature years and

addressing a variety of situations which called forth a variety of responses.

As I stressed in chapter I, it is important that we recognize the experiential dimensions and foundation of Paul's theology. Fifty years ago Adolf Deissmann was protesting against a doctrinaire approach to Paul – as though his theology and religion revolved round some doctrine (justification, redemption, or whatever), as though his Christ-centredness could be reduced to a Christology.[2] The protest was well made, and although it can of course be pressed too far, it needs to be frequently reiterated. Insightful as it is to present Paul's theology as a set of variations on his doctrine of justification, we will deceive ourselves if we think that we have thereby penetrated to the living heart of his faith. And, important as it is to trace the sources and antecedants of Paul's theology in its present form, it is hardly satisfactory to treat such expressions as christological titles and hymns as little more than the evolutionary product of a process of literary natural selection – a tendency unfortunately still with us. Perhaps the classic example of the failure to appreciate the extent to which Paul's theology is the expression of his experience is the *doctrine* of predestination. So far as Paul is concerned the idea of election speaks neither of an immutable law of God nor of an implacable law of nature, but is simply, in Otto's words, 'an immediate and pure expression of the actual religious experience of grace'.[3] This continuing 'experience of grace' is so much the heart and foundation of Paul's theology and religion that we will never understand him unless we give full weight to its contribution. I hope that the present section of this study will demonstrate something of *the fundamental role of experience, not least the experience of grace, in the shaping of Paul's theology.*

Obviously central to Paul's religious experience is his experience of Christ, expressed particularly by his 'in Christ', 'in the Lord' language. We could begin by plunging directly into this material, as Deissmann did; but the thought and conceptualizations are difficult for us to grasp, and it will be more helpful I think to approach it less directly, after dealing with more familiar material. Also fundamental to Paul's religious experience was his eschatological consciousness. We have already investigated part of this strand in chapter V, but it will be more convenient to return to it in chapter X. We will start therefore with Paul's understanding of the charismatic Spirit, dealing particularly with *charismatic phenomena* similar to those already discussed in chapters IV and VII. One of the questions raised by our study of Acts was where and how such a diverse range of charismata could be integrated into a continuing community and its worship. Paul is very conscious of the corporate dimensions of charismatic experience, and in examining Paul's concept of the body of Christ we will uncover his answer to the problem of how to *regulate* the charismata. We will then be in a better position to begin our exploration of Paul's 'Christ-mysticism'. In so doing Paul's answer to the other problem raised by Luke's Acts will take shape, and hopefully the *distinctiveness* of Christian religious experience for Paul will become clearer.

§37. SPIRIT AND GRACE

The two words which Paul uses more than any other to describe the believer's experience of God are 'Spirit' and 'grace'.

37.1 *Spirit* (πνεῦμα – *pneuma*) for Paul is essentially *an experiential concept*: by that I mean a concept whose content and significance is determined to a decisive degree by his experience. Long ago Gunkel demonstrated beyond dispute that 'the root of Paul's πνεῦμα teaching lies in the *experience* of the apostle'.[4] And my own earlier study of the conversion-initiation passages in Paul made the same point in its own way.[5] One only needs to read such passages as Rom. 5.5; 6.1ff.; 8.9, 14; I Cor. 1.4–9; 6.9–11; 12.13; II Cor. 1.21f.; 3; Gal. 3.1–5; 4.6f.; Col. 2.11ff.; I Thess. 1.5f. (Titus 3.5–7) and the point becomes clear. The Spirit is that power which operates on the *heart* of man – the 'heart' being the centre of thought, feeling and willing, the centre of personal consciousness, what we might call 'the *experiencing* I'.[6] The Spirit is that power of inner life which leaves far behind all the merely ritual and outward and makes a faith in God and worship of God existentially real (Rom. 2.28f.; II Cor. 3; Gal. 4.6; Phil. 3.3; Eph. 1.17f.). The Spirit is that power which transforms a man from the inside out, so that metaphors of cleansing and consecration become matters of actual experience in daily living (I Cor. 6.9–11). The Spirit is the source of that wave of love and upsurge of joy which overwhelms the forces that oppose from without (Rom. 5.5; I Thess. 1.5f.). The Spirit is the power that liberates from a rule-book mentality of casuistry and fear (Rom. 8.2, 15; II Cor. 3.17), so that ethical decisions become a matter of inward conviction and spontaneous love, of walking by the Spirit, rather than of unquestioning obedience to a law (Rom. 7.6; II Cor. 3.3; Gal. 5.25; Col. 2.11; see further below §40.5).

From such passages as these it will also have become clear that although in Paul's view the Spirit operates in and from a man's heart, we are not describing something hidden in the secret depths, a religion of mere inwardness and 'closet piety'. On the contrary, the Spirit is a power whose operation in the heart of a man cannot be concealed. In Paul, as elsewhere in the NT, the Spirit is understood as 'something whose reception may be verified'.[7] He is that baptismal water into which the whole person is publicly plunged (I Cor. 12.13), that seal which marks the believer as Christ's property for all to see (II Cor. 1.22; Eph. 1.13). Hence Paul can remind his Galatian readers of their reception of the Spirit as an event well remembered by them all (Gal. 3.2). So too it is the (manifest) presence of the Spirit which defines and determines the sphere of being 'in Christ' (Rom. 8.9), just as it is obedience to the inner promptings of the Spirit which defines and determines sonship (Rom. 8.14).[8]

It is our task in these chapters to investigate more closely the manifestations of the Spirit, and in particular (chapter X), to investigate in what way it is true for Paul that the presence of the Spirit 'may be verified'. For the moment it is enough that the experiential dimension of Paul's Spirit talk be recognized as a basic fact of his whole religion and theology.

37.2 *Grace* (χάρις – *charis*). 'In Paul *charis* is a central concept that most clearly expresses his understanding of the salvation event',[9] that is, as an act of wholly unmerited generosity on God's part. It is important to grasp from the outset that for Paul 'grace' does not mean an attitude or disposition of God; it denotes rather the wholly generous *act* of God; 'grace is *God's eschatological deed*'.[10]

Thus, in the first place, it is used of the historical event of Jesus Christ (II Cor. 8.9; see also Rom. 5.15; Gal. 2.21; Eph. 1.6f.). But for Paul grace is not merely an act of God in the past; it is also and more characteristically, the act of God in the present. Thus it denotes, secondly, 'the grace of conversion' – the decisive movement of the divine within and upon a man establishing a positive interaction and relation between God and the man of faith (see especially Rom. 3.24; 5.15, 17, 20; I Cor. 1.4f.; 15.10; II Cor. 6.1; Gal. 1.6, 15; 2.21; Eph. 2.5, 8). Even a brief study of these passages will reveal two important points: that for Paul grace is not something merely believed in but something experienced; and that what is experienced is that same transforming power experienced in the heart of the believer at which we have already glanced (§37.1). For Paul grace means *power*, an

otherly power at work in and through the believer's life, the *experience*
of God's Spirit.[11]

Thirdly, grace describes not merely the past act of God initiating
into the life of faith, but also the present continuing experience of a
relationship with God sustained by divine power (Rom. 5.2; cf. Col.
3.16), rather than by legal enactment (Gal. 5.4). Grace denotes that
enabling which rises above the power of sin and law (Rom. 5.21; 6.14),
an enabling that makes for 'sincere and godly singleness of mind' (II
Cor. 1.12), a power that enables Paul to treat physical infirmity as a
matter of praise rather than of complaint (II Cor. 12.9).[12] No one can
read such phrases as 'all grace abounding to you', 'the surpassing
grace of God upon you', the richness of God's grace lavished upon us'
(II Cor. 9.8, 14; Eph. 1.7f.) without realizing that we are dealing with
an experiential concept of great moment. Moffatt speaks fittingly of
the consciousness of 'a full tide (which) flowed into their little lives
from the great ocean'.[13] '*Grace*' *was for Paul a tangible and verifiable
reality as much as its correlative* '*Spirit*' (II Cor. 8.1). From this it follows
incidentally that Paul's greetings and benedictions at the opening
and close of his letters are no mere formality: the typical Greek
literary form χαίρειν (greeting!) has been replaced with χάρις, and the
concluding benediction ('Grace be with you' in its simplest form) is
even more original.[14] This is because Paul's most earnest and constant
wish for his converts is that they may experience grace, may know
ever afresh the gracious power of God existentially moving in and
upon their lives.

Fourthly, the more general experience of grace takes different
forms in individual cases. Grace can also denote particular acts of
God. Paul not infrequently speaks of 'the grace given to me/you'
(Rom. 12.3, 6; 15.15; I Cor. 3.10; Gal. 2.9; Eph. 3.2, 7f.; also Rom.
1.5).[15] In each case he is talking about some sort of commission or
enabling for some service. And in each case there is implied some
consciousness of that commission or enabling: it is an inward compulsion laid upon him – in Paul's case a continuing compulsion.
Moreover, the way in which he speaks in Rom. 12.3–8 ('the measure
of faith', 'according to the grace given to us', 'in proportion to our
faith')[16] suggests that so far as Paul is concerned believers should have
some sort of *awareness* of the particular manifestation of grace in their
lives – what it is, what are its limits, when it ends (see further below
§39.4).

Fifthly, a not unnatural extension of usage is to speak of the
particular ministry or service to which grace/Spirit inspires and
which grace/power enables as itself 'grace' (I Cor. 16.3; II Cor. 1.15;

8.1;[17] 8.4, 6f., 19; Eph. 4.29). In each case 'grace' is used of the actual, visible outworking of divine grace in a particular manifestation.

From this brief review of Paul's use of *charis* four important points emerge.

(*a*) Grace is a dynamic concept – the act of God for, in, and through man. Where it describes the act of God in and through men it overlaps with the concepts 'power' and 'Spirit'. Indeed, it is often more or less synonymous with these terms and shares with them the character of being concepts of experience. It always, of course, carries with it the thought of God's unmerited generosity. It is the word that Paul at once turns to when he attempts to express his sense of humility and wonder at *the dynamic experience of being taken hold of, upheld and used by God*.

(*b*) There is no sharp line of distinction between the different uses we have outlined above. 'The grace of God in Christ' (Rom. 5.15; Gal. 2.21; Eph. 1.6f.) denotes both the historical event of Christ's death and resurrection, and the experience of grace in the here and now. So too the grace of Paul's conversion is not something different from the continuing grace outworking through his present ministry (I Cor. 15.10); as Paul's conversion was not something different from his call, so the grace which transformed him was not something different from the grace 'working with him'. So too the continuing experience of grace comes to individual expression in particular enablings and inward compulsion to some activity or service. Unlike his near contemporary Philo, Paul never uses *charis* in the plural, always singular. *All grace, including its particular manifestations, is the one grace of God*.[18]

(*c*) Grace is always *God's* action. Several times Paul speaks of grace as given to men (Rom. 12.3, 6; 15.15; I Cor. 3.10; Gal. 2.9; etc.). But he never means that grace somehow becomes man's possession, something he has at his disposal to use at his own will. It is *always God's action through him*.[19] Whereas Philo speaks of grace(s) as the natural equipment of men – for example, seeing, hearing, reason are χάριτες for Philo – for Paul grace (always singular) is always the act of God.[20] Even in the single occasion when he uses a personal pronoun with *charis* ('your gracious act' – I Cor. 16.3),[21] it is precisely the same grace on which he enlarges in II Cor. 8 – 'the grace of generosity' (8.1) coming to concrete expression in their contribution to Paul's collection. When Paul uses the phrase 'given to' the emphasis is not on the preposition or the recipient but on the verb – grace as an unmerited act of boundless generosity – the givenness of grace.

(*d*) It follows that in a very real sense *the whole of life is for Paul an expression of grace: all is of grace, and grace is all.* This means that the particular manifestations of grace are the more visible embodiments of a power out of which the believer in fact lives all the time; they are that inward power coming to conscious outward expression (conscious in that they are recognized as grace, the gracious action of God). Grace then does not manifest itself only in particular compartments of the believer's life; and the particular conscious experiences of grace are not the only operations of grace in his life.[22] All is of grace and grace is all. At the same time this does not mean that the believer is necessarily different from the unbeliever, as though an aura of 'grace' hung always around him, or he had to confine himself only to a narrowly circumscribed mode of living which could be legitimated as 'gracious'. As the discussion of I Cor. 8; 10 and Rom. 14 makes clear, grace does not cut a man off from social contact and the life of the market place. The man of faith is different, but only in that there is a dimension to his existence which determines all (Rom. 5.2; I Cor. 10.26); there is an energizing of his existence whose source is God (e.g. Rom. 5.21; 6.14; II Cor. 12.9; Gal. 5.4); there is a direction to existence which is the glory of God (Rom. 14.6ff. – 'he gives thanks (εὐχαριστεῖ) to God'; I Cor. 10.31). Grace gives the believer's life both its source, its power and its direction. All is of grace and grace is all.

§38. CHARISMA, CHARISMATA AND PNEUMATIKA

Granted then that the experience of Spirit and of grace is fundamental to Paul's life as a Christian, we must go on to ask how that Spirit and grace came to particular expression in the lives of Paul and his converts. What experiences, what aspects of the experience of life as a believer did he recognize as expressions of Spirit and grace? We attempt to answer this question by examining those words which themselves mean 'expression of Spirit' and 'expression of grace' – πνευματικόν (*pneumatikon*) and χάρισμα (*charisma*). The latter is the more important of the two for Paul and we give it the centre of attention.

38.1 Χάρισμα, *charisma*, is a distinctively Pauline word. Of the seventeen occurrences in the NT only one comes from outside the Pauline corpus, and that from a typically Pauline passage (I Peter 4.10). When we spread the comparison further the newness and distinctiveness of Paul's usage becomes even clearer. He does not owe the concept to the OT: *charisma* occurs only twice in LXX and then only as variant readings;[23] indeed, it may be that Paul's choice of *charisma* is partly motivated by a desire to mark off the new experience of grace from the OT religion of law and ritual.[24] Josephus does not use the word at all, and the only two occurrences in Philo are in reference to creation,[25] whereas Paul confines its use to the relation between God and man.[26] The only other near parallel is in the Sibylline Oracles (II.54), of indeterminate date, while the handful of examples in secular Greek are all much later than Paul.[27] In post-Pauline Christian usage the characteristic Pauline sense is almost completely lost.[28] In short, *'charisma' is a concept which we owe almost entirely to Paul.* This is significant, since it means that the main influence determining Paul's choice of the word is his own experience, the creative experiences which it describes.

38.2   *Charisma in general – the range of meaning.* In its range of meaning *charisma* overlaps to a considerable degree with *charis*.[29] In Rom. 5.15f. *charisma* seems to denote both the gracious act of God in Jesus and its effect on men in terms of acquittal.[30] In Rom. 6.23 *charisma* is used as a summary word for all that God's unmerited generosity accomplishes in and for the believer; 'the free gift of God is eternal life' – the thought being more of the gracious gift than of the gracious act.

Second, *charisma* is used twice of particular gifts given to the believer. In II Cor. 1.11; although the second half of the verse is confused, *charisma* must refer to the divine deliverance from deadly peril just mentioned (1.10).[31] Whether the peril was some serious illness or an external threat, Paul expresses his conviction that it was only divine power which saved his life, either by operating directly in him (cf. II Cor. 12.9), or by inspiring some human intervention. *Charisma* here then is a particular action of God on Paul's behalf either directly in Paul himself or through the circumstances that brought him deliverance.[32]

In I Cor. 7.7 Paul regards celibacy as a *charisma*: the enabling to refrain from sexual relations within marriage, and to restrain the sexual appetite when unmarried, Paul regards as something given by God.[33] It is not the celibate state which is the charisma, but the enabling to say 'No' to sexual passions – an enabling which Paul experiences as something not in his own strength but as given from beyond. Notice that, contrary to frequent assertion,[34] Paul does not call marriage a charisma. When Paul says, 'Each has his own charisma from God, some one, some another', he means simply that some have the gift of continence; others who do not have this gift are well advised to marry, for assuredly they will have some other gift from God.[35] What other gifts he had in mind, whether the sort of charismata he itemizes in I Cor. 12 or a broader spectrum, we cannot tell. The latter seems more probable.

Third, *charisma* as a particular manifestation of grace within the context of the community of faith – Paul's most frequent usage. Rom. 11.29 – 'the charismata and the call of God are irrevocable'. Charismata here could refer to the peculiar favours granted to Israel in times past – the sonship, the glory, the covenants, the law, the worship and the promises (9.4). But would Paul describe the law as an 'irrevocable gift'? In the context of 11.28f. 'charismata' appears together with 'call' as an explanation of the word 'election'. It therefore probably refers to the *acts* of grace whereby God made Israel's calling and election sure – God's gracious action on behalf of Israel.[36]

The remaining passages all refer to the Christian community and only in this context does Paul go into detail and give instances of the sort of charismata he has in mind. We shall note the more general allusions and then in the subsequent paragraphs of this chapter look at Paul's examples of charismata within the community more closely. Rom. 1.11 – Paul longs to see the Romans 'that I may impart to you some spiritual gift (τι χάρισμα πνευματικόν) to *strengthen* you'. Paul uses μεταδίδωμι (give a share of) because he himself expects to benefit from the charisma as well (hence v. 12). That Paul has any one particular charisma in mind is doubtful;[37] he is simply expressing his confidence that when they come together God will minister through him in a particular way for their mutual benefit. I Cor. 1.7 – Paul expresses his pleasure that from their conversion the Corinthians had been rich in experiences of inspired speech and knowledge, so that in fact they were constantly enjoying the full range of spiritual manifestations. Paul clearly has in mind the sort of charismata which he lists in I Cor. 12.8–10.[38] We will leave consideration of the two occurrences of *charisma* in the Pastorals till chapter XI.

38.3   Πνευματικός, *pneumatikos*, is almost as distinctively Pauline as *charisma*, at least within early Christian literature (elsewhere in the NT only in I Peter 2.5). But it is used elsewhere in somewhat parallel fashion,[39] and plays a key role in the incipient gnosticism of Paul's own time – a fact which emerges most clearly from Paul's own use of the word in I Cor. 2.13ff.;[40] 14.37 and 15.44ff.[41] (see also Jude 19). In consequence *pneumatikos* is less able to provide a vehicle for the distinctive Pauline emphases than *charisma*.

Nevertheless, it is quite an important word for Paul, since it expresses so clearly the sense of belonging to Spirit, embodying Spirit, manifesting Spirit, of the essence or nature of Spirit.[42] As an adjective its range of usage is rather different from that of *charisma*. Paul uses it in three main ways – (*a*) as an adjective (spiritual something), (*b*) as a masculine noun (spiritual man, *pneumatiker*), and (*c*) as a neuter plural noun (the spirituals, spiritual things).

(*a*) In Rom. 1.11 *pneumatikon* qualifies *charisma*, a striking double emphasis underlining Paul's conscious dependence on the Spirit and grace for any benefit he can bring to the believers at Rome.[43] Rom. 7.14 – the law is 'spiritual' in the sense that it derives from the Spirit (given to men by inspiration/revelation) and was intended to address men at the level of the Spirit (cf. Rom. 8.4). I Cor. 15.44, 46 – the resurrected body is 'spiritual' in that it embodies the Spirit, the Spirit is its life principle, the unifying centre and motivating force of its existence. Eph. 1.3 – the blessings are 'spiritual' in that they derive from the Spirit and take their character from the Spirit. Col. 1.9 speaks of a 'spiritual understanding', implying a charismatic insight given by the Spirit (see below §40.5). And Eph. 5.19; Col. 3.16 speak of 'spiritual songs', that is of songs prompted by the Spirit and manifesting his inspiration (see below §41.5).[44]

(*b*) Some Christians are spiritual men' (οἱ πνευματικοί) and others not; that is, they are possessed by and manifest the Spirit more than others, or in a manner not yet experienced by others (I Cor. 2.13, 15; 14.37; Gal. 6.1). This is a claim made both by Paul's opponents in Corinth and by Paul himself! We will investigate it more fully in chapter IX (§48).

(*c*) In I Cor. 9.11 τὰ πνευματικά is used in contrast to τὰ σαρκικά, denoting in both cases the whole range of activities, attitudes, experiences, etc. which draw their significance from the Spirit in contrast to those which draw their significance from the merely physical, human and worldy (σάρξ); not so very different is the similar contrast in Rom. 15.27. In I Cor. 12.1; 14.1 and probably 2.13 *pneumatika* is used with more restricted reference to spiritual gifts, synonymous with *charismata*.[45] Of the two words the latter seems to be Paul's preferred choice (cf. e.g. Rom. 1.11; 12.6; I Cor. 1.7). The Corinthian situation and the way in which Paul introduces the subject in I Cor. 12.1 suggests strongly that τὰ πνευματικά is the description used by the Corinthians, emphasizing the pneumatic character of their experiences.[46] But Paul is not critical of this use of *pneumatika* (as 14.1 indicates),[47] and even if elsewhere he prefers to underline the gracious character of charismatic experience,[48] he fully shares the Corinthian understanding of charismata as gifts of the

Spirit (I Cor. 12.4) and underlines this belief on his own account (12.7ff., 11).[49]

All these references are somewhat fragmentary and shed only fitful light on our subject. If we are to gain a fuller and more coherent insight into Paul's evaluation of charismatic experience we must pay special attention to his more comprehensive treatment of charismatic phenomena within the Christian community – making particular but by no means exclusive use of his lists of *charismata/pneumatika* in Rom. 12.6–8 and I Cor. 12.8–10.

§39. MIRACLES

39.1　Paul uses four different phrases to describe the distribution and diversity (διαιρέσεις)[50] of gifts mentioned in I Cor. 12.4–10 – *charismata*, acts of service (διακονίαι), activities (ἐνεργήματα), and manifestation of the Spirit (φανέρωσις τοῦ πνεύματος).[51] These are all alternative ways of describing the whole range of spiritual gifts: *all* the charismata are acts of service, *all* are actions wrought by God, *all* are manifestations of the Spirit for the common good (12.7; cf. Eph. 4.12). We start with ἐνεργήματα and pick up the other phrases in due course.

The ἐνεργεῖν word group is normally used for the operations of the divine (or demonic). Paul is no exception.[52] Paul's description of charismata as ἐνεργήματα is deliberately chosen therefore to underline his conviction that all charismata are effected by divine power; *the utterances and actions he goes on to list are only charismata in so far as they are the action of God's Spirit in and through the individual*. This is made even more explicit in I Cor. 12.6b – 'God who brings about (ἐνεργῶν) all these things in each case/person'. And just in case the point be forgotten he repeats it in 12.11: 'all these charismata are the work of one and the same Spirit (ἐνεργεῖ)'. It is also relevant to notice that ἐνέργημα means properly 'what is effected', 'the act', 'action', rather than the acting (ἐνέργεια – 'activity'). 12.10a warns us against pressing the distinction too far. But the point nevertheless emerges that when Paul speaks here of charismata he is thinking of concrete actions, actual events, not of latent possibilities and hidden talents. *Charisma is an event, an action enabled by divine power; charisma is divine energy accomplishing a particular result (in word or deed) through the individual*.[53]

39.2　*Dunameis* (δυνάμεις – I Cor. 12.10, 28f.). Although all charismata are ἐνεργήματα, the word is also very naturally used for particular charismata[54] – viz., those charismata which are most obviously a display of divine power, that is, miracles.[55] So in 12.10 we read, 'To another is given the operation of miracles (ἐνεργήματα δυνάμεων)'. That there is here a certain redundancy of expression is indicated by the parallel allusion in 12.28f., where *dunameis* alone obviously means the same thing. In both cases *the charisma is the actual miracle, or the miracle working power operating effectively in a particular instance.* That miracles took place within Paul's ministry and the Pauline churches, just as in Jesus' ministry and that of the early Palestinian communities, there can be no doubt. We have the first hand testimony of Paul himself, the only assuredly eyewitness accounts we possess (see particularly Rom. 15.19; II Cor. 12.12; Gal. 3.5).[56] What these *dunameis* included we are unfortunately now unable to determine. In the Synoptics *dunameis* is used for the whole range of Jesus' healings and also for the 'nature miracles' (though probably only by the evangelists).[57] Paul, however, seems to distinguish *dunameis* from 'gifts of healing' in I Cor. 12.9f., and it may be that in *dunameis* he is thinking primarily of exorcisms.[58] Yet demon possession as such does not feature prominently in Paul's thought (cf. I Cor. 10.20f.; Eph. 2.2); he thinks rather of spiritual powers in heaven operating through the (personified) power of sin, law and death, and behind the pagan cults and authorities (see below n.98). All men are subject to these powers and liberation from their dominion comes only through the power of the Spirit (see particularly Rom. 6–8 and below §53). Nevertheless, it is possible that he has exorcisms particularly in mind here (cf. Acts 16.18; 19.12ff.). Nor may we exclude the possibility that *dunameis* here includes 'nature miracles'.[59] Be that as it may, by *dunameis* Paul is evidently thinking of *events in which people (and things?) were visibly and beneficially affected in an extraordinary way by a non-rational power through the medium of Paul and other believers.*

39.3   *Gifts of healing* (χαρίσματα ἰαμάτων – I Cor. 12.9, 28, 30) requires little comment. No doubt the sort of healings we have already observed in the ministry of Jesus and in Acts are in Paul's mind (see above §§12.3, 30.1) – though whether we are dealing simply with what would now be called psychosomatic illnesses we cannot tell. Again it is worth pointing out that in I Cor. 12.9, 28, 30 we have first hand testimony to the fact that there were cures and healings experienced in the Pauline communities for which no natural or rational explanation would suffice – they could only be put down to the action of God. Also worthy of comment is the repetition of *charismata* and the use of the plural (the first three *charismata* listed in 12.8ff. are all

singular): 'to another gifts of healings'. The charisma is not a healing
power which is effective for all (sorts of) illnesses; it is *the actual healing
itself*. As there are many (different) illnesses, so there are many
(different) healing charismata.[60]

39.4   *Faith* (πίστις – I Cor. 12.9; Rom. 12.3, 6). Under miracles we
must include the third member of the I Cor. 12.8–10 list – faith. As
almost all commentators recognize, 'faith' here can hardly denote
justifying faith – that active attitude and openness to God which is the
basis of the believer's whole relationship with God and which Paul
deals with so powerfully in Rom. 3.22–5.2 in his exposition of Hab.
2.4: 'the just man by faith shall live' (Rom. 1.17). It must rather
signify more concentrated experiences of faith which arise out of the
believer's general relationship with God in particular situations –
faith 'so as to move mountains' (I Cor. 13.2 – clearly recalling the
words of Jesus – Mark 11.23f. par.; cf. Mark 9.23; Matt. 17.20/Luke
17.5f.).[61] Hence it is a charisma which may be given only to some
('to another, faith' – I Cor. 12.9);[62] hence too the association with
the next two charismata in the list: gifts of healings and operations of
miracles. Paul presumably has in mind that mysterious surge of
confidence which sometimes arises within a man in a particular
situation of need or challenge and which gives him an otherly certainty and assurance that God is about to act through a word or
through an action (such as laying hands on someone sick).[63] Jesus
certainly knew such experiences in his own ministry (cf. e.g. Mark
3.5; 5.36; 9.23ff. – though see above §12.4) and recognized the same
sort of bold assurance for particular needs in others (cf. Matt. 8.10/
Luke 7.9; Matt. 15.28). The same was true in the earliest community
and mission (cf. Acts 3.6f.; 14.9f.; also 6.5, 8; 11.24). And similar
experiences of faith to heal or be healed being given from beyond are
familiar to us from the history of Christianity.[64]

We should, however, note that in Rom. 12.3 Paul thinks of such
faith in connection with charismata in general.[65] There he encourages the Roman Christians to think with sober judgment about their
charismatic role within the body of Christ. The 'measure' they are to
use is the faith which God has dealt out to each.[66] It can serve as a
measure precisely because it is *that assurance that God is speaking or acting
through the charismatic's words or actions*. This recognition that the
charisma is *God's* act should prevent inflated opinions and self-
important posturing and enable a sober estimate of one's role within
the community.[67] So too in Rom. 12.6 the charisma of prophecy has
to be exercised according to the proportion of the individual's faith

(κατὰ τὴν ἀναλογίαν τῆς πίστεως). By 'faith' here again Paul presumably is thinking of a believer's confidence that God's Spirit is speaking in the very words he is then uttering. Paul's counsel therefore is to the effect that the man who speaks under inspiration should speak only when conscious of his words as inspired and should presumably cease to speak when that sense of inspiration ceases, that is, when he ceases to be confident that God is speaking through him (cf. I Cor. 14.30, and see further below §48.1).[68] Finally, we may note that in Paul's view charismatic faith also has a role in the determining of conduct as well as in the exercise of charisma (Rom. 14.22f. – see further below p. 233).

§40. REVELATION

40.1   Paul also describes charismatic phenomena as 'the manifestation of the Spirit' (ἡ φανέρωσις τοῦ πνεύματος – I Cor. 12.7). Here φανέρωσις (phanerōsis) is not merely a gift which some have, but each charisma is a manifestation of the Spirit: 'In each of us the Spirit is manifested in one particular way' (NEB). Here too it is clear that what is being described is not some hidden talent or latent faculty, but a particular action or utterance which can be described as manifest or open, or which makes manifest, discloses. *The manifestation of the Spirit is the actual action or utterance itself in its character as revelation.*

But does the phrase mean 'that which manifests the Spirit', or 'the manifestation which the Spirit produces'? Despite a long standing dispute among commentators it is in fact difficult to exclude either sense. The Spirit is undoubtedly thought of as the author and giver of the charismata – a point repeatedly emphasized in the immediate context (vv. 3, (4), 8, 9, 11). But without an object *phanerōsis* is a vague and incomplete concept (manifestation of what?); and in the only other use of the word in the NT the accompanying genitive is certainly objective (II Cor. 4.2: 'manifestation of the truth' – the truth is that which is manifested). It is quite likely that Paul was being deliberately ambiguous, his thought being that *the Spirit reveals himself* in the charismata.[69] As we shall see later, this phrase introduces us to the important idea that *there are certain (kinds of) action and utterance which demonstrate the Spirit's presence and activity.* It is important to realize that in Paul's view the sort of charismatic action and utterance which he lists in I Cor. 12.8–10 are in some sense an evidence, a disclosure, a making visible of the Spirit. But as we shall also see below, there is much more to be said (chs. IX and X).

Like the other generic words in I Cor. 12.4–7, *phanerōsis* can also be used for particular charismata – those whose character as revelation is more immediate and more clearly marked. In point of fact Paul uses φανέρωσις itself on only one other occasion (II Cor. 4.2). But the verb φανερόω, and the near synonyms 'reveal' (ἀποκαλύπτω) and 'revelation' (ἀποκάλυψις), bring us into a very broad range of religious experience which we can therefore properly discuss under the heading of 'revelation'.

40.2 *The revelation of Christ.* The most important event of revelation for Paul is *the eschatological event of Christ*, unveiling the mystery of God's final purposes (see especially Rom. 16.25f.; Eph. 3.3ff.; Col. 1.26f.).[70] The revelation is not just the making known of some philosophical fact which gives information about the construction of the cosmos or the schedule of the eschaton; the mystery is Christ himself.[71] Christ in himself, in his death and present life, reveals God's final way of righteousness (Rom. 1.17; 3.21; Gal. 3.23); Christ in himself, in his life beyond law, reveals God's end-time way for Jew and Gentile (Eph. 1.9; 3.6; cf. Rom. 11.25); Christ in himself, in his life beyond death, reveals God's eschatological way to wholeness (Rom. 8.17ff.; I Cor. 2.7; Col. 1.27).[72]

Revelation therefore is not merely an event of the past, confined to the irretrievable pastness of history. Nor is revelation limited to the past events of Jesus' life, death and resurrection. For Paul *the act of revelation takes place wherever Christ manifests and makes himself known*, whether in his parousia (I Cor. 1.7; II Thess. 1.7) or now through the gospel (Rom. 1.17; 16.25f.; I Cor. 4.1; II Cor. 2.14; 4.4ff.; Eph. 3.7ff.; 6.19; Col. 1.24–8; 4.4).[73] For Paul himself in particular it took place pre-eminently in his conversion – the 'revelation of Jesus Christ' (Gal. 1.12, 16 – see above pp. 105f., 108) and the use of revelation language when talking about the gospel and the object of his ministry shows how much Paul was influenced in his thinking by his own experience.[74] For Paul, in other words, conversion involved an act of revelation, Christ making himself known through the gospel and being recognized in the reality of his risen life and eschatological significance. Revelation here therefore is conceived as an event which enlightens the mind and heart (man as a thinking, feeling, willing being), and does so in such a far reaching and penetrating manner that the whole self-understanding, world-view and life-style is transformed and reoriented in accordance with its light.

40.3 *Vision and ecstasy.* Revelation is not confined to the experience of conversion or the proclamation of the gospel.[75] Paul himself enjoyed many other and diverse experiences of revelation throughout his Christian life, and expected that other believers would enjoy similar experiences: experiences in which insights into cosmological and divine realities were given to the believer, and experiences in which particular issues and problems of conduct and daily living were resolved for the believer.

Among his particular revelations Paul includes ecstatic and visionary experiences – the 'visions and revelations' of II Cor. 12.1 (= 'revelations' 12.7). 'Vision' emphasizes more the experience of seeing, and 'revelation' the experience of hearing; but in fact the words are near synonyms here,[76] and together as a hendiadys designate a range of visionary and auditory experiences. That Paul has in mind ecstatic experiences is clearly shown by the one example he cites (12.2–4) – an experience which he himself had enjoyed fourteen years earlier – the time note obviously indicating a real experience and not merely a symbolical or hypothetical account.[77] The characteristics of ecstasy are clearly marked.

(a) Verses 2, 3 – 'whether in the body or out of it, I do not know – God knows'. In his experience Paul had been so carried out of himself, and lost his normal consciousness of bodiliness to such an extent that he was not sure whether he had left his body behind. His consciousness was so focussed on the sensation of being 'caught up', on the visionary awareness of being in the 'third heaven', in 'paradise',[78] and on what he heard, that in looking back he could recall nothing of his normal bodily sensations. Whether the feeling of being caught up included a consciousness of soaring through the lower levels of heaven (first and second heaven) is not clear;[79] but certainly we must assume that he saw something at least of what Jewish tradition had come to regard as the inhabitants and 'furniture' of heaven (angels, the righteous, 'the Lord' on his throne, etc. – cf. Acts 7.56; Rev. 4.1ff.).[80] At all events this sort of lapse of normal consciousness is an indisputable mark of ecstasy. Such 'out of the body' experiences are well known within mystic tradition and shamanism.[81]

(b) 'The objectifying of the I' (Lindblom). The use of third person ('I know a man in Christ' – v.2) could be simply stylistic,[82] and it may be partly explained by Paul's desire to give little personal weight to such experiences.[83] However, taken together with the uncertainty of his bodily relation to the experiences, it probably denotes, in part at least, that curious ambivalence of the ecstatic's consciousness, where the experience is in some way objective, where he can as it were observe himself undergoing the experience, and can ask him-

self, 'Is this really me who is seeing and hearing these things?' Such
'objectifying of the I' is typical of mystical and ecstatic experience.[84]

(c) 'He heard unutterable utterances (ἄρρητα ῥήματα) which a man
may not put into words' (v.4). The 'unutterable utterances' may
simply mean divine secrets which the recipient is strongly forbidden
to divulge – 'words so secret that human lips may not repeat them'
(NEB).[85] Any attempt to identify this secret information with one of
the particular mysteries (e.g. Rom.11.25f.; I Cor. 15.51ff.) or
revelations (e.g. Gal.2.2) which Paul mentions elsewhere hardly does
justice to Paul's language; although we may more credibly refer to I
Cor.2.10 – 'the depths of God'.[86] It is likely, however, that the
phrase includes also a sense of the impossibility of putting such an
experience of the world beyond into the words of this world. There
had been a genuine and deeply significant communication, but the
most important part of it had been at a non-verbal, non-rational
level – 'things beyond our seeing, things beyond our hearing, things
beyond our imagining' (I Cor.2.9 NEB). This too is characteristic
of mystical and ecstatic experiences.[87]

How typical or untypical was this experience for Paul? Was he
subject to frequent experiences of ecstasy? The evidence is not at all
clear cut on this point. We will review it briefly. First, II Cor.12.1, 7.
On the one hand Paul speaks of 'visions and revelations' (12.1) and
'revelations' (12.7) in the plural. The ὑπερβολὴ τῶν ἀποκαλύψεων of v.7
probably denotes 'extraordinary character, magnificence of revelations' (NEB, JB), rather than 'excess, abundance of revelations'
(RSV).[88] But either way Paul had known some very striking experiences of ecstasy in his life 'in Christ'. On the other hand, it is probably significant that he goes back fourteen years to choose an example
of one of his revelations. This surely indicates that the 12.2–4
experience was something out of the ordinary for Paul.[89] The intervening visions and revelations had not been quite so extraordinary.
Moreover, as we shall see in chapter IX (pp.267, 274f.), Paul's language (ὑπερβολὴ τῶν ἀποκαλύψεων) has almost certainly been provoked
by the charges and taunts of the pseudo-apostles who threatened his
work and authority in Corinth. The ὑπερβολή may therefore be a
somewhat exaggerated claim (he has to go back fourteen years to
find a really impressive revelation); in less contentious circumstances
Paul would perhaps have been content with a more modest claim.

Second, II Cor.5.13: 'if we are beside ourselves, out of our senses
(ἐξέστημεν) it is for God; if we are in our right mind (σωφρονοῦμεν) it is
for you'. ἐξίστημι properly denotes an experience of dissociation (the
verb means literally 'to stand outside of oneself'). The immediate

contrast with σωφρωνέω (be of sound mind, so, be sensible, serious) indicates an experience divorced from the rational mind. And the fact that Paul mentions the ἔκστασις (ecstasy – the noun from ἐξίστημι) as a potential matter for boasting shows that we are back in the contentious atmosphere of II Cor. 10–13; that is to say, Paul has in mind the sort of experiences of which the Corinthians made so much, and particularly, no doubt, the 'visions and revelations' of II Cor. 12.1 – for of all the matters mentioned in II Cor. 10–12 about which Paul could boast, the 'revelations' of II Cor. 12.1–4, 7 are most appropriately alluded to as ἔκστασις.[90]

Third, Paul's considerable glossolalic experience (I Cor. 14.18) may have included ecstatic elements. This is suggested particularly by the parallel between II Cor. 5.13 and I Cor. 14.2, 14ff.: the dissociation phenomenon is the same – the rational mind plays no part in speaking in tongues and gains no benefit from it (I Cor. 14.14ff.); and the contrast between experiences which belong to one's private relationship with God rather than to the public assembly is very close (I Cor. 14.2). But we must return to this question later (§41.7).

Fourth, more questionable is Schmithals's equation ἐξιστάναι = φανεροῦσθαι. On the basis of the parallelism between II Cor. 5.11a and 5.13 he argues that 'φανεροῦσθαι means a making manifest of the Pneuma in ecstasy'. Following from this he asserts that φανερόω in II Cor. 11.6 also alludes to ecstatic manifestation of knowledge.[91] This is certainly possible in view of the situation in Corinth, but may be reading too much into Paul's language without sufficient justification.

Fifth, again in view of the state of affairs in Corinth, it is possible that the μεταμορφοῦσθαι of II Cor. 3.18 ('changed into his likeness from one degree of glory to another') includes experiences of ecstasy.[92] But although metamorphosis is a familiar idea in the Hellenistic mystery cults, Paul's thought is primarily influenced by Jewish apocalyptic (see particularly II Bar. 51.3, 10) and belongs more to his own special brand of mysticism than to controversy over the value of ecstatic experience (cf. Rom. 8.29; 12.2; I Cor. 15.51ff.; Gal. 4.19; Phil. 3.10, 21).[93]

All in all then it is clear that Paul was no stranger to ecstatic experience; but that such experiences were frequent or greatly exalting we cannot say.[94] The question of real moment however, is whether they were important to Paul (few or many, seldom or frequent). Was Paul an ecstatic? Did he root his authority and missionary compulsion in such experiences? Were they essential to his piety? Paul's position on these questions is quite clear-cut and decisive; we shall return to them in due course (§§55, 56.3).

40.4 *Knowledge and wisdom.* The believer may also experience particular revelations of a more rational kind, where the unveiling of insight or information takes place on the level of the mind and understanding. This is certainly the implication of Paul's association of revelation with prophecy in I Cor. 14.6, 26, 30, for in that chapter prophecy is characterized precisely as communication at a rational level in explicit contrast with the complete non-rationality of glossolalia (14.6–25). Revelation is clearly understood here as something which speaks to man's understanding as well as his spirit. This is also the case in Gal. 2.2 ('I went up to Jerusalem by revelation' – κατὰ ἀποκάλυψιν); it is quite likely that Paul has in mind here a specific command addressed to himself by a prophetic oracle given out under inspiration, whether in the worship of the assembly or in a less formal gathering for prayer (cf. Acts 13.2; 16.6f.; see above pp. 172f., 176f.).

A survey of rational revelations must include discussion of Paul's understanding of 'knowledge' (γνῶσις – *gnōsis*) and 'wisdom' (σοφία – *sophia*); their place within the revelation-mystery complex of ideas is sufficiently evident from I Cor. 2.7, 10 (part of the discussion of *sophia* in I Cor. 1.17–2.16) and I Cor. 13.2; 14.6. And he specifically includes 'word/utterance of wisdom' and 'word/utterance of knowledge' (λόγος σοφίας, λόγος γνώσεως) among the charismata of I Cor. 12.8–10. To understand what Paul means by these latter phrases we must clarify his understanding of *gnōsis* and *sophia*.

Gnōsis and *sophia* however present us with special difficulties. It is not easy to gain a clear idea of what Paul means by them. This is because, in the Corinthian letters in particular, they are not Paul's own choice of expression; his use of them has been determined in large measure by the situation which he addresses at Corinth. As is now widely recognized within NT scholarship, *gnōsis* and *sophia* are the *slogans of the faction opposing Paul in Corinth.*[95] It is because his opponents claim to possess *gnōsis* and *sophia*, and deny them to others (including Paul), that Paul has to take up the concepts in the first place. This is why *gnōsis* keeps recurring within the Corinthian letters and only rarely elsewhere, and why I Cor. 1–3 is so dominated by discussion of *sophia*.[96]

The importance of knowledge for the Corinthians is indicated by I Cor. 13.2, 8; II Cor. 8.7; 11.6, and especially I Cor. 8. It was evidently the Corinthians' proud boast that they 'possess knowledge' (8.1). What was this knowledge? Fortunately the chapter gives us some clues. The knowledge in this case is that 'idols count for nothing in the world'; 'there is no God but one' (8.4).[97] Knowledge here then is an insight into the real nature of the cosmos – a recognition in particular of the relationship between the material idol and the spiritual beings that people the cosmos ('gods many and lords many' – 8.5; 'demons' – 10.20).[98] If we may generalize on the basis of such little information and tentatively in the light of later gnosis,[99] we may infer that *gnōsis* for the Corinthians was charismatic insight into the real nature of reality, into the structure of the cosmos and the relationships of divine and human, spiritual and material within that cosmos. Of equal importance is the fact that this knowledge was not purely speculative but had a practical outworking. In the Corinthian case knowledge enabled the Corinthians to join in the social activities and feasts of the pagan temples (8.10) without qualm or reservation. *Gnōsis* we might say was a charismatic 'world view' with distinctive ethical corollaries.

From this we can deduce Paul's understanding of *gnōsis* in I Corinthians and in particular his understanding of 'utterance of knowledge' in I Cor. 12.8. Two possibilities are open to us. On the one hand Paul evidently shares at least some of the Corinthians' understanding of *gnōsis*. He regards Corinthian *gnōsis* as an enriching (I Cor. 1.5 – ἐπλουτίσθητε; II Cor. 6.6; 8.7; 11.6), and shares the attitude of Corinthian *gnōsis* to idols and to meat used in temple sacrifices (8.1, 4 – he agrees with the Corinthian assertions; 10.25ff.; cf. Rom. 14.14). It is true that for Paul the much more important *gnōsis* is knowledge in the more OT, experiential (rather than speculative) sense of personal relationship with Christ (Phil. 3.8; so also II Cor. 2.14; 4.6; 10.5).[100] But in I Corinthians when the noun is used it is the more speculative *gnōsis* which is always in mind, and it is quite likely in this sense that Paul speaks of *gnōsis* in 12.8 and 14.6, as 13.2, 8 seem to confirm. 'Utterance of knowledge' may therefore quite properly be understood as a word spoken under inspiration giving an insight into cosmical realities and relationships – a word which bears a practical application within itself or from which a course of conduct is readily inferred.[101] For example of such a 'word of knowledge' given out at Corinth we probably need look no further than I Cor. 8.4: the statement that 'an idol is nothing in the world' (οὐδὲν εἴδωλον ἐν κόσμῳ) in its brevity and somewhat cryptic character has the distinct ring of an oracular saying.

On the other hand it may be that 'utterance of knowledge' expresses more of Paul's reaction against Corinthian *gnōsis* than his agreement with it[102] for in I Cor. 8.2 he contrasts Corinthian *gnōsis* with the knowledge that ought to characterize the believer: 'If anyone thinks he knows (something) he knows nothing yet in the true sense of knowing' (ἔγνω καθὼς δεῖ γνῶναι). What Paul means is perhaps

clarified by the similar contrast in I Cor. 2.12: 'We have received not
the spirit of the world but the Spirit which comes from God, so that
we may know the things given us by God'. 'Word of knowledge' here
then would denote some charismatic insight into 'the things given us
by God' (τὰ ὑπὸ τοῦ Θεοῦ χαρισθέντα ἡμῖν), that is, some understanding
of the relationship of God to the believer(s), some recognition of the
charismatic dimension (τὰ χαρισθέντα) to the believer's life individually
or as a community. Since 'knowledge' in this more OT sense includes the overtones of 'acknowledgement'[103] we may assume that
some practical application of the *gnōsis* was explicit or implicit in the
'word of knowledge' – some outworking of love in contrast to the
divisive consequences of the Corinthian *gnōsis* (cf. I Cor. 3.3; 8.1ff.;
13.2, 4ff.).

We are in a stronger position when it comes to determining the
sense of *sophia*. From I Cor. 1–3 we can recognize both the Corinthian concept of wisdom (at least as Paul sees it) and the very different understanding of wisdom proposed by Paul. Paul in fact uses
the term *sophia* in four different ways – two bad senses and two good
senses.[104] Wisdom is used in a bad sense first as rhetorical skill or
eloquence (1.17 – ἐν σοφίᾳ λόγου; 1.19f.; 2.1, 4f.). The danger in this
sophia is that faith becomes a matter of rational persuasion and superficial impression rather than of existential encounter with the Spirit and
power of God (1.17, 22ff.; 2.4f.). Dangerous at a more fundamental
level is wisdom, secondly, in the sense of worldly wisdom (σοφία τοῦ
κόσμου – 1.20ff.; 2.5f., 13; 3.19; II Cor. 1.12; cf. Col. 2.23); that is,
the wisdom which judges the gospel and all claims to truth by human
standards (2.13 – ἐν διδακτοῖς ἀνθρωπίνης σοφίας λόγοις), by the values
of this age (2.6), in terms of what a purely this-worldly appetite and
ambition counts as important (II Cor. 1.12 – ἐν σοφίᾳ σαρκικῇ). To
what extent this is a fair representation of the Corinthian view of
sophia it is not possible to say. Corinthian *sophia* was presumably a
rather sophisticated intellectual conceptualization of human existence
as dominated by 'the rulers of this age' (2.6), with the prospect of
liberation and escape envisaged in terms probably of mystic or
ecstatic experience. Certainly the use of πνευματικός (spiritual) in
2.13, 15; 3.1; in 12.1; 14.1, 37, and in 15.44, 46 – in all three instances Paul picking up the language of his opponents – strongly
suggests a link between *sophia*, ecstatic experience (12.2, etc.), and
affirmation of an experience of resurrection life in the here and now
which renders nonsensical any talk of a still future resurrection of the
body.[105]

The two good senses of *sophia* in I Cor. 1–2 are neatly expressed by the German words *Heilsplan* and *Heilsgut* (plan of salvation and benefits of salvation). The senses merge into each other, but the former comes to clearest expression in 2.6ff. – God's wisdom is his plan to achieve salvation through the crucifixion of Jesus and through the proclamation of a crucified Christ (1.20–5); the latter is more clearly expressed in 1.30 – Christ has become our wisdom, (that is) our righteousness, consecration and redemption. *Sophia* here has almost the same range of meaning as the larger concepts of 'revelation' (see above, particularly §40.2) and 'grace' (II Cor. 1.12 – 'not by human wisdom but by the grace of God'). It is both the rational recognition or acceptance that God's plan of salvation works through a man crucified in the past, but it is also a recognition arrived at and confirmed through the existential experience of saving power in the here and now through the proclamation of this crucified Christ. Thus the two good senses of *sophia* can be matched with and set against the two bad senses. Against the wisdom of this world Paul sets the crucified Christ; and against the wisdom of words Paul sets the power experienced through the gospel of the cross (1.17f., 22ff.; 2.4f.).

Wisdom then for Paul is not like the Greek *gnōsis* – an insight into the true reality of what is; *sophia* is a much more Jewish concept – the recognition of the activity of God, in particular *the recognition that God's salvation-history centres on the crucified Messiah*. But it is not merely a rational acknowledgment; it includes *experiential participation in that salvation-history*, the actual experience of God's saving power in the here and now – the 'demonstration of the Spirit and power' (2.4). It is important that these two elements be held together: Paul proclaimed Christ crucified not simply because the paradox of the cross had come home to him with the force of revelation; but also because through the proclamation of the cross he and others had begun to experience 'the power of God effecting salvation in and for the believer' (Rom. 1.16). At the same time, Paul's *sophia* theology was not based solely in an experience of power, but on experience occasioned by the preaching of the Crucified One.[106] We shall examine the wider ramifications of this in chapter X.

In the light of this, what does Paul understand by a 'word of wisdom'? It probably means simply some charismatic utterance giving an insight into, some fresh understanding of God's plan of salvation or of the benefits it brings to believers. In view of the antitheses drawn so sharply between worldly wisdom and the word of the cross in I Cor. 1–2, Paul may think of the 'word of wisdom' as an inspired proclamation with saving power. In this case 'word of wisdom' would be the sort of charisma which brought a man recognition as an

evangelist; whereas 'word of knowledge' sounds more like the charisma of a teacher. Alternatively, bearing in mind the Jewish tradition
of wisdom teaching most clearly evidenced in Proverbs and Ecclus.
1–42, 'word of wisdom' may be thought of as some kind of practical,
even earthy advice, though presumably inspired advice arising out of
recognition of God's *Heilsplan* and *Heilsgut*. In this case 'word of
wisdom' and 'word of knowledge' would be virtually synonymous –
simply variant expressions of the same sort of charisma picking up
both the key words of the opposing Corinthian faction.[107]

One last question on this subject: Does Paul regard *gnōsis* and
sophia as such as charismata? The broad parallel between *sophia* on
the one hand and 'revelation' and 'grace' on the other (see above
p.220), and the use of *gnōsis* in I Cor. 1.5; 13.2, 8; 14.6 would make
an affirmative answer possible. Yet there can be little doubt that in I
Cor. 12.8 Paul deliberately speaks of '*word* or *utterance* of wisdom/
knowledge', rather than of 'wisdom' and 'knowledge' *per se*. The
phrases are almost certainly aimed at the gnostic faction in Corinth.
In direct contrast and by way of rebuke to those who make proud
boast of their possession of knowledge and wisdom, Paul *confines* the
charisma to the *actual utterance* which expresses (some aspect of) knowledge and wisdom.[108] The charisma of God is no possession of man to
be used at his will; it is the particular word given in a particular
instance and is 'mine' only in the act and moment of uttering it.
Similarly in I Cor. 14.6 Paul has in mind a particular expression. It
follows that *for Paul wisdom and knowledge as such are not to be thought of
as charismata; only the actual utterance which reveals wisdom or knowledge to
others is a charisma.*

Finally we should briefly consider Eph. 1.17ff.: Paul's prayer is
that 'God may give you a spirit of wisdom and revelation in the
knowledge of him, having the eyes of your heart enlightened, that
you may know what is the hope to which he has called you, . . .'
Of particular note is the unusually high concentration of revelation
words – wisdom, revelation, knowledge (ἐπίγνωσις), and enlighten
(φωτίζω). Two other points may be mentioned. First, two different
moments of revelation are envisaged here: an experience of enlighten-
ment in the past (presumably conversion), whose light still illumi-
nates the present (πεφωτισμένος – perfect tense);[109] and the prayed for
possibility of further illumination in the future given by the Spirit.[110]
This brings us, second, to the question, What kind of revelations are
prayed for? The answer seems to be that Paul envisages experiences
or insights or utterances unveiling some aspect of the mind and plan
of God ('Spirit of wisdom and revelation' – cf. I Cor. 12.8; 14.6, 26;

Rev. 4ff.), which arise out of a living relationship with God and deepen that relationship existentially ('in the knowledge of him'),[111] and which result in a fuller cognizance *and* experience of ('that you might know')[112] 'the hope to which he calls you . . . the wealth and glory of his power towards us who believe'. That is, he has in mind revelations both rational and existential. This certainly does not mean that Paul envisages growth in knowledge as a series of cataclysmic and ecstatic experiences, though these cannot be excluded; we are probably nearer Paul's mind if we understand the growth in knowledge coming about through not infrequent experiences of illumination and fuller insight, whether in private study and devotion or in the (charismatic) assembly (cf. Philemon 6).

40.5   *Guidance.* Still under the heading of revelation, and difficult to distinguish clearly from the material just examined,[113] is revelation experienced as *guidance*, as *assured conviction regarding God's will in matters of ethical conduct and decision.* 'Reveal'/'revelation' may itself be used in this sense in two places – Gal. 2.2 and Phil. 3.15. The 'revelation' which led Paul to go up to Jerusalem (Gal. 2.2) could have come through prophecy (cf. I Cor. 14.6, 26, 30 and above p.217); but equally well ἀποκάλυψις could denote a personal vision or dream (cf. II Cor. 12.1ff., and above on Acts pp.177ff.), or simply a firm conviction in his own mind which he attributed to the Spirit.[114] In Phil. 3.15 'revelation' is conceived as a God-given conviction as to the truth of Paul's attitude and conduct: viz., that 'perfection', or better 'maturity', is a matter of *becoming*, not something already attained – a conviction, that is, as to life-style and conduct.[115] It should be noted that Paul envisages any (τι) believer as the recipient of such revelation; it is not the peculiar prerogative of apostle or prophet.

We are here touching the fringes of a fairly large subject – that of Pauline ethics.[116] There is no need for us to investigate it in any depth. But we must pause long enough to make clear *the charismatic dimension of Paul's ethics.*

(*a*) Christian conduct is conduct determined by the Spirit. Believers are characterized as those who walk by the Spirit (Rom. 8.4 – περιπατοῦντες κατὰ πνεῦμα; Gal. 5.16 – πνεύματι περιπατεῖτε); who are led by the Spirit (Rom. 8.14; Gal. 5.18 – πνεύματι ἄγοντες);[117] who order their lives by the Spirit (Gal. 5.25 – πνεύματι στοιχῶμεν!). That day to day conduct is in mind here can scarcely be doubted; it is explicit in the choice of the metaphor 'walk' and by its use elsewhere in Paul (Rom. 6.4; 13.13; 14.15; I Cor. 3.3; 7.17; etc.).[118]

(*b*) What Paul means by this in practice comes to clear expression in the sharp antithesis he draws between law and Spirit. Rom. 7.6: Christians are defined precisely as those who are 'discharged from the law . . . so that we serve *not* under the old written code but in the new life of the Spirit'. II Cor. 3.6: the new covenant is characterized *not* by a written code, but by the Spirit; 'the written code kills, but the Spirit gives life'. See also Rom. 6.14 (not law but grace); 8.2; Gal. 5.16 (where the answer to libertinism and antinomianism is not law but Spirit). In these passages Paul clearly has in mind the tremendous sense of liberation and renewal which the experience of God's grace/Spirit brought to him; the *life* of the Spirit had set him free from the letter of the law (cf. Rom. 8.2; II Cor. 3.17; Gal. 5.1, 13). In particular, it is clear from Rom. 2.28f.; II Cor. 3.3 and Phil. 3.3 that Paul identified this experience of new inner vitality towards God with the prophetic hope of a circumcised heart, the eschatological hope of the law written *within* (II Cor. 3.3 specifically alludes to Jer. 31.31–4).[119] Hence worship was no longer a matter of obligation and requirement, but a *spontaneous* urge to praise God (Phil. 3.3). In ethics for Paul the primary driving force was no longer obedience to a written law, but *obedience to an inward compulsion* (the law written on the heart, the law of the Spirit). This inward conviction shaping both motive and action he also refers to as 'the mind of Christ' (I Cor. 2.16; Phil. 2.5),[120] and in Rom. 14.22f. as the 'faith/conviction (πίστις) that you have', that is, concerning a particular issue of Christian conduct. Indeed Paul goes so far as to assert that 'whatever (decision, conduct) does not emerge from conviction is sin' (Rom. 14.23).[121] Conduct as well as charisma is to be determined by 'the measure of faith' (Rom. 12.3 – see above pp. 211f.).

(c) Here too we must note Paul's use of δοκιμάζειν (*dokimazein*), which refers to ethical decision making in Rom. 2.18; 12.2; 14.22; Eph. 5.10; Phil. 1.10 (cf. Col. 1.9f.). The word means properly 'to test, and if the test warrants it, to approve'.[122] That the same law/Spirit antithesis is in Paul's mind in the use of this word is implied by Rom. 2.18: the Jew is able to make his moral distinctions and approve what is right because he receives instruction from the law. But the Christian's capacity for ethical decision depends rather on 'the renewal of his mind' (Rom. 12.2). By this last phrase Paul evidently has in mind that fundamental reshaping and transformation of inner motivations and moral consciousness (νοῦς)[123] which he elsewhere thinks of as the writing of the law in the heart, and as the work of the eschatological Spirit (II Cor. 3.3).[124] It is not something accomplished once and for all at any one time (conversion or in subsequent experiences); Paul understands it rather as a process (μεταμορφοῦσθε –

present). *Dokimazein* therefore does not mean here 'testing',[125] testing, that is, by some norm or standard whether implanted once for all within or inscribed on tablets of stone without. It denotes rather a spontaneous awareness of what is God's will in the concrete situation and the ethical dilemma of the ever new here and now, and a recognition and approval of that will as good, acceptable and perfect. Cullmann defined this charisma of revelation well:

The working of the Holy Spirit shows itself chiefly in the 'testing' (δοκιμάζειν), that is in *the capacity of forming the correct Christian ethical judgment at each given moment* . . . This 'testing' is the key to all Christian ethics . . . Certainly of moral judgment in the concrete sense is in the last analysis the one great fruit that the Holy Spirit . . . produces in the individual man.[126]

It is no objection to this understanding of *dokimazein* that in Phil. 1.9f. Paul thinks of *dokimazein* as the consequence of 'abounding love'.[127] For the overflow of love in the heart is but another way of talking about the experience of grace/Spirit (cf. particularly Rom. 5.5); it is the inner compulsion of love (or Spirit) which expresses itself in acts of love (or walking κατὰ πνεῦμα) (cf. Rom. 8.4 with 13.8–10; Gal. 5.13f. with 5.16ff.). For Paul love is not so much a moral principle to be discerned and then applied in each individual case. It is much more the inner compulsion of God's Spirit coming to concrete expression in loving word and act.[128] So in Phil. 1.9 the way in which Paul conceives love overflowing into *dokimazein* is through ἐπίγνωσις (knowledge – see above pp.221f. and n.111) and αἴσθησις, where αἴσθησις probably means a more inspirational (charismatic) perception, sense or feeling for what is right and appropriate in the given situation.[129] Likewise in the parallel passage in Col. 1.9f., a lifestyle and conduct 'worthy of the Lord' is possible only for the man who is 'filled with the knowledge (ἐπίγνωσις) of his will in all spiritual wisdom and understanding' (ἐν πάσῃ σοφίᾳ καὶ συνέσει πνευματικῇ); πνευματικῇ, in the position of emphasis, characterizes the believer's wisdom and understanding as charismatic, revelatory, in contrast with all merely human equivalents (2.18, 23; cf. I Cor. 2.5f., 13; II Cor. 1.12).[130]

All this does not mean that Paul's ethic is solely enthusiastic, depending on some 'inner light', or ever fresh revelations. The law still stands as God's standard of righteousness, as the individual commands which pepper the second half of Paul's letters[131] and such passages as Rom. 3.31; 7.12–14; 8.4; 13.8–10 indicate; and Paul also speaks of the 'law of Christ' as a norm for relationships (Gal. 6.2; cf. I Cor. 9.21). His ethical teaching can be fairly described as an ellipse round the two foci, the mind of Christ and the law of Christ.[132] Paul was well aware of the dangers of a liberty which degenerated into license (Gal. 5.13ff.). Nevertheless, it is not the individual commands and exhortations which give Paul's ethic its distinctive character; there is nothing in his catalogue of virtues and house rules which distinguishes them from Stoic and Jewish formulations.[133] *The distinctive element in Paul's ethics is the charismatic recognition of God's will and the inward compulsion of love.*[134]

Here again we must guard against the tendency to play down or ignore the reality and vitality of Paul's experience of God. And not simply *Paul's* experience: when Paul urged his readers to walk by the Spirit and be led by the Spirit we must presume that they shared something at least of the vitality of that experience.[135] The Spirit here cannot be reduced to some rationally construed claim of God, nor love to a generalized ethical principle. Both denote the particular conviction and compulsion in a given situation, not necessarily independent of external norms but not necessarily dependent on them either. In a similar way the attempt to reduce Paul's concept of guidance to the level of Bible study misunderstands Paul at a fundamental level and runs a grave risk of falling back into the Jewish formalism[136] from which Paul's experience of the Spirit liberated him.

40.6   Finally under the heading of revelation, we must note the use of φανερόω in II Cor. 2.14; 3.3; 4.10f. – particularly 4.10f.: '. . . always carrying in the body the death of Jesus, so that the life of Jesus may also be manifested (φανερωθῇ) in our bodies. For while we live we are continually being handed over to death, for Jesus' sake, so that the life of Jesus may be manifested (φανερωθῇ) in our mortal flesh'. We touch here the deeper layers of Paul's so-called 'Christ-mysticism', and we must delay further consideration of these passages till chapter X. For the moment we must simply note that Paul conceives of revelation as taking place also through the character of his life and ministry. God and the risen Jesus manifest themselves not only in vision, or prophetic utterance, or charismatic conviction, but through Paul's very existence in its character of dying and living. There are important corollaries here for the understanding of religious experience and of the charismatic Spirit which we shall explore in chapter X.

§41. INSPIRED UTTERANCE

'Spirit and speaking belong together.'[137] This was true of the earliest community, as we saw above (pp. 170f.); and it is certainly true for

Paul. For Paul it was a matter of first importance that the Spirit inspires the believer to speak out. Revelation is not confined to visions with their 'unutterable utterances', nor inspiration to motivation and conduct. *Charis*, more often than not, will come to expression in the charisma of inspired speech. This point has already been illustrated by our examination of the phrases *utterance of wisdom, utterance of knowledge* (§ 40.4 above): it is not *sophia* or *gnōsis* which is the charisma so much as the inspired utterance which gives some insight into 'the depths of God' (I Cor. 2.10), and/or some counsel arising out of divine *sophia* or *gnōsis*. We need say no more about these charismata.

41.1   Proclamation. Of central importance for Paul was his firm conviction that his own preaching of the gospel was charismatic; that is, in particular instances he could remember and name, his preaching was not with words of his own choice and their effect on his hearers owed little or nothing to him. The key passages here are I Thess. 1.5f. and I Cor. 2.4f. I Thess. 1.5 – the gospel came to the Thessalonians not in word only but in power and in the Holy Spirit and with full conviction (πληροφορία). That is to say, their experience of the gospel was not simply that of hearing Paul speaking, or of being persuaded by the logic of what he said. Paul spoke, it was his words that were heard; but the experience was that of being addressed by God's Spirit, of being grasped by divine power, of being convinced beyond doubt of the existential truth of what Paul said quite apart from any considerations of reason or logic.[138] The gospel was experienced not as a human word from without, but as a divine energy within (2.13). Their joy on receiving the word was not the pleasure of mind or body ('in much affliction'); it was 'joy of the Holy Spirit', charismatic, inspired joy (1.6).

A similar contrast is drawn between human word and divine power, but with much greater sharpness, in I Cor. 2.4f.; 'my speech and my message were not in persuasive words of wisdom ('did not sway you with subtle arguments' – NEB), but in demonstration (ἀποδείξει) of Spirit and power, so that your faith might not rest in the wisdom of men but in the power of God'. Particularly interesting is Paul's use of the word ἀπόδειξις, the sole occurrence in the NT. It is a more or less technical term in rhetoric and denotes a compelling conclusion drawn out from accepted premises.[139] But Paul's point is precisely that the ἀπόδειξις of his message was nothing to do with his skill as a rhetorician, nothing to do with arguments and proofs; it was ἀπόδειξις of Spirit and power. That is to say, their experience was not so much of intellectual persuasion, but rather of being grasped by divine power, of being compelled with a whole-hearted conviction to accept and affirm Paul's message, despite Paul's obvious deficiencies as a rhetorician! The impact of Paul's message at a non-rational level was so over-whelming and compelling, so conscious were they of the power of God, that aesthetic distaste for Paul's style and logic counted for nothing.[140] We should note that the combination of divine power and human deficiency and weakness is important for Paul; it is power *in weakness, through weakness* which distinguishes Paul's understanding of *charisma* from that of his Corinthian opponents (cf. I Thess. 1.6 – joy even in affliction).[141]

Other passages in which Paul emphasizes the charismatic power of inspired proclamation are Rom. 1.16 ('power into salvation'); II Cor. 4.4–6 (cf. 3.18); Eph. 6.17 ('for sword, take that which the Spirit gives you – the words that come from God' NEB, cf. JB).[142] In Rom. 15.18 he draws attention to the power of the Spirit which accompanied his proclamation by word and deed; so too the Galatians experienced both Spirit and the outworking of this power in miracles when they received the gospel (Gal. 3.5).[143] Elsewhere Paul's thought focusses not so much on the impact of his gospel as on his dependence on inspiration in preaching – particularly Eph. 6.19 ('pray for me, that I may be given a word when I open my mouth to speak, and may boldly (ἐν παρρησίᾳ) make known the mystery of the gospel') and Col. 4.3. Similarly, Paul is conscious that the openness,[144] the boldness (παρρησία) with which he has spoken in the past is itself a charisma, something given with the inspired utterance (II Cor. 3.12; Eph. 6.19f.; I Thess. 2.2; cf. Philemon 8; and see above p. 171).

41.2 *Prophecy* (προφητεία – Rom. 12.6; I Cor. 12.10; 13.2; 14.6; I Thess. 5.20). If the inspired utterance of the gospel plays a role of critical importance in creating the community of faith (Rom. 10.17), the inspired utterance of prophecy plays the equivalent role in building it up. The importance of prophecy for Paul can easily be demonstrated. In all the various lists and discussions of charismata in Paul's letters the only constant member is 'prophecy' or 'prophet' (Rom. 12.6–8; I Cor. 12.8–10, 28ff.; 13.1–3, 8ff.; 14.1–5, 6ff., 26–32; Eph. 4.11; I Thess. 5.19–22).[145] And whenever Paul makes any attempt to classify the gifts in terms of importance, prophecy is given preference over all the rest (I Cor. 14.1 – 'Make love your aim and earnestly desire the spiritual gifts, especially that you may prophesy' (RSV); I Thess. 5.19f. – 'Do not stifle inspiration, and do not despise prophetic utterances' (NEB)); only in the two passages where Paul speaks of gifted men (prophet) rather than of the gift (prophecy) do prophets fall into second place – behind apostles (I Cor. 12.28; Eph. 4.11; cf. Eph. 2.20).

What was prophecy in Paul's view? Does he in fact think of it as inspired utterance? The question arises because in the Greek world προφήτης did not necessarily denote someone who spoke under inspiration. In particular Plato carefully distinguished two kinds of prophecy.[146] One was mantic prophecy, the prophecy of *inspiration*, where the prophet was possessed by the god and became only a mouthpiece for the divine utterance. The other was the prophecy of *interpretation*, the conscious art of the augur, where prophecy was an acquired skill, the ability to interpret signs and omens, and where the prophet remained quite self possessed. Thus in the case of the most famous of the Greek oracles, at Delphi, there was a clear difference between the Pythia who spoke in a state of ecstasy, and the prophet whose task it was to interpret the Pythia's saying to the inquirer, the one speaking under divine constraint, the other using rational discernment.

The relevance of these distinctions to the question above becomes apparent as soon as we realize that Paul, unlike Luke, seems to make an analogous distinction between glossolalia and prophecy. He certainly goes out of his way to distinguish and distance prophecy from ecstatic inspiration. He never uses words like μάντις and ἐνθουσιασμός for Christian prophecy. On the contrary, it is clear from I Cor. 14.15, 19 that he prizes prophecy because it is a 'speaking with the mind' in contrast to the non-rational utterance of glossolalia, (and the 'unutterable utterances' of II Cor. 12.4). Similarly in 14.23f. it is only glossolalia which the unbelieving outsider describes as madness; even if 'all are uttering prophecies' (at the same time?) the response is very different. In consequence there has been a tendency in some quarters to understand prophecy in the Pauline churches more in terms of the second kind of prophecy distinguished by Plato – that is, prophecy simply as preaching, as exposition of previous revelation, as interpretation of traditional material (OT and traditions about Jesus) for the new times and situations of these churches.[147]

But this will not do. (1) For Paul prophecy is a word of revelation. It does not denote the delivery of a previously prepared sermon; it is not a word that can be summoned up to order, or a skill that can be learned;[148] it is a spontaneous utterance, a revelation given in words to the prophet to be delivered as it is given (14.30).[149] At this point Paul stands wholly within the (Hebraic) tradition of prophecy as inspired utterance.[150] (2) The parallel with Plato's distinction between prophecy of inspiration and prophecy of interpretation breaks down. Prophecy is not to glossolalia as interpretation is to inspired utterance. Glossolalia does require interpretation, but that is a separate charisma from prophecy ('interpretation of tongues' – see below §41.8). In fact prophecy itself requires some sort of evaluation ('discerning of spirits' – see below §41.3), so that Pauline prophecy is, if anything, more analogous to prophecy of inspiration in Plato's distinction. (3) The parallel also breaks down because it is not Paul's intention to set 'speaking with the mind' and 'speaking with the Spirit' in antithesis. As I Cor. 14.19 makes clear, the antithesis is between 'speaking with the mind' and 'speaking in a tongue'.[151] That is to say, he contrasts prophecy and glossolalia not as to inspiration, but as to intelligibility: prophecy is as much inspired speech, as much a 'speaking with the Spirit', as much a charisma, as glossolalia; the difference is that glossolalia is unintelligible whereas prophecy is intelligible (with the Spirit *and* with the mind). (4) Finally we may recall Paul's counsel to the Romans, that prophecy should be 'according to the proportion of faith'. As we saw above (§39.4) this last phrase is best understood as a reference to the speaker's consciousness and confidence of inspiration. When that sense of inspiration ceases he should desist (cf. I Cor. 14.30). In short, *prophecy in Paul cannot denote anything other than inspired speech.* And prophecy as charisma is neither skill nor aptitude nor talent; the *charisma is the actual speaking forth of words given by the Spirit in a particular situation and ceases when the words cease.*

Why is prophecy so important for Paul? The one sentence answer is, Because it builds up (οἰκοδομεῖ) the assembly (I Cor. 14.4). We shall see in chapter IX how fundamental this principle of οἰκοδομή is to Paul (§49.2). In the meantime, because Paul spends so much time speaking about prophecy in I Cor. 14, we are in a position to see what 'building up' actually means in the case of prophecy.

(a) 14.3, 31 – he who prophesies speaks words of upbuilding, and encouragement and consolation (οἰκοδομὴν καὶ παράκλησιν καὶ παραμυθίαν). It is difficult to distinguish the last two words: both include the ideas of admonition and comfort.[152] Prophecy builds up because the inspired utterance speaks to the situation of need in the assembly at the time, whether the need be for a word of understanding sympathy (cf. I Cor. 12.26a), or for a word of challenge and rebuke to careless or slipshod or detrimental activities (cf. Rom. 12.8; and as example of such exhortations, I Cor. 1.10; II Cor. 10.1ff.; Phil. 4.2; or perhaps Paul is thinking of more general, less specific exhortations like Rom. 12.1f.; 15.30; Eph. 4.1ff.; I Thess. 4.10f.). That Paul could so describe prophecy strongly suggests that he had experienced or witnessed such prophetic utterances in the various assemblies (cf. II Cor. 1.3ff.).

(*b*) 14.6, 26, 30 – prophecy built up because it often came as a word of revelation. The frequency with which Paul speaks of revelation in I Cor. 14 indicates that it was a regular feature of the assembly and a typical form of the inspired utterances for Paul.[153] Indeed prophecy and revelation are near synonyms in 14.26–32. Our study of the charisma of revelation above gives us some ideas of what Paul has in mind in these passages: the word of revelation would shed new light on the salvation event of Jesus Christ, or on the relation between the exalted Lord and his community or the cosmos, whether present or future, or would reveal some practical course of action for an individual or group. It would include both fore-telling and forth-telling. We certainly cannot assume that prophecy concerned itself only with laying down and elaborating matters of doctrine (prophecy as the raw material of systematic theology); or only with giving advice on day to day matters of ethical concern and decision. The breadth of Paul's concept of revelation was something we noted above, and we cannot assume any less for prophecy.

Prophecy as revelation may of course overlap with prophecy as exhortation and consolation; the revealing word may also be a challenging or comforting word. Within the Pauline corpus we have one fairly certain example of a prophetic revelation which would bring comfort – I Thess. 4.15ff. Paul passes on to the Thessalonians a word of prophecy ('a word of the Lord');[154] it had been revealed to him in verbal (rather than visionary) form that those believers who died before the parousia would not thereby be disadvantaged or left behind, but would in fact forestall those left alive for they would rise and be with the Lord in the air first. Perhaps the 'mystery' of I Cor. 15.51f., and even the 'mystery' of Rom. 11.25f., were similarly unveiled to Paul by a prophetic word given directly to himself or through another; though in view of its scriptural 'proof' the latter is probably best taken as a 'teaching' rather than a prophecy (see below §41.4).

(*c*) I Cor. 14.22 – prophecy also builds up because it serves as 'a sign for believers'. The connection of thought in these verses, 14.20–5, is not at all self-evident and has caused much confusion. The exegesis becomes clearer if we assume that the passage is polemically directed against those in Corinth who regard speaking in tongues too highly. As the form of v. 22 suggests, this faction have maintained that glossolalia is a sign for believers, that is, a proof of pneumatic status and authority.[155] Paul refutes this. The only relevant passage in the law which mentions unintelligible utterance is Isa. 28.11–12: to those who have paid no heed to God's (intelligible) word through the prophets, God will speak through the Assyrian invaders; in other words, the alien tongue of the invading army will be an expression of God's judgment on Judah. Thus the unintelligible utterance of glossolalia is a sign not for believers but for unbelievers – a sign of divine judgment, not of divine pleasure – a sign, that is, not of their closeness to God but of their distance from God.[156] If we are right so far, it means that Paul does not take up the Corinthians on their own terms; if it is a question of self-edification then he has already granted that glossolalia serves this end (I Cor. 14.4). But in the assembly the chief object is the edification of others (14.1–5), and judged on these terms he has already shown that glossolalia serves no useful purpose (14.6–19). The only purpose of glossolalia so far as others is concerned is as a sign of judgment on unbelief (14.21–22a).[157] The irony is that only faith recognizes a 'sign' to be such. So even if the whole assembly speaks in tongues[158] the unbeliever receives no revelation; it does not bring home to him his unbelief; the only significance he draws from it is that they are all mad (v. 23). In short, glossolalia in itself serves no useful purpose whatsoever in the assembly, far less as a sign of superior spirituality and authority. The only role which can be claimed for it from the law is that of serving as a sign of judgment on unbelievers; but glossolalia fails to fulfil even that role since his unbelief prevents the unbeliever from recognizing it as a sign (cf. Matt. 12.39/Luke 11.29).

That which can be described as a sign is prophecy[159] but 'sign' in what sense? It cannot be sign of judgment as in v. 22a;[160] for then Paul could not deny it that role in respect of unbelievers (v. 22b), since in vv. 24f. prophecy serves precisely as a sign of judgment to unbelievers in their unbelief; the prophetic words bring conviction of divine judgment on the secrets of their hearts. The parallel between glossolalia and prophecy at this point means only that both are a sign – not a sign of judgment, but a sign. Prophecy is a sign, as glossolalia is a sign, in that both reveal God's attitude – the one God's attitude towards (wilful) unbelief (hence a sign of judgment), the other God's attitude towards faith. Prophecy by its inspiration *and* content reveals that God is present in the midst of the assembly – even the unbeliever confesses this (vv. 24f.). As glossolalia confirms the unbeliever in his unbelief (v. 23 – 'You are mad' = God is *not* here), so prophecy confirms the believer in his faith (v. 25 – God is here).[161]

In short, Paul's description of prophecy as a sign for believers is determined almost entirely by the contrast he wishes to draw with glossolalia. 'Sign for believers' is simply another way of saying prophecy is of value in the assembly whereas glossolalia in itself is of no value whatsoever in the assembly. What this means in particular instances we have to glean from other descriptions of prophecy in this chapter – vv. 3, 6, 26, 30f. (see above), not excluding vv. 24f. (see below).

(d) 14.24f. Although the formulation of this passage is determined by the contrast just examined, we would not be unjustified in recognizing here a further way in which prophecy builds up the assembly. In vv. 24f. prophecy lays bare the secrets of the unbeliever's heart. But no doubt Paul knew of many instances when a prophetic word within the worshipping assembly had brought conviction and a deeper humbling and commitment to a believer or group of believers. We saw in chapter IV that a charismatic insight into the innermost heart of certain individuals was one of the characteristics of Jesus' prophetic ministry – as indeed of the phenomenon of (charismatic) prophecy wherever it appears within the history of religions.[162] Almost certainly this is what Paul has in mind here – various cases where the words which the prophet felt compelled to speak had struck home with (humanly) unexpected and unintended relevance and force in the consciences and hearts of particular individuals.[163] Perhaps we should recognize some such prophetic words in those passages which Käsemann has designated 'sentences of holy law' – particularly I Cor. 3.17; 14.38; 16.22a; Gal. 1.9; cf. I Cor. 14.13, 28, 30, 35, 37.[164]

If we are rightly interpreting the mind of Paul at this point (I Cor. 14.24f.), then we gain an important insight into the importance of prophecy for the Christian community. Prophecy prevents a man pretending to be other than he is – prevents the believer hiding behind a mask of pretended righteousness, of apparent spirituality. At any time the prophetic word may expose him for what he is. He dare not take refuge in the image he portrays to the world, in his reputation, in arguments of self-justification. Where the prophetic Spirit is present honesty with oneself and about oneself is indispensable (cf. I Thess. 2.4).[165] Moreover, and more important, whereas glossolalia draws the hearers' attention to the speaker by giving an impression of spirituality (as presumably the Corinthian faction thought) or of madness (I Cor. 14.23), prophecy makes the hearer conscious only of God (14.24f.).[166] In short, *prophecy edifies because it does not exalt man but humbles him, making him aware that he stands before God in all his vulnerability.*

To sum up, Paul values prophecy so highly because it is not only a charisma, but a charisma which more than any other builds up the community of believers in their faith and common life and worship. It has this effect because, unlike glossolalia, it speaks to other men and speaks to the *whole* man.[167] That is to say, prophecy communicates at the level of the mind; it does not absolve the believer or the believing community from reasoning about their faith; on the contrary, where prophecy is active the community is compelled to think about its faith and life even more (see further below §§41.3, 49). But at the same time prophecy does not permit faith to be solely a matter of rational thought. For in a wholly existential way prophecy opens up the community to itself and the believer to himself; it makes the believer conscious of wider dimensions of reality and sets him in the context of ultimate reality; it makes him aware that he stands naked in the presence of God himself. This charisma is the guarantor of spiritual health and growth. Without it the community cannot exist as the body of Christ; it has been abandoned by God.

41.3   *Evaluation of inspired utterances* (διακρίσεις πνευμάτων – I Cor. 12.10). It is important to realize at the outset that *this gift* ('discerning of spirits' AV) *forms a pair with prophecy*. It is not to be thought of as an independent gift;[168] rather it provides a *test* of prophetic utterance and a *control* against its abuse (so I Cor. 14.29) – the equivalent in fact to the role filled by 'interpretation of tongues' in relation to glossolalia (12.10; 14.27f.).[169]

But what is 'discerning of spirits'? The precise sense Paul intends by each of the words is not entirely clear. The use of πνεῦμα in the plural is striking, and the related plurals in 14.12, 32 (also '*my* spirit – 14.14) have caused some perplexity. Either Paul's language reflects the view that there are many spirits at large, any one of which may take possession of a man and so become 'mine' (cf. I John 4.1ff.).[170] Or he is using πνευμάτων (spirits) in the sense of πνευματικῶν (spiritual gifts)[171] – just as he can use *charis* and *charisma* synonymously (see above §§37.2, 38.2). With διακρίσεις (*diakriseis*) the almost unanimous opinion has been that it denotes *distinguishing* between (different) spirits (RSV, NEB); that is, charismatic discerning as to whether the source of inspiration is good or evil (whether 'from God' or 'of antichrist' in the language of I John 4.2f.).[172] But recently the case has been strongly argued that *diakrisis* denotes rather *interpretation* of inspired revelations, on the analogy of the ability to interpret dreams and oracles.[173]

In fact there may be little ground for dispute between these two sets of alternatives. Paul's meaning may be less precise than either and so be able to embrace the different nuances of each. The key to

correct exegesis here, as so often in I Corinthians, is an appreciation
of the situation addressed by Paul.[174] It is evident from I Cor. 14.12
that the Corinthians were eager to experience inspiration ('eager for
spirits'), particularly the inspired utterance of glossolalia (14.6-12).
We may assume from the implied rebuke of 12.2 that this frequently
involved the assembly (or certain members) working themselves up
into a state of spiritual excitement, leaving themselves open to passions and powers (spirits?) which swept them away (ἤγεσθε ἀπαγόμενοι
– 12.2) in an outpouring of glossolalic ecstasy, and which brought no
benefit to other believers let alone unbelieving outsiders (cf. 14.23 –
μαίνεσθε – see above n. 161; 14.27f.; 14.33a – 'disorder, confusion';
14.40).[175] Paul's response is twofold: he does not forbid or reject
inspired utterance out of hand, but stresses the superior value of intelligible speech (14.14–25); and he recommends certain controls to
prevent the 'eagerness for spirits' from degenerating into an abandonment to any and every impulse of inspiration (14.26–33). It is in this
latter role that the charisma *diakrisis pneumatōn* comes into its own
(14.29 – διακρινέτωσαν). In this context *diakrisis pneumatōn* is best understood as *an evaluation, an investigating, a testing, a weighing of the prophetic
utterance* by the rest (of the assembly or of the prophets) to determine
both its source as to inspiration and its significance for the assembly
(source and significance being two sides of the one coin, so that the
evaluation includes both interpretation of spirits = spiritual utterances, and distinguishing of spirits = sources of inspiration). That it
is described as a charisma presumably means that the evaluation was
not simply a matter of logical and rational analysis but ultimately a
sense shared by (most of) those involved that this word was (or was
not) a word of the Spirit and that the significance discerned in it was
in accord with the mind of the Spirit (cf. I Cor. 2.16; 7.40).

   This interpretation finds confirmation from three other closely
related passages. (*a*) I Cor. 12.3. It would be difficult to deny that this
verse provides one particular rule of thumb for evaluating spiritual
utterances. It is quite likely, though many disagree,[176] that during
the Corinthian worship some member(s) of the assembly had cried
out under inspiration, 'Jesus be cursed!' Possibly there were those at
Corinth influenced by gnostic ideas of the fundamental impurity of
matter who consequently maintained a distinction between the man
Jesus and the heavenly spiritual being Christ: to identify this Christ
with the physical human being Jesus seriously dishonoured Christ
and put the whole (gnostic) way of salvation in question, hence,
'*Jesus* be cursed!', '*Christ* is Lord!'.[177] In the Christian community at
Corinth, already heavily influenced by gnostic-type ideas at other

points (see above pp.120f. and §40.4), such an utterance as 'Jesus be
cursed!' would not be recognized immediately as false teaching,
especially if it was spoken under inspiration in the assembly. So the
question was put to Paul,[178] and Paul in a single sentence gives an
easy test to apply to such cases. Where the subject matter of inspired
utterance is the relation between the earthly Jesus and the exalted
Lord, the mark of the Spirit is the confession '*Jesus is Lord!*'[179]
Alternatively, if this explanation is too sophisticated and the theology
implied too advanced for the time, we may simply have to recognize
I Cor. 12.3a as the cry of pneumatic licence rather than of gnostic
Christology.[180]

Here then we have one example of evaluating spiritual utterances,
a case of determining whether the utterance in question was from the
Spirit of God or from other sources ('distinguishing spirits'), and
whether therefore any heed should be paid to it. Obviously the rule
of thumb arrived at here would not be of very wide application (not
many inspired utterances would run so sharply counter to the basic
kerygma); so we must assume that it is a particular application of a
wider test (the criterion of kerygmatic tradition – see below §49.2).
But that 12.3 provides *a* test of inspiration can hardly be doubted.[181]

(*b*) I Cor. 2.13: 'we speak of the things given us by God not in
words given us by human wisdom but in words given us by the Spirit,
πνευματικοῖς πνευματικὰ συνκρίνοντες'. Once again it is not precisely clear
what Paul means by this last phrase: perhaps, 'comparing the
spiritual gifts and revelations (which we already possess) with the
spiritual gifts and revelations (which we are to receive) and judging
them thereby' (cf. II Cor. 10.12);[182] alternatively, 'interpreting
spiritual truths by means of spiritual words';[183] or again, 'interpreting spiritual truth to those who have the Spirit' (NEB, so RSV).[184]
That some sort of evaluation of *pneumatika* is envisaged is clear
enough from the context;[185] the end in view being that believers
might come to know (that is come to a better understanding and
fuller experience of) the things given them by God (2.12).

Furthermore, that συγκρίνω denotes evaluation in order to reach a
decision concerning (that is, judgment), is suggested by vv. 14–15
and the parallel use of ἀνακρίνω in these verses.[186] *Pneumatika* (spiritual
things/gifts) should be subjected to scrutiny and evaluated, but not
pneumatikoi (spiritual people). The charisma of evaluating does not
include the passing of opinions about this or that man's worth or
status; it is confined to the investigation and evaluation of particular
charismata on the occasion of their manifestation. We may note in
passing that a similar but more far-reaching restriction on *diakrisis* is

spelled out in Rom. 14: it must *not* be exercised over matters of valid disagreement (14.1, 14),[187] for such evaluation inevitably leads some believers to pass judgment (κρίνω) on others (14.3f., 13), a prerogative reserved for God alone (14.10; I Cor. 4.3f.). The only *person* with respect to whom the believer should exercise *diakrisis* is himself (I Cor. 11.31; so 11.28; II Cor. 13.5; Gal. 6.4).

(c) I Thess. 5.19–22 – 'Do not stifle inspiration, and do not despise prophetic utterances, but bring them all to the test (πάντα δὲ δοκιμάζετε) and then keep what is good in them and avoid the bad of whatever kind' (NEB). As most commentators agree, these verses form a single unit. The admonition to 'test everything' is not simply a general homily loosely or accidentally attached to the word about prophecy. Paul no doubt knew both from the history of Jewish prophecy (see above p. 175 and n. 87) and from his own experience how the prophetic spirit could be abused (cf. II Thess. 2.2). He would hardly insist on prophecy being given a completely free rein without adding some qualification. 'Test everything' obviously provides that cautionary qualification (cf. I John 4.1 and *Didache* 11.11, where δοκιμάζειν is used in the same sense of a control to which prophets and prophetic utterances must be subjected).[188] So too vv. 21b–22 are almost certainly a continuation of the same theme. Paul may well be echoing a saying (of Jesus?) about money changers – that is, those who have learned to distinguish good (that is, genuine) money from bad (that is, counterfeit).[189] If 'the good' means 'the genuine', then what Paul is talking about is a testing which determines the source and nature of the inspired utterance ('discerning of spirits'). Furthermore, in v. 22 'evil' is probably to be taken as an adjective rather than a noun – 'every bad kind' (that is, of prophecy).[190] I Thess. 5.21a therefore stands in the same relation to 5.20 as I Cor. 12.10c to 12.10b, or I Cor. 14.29b to 14.29a.[191] Prophecy is to be strongly encouraged in the assembly, but only when the prophetic utterances are subjected to evaluation by the community, an evaluation aimed at determining whether the word is a genuine word of the Spirit, or a word to be ignored and rejected.

To sum up, 'discerning of spirits' is to be understood as *evaluation of prophetic utterances, an investigating and interpreting which throws light on their source and their significance.* The importance of this charisma as a regulative force within the charismatic community can hardly be overemphasized, and we must return to it when we discuss the communal dimension of the charismata in chapter IX.

41.4   *Teaching* (διδαχή – I Cor. 14.6, 26). In Paul's view the activity of teaching (διδάσκων) is also a charismatic act (Rom. 12.7). Paul certainly uses the noun in a non-charismatic sense for a body of teaching, something his readers already accept and can therefore use as a check on beliefs and life (Rom. 6.17, 16.17). But in I Cor. 14.6, 26 he obviously has in mind *particular* teachings. That a charismatic insight is in view is strongly suggested by the companion contributions to the assembly's worship listed in vv. 6 and 26; v. 6 – revelation, knowledge, prophecy;[192] in v. 26 both 'hymn' and 'teaching' are probably thought of as spontaneous utterances, as 'revelation' and certainly 'tongue' and 'interpretation' are. Note also Col. 3.16 – 'teaching . . . one another with psalms, hymns and spiritual songs . . .'. As suggested above (p.186) the particular insights of teaching are probably to be distinguished from the particular utterances of prophecy in that prophecy would express a new word from God as such, whereas teaching would tend to denote more *a new insight into an old word from God*, into the traditions already accepted by the community as authoritative in some degree – viz., OT writings, tradition of Jesus' sayings, the gospel which they initially received (cf. I Cor. 11.2, 23; 15.3; II Thess. 2.15, 3.6).[193] Thus in Col. 3.16 the 'teaching' arises out of 'the word (λόγος) of Christ dwelling in you . . .'.

Such *charismatic exegesis* may be found in some of Paul's use of the OT – for example, Rom. 11.25ff.; I Cor. 9.8ff.; Gal. 3.8. Other expositions of OT passages are much more contrived and cannot be regarded as spontaneous insights (particularly Rom. 4.3–22; I Cor. 10.1–4; II Cor. 3.7–18; Gal. 4.21–31); but even in these cases Paul probably regarded the initial insight specifically as a charisma.[194] So too in I Cor. 14.6, 26 we should not exclude the possibility that the 'teaching' envisaged was an elaboration by the individual of an insight received some time prior to the assembly.[195] An example of charismatic instruction (παραγγελία) possibly based on a Jesus-word may be indicated in I Thess. 4.2. The word in question would probably be the same dominical logia which form the basis of his teaching in I Cor. 7 (that is, 7.10 – cf. I Thess. 4.3ff. with I Cor. 7) and I Cor. 9 (that is, 9.14 – cf. II Thess. 3.6ff. with I Cor. 9.15ff.).[196] That Paul is referring to instructions given under inspiration is probably indicated by the phrase 'through the Lord Jesus'.[197] Elsewhere in Paul the phrase often teeters on the brink of denoting an experience of God, of grace, of inspiration, and in Rom. 15.30; II Cor. 4.5; Gal. 1.1 and I Thess. 4.2, it seems to fall over the brink. However, the classic example of charismatic interpretation of a saying of Jesus, and its consequent reinterpretation of OT tradition, is probably Stephen's treatment of Jesus' words about the destruction of the temple and its restoration

(Acts 6.14 and 7.2–53).[198] If these inevitably tentative suggestions are justified, then it strengthens the claim that in Paul's understanding 'teaching' included both a recognition of traditional material as authoritative and an appreciation of the need for it to be interpreted and applied charismatically to the ever changing needs and situations of the believing communities (see further §§48.2, 58.2).

41.5   *Singing.* It is clear from I Cor. 14.15 that Paul recognizes a kind of *charismatic hymnody* – both a singing in tongues[199] (here = 'with the Spirit') and a singing with intelligible words ('with the mind'). Since Paul in this context seems to be thinking solely of inspired utterance, whether edifying the mind (prophecy)[200] or leaving it unfruitful (glossolalia), we must presume that both types of singing envisaged in 14.15 were spontaneous.[201] The same is likely to be true of the 'hymn' ($\psi\alpha\lambda\mu\acute{o}s$) in 14.26; although the possibility cannot be excluded that Paul is thinking also of a previously prepared (or inspired) song, or a psalm already known to the congregation.[202]

In the parallel passages, Eph. 5.19/Col. 3.16, Paul mentions three forms of singing – 'psalms, hymns and spiritual songs'. That Paul again has in mind charismatic singing is strongly suggested by three factors. The first is the preceding verse in Ephesians – 5.18f.: 'Do not get drunk with wine . . . but be filled with the Spirit, addressing one another in psalms, . . .'. This admonition is prompted presumably by a situation, actual or threatened, like that in I Cor. 11.20ff., where the common meal and Lord's Supper witnessed scenes of drunken roistering. Paul does not forbid all spontaneous singing, but urges a spontaneity that comes from the impulse of the Spirit and not from the stimulus of drink. The single voice evoking a particular theme or the whole assembly picking up a well-known chant or refrain would have some similarity (warmth and cheerfulness) to what today would be a sing-song round the piano in the village pub; but the inspiration behind the singing and the content of the words would no doubt be very different (5.19 – 'wholeheartedly to the Lord')!

Secondly, the same note of divine givenness, of impulse and theme coming from beyond, is struck in Col. 3.16 by the piling up of charismatic phraseology – 'word of God', 'in all wisdom', 'with grace'.[203] And thirdly, the word 'spiritual' used in both passages characterizes the song so described as one prompted by the Spirit and manifesting the Spirit.[204] It is not at all clear whether Paul in using three different terms intends any distinction between them,[205] so that the adjective ('spiritual') probably embraces all three nouns.[206]

Yet, even if 'spiritual' belongs solely to 'songs', the distinction between the first two members (psalms and hymns) and the third
(spiritual songs) would be not between established liturgical forms
and spontaneous song, but presumably between spontaneous singing
of intelligible words or familiar verses, and spontaneous singing in
tongues.[207]

We have no examples of glossolalic hymnody in the NT, but research over the past fifty years has uncovered a number of hymnic
forms (e.g. I Tim. 3.16; Phil. 2.6–11; Col. 1.15–20; Eph. 5.14), and
we may recognize in some of Paul's doxologies and other expressions
of deep feeling, utterances typical of the cries which must have
punctuated the worship of the Pauline assemblies (Rom. 11.33–6;
Gal. 1.5; Eph. 3.21; Phil. 4.20; (I Tim. 1.17; 6.15f.); II Cor. 1.3f.;
Eph. 1.3ff.; Rom. 7.25a; I Cor. 15.57; cf. Rev. 4.8, 11; 5.12f.; 7.10,
12; 11.15, 17f.; 15.3f.; 19.6–8).[208]

It is worth noting the verbs Paul uses with the three nouns –
'speaking to each other' (Eph. 5.19), 'teaching and admonishing one
another' (Col. 3.16). These indicate that the 'psalms, hymns and
spiritual songs' were not only vehicles of praise ('to the Lord', 'to
God'), but served also as a means of instruction (more easily remembered perhaps than a word of teaching – e.g. Col. 1.15–20), and
as a means of warning and encouraging (less personal and less painful
perhaps than a word of prophecy – e.g. Eph. 5.14).

41.6 *Prayer.* It is somewhat surprising that Paul never designates
prayer as a charisma, at least not in so many words.[209] On the other
hand, prayer for Paul is never simply a matter of saying (set) prayers;
prayer is praying, praying about particular people and particular
situations.[210] So there is inevitably a large degree of spontaneity
about all prayer for Paul. But in addition there is a praying which is
determined wholly by the Spirit, where the words and sentiments
come to the pray-er's lips as given from God – inspired utterance.
That is the implication in I Cor. 11.4f., 13, where praying and
prophesying are probably both to be thought of as charismatic
speech. Earlier in the same letter devotion to prayer is the other side of
the charisma of voluntary celibacy (I Cor. 7.5, 7 – see above pp. 206f.).
In Eph. 6.18 there is the exhortation specifically to 'pray at all times
in the Spirit' – 'pray on every occasion in the power of the Spirit'
(NEB): that is, in every specific situation hold yourselves open to the
prayer of the Spirit (cf. Eph. 5.18ff.; and see below Rom. 8.15f.,
26f.).[211] And in I Cor. 14.14–17 it is clearly prayer as inspired utterance which is in mind, both prayer in tongues and rational prayer.

Above all we have Paul's familiarity with the *abba*-prayer of Jesus
(see above §4) in Rom. 8.15f. and Gal. 4.6 and his description of
Spirit prayer in Rom. 8.26f.

Rom. 8.15f.: 'The Spirit you have received is not a spirit of slavery
leading you back to a life of fear, but a Spirit that makes us sons, enabling us to cry "Abba! Father!" In that cry the Spirit of God joins
with our spirit in testifying that we are God's children . . .' (NEB).
The suggestion has frequently been aired that Paul is thinking here of
liturgical usage in the assembly's prayers, perhaps specifically of the
Lord's Prayer (Luke 11.2).[212] This is unlikely.[213] The central theme
in these verses, as probably also in Gal. 4.6,[214] is the filial consciousness and assurance of the believer,[215] and the 'Abba' almost certainly
refers to a spontaneous expression of this sense of sonship in a cry of
exultation and trust – an inspired utterance. For one thing, a contrast
is drawn with 'a spirit of slavery' and 'a life of fear' (8.15), where
Paul most probably has in mind that inner questioning which so
often underlies a religious man's boasting – the inner insecurity and
lack of trust in God which seeks security in the letter of the law and
the conformity of ritual.[216] By contrast 'Spirit of sonship' must refer
to that inner confidence of belonging to God which is not the product
of anxious striving, but the given starting point of conduct (8.14) and
prayer.[217] Assurance for Paul, in other words, is not a matter of
arguing oneself back into belief, as though belief were simply a
rational matter, the acceptance of certain propositions. Nor is assurance a matter of suppressing inner doubts and questions in blind conformity to tradition, however hallowed. Assurance is *the consciousness
and confidence of sonship*. God does not only want men to be his sons;
he wants them to know it.

Second, the verb Paul uses in describing the *abba*-prayer both in
Rom. 8.15 and Gal. 4.6 is a very strong one – κράζειν – to cry out. It
can be used of a solemn proclamation (as in Rom. 9.27), but elsewhere in the NT its regular sense is 'to cry out loudly', so that it can
be used for the screams and shrieks of demoniacs (Mark 5.5; 9.26;
Luke 9.39).[218] The context of Rom. 8.15 and Gal. 4.6 suggests that
κράζειν in these verses has more of the latter sense than of the former –
that is, a cry of some intensity, probably a loud cry, and perhaps (but
less likely) an ecstatic cry.[219]

Third, 'in this cry the Spirit bears witness (συμμαρτυρεῖ) with our
spirit that we are God's children' (Rom. 8.16). The assurance of sonship is not a conclusion or inference drawn from the fact that the
community says 'Abba'. It is rather an inner confidence borne in
upon the believer by the consciousness that it was not simply he him-

self and of himself that had cried 'Abba' (κράζομεν – Rom. 8.15); the word was something given him, uttered through his lips by the Spirit (κρᾶζον – Gal. 4.6).[220] In this verse the twin aspects of *charismatic* (as distinct from ecstatic) *consciousness* come to fairly clear expression: not only *the consciousness of being moved upon by divine power*, of words being given, of God acting through words or actions, but also *the conscious willingness to be so used, the awareness and acceptance of the words and actions as one's own*; in a word, *the consciousness of partnership, of cooperating with God, of grace*. In both Rom. 8.15f. and Gal. 4.6 therefore it is clear that Paul is speaking of prayer as inspired utterance.

In Rom. 8.26f. also Paul seems obviously to be speaking of charismatic prayer. But what sort of prayer is this which is the complement of the believer's inability to pray aright ('We do not know how we ought to pray'), and which comes to expression in wordless groans ('but the Spirit himself intercedes on our behalf with inarticulate groans – στεναγμοῖς ἀλαλήτοις)? Some have suggested that Paul is not actually speaking of the prayer of believers, but of the Spirit's intercession on our behalf in the heavenly sphere.[221] But the role of heavenly intercessor is filled by Jesus (Rom. 8.34); for Paul the characteristic work of the Spirit is not apart from believers but in and through them. This is particularly clear in Rom. 8.26f. where the thought follows on closely from 8.15f., as commentators frequently recognize.[222] Others have taken the στεναγμοῖς ἀλαλήτοις as glossolalia, either the worldless stammering of ecstasy,[223] or with ἀλαλήτοις understood in the sense of 'unutterable' rather than 'wordless', 'not unspoken but unspeakable'.[224] But neither of these interpretations fits well with Paul's understanding of glossolalia as spoken language, albeit the language of angels (see below §41.7), and we may not assume, as Käsemann does, that the abuse of glossolalia in Corinth either was repeated in Rome or had wholly determined Paul's train of thought here. Would his Roman readers have understood such an allusion? His Spirit talk in the Romans letter is remarkably unguarded if 'enthusiasm' posed the very same threat in Rome as in Corinth (cf. Rom. 7.6; 8.2, 14), and his brief treatment of charismata in Rom. 12 contains no allusion whatsoever to glossolalia (though see further §46.2). It is probably better therefore to take στεναγμοῖς ἀλαλήτοις in a broader sense, so that it does not exclude glossolalia but may not be confined to it (cf. RSV – 'sighs too deep for words').[225] What Paul seems to have in mind is the only form of prayer left to the believer when he comes to the end of himself, frustrated by his own weakness (cf. Rom. 7.24; II Cor. 5.4) and baffled by his ignorance of God and of God's will. As he longs for the yet to be, the full adoption of sonship, the wholeness of redemption (Rom. 8.22f.; cf. I Cor. 13.12), the only way his consciousness of God, that is of the first fruits of the Spirit (Rom. 8.23), can come to expression is in an inarticulate groaning which confesses both his weakness and his dependence on God. Here again we see the two sides of charismatic consciousness, for Paul at any rate – *the consciousness of human impotence and the consciousness of divine power in and through that weakness* (cf. II Cor. 12.9f.).[226] It is this consciousness that the Spirit is acting in and through his complete impotence at the most fundamental level of his relationship with the Father which gives him confidence that the Spirit is at work in all his other relationships and circumstances (Rom. 8.28 – 'in everything he (the Spirit) cooperates for good with those who love God' – NEB).[227]

We have still to look at Paul's understanding of glossolalia; but it is already clear that *charismatic prayer played an important part in Paul's life as a Christian.*

41.7   *Glossolalia* (γένη γλωσσῶν – I Cor. 12.10, 28; γλῶσσαι – I Cor. 12.30; 13.1, 8; 14.5f., 18, 22f., 39; γλῶσσα – I Cor. 14.2, 4, 9, 13f., 19, 26f.).

What was Corinthian glossolalia? What did *Paul* think glossolalia was? These are two separate questions; but by the nature of the evidence it is not easy to keep them disentangled. Was Corinthian glossolalia 'the broken speech of people in ecstasy',[228] and did Paul recognize it to be such ('ecstatic utterance' – NEB)? Or did he think of it as a heavenly language or variety of heavenly languages?[229] Or did he think of glossolalia as 'the miraculously given ability to speak a human language foreign to the speaker'?[230]

There are some indications that the Corinthian glossolalia was indeed 'ecstatic utterance', measured in value by them precisely by the intensity of the ecstasy which produced it and by the unintelligibility of the utterances.[231] For one thing Paul's contrast between prophecy and glossolalia is between two forms of inspired speech; glossolalia is something more than inspired speech as such, it is inspired speech 'without the mind', that is mindless utterance (14.15, 19). Furthermore, we have already seen above (p. 234) that the picture of the Corinthian assembly which emerges from 12.2f.; 14.12, 23, 27f., 33a, 40 is one of confusion and disorder, with a substantial number of the congregation evidently working themselves up into a state of spiritual ecstasy endeavouring to become vehicles of inspired utterance. These features of Corinthian glossolalia are too reminiscent of the mantic prophecy of the Pythia at Delphi (see above §41.2) and the wider manifestations of ecstasy in the worship of Dionysus,[232] so that the conclusion becomes almost inescapable: glossolalia as practised in the assembly at Corinth was a form of ecstatic utterance – sounds, cries, words uttered in a state of spiritual ecstasy.

Yet the more one recognizes the ecstatic character of Corinthian glossolalia, the more remarkable becomes Paul's otherwise positive assessment of glossolalia. Mindless ecstasy may characterize Dionysiac worship but it should not characterize Christian worship (12.2); glossolalia is to be strongly discouraged in the assembly (14.5–12, 19). Nevertheless, he allows glossolalia a role in the assembly (14.27f., 39). Certainly he ranks glossolalia last in his two listings of charismata (12.8–10, 28), and evidently regards it as a somewhat childish gift, or at least a gift which appeals to the child more than the man (14.20, cf. 13.11). Nevertheless he does regard it as a charisma. As for Paul himself, he does not value ecstatic experience very highly (II Cor. 12.1ff. – see below §55), and would rather speak five words with his mind in the assembly than ten thousand words in a tongue (14.19)![233] Yet he speaks in tongues a great deal (more than all the Corinthians! 14.18), and is very willing for the Corinthians to experience this charisma (14.5).[234] It looks very much therefore as though Paul knows and values a form of glossolalia which is not so 'abandoned' as the Corinthian glossolalia – a glossolalia which can be readily controlled (14.28 – the glossolalia which is to be permitted is glossolalia which can be restrained when its utterance would be inappropriate); a glossolalia which is a speaking of actual words (14.19); a glossolalia, that is to say, which was ecstatic only in the technical sense of being automatic speech in which the conscious mind played no part, but not ecstatic in the more common sense of 'produced or accompanied by exalted states of feeling, rapture, frenzy'.[235]

Can we clarify Paul's concept of glossolalia further? Was it simply a speaking of words (14.19), or were the words syntactically connected? In other words, did he think of glossolalia as a *language*? And if so, did he think of it as human (foreign) language, or as language spoken nowhere on earth, that is, heavenly language(s)? The answer to the first question is straightforward: Paul thought of glossolalia as language. (1) This is the most obvious and regular meaning of γλῶσσα in NT and Greek literature generally,[236] and it is quite clear from I Cor. 12.28, 30 that 'tongues' (γλῶσσαι) is simply an abbreviation for 'different tongues' (γένη γλωσσῶν) = different languages.[237] (2) The gift which accompanies glossolalia is 'interpretation' (ἑρμηνεία – see below §41.8). In biblical Greek the regular and characteristic sense of ἑρμηνεία and its cognates is 'translation'. The implication is strong therefore that for Paul 'interpretation of tongues' means 'translation of languages'.[238] (3) The only passage in the OT which throws light for Paul on the function and purpose of glossolalia is Isa. 28.11f., where ἑτερογλώσσοι (strange languages) is obviously taken as the counterpart of γλῶσσαι (14.21f. – '"In strange languages . . ." says the Lord. Therefore tongues . . .').

It is evident then that Paul thinks of glossolalia as language. But can we go on from that to conclude that he equates glossolalia with 'human language foreign to the speaker' (Gundry)? I think not. (1) 13.1 – 'tongues of men and tongues of angels'. Since he is presumably thinking throughout 13.1–3 of different types of charismata as such, 'tongues of men' will denote not simply 'ordinary human speech',[239] but inspired speech of different kinds in the vernacular (see above §41.1–6); while 'tongues of angels' will be Paul's and/or the Corinthians' description of glossolalia. In 13.2 he picks out the highest kind of the former (prophecy), while presumably 'all mysteries (cf. 14.2) and all knowledge (cf. above §40.4)' pick out the highest benefits that the Corinthians (claim to) derive from spiritual ecstasy and ecstatic glossolalia. (2) 14.2 – the glossolalist 'speaks mysteries (μυστήρια) in the Spirit'. Μυστήριον in Paul 'always has an eschatological sense';[240] it means simply God's eschatological secret, God's secret purpose. Usually Paul uses the word of the mystery of God's secret purpose now revealed in Christ and the gospel (see above §40.2). But in 14.2 the sense is of heavenly secrets not yet revealed or in unrevealed form (cf. II Cor. 12.4); that is, mysteries of which only the angels in heaven have knowledge. Paul thus characterizes the glossolalist as holding a secret conversation with God (he speaks to God – 14.2); the subject matter is the eschatological secrets known only in heaven; so presumably the language used is the language of heaven (cf. Rev. 14.2f.).[241] (3) The analogy Paul uses in 14.10f. between glossolalia and foreign language cannot be taken as evidence that Paul thought of glossolalia as foreign language.[242] Paul would not have used foreign or 'different languages' (γένη φωνῶν) as an *analogy* (both unintelligible speech) if he had thought glossolalia was itself a foreign language.[243] That which is not self-evident (the uselessness of unintelligible glossolalia in the assembly) is illuminated by that which is self-evident (the uselessness of unintelligible foreign language in the assembly). In short, the most obvious conclusion is that Paul thought of glossolalia as speaking the language(s) of heaven.

Two final questions must be asked: Why does Paul value glossolalia? and, Was glossolalia a peculiarly Corinthian phenomenon, or was it more widespread throughout the early churches? The answer to the first is twofold. Paul values glossolalia because it is a charisma, inspired utterance, the Spirit speaking through him.[244] Whether he has confused a purely psychological phenomenon with a divine charisma is not something we are now in any position to determine. Certainly his distinction between ecstatic glossolalia and a more controlled speaking in tongues (see above) shows that he was not lacking in critical discrimination in such matters (see further below §§46–49). On the other hand it is only in comparatively recent times that we have become aware of the capacity of the subconscious to manifest itself in ways often strange to and unexpected by the conscious mind. However, in the end we can do no more than state it as Paul's opinion that there was a kind of glossolalia which was *a manifestation of the Spirit*, a charisma of God.

The other reason why Paul values glossolalia is because it is for him primarily a kind of prayer – 'he who speaks in a tongue speaks not to men but to God' (I Cor. 14.2) – which may take the form of spoken prayer ('pray with the Spirit' = inspired prayer; 'bless with the Spirit', that is, praise God in inspired speech; 'give thanks' – 14.14–17), or of sung praise ('sing with the Spirit' = inspired hymnody – 14.15). It is presumably as Spirit-inspired prayer that glossolalia 'edifies' the tongues-speaker; and here we may draw in Rom. 8.26–8, even though that is not talking about glossolalia as such (see above §41.6). *He who experiences glossolalia (or wordless groans) experiences it as effective communication with God.* The prayer which he finds himself unable to utter the Spirit utters through him, giving him the sense of communing with God, the confidence that God knows his situation and needs better than he does himself, the assurance that God's Spirit is directing his course and its circumstances.[245]

Was glossolalia a peculiarly Corinthian phenomenon, or was it more widespread throughout the early churches? The failure of Paul to use the phrase 'speak in (different) tongues' outside of I Corinthians is of course of little weight in itself. As has often been pointed out, he mentions the Lord's Supper in only one letter as well (I Cor.), but we certainly cannot conclude that the Lord's Supper was 'a peculiarly Corinthian phenomenon'. The Lord's Supper and glossolalia are discussed in I Corinthians because the Corinthians abused both, not because they monopolized either. Other possible allusions to glossolalia include Rom. 8.26 (Spirit prayer as 'inarticulate groans') and Eph. 6.18 ('pray at all times in the Spirit');[246] also Eph. 5.19 = Col. 3.16 ('spiritual songs'),[247] I Thess. 5.19 ('Do not quench the Spirit'), and possibly II Cor. 5.4 (cf. Rom. 8.23, 26).[248] But in every case the

allusion seems to be much more general, probably including glossolalia, but hardly confined to it – charismatic prayer and singing of all
kinds (Eph. 6.18; 5.19 = Col. 3.16), no doubt engaging the same
range of emotions as the *abba*-prayer (Rom. 8.15; Gal. 4.6), but taking a variety of vocal expression, and not simply glossolalia (e.g. the
'Abba' *cry*, and the 'inarticulate groans' of Rom. 8). The reference
in I Thess. 5.19 is even less restricted: no flame which the Spirit
kindles in the assembly is to be quenched, including glossolalia no
doubt, but many other charismata as well.[249]

In addition we may remind ourselves that Luke was familiar with
accounts of glossolalia in the primitive Palestinian community and its
early mission (see above §§26.3, 34). Furthermore, Jude 19f. seems
to have in mind a situation very similar to that in Corinth. He
castigates his opponents as 'worldly-minded, lacking the Spirit'
(ψυχικοί, πνεῦμα μὴ ἔχοντες); clearly they have laid claim to be
pneumatikoi, denying the epithet to others. Jude will have none of this
(cf. I Cor. 2.13–15). At the same time he encourages his readers to
'pray in the Holy Spirit' (v. 20; cf. I Cor. 14.15; Eph. 6.18). His aim
seems to be to achieve the same sort of charismatic balance that Paul
strives for in I Cor. 14. A reference to charismatic prayer, including
glossolalic prayer, may therefore be presumed for Jude 20.[250] Finally
we may draw attention to the significance of Mark 16.17: 'These
signs will accompany those who believe: in my name they will
exorcise demons; they will speak in (new) tongues . . .'. The passage (Mark 16.9–20) is universally accepted as a second-century
addition to Mark's gospel, and it is fairly clear that it is modelled on
the accounts of apostolic Acts, particularly Luke's (e.g. Acts 2.4–11;
16.18; 28.3–6).[251] The significance of the reference is then that, with
the Christian mission probably already a century old, speaking in
tongues was regarded as a typical sign of the gospel's expansion in the
first century and perhaps also in the second.[252] I conclude therefore
that glossolalia was a phenomenon familiar among both Jewish and
Hellenistic Christians of the first century and beyond, that it was
recognized as a manifestation of the Spirit, and that it held a place of
some significance within individuals' lives and within the Christian
mission.

41.8   *Interpretation of tongues* (ἑρμηνεία γλωσσῶν – I Cor. 12.10; 14.26;
(δι)ερμηνευτής – 14.28; διερμηνεύω – 12.30; 14.5, 13, 27). If we have
rightly grasped the nature of Corinthian glossolalia and Paul's
understanding of the charisma of tongues, the meaning of the accompanying gift, interpretation (ἑρμηνεία) of tongues, poses no difficulty.

As we noted above, the regular and characteristic sense of ἑρμηνεία and its cognates in biblical Greek is 'translation'. But, as any translator knows, translation is not a matter simply of substituting words in one language for words in another – far from it. Since the nearest equivalent words in two languages often have a very different semantic range, and since the idioms and flexibility of two languages are never the same, even so-called literal translation involves a fair degree of interpretation. And good translation involves a considerable degree of interpretation; good translation is interpretative translation. Judaism was already familiar with this: the LXX (Hebrew into Greek) is an interpretative translation (cf. ch. VII n. 139 above); the Targums were Aramaic paraphrases of the Hebrew texts. In other words, there is no real boundary line between 'translation' and 'interpretation' – as is confirmed by the semantic range of (δι)ερμηνεύειν within biblical Greek itself (see II Macc. 1.36; Job. 42.18 (17b); Luke 24.27). Moreover, the more we recognize Hellenistic influence on Corinthian glossolalia, the more seriously we have to consider the basic meaning of the word in wider Greek thought – viz., 'to interpret, expound, explain'. In particular, the relation between 'glossolalia' and 'interpretation' so closely parallels that between what we distinguished above as the 'prophecy of inspiration' and the 'prophecy of interpretation' (§41.2) that it becomes difficult to deny a close equivalence of function between, for example, the prophet who interpreted the utterances of the Pythia at Delphi and the interpreter of tongues at Corinth.[253]

Word study, however, takes us only so far. The realities of the situation at Corinth throw further light on the nature of this gift. Above all we must notice that 'interpretation' is not an independent gift; it is precisely interpretation *of tongues*. The two go together – tongues and interpretation, the two sides of the one coin. So closely interconnected are they that Paul will not conceive of the one without the other in the assembly (I Cor. 14.5, 13, 27f.). This brings to light an unresolved tension in Paul's treatment of these two charismata. Glossolalia is a charisma, an act of *service* (I Cor. 12.5), a 'manifestation of the Spirit *for the common good*' (I Cor. 12.7); the speaker in tongues is a member of the body of Christ, as indispensable in his function as all the others (12.14–30 – see below §45.2). And yet glossolalia is not to be encouraged in the assembly, only permitted (14.39); and if the decision rested solely with Paul even that permission would be almost completely withdrawn (14.19). In what sense then is glossolalia a gift for the service of the body of Christ, 'for the common good'? And if the reply be given, 'It benefits the assembly through the accompanying interpretation' (14.5), the question then becomes, Why is this somewhat cumbersome two-stage gift necessary? If the Spirit wishes to edify the assembly, why tongues at all? Why not simply a word of prophecy or praise in the common language of the assembly (14.4)? The 'mind of Christ' is somewhat obscure at this point, and Paul does nothing to clarify it.[254] Indeed the conclusion suggests itself that Paul is trying to rationalize a form of charismatic worship in Corinth with which he is not altogether happy – that he is trying to control what he could not forbid (since it would strain his authority beyond breaking point), namely the rather selfish expression of a form of spiritual enthusiasm which brought no benefit to the assembly. If this is so, then *interpretation of tongues' is to be seen in the first instance as the assembly's control over glossolalia*, its safeguard against possible abuse, a further check on the already limited role Paul permits for glossolalia in the assembly; in other words, even the few glossolalic utterances allowed in the assembly must each be balanced immediately by an inspired utterance in the vernacular.

What this may mean is that in the reality of the Corinthian situation 'interpretation of tongues' amounted to nothing more than the first utterance in the vernacular which followed an utterance in a tongue.[255] For Paul, of course, interpretation of tongues is a charisma, an inspired utterance, not simply some form of rational discernment[256] – how one could rationally discern a 'mindless utterance' is a puzzle in itself: 'there is no dictionary of glossolalia'.[257] He may well have thought of it as a kind of mind-reading – prophetic insight, clairvoyance, or telepathic thought transference,[258] or whatever. But perhaps he simply assumed, or encouraged the assumption for the sake of good order, that whatever inspired utterance in the vernacular followed the 'tongue', that was the interpretation. At all events, by insisting on this companion gift Paul achieves a control over that gift which at first seems most to express the nature of charisma (by its manifest inspiration), but which in fact least expresses the real purpose (for Paul) of charisma, as gift from God *for others*. This latter aspect comes to clearest expression in the charismata to which we now turn.

§42. SERVICE

We have so far examined charisma as display of energy (ἐνέργημα), as revelation (φανέρωσις), and as inspired utterance. The other general word Paul uses in I Cor. 12.4–7 to describe the manifestation of grace is *service* (διακονία – *diakonia*) – 12.5: 'there are varieties of service but the same Lord'. *Diakoniai* here obviously does not refer to ecclesiastical offices or regularly appointed ministries.[259] The different utterances and actions which are listed in 12.8–10 include occasional contributions to the worship of the community as well as the more regular contributions by those recognized as prophets, teachers, etc. (I Cor. 12.28). *Diakoniai* therefore denote *the actual contributions themselves*, and is best translated '*acts of service*', or 'ways of serving'.

42.1   *Diakonia* (διακονία – Rom. 12.7; cf. I Peter 4.11). Although all charismata are *diakoniai*, *diakonia* can also be used of course for particular charismata, actions whose divine prompting is evidenced not by inspired speech or displays of power, but precisely by *their character of service*: that which serves the needs of fellow believers or the community life. Examples of such *diakoniai* are to be found elsewhere in Paul's letters. On several occasions *diakonia* denotes the collection for the church in Jerusalem (Rom. 15.31; II Cor. 8.4; 9.1, 12f.). In II Cor. 11.8 Paul's own ministry in Corinth is called an act of service to the Corinthians, particularly by virtue of the fact that he did not look to the Corinthians for any financial or material support. I Cor. 16.15 speaks of the service rendered by Stephanas and his family to the saints – that is, presumably, hospitality, since it is a household ministry; it is very likely that the Corinthian church met frequently in Stephanas's house. Even in II Tim. 4.11 Mark's *diakonia* is the particular service of assisting the imprisoned Paul in some way, most likely in his personal affairs.[260] In all these cases Paul has in mind particular acts of service. However, he also uses *diakonia* for a more sustained act of service, a *ministry*; it is in this sense that he uses the word for his own ministry as a whole (Rom. 11.13; II Cor. 3.8f.; 4.1; 5.18; 6.3; cf. II Tim. 4.5).[261] *Diakonia* in Rom. 12.7 probably falls somewhere in the middle of this spectrum of meaning – denoting neither an isolated and individual act of service nor a ministry taking up the energies of a whole life. It is best taken to mean a particular kind of service for which the same individual is regularly responsible, or regular acts of service of different kinds undertaken by the same person. It should be noted however that the charisma of *diakonia* here does not signify a particular office (diaconate) or acts of service undertaken as a community appointment or even at the community's behest. Stephanas and his household had after all *taken upon themselves* (ἔταξαν ἑαυτούς – literally, 'appointed themselves to') the service of the saints (I Cor. 16.15).[262] There *diakonia* was a charisma not because it was a community office or appointment, but because it was a spiritually sensitive recognition of and response to a particular need or lack within the community. Thus also in Rom. 12.7, *the charisma is the activity of serving, recognized to be a charisma, of divine prompting, precisely because of its character as service* (but see further below §43.5).

42.2   *Giving and caring.* Also to be considered under the heading of 'service' are the last three charismata mentioned in Rom. 12.8 – μεταδιδούς, προϊστάμενος, ἐλεῶν – and two of the last three members of the I Cor. 12.28 list – ἀντιλήμψεις and κυβερνήσεις. Μεταδιδούς means 'giving', or more precisely, 'giving a share of, sharing'. It can be used of giving a share in the gospel (I Thess. 2.8), or in a particular *charisma* (Rom. 1.11); but here it probably refers to the sharing of food or possessions within the community (ἁπλότητι – 'with generosity').[263] It is a charisma not simply because it involves giving – that may mean nothing in fact (I Cor. 13.3). It is a charisma because it is a giving which has the character of sharing what is of value to both, because it is a giving which is sincere, without ulterior motives or secondary objects (ἁπλότητι) beyond that of the desire to share what one has with those who have not.[264] The highest expression of this charisma in the eyes of the Corinthians would no doubt be a giving which was as eye-catching as glossolalic ecstasy – viz., a giving away of one's property (literally bit by bit – cf. Acts 2.45; 4.34–7), and a giving of oneself in martyrdom or self-immolation (self burning) (I Cor. 13.3).[265] It should be noted that Paul does not commend such action, or describe voluntary poverty and martyrdom as charismata; he cites them only as the most extreme form that charismatic giving could take: even that sort of action can be loveless and graceless, that is, not really a charisma.[266]

We look next at the closely related charisma of ἐλεεῖν. Ὁ ἐλεῶν could refer to acts of mercy in general,[267] but Paul probably has in mind almsgiving in particular.[268] The importance of 'poor relief' as an important expression of piety was part of Christianity's heritage from Judaism.[269] So too the exhortation to give 'cheerfully' (ἱλαρότητι – from which comes our 'hilarity') was common to Jewish and Christian 'wisdom' (Prov. 22.8 LXX; Ecclus. 35.8; *Leviticus Rabbah* 34.9; II Cor. 9.7).[270] This does not mean, however, that either the act or the exhortation is nothing more than a formal carry over from Judaism. In the Pauline literature, apart from Rom. 12.8, 'mercy' always refers to God's mercy, particularly God's mercy in the present age to believers, not least to Paul himself.[271] We may infer therefore that for Paul giving to the poor is a charisma *only in so far as it is a reflection of God's unmerited generosity in Christ,*[272] an act of concern for the needy freely willed and cheerfully carried through rather than as a duty.

What charisma Paul refers to with προϊστάμενος is not entirely clear. In the NT προΐστημι appears only in the Pauline literature; but it occurs frequently outside the NT. It can mean (a) 'rule, lead, direct, conduct, manage'; (b) 'protect, represent, care for, help'; (c) 'devote oneself to, concern oneself with, engage in'.[273] What sense does Paul intend for Rom. 12.8?

(a) ὁ προϊστάμενος could mean 'he who rules', 'leader' (NEB), in the sense of presiding over the worship or managing the community's common affairs.[274] For one thing, in I Tim. 3.4f., 12 the verb must denote some exercise of authority over children and management of a household (note the ἐν ὑποταγῇ, 'in submission', of I Tim. 3.4); in the social circumstances of the day the head of a household was just that – head and master (cf. e.g. Mark 14.14; Eph. 5.22–5; Col. 3.18–4.1). Moreover, in the parallel passage in I Thess. 5.12 προϊστάμενος is linked with νουθετοῦντας (admonish), which implies some exercise of authority, the authority of greater experience, or of superior knowledge or wisdom (cf. I Cor. 4.14).

(b) Alternatively ὁ προϊστάμενος could mean 'he who gives aid' (RSV), or better, 'he who cares for others', very likely with reference to those who took it upon themselves to care for and protect more defenceless members of the community (widows, orphans, slaves, strangers).[275] For one thing, the sense 'care for' is an integral part of the father's responsibility in the I Timothy passages above,[276] and for another, in Rom. 12.8 προϊστάμενος is set between two words which denote forms of aid-giving (μεταδιδούς and ἐλεῶν), and is therefore likely to bear a similar meaning. This last is probably the most weighty consideration,[277] and may be decisive also in the case of I Thess. 5.12.[278] The three words in Rom. 12.8 therefore probably run into each other and together cover the whole range of the early community's 'welfare service': μεταδιδούς – distribution of food and clothing; προϊστάμενος – championing the cause of those who had no natural mentor to speak and act for them; ἐλεῶν – the giving of financial aid.[279]

The ἐν σπουδῇ which Paul attaches to προϊστάμενος is probably best translated 'with zest': 'he who cares for others, acts on behalf of others, let him do it with zest'.[280] In other words, it is a charisma not simply because it involves helping others, but because it is *an expression of the vitality of the community as community*. It is the common life, the shared Spirit (κοινωνία) expressing itself in a loving and vigorous concern for the less fortunate (cf. I Cor. 12.25f.; see below §45). The same applies if προϊστάμενος is taken in the sense of leadership: the charisma is not simply the exercise of leadership, but giving a lead with zest, so that the worship and affairs of the community of believers expresses the new creation vitality and energies of life in Christ.

Finally we must again draw attention to the significance of the fact that the *charismata* are expressed by means of verbs in participial form: 'he who shares, he who cares, he who gives'. In other words, the charisma in each case is the sharing, caring, giving. It does not designate an official position which involves these acts; it designates the acts themselves.[281] The present participles could include indivi- dual acts;[282] but they probably denote more regular ministries within the community. Yet there is no suggestion that these acts or ministries could only be entered upon by permission or authorization of the community. These appear to be charismatic ministries in the sense that they are undertaken at the urging of love and concern and in the strength of that inspiration, rather than as a community or official appointment. The community may however be called upon to *acknowledge* that these ministries are charismata of the Spirit and therefore worthy of respect (I Thess. 5.12), just as Paul urges the Corinthians to recognize and acknowledge the divinely given authority of Stephanas in a ministry which he had taken upon him- self (I Cor. 16.15f. – see further below, §48.3 and pp.292f.).

42.3 *Helping and guiding.* Ἀντιλήμψεις and κυβερνήσεις from I Cor. 12.28 need not detain us long. Both occur only once in the NT, but the former is well known in the LXX and the current speech of Paul's day in the sense 'help, assistance';[283] and the latter is known in the sense 'steering, directing, governing', a metaphor drawn from the important role of the helmsman (κυβερνήτης) in steering a ship (cf. Acts 27.11; Rev. 18.17).[284] It is difficult to define them more closely. Ἀντιλήμψεις is best translated 'helpful deeds' (Arndt & Gingrich), and presumably covers the same sort of activities as those denoted by the last three members of the Rom. 12.8 list (cf. Acts 20.35).[285] Κυβερνήσεις must denote some kind of activity which gives direction. It could be translated 'giving counsel' and include wise advice to puzzled individuals, but the metaphor (steering a ship) suggests that it is directing the community which Paul has in mind. 'Administra- tion' errs on the other side by prompting the inference that the early churches were already seen as 'administrative structures', 'institu- tions'. Perhaps we should strive for nothing more precise than 'giving guidance', since its object can embrace both the affairs of the com- munity and individuals within it.[286] If προϊστάμενος has the sense of leadership (though see above §42.2), then κυβερνήσεις would obviously refer to similar functions. More probable is a link between ἀντιλήμψεις and κυβερνήσεις and the (later) more established positions of deacon and overseer respectively (Phil. 1.1; I Tim. 3.1ff., 8ff.)[287] – in the sense that the activities of helping and guiding others came to be recognized as requiring a more regular sort of ministry (see further below pp.288f.).

Two other points are worth noting. First, both words refer to functions, actions, rather than to people. The list of I Cor. 12.28 changes after the first three items, from an ordered hierarchy of people ('first apostles, second prophets, third teachers') to a fairly random collection of actions ('then miracles, then gifts of healing, helpful deeds, giving guidance, different kinds of tongues').[288] *The charismata are the functions, not the people*; they are the activities not a number of offices.[289] In fact, only the second half of the list in I Cor. 12.28 can properly be said to speak of charismata.[290] So, for example, it is prophecy which is the charisma not the prophet, and in 14.1 Paul encourages the Corinthians to aim at the charisma of prophecy not at a hierarchical position labelled 'prophet'.[291] We will return to an examination of the relation between 'office' and charisma in chapter IX. Second, both words are in the plural. The charismata therefore are the concrete deeds of helpfulness, the actual giving of guidance on different occasions.[292] The same is true for the rest of the charismata in the I Cor. 12.28 list – the charisma is the actual miracle, the actual healing, the particular tongue/language. Charisma in other words is *not a latent power or ability* which may be sometimes displayed and sometimes not. *Only the actual deed or word is the charisma.* And, strictly speaking, the speaker or the doer only 'possesses' the charisma in that instant.

§43. CONCLUSIONS

43.1 *Charisma can only be understood as a particular expression of charis*; this was why we had to study *charis* first. In the same way *pneumatika* can only be understood as a number of individual embodiments of *pneuma*. 'The gift is inseparable from the gracious power which bestows it . . . it is indeed the manifestation and concretion (sic!) of this power.'[293] This is implied both by the semantic relation of the two pairs of words, by the fact that *charisma* obviously overlaps with the latter end of the range of meaning of *charis* examined above in §37.2 (cf. e.g. Rom. 1.11 with Eph. 4.29, and Rom. 12.6ff. with II

Cor. 8.1, 4, 6f.), and by the way in which Paul specifically associates the words in Rom. 12.6 and I Cor. 1.4–6; 12.1, 4, 7, 11 (cf. I Peter 4.10).[294] This relation between grace and gift is of central importance if we are to enter into Paul's understanding of charismatic experience.

43.2   It means in the first place that *charisma is always an event, the gracious activity* (ἐνέργημα) *of God through a man*. It is the actual miracle, the healing itself, the particular experience of faith; it is the actual revelation as man experiences it, the very words of wisdom, prophecy, prayer, etc. themselves, the particular act of service as it is performed. Charisma is not a possession or an office; it is a particular manifestation of grace; the exercise of a spiritual gift is itself the charisma. Charisma is never, strictly speaking, *my* charisma; it is given to me only in the sense that God chooses to act through me for others. Indeed, in an important sense charisma is not given to me at all, but only to the one whom the charisma serves.[295] Charisma is not something an individual can put in cold store, as it were; it is the experience of grace and power *in a particular instance and only for that instance*. We shall have to return to this point in chapter IX (§45.2).

43.3   It means, secondly, that charisma is always a specific act of *God*, of God's Spirit through a man. It is the activity of *God*, the manifestation of the *Spirit*; it is the demonstration of Spirit and power (I Cor. 2.4), that is, the experience of being grasped by an otherly power, and, in the case in point, of being compelled to acknowledge the truth of Paul's message and to recognize in that power the action of the one of whom the message spoke. That is to say, charisma is *not* man's response to grace. It is God's grace itself coming to visible expression. Hence charisma should not be understood as the *consequence* of charis, nor charis as the *presupposition* of charisma.[296] It follows that the exercise of charismata does not presuppose or depend on a 'state of grace', nor on the charismatic's having reached a certain degree of sanctification;[297] *charisma is something given, something unachieved, uncontrived*. Nor again does the manifestation of charismata make the believer more holy.[298] *There is no immediate causal connection between charisma and sanctification* (ἁγιασμός).[299] The Corinthian church itself is evidence enough on that score (cf. I Cor. 1.7 with 3.1ff.). Conversely of course the presence of charismata is not in itself a sign of *im*maturity. Quite the contrary: *charisma is the inevitable outworking of charis*; if there is no charisma, there can be no charis. The Corinthian immaturity displayed itself in their *attitude* to the charismata: that is, their too high regard for particular gifts and their lack of love and control in the manifestation of them (see further below §46.1).

43.4   It means, thirdly, that *charisma* is typically an *experience*, an experience of something being accomplished through me – an experience of grace. In all the charismata we have examined above *the consciousness of grace and of the otherness of grace* is strongly implied. What we have seen in fact are different experiences of grace – the experience of a gracious power that heals, the experience of grace to trust, of being enabled to believe, the experience of the grace of revelation, of being permitted to see into realities beyond sight and mind, of being given to participate in God's wise plan of salvation, of being made aware of God's will in moments of decision, the experience of the grace of boldness in preaching, of the givenness of words in prophecy, praise and prayer, the experience of the grace of assurance of sonship in the cry 'Abba' which comes through my lips and is wholly my cry but is prompted by one who is other than myself, the experience of grace enabling to share and care, to help and counsel. *Charisma is the experience of grace given* (Rom. 12.6). Each consciousness of grace Paul attributes to the charismatic Spirit.

43.5   It means fourthly, that *charisma is not to be confused with human talent and natural ability*; nowhere does charisma have the sense of a human capacity heightened, developed or transformed.[300] As Gunkel (and Wetter) long ago demonstrated so clearly against the earlier idealistic view of F. C. Baur, so far as Paul was concerned charismata are the manifestation of supernatural power.[301] Charisma is *always* God acting, *always* the Spirit manifesting himself. Charisma emerges from the new life begun by the gracious act of God and as an expression of that grace. The justified refusal to distinguish between 'natural' and 'supernatural'[302] – justified in relation to any attempt to interpret religious phenomena today (cf. above pp. 72ff.) – should not blind us to the fact that for Paul *every* charisma was supernatural. *The character of transcendent otherness lies at the heart of the Pauline concept of charisma.* It was not a matter of some otherwise quite ordinary activities and abilities being hailed as charismata simply because they were done within the community.[303] The 'infinite qualitative distinction' (Kierkegaard) between divine and human means that every expression of grace is always something *more* than human. Charisma may of course chime in with an individual disposition and temperament, and will certainly make use of natural abilities (even glossolalia makes use of the vocal chords); the expression of divine power through the human frame will certainly be tempered in some degree by the body's limitations. But the charisma itself can properly be exercised only when it is recognized as the action of the Spirit, for *charisma is characterized not by the exercise of man's ability and talent but by unconditional dependence on and openness to God.* So one can exercise even such charismata as celibacy, teaching, giving to the poor, helping, only when one recognizes that they are not something performed in one's own power, but only when one stands in conscious dependence on God. 'Do you give service? Give it as in the strength which God supplies' (I Peter 4.11 NEB).[304]

43.6   We must note also *the diversity of charismata*. It is sometimes assumed that a list like I Cor. 12.8–10 is a complete or at least sufficiently comprehensive inventory of the charismata that Paul expected in all his churches.[305] But (1) it will have become clear how much that list in particular *was determined by the particular situation at Corinth*. Paul mentions only such charismata as are immediately relevant to the community he addresses, some by way of recognition of Corinthian charismata (gifts of healing, miracles, faith, prophecy, tongues), some by way of correction of Corinthian abuse (*word* of wisdom/knowledge, evaluation of inspired utterance, interpretation). It was not intended as a full or model list for all churches. (2) When we look beyond the immediate Corinthian discussion and draw in Rom. 12.6–8, it becomes evident that in these lists Paul is not drawing from a limited pile of specified charismata, nor indeed is he drawing from a large pile of well defined spiritual operations. The variety of terminology and the overlap between different gifts (prophecy and exhortation; service, helpful deeds, sharing, caring, and giving; utterance of wisdom, utterance of knowledge, and teaching) makes it clear that Paul has in mind a wide range of charismatic phenomena and that these lists are *only a selection* of typical and often not very clearly circumscribed manifestations of grace. Our own investigation in this chapter underlines something of the actual range and diversity of charismata as envisaged by Paul, though since he himself never attempted a detailed topography of charismatic phenomena a comprehensive and final mapping out of Paul's theology here is not possible.

43.7   It follows from this that *charisma does not belong exclusively to the sphere of church or worship*. As all is of grace (see above pp. 204f.), so grace may manifest itself in many different ways in all sorts of circumstances. It is true, as we have already seen, that Paul thinks of charismata primarily in the context of the community of faith, but as a general definition charisma does not mark off a sacred from a secular section of life, or private from public.[306] As Rom. 12.1ff. makes clear, *the believer's spiritual (and charismatic) worship involves the totality of his relationships in this age* (cf. Rom. 1.9; Phil. 3.3).[307] Similarly in Col. 3.16f. Paul's thought runs directly and without break from singing psalms, hymns and spiritual songs, to the wider activities of every day life,[308] and then on to the mutual responsibilities of every day human relationships (cf. Eph. 5.18ff.). The range of charismata we have examined above stretches far beyond the gatherings for worship, and the particular charismata which come to expression in the Sunday assembly are simply particular manifestations of that grace which is always at work in the believer's life and which may come to expression in any number of different ways in the believer's daily life. *Not simply worship, but all life is to be lived in conscious dependence on God*, open to that charisma, that manifestation of grace which at any time may transform attitudes, relationships, situations in the direction of God's good, acceptable and perfect will. The grace of God does not recognize human distinctions between 'sacred' and 'secular'.

43.8   It also follows that *the experience of grace in Paul may not be narrowed or confined within some sacramental system or channelled through some priestly hierarchy. Paul indeed knows nothing of sacramental grace as such*. He nowhere speaks of baptism or the Lord's Supper as a charisma. Of course baptism plays a part in the experience of conversion-initiation, but the primary connection is between Spirit and faith (Gal. 3.2ff.).[309] The Lord's Supper does bring to visible expression the oneness of the Christian community in their experience of the one Christ (I Cor. 10.16f.), but again there is no suggestion of an experience of grace which is peculiarly and exclusively mediated through the ritual act.[310] It must now be clear that *for Paul the experience of grace is not only manifold and varied but is also frequently direct and unmediated*. Indeed *charisma* by definition is such an experience. Within a community of course, one experiences the benefits of charismata through others – the grade of community is the mutual interdependence of charismatic fellowship (see below §45). Within community baptism and the Lord's Supper play a part in bringing that grace to visible expression, but to attempt somehow to depict the sacraments in Paul as the chief or sole channels of grace would be to fly in the face of all the evidence reviewed in this chapter.[311]

43.9   Finally, we must sum up our results so far as a comparison of the charismatic experience of Jesus and of Paul is concerned. We cannot of course make the comparison at the level of the particular *concept* of *charisma*, since that term is peculiarly Paul's both in the meaning he puts into it and in the range of its application. But we can make the comparison at the level of the charismatic phenomena and characteristics such as we discussed in relation to Jesus (chapter IV). Here we can see that *Paul is both more of a charismatic and less of a charismatic than Jesus.* On the one hand Paul experienced *more* in the way of visions and ecstasy than Jesus (see above §15). On the other hand, Paul's mission was characterized by healings and exorcisms to a *lesser* degree than Jesus' ministry. More important, Paul does not seem to have attributed the same eschatological significance to exorcisms as did Jesus (see above §8); even more than Jesus Paul plays down the significance of the miraculous and emphasizes the centrality of the charisma of inspired utterance (prophecy). At the same time, none of Paul's inspired utterances surpass those of Jesus in the degree of authority and of self conscious authority implicit in them. So much by way of phenomenological parallels. The deeper theological issue of whether Paul's charismatic experience was on the same level as Jesus' or puts Paul on the same level as Jesus must await the further analysis of chapter X.

IX

THE BODY OF CHRIST –
THE CONSCIOUSNESS OF COMMUNITY

§44. INTRODUCTION

So far in Part III we have examined Paul's understanding of religious experience in terms of Spirit and grace – the consciousness of grace. Our study has hardly been exhaustive; but by confining ourselves to the task of defining what *charisma* means in each case, and by examining the different ways in which Paul found grace to manifest itself in his and others' experience, we have at least been able to see something of the essence of charismatic experience and something of its diversity for Paul. It also became increasingly evident as chapter VIII developed that charisma and community belong together. Charismatic experience was doubtless possible outside the community's worship (e.g. Rom. 8.26f.; I Cor. 14.18f.; II Cor. 1.11;[1] and see above §43.7); but it is significant that in his major discussions of charismata Paul always and explicitly relates them to the Christian community (Rom. 12.1–8; I Cor. 12–14; see also Eph. 4.1–16).[2] It is this *corporate dimension of religious experience* in the Pauline writings which we must now examine more closely.

We will look first at the relation between Spirit, charisma and community – *the charismatic community*. This last phrase however brings together two dynamic concepts whose interaction may seem to throw them apart rather than to bind them more closely together. Hence we must ask whether 'charismatic community' denotes the living reality of the Pauline churches, or whether it is merely a catchy phrase, an impractical ideal of Paul's. Do the Pauline congregations demonstrate that charisma and community can integrate? When the individual believer is not regarded as a merely passive recipient of grace from others, when each is encouraged to see himself as a channel of grace to the rest, does that in practice make for unity or for disunity? Questions of this sort arose in our study of Luke's account of the primitive Christian communities (see above §§31.3, 32.1), though Luke unfortunately made no attempt to answer them. Fortunately (for us!) they arose in acute form in the Pauline churches (*charismata as a threat to community*), and Paul's attempt to grapple with the problems, to control the charismata, is highly instructive. Whether he succeeded in another question; indeed, whether the Pauline ideal of charismatic community must always give way in practice to a hierarchical authority structure is a tantalizing question which, as we shall see in chapter XI, is raised by the Pastoral epistles, the last contributions to the Pauline corpus, and which is still very much alive today.

§45. THE CHARISMATIC COMMUNITY

Religious experience is never reducible in Paul to an individualistic pietism – what one does with one's aloneness before God. On the contrary, *the corporate dimension of religious experience is integral to Paul's whole understanding of the divine-human relationship*. And when we talk about community with reference to Paul we are in fact talking about the *experience* of community. At the heart of the coming together of believers in the churches of the Pauline mission was the shared experience of God's Spirit.

45.1 *Spirit as a shared experience*. It is not difficult to demonstrate that not only is the Spirit an experiential concept in Paul (see above §37.1), but in addition it denotes a *shared experience*. Only rarely does he speak of the Spirit in individual terms (I Cor. 7.40, perhaps 14.14?) His regular usage is in terms of 'us' and 'you' (plural) – Rom. 5.5; 7.6; 8.9, 11, 15, 23, 26, etc. and in almost every case he is appealing to a shared experience. He did not need to enlarge on these (to us often enigmatic) references to the Spirit. His converts knew from their own experience what he was talking about – be it the experience of overflowing love (Rom. 5.5), of guidance (Rom. 7.6), of crying 'Abba! Father!' (Rom. 8.15), or whatever. For all its diversity there was a common denominator in their experience of the Spirit at conversion-initiation to which Paul could recall his converts (e.g. II Cor. 1.21f.; 4.6; Gal. 3.2ff.), so much so that the common experience of the Spirit could stand as the one necessary and sufficient term in Paul's definition of belonging to Christ (Rom. 8.9).[3]

A phrase which expresses better than most the corporate dimension of the experience of Spirit and its importance for the early

Pauline churches is ἡ κοινωνία τοῦ ἁγίου πνεύματος (II Cor. 13.13/14;
Phil. 2.1). Frequently understood in the sense 'the fellowship created
by the Holy Spirit', it really means *participation* in the Holy Spirit',[4]
and denotes precisely the shared experience of that which is possessed in common – the experience of grace underlying all its diverse
manifestations. In II Cor. 13.13/14 the third phrase of the triad denotes the concrete realization in experience of the grace manifested by
Jesus and the love exercised by God. Paul's prayer is in effect that the
experience of divine love and grace which is the common bond of
believers may be enjoyed by all his readers. In Phil. 2.1 the experiential content of the phrase is more marked. In a series of affective
phrases[5] Paul appeals to the warmth and vitality and unifying force
of the Philippians' common experience against all tendencies to self-
seeking and friction. Only if the Spirit was a common factor in their
experience, only if κοινωνία πνεύματος spoke to an actual experience
of grace and power shared by all his readers, could Paul make this
appeal or hope for its success.

That the shared experience of the Spirit was fundamental to the
unity of the early Christian communities comes to clearest expression
in I Cor. 12.13 and Eph. 4.3. In the former passage the theme of unity
dominates the immediate context (v. 11 – 'one and the same Spirit';
v. 12 – 'one body'; v. 13 – 'one Spirit . . . one body . . . one
Spirit'). What is frequently overlooked, however, is the point that the
unity of the Spirit is the determinative factor; *the unity of which Paul
speaks is in the first instance the oneness of their common experience of new life.*
The dispute as to whether Paul thinks of the body of Christ coming
into existence through Spirit-baptism[6] or conceives rather of the body
of Christ as an individual or cosmic entity with an existence prior to
the incorporation of any individual into it,[7] does not affect the point
being made here. In existential terms the Corinthians' experience of
the one body of Christ was a function of, determined by their experience of the one Spirit. Paul does not appeal here to the unifying
influence of a christological concept but to the common experience of
grace.[8] Nor, we may add, does he appeal to the unifying influence of a
ritual action. Despite commentators' continued reference of the verse
to the sacrament of baptism without question[9] I remain convinced
that, whatever the reference to the sacrament as such, the primary
reference in 12.13a is to the experience of the Spirit, as vv. 11 and 13c
surely confirm (cf. Gal. 3.26ff.).[10] Paul does not say 'one baptism,
therefore one body', but 'one *Spirit,* therefore one body'. The Corinthians knew they were members of the one body because the metaphors of being 'baptized in one Spirit' and of being 'drenched in one

Spirit' were living realities in their common experience and memory ('all').

The same point emerges, though in a less clear cut manner, from Eph. 4.3f. The unity of the church is in immediate terms the unity of the Spirit[11] – the reference being to the unifying force of a common experience of Spirit. Paul's choice of verb is instructive – τηρεῖν (maintain, preserve): the unity of the Spirit is not something yet to be created, far less is it something which they themselves create; all the Ephesians can do is to either preserve it or destroy it. This is because the unity of the Spirit is something given: the experience of grace shared by those who came to faith in Christ provides the starting point and basis of community.[12]

To some it may seem trite and obvious, but today it can hardly be stressed too much that *fundamental to Christian community for Paul was the shared experience of Spirit/grace*. Without this, 'fellowship' (κοινωνία) lacks all substance; it remains a jargon word or ideal and never becomes an existential reality. So too unity hinges on this common experience. There can be structural unity or formal unity; but without a common experience of grace (emphasis on both 'experience' and 'grace') unity can never be a living reality. In the Pauline 'model' of church this emphasis must of course be integrated with others; but it dare not be lost sight of, otherwise the 'model' is unworkable.

45.2 *The body of Christ as charismatic community*. If it is the (experienced) Spirit who creates community in the first place, so it is the Spirit experienced in charismata who sustains community. This comes out with greatest force in Paul's exposition of the church as body in I Cor. 12.14–27. Whatever other influences shaped Paul's concept of the church as the body of Christ,[13] it is clear that in this passage the dominant influence is the typical Stoic use of the metaphor of the body to describe the relationship between individual and society.[14] In Paul's development of the metaphor, however, it becomes an expression not simply of community but specifically of *charismatic community*.[15]

Notice, first of all, that Paul is here describing *the local church* at Corinth. When he says to the Corinthians 'you are Christ's body' (12.27) he is not thinking of 'the universal church', nor does he mean 'you at Corinth are part of the international fellowship of Christians'. His thought is rather that the Corinthian believers are the body of Christ in Corinth.[16] This is wholly of a piece with Paul's use of ἐκκλησία (church). At this stage it is only rarely (if at all) that he speaks of 'the church' (singular) referring to *all* believers. In his earlier letters 'the church' almost always means all the Christians living or gathered in one place;[17] hence the regular use of the plural – 'the churches' in Judea, Galatia, Asia, etc. (Rom. 16.16; I Cor. 7.17; 16.1, 19; II Cor. 8.18f., 23f., etc.). Thus there is no question of applying the metaphor of I Cor. 12.14ff. as though the Corinthians formed only a part (a leg or an arm) of the wider church (the universal body of Christ). Since it is clear that vv. 15ff., 21ff. are directed to the inferiority and superiority complexes created by the gnosticizing faction in Corinth,[18] it is also clear that the whole development of the metaphor applies to the Corinthians situation as such; that is, *it is the Corinthian assembly as such which Paul calls 'Christ's body'*. We must not overemphasize this, as though Paul thought solely in terms of isolated and independent Christian communities.[19] Nevertheless it does mean that Paul did not see the Christian community at Corinth as dependent on other churches for its life and worship as community, far less on some central organization in Jerusalem or Antioch.[20] The manifestation of Christ's body in Corinth depended solely on the proper functioning of the church in Corinth.[21]

Second, membership of the body means *charismatic membership*. The many members who make up the one body (I Cor. 12.14) are not simply individual believers, but individual believers *as charismatics* (vv. 4–11, 27–30) – that is, believers through whom the Spirit of grace may manifest himself in diverse ways at any time.[22] So too in Rom. 12 the charisma is nothing other than the function ($\pi\rho\hat{a}\xi\iota\varsigma$ – v. 4) of the member as member in the body of Christ.[23] It is of central significance to Paul's concept of the body of Christ then that each member 'has' his own gift (Rom. 12.3ff.; I Cor. 7.7; 12.7, 11 – 'to each . . . to each'; so I Peter 4.10); no member lacks a manifestation of grace;[24] no member can refuse the contribution to the worship or the life of the community which the Spirit would make through him without thereby 'quenching' the Spirit (I Thess. 5.19) and thereby ceasing to function as a member of the body. Not all of course 'have' the same charisma (Rom. 12.4; I Cor. 12.17, 19); and no individual manifests all the charismata (I Cor. 12.18, 20, 29f.); but each is a member of the body only in so far as the Spirit knits him into the corporate unity by the manifestation of grace through him. To have the Spirit is to experience the power of grace constantly seeking to come to concrete expression. I Cor. 12.15ff. therefore should not be understood as Paul taking the part of the non-charismatic against the charismatic – *all* are charismatics (vv. 7, 11).[25] At no time does Paul conceive of two kinds of Christians – those who minister to others and those who are ministered to, those who manifest charismata and those who do not. *To be Christian is to be charismatic; one cannot be a member of the body without sharing the charismatic Spirit.*

Third, as Paul's concept of the body of Christ is dynamic, so his understanding of membership of the body is dynamic. There is no such thing as passive membership, no catechumenate or training time. Initiation into the body (Spirit-baptism – I Cor. 12.13) is initiation into active membership.[26] To belong to the body is to have a function ($\pi\rho\tilde{\alpha}\xi\iota\varsigma$) within the body (Rom. 12.4), a contribution which the member must make; otherwise the health of the whole suffers. The less spectacular and so apparently less effective and important charismata, are in fact every bit as important, indeed if anything *more* important for the welfare of the whole (I Cor. 12.21ff.). Every charisma, every manifestation of grace is *indispensable*, for *the Spirit's gifts are the living movements of Christ's body.*

So too the interdependence of members is a dynamic process. When Paul speaks of the functioning of the members of the body he is not thinking of individuals with set functions.[27] As each charisma is a new act of grace, so the *unity* of Christian community cannot be a static state; rather it is *an ongoing creative event, constantly dependent on the Spirit manifesting his manifold interacting charismata.*[28] The unity of today does not guarantee the unity of tomorrow – that depends on ever new charismata bringing about that unity through their mutual interaction. We may go so far as to say that in Paul's view there is no body and no unity apart from charismata. (The Spirit of) Christ manifesting himself through different members of the community in dynamic mutual inter-dependence *is* the body (12.12).[29]

It follows, fourthly, that the *the charismatic as charismatic does not exist for himself but only for the community.* 'The Corinthians are fundamentally and primarily the body of Christ and only in a secondary way individual members.'[30] If we are to appreciate Paul's emphases, the charismata are never to be thought of as given *to* the individual, far less for his own personal advancement or pleasure; on the contrary, that is the very antithesis of community (14.2ff.).[31] Rather the charismata are always to be seen as *service* ($\delta\iota\alpha\kappa\nu\nu\iota\alpha$ – 12.5; see above pp. 249f.), as *gifts for the body*, given to, or better, *through* the individual 'for the common good' (12.7).[32] This is why there is no place for false modesty or inferiority complexes (12.15f.), no place for pride or superiority complexes (12.21ff.; see also Rom. 12.3). Whatever the gift, it is the Spirit's work; whatever the gift, it is necessary to the body. Through whom it is given does not matter. In terms of community, the charisma is more important than the charismatic as such.[33] Thus the concern of the individual should be solely to play the part given him in any particular instance and to encourage others to play theirs (cf. I Cor. 12.25f.). For, as the health of the whole depends on the proper functioning of each member, so the health of each member depends of the proper functioning of the whole. No personal flights of spirituality can free the individual from his responsibility to the community or from his dependence on the community. Thus the emphasis of Rom. 12.5 – 'We, though many, are one body in Christ, and individually members of one another'.[34]

45.3   To *sum up*, Paul sees the corporate dimension of Christian experience and life in terms of charismatic community. If *unity in diversity* is the keynote of the body metaphor in Rom. 12 and I Cor. 12, it is important to recall that both terms denote experience of Spirit – unity, the experience of Spirit in its *common* character as *grace* (§45.1), diversity, the experience of Spirit in its *variety* as *charismata* (§45.2). To put it another way, the church consists of κοινωνία (sharing) in both its passive and active senses – 'sharing' in the sense of the shared experience of grace which brings different individuals together into community in the first place, and 'sharing' in the sense of each contributing the different charismata to the common life of worship and service. Thus, to say that for Paul the church is a charismatic community means that the body of Christ in Corinth or Rome or Thessalonica or wherever is Christ's Spirit binding believers together and building them up through the wide range of his manifestations of grace. It means that each member of that community of faith has a function within the life of that community, a contribution necessary to the well-being of the whole. It means that charismata are indispensable to community, that community is a reality only when it is charismatic community,[35] that community consists in the dynamic mutual interdependence of the whole on the one and the one on the whole. It means that believers are members of the community only as charismatics; that they are charismatics only as members of the community. It means that the unity of the church is not destroyed by this diversity; on the contrary, it depends on the proper functioning of the whole range of diverse charismata; without the diversity of the charismata there can be no unity.[36] In a word, *the church as charismatic community means unity in and through diversity – the unity of charis in and through the diversity of charismata.*

§46. CHARISMATA AS A THREAT TO
COMMUNITY

So much for the theory, what about the practice? How did Paul's
concept of charismatic community work out in the churches he himself established? The evidence relating to this question in the Pauline
letters is fragmentary and allusive, and a proper study of it would
involve discussion of some far reaching issues on the state of affairs
and the nature of the Christianity in these places. We can only look
briefly here at the passages which are of immediate relevance to our
question.

46.1   *Corinth.* We start with the correspondence which spells out
Paul's concept of charismatic community most fully. In view of the
'ecclesiology' we have sketched out above (§45.2) it is a very striking
fact that each one of the extant letters sent to the Corinthian church
during the first decades of its life is addressed to a church threatened
by schism in one degree or another (I Cor.; II Cor. 1-9; 10-13; I
Clement).

(*a*) The Corinthian church of I Corinthians. That the church in
Corinth was threatened by *de facto* schism is clear enough, particularly from I Cor. 1.10ff.; 11.17ff. Our investigation in chapter VIII
also made it quite clear that charismata constituted part of that
threat; or, to be more precise, the attitude to charismatic phenomena
and conduct arising out of charismatic experience constituted the
chief threat to the unity and community of the Corinthian church
(see above §§40.4, 41.2, 3, 7). It was the value put on 'knowledge'
and 'wisdom' by the self-styled *pneumatikoi* (spiritual men) which
Paul saw as the root of the problem in I Cor. 1.17–4.21. It was this
'knowledge', and probably its particular expression in the 'word of
knowledge', 'an idol is nothing in the world' (I Cor. 8.4), which had
led to the inconsiderate conduct on the part of the knowledgeable ones
in the matter of food offered to idols (I Cor. 8.10). It was the Corinthians' eagerness for spirits (I Cor. 14.12), that is, for the experiences of
inspiration and ecstasy, which was undoubtedly the cause of the disorder and confusion in the assembly (I Cor. 14.33a). Finally we might
note the significance of I Cor. 13.4–7. The whole chapter is obviously
aimed at the Corinthians' over-evaluation of charismatic phenomena,
particularly glossolalia, prophecy and knowledge;[37] and set as they
are between the more obviously polemical passages, vv. 1–3 and 8–13,

it must be judged more than likely that Paul intends vv. 4–7 to serve the same purpose.[38] In that case it follows that in Corinth charismatic experience had given rise to impatience and unkindness, jealousy and boastfulness, arrogance and rudeness, selfishness and irritableness, resentfulness and delight in the failings of others. In other words, far from expressing the unity of the Spirit, charismatic phenomena in Corinth had in actual fact expressed lack of love, lack of faith, lack of hope; far from building up the Corinthian community, charismata constituted one of its chief threats.

(*b*) The Corinthian church of II Corinthians. The situation confronting Paul in Corinth at the time he wrote II Cor. 10–13 was even more serious. Without entering into the lively debate as to the precise nature of that situation and other related issues, I need only say that the contributions of Käsemann and Barrett in particular seem to me to provide the most coherent and plausible reconstruction.[39] Evidently several envoys from Jerusalem ('false apostles' – II Cor. 11.13) had appeared on the scene, intent on bringing the Corinthian church within Jerusalem's 'sphere of influence'. In order to achieve this aim they had felt it necessary to attack Paul's authority and apostolic status. The result had been to confuse and divide the Corinthian church, or, probably more exactly, to deepen the divisions already evident in I Cor., and also to impose severe strain on the relationship between Paul and the church of Corinth (II Cor. 1.15–2.11, 17–3.1; 7.2–13; 10–13). At the heart of the problem was the impressiveness of the false apostles' charismata: their speech was obviously inspired, probably often ecstatic – beside which Paul's preaching seemed dull in comparison (II Cor. 10.10; 11.16); they enjoyed an abundance of visions and revelations (12.1); their apostleship was proved beyond dispute by 'signs and wonders and miracles' (12.12); it was no doubt the manifest superiority of their charismatic experience which enabled them to act towards the Corinthians in an arrogant way and to batten on Corinthian hospitality – beside which conduct Paul's refusal to accept support was taken as a confession of his deficiency in spiritual experience (11.7–21). Here again then the threat to the Christian community in Corinth centred largely on the role and importance attributed to charismatic phenomena in the Corinthian church.

(*c*) The Corinthian church of I Clement. Whether the threat to which Clement of Rome addressed himself in the 90s also hinged on charismata and their role in the church at Corinth we cannot tell now with any certainty; but it may indeed be the case that the deposing of the erstwhile leaders by younger members (I Clem. 3.3;

44.6) was occasioned by the latter's over-evaluation of charismata of speech and knowledge (cf. 21.5; 48.5; 57.2).[40] We do not know what happened in the forty years that intervened between Paul's correspondence and that of Clement. But it is quite possible that Corinth provides one of the earliest examples of what we might call the cycle of Christian corporate experience familiar to us from Christian history: dynamic spiritual experience and vigorous growth, followed by a progressive settling and quieting down into respectability and more regular and established patterns, followed by restiveness and quest for renewal and the freshness of first hand experience on the part of the emerging new generation.[41] Be that as it may, it must be said that the reality of the Corinthian church both in the 50s and in the 90s puts a largish question mark against the practicability of Paul's vision of charismatic community (see further below §57).

46.2   *Rome.* The other letter from this period of Paul's life in which he enlarges on his concept of the charismatic community is Romans.[42] Here we are on much less certain ground: Paul does not know the Roman church at first hand, and he does not say very much about what is happening there. But it is clear enough that Paul was aware of strong disagreements and quarrels that threatened the peace and unity of the Christian community in Rome (see particularly 14; 16.17–20).[43] Whether or to what extent charismata played a part in all this is very much an open question. What we can say is that Paul seems to think in terms of a group or faction in Rome who shared at least some of the attitudes and values of the Corinthian gnostics (cf. Rom. 6.1 and I Cor. 5–6; Rom. 13.13 and I Cor. 11.17–22; Rom. 14.1–15.6 and I Cor. 8; 10.23–33; Rom. 16.17f. and I Cor. 1–4).[44] In particular we may notice Rom. 6.4f., where Paul deliberately refrains from stating that believers already participate in the resurrection of Christ (as they do his death) – participation in Christ's resurrection is still outstanding and future.[45] This reserve is quite likely to have been occasioned by the danger, real or suspected, of a gnostic or enthusiastic view of the resurrection such as we find in I Cor. 15.12.[46] So too Rom. 8.26f., though not specifically speaking of glossolalia (see above p.241), may nevertheless be a sharp reminder to any who thought the Spirit's inspiration was a mark of salvation already realized instead of the sighing of the creature still awaiting bodily redemption, the full realization of the new creation (cf. 8.15ff.).[47] In view of such parallels, the further parallel between Rom. 12.1–8 and I Cor. 12 assumes some significance.[48] We may draw

particular attention to Rom. 12.3: 'Do not be conceited or think too
highly of yourself'. Although Paul as a good pastor addresses the exhortation to 'everyone', the immediate context and the consequent
parallel with I Cor. 12.21ff. (cf. I Cor. 13.5; II Cor. 11.20) suggests
that Paul's primary target is any whose conceit is in direct proportion
to the large measure of grace they believe they experience, that is, in
direct proportion to the importance of the charismata which they
manifest.[49] Thus, in Rome too, charismata may have been more of a
disruptive element than a unifying factor; or, at least, Paul may have
seen this as a prospective danger.

46.3   *Thessalonica.* We complete our survey for the time being with a
glance at the earliest of Paul's writings – Thessalonians and Galatians.
There is much to be said for the view that Paul was faced in Thessalonica with a situation somewhat similar to that in Corinth – a situation where the charismatic enthusiasm of some had again got out of
hand.[50] In particular, the parallels between I Thess. 1.5; 2.3–12 and
such passages as I Cor. 2.4; 4.15; II Cor. 4.2; 11.9; 12.12, strongly
suggest that Paul was faced with similar charges and criticisms as
those levelled against him by the Corinthian gnostics: for all the
effectiveness of his ministry he lacked power and presence, he lacked
the more striking charismata.[51] I Thess. 5.19–22 is clearly addressed
to a charismatic community[52] which was experiencing some tensions.
On the one hand were those who were in danger of 'despising' prophetic utterance – presumably because the prophecy experienced at
Thessalonica was usually of an ecstatic nature.[53] On the other hand,
there were those – presumably the ecstatic prophets – who needed to
be reminded that prophetic utterance must be tested and evaluated.
The clearest evidence of all for our purposes is II Thess. 2.2: 'I beg
you, do not suddenly lose your heads or alarm yourselves, whether
at some oracular utterance (διὰ πνεύματος) or pronouncement (διά λόγου)
. . .' (NEB). By διὰ πνεύματος Paul obviously has in mind some form
of words spoken under inspiration (cf. the use of πνεῦμα in I Cor.
14.12); if the next phrase denotes inspiration of a rational kind (cf. I
Thess. 4.15), then διὰ πνεύματος would refer to some kind of ecstatic
utterance – though not necessarily glossolalia since a verbal revelation may be implied in v. 2c ('The day of the Lord has come')[54] –
at all events, an utterance whose manner and/or content seemed
plainly to indicate, 'This is the ultimate, the eschatological experience
of God'. Presumably such a prophecy had been given in the Thessalonian assembly by one of the ecstatic prophets,[55] with the consequence outlined in II Thess. 3.6–11. If this analysis is correct, then

here again is a church where charismatic experience had had divisive and *un*edifying results: Paul was regarded in a rather condescending manner by those who enjoyed striking charismatic experiences and who took such charismata as a criterion of spiritual worth; the church was divided on the value of experiences of Spirit and particularly on the value of prophecy, because its most frequent manifestations lacked control; a section of the congregation had been so impressed by some inspired utterance(s) that they had adopted a manner of life which dishonoured Christ and made them a burden rather than a benefit to the community. In short, in Thessalonica charismata were threatening the unity and fellowship of the Christian church.

Some would find in the letter to the Galatians evidence of a similar danger to the church there (particularly 3.2, 5; 5.13, 25f.; 6.1ff.).[56] But the conclusion of a threat to community from charismatic enthusiasts or gnostics cannot be read out from these passages with much conviction – although the whole section, 5.13–6.10, shows that Paul was not unmindful of the danger.[57]

46.4   I conclude then that Paul's theory of a Christian community bonded together into a developing unity by the diversity of charismata did not translate very well into practice. Out of the sparse information which comes to us from this period it would appear that three out of the four churches with whom Paul was in correspondence were in one degree or other threatened by the presence of (certain) charismatic phenomena. Charismata which were intended for the building up of community seemed rather to be destroying it (cf. II Cor. 10.8; 13.10).[58]

Before we move on to the next stage of the discussion we should perhaps pause to clarify one point. We have spoken throughout this section of charismata as a threat to community. Someone might object, not without justification, that this is a wrong use of the word 'charisma'. Charisma by definition is the manifestation of grace – in community terms the individual member's Spirit-given function within the body. Anything which threatens the community, which tends to destroy the oneness of the body, is *ipso facto* not a charisma, not of the one Spirit. However, the issue here cannot be solved merely by repeating definitions, and the impeccable logic of this line of reasoning should not be permitted to obscure the real problem – the problem which we dubbed in §31.3 'the problem of false prophecy': when is an inspired utterance (or action) *not* a charisma? Clearly there were those in Thessalonica, Corinth and probably Rome, who

believed that their inspiration was of God, but whose words and
actions Paul judged to be detrimental to the Christian community.
Since, therefore, the experience of inspiration in itself was no guarantee that God was its source (I Cor. 12.2f.), the practical problem was
to know when an inspired utterance or action was a charisma and
when not. Who was to say? By what criterion could a judgment be
made?

That the problem was not simply a matter of definition becomes
even clearer when we consider such passages as I Cor. 13.1–3, 8ff. and
I Cor. 1.5, 7 with 3.1ff. Paul does not dispute that the Corinthians
experienced genuine charismata, including prophecy, faith, giving.
But *even genuine charismata of the most striking nature when exercised without
love made for strife within the community and stunted the growth of the body.*[59]
The seriousness of the danger to the charismatic community and of
the problem thereby posed should not be underestimated. How then
were even the genuine charismata to be controlled? Who was to
evaluate the contribution of a charismatic as he functioned within
the community? How was such an evaluation to be reached? These
questions bring us back to the next stage of our study.

§47. THE EXERCISE OF AUTHORITY IN THE COMMUNITY: APOSTOLIC AUTHORITY

47.1　Since R. Sohm first posed the question of how charismatic
organization and ecclesiastical law were related within the early
church,[60] this question has proved to be one of the thorniest problems
for those concerned with the historical and theological evaluation of
primitive Christianity, the subject of continuing and often heated
debate, no doubt because of its potential repercussions for dogmatic
ecclesiology. It is not surprising that O. Linton in his valuable review
of research into 'the problem of the early church' from 1880 to 1931
ended by posing the question afresh: 'How do Spirit and office stand
in relation to each other in early Christianity?'[61] It has been principally in these terms, that is, on the relation between Spirit and office
or between charisma and office, that the debate has continued. For
some the answer was simply a matter of disentangling Harnack's distinction between 'religious' (or 'charismatic') ministries which were
universal in scope (apostles, prophets, teachers) and 'administrative'
ministries which were purely local (presbyters, bishops, deacons),[62]
and re-ordering the elements into a sharp distinction between charisma and office in which the former was clearly subordinate to the
latter.[63] Most, however, have recognized that charisma and office

could not so readily be set in antithesis in historical and exegetical analysis. On the contrary, such analysis led to the conclusion that charisma implied office, that office expressed charisma.[64]

The most penetrating contributions to the debate in recent years have come from E. Schweizer[65] and E. Käsemann,[66] whose insights both stem basically from the recognition of the nature of charisma as the particular action of God in a given situation (see above §43):[67] thus Schweizer – 'with Paul charism and ministry are both regarded essentially as an event, as something that takes place';[68] Käsemann – 'The Apostle's theory of order is not a static one, resting on offices, institutions, ranks and dignities; in his view, authority resides only within the concrete act of ministry as it occurs'.[69] A significant indication of the direction in which the debate is now moving are the two most weighty contributions from the Roman Catholic side in recent years: H. Küng, who emphasizes the continuing charismatic structure of the church,[70] and G. Hasenhüttl, whose provocative title, *Charisma, Ordnungsprinzip der Kirche*, tells its own tale.[71] In view of the increasing importance of Pentecostalism within Christianity today, and of the increasing influence of Pentecostal teaching not least on Roman Catholicism itself,[72] the question of Spirit and office, of charisma and order, is still very much alive and flourishing.

Obviously we cannot enter into the debate here in an extensive way. Our subject is the religious experience of earliest Christianity, and we must confine ourselves to the examination of how Paul envisaged the exercise of authority in the community in relation to the charismata, particularly in view of the dangers of charismatic anarchy outlined above (§46). The questions which arise for us are: *Did Paul regard authority as a charisma or as a function of office?* – that is, was a pronouncement authoritative in virtue of the speaker's office or in virtue of his inspiration at the time of speaking? And *in whom did Paul reckon authority was vested?*: in an individual over or in the community, in a group within the community, in the community itself, or in some combination of these? Since it is impossible to hold these two questions apart we will tackle them by examining the last named alternatives in turn: the authority of the apostles; the authority of different ministries; the authority of the community.

47.2 *Who were the 'apostles' of I Cor. 12.28?* I Cor. 12.27f. – 'Now you are Christ's body, and each one of you members of it. And God has appointed in the church first apostles, second prophets, third teachers . . .'. Here is the obvious place to start. Paul reminds the unruly members of the Corinthian church that while all members are mutually indispensable, nevertheless a certain ranking in importance attaches to three of the functions God gives to men within the Christian community. In the first place stand apostles (see also Eph. 4.11). But who were these apostles? and what was their authority?

Who were the apostles of I Cor. 12.28? A study of Paul's use of the word 'apostle' reveals that he does so in two positive senses. First, as all agree, it can be used in the sense of 'delegate, envoy or messenger' – II Cor. 8.23; Phil. 2.25. Clearly that is not the sense intended in I Cor. 12.28, since the authority of the delegate is authority to represent his community *elsewhere*; whereas in I Cor. 12.28 we are talking about apostles set *in* the church = the local community (see above pp. 262f.).

Second, elsewhere, and leaving aside II Cor. 10–13 for the moment, 'apostle' always refers to what we might call apostle in the I Cor. 15.7–9 sense, apostles of Christ rather than delegates of a church – that is, a limited circle of individuals (though much wider than 'the twelve'), a select circle which was soon closed, though not before Paul had been added to it by the abortion of his conversion (see above §18.3). If we may take Paul as typical,[73] we can slightly elaborate our conclusions of chapter V and list the key characteristics of apostleship (in the second sense) as follows: (1) they had been commissioned personally by the risen Jesus in a resurrection appearance (I Cor. 9.1; 15.7; Gal. 1.1, 15f.; I Thess. 2.6/7 – 'apostles of Christ'); (2) they were missionaries and church founders (Rom. 1.5; 11.13; 15.20; I Cor. 3.5f., 10; 9.2; 15.9ff.; Gal. 1.15f.); (3) theirs was a distinctively and decisively eschatological role (Rom. 11.13ff.; 15.15f.; I Cor. 4.9; 15.8; Eph. 3.5). We should note that all three elements were integral to Paul's understanding of apostleship (in the second sense). Hence the distinction observable between Paul's fellow workers – between Barnabas and Silvanus on the one hand, and such as Timothy and Epaphras on the other. No doubt one or other of the latter group had taken part with Paul, like Barnabas and Silvanus, in the founding of new churches, and perhaps had even founded churches independently of Paul; yet the title 'apostle' is withheld from them (notably in II Cor. 1.1; Col. 1.1; cf. Phil 1.1) – no doubt because they could not trace their commissioning back to an appearance of the risen Jesus.[74] Hence too, perhaps, Paul's hesitation about recognizing the apostleship of James, since he was not properly speaking a missionary and founder of new churches.[75] Hence too the question of other apostles in the future or of successors to the original apostles was one which never occurred to Paul – there could be, almost by definition, no successor to the *eschatological* apostles, since their work spanned the interval between resurrection and parousia; they were the last act in the arena before the end (I Cor. 4.9).[76]

There can be little doubt that 'apostles' in I Cor. 12.28 means apostles in the second sense.[77] Notice again that he is speaking of the local church – here the church in Corinth. This does *not* mean that each local community produced its own apostles to exercise authority within the community – Paul never uses 'apostle' in this sense. Nor does the term 'apostle' in I Cor. 12.28 refer to '*all* the apostles' of I Cor. 15.7. Rather Paul refers to the particular apostles who established the church in question. The founder of a new community continued to have authority within that community. In other words *the apostle exercised authority within a community not as an 'apostle of the universal church', but as founder of that community*; his authority as apostle in a church sprang from his work in bringing that church to birth. So we find in I Cor. 4.15 – 'You may have countless tutors in Christ, but you do not have many fathers; for it was I who became your father in Christ Jesus through the gospel', and in I Cor. 9.2 – 'If others do not accept me as an apostle, you at least are bound to do so, for you are yourselves the very seal of my apostolate in the Lord' (NEB). Contrary then to still widespread opinion, apostles, in Paul's view at least, were no figures commanding authority in any and every church; their authority was limited to their sphere of operation, to the churches they founded (Gal. 2.9).

This delimitation of apostolic authority comes out most clearly in II Cor. 10–13. It was precisely the attempt of apostles of the *Jewish* mission to exercise authority *in Corinth*[78] that Paul resisted so strongly. On what grounds Paul's opponents claimed apostolic authority is not entirely clear. On one view they called themselves apostles in part at least because they were representatives of the apostles in Jerusalem (the 'super apostles' of 11.5; 12.11).[79] Here the concept of apostleship would be derived primarily from the Jewish *shaliah* – an envoy with the full authority of the one who sent him and whom he represented: as the rabbis said, 'The one sent by a man is as the man himself'.[80] The authority claimed by Paul's opponents in II Cor. 10–13 on this view, therefore, was the authority of the Jerusalem apostles. Paul contested this claim on two grounds: first Jerusalem could not exercise apostolic authority in Corinth; the only one who could exercise such authority was the one who brought the gospel to them in the first place, the founder of the church (10.13–16; 11.2; 12.14).[81] Second, his opponents' claim to apostleship was an inadmissable confusion of the two senses of 'apostle' which he himself so clearly distinguished (see above p.273) – a confusion between apostles as sent by men or

church, and apostle as sent by the risen Lord. The conduct of Paul's
envoy (Titus) was in marked contrast to the conduct of Jerusalem's
envoys (12.17).[82] The sort of authority they claimed belonged only
to those sent by the risen Christ (Rom. 10.15; I Cor. 1.17). Since
therefore they had stepped so far beyond the bounds of what authority they could claim, they were to be classed not as apostles, but as
'false apostles' (11.13).

Alternatively, it is possible that the 'false apostles' were none other
than the 'super apostles' (see above n. 79), and that their claim to
authority rested not on a commission from Jerusalem but on a commission from Christ himself – 'apostles of Christ' (10.7, 11.13)[83] – that
is, they claimed to belong in effect to the I Cor. 15.7 circle of apostles.
To the extent that Paul recognized this claim his arguments outlined
in the previous paragraph still applied: even 'apostles of Christ' had
no apostolic authority in churches founded by others, outside the
mission,[84] or 'sphere' (NEB) or 'province'[85] assigned them by God
(10.13–16, cf. Rom. 15.20). But in point of fact he did not recognize the
claim: they were false apostles, deceitful workmen, servants of Satan;
their claim to be apostles of Christ was only a masquerade, like Satan's
disguising himself as an angel of light (11.13ff.). In other words, Paul
did not accept their claim to a resurrection appearance and commission from the risen Christ. Their 'visions and revelations' (12.1),
on which they doubtless based their claim, were not at all the same
thing.[86]

These two alternatives are of course not mutually exclusive. But
we need not come to any decision on that here. Either way our understanding of 'apostles' in I Cor. 12.28 is confirmed. In short, *the apostles
whom Paul ranks first in the body of Christ in Corinth are the founders of the
Corinthian church* – that is, presumably, Paul and Barnabas (I Cor.
9.6).[87] As apostles they provided a link not so much between the local
church and other churches elsewhere (the universal church)[88] as
between the local church and the gospel (see further below).

47.3   *What was Paul's conception of apostolic authority?* (a) Whence was
it derived? (b) What limits did he set to it? Here again we may take
Paul as a model: presumably he tried to live out his concept of
apostolic authority in his relation with his own churches.[89] Thus we
are not surprised that Paul quite often speaks to his converts with the
distinct tones of authority – sometimes giving orders (παραγγέλλω – I
Cor. 7.10; 11.17; I Thess. 4.11; II Thess. 3.4, 6, 10, 12), sometimes
admonishing (νουθετέω – I Cor. 4.14; Col. 1.28), sometimes commanding (διατάσσω – I Cor. 7.17; 11.34; 16.1), sometimes threatening

(I Cor. 4.21; II Cor. 10.6, 8ff.; 13.1ff.). It is noticeable that his tone becomes most authoritative when either his gospel is threatened (II Cor. 11.1ff.; Gal. 1.6–9; 2.3ff., 11ff.; 3.1ff; 4.8ff.; 5.2ff.) or when the unity of one of his congregation is threatened (I Cor. 5.1–5, 9ff.; 10.14, 25ff.; 11.17ff.; 14.26–33, 39f.; II Cor. 6.14; II Thess. 3.6ff., 14f.). His authority, as he himself explicitly states, is authority for building up not for destroying his churches (II Cor. 10.8; 13.10).

(a) What was the source of Paul's apostolic authority? From where did Paul derive his authority as apostle? He derived it firstly from *his personal commissioning by the risen Lord and by the success of his commission in the case of the particular congregation addressed by him.* Our discussions in chapter V and above (§47.2) are enough to validate our answer. I need only underline that both parts of the answer go together in Paul's mind. Not just the commissioning by the risen Jesus gave Paul authority over his converts, but its manifest effectiveness in their case. Those who had once experienced the authority of his apostolic commission in their conversion could not thereafter deny it without denying their own existence as Christians (see particularly I Cor. 9.1f.; II Cor. 3.2f.; 11.2). Having once become their father through the gospel he had a continuing paternal responsibility to supervise their growth (see particularly I Cor. 4.14f.; II Cor. 12.14; I Thess. 2.11).[90] II Cor. 10.13–6 may well mean that in Paul's view the effectiveness of an apostle's work provided the measure and marked out the extent of his authority (see above nn. 84 and 85).

The apostle, secondly, derived his authority from *the gospel.* 'There is no apostolic authority which the apostle might possess apart from his message'.[91] This answer is of course wholly bound up with the first, but it requires separate emphasis. It was because the gospel had come to him with the force of personal revelation, had proved so liberating and dynamic in his own case (Rom. 1.1; 2.16 and 16.25 – 'my gospel'; 10.15), *and* had proved its divine origin in the case of his converts, that he could neither yield on it himself or bear to see his converts abandon it (see particularly Gal. 1.6ff., 15f.; 2.3ff.; 3.1–5; 5.2ff.). As von Campenhausen notes:

he abandons any and every conceivable authority, in principle even his own, the moment it runs counter to the 'gospel' . . . The authority of the apostolic man is wholly bound up with the scandalizing truth of the message through which it exercises its effect, and from which by its very nature it cannot be separated.[92]

We should add that Paul recognized the importance of his gospel being confirmed by the other apostles, particularly those in Jerusalem (Gal. 2.2, 7ff.); but the important word is '*confirmed*' – even the Jerusalem 'pillar apostles' added nothing to him (Gal. 2.6). In other words, Paul's apostolic authority at this point derived directly from the 'revelation of Jesus Christ' (Gal. 1.12) and not from a previous apostle or apostolic council.

The apostle, thirdly, derived his authority from *tradition*. Or to be more precise, otherwise we shall contradict the last point, Paul regarded himself as apostle as *mediator of authoritative tradition* (I Cor. 7.10; 9.14; 11.2, 23; 15.3; Phil. 4.9; II Thess. 2.15).[93] This did not necessarily conflict with the charismatic authority which derived from new revelation.[94] The essential point for Paul was that it derived from the Lord (I Cor. 7.10; 9.14; 11.23); a tradition initiated by man was without validity (Col. 2.8).[95] Even where he had, or at least referred to, no dominical word for authorization, he quite often expressed the instruction as a call to imitate his own conduct (I Cor. 4.16; 11.1f.; Phil. 3.17; 4.8f.; II Thess. 3.6ff.), which was itself an imitation of Christ's (I Cor. 11.1; cf. Phil. 2.5; I Thess. 1.6). And since the authority behind this admonition derived not simply from Paul as apostle but directly from the superior authority of Christ,[96] he could refer them directly to the Jesus' tradition without reference to his own authority (Col. 2.6; Eph. 4.20). Here too we may add that the practices of other churches could be called upon to back up his instructions by way of confirmation (I Cor. 4.17; 7.17; 11.16; 14.33; cf. I Thess. 2.14); but the churches in question were the churches established by Paul, and their obedience only confirmed Paul's apostolic authority; his authority did not stem from them.

We can see then that *Paul derived his authority as apostle not from the inspiration of the present but from the decisive events of the past which remained determinative for believers*: specifically, (1) words of the earthly Jesus and his overall example of humility and service; (2) a once-for-all revelation or appearance of the risen Jesus commissioning him with the gospel to the Gentiles; (3) the conversion and establishment of the congregation addressed through his ministry. It was important to him that the authority of his gospel was *confirmed* by the rest of the apostles, and that the authority of his instructions were *confirmed* by the other churches of his mission – for the unity of Christianity as a whole was precious to him; but his authority as apostle in a particular situation did not derive from any other Christian, church or apostle outside that situation.

(*b*) Lastly we must ask how Paul exercised his authority in practice. What limits did he set to it? Three points call for comment. First, an analysis of the authority words mentioned earlier reveals that he used them relatively seldom as a means of expressing his own authority.[97] He talked of his converts' obedience (ὑπακούω, ὑπακοή) quite often, but usually of their obedience to Christ or to the gospel, only occasionally of their obedience to himself (II Cor. 7.15; 10.6(?); Phil. 2.12; II Thess. 3.14; Philemon 21). Ἐντολή (order, instruction) occurs twice (I Cor. 14.37; Col. 4.10), but he deliberately refrained from using one of the strongest words available to him – ἐπιταγή (command);[98] thus II Cor. 8.8 – 'not as a command' (cf. I Cor. 7.6, 25). More significant still, he emphasized his authority as such (ἐξουσία) only when left no alternative by the false apostles in Corinth (II Cor. 10.8; 13.10); otherwise he only mentioned it as something which he refused to use (I Cor. 9.4ff., 12, 18; II Thess. 3.9; cf. I Thess. 2.6f.), even when it was backed by a specific command of the Lord (I Cor. 9.14). Perhaps most striking of all is the word which he prefers above all others – παρακαλέω (exhort – 23 times) – a word he could use also when addressing the Lord (II Cor. 12.8)! *The great bulk of Paul's ethical instructions in his letters are more the exhortations of a fellow believer than the commands of an apostle* (see particularly Philemon 8ff., and further below).[99]

Second, von Campenhausen's excellent treatment of the subject shows *how careful Paul was to circumscribe his own authority by the freedom of his converts.*[100] He did not develop his authority in the obvious way by building up a sacral relationship of spiritual control and subordination. On the contrary he deliberately set his face against such a possibility. 'Christ has set us free, to be free men (Gal. 5.1 NEB); 'Do not become slaves of men' (I Cor. 7.23); 'Not that we lord it over your faith; we work with you for your joy . . .' (II Cor. 1.24 RSV); 'I preferred to do nothing without your consent in order that your goodness might not be by compulsion but of your own free will' (Philemon 14). Paul 'cannot simply give orders . . . The congregation of those who possess the Spirit must follow him in freedom . . .'.[101] By no means does Paul cling to authority as his sole and final prerogative. By no means does he set himself over against his congregations in an authoritarian way.[102] On the contrary, those who have once proved and validated his apostleship by their conversion must continue to prove and validate the authority which stems from that relationship thus established. In this dynamic relationship his congregations are also responsible and must share in the exercise of authority; so for example, I Cor. 5.3–5; II Cor. 2.6–8. 'By thus appealing to the congregation's own judgment and sense of responsibility he takes their freedom seriously, possibly indeed more seriously than they themselves had expected'.[103]

Third, Paul seems to recognize that *apostolic authority is not limitless in its scope.* Its exercise is restricted to those matters which arise immediately out of his commission, the available dominical tradition, and his founding of the church in question (hence p.276 above). Beyond or outside such matters he is as dependent on the inspiration of the Spirit and on its evaluation by the congregation as anyone else who 'has the Spirit', is 'spiritual', or is given a charisma of prophecy or teaching. Thus in looking forward to his visit to a church he did not found, he does not think in terms of apostolic instruction, but rather speaks of the charisma which he confidently expects to be given through him for their mutual benefit (Rom. 1.11); whereas he never speaks of apostleship or apostolic authority specifically as a charisma[104] – *charis* (Rom. 1.5), but not *charisma*.[105] Again, in I Cor. 7, when he leaves behind the guide-lines of dominical tradition, he does not command but merely profers his opinion (γνώμη – I Cor. 7.25, 40; so II Cor. 8.10). To be sure he is confident in his own mind that his opinion is informed by the Spirit (I Cor. 7.40), but even so that does not give him the right to exalt his inspired opinion into an apostolic command.[106] Indeed, even where he is certain that his instructions are a 'command of the Lord', he still does not expect them to be obeyed merely on his word; first they must be recognized as the Lord's command and then obeyed on that basis (I Cor. 14.37f.). So too in I Thess. 4.2, 15 we should probably recognize the authority of the teacher and the prophet speaking under inspiration rather than the authority of the apostle (see above pp. 230, 237); as in I Cor. 14.37f., his appeal in I Thess. 4.2–8 is both to his own inspiration (v. 2) but also to the Spirit in his converts (v. 8). In all these cases the authority which stems from the founding of a church in the past gives way to the authority of a charisma in the here and now; where the former can command within its limits, the latter can only invite evaluation and response on that basis (see further below §§ 48.1, 49.2).

In short, it follows that *as apostolic authority stems directly from certain decisive events and words of the past, so the exercise of that authority is limited by these same events and words*: only where these events and words speak immediately to the issue at hand can the apostle speak as apostle. Even within these limits Paul is conscious that his relationship with the community in question is a living and dynamic one, that they share the same Spirit and the same freedom, that he stands *within* the charismatic community even as apostle (I Cor. 12.28; cf. 5.3); consequently wherever possible he encourages his congregations to share in the exercise of an authority which in principle is his alone. Outside these limits Paul recognizes that he is just one 'spiritual man' (*pneumatikos*) among many spiritual men; like them he must depend on the charisma of the Spirit for any word of authority; like them he must submit that word to the judgment of the charismatic community at large (I Cor. 2.12ff.).

We can now give a first preliminary answer to the question of how Paul met the charismatic threat to community. Where charismata were being used in a way which threatened the *gospel*, as in II Cor. 10–13 (particularly 11.4), Paul did not hesitate to 'pull all the rank' he could, even though he found it almost wholly distasteful. Where charismata were part of a threat to *the unity of one of the churches he had founded* (Corinth, Thessalonica), he was able by virtue of that fact to speak as their apostle on the various interlocking issues; in some instances giving authoritative instruction by direct application of the gospel or dominical tradition (as in I Cor. 4.14–21; 6.9–20; 11.17–34, and probably II Thess. 3.6–13); in others encouraging their participation in the exercise of authority (I Cor. 5.1–5; II Cor. 2.6–8), or submitting his exhortations to their own evaluation less as an apostle and more as one *pneumatikos* among others (I Cor. 2.12–16; 7.25–40; 14.29–33a, 37f., and probably I Thess. 4.2–8). *Apostolic authority, therefore, provided one control on the charismatic threat to community* – an authority which as such was not itself charismatic.

§48. THE AUTHORITY OF OTHER MINISTRIES WITHIN THE PAULINE CHURCHES

When we look beyond apostles, other regular ministries come at once into view – prophets, teachers (I Cor. 12.28), overseers, deacons (Phil. 1.1), evangelists, pastors (Eph. 4.11), and possibly others beside.

48.1   *Prophets*. It is quite clear from I Cor. 12.28 and (probably) 14.29ff. that in Corinth at least there was a fairly well defined circle of recognized prophets.[107] We may presume from this, from Rom. 12.6, and from the key role Paul gives to prophecy in the building up of community (I Cor. 14), that there were a number of prophets within each or most of the Pauline congregations. There is certainly no evidence in the Pauline literature to support Harnack's view that the prophets of I Cor. 12.28 were wandering prophets who moved from community to community,[108] although this does not exclude the possibility that there were such (cf. Acts 11.27; 15.32).[109] It is possible that the group in Corinth included women (I Cor. 11.5), but Paul is probably thinking here only of occasional and not of regular prophesying.[110]

What authority did the prophets have? From where did they

derive it and how was it exercised? The little evidence we have is nevertheless fairly explicit. *The authority of the prophet was authority to prophesy under inspiration; his authority was the authority of his inspiration and did not extend beyond his inspiration.* Hence the injunction that prophecy should always be in accordance with the measure of the prophet's faith (Rom. 12.6) – that is, he should not speak beyond the limits of his inspiration, without the (divinely given) confidence/ faith that his words were God's words (see above §39.4). Hence, too, one prophet must give way to the inspiration of another (I Cor. 14.30;[111] 14.32(?)[112]) – the individual prophet as prophet was subject to the charisma of prophecy.

At the same time, the inspiration of the individual was subject to the evaluation of 'the others' (I Cor. 14.29) – that is, probably, the other prophets,[113] though it is possible that Paul means the community as a whole (cf. I Cor. 2.13ff.; I Thess. 5.21 – see below §49.1).[114] The authority of the prophets therefore included *authority to evaluate the oracle of another prophet*, or indeed, no doubt, any other prophecy – evaluation involving discussion (presumably) leading to some sort of agreed judgment on the origin and significance of the oracle (see above §41.3).[115]

In the light of these brief considerations we may characterize prophetic authority as follows: (1) Prophetic authority did not derive from an appointment to the rank of prophet whether by apostle or by community. *Prophetic authority derived only from prophetic inspiration.*[116] The community did not install a man into a prophetic 'office' and then allow him to prophesy; on the contrary, the community simply recognized a man as a prophet because he already prophesied regularly. Or to put it more succinctly: a man did not prophesy because he was a prophet; rather he was a prophet because he prophesied. (2) *Prophetic authority was not confined to the prophets.* Only an apostle could exercise apostolic authority; but anyone might prophesy. Paul clearly expected that other members of the assembly other than the prophets would be inspired to prophesy (cf. 14.5, 24, perhaps 31);[117] in such cases their prophecies would be every bit as authoritative as those of the prophets, since authority lay in the prophesying and not in the prophet. The only difference between the prophet and other members of the assembly was that he prophesied regularly and they only occasionally (otherwise they too would be recognized as prophets). (3) Even more than in the case of Paul's apostolic authority, *the prophetic authority was subject to the assessment of the wider community* (whether the community as such or the prophets in particular). The individual's own sense of inspiration might be authority enough for his speaking out; but the authority which that utterance carried for the community depended on a wider sense of inspiration – on its source being recognized as the Spirit of Christ and its significance recognized as the mind of Christ (cf. I Cor. 2.16; 7.40).

In short, for Paul prophetic authority is charismatic authority; it is not the authority of office; it is not something possessed; it exists only in each charisma of prophecy, or communally in the act of evaluation. The authority belongs to the charisma and nowhere else; but because of its communal dimension it is able to control the threat posed to community by a selfish inspirationism.

48.2 *Teachers.* I Cor. 12.28 also implies that in Corinth there was a recognized group of teachers; see also Gal. 6.6.[118] The evidence is even less than before, but it would appear that teachers had a twofold function in the Pauline communities. First, theirs was the responsibility of *passing on the tradition*, received presumably, in the first instance at least, from the founding apostle – that is, in particular, the tradition of kerygma and Jesus' words (cf. Rom. 16.17; I Cor. 4.17; 11.2; Col. 1.28; 2.7; II Thess. 2.15; 3.6).[119] The necessity of such a role was obvious for one as conscious as Paul of his continuity with those in the faith before him (I Cor. 11.23; 15.3; Gal. 2.2, 7ff.). Indeed, the importance of the teaching function itself within the Pauline communities is one of the clearest examples of his debt to Jewish Christianity and Judaism[120] – although his choice of κατηχέω (give instruction – I Cor. 14.19; Gal. 6.6), a word hardly known in the religious vocabulary of Judaism, may imply an attempt on Paul's part to indicate the distinctive nature of Christian instruction.[121]

The second function of the teacher was the *interpretation of tradition*, and thus its development. The most obvious need would be for the interpretation of LXX passages as prophecies of Jesus;[122] but new situations and issues would require fresh interpretation of the Jesus and kerygmatic traditions too, especially if a word of prophetic guidance was lacking (for examples see above §41.4). Here the 'model' would more likely be the charismatic interpretation of Jesus (see above §13.3) than the rabbinic authority of learning and precedent. That such exegesis would be open to the charge of special pleading is obvious from Paul's treatment, for example, of Gen. 12.7 etc. in Gal. 3.16, of Hab. 2.4 in Rom. 1.17ff., and of Gen. 15.6 in Rom. 4 (contrast even within the Christian interpretative tradition, James 2.22f.). But this simply emphasizes that the authority of such exegesis lay not so much in its logic as in the charisma of the act of teaching. In terms of the NT as a whole we may say that if Revelation is the classic expression of (apocalyptic) prophecy, so Hebrews is the classic expression of a teacher's interpretation of the OT cult and Matthew of a teacher's passing on and interpretation of the Jesus tradition.

If this is a fair, though inevitably speculative, outline of the teaching function within the Pauline churches, we can draw some conclusions about the authority of teachers within their communities. (1) *The teaching function had more the character of 'office' than any other of the regular ministries.* For it was constituted not merely by the charisma of the moment but primarily by the tradition from the past. The role of teacher would therefore almost certainly be limited to those who had ability to retain, understand and teach that tradition. It would involve learning and studying, and would thus more or less from the first be a part or full time work or 'profession', with teachers dependent for their material support on their fellow Christians, particularly those whom they taught (Gal. 6.6). Moreover, the passing on of tradition, in so far as it was merely passing on, would not necessarily require an ever fresh charisma (though see above §43.5). In this role *the teacher's authority would be the authority of his tradition* – no more and no less; and the community would not be subject to the authority of an 'office', but both teacher and community would stand together under the authority of the tradition.

(2) To the extent that both were mediators of tradition the roles and authority of apostle and teacher were very similar. But beyond that the similarity ceases. Unlike the apostle the teacher's authority lay not in his unique personal relation to the risen Jesus, not in his appointment, far less his 'office', but only in his teaching. The apostle could command and give orders; the teacher could only teach. Moreover, the relation between teacher and community was not so personalized as the relation between apostle and community. Where a teacher-pupil relationship, such as we find in Judaism between rabbi and pupil,[123] developed in Corinth,[124] Paul was quick to denounce it, and to rally the community as a whole under the one banner of Christ (I Cor. 1.10–17). For the teacher did not have his own teaching or an independent tradition, only the tradition shared by all the other churches.[125] And his authority as teacher was limited to the function of passing it on.

(3) *As the teacher moved beyond the simple passing on of tradition to its interpretation, so the locus of his authority moved more from tradition to charisma.* Here his authority was more like that of the prophet than that of the apostle. As the prophet depended for authority to prophesy on the charisma of faith (Rom. 12.6), so the teacher depended for authority to teach on the charisma of teaching (Rom. 12.7).[126] The

development and giving out of the interpretation would not necessarily depend on a charisma at that time, but the authority of that interpretation would depend on whether the insight which led to it was given by the Spirit or not – that is, it was ultimately charismatic authority (see again §41.4). Presumably, like prophecy, such a word of teaching was subject to the judgment of the wider community (at large? or as represented by the teachers in particular?). Nothing is said about this, but in so far as Paul's 'opinion' in I Cor. 7.25, 40 was Paul speaking as teacher rather than apostle, the inference seems to be justified (see above p.279).[127] In this way any tendency to more extravagant flights of exegetical fancy would be subject to check and control – the yardstick being the tradition itself first taught by the apostle (Rom. 16.17f.).

(4) Finally we may note that as prophecy was not limited to the group of prophets, so *teaching was not limited to the group of teachers*. The tradition was shared by all, and known in its essentials by all. So any member might be given a charismatic interpretation for the benefit of the whole assembly (I Cor. 14.26). Indeed, according to Col. 3.16, the community as a whole had the responsibility of teaching. Presumably anyone who showed himself knowledgeable about the tradition and who regularly manifested the charisma of teaching would be recognized as a teacher; although, in view of the more 'professional' character of his work, perhaps his recognition as a teacher was more formal than in the case of a prophet. Even so, I repeat, his authority as teacher would lie only in the tradition and in his teaching and not in his office or 'professional capacity'.

In short, the teaching function provided *an indispensable complement to prophecy; the normative role of the gospel and of Jesus' words provided an invaluable control on charismatic excess*. As Greeven puts it: 'Prophecy without teaching degenerates into fanaticism, teaching without prophecy solidifies into law'.[128] Yet we should also not forget that Paul ranks prophecy above teaching: teaching preserves continuity, but prophecy gives life; with teaching a community will not die, but without prophecy it will not live.[129]

48.3   Were there *other regular ministries* in the Pauline churches apart from prophets and teachers? In particular, was there a regular role of leading a community and its worship which was fulfilled by a recognized group in each congregation? At first sight the answer is an obvious Yes, with reference particularly to the 'overseers' of Phil. 1.1 and the 'pastors' of Eph. 4.11. But a closer examination of the evidence available reveals a rather different picture.

(a) *Paul consistently avoids using words which in Judaism denoted leadership of worship or of synagogue or priestly office.* There seems to be no individual in the Pauline churches who was the equivalent of the ἀρχισυνάγωγος (leader or president of a synagogue).[130] The word which denotes the president's assistant (ὑπηρέτης – Luke 4.20) is used only once, of the work of Paul, Apollos and Cephas, and there in its broader, non-liturgical sense (I Cor. 4.1).[131] Elders (πρεσβύτεροι) formed the governing body of a Jewish congregation, and the leadership of the Jerusalem church under James was probably already modelled on that pattern (see above §32.3), but the word never once appears in the Pauline corpus before the Pastorals.[132] Finally, there is λειτουργία (service), which in the LXX regularly denotes the ceremonial service performed by the priest. Paul uses λειτουργός once of his own ministry in a metaphorical way (Rom. 15.16). But five out of the other six uses of the same word group apply to the service of the whole congregation (Rom. 15.27; II Cor. 9.12; Phil. 2.17(?), 25, 30).[133] In speaking of the work of other individuals and associates within their churches Paul consistently avoids these words.

(b) This silence becomes all the more eloquent when we realize that *nowhere in his letters*, with the probable exception of Phil. 1.1 (see below pp. 288f.), *does Paul address one single class or group of people as though they were responsible for the organization, worship or spiritual wellbeing of others.*[134] The significance of this becomes plain again from I Corinthians, where repeatedly there are situations which would seem to cry out for a leader or organizing group, and yet Paul says nothing of such leadership or to encourage its appointment: I Cor. 5.3–5; 6.1–8 – no group to whom disputes could be referred, no elders to act as judges, only the expectation that in the event someone would be given the necessary wisdom to judge rights and wrongs (6.5); 11.17–34 – no president of the common meal and the Lord's Supper; 14.26–40 – no leader to regulate worship, except that the prophets (probably) regulated their own charismata on behalf of the whole; 16.1f. – no one to organize the collection, so that Paul has to give the most basic instructions.[135] The implication is plain: if leadership was required Paul assumed that the charismatic Spirit would provide it.

(c) Other words and passages allude to a variety of more or less regular ministries, and are often taken to denote not merely service of the community but a particular *office* within the community. In Rom. 12.6–8 Paul refers to various regular ministries, apart from prophet and teacher. These include 'he who exhorts': although 'exhortation' was one expression of the prophetic charisma (see above pp. 229f.), Paul envisages that there will be some who contribute regularly in more limited ministries of the spoken word. The presence of prophets does not make these more limited ministries any less important or necessary. He also thinks of others through whom the prompting of the Spirit expresses itself in different kinds of service – giving and caring (see above §42.2). None of these activities can properly be termed 'offices'.

In I Corinthians the only possible candidates are the ἀντιλήμψεις and κυβερνήσεις of I Cor. 12.28, and the service (διακονία) of Stephanas in I Cor. 16.15. But as we have seen in chapter VIII, the first two words denote actions not people (helpful deeds, giving guidance – §42.3), and the second of these cannot refer to community leadership as exercised by a recognized group or individual, otherwise Paul must have referred to them in some of the instances mentioned above (p.285). Far less can they denote offices to which the Christian had to be elected before he could exercise them.[136] As for Stephanas's 'service of the saints', we recall that this was a particular task or area of *service* which Stephanas and his household *had taken upon themselves* (ἔταξαν ἑαυτούς – see above §42.1); that is, Paul had not appointed them to it.[137] And Paul asks the community not to regularize their ministry by formal ratification, far less to appoint Stephanas (and his household!) to an office ('deacon'), but rather to recognize and submit themselves to the manifestly charismatic authority which they *already* exercised in the work they did (I Cor. 16.16, 18).[138] This was the authority of regular ministry, not just of an isolated act; but presumably it was limited to their particular task(s), otherwise we might have looked for an appeal or reminder or instruction to Stephanas in the various situations mentioned above. The same must apply to Fortunatus and Achaicus, as indeed to 'every fellow labourer and hard worker' (16.16).[139] *Wherever* some particular charisma of service was manifested through the same individuals in a regular way the community should recognize that here were men (and women) whose lead should be followed *in these areas of service*.

When we turn from I Cor. 16.15ff. to I Thess. 5.12ff., we notice that the charge Paul lays upon the 'brothers' at Thessalonica is very similar to that laid upon the Corinthians. There were certainly those at Thessalonica who laboured among the community, cared for them in the Lord and counselled them, and this group was not co-terminous with the 'brothers' who are addressed. But to assume that this group was a small one, that these were all fairly well defined functions, and that they had to be appointed to the 'offices' in question before they could exercise them, goes far beyond the text. More likely Paul has in mind the 'activists' (like Stephanas) who form the core of any community like that at Thessalonica, and whose only 'qualification' is the hard work and service they take on.[140] It would certainly be hard to divide up the words used by Paul into different and distinct ministries (κοπιῶντες, προϊστάμενοι, νουθετοῦντες). More likely Paul chooses words which adequately cover the range of activities he has in mind. And the words themselves can hardly denote a closed group or activities undertaken only by apostolic or community appointment: as the use of νουθετέω in 5.14 makes clear, the task of counselling was not confined to a handful of 'leaders' but was a *community* function (see also II Thess. 3.15); in a charismatic community the Spirit might inspire each and any to admonish his fellow believers (Rom. 15.14; Col. 3.16).[141] We should probably conclude therefore that those mentioned in I Thess. 5.12 were the ones who were most active in the life of the Christian community, who undertook their service at the instigation of the Spirit and *whose only authority was that of some particular charisma(ta) manifested in a regular ministry*.

Another passage which on the face of it could suggest a leadership group within a Pauline community is Gal. 6.1: who were the *pneumatikoi* (spiritual men)? Paul's use of the word in I Cor. 2 suggests itself as the most obvious guide. There the spiritual ones are those who 'have received the Spirit' (2.12), that is Christians in general (cf. Rom. 8.9; Ignatius, *Eph.* 8.2).[142] But two points must be made to clarify Paul's meaning. First, he is speaking polemically against the Corinthian gnostics who presumably confined the word to those possessing wisdom and knowledge; Paul replies, 'All who have the Spirit are spiritual'. Yet, secondly, at the same time, Paul himself qualified the application of the word in the verses that follow (3.1ff.): all Christians are spiritual (*pneumatikos*) except those who show themselves to be unspiritual by living according to the flesh (*sarkinos/sarkikos*). In other words, Paul uses 'spiritual' in two senses and rejects a third: 'spiritual' = Christians, those who *have* the Spirit; 'spiritual' = Christians who are *walking* according to the Spirit and not according to the flesh, demonstrated particularly by their love and concern for the community (see below §49.2); 'spiritual' does *not* denote a distinct group of Christians marked out by special, striking and more esoteric charismata.[143] In short, for Paul it was not an additional experience or further initiation (or appointment) which makes a man spiritual, though some members of their community by their lack of love and quarrelling might thereby demonstrate their *un*spirituality. Returning to Gal. 6.1, we may conclude: the *pneumatikoi* are not a faction within the Galatian church like the Corinthian gnostics – the tone is hardly sarcastic or disapproving;[144] and it is unlikely that

the word refers to a group of leaders (overseers, pastors) as such;[145]
rather they are the community at large (cf. νουθετέω above), or more
precisely, *all who are walking by the Spirit* (Gal. 5.16–25) and not giving
way to self-conceit, destructive and uncharitable criticism of others or
envy (5.13ff., 26; 6.3).[146]

E. E. Ellis has recently argued that συνεργός (co-worker),[147]
ἀδελφός (brother) and διάκονος (servant) all denote special classes of
workers whom Paul associated with himself in his mission. But such
an interpretation imposes a narrowing of Paul's meaning which the
texts cited do not justify. Συνεργός denotes simply someone who had
worked with Paul at one time or another, and no more denotes a
particular class of work or type of association than συνστρατιώτης (fellow
soldier – Phil. 2.25) or σύνζυγος (yokefellow – Phil. 4.3).[148] The only
official and specific associations are the 'apostles (= delegates) of the
churches' (II Cor. 8.23; Phil. 2.25). The case for recognizing a class
of 'brothers' is almost wholly unconvincing. In every instance cited
by Ellis 'brothers' almost certainly means 'fellow Christians'.[149] The
case for regarding διάκονος as a special class of worker is certainly
stronger, in view of Phil. 1.1, but apart from that reference, the word
makes better sense as a general description of *anyone whose activity
served Christ, the gospel, or one of his churches*.[150] This is why Paul can use
it equally of his own ministry (I Cor. 3.5; II Cor. 3.6; 6.4; Eph. 3.7;
Col. 1.23, 25) as of the work of others (Rom. 16.1; II Cor. 11.23; Eph.
6.21; Col. 1.7; 4.7; I Thess. 3.2). In none of these cases can it be
taken to signify a specific kind of service, let alone a particular office
or position within the churches (cf. Rom. 13.4; II Cor. 11.5!).[151] In
these passages διάκονος no more signifies 'a special class of co-worker'
than δοῦλος (slave – Rom. 1.1; II Cor. 4.5; Gal. 1.10; Eph. 6.6; Phil.
1.1; Col. 4.12).[152]

But what about the overseers and deacons (ἐπίσκοποι καὶ διάκονοι) of
Phil. 1.1? It is quite clear that these are distinct groups within the
church at Philippi, otherwise Paul's singling them out from the
Philippian Christians in general has no meaning.[153] Probably too
they had fairly clearly recognized functions, as the use of the nouns
rather than a phrase like 'those who serve' (οἱ διακονοῦντες) or 'those
who engage in service' (διακονία) suggests. What these functions were,
however, and whether they were narrowly specified and defined, it is
not possible to say with any certainty. 'Επίσκοπος is best translated
'*overseer*', and must refer to *some leadership role* and/or administrative
or financial responsibility (cf. James 1.27 – ἐπισκέπτεσθαι).[154] To
associate the overseer with leadership of the ceremony of thanksgiving
(eucharist) is a gratuitous assumption;[155] as is the equation of over-

seer with elder.[156] It is more probable that in Philippi the vague area of service indicated in I Cor. 12.28 by κυβερνήσεις (giving guidance) had cohered into a particular ministry. As for the deacons, they may have been (local) preachers (cf. 1.5 – overseers as well?).[157] But the choice of name (servant) suggests something more in the line of what I earlier called 'welfare service':[158] viz., that particular area of διακονία which is denoted in I Cor. 12.28 by 'helpful deeds', and in Rom. 12.8 by 'sharing, caring and giving' (see above §42.2, 3). Again in Philippi these more diverse and unspecified services seem to have cohered into a more distinctive ministry.[159] More than this we cannot say. We certainly cannot assume from the words in the Pastorals and in later Catholicism that already in Philippi these ministries were offices to be filled by appointment and ordination.[160] The pattern of charisma and ministry in the other churches which Paul established suggests rather that these were charismatic ministries which the individuals concerned had taken upon themselves and whose role as regular ministries was recognized by the church in Philippi (cf. above §48.1, and pp.286f.).

No further light on these issues can be shed by Col. 4.17, where the community is called upon to urge Archippus: 'Attend to the ministry (διακονίαν) which you received in the Lord (παρέλαβες ἐν κυρίῳ), and discharge it to the full'. Was this a regular ministry which the community already recognized, or a particular act of service to which he had been publicly called, perhaps through a word of prophecy (ἐν κυρίῳ)?[161] We cannot say. Firmer conclusions (e.g. that this was an official ministry (diaconate) to which Paul had appointed him) have no real foundation in the text.[162]

Finally we have the evangelists and the pastors of Eph. 4.11. 'Evangelist' clearly denotes a preacher of the gospel. If they were primarily missionaries,[163] then their prominence (third in the list) supports the view that the apostles (I Cor. 15.7) were beginning to die off, or were already dead.[164] But they may have functioned simply as evangelistic agents of the local church in the surrounding district. 'Pastor' probably signifies the sort of function elsewhere covered by the word προΐστημι (care – Rom. 12.8; I Thess. 5.12).[165] If 'apostles and prophets' belong to an earlier day (as could well be implied by Eph. 2.20), then we may already have reached the time when charismatic ministries began to give way to more regulated functionaries (see further below §57.2).[166] Yet we must also note that both words denote functions rather than 'offices' and are not yet established titles;[167] the thought is still thoroughly Pauline at least to the extent that the ministries are not confined to a few – each member has his part to play (v. 16), that is, in its context, his ministry for the benefit of the whole.[168]

48.4 To *sum up*, as well as individual charismatic acts and utterances *Paul recognizes the importance of regular ministries within the charismatic community*. The ones to which he gives particular prominence in the central period of his apostolic work were the ministries of the word, of prophet and teacher, the interaction of new revelation with old.[169] Other regular ministries were at this stage much more diverse – as diverse as the situations and the individuals involved (Rom. 12.6–8; I Cor. 16.15–18; I Thess. 5.12) – although with the passing of the years regular ministries known as overseers and deacons emerged at Philippi, and as the founding era of apostles and prophets began to wane, more established functionaries appeared in the churches of Asia Minor (evangelists, pastors and teachers). But *in the earlier years of the Hellenistic mission there were no specific and well defined ministries apart from those of prophet and teacher*. On the contrary, the tremendous variety of words used by Paul[170] indicates a whole range of activities and services which overlapped and which could not be clearly distinguished.[171] Such ministries were open to all,[172] for they were essentially charismatic ministries, that is activities for which no further qualification was needed than obedience to the inspiration of the Spirit.[173] When such a ministry was undertaken regularly, whether intensively over a short period (for example, working with Paul), or less intensively over a longer period (as presumably Stephanas), the congregation could be called upon to recognize and respect the individual concerned as prophet or teacher or simply one who engaged in a regular form of service. Indeed, the fact that Paul urges both Thessalonians and Corinthians to acknowledge the ministries of men like Stephanas shows that Paul regarded such *regular* ministries as of no little importance within the ongoing life of his churches. *For Paul the body of Christ grows not simply out of a series of unrelated acts of ministry but through regular ministries as well.*

At the same time, it is also important to underline *the charismatic character of these ministries*. They should certainly not be designated 'offices'; for 'offices' signify positions where certain privileges and authority are reserved for an appointed few, positions with well defined responsibilities which the 'officials' can only begin to exercise on appointment; whereas in the charismatic community *all* may be prompted by the Spirit to exercise any ministry, and the recognition by the community of regular ministries is precisely a *recognition* of authority *already* manifested in each charismatic act of service.

Within the Pauline churches the only ministries which *begin* to fall within this definition of 'office' are apostles and teachers; but since apostles by (Paul's) definition were unrepeatable (eschatological apostles), and since teaching included charismatic teaching, the word 'office' is best avoided completely in any description of the Pauline concept of ministry.[174] As for authority and continuity, in Paul's view *that lay primarily in the Spirit* ever freshly creating a new word (prophecy) and in the gospel tradition first brought by the apostle and passed on by the teacher. In short, *authority was essentially charismatic authority: only he who ministered could have authority and that only in the actual exercise of his ministry.*[175]

How then did Paul think the threat of charismatic excess within his communities could be controlled? The prophets provided part of an answer (§48.1), but the prophets were themselves charismatics. Gospel tradition provided another part of the answer (§48.2), but teachers could handle the tradition charismatically, that is creatively. Other regular ministries of diverse nature also played a part, but these too were essentially charismatic ministries (§48.3). How else could controls be applied? Not by a concept of office. How then? This question brings us to our last section.

§49. THE AUTHORITY OF THE COMMUNITY AND ITS CRITERIA OF ASSESSMENT

49.1   *The authority of the community.* Where in the community did the authority lie that could regulate the charismata? Partly in the founding apostle(s) (§47); partly in the regular ministries which emerged within the communities (§48); but partly also in the community itself. It is important to realize that in Paul's view *the community as such had an authoritative role in ordering its worship and affairs.* We have already touched on this at various points and we need only elaborate our earlier findings briefly.

(1) *Paul never addresses himself to a leadership group within a community* (apart from Phil. 1.1). His instructions and exhortations are generally addressed to the community as a whole. This can only mean that responsibility for responding to such exhortations lay with the congregation as such and not merely with one or two individuals within it.[176] Hence the lack of mention of any leadership group, overseer or whatever, in situations like those outlined in I Cor. 5; 6; 11; 14; 16. Paul does not even seem to envisage the prophets giving a lead,[177]

their authority as prophets lying solely in their charisma of prophecy and evaluation of inspired utterances.

(2) Paul's understanding of the local church as the body of Christ necessarily implies *each member* having a *function* within that congregation and a *responsibility* for its common life and worship (cf. I Cor. 12.25f.). Hence the exhortations to *all* the members of different communities to teach, admonish, judge, comfort (Rom. 15.14; I Cor. 5.4f.; II Cor. 2.7; Col. 3.16; I Thess. 5.14).[178]

(3) The community as a whole are 'taught by God' (I Thess. 4.9), they all participate in the one Spirit (κοινωνία), they are all men of the Spirit (*pneumatikoi*).[179] As such they have authority to regulate and exercise judgment concerning the charismata (I Cor. 2.15). Hence even Paul himself does not hesitate to submit his opinions to them: in I Cor. 14.37 even though he is certain that his counsel is a 'word of the Spirit' (2.13) he still expects the Corinthians to exercise judgment concerning it – for that is why they have received the Spirit, precisely 'in order that they might know/recognize all that God gives them by his grace' (2.12; cf. Phil. 3.15). Hence too, not only the prophets have responsibility to evaluate individual prophecy (I Cor. 14.29) but the community also has responsibility both to encourage prophecy and to 'test everything', including prophecy (I Thess. 5.20f.).[180] Not least in importance is the community's responsibility to recognize and acknowledge the manifest charismatic authority of those who do not spare themselves in the service of the church and to encourage them in these more regular ministries (I Cor. 16.15–18; I Thess. 5.12f.; cf. Phil. 2.29f.). In the light of these considerations I Cor. 14.16 gains a new significance. The 'Amen' which the congregation utters after a prayer or prophecy is not just a formal liturgical assent; it indicates rather the importance Paul attaches to the community's members being able to understand and to give assent to what is said in its worship.[181] 'The responsibility of the church as a whole to hear, understand, test and control is underlined'.[182]

If Paul's intention was for the charismatic community to administer its own affairs in the same manner as it worshipped, as we may assume, then we may find his guide lines for the ordering of congregational affairs in I Cor. 14.26ff. That is to say, in meetings where there was confusion or uncertainty over some issue, some individual might feel himself inspired to give a lead – for example, by a word of practical wisdom (cf. I Cor. 6.5), a word of counsel (κυβέρνησις), a prophet speaking in the name of the risen Lord, a teacher referring to some word in the kerygmatic tradition. Alternatively the community might call on those who had already demonstrated their spirituality by their hard work, love and service, like Stephanas, to give some lead. The counsel would then be assessed and discussed, presumably until the congregation felt that they knew the mind of Christ in the matter (cf. II Cor. 2.6; also Rom. 1.11f.; 12.1f.; 15.14; Phil. 1.9–11; 2.1ff.; I Thess. 4.18; 5.11, 19f.).[183]

But how did they make such assessments? What criteria did they use?

49.2   *The criteria of assessment.* In the course of the three chapters given over to the discussion of the charismata (I Cor. 12–14), Paul highlights three criteria which should enable the community to evaluate charismatic contributions to its life and worship.[184]

(a) *The test of kerygmatic tradition* – I Cor. 12.3. Inspiration alone is no proof that the inspiration is by God's Spirit (12.2). It must be tested, evaluated (see above §41.3). In this instance the yardstick is a fairly basic expression of the gospel – 'Jesus is Lord' (cf. Rom. 10.9; II Cor. 4.5) – that is, it is drawn from the kerygmatic tradition. If an inspired utterance confirms or is in accord with the gospel by which they are converted it can be concluded that the oracle is of God. If however, the utterance runs counter to that gospel it is to be rejected.[185]

Paul of course does not intend this to be the only test which arises out of the gospel: the particular rule of thumb which he applies in I Cor. 12.3 is very probably determined by the situation which had arisen in Corinth – a charismatic crying out 'Jesus is accursed' under obvious inspiration but in the Christian assembly (see above pp. 234f.). Throughout Galatians on the other hand the test which arises out of the kerygma is the test of Christian *liberty* rather than of Christology – a test which he applies again and again with powerful effect (Gal. 1.6ff.; 2.3ff., 14ff.; 3.1ff.; 4.1ff.; 5.1ff.).

In addition, it is just possible that in I Cor. 2.13 Paul envisages a testing which consists in 'comparing spiritual gifts with spiritual gifts and judging them thereby' (see above ch. VIII n. 184) – that is, previous charismata assessed and proved become precedents by which to judge new charismata; note too the appeal which Paul makes several times in I Corinthians to the practice of his other churches (see further above p. 277). This would not mean that Paul envisaged tradition as a steadily expanding rule book of precedent and law for all situations and occasions. That which remained normative was the *kerygmatic* tradition – the gospel and teaching which brought their church into existence (I Cor. 11.2, 23; 15.3; II Thess. 2.15).[186] Earlier and other charismatic interpretations of that tradition might provide guide-lines and limits for fresh interpretations of that kerygmatic tradition in different circumstances. But *the authority belonged in an unparalleled way to the message of the first witnesses.* Indeed, if we take the implication of I Cor. 15.6b aright, even the central affirmation of the kerygma is in principle subject to an independent testing which goes behind the kerygma to those who were eyewitnesses of the decisive salvation-history events (see also above §41.4).

(*b*) *The test of love* – I Cor. 13. Love (ἀγάπη) is one of the most important words in the Pauline vocabulary: it appears 116 times in the NT, 75 of them in the Pauline corpus (nearly two-thirds). From the centrality of the 'hymn to love' in I Cor. 13 within the discussion of charismata in the Christian community (see above n. 37), it is clear that love for Paul is a crucial test of charismatic phenomena.[187] Without love, even the most soaring experiences of worship and devotion are meaningless jangle (13.1).[188] Without love, even prophecy and the most profound insights into God's mysteries, even faith to do what seems impossible,[189] makes the charismatic no better (13.2). Without love, even the most self-sacrificing service to others improves him in no way (13.3).[190] In short, *even man at his religious best, at the limit of charismatic possibility, if in all that he lacks love, does neither himself any good* (*nor presumably his community*).

Notice that Paul does not think of love here as a charisma;[191] he thinks of it rather in terms of the individual's character (vv. 4–7; 'I am nothing' – v. 2; 'I am none the better' – v. 3).[192] Love here is the power which transforms character and which motivates the transformed character. It is another aspect of the power of grace. The Spirit which manifests itself as charisma in the concrete situation of community manifests itself as love in the character of the charismatic. It is impossible to experience love without charisma, since the loving character inevitably expresses itself in loving action, of service or whatever, and that is charisma as much as glossolalia or prophecy. But *it is only too possible to experience charisma without love* (I Cor. 3.1–4; 13.1–3; cf. Rom. 14.15), or for love to be hypocritical (Rom. 12.9; II Cor. 6.6).[193] The problem and the danger of charisma is that it can function purely at the level of the emotional and non-rational (glossolalia) or of the emotional and rational (prophecy) and lack all moral and ethical character. Only when charisma is manifested *as the expression of grace*, that is, in humble, selfless love, only then will it benefit either the individual or the community. Hence the necessary test, since charisma without love is profitless. The test is simply the test of character: vv. 4–7 – whoever is charismatic and yet impatient, unkind, envious, conceited, etc. – and such traits cannot be concealed for any length of time in a small group like a house church – his charisma may have to be discounted or even disregarded as *a gift the community can do without* – for the sake of the individual in question. It was by this test, among others, that the false apostles of II Cor. 10–13 demonstrated their lack of divine commissioning: in particular, it highlighted their arrogant boasting.[194]

In Galatians 'the fruit of the Spirit' plays the same role as 'the hymn to love' in I Corinthians. For most of the letter Paul has been concerned to make the Galatians aware of their loss of liberty by lapsing into legalism. But in 5.13 he turns to the opposite danger – of losing liberty by selfish unconcern for others. In 5.22f. he gives a brief character sketch of the man of the Spirit – and the most choice fruit is love[195] – that is, love is not so much an act of man's will (cf. I Cor. 13.3) as the power of the Spirit which engages and moulds both man's emotions and his will. So here the spiritual man is not the one who insists on his liberty to indulge his own desires, but who limits his liberty by love of his neighbour and who expresses his liberty by serving his brother.[196] The lesson has been well learned elsewhere in the churches of the NT (Matt. 7.15–23; cf. Jer. 23.9–15; 29.15–23; *Didache* 11.8; Hermas, *Mand.* XI.8). *The proof of the spiritual man is not so much charisma as love.*[197] Both are necessary to the individual (as a member of the church) and to the church; but only when charisma is the expression of love of neighbour is it to be welcomed and valued; whereas when charisma lacks love it becomes a threat to community and a spiritual menace to the charismatic himself.

(c) *The test of* οἰκοδομή (*oikodomē* – building up). The metaphor of the church as a house or temple in process of being built is one to which Paul frequently reverts. Paul sees his own task essentially as a founder and builder of churches (Rom. 15.20; I Cor. 3.9f.; II Cor. 10.8; 12.19; 13.10; cf. Eph. 2.21) and his readers are reminded to ensure that what they do helps build one another up towards the ideal of a community whose mutual concern wholly expresses the Spirit and love of Christ (Rom. 14.17ff.; 15.2ff.; I Cor. 10.24; Eph. 4.29; Phil. 2.4; I Thess. 5.11).[198] In I Corinthians in particular *oikodomē* is applied as a test in several of the disputes which threaten the unity of the Corinthian church: by implication in 3.16f., specifically in the dispute about the rightness or wrongness of eating the sacrificial meat of pagan temples (8.1 – '"Knowledge" breeds conceit; it is love that builds'; 10.23 – '"All things are lawful", but not all things build up'),[199] and above all in I Cor. 14, where the noun and verb together occur seven times.[200] Thus in 14.3ff., 12, 17 it is by the test of *oikodomē* that prophecy proves to be superior to glossolalia –

for in glossolalia a man may speak to God in a way which makes for his own spiritual growth, but in prophecy God speaks to the community as a whole, instructing mind and will as well as stirring the emotions. So too in 14.26 the whole service of worship in all its parts must be measured against the yardstick of *oikodomē*: two or three glossolalists may speak in tongues (since they have no other charisma to offer(?)), but no more, and even then only if the tongues are interpreted (see above pp. 247f. and ch. IX n. 113) – otherwise the congregation as a whole will derive no benefit from them; two or three prophets may prophesy, but the rest must exercise the charisma of evaluation so that the community as a whole may get the most out of the prophecy and may not be misled by false prophecy. So too the reason why Paul is so confident that his instructions are 'a command of the Lord' (14.37) is because they pass the test of *oikodomē* – they so obviously are for the community's benefit; anyone who fails to recognize them as such thereby demonstrates his *unspirituality* by the same criterion – in which case he is not acknowledged by God and any charisma he claims should not be acknowledged by the community (14.38). Again the reason why Stephanas and the others should be given respect and their lead followed (16.15ff.) is obviously because they have so fully proved themselves by the test of *oikodomē*, by their service to and hard work on behalf of the community. Finally we should note that the missionary dimension of proclamation and prophecy is integral to Paul's concept of *oikodomē* (cf. I Cor. 3.5ff.; II Cor. 10.8; 12.19; 13.10). So in I Cor. 14.22–5 it is precisely the effect of the inspired utterances on *the outsider and unbeliever* which provides the test of *oikodomē* for these utterances. *What the outsider finds wholly meaningless cannot edify the church*; and conversely, that which builds up the church is precisely that which makes the outsider aware of his true nature and aware of God's presence in the community.[201] In short, since charismata are the functionings of the body of Christ, 'acts of service' (διακονίαι) given by God's Spirit to build up the charismatic community in unity of love and purpose,[202] *whatever does not build up, whatever word or action destroys the congregation's unity or causes hurt to its members or leaves the outsider merely bewildered, that word or action fails the test of* oikodomē, *and should be ignored or rejected, no matter how inspired, how charismatic it seems to be.*[203]

These then are the tests which Paul himself applies in assessing charismatic questions, and doubtless these are the criteria which he expected his churches to use when making such assessments. Taken together they provide quite a comprehensive yardstick. It should, however, be stressed that as developed by Paul they do not provide any hard or fast rules or rubrics or laws.[204] The test of kerygmatic tradition could most easily degenerate into a set rule of faith; but at this stage confessions were more in the nature of slogans than dogmas, slogans which needed to be interpreted afresh in different situations.[205] And the tests of love and *oikodomē* are criteria which by their very nature could not be used in an arbitrary or casual or legalistic way. In other words, *the application of such criteria in assessing charismata would have itself to be charismatic* – that is, carried through in conscious dependence on the grace of God and the inspiration of the Spirit.

§50. CONCLUSIONS

50.1 *Paul thinks of each of his churches as a charismatic community.* His vision of the structure of the Christian community is 'one of free fellowship, developing through the living interplay of spiritual gifts and ministries, without benefit of official authority or responsible "elders"'.[206] Charismata are not some optional extra which a church may lack and yet remain the body of Christ. On the contrary, *charismata are the living actions of the body of Christ. The body of Christ only comes to realization in any place through the manifestations of grace.* 'Body of Christ' and 'charismatic community' are synonymous expressions of Paul's ecclesiology. Without community, charisma is both rootless and fruitless; but without charisma, community is both graceless and lifeless. The cautionary conclusion to his discussion of charismata in I Cor. 12–14 (14.39f.) is in no sense an instinctive denial of the logic of his position. Throughout these chapters his position is consistent: a strong encouragement of all charismata which benefit the community (note particularly 14.1, 26ff., perhaps also 12.31?). Where the danger of abuse was not so great (though still present), his encouragement is even bolder: I Thess. 5.19f. – no flame is to be quenched, all are to be open to the inspiration of the Spirit; charismata are so fundamental to the life of the Christian community that the cold water is to be kept strictly in reserve.[207]

From all this the character of Christian community for Paul begins to take on clear features. Christian community is not primarily a sociological entity – the people who come together Sunday by Sunday (far less the institution at the corner); *Christian community exists only in the living interplay of charismatic ministry, in the concrete realizations of grace, in the actual being and doing for others (not simply for oneself) in word and deed.*[208] Nor is Christian community primarily an enthusiastic conventicle or camp-meeting of believers concerned only for richer experiences of holiness or power;[209] *Christian community consists rather in the fullest possible exercise of the gifts that build up;* usually the more striking or extraordinary the gift the *less* valuable it is – it is serving rather than lording that counts, building up rather than flying high. Christian community is not sacerdotal in the sense that only some have particular functions, only some have ministry; charismata are many and various, and *all are charismatics, all have ministry* – for Paul the Spirit has surmounted the old Jewish distinction between priest and people and left it behind. Some will have a more *regular* ministry which the community should recognize and encourage; but the idea of mono-ministry, of all the most important gifts concentrated on one man (even an apostle) is foolish nonsense to Paul (I Cor. 12.14–27). Again, Paul has no concept of office whereby authority attaches to position rather than to charisma; 'only he who ministers can have authority and that only in the actual exercise of his ministry'.[210] Consequently Paul has no concept of a hierarchy of offices; *community is dependent only and immediately on Christ the Lord and his Spirit*; some charismata are more important than others, but any man or woman may be called to exercise any ministry either occasionally or regularly.[211] So too Christian community is not primarily sacramental in character; baptism and the Lord's Supper express community and thereby consolidate community, but they neither create it nor do they form its basis; as all Christians as members of a Christian assembly are charismatics, so *all have immediate access to grace, all may be the channel and instrument of grace to others*. And although the most edifying charismata and charismatic ministries are ministries of the spoken word, it is not an adequate description of Paul's ecclesiology to say that the church 'ever becomes the Body of Christ through Word and Sacrament'.[212] *Each church becomes Christ's body through charisma – not just through any particular charisma or charismatic ministry, but through the interaction of the whole range of charismata,* manifesting the unity of grace through the diversity of grace's gifts. In short, *charisma is more fundamental to community and unity than either office or sacrament.*

50.2   At the same time Paul is well aware of the dangers of charismatic enthusiasm, of the few thinking themselves somehow specially endowed over the many, of spirituality being seen in terms of esoteric experiences instead of service to the whole community. Consequently he takes care to mark out the checks and controls which, if observed, should prevent the liberty of the Spirit degenerating into a licence for selfishness. In the first place *the charismata include their own safeguards.*[213]

In the Rom. 12.6–8 list it is the 'measure of faith' (12.3). In the I Cor. 12.8–10 list each group provide their own control: only the *utterance of wisdom/knowledge* is the charisma; *dunameis* and healings are dependent on faith; prophecy is qualified by evaluation of inspired utterances, tongues by the interpretation of tongues. In the second place comes *apostolic authority*, which is able to command respect by virtue of the apostle's unique commission and of the unique relation he has to one of his churches as its founder.[214] Third, the *regular ministries*, particularly of prophets and teachers, are able to exercise some control over particular utterances and teachings by virtue of their greater experience of these gifts. Fourth, *the community as a whole* has the authority to evaluate its words and actions by *the criteria of kerygmatic tradition, love and* oikodomē.

Paul therefore conceives of authority in dynamic terms, not in terms of office or fixed form. The exercise of authority in the Pauline communities was one of *ongoing dialectic* – between the more formal authority of apostle as apostle and the kerygmatic tradition on the one hand, and the charismatic authority of all ministry within the community and of the community itself on the other; between the individual with his word or act containing its authority within itself as charisma, and the community with its responsibility to test and evaluate all charismata; between the decisive salvation-history events of the past (resurrection appearance commissioning and kerygmatic tradition) and the new situations, problems and demands requiring new revelations and fresh interpretation of the tradition. This vision of the charismatic mutual interdependence and dynamic interaction of both ministry and authority is a striking one; its realization would clearly depend on a sensitiveness to the direction of the Spirit and a deliberate restraint on self-assertiveness on the part of all members of the community at all times. Did the vision ever become reality? Did history prove its impracticality? We will return to these questions in our concluding chapter.

50.3   Finally we may sketch out a comparison between Jesus' concept of discipleship (see above §13.4) and Paul's concept of charismatic community. The comparison is most illuminating at three points. (1) Paul conceived of a community of charismatics where each depended on all the rest for his own upbuilding and the upbuilding of the whole. Jesus did not form a community properly speaking; the life and growth of the circle round him depended solely on him for teaching and prophetic ministry (2) In Paul's community all might exercise authority immediately from God and the community as a whole had an authoritative role. For the disciples of Jesus there was only one authority – Jesus; and any authority they were given to exercise was derived from him. The nearest parallel to Jesus in the Pauline communities was the apostle(s); but their authority derived from the past revelation and the founding of the community in the past – they had no primacy or centrality so far as fresh revelation was concerned. (3) Jesus' group of disciples existed not for themselves but for eschatological mission. The Pauline communities retained the emphasis on mission, but were to a much larger extent concerned for themselves and for their own upbuilding as focal points of the diverse grace of God.

In short, where Jesus' presence seems to have sufficed for his own disciples and to have made the formation of community unnecessary, for Paul the only way in which the eschatological grace of God could come to full expression was precisely through community. *Only a charismatic community functioning as such could hope to manifest adequately the same grace that God manifested in the one man Jesus.* This conclusion points the way forward to our next chapter.

X

THE SPIRIT OF JESUS –
THE CONSCIOUSNESS OF CHRIST

§51. INTRODUCTION

Is religious experience self-authenticating? We have seen how fundamental experience of God's Spirit and grace is for Paul's whole
religion both in belief and practice. We have studied the diversity of
experience to which he attaches the name *charisma*. We have indicated how important charismatic experience is if Christian community
is to be a living reality. But the more emphasis we give to such experience the more pressing becomes our question: Is religious experience self-authenticating? Or to narrow the question to the limits
of our present study: *What was it in Paul's religious experience which
authenticated it as distinctively Christian experience, that is, as experience of
'the God and Father of our Lord Jesus Christ'?* We can put that question
to Paul with some hope of an answer because he was by no means
oblivious to the issues involved. His recognition of the 'problem of
false prophecy', and his encounter with the 'false apostles' at Corinth
must have made him aware, if it was not already obvious to him, that
there are religious experiences and religious experiences, and some
can provide a basis for life and authority, while others are at best
little more than an exercise in self-delusion. We must therefore inquire more closely into the nature of religious experience for Paul, and
ask whether there was for Paul anything distinctive in his religious
experience which marked it off for him as Christian.

We have already answered the question in part. In chapter V we
saw how Paul fought to maintain the distinctiveness of his experience
of the risen Christ in the resurrection appearance which commissioned him as an apostle. But we saw too that for Paul that experience
was distinct not only from the experience claimed by the 'false
apostles', but distinct from his own later spiritual experiences as well.
The question then becomes, *Did Paul regard his subsequent spiritual experience as distinct from that of the 'false apostles', and if so how?* In chapter

IX we saw how Paul tackled the problem of false prophecy at the communal level. But the failure of Paul's vision of charismatic community to outlive him, as we shall see (§57), shows how fragile any structure is which must continually grow afresh out of religious experience. So here too further inquiry is called for into the nature of that experience. And the question can be posed thus: *What is the distinctive character of the religious experience which provides a basis for Christian community?*

§52. THE AMBIGUITY OF CHARISMATIC EXPERIENCE

Those who have followed the investigation through to this point will already realize that *for Paul there is nothing distinctively Christian in charismatic phenomena as such.* His confrontation with the gnostic faction and 'false apostles' at Corinth will have made this obvious. But since 'charismatic' and 'charismata' can so easily become unthinking slogans and emotive catchwords, it is worthwhile to pause and underline the fact that *charismatic phenomena were as widespread outside early Christianity as inside the Pauline churches.* Indeed there are an abundance of reports and claims of charismatic phenomena in the literature of this whole period. We need mention only a few examples to establish our point.

52.1 *Healings and wonders outside Christianity.* Jesus was not the only Galilean charismatic with a reputation in Judaism as a worker of miracles. A storm is said to have subsided in answer to the prayers of Rabbi Gamaliel (*c.* 90–130 AD); rain miracles were attributed to Honi the Circle Drawer and Hanina ben Dosa; and in addition Hanina was credited with various healings and a miraculous dispensing of bread.[1] Outside Judaism, both Vespasian and Hadrian were supposed to have cured the blind and the lame by touch and by spittle. And many cures were attributed to Asclepius, the god of healing; indeed one of the most interesting inscriptions to be retrieved from the past is a list of the cures worked in the Asclepium at Epidauros, the most renowned of his sanctuaries, justly dubbed by Oepke as 'an ancient Lourdes'.[2]

There is no lack of wonders and prodigies. For example, Julius Obsequens in his *Prodigiorum Liber* (fourth century AD) enumerated in chronological order the portents which occurred from the year 190 (249?) to the year 12 BC, using the first-century historian Livy as his principal source;[3] and A. Giannini has made an extensive collection from ancient authors of miracles related to water, animals, plants, etc.[4] To cite but two examples which best fall under this heading, and which are of special interest to NT scholarship: Lucian of Samosata passes on reports of a Babylonian who flew, walked on water and walked slowly through fire;[5] and Dio Cassius in his *History* tells how Numerius Atticus, a senator and ex-praetor, swore that he had seen Augustus ascending to heaven after the manner of which tradition tells concerning Proculus and Romulus – a testimony which was taken as confirmation of Augustus's immortality.[6]

52.2 *Dreams, epiphanies and visionary experiences outside Christianity.* Dreams had long since been given a revelatory significance both within Judaism and without, and the same obviously held true for visionary appearances of divine beings; in Judaism of course the epiphany would be that on an angel, whereas in Hellenism it could be one of the ancient gods or the deity of the mystery cult.[7] As to the 'visions and revelations' of II Cor. 12.1ff., and in particular the example Paul cites, again parallels are not lacking both in Judaism and elsewhere.[8] As good examples we may mention *The Ascension of Isaiah* 6–11,[9] where Isaiah ascends through the seven heavens and receives revelation of future redemption through Christ;[10] and particularly the vision of *Poimandres*, the first tractate of the Hermetic writings. The climax is the description of the soul's ascent through the different 'zones' until stripped bare of all his lower powers he 'enters the eighth nature, possessing only his own proper power'. There 'he hymns the Father' and 'hears a kind of sweet sound of certain Powers, who dwell above the eighth nature, as they praise God'. Then ascending still higher, he and those with him become themselves Powers and 'enter into God. Such is the blissful goal of those who possess knowledge (*gnōsis*) – to become God'. The vision ends with the seer's commission to save mankind; he went forth and 'began to preach to men the beauty of piety and of knowledge (*gnōsis*)' (*Poimandres* 24–27).[11]

We have little literary evidence of the mystical experiences which presumably came to many of the initiates to the mystery religions; but the enigmatic description of Lucius's experience in his initiation to the cult of Isis may probably be taken as typical:

I approached the very gates of death and set one foot on Proserpine's threshold, yet was permitted to return, rapt through all the elements. At midnight I saw the sun shining as if it were noon; I entered the presence of the gods of the underworld and the gods of the upper-world, stood near and worshipped them.[12]

52.3 *Ecstasy and inspired utterance* were also well known in religious experience outside new born Christianity.[13] Within Judaism we should mention especially Philo (*c.* 20 BC – *c.* 45 AD). As R. Meyer notes: 'Philo discusses the nature of prophecy with extraordinary frequency – a sign that he himself had inner pneumatic experiences'[14] – as indeed Philo himself testifies.[15] His most explicit treatment comes in *Quis Rerum Divinarum Heres*, where he discusses the 'ecstasy' of Abraham (Gen. 15.12 LXX). In view of the importance of prophecy in Paul's treatment of charismatic experience it is worth quoting Philo at some length:

> A prophet (being a spokesman) has no utterance of his own, but all his utterance came from elsewhere, the echoes of another's voice . . . he is the vocal instrument of God, smitten and played by his invisible hand . . . This is what regularly befalls the fellowship of the prophets. The mind is evicted at the arrival of the divine Spirit, but when that departs the mind returns to its tenancy. Mortal and immortal may not share the same home. And therefore the setting of reason and the darkness which surrounds it produces ecstasy and inspired frenzy . . . The prophet, even when he seems to be speaking, really holds his peace, and his organs of speech, mouth and tongue, are wholly in the employ of Another, to show forth what he wills. Unseen by us that Other beats on the chords with the skill of a master-hand and makes them instruments of sweet music, laden with every harmony (259–66).[16]

Moreover, despite the strong view, particularly in rabbinic Judaism, that the prophetic Spirit had been withdrawn from Israel (see above ch. III n.60 and ch. IV n.81), there was no lack of Jewish charismatics claiming prophetic inspiration within the Jewish mission.[17] As to Paul's understanding of glossolalia as the language of heaven, we may note, for example, that Rabbi Johanan ben Zakkai (died about 80 AD) was credited with understanding the speech of the angels,[18] and in the *Testament of Job* 48–50 Job's first daughter raised to God 'a hymn after the angelic hymnody', the second 'received the dialect of the principalities', and the third spoke 'in the dialect of the Cherubim'.[19]

Greek religion too was no stranger to ecstasy and inspired speech. According to Socrates in the *Phaedrus*, 'Our greatest blessings come to us by way of madness provided the madness is given us by divine gift'. And he goes on to distinguish four types of this 'divine madness': (1) prophetic madness, whose patron God is Apollo; (2) telestic or ritual madness, whose patron is Dionysus; (3) poetic madness, inspired by the Muses; (4) erotic madness, inspired by Aphrodite and Eros.[20] We have already briefly noted Plato's description of mantic prophecy with particular reference to the Pythia at Delphi (see above §41.2), and we need add little more beyond the observation that the prophecies were always given in the first person, never the third – the god being understood to take possession of the Pythia's vocal organs and speak immediately through her.[21] Delphi was the most famous of the Greek oracles, but there were many others, and many independent prophets beside.[22] Perhaps it is worth citing the comments of Celsus in the second century, passed on to us by Origen:

There are many who, although of no name, with the greatest facility and on the slightest occasion, whether within or without temples, assume the motions and gestures of inspired persons . . . They are accustomed to say, each for himself, 'I am God; I am the Son of God'; or, 'I am the Divine Spirit' . . . To these promises are added strange, fanatical, and quite unintelligible words, of which no rational person can find the meaning: for so dark are they, as to have no meaning at all . . .[23]

As to the ritual madness of the followers of Dionysus we need refer only to the classic work of E. Rohde. The principal feature of Dionysiac festivals was the wild dance of the devotees to the sound of flute, drum and cymbal. The purpose of the dance was to induce a state of frenzy and possession, in which condition of ecstasy (ἔκστασις) they became 'full of the god', possessed by the god (ἐνθουσιασμός); as ἔνθεοι they were completely in the god's power, their words and actions were the god speaking and acting through them.[24] The parallels between such madness and the ecstatic behaviour of the Corinthians (I Cor. 14.23 – 'You are mad') should not be ignored (see above p. 234).

Finally, lest it be concluded that the chief parallels between Christian charismata and charismatic phenomena in the ancient world lie in the area of the ecstatic and enthusiastic, I must point out that prophetic insight and prophetic foresight was also familiar to classical antiquity (telepathy, clairvoyance, precognition).[25] In particular, I may draw attention to parallels with the more rational inspired speech which Paul regards more highly than ecstatic speech by reason of its power to convict (I Cor. 14.24f.). Thus Alcibiades testifies, 'Socrates makes me confess that I ought not to live as I do, neglecting the wants of my soul';[26] and Epictetus says of Musonius Rufus, a Stoic contemporary of Paul, 'He spoke in such a way that each of us sitting there felt he was somehow being accused; he had such a grip of things, such power to make each of us see his personal wrongdoing'.[27]

52.4 Apollonius of Tyana. One of the most famous charismatic figures of this period was Apollonius of Tyana, of particular interest to us since he must have been a near contemporary of Paul. It may be of value to take this one figure and outline the sort of charismatic phenomena which were attributed to him by his third-century biographer Philostratus.[28] These include healings of various kinds, including exorcisms (III.38–40; IV.20; VI.43), and one instance of raising a girl from the dead (IV.45 – though Philostratus speaks of 'her apparent death'). More in the line of wonders are his interview with the spirit of Achilles (IV.16), the way in which Apollonius miraculously frees himself from his fetters (VII.38 – whereupon Damis, his companion, recognized for the first time the godlike and superhuman nature of Apollonius), and his ability to transport himself miraculously from one place to another (IV.10; VIII.5, 8, 10–12). In addition, Apollonius is a witness to the Indian Brahmans' ability to levitate (III.15). In his introduction Philostratus refers to 'Apollonius's frequent presentiments and prophecies' (I.2), and includes accounts of dreams from which Apollonius is able to determine the will of the gods (I.23; IV.34), and various instances of clairvoyance and pre-vision (IV.18, 43; V.11–13, 18, 24, 30; VI.3.32; VII.10, 41; VIII.26; cf. III.16). Lastly we may mention his charismatic authority (I.17 – 'his sayings had the ring of commandments issued from a throne'), and his gift of 'interpretation of tongues' (I.19 – 'I understand all languages, though I never learned any of them').

52.5 *Conclusion.* I have selected these examples with great freedom, and have not attempted a critical examination of the literature or of the phenomena themselves. That would be quite beyond the scope of this work. It should however be pointed out that there was great diversity of opinion in the ancient world on the value and authenticity of such claims and experiences. R. M. Grant comments that 'credulity in antiquity varied inversely with the health of science and directly with the vigour of religion';[29] and while there was a more or less sustained philosophical critique and scepticism, particularly of the grosser wonders, from the sixth century BC onwards, it always had to fight for its life in the face of popular superstition. Here are but a few examples. Dodds quotes 'the cool judgment of Cicero that "few patients owe their lives to Asclepius rather than Hippocrates"', and notes that the critique of dreams goes back to Heraclitus's observation that 'in sleep each of us retreats into a world of his own'.[30] Perhaps the sharpest onslaught on religious superstition came from Lucian of Samosata (second century AD), particularly in his attacks on naïve belief in wonders (*Philopseudes, Lover of Lies*) and the techniques of oracle prophecy.[31] Certainly one of the highlights of the whole period was Seneca's 'sending up' of the official deification of

the Emperor Claudius (54 AD).[32] Among the more serious repercussions of the whole debate were the affects on religious propaganda,
evident in the clear tendency of apologists to present their heroes,
whether Socrates or Heracles on the one hand or Moses on the other,
as 'divine' by virtue of their wisdom rather than any miracle working
power.[33] That Paul's confrontation with the Corinthian gnostics and
'false apostles' belongs somewhere within this debate should be
sufficiently evident without further discussion (I Cor. 1.18–4.21; II
Cor. 2.14–4.6; 10–13); at all events we cannot stop here to pursue the
issue more closely.[34] But, hopefully, enough has been said to show that,
(1) there was no lack of claims to phenomena outside early Christianity which paralleled the Pauline charismata in varying degrees
of closeness; (2) Christian claims to charismatic experience would very
likely be accepted uncritically by large numbers at the popular level
and measured against the parallel phenomena in other cults; and (3)
the philosophical critique of miracle would find no greater credibility
in the Christian claims than in those of other religious propagandists
(cf. Acts 17.32).[35]

In short, *there was nothing distinctively Christian in charismatic phenomena themselves.* When we set early Christianity in the context of its
times, the full ambiguity of the charismata becomes apparent. Even
the emphasis that *charisma* is the experience and expression of grace
is not in itself sufficient to distance Christian charismata from similar
phenomena outside Christianity, since all inspiration comes as an
experience of receiving a gift from beyond, of something given and not
achieved. This does not mean that charismata cease to be important
within the Pauline community. Not at all! nothing of what was said
in chapters VIII and IX is affected by our present conclusion: *the
ambiguity of the manifestation of the divine does not make that manifestation
any less essential to spiritual and community life.* What our conclusion
means is this: (1) charismata in themselves could not be taken as a
mark of specifically Christian experience or of a higher stage of experience within Christianity (against the Corinthian gnostics) or of
special commission as a servant of Christ (against the Corinthian
'false apostles'). In other words, the *danger* of charismatic experience
and the need for *controls* on charismata within the Christian community is confirmed and underlined (ch. IX). (2) Since charismatic
experience as such does not bring us to the heart of distinctively
Christian experience for Paul we must dig more deeply and pursue
our quest into other aspects of Paul's religious experience.

§53. THE ESCHATOLOGICAL SPIRIT

The most obvious place to begin this stage of our inquiry is in the area of eschatology. In chapter III we saw that Jesus' claim to be *already* manifesting the power of the *eschatological* kingdom was a key aspect of his distinctive claims for both himself and his mission. In chapter V we saw that a distinctive feature of Paul's consciousness of commission was his sense of *eschatological* apostleship, of having a decisive role to play in bringing about the climax and conclusion of God's purposes in this age. In chapter VII we had to give first place to the eschatological enthusiasm of the earliest Jerusalem community in our description of its religious experience. The question naturally follows: Does the eschatological dimension of Paul's religious experience in general mark it off from the religious experience of the ancient world? Is there a distinctively Christian element in the religious experience which Paul describes in his letters?

53.1   *The already–not yet tension of Christian experience.* The most characteristic feature of Christian experience viewed from this angle is for Paul the tension between realization and unfulfilment, the tension between the already of Jesus' resurrection and the not yet of his parousia. For Paul the believer is caught in the interval between fulfilment and consummation, in the overlap of the present age and the age to come, where the final work of God has *begun* in him but is not yet completed (Phil. 1.6).[36] We will briefly review the evidence in Paul for the *eschatological tension* of his experience and that of his converts.

On the one hand, Paul believed that in Christ's death and resurrection the bell for the final lap of this world's history had sounded, the imminent End had begun decisively to influence history's course.[37] He felt that by his encounter with the risen Jesus someone, something from the future, the power of the age beyond death, had entered his own experience and radically altered it. If anything makes this clear, this overwhelming sense of eschatological newness, it is the way in which Paul ransacks his vocabulary to find appropriate language – metaphors adequate to express this utterly new dimension to his own experience and that of his converts. So we find metaphors drawn from the law court (justification), from the slave market (redemption), from warfare (reconciliation), from everyday life (salvation = wholeness, health; waking up, putting on new clothes, invitation to a banquet), from agriculture (sowing, watering, grafting, harvest), from commerce and trade (seal, down-payment, accounting, refining, building), from religion (circumcision, baptism, purification, consecration, anointing), and, most significant of all, from the major events of life and world history (creation, birth, adoption, marriage, death, resurrection).[38] The list could be extended.

What prompted such a range and variety of metaphors? Not merely an agile mind and vivid literary style. These are the product of great and deep experience. Through them a profound and many faceted experience of God struggles and strives to find adequate expression. Something decisive had happened, something quite new and unthought, lifting the believer's life into a whole new plane of existence; one does not, after all, use metaphors like liberation, creation, birth, marriage and death to describe everyday occurrences, only for once-in-a-lifetime events which shape all subsequent experience of reality. No verse expresses this sense of already participating in the newness of the End, of old narrow ways ended and new panoramas opened up on a cosmic scale, than II Cor. 5.17: 'When anyone is united to Christ, there is a new creation; the old is finished and gone, everything has become fresh and new (τὰ ἀρχαῖα παρῆλθεν, ἰδοὺ γέγονεν καινά)'.[39] It would be instructive to pause longer and let some of these metaphors from a distant age unfold their meaning and eschatological significance more fully, but space does not permit. It must suffice to note that at the heart of them all is *the consciousness of a radically new relationship with God determining the whole of life's course by the light of the imminent End.*

On the other hand, Paul never allowed the exciting newness of the already to silence the promise and warning of the not yet. Paul never allows the tension between the two to slacken. This is sufficiently clear from his use of the same metaphors. For the most part he prefers to speak of the believer as already *justified* (e.g. Rom. 5.1); but in Gal. 5.5 he talks of righteousness as something still awaited and hoped for. In one sense believers already have *redemption* (Rom. 3.24; Eph. 1.7; Col. 1.14); but in another they still await redemption, that is redemption of the body (Rom. 8.23; Eph. 1.14; 4.30). *Salvation* is essentially an eschatological good, something still awaited; wholeness belongs to the not yet (e.g. Rom. 5.9f.; 13.11; I Thess. 5.8f.), hence the striking use of the present tense of the verb in I Cor. 1.18; 15.2; II Cor. 2.15: believers are in the process of being saved. At the same time Paul can exclaim, '*Now* is the day of salvation!' (II Cor. 6.2) – the eschatological thrill and urgency of these words is unmistakable – and Eph. 2.5, 8 can even speak of Christians as those who have been saved (perfect tense).[40] In other words, salvation is an ongoing process, but it has begun and begun decisively (cf. Phil. 1.6). Again in one sense believers have already '*put on*' Christ (Gal. 3.27); but in Rom. 13.14 Paul exhorts his readers to 'put on the Lord Jesus Christ' as something not yet fully accomplished (see also Col. 3.9f.). It is unnecessary to labour the point, but it may be worth further illustrating it from three of the most striking metaphors. (1) *Adoption* (υἱοθεσία) is one of the best examples of the already–not yet character of the believer's present life, because Paul uses the same word in the two different senses within a few verses of each other. Rom. 8.15 – 'You did not receive the spirit of slavery to fall back into fear, but you received (aorist tense) the Spirit of sonship/adoption (πνεῦμα υἱοθεσίας)'; Rom. 8.23 – We too, like creation, 'groan inwardly as we wait for adoption as sons (υἱοθεσίαν)'.[41] (2) In two passages Paul makes vivid use of the *marriage* metaphor. I Cor. 6.17 – as union between a man and woman makes them one flesh, so union between the believer and his Lord makes them one Spirit (see further below p.323). But in II Cor. 11.2 Paul likens conversion not so much to marriage as to betrothal of marriage; the believer's life on earth is like the ongoing preparation for the not yet consummation of marriage itself. Even more striking is Eph. 5.25–7: the spiritual cleansing which comes through the gospel is like the actual bridal bath which the bride takes before her wedding; the church is as it were a bride purified and on her way to the wedding ceremony at the parousia.[42] (3) Finally, we might notice that whereas in Colossians Paul can happily speak of *resurrection* as in some sense already past for the Christian, since he shares in Christ's resurrection (Col. 2.12; 3.1), in his earlier letter to the Romans he thinks of resurrection as still future, for only in the resurrection of the body will the whole man be conformed to the resurrection of Christ (Rom. 6.5; 8.11, 23).[43] In all these metaphors *the two-sidedness of Paul's eschatological consciousness* is clearly evident. The cry of exultant joy at liberation from previous bondage is always balanced by the sigh of frustrated longing for complete release into the full liberty of sonship.

53.2   *The Spirit as the key to the eschatological tension of Christian experience.* In Paul's view it was precisely the coming of the Spirit which set up the already–not yet tension in the believer's life. For *the Spirit is the future good which has become present for the man of faith – that power of the not yet which has already begun to be realized in his present experience.*[44] He is 'a Spirit that makes us sons' (πνεῦμα υἱοθεσίας) in anticipation of and with a view to full sonship at the eschaton (Rom. 8.15, 23). As in the case of Jesus (see above §§8.3, 5; 16.3, 4), the Spirit is the powerful manifestation of the future rule of God in and through the present life of faith (Rom. 14.17; I Cor. 4.20).[45] To experience the Spirit is to begin (but only begin) to enter upon the inheritance of sonship (Rom. 8.15–17; I Cor. 6.9–11; 15.42–50; Gal. 4.1–7; 5.16–25; Eph. 1.14; cf. Titus 3.5–7).[46]

The clearest expression of this emphasis is Paul's use of the metaphors ἀπαρχή (first-fruits) and ἀρραβών (first instalment). The Spirit is the first-fruits, that is, first sheaf[47] of the harvest of the End, that is the *beginning* of the eschatological harvest of redemption (Rom. 8.23). The commercial metaphor (ἀρραβών) is to the same effect: the Spirit is the first instalment, down payment, guarantee of the complete inheritance which awaits the resurrection of the body (II Cor. 1.22; 5.5; Eph. 1.14). Both metaphors speak of a beginning, a first act, which looks forward to and anticipates a future completion: the first-fruits are the first reaping of the complete harvest; the handing over of the 'first instalment' is an act which engages the giver to something bigger.[48] In both metaphors that which is given is a part of the whole: in a transaction the ἀρραβών is the same material (money, cloth, or whatever) as the total payment; the total harvest is made up of sheaves just like the one used as the ἀπαρχή. So for Paul *the gift of the Spirit is the first part of the redemption of the whole man, the beginning of the process which will end when the believer becomes a spiritual body*, that is, when the man of faith enters into a mode of existence determined solely by the Spirit.[49] The present experience of the Spirit's power is only a foretaste of that future. The already–not yet tension is set up precisely by the fact that the Spirit by his coming begins to reclaim man for God, to contest the sway of man's selfish passions, his self-sufficiency and self-indulgence, and, if man wills, to defeat them.

The Spirit then is that power which earlier men of faith had assumed must be reserved for the age to come. The first Christians' experience of an inner power that transformed and made new was such that they could only conclude: This is the power of the new age, this is the eschatological Spirit. The Spirit was the presentness of future blessing. The Spirit was that power of the resurrection age already experienced and active to make its recipients fit for that age yet to come. Here a Pauline answer begins to emerge to our opening questions: *the charismata must be set and seen within the context of the fundamental eschatological tension of Christian experience.* Anything which breaks or slackens or ignores this tension makes either for an instability and fluctuation of experience, or for a rigidity and formalizing of experience, both of which are potentially dangerous to the individual and hence to his community. He dare not over-emphasize the already and forget the not yet; but neither should he over-emphasize the not yet and fail to appreciate the already. *We can begin to understand the charismatic Spirit only if we recognize him as the eschatological Spirit.*[50]

53.3   *The warfare between Spirit and flesh.* The eschatological tension comes to its sharpest existential expression for Paul in the believer's recognition that he is *a divided man*, a man of split loyalties. He lives in the overlap of the ages and belongs to both of them *at the same time.* So long as this age lasts he has a foot in both camps – both sinner and justified *at the same time.* As a 'living soul' he is of the stock of 'the first Adam', but as one who experiences the 'life-giving Spirit' he belongs *also* to 'the last Adam' (I Cor. 15.45).[51] As a Christian he has the Spirit, is 'in Christ' (Rom. 8.9); but *at the same time* he is still flesh, still part of the world (Rom. 6.19; I Cor. 1.29; 6.16; 7.28, etc.), still living in some sense at least 'in the flesh' (II Cor. 10.3; Gal. 2.20; Phil. 1.22).[52] Consequently the Spirit's redeeming work has only *begun* and is *necessarily incomplete* (Phil. 1.6): for the Spirit has come to take possession of the whole man, man as body (cf. I Cor. 6.19); but the present body is still the mortal body, still the body of flesh (Rom. 6.12; 7.24; 8.10f.). Only at death or parousia will the Spirit's work be complete, for only then will the believer cease as flesh and his body be raised as a *spiritual* body (Rom. 8.11, 23; I Cor. 15.44ff.; Phil. 3.21); that is, only then, for the first time, will the Spirit extend his sway fully to the *whole* man. But in the between time of the present the believer is a divided man, and his entire experience in the present is characterized not only by eschatological tension, but by *warfare* – warfare between the forces of the old age and those of the new, warfare between the desires of his Adamic nature and the power of the last Adam, warfare between the flesh and the Spirit.

The clearest expression of Paul's thought at this point is Gal. 5.13–26 and Rom. 7.13–8.25. First Galatians 5 reads:

Walk by the Spirit and do not fulfil the desires of the flesh (ἐπιθυμίαν σαρκός). For the desires of the flesh are against the Spirit and (the desires of) the Spirit are against the flesh; for each is in conflict with the other, so that what you will to do you cannot do (vv. 16f.).

If we owe our life (as believers) to the Spirit, let the Spirit also direct our course. Let us have no self-conceit, no provoking one another, no jealousy of one another (vv. 25f.).

Here, without dispute, Paul is talking to and about believers. Equally clearly he is speaking about Christian *experience* – as the talk of 'desire' and 'walking by the Spirit' indicates.[53] Christian experience is one of conflict between flesh and Spirit, a conflict, that is, between the believer's desires as a man of this age (particularly his self-indulgence and self-sufficiency) and the compulsion of the Spirit – a real conflict which either side may win in any particular instance, so that the believer has constantly to be exhorted to follow the direction of the Spirit. Most striking of all is the last clause of 5.17: the conflict takes place' ἵνα you may not do what you want to do'. The ἵνα could be taken in a final sense ('in order that').[54] But final ἵνα makes for a very compressed sense; and does Paul intend to say that the Spirit fights against the flesh in order to prevent the believer doing what he wants to do (cf. Rom. 7.15f., 18–21)? More appropriate to the movement of the thought is ἵνα with consecutive force – 'so that what you will to do you cannot do' (NEB).[55] That is to say, the two dimensions of the believer's existence run counter to each other and prevent his living wholly in one or other; the Spirit prevents his fleshly desires coming to effect, but so too does his fleshliness prevent the Spirit inspired desires coming to effect. The consequence of this warfare between flesh and Spirit is *continuing frustration* since the believer finds himself torn in two by conflicting desires and impulses.

More disputed is the place of Rom. 7.14–8.25 in Paul's thought. The majority of modern commentators take the second part of chapter 7 as Paul's description of 'man under the law'.[56] With such a view I find myself in substantial disagreement; but I cannot enter into all the necessary and detailed exegesis and discussion here and may mention only briefly the most crucial points.[57]

(1) Kümmel repeatedly insists that the condition depicted in Rom. 7 is different from that presupposed in Rom. 6 and 8.[58] But in that case Rom. 7.7–25 becomes an unnecessary interruption and digression in Paul's train of thought, much more suited to the context of Rom. 2–3 than that of 6–8. Yet Romans is a much more carefully planned work than any of his other letters, so that it is more likely that 7.7–25 belongs where it does by deliberate choice. In which case it is probable that Paul's thought flows consistently from Rom. 6 through 7 to 8[59] – in the course of which he looks *in turn* at the Christian in relation to three key realities of his experience: to sin (6), to sin and the law (7), to the law and the Spirit (8.1–8), to the Spirit (8.9–30); not that he is able to compartmentalize the discussion quite so neatly, as we shall see. The difference between 7.7–25 and the rest of Rom. 6–8 therefore probably denotes *not* different conditions, but the *same* condition viewed from different aspects; so that the 'wretched man' of Rom. 7 is the believer seen *only* in terms of the flesh, law and

sin, and Rom. 7.7–25 describes a *continuing* dimension of the believer's experience, *even as a believer*.

(2) There is nothing in Rom. 7 which demands that the frequently repeated 'I'/'me' (about twenty times) be understood in a way which distances Paul from the experience he is describing. It is certainly quite probable that in 7.7–13 at least he is describing *typical* experience of an 'I';[60] but the existential anguish and frustration in vv. 15ff. and 24 is too real and too sharply poignant to permit any reduction of the 'I' to a mere figure of style. Whatever else this is, it is Paul speaking from the heart of *his own* experience.[61] If the 'I' is typical, then Paul most probably uses it because he knows *his* experience is typical, and not, surely, because it denotes the experience of Everyman *except* himself!

(3) If the passage gives expression to Paul's own experience, it cannot refer to Paul's pre-Christian experience. There is nothing of such anguish and frustration in other passages where he speaks explicitly of his 'former life' – quite the reverse (Gal. 1.13f.; Phil. 3.4–6). Rather with Rom. 7 we listen in to a man in conflict with himself, a man, in fact, in the throes of the very conflict we have described above (pp. 312f.). To be sure Paul expresses himself in very strong terms (7.14 – 'sold under sin'; 7.23 – 'captive by means of the law of sin'); but what comes to the surface here is Paul's consciousness of the paradox of the believer's present condition, the consciousness of his fleshliness, of his belonging to the world as flesh, even as a believer. It is this consciousness which rends the cry from his throat in 7.24 – 'Miserable creature that I am! Who will deliver me from this body doomed to death?' – the cry not so much of despair as of *frustration* – the frustration of one who has to try to follow the leading of the Spirit while still in the flesh, the anguish of trying to express the life of the Spirit through the body of death, the longing for the life of the Spirit to have a *spiritual* body as its embodiment and means of expression (cf. Rom. 8.22–23; II Cor. 5.4). In a word, it is not the cry of the not yet believer for the freedom of the Christian; rather it is the cry of the already believer for the full freedom of Christ. The language of Rom. 7.14ff. is certainly strong, but not so very much stronger than that of Gal. 5.17 (see above p. 313).

(4) The passages which most clearly express Paul's meaning in the whole section are 7.25b and 8.10. 7.25b – 'This is the most telling passage of all. Notice that one and the same man serves both the law of God and the law of sin, that he is righteous and at the same time he sins' (Luther on 7.25). The significance of 7.25b is that it comes *after* 7.25a and that it is the conclusion to chapter 7 as a whole.[62]

Even after the shout of thankgiving Paul still has to confess, 'I, I my-self, serve the law of God with my mind, but with my flesh I serve the law of sin'.[63] The 'mind' here must be the mind renewed by the Spirit (cf. Rom. 12.2), since Paul nowhere else speaks so positively of the 'natural' mind.[64] 'Mind' is then more or less synonymous with 'the inner man' (ὁ ἔσω ἄνθρωπος) of v. 22, a phrase which most probably also refers to the believer as part of the new age, belonging to the last Adam (so II Cor. 4.16; Eph. 3.16; cf. Gal. 3.27 with Rom. 13.14; Col. 3.9f.; Eph. 4.22ff.).[65] Hence both before and after v. 25a Paul expresses his experience *as a believer*. It is as one who knows Christ as Lord that Paul confesses, 'I with my flesh, as flesh, go on serving the law of sin'. Here then is Paul's conclusion to his discussion of the Christian's relation to sin and the law; it is not a relation which has been left behind, rather it is a relation which continues even for the man who also experiences the Spirit.[66] The antithesis between the inward man and the flesh is not overcome and left behind, it con-tinues through and beyond the shout of thanksgiving – as a continu-ing antithesis between mind and flesh. In short, *the warfare does not end when the Spirit comes; on the contrary, that is when it really begins.*[67] Service of the law of God means victory for the Spirit; service of the law of sin means victory for the flesh; and there is no battle in which the flesh is wholly the loser till the last battle. This is the paradox and ten-sion of the believer's experience so long as this age lasts – *simul iustus et peccator.*

(5) At first sight 8.1ff. seems to speak of a wholly different ex-perience. In fact, however, these verses only elaborate the other side of the paradox. 8.2 cannot denote complete liberation from the power of the flesh and of death – even men of the Spirit die (I Thess. 4.13; I Cor. 15.26)! Rather v. 2 speaks of an experience where with the coming of the Spirit the law of sin is no longer the sole determiner of present conduct or the final determiner of ultimate destiny. And in 8.4ff. Paul does not contrast believer with unbeliever,[68] rather *he confronts the believer with both sides of the paradox, both sides of his nature as believer* – as again most forcefully in 8.12f. If he lives solely on the level of the flesh, solely as flesh, then his ultimate destiny is death (vv. 6ff., 13a; Gal. 6.8a). But if he allows his walk to be determined by the Spirit then his ultimate destiny is life – life in death, life through death, life beyond death (vv. 6, 10f., 13b; Gal. 6.8b). In v. 10 this continuing paradox of flesh and Spirit, death and life comes to clear expression: 'If Christ is in you, the body is dead because of sin, but the Spirit is life because of righteousness'.[69] The body is dead because the Christian is still as flesh a member of the first Adam – dead

towards God, dead in sin, heading for death; the 'body' of which Paul speaks in 8.10 is the same 'body of death' of which he spoke in 7.24. But the Christian *also*, at the same time, has the Spirit, also shares the life of the last Adam, the life-giving Spirit; as such he is alive towards God, dead to sin.[70]

To sum up, we have not yet finished with Rom. 8, but already it is clear that *in no other place does Paul describe so fully the moral experience of the Christian as in Rom.* 7.14–8.25. In these verses the believer's experience is clearly depicted as an experience of warfare between flesh and Spirit. It is not a warfare from which the believer can distance himself and take sides as though he were a neutral observer or umpire. On the contrary, he finds himself on *both* sides; as believer he lives on both levels, flesh and Spirit, *at the same time*; the division runs right through the believing 'I'.[71] It is because he lives on two levels at once that he has constantly to choose between the two levels – flesh or Spirit. 'I' in my 'inner man', as renewed mind, as man of Spirit, have to choose against 'I' as flesh. By the power of the Spirit it can be done. But the choice has to be made, and made repeatedly if life and not death is to triumph at the last. In short, if 7.24 is the believer's life-long cry of frustration, 7.25a is his thanksgiving of eschatological hope, and 7.25b his calm realism for the present in the light of both.

53.4   Here then in the already–not yet tension of the believer's experience and in its character as warfare between flesh and Spirit, *the distinctiveness of Paul's understanding of religious experience begins to assume a clearer shape*. It is the manner in which Paul maintains the tension so firmly that sets his soteriology apart from that of his Jewish and gnosticizing contemporaries. Gnostics were certainly aware of an antithesis between flesh and spirit, but it was an antithesis which had been overcome. Flesh and spirit did not mark a division which ran through the gnostic 'I'; rather for the gnostic the true 'I' was a prisoner incarcerated within the flesh. This is why he could either glut the body or starve it; for what he did with his body made no difference to his true self. Hence the attitude attacked by Paul in I Cor. 6.12ff. Hence too the attitude rebuked in I Cor. 3.1ff.; 4.8: the gnostic believed that with the acquisition of knowledge and wisdom his salvation was already assured – already he was spiritual, already mature, already full, already reigning.[72] In other words, they overemphasized the already and largely ignored the not yet.

It is somewhat ironical that the same mistake appears on both sides of the History of Religions school in their interpretation of Paul.

Thus, for example, Bousset could speak of Paul's 'consciousness of the perfection of his present Christian state'; 'the natural being has completely died in him'.[73] And Schweitzer could write, 'As a consequence of being in the Spirit, believers are raised above the limitations of the being-in-the-flesh'.[74] But this is never Paul who speaks thus. He certainly was conscious of his 'being in the Spirit', or rather of the Spirit being in him (the already); but he was also all too conscious of his fleshness, his all too earthly desires and self-concern (cf. e.g. Rom. 8.13; Phil. 3.8–14; Col. 3.5); 'the "Pneumatiker" is confined within the eschatological "Not yet"'.[75] *It is precisely this not-yetness which distinguishes Paul's understanding of redemption from that of his gnostic opponents.* Whereas for them perfection was a present reality, since the body did not matter; for Paul perfection was not yet, precisely because the body was yet to be redeemed (Rom. 8.11, 23ff.; I Cor. 15.44–9; Phil. 3.10f.).[76]

If it is the not yet emphasis which separates Paul from the more gnostic ideas circulating in his churches, *it is the already emphasis which distinguishes him from most of contemporary Judaism.* The messianic expectations which characterized main stream Judaism looked to an eschatology which lay wholly in the future. So too apocalyptic hope was consumed by a yearning for the imminent intervention of God and had no gospel of the present. Paul however, is typically Christian in his belief that the last days have already begun, the eschatological Spirit is already the portion of believers; with the resurrection of Jesus the end-time resurrection has already begun. For Paul the gospel is rooted in the Christ who has already come. His hope for the future springs from his faith in the Christ event of the past, and from his experience of the Spirit in the present.

Only in one section of Judaism do we find a parallel to Paul's eschatological tension – and that is in the Qumran sect. As we have seen above (pp. 162f.), they were an eschatological community with several points of similarity with the early Jerusalem church. The parallel with Paul's already-not yet tension is even more striking. I am thinking particularly of the instruction on the two Spirits given in the Rule of Qumran (IQS 3.13–4.26).[77]

And he (God) allotted unto man two Spirits
that he should walk in them until the time of his visitation;[78]
they are the Spirits of truth and perversity
                    . . .
Dominion over all the sons of righteousness
is in the hands of the Prince of light;
they walk in the ways of light.

All dominion over the sons of perversity
is in the hand of the Angel of darkness.
And because of the Angel of darkness
all the sons of righteousness go astray;
and all their sins and iniquities and faults,
and all the rebellion of their deeds,
are because of his dominion (3.18–21).

Till now the Spirits of truth and perversity battle in the hearts of every man
(4.23).[79]

The parallel is not close verbally (Spirit/flesh; two Spirits), and the
attitude to the law which is bound up with this experience is very
different from Paul's;[80] but in existential terms the same sort of
religious experience is clearly being described. More to the point,
within the context of Qumran self-consciousness this existential conflict was bound to be understood in eschatological terms; the two
Spirits dualism does not simply divide men into two classes but runs
through the heart of every man, including 'the sons of righteousness'!
In view of this parallel we cannot say that we have uncovered the
distinctive nature of Christian experience for Paul. We must therefore
pursue our inquiry still further and examine more closely the two
ends of the eschatological tension, the two sides of the paradox of
Christian experience – Spirit and flesh, life and death.

§54. THE SPIRIT OF JESUS

As we have seen, the already element in Christian experience is
understood by Paul primarily in terms of the eschatological Spirit.
When we subject his concept of Spirit to closer scrutiny a distinctively
Christian feature at once becomes evident: for Paul the Spirit is *the
Spirit of Jesus*. It was the same eschatological Spirit that the prophets
looked forward to – the same power Paul's converts had experienced
liberating them from slavery to the law, flooding their hearts, transforming their attitudes (I Thess. 4.8 alluding to Ezek. 37.14; II Cor.
3.3, 6 alluding to Jer. 31.31–3; Ezek. 36.26; Rom. 5.5 echoing Joel
2.28). It was the same Spirit that anointed Jesus (II Cor. 1.21).[81] But
now for Paul it has somehow become 'the Spirit of Christ' (Rom. 8.9),
'the Spirit of God's Son' (Gal. 4.6), 'the Spirit of Jesus Christ' (Phil.
1.19).[82] What does he mean by this? Why does he bring Spirit and
Jesus together in this way? What is the significance of these preposi-
tional phrases?

54.1 *Jesus as the definition of the Spirit*. The first answer which springs to view is that at several crucial points in his letters Paul characterizes Christian experience of Spirit in terms of Jesus. When he wants to mark off the religious experience of himself and his converts from that claimed by his opponents or from a less than Christian experience, it is what we might call the *Jesus-character* of Christian experience which he seizes upon.

I refer first to I Cor. 12.3, which we have already discussed (pp. 234f.). Paul, as we have seen, was clearly aware that there was nothing distinctively Christian in ecstatic and charismatic experience (12.2). Consequently he at once attempts to define more closely the character of Christian charismatic experience. The mark of inspiration by the Spirit of God is the confession of Jesus as Lord. Whatever inspiration denies the kerygma of Jesus' death and resurrection, by that fact declares its source to be other than the Spirit. It should perhaps be reiterated that Paul is talking in experiential terms here. The confession of Jesus' Lordship is not a dogmatic statement, the logical conclusion of argument or persuasion; it is a charismatic conviction born of inspiration and expressed in words given from beyond. It is thus a direct and immediate manifestation of Spirit. Notice then the significance of Paul's claim: the range of possibly authentic experiences of inspiration has been narrowed to those experiences which affirm or accord with and do not deny the kerygmatic tradition about Jesus. This means that in Paul's view the Spirit has been limited or has limited himself in accord with the yardstick of Jesus. *The power of God has become determined by its relation to Jesus.*[83]

I think secondly of Rom. 8.14ff. (see above pp. 21f., 240f.). Here again Paul is striving to express something of the distinctive character, of Christian experience – here as the experience of being led by the Spirit, of walking according to the Spirit rather than in accordance with the flesh. This distinctiveness he expresses in terms of sonship: 'All who are led, or moved (ἄγονται) by the Spirit of God are sons of God'.[84] Then in a most striking way he goes on to elucidate sonship in terms of experience.[85] Moreover, the experience is the very experience of prayer which characterized Jesus' own relationship with God – 'Abba! Father!' (see above §4). And Paul is clearly aware of this since he draws the conclusion from it that those who so experience the Spirit are not only sons, but heirs – that is, *fellow heirs with Christ* (8.17); the shared experience denotes a shared relationship.[86] Here again therefore we have Paul describing an existential experience (the charismatic awareness of sonship), which is the mark of the Spirit of God, and which marks out the Spirit as distinctively the Spirit of sonship, the Spirit of God's Son (8.15; Gal. 4.6f.). Again the significance of Paul's thought here is clear enough. In Paul's view experiences of God's Spirit can be more narrowly delimited in the light of Jesus' own experience of God and relation to God. The Spirit of God can be more precisely defined as the Spirit of Jesus' own relationship with the Father and as the Spirit which both brings about the same relationship for believers and makes it existentially real. In short, we might say that *for Paul the character of the Spirit has taken its 'shape' from the impress of Jesus' own relationship with God.*

Thirdly, we have II Cor. 3.18. The verse comes in a section which is the focus of much debate at the present time. It must suffice here to note the wide agreement on all sides that chapter 3 is part of a Pauline polemic or defence against other missionaries, presumably Jewish Christians, who in Paul's view overemphasized the continuity between Judaism and Christianity.[87] In particular, they must have insisted that the revelation, the law, given through Moses remained binding and normative for Christians (3.3, 6ff.). In response Paul insists that Christianity is quintessentially a religion of Spirit rather than of law (vv. 3, 6), the fulfilment of the prophetic hope for the new age (Jer. 31.31ff.). Then in the following allegorical exposition of Ex. 34.29–35 (vv. 7–18) he proceeds to equate allegorically this Spirit with Yahweh (vv. 16ff.) as the source of glory.[88] The contrast here is twofold: under the old covenant only Moses had direct access to the divine presence, and its effect on Moses was transient (the glory soon faded); but now Christians, *all* Christians (v. 18),[89] can experience the divine presence directly in the Spirit, and the effect of the Spirit on their lives is sustained and increasing (they are being transfigured into the likeness of the Lord from one degree of glory to another – v. 18).[90] The point for us is the way in which Paul expresses what is for him the distinctive work of the eschatological Spirit as experienced by Christians: viz., the Spirit transforms believers into the image of Yahweh. Now, by 'image of God' Paul is clearly thinking primarily of Jesus (so explicitly in 4.4; see also Col. 1.15).[91] That is to say, the distinctive mark of the eschatological Spirit is an immediacy of relationship with God which makes the believer more like Jesus (if we may use such simple, pietistic language). Here once again then relationship with God is seen in terms of experiencing the Spirit,[92] but once again the experienced Spirit is seen in terms of Jesus. *Only that power which reproduces the image of Jesus Christ is to be recognized as the power of God.*[93]

This 'transformation into the image of Christ' motif is a characteristic feature of Paul's thought, and he usually expresses it in terms of the Spirit. In Rom. 8.29 the flow of thought from 8.28 implies that the process of 'being conformed to the likeness of God's Son' is the effect of the Spirit cooperating in everything for the good of those who love God.[94] This passage is particularly interesting since it draws together the thought of Rom. 8.14ff. and of II Cor. 3.18: to experience the Spirit's working is not only to experience sonship but also to become more like the Son, to take on increasingly the family likeness. When we turn to I Cor. 15.49 it becomes clear that for Paul this process is only completed at resurrection or parousia. The 'image of the heavenly man' is precisely the spiritual body (vv. 44f.). That is, *the model and goal of an existence wholly determined by the Spirit is the risen Christ*. Other variations on the same theme are the idea of 'putting on Christ' (Rom. 13.14; Gal. 3.27), which is probably a near synonym for 'receiving the Spirit',[95] and the somewhat confused metaphor of Gal. 4.19 where Paul talks of Christ being formed in his converts. This last verse must mean that Paul was looking and longing for the time when the life of Christ would come to full expression in them[96] – that is, the characteristics of Christ's life would be reproduced in them.

Finally, we should mention also the second and third criteria of assessing charismata (see above §49.2). If the Spirit attests his activity above all by love, then we should recall that *the* expression of love for Paul is Christ dying for sinners (Rom. 5.8). Thus we might legitimately infer that Paul intends the 'hymn to love' and the 'fruit of the Spirit' (I Cor. 13.4–7; Gal. 5.22) as 'character sketches' of Christ. In that case it follows that for Paul the distinguishing and delimiting mark of the Spirit is again the image or character of Jesus; *to be spiritual is to be like Christ*; to express 'the mind of Christ' is to fulfil 'the law of Christ' (Gal. 6.1f.; Rom. 15.5 – κατὰ Χριστὸν Ἰησοῦν; cf. above pp. 224f.).[97] As for the criterion of *oikodomē*, the outworking of love at community level, it follows that to build up the community means to make it more fully the corporate embodiment of Christ (cf. Eph. 4.12f.). *If the body of Christ is recognizable only where the Spirit manifests himself charismatically in community* (see above §45.2), *so the Spirit is recognizable only where the community of the Spirit manifests the character of Christ*.

In short, Paul in effect looks round at all the various manifestations of the Spirit claimed by his converts and his opponents and says firmly, 'The yardstick is Jesus'. *The character of the Christ event is the hallmark of the Spirit*. Whatever religious experience fails to reproduce this character in the individual or community, it is thereby self

condemned as delusory or demonic; it is not the work of the eschatological Spirit. For the eschatological Spirit is no more and no less than
the Spirit of Christ.

54.2   *Christ the life-giving Spirit.* Paul can express the relation of the
Spirit to Christ not simply in terms of definition, but also as an equation: 'the last Adam became life-giving Spirit' (I Cor. 15.45).[98] By
'last Adam' Paul obviously means the risen Jesus, the risen Jesus as
the beginning of a new race of men, the first born of a new family of
man (Rom. 8.29; I Cor. 15.20ff.); as the first Adam came to be as a
living soul by creation, so the last Adam came to be as life-giving
Spirit by the resurrection.[99] By 'life-giving Spirit' Paul is just as
obviously speaking in terms of the religious experience of believers;
the 'life-giving Spirit' is that power which believers experienced as
new life, liberating life, life from the dead (Rom. 8.2; II Cor. 3.6ff.).[100]
The point for us is that *Paul equates the risen Jesus with the Spirit who
makes alive.* He does not say that Jesus by his resurrection became a
spiritual body (though that is implied in the context). He does not
say that Jesus by his resurrection became a living spirit (though that
would have made a better parallelism in v. 45). He deliberately says
that Jesus by his resurrection became that Spirit which believers
experience as the source and power of their new life and new relationship with God. As from his resurrection Jesus may be known by
men only as life-giving Spirit.

But conversely, since an equation can be read both ways, it also
follows that Spirit has become last Adam, that life-giving Spirit may
be known only as last Adam. This means, first, that as from the resurrection the Spirit is to be characterized as that power which conforms men to the family image of the last Adam (see above pp. 320f.), a
process already in train in believers (see further below §55.2), and
one which the Spirit will bring to completion in the resurrection body
(15.44–9). But in addition, it means, secondly, that the Spirit not
only creates the character of Christ in believers, but also *the Spirit has
himself taken on the character of Christ.* In short, if the risen Jesus is experienced now only as life-giving Spirit, so Spirit is experienced now
only as last Adam.

Notice what Paul is doing here. He is both describing the mode of
existence now enjoyed by Jesus, *and* he is specifying the character of
Christian experience, and all at the same time.[101] Of course he is
speaking primarily in existential rather than in ontological terms.
Jesus still has a personal existence; there is, we may say, more to the
risen Jesus than life-giving Spirit (cf. e.g. Rom. 1.3f.; 8.34; I Cor.

15.24–8).[102] But so far as the religious experience of Christians is concerned Jesus and Spirit are no different. The risen Jesus may not be experienced independently of the Spirit, and any religious experience which is not in character and effect an experience of Jesus Paul would not regard as a manifestation of the life-giving Spirit. This presumably is part of the reasoning behind Paul's restriction of resurrection appearances to a unique few and to a unique period: apart from these extraordinary manifestations the risen Jesus may now be experienced only pneumatically, charismatically, as a manifestation of Spirit. At the same time the identification of Spirit and risen Jesus in experience means that Paul can clearly mark out the limits of charismatic experience: only that experience which embodies the character of Christ is experience of Spirit. *If Christ is now experienced as Spirit, Spirit is now experienced as Christ.*

This conclusion is confirmed by Rom. 8.9–11; I Cor. 6.17; 12.4–6, and probably Paul's uses of the 'in Christ' formula, though *not* II Cor. 3.17.[103] In Rom. 8.9–11 Paul rings the changes on a sequence of phrases which all denote the same experiential reality: '*Spirit of God* dwells in you' = you 'have the *Spirit of Christ*' = '*Christ* is in you'. Here again Spirit and Christ are equated at the existential level ('in you'). One cannot experience Christ without experiencing Spirit. Or to put it more accurately: one cannot experience Christ except as Spirit, which also means that one cannot experience Spirit except as Christ. Here again the distinctive mark of the Christian is experience of the Spirit (8.9), but not merely experience of Spirit – that is, of inspiration, of charismata; *the distinctive mark of the Christian is experience of the Spirit as the life of Christ* (cf. II Cor. 13.5; Gal. 2.20; Col. 1.27; Eph. 3.16f.).[104]

I Cor. 6.17 – 'He who is united to the Lord is one Spirit'. The sentence is constructed on the parallel of Gen. 2.24: in marriage the two became one – that is, literally, one flesh (6.16); the flesh is the medium of this oneness – that is, not just as physical union, but as a harmony of earthly desire and personality.[105] If their union is a living reality, then the two fleshes/personalities mingle and merge and complement, so that the resulting one flesh/personality is richer and fuller. So it is with the believer's relation with Christ, but here the medium of union is the Spirit.[106] The one Spirit which unites believers is precisely the reality of their union with Christ, and the reality of that union is demonstrated by whether or not they begin to take on the character of their heavenly partner.

I Cor. 12.4–6 – the significant thing here is that each verse refers to the same range of charismatic manifestations. As the whole range of spiritual gifts can be described alternatively as charismata, services, activities, so their source can be described equivalently as 'the same Spirit', 'the same Lord', 'the same God'. That is to say, charismatic experience for Paul is ultimately the experience of a *power* which is *divine* and which *bears the character of Jesus the Lord.*[107]

Finally we may mention the 'in Christ' formula in Paul. I cannot here enter into the debate about this phrase,[108] nor stay to elaborate a somewhat contentious thesis, since it would consume too much space and do little to advance the present study. It does however seem to me, particularly in view of our exposition of the charismatic Spirit in Paul, that in various passages 'in Christ' (or 'in the Lord') refers not so much to the objective saving work of Christ,[109] not so much to the community of faith,[110] not so much to the idea of Christ as a corporate personality,[111] or (mystically) as a sort of atmosphere in which Christians live,[112] but rather denotes religious experience (or a particular religious experience) as experience of Christ – deriving from Christ as to both its source and its character.[113] In all the passages noted, 'in Christ' or 'in the Lord' expresses not merely a rational conviction, but something more – a sense that Christ is thoroughly involved in the situation or action in question – *a consciousness of Christ.*[114]

In short, in all these passages mentioned in this section, the religious experience spoken of is *experience of Spirit identified and distinguished as experience of Christ.* The Christian's consciousness of grace and consciousness of community is also and definitively consciousness of Christ.

54.3 *Conclusion: Jesus the personality of the Spirit.* In many of the passages discussed it is evident that 'Spirit' is a very plastic concept which Paul adapts and uses as his text requires (particularly I Cor. 6.17; 15.45). But he does not make of it a wax face which may be moulded into any number of characters. Rather his experience has made him see it more as a sort of mask which has been assumed by Christ, and which has taken on his characteristic features. I say his experience has showed him this, because it has also become evident that *when Paul wants to find the distinctive mark of Spirit-given experience, he finds it not in the charismatic Spirit as such, nor in the eschatological Spirit as such, but in the Jesus Spirit, the Spirit whose characteristics are those of Christ;* he experiences the Spirit as a power which owns the Lordship of Jesus, which reproduces for the believer Jesus' relationship of sonship with the Father, which creates the believer's character afresh after the pattern of Christ.[115] The only charismata, the only charismatic

Spirit Paul wants to know about is the Spirit of Christ, that is Christ the live-giving Spirit.

It is clear that in presenting the relationship of Jesus and the Spirit in such dynamic terms Paul has taken a bold and decisive step forward in Judaeo-Christian thinking about the Spirit of God and about religious experience. The process of defining *ruah* and *pneuma* more and more closely (from ecstatic to ethical to eschatological) reaches its climax when Paul defines the Spirit as no more and no less than the Spirit of Jesus. The rationale of Paul's conclusion seems to be as follows. In his life on earth Jesus was a man determined by the Spirit – he lived 'according to the Spirit' (Rom. 1.3f.);[116] but in the resurrection the relationship was reversed and Jesus became the determiner of the Spirit.[117] In a sense we may say that Jesus was so wholly determined by the Spirit of God that the character of Jesus[118] became the clearest possible visible expression of the Spirit – not merely his actions and words, but *Jesus himself* became *the* charisma of God (cf. above p.202, also §40.2). And so the character of Jesus became as it were the archetype which the eschatological Spirit filled, the 'shape' which the Spirit took on as a mould, the shape which the Spirit in turn stamps upon believers. To change the metaphor slightly: in Paul's view the man Jesus became a sort of funnel or nozzle through which the whole course of salvation history flowed – whatever passed through that nozzle came out at the other end in the shape of Jesus, transformed into his image. This includes such concepts as covenant and sonship, but also and in particular, the key words used to denote the revelatory activity of God in the OT – Wisdom, Word, Spirit. Because for Paul, and the early Christians in general, Jesus was *the* revelation of God (see above §40.2), these words took on the shape of Christ, were identified with Christ – Christ the Wisdom of God (I Cor. 1.24 – see above p.31 and §40.4), Christ the Word of God (John 1.1–18), Christ the Spirit of God (I Cor. 15.45). By identification with Christ these hitherto impersonal (though sometimes personified) concepts gained character and personality – the character and personality of Christ.[119] In Paul then *the distinctive mark of the Spirit becomes his Christness. The charismatic Spirit is brought to the test of the Christ event.*[120] The touch of the Spirit becomes finally and definitively the touch of Christ. In brief, the dynamic of the relationship between Spirit and Jesus can be expressed epigrammatically thus: *as the Spirit was the 'divinity' of Jesus* (see above §16.6), *so Jesus became the personality of the Spirit.*

To extend these reflections more systematically into an inquiry into the traditional Christian doctrine of the Trinity, or even into its roots in the NT, lies outside the scope of the present work.[121] We may, however, pause long enough to make two brief points which are of more immediate relevance to us here.[122] First, so far as Paul is concerned, there is what might be called a *'Trinitarian' element in the believer's experience*. It is evident from Paul that the first Christians soon became aware that they stood in a dual relationship – to God as Father, and to Jesus as Lord. This relationship and awareness of it was attributed by them to the Spirit (Rom. 8.15f.; I Cor. 12.3). That is to say, Christians became aware that they stood at the base of *a triangular relationship* – in the Spirit, in sonship to the Father, in service to the Lord. Second, if such are indeed the roots of the Trinitarian doctrine, then it follows that the doctrine of the Trinity is grounded in *experience* – and in experience of Spirit, Spirit as Spirit of sonship, Spirit as Spirit of the Son. To say that the first Christians 'experienced the Trinity' would be inaccurate; they experienced *Spirit*, who made them conscious of their dual relationship as men of Spirit.[123] Trinitarian theology should always bear in mind this primacy of early Christian experience, and return to it rather than to old dogmas as the starting point for fresh definitions. It is when Trinitarian theology looses itself from these anchor points and attempts to soar into the realm of speculative metaphysics that theology itself becomes unreal. As scholastic enterprise elaborated the experience of grace into the doctrine of predestination (see above p. 200), so it elaborated the experience of sonship into the doctrine of the Trinity. And in both cases it may be argued that the net result has been more to retard the gospel than to advance it.

§55. SHARING IN CHRIST'S SUFFERINGS

When studying Rom. 8.10 we saw how the flesh/Spirit tension of the believer's experience could be re-expressed by Paul as the paradox of death and life. In §54 above we have discovered what was the distinctive element on the one side of the paradox: the Spirit was the Spirit of Christ, the new life was experienced as the life of Christ. What of the other side of the paradox? How does death play a part in Christian experience?

55.1 *Suffering and death as the necessary complement to life.* For Paul, the Christian life is a continuing experience of death as well as of life (Rom. 7.24; 8.10, 13 – see above §53.3). 'Sanctification' is a process of both life and death; death is working out in the believer as well as life. This is the consequence of his divided state: although as a member of the last Adam, as belonging to Christ through the Spirit, he is living; at the same time, as a member of the first Adam, as belonging to the world as flesh, he is dying. A particular expression of this is the suffering of the believer.

It is not unimportant to recall at the outset that the role which Paul attributes to suffering and death in his soteriology is in no sense a matter of mere theory. Paul's understanding of suffering stems from his experience of suffering.[124] By any account his whole ministry was characterized by considerable personal suffering.[125] We should also note that Paul did not regard suffering as something peculiarly apostolic or especially his own, despite his 'suffering Servant' concept of eschatological apostleship (see above §20.2). Suffering was something *all* believers experienced – an unavoidable part of the believer's lot – an aspect of experience as Christians which his converts shared with Paul: Rom. 5.3 ('we'); 8.17f. ('we'); II Cor. 1.6 ('you endure the same sufferings that we suffer'); 8.2; Phil. 1.29f. ('the same conflict which you saw and now hear to be mine'); I Thess. 1.6 ('imitators of us and of the Lord'); 2.14 ('imitators of the churches of God in Judea; for you suffered the same things'); 3.3f. ('our lot'); II Thess. 1.4ff.[126]

Paul's attitude to suffering is nothing if not positive. He does not merely endure it in stoical fashion. He welcomes it and rejoices in it (see particularly Rom. 5.3; II Cor. 12.9). Nor is he merely 'whistling in the dark to keep his spirits up', or making a laboured virtue out of painful necessity; far less is this the tormented pleasure of a masochist. On the contrary, *Paul rejoices in his sufferings because he sees in them the expression of life*. Suffering is not some defect in God's way of salvation – it is part of the saving process itself. Suffering is the necessary outworking of the not yet of salvation. It is the inevitable consequence of the life of the Spirit having to express itself through the body of death.

The clearest expression of Paul's thinking on this point is II Cor. 4.7–5.5. I refer for the moment particularly to vv. 11 and 16: v. 11 – 'While still alive, we are continually being handed over to death for Jesus' sake, so that ($\ddot{\iota}\nu\alpha$) the life of Jesus also may be revealed in our mortal flesh'. Two thoughts are linked here. First, that the experience of suffering is the experience of the power of death continually asserting itself over its continuing domain – the flesh, the mortal body. Second, that if the life of Jesus is to achieve visible expression in the believer's life that can only be through the body[127] – but that means through this body, the body of flesh, the body of death.[128] Now notice how Paul links these thoughts – by ἵνα; death must have its say in the believer's experience *in order that* the life of Jesus may come to visible expression also; *the life of Jesus manifests itself precisely in and through the dying of the body*; life and death are two sides of the one process. So in v. 16 – 'Though our outward humanity is wasting away, yet day by day we are being inwardly renewed'. There is no dualism here. Paul has in mind the same split in the believer's 'I' which we noted in Rom. 7 (see above p. 316).[129] 'I' as flesh am dying; 'I' as man of Spirit am living. But it is the same 'I': my renewal by the Spirit in my relatedness to God takes place in and through the wasting away of me in my relatedness to the world.[130] Nor should we think that Paul is here retreating into mystical inwardness or etherealizing the concept of suffering. On the contrary, his thought is entirely 'worldly'. For *it is only by living out one's relatedness to the world that the process of decay which makes manifest the life of the Spirit can go forward.* To live *in* the world of course does not mean to live *for* the world, and there is always the danger that 'in the flesh' (Gal. 2.20) may become 'according to the flesh' (Rom. 8.4f., 13); but that is the risk the believer must take if the process of life and death is to be advanced in him.

In Rom. 5.2ff. a closely parallel line of thought is briefly elaborated. The key point is the eschatological dimension of the believer's sufferings. Suffering and hope go together. Suffering does not contradict or deny hope. On the contrary, hope arises together with suffering (vv. 2f.); indeed hope arises out of suffering (vv. 3ff.). Suffering has a *creative* role for Paul (κατεργάζεται). Out of a life lived in this world it produces a life lived in dependence on God.[131] The creative role of suffering and the creative role of the Spirit (v. 5) are two sides of the one process. So too in Rom. 8.17, note particularly the εἴπερ ('provided that')[132] and the ἵνα ('in order that') – 'fellow heirs with Christ, *provided that* we suffer with him *in order that* we may also be glorified with him' (see also II Cor. 4.17f.; II Thess. 1.4f.). Suffering is the way to glory. Hence, in Rom. 8.26 the eschatological and charismatic prayer of the spiritual man is precisely *not* a new language which sets aside his physical weakness, precisely *not* the mature dialogue of the gnostic with divine powers, but rather the very inarticulate groaning of his this-worldly weakness.[133]

A striking variation on the theme occurs in II Cor. 4.12 and Gal. 4.19. Elsewhere Paul has portrayed death and life as two sides of the one process in himself or in believers generally; but here he thinks of death and life as two sides of the relation between himself and his converts – death in us, life in you (II Cor. 4.12). In the confused metaphor of Gal. 4.19 Paul depicts himself as a woman in labour, endeavouring to bring to birth Christ in his converts, that is, presumably, to bring the life of Christ to visible expression in the lives of his converts (see above §54.1). Here again the basic thought is that suffering is the necessary complement to life – Christ comes to birth in them out of Paul's sufferings.[134] The effect of death exerting its sway over Paul is life for his converts (II Cor. 4.12) – an unexpected twist to the idea of charismatic community.

Finally we may turn to II Cor. 4.7; 12.9f.; 13.3f., where Paul plays upon the paradox of weakness and power in his own life. Here more than anywhere else Paul is striving to express the distinctiveness of the not yet. As we have already seen (§46.1), his opponents of II Cor. 10–13 based their claim to apostolic authority on their impressive charismatic experiences – the signs of apostleship (12.12). Consequently they despised Paul as weak and of no account (10.10; 11.21). Clearly in their view weakness – including here physical weakness,[135] 'lack of presence' (NEB), poor speech – was the denial of power. Weakness denoted the absence of Spirit; divine power would naturally manifest itself as such. Paul's response is memorable and of lasting importance. Divine power does not manifest itself by making the believer powerful, but as *power in weakness*; only so may it be recognized as *divine* power (4.7; 13.3f.). Weakness does not hinder or prevent the manifestation of power; on the contrary it is the necessary presupposition of power, the place wherein and the means whereby divine power is revealed on earth (12.9).[136] This was the lesson Paul had learned when, on his first visit to Corinth, he had seen the gospel working powerfully, not despite but *through* his weakness (I Cor. 2.3ff.)[137] – this is why he does not hesitate to characterize the kerygma as the gospel of the *weakness* of God (I Cor. 1.25; cf. above p. 220).[138] And the same conclusion had been driven home to him by the answer given to his thrice repeated prayer for deliverance from his physical weakness: *power does not drive out weakness; on the contrary, it only comes to its full strength in and through weakness* (12.9). In other words, the paradox of the already-not yet of eschatological tension, of life in death, is not surmounted by the charismatic Spirit. On the contrary, charismatic experience which tries to leave this paradox behind is potentially disastrous; power without weakness is destructive; only charismata which manifest power in weakness build up the community (10.8; 13.10).[139] This is clearly why Paul *never* boasts of his charismata, but rather of his weakness (11.30), for it is only when he is conscious of his own weakness, that is, when he is not seeking to manipulate or direct the power of God in any way – only then (note again the ἵνα) can God's grace and power fully rest upon him and manifest itself through him (12.9).[140] 'For when I am weak, then I am strong' (12.10).

The distinctiveness of Paul's understanding of the charismatic Spirit over against that of his Corinthian opponents is therefore quite plain. Where they thought of the Spirit as a power of the already which swallows up the not yet in forceful speech and action, Paul thought of it as a power which reinforces the not yet. Where they glorified in the power that came to perfection in ecstatic experience, Paul looked instead to the power that came to perfection in weakness. Paul was no ecstatic, living out of experiences which took him out of this world.[141] In his experience the Spirit of Christ had not obliterated the antithesis of power and weakness, he had sharpened it.

Here then is a clear answer to our question about the distinctive character of Christian experience for Paul. In the analysis of religious experience which his own ministry forced upon him, *that which he focused upon as distinctively Christian was charismatic power in and through human weakness.* We could almost leave it at that were it not for the fact that when we set this Pauline emphasis within the wider thought of his times several striking parallels jump at once into view. For example, Philo allegorizes the burning bush as a message to a suffering nation: 'Do not lose heart, your weakness is your strength . . .'.[142] And Pliny in a letter to Valerius(?) Maximus quotes as though a proverbial saying: 'We are never so virtuous as when we are ill'.[143] H. D. Betz in fact maintains that as ἀσθενής (weak) Paul actually corresponds to the type of the oriental *Goeten* (magicians, sorcerers), though the parallel between the Lucian passages he cites and II Cor. 12.9 is hardly close, either in content or in context.[144] Nevertheless the point remains that Paul was neither the first to make the experiential discovery of the paradox, strength in weakness; nor was he the last.

There is, however, one strand of Paul's thought on this subject still to be examined, and it is this which brings us to the heart of the distinctive character of Paul's experience of weakness, suffering and death.

55.2   *The fellowship of Jesus' sufferings.* For Paul not only is the power which he experiences the risen life of Christ, but the suffering which he undergoes is somehow the suffering of Christ given over to death. Thus in II Cor. 13.3f. when he explicitly responds to the Corinthian challenge for *proof* (δοκιμή) that Christ speaks through him, the most striking thing he says is v. 4b – 'we are weak in him' – *not*, we are weak in ourselves, but strong in him. *The character of the experience in which Christ speaks through a man is determined by the character of the Christ who speaks.* And the key fact here is that Christ remains the Crucified even though he now lives by the power of God (v. 4a).[145] *To experience the exalted Christ therefore is to experience not merely new life but new life which is life through death, life out of death, and which always retains that character.* As soon as the exalted Christ is separated from the crucified Jesus, charismatic experience loses its distinctive Christian yardstick.[146] As soon as charismatic experience becomes an experience only of the exalted Christ and not also of the crucified Jesus, it loses its distinctive Christian character. In Paul's view, religious experience for the Christian is not a matter of Christ taking him out of his weakness and leaving it behind in experiences of inspiration and ecstasy; on the contrary, Christ is present in his weakness – *his weakness is part of his experience of Christ.*

This theme, that in his own sufferings the believer is somehow sharing in Christ's sufferings, runs consistently through Paul's letters. It is probably implied by the construction of I Thess. 1.6: the Thessalonians' sufferings were an imitation of the Lord's. The gospel manifested itself in them not simply as joy, but as joy in suffering – an experience which they shared with the missionaries who brought them the gospel and with Jesus himself.[147] Paul's thought here may be simply: As Jesus was persecuted, so will his followers. But elsewhere Paul is in no doubt that Christian's sufferings are actually part of Christ's sufferings.[148]

In Gal. 2.19/20; 6.14 and Rom. 6.5 Paul's choice of tense is striking. In talking about the believer's existential relation to the cross or death of Christ he uses a *perfect* tense rather than an aorist. Gal. 2.19/20 – 'I have been crucified with Christ', that is, not as a once for all act in the past, finished and left behind (the force of the aorist); on the contrary, I am in that state still (the force of the perfect) – I have been nailed to the cross with Christ and in effect *am still hanging there.* The experience of 'Christ in me' is the experience of death as well as of life – *of Christ's death as well as of Christ's life.* Galatians 6.14 is to be understood similarly.[149] Rom. 6.5 reads – 'We have become one (σύμφυτοι γεγόναμεν) with the very likeness of Christ's death; in which case we shall also become one with the very likeness of his resurrection'.[150] What Paul means here is this: until believers are conformed in the future resurrection to Christ in his risen state, they must be conformed to Christ in his death. He has no doubt that believers will experience a resurrection which will in effect be precisely like Christ's. And what gives him assurance in this belief is the fact that he is already experiencing a death which in effect is precisely like Christ's. Both life and death are part of his experience as a Christian, and *both the life and the death are closely patterned on the death and life out of death of Jesus.* It should be observed that in these three passages the dying is thought of in more ethical terms – dying of the old self, dying to the law, dying to the world. Elsewhere the idea of death is expressed more in terms of physical weakness and suffering. But in Paul's mind there is no clear line of distinction between these two, as his concept of 'flesh' (see above n. 105 and below p. 336) and such passages as I Cor. 6.12–20; 7.32ff.; 9.26f. indicate.

In Rom. 8.17 and II Cor. 1.5 the same theme is mentioned in a brief and unemphatic way which shows how integral to Paul's soteriology it was. In Rom. 8.17 believers must suffer *with Christ* if they are to be glorified with him.[151] The context shows that in Paul's mind Christian suffering is part of the death throes of the present age, part of the messianic woes which will introduce the new age (see above n. 134). But he probably understands Christ's death too in terms of the messianic woes.[152] That is to say, in so far as the new age is already present in the Spirit the messianic woes are complete. But in so far as the old age still lasts, they are incomplete. In the event this means that those who experience the Spirit of the new age experience the sufferings of the old age *as the messianic woes* – as a suffering of what Jesus suffered – as a dying of the old age and as a dying with the old age. Those who are sons through receiving the Spirit of sonship (8.15) must experience the same transition and transformation to full sonship (8.23) that Jesus himself experienced (Rom. 1.3f.) if they are indeed to be fellow heirs with him – that is, through death and resurrection, or rather through *his* death and resurrection, since *no other death has opened the way to resurrection.*

Even bolder is II Cor. 1.5 where Paul identifies his sufferings as a *sharing* in Christ's sufferings.[153] The sufferings experienced by Christ did not end on the cross. So long as the old age lingers on, its concluding sufferings which Christ's death began are incomplete. So that those who are Christ's and who suffer in this world suffer as Christ's and share Christ's sufferings.[154]

The boldest expression of this thought comes, however, in Col. 1.24: Paul's own sufferings complete what is lacking in Christ's afflictions.[155] Here again the thought is of the sufferings of the end-time,[156] and here the tension implicit in the earlier verses becomes explicit: viz., on the one hand, Christ has already undergone the messianic woes – they are by definition the Christ's sufferings; what needed to be done to bring in the new age has been done. But on the other hand, the new age has not yet arrived; believers experience the risen life in Christ, with Christ (Col. 2.12f.),[157] but suffering continues. The only resolution of the paradox is *to recognize Christ in the experience of suffering as well as in the experience of life*. There is no need to press for the full-scale mystical interpretation of Deissmann and Schneider[158] to recognize the probability that this conclusion of Paul's was not simply a logical deduction but a sense that the power of the crucified and risen Christ was working out through the dying away of the old nature and his mortal body as well as in the renewing of the new nature (Col. 3.9f.) – in a phrase, the consciousness of Christ in his suffering as well as his renewal.

Perhaps the two most striking variations on this whole theme are to be found in II Cor. 4.10 and Phil. 3.10f. It is particularly significant for our study that both passages come in polemic or apologetic contexts, where Paul seems to be striving to express in words where it is that his experience of Christ and the ministry it brings differs from those who disagree with or oppose him. We have already noted the polemical thrust of II Cor. 3 (see above p. 320), and it continues to shape the development of Paul's thought in II Cor. 4 (see also pp. 329f. above). 4.10: 'Wherever we go we carry death with us in our body, the death that Jesus died (τὴν νέκρωσιν τοῦ 'Ιησοῦ), that (ἵνα) in this body also life may reveal itself, the life that Jesus lives (ἡ ζωὴ τοῦ 'Ιησοῦ)' (NEB). Here the paradox of death and life in Paul's experience is explicitly understood in terms of *Jesus*' death and life. It is not simply that the daily renewal of the 'inward man' is the outworking of the risen life of Christ, but the withering away of the 'outward man' (4.16) is the outworking of the death of Christ. The death of Christ was not merely an event of the historical past, some legal act as it were once performed and complete in itself; it is also a process – the dying of Christ in his identification with human nature, as coming to concrete realization in the actual experience of Paul.[159]

The particular polemical point of this verse probably comes in the ἵνα. It is quite likely that the phrase 'the life of Jesus' was a slogan of Paul's opponents,[160] in which case Paul's point is that experience of Jesus' life does not mean that experience of death and of dying is a thing of the past. On the contrary, it is only through the experience of death, of *Jesus*' death *as a continuing experience of this bodily existence*, that it is possible for the life of Jesus to be manifested in this present body. The continuity of thought from II Cor. 3.18 through II Cor. 4 implies that in Paul's mind this is what the experience of transformation into Christ's image means for the believer. To become like Christ is not to be exempt from suffering and death: rather, it means precisely becoming like Christ in his death as well as in his life beyond death – to experience Christ's life through the experience of his death.[161] In short, once again Paul senses in a half-conscious or semi-mystical way that *Christ stands on both sides of the death-life paradox of the believer's experience*; he experiences Christ as the Crucified as well as the Exalted; indeed, it is only when he experiences Christ as crucified that it is possible for him to experience Christ as exalted, only when he experiences death as the dying of Christ that it is possible to experience the risen life of Christ.

Finally we consider Phil. 3.10f. Paul's ardent desire is that he may come to know Christ. What he means by this is explained more fully in the following phrases.[162] To know Christ is to experience[163] the power of his resurrection and a participation in his sufferings in a growing conformity to his death, thereby attaining the resurrection from the dead. It is clear from the context that Paul is here describing what is distinctive about his Christian experience as against his pre-conversion experience within Judaism (3.4ff., cf. vv. 7–9), and prob-ably also what is distinctive in his experience of Christ over against the claims of gnostic-type elements in Philippi (3.10f., 12ff.).[164] Notice then that (1) religious experience for Paul is an experience not only of life but of suffering and death. He does not see suffering as a temporary antecedent to resurrection power: he mentions the experience of suffering and death *after* the talk of experiencing resurrection power. Experience of resurrection power does not leave suffering and death behind; *the power of Christ's resurrection manifests itself precisely in and through the fellowship of his sufferings*. Both sides of the death-life paradox remain in full force in the believer's experience till the end; he must experience the full outworking of death as well as of life if ($\epsilon\check{\iota}$ $\pi\omega\varsigma$) he is to experience the resurrection from the dead.[165] But (2) it is not any suffering that Paul has in mind. It is suffering which can be recognized as a participation in Christ's suffering, suffering which can be characterized as a 'becoming like Jesus in his death'.[166] Only Christ's death has resulted in resurrection. So *only those who suffer his death will attain the resurrection from the dead that he already enjoys*. Consequently we see emerging again as the distinctive feature of Christian experience, the awareness that life cannot be separated from death in the believer's experience so long as this age lasts, but also that Christ is involved both in the believer's dying as in his new life. For Paul, religious experience is quintessenti-ally a sense of identity with Christ in his dying as well as his rising again – a consciousness of Christ in his life through death.

55.3   *Corollaries and clarifications.* To restate Paul's various statements
on this theme of suffering Christ's death is comparatively easy. To
get inside these statements and begin to understand what is one of
the profoundest elements in Paul's religion and theology is far from
easy. It would be a bold man who claimed to know Paul's mind with
any precision on this subject. Nevertheless, the attempt must be made.
But first, four clarificatory points must be taken into account.

First, Paul speaks of death as a past event in the believer's experience: at conversion-initiation the convert died to sin (Rom. 6.2ff.;
Gal. 2.19a; Col. 2.11ff., 20; 3.3). But in the light of the evidence
reviewed above it becomes clear that the 'dying' of conversion-
initiation is only the *beginning* of a process of death – the initial
identification with Christ in his death and life so that his death and
life may work themselves out in the believer. Conversion is a *decisive*
event of the past – there is no question on that score so far as Paul is
concerned (see above §53.1). But this certainly does not mean that
the believer's old nature (attitudes, values, desires, etc.) are dead, or
that he is dead to them – very much to the contrary. The dying of the
old nature and the dying to the old nature is *a life-long process* which
will not be completed till the death or transformation of the body.
Conversion means not so much a once for all dying and coming to
life as the entry into the convert's experience of death and life, of
Christ's death as well as his life. This is why in Romans, Galatians
and Colossians Paul follows up these bolder statements about conversion with exhortations which on the face of it seem to contradict
them. So, for example, Rom. 6.11 does not mean, '*Pretend* you are
dead to sin; assume that you can no longer sin', but rather, Recognize
the death at work in you and the life at work in you, and choose the
death and life of the Spirit rather than the life and death of the flesh
(cf. Gal. 5.16ff.; Col. 3.5ff.).[167]

Secondly, the initial dying with Christ is linked in Rom. 6.4 and
Col. 2.12 with baptism. But the major development of the theme of
suffering and dying with Christ reviewed above is not dependent on
the metaphor or event of baptism.[168] It would therefore be a mistake
to seek elucidation of Paul's experience by constantly harking back
to his baptism; it was much too contemporary, too day-to-day an
experience for that. On the other hand, we dare not ignore a point
which such interpretation is attempting to undergird – viz., that there
is a corporate dimension to the experience of dying with Christ.[169]
As the manifestation of the grace of Christ can only come to full
expression now in charismatic community (chapter IX), so the
manifestation of the death and life of Christ can only come to full

expression in the community of those who share in that death and life.

Thirdly, we should perhaps attempt to clarify what appears as a curious ambivalence in Paul's thinking about the life of this world, about the flesh, the physical body: viz., he thinks of the flesh as a continual source of danger and of potential disaster, and yet he sees it at the same time as the locus of divine revelation. The paradox comes to sharpest expression in II Cor. 12.7ff., where weakness is seen both as the work of Satan and as the medium of divine power. No doubt this positive/negative attitude emerges because of Paul's recognition that life here and now cannot be lived out of the body, apart from the flesh, *in absentia* from the world. But it does mean that exegesis of Paul has to work with some such distinction as that between life *according to* the world/flesh and life *in* the world/flesh – the one to be resisted, the other inevitable for man as a human being (as above p. 328).[170] In fact Paul does not always observe this distinction, using 'in the flesh' both for the life which the believer no longer leads (Rom. 7.5; 8.9) and for his present life (II Cor. 10.3; Gal. 2.20; Phil. 1.22, 24; Philemon 16), and thereby underlining the paradox of 'life in the flesh' – that it is precisely in and through the medium which attaches the believer most firmly to this world and which most threatens the believer's spiritual life that the life of the Spirit manifests itself most fully.[171] In other words, Paul recognizes that life here and now must be lived in some sense in the flesh, to some extent in terms of the flesh, and *to that extent he welcomes worldly existence, for only so can the death of Jesus work out through him, only so can the character of Christ as the Crucified become visible through him* (hence the calm realism of Rom. 7.25b). At the same time life *in* the flesh can very easily and quickly (and unconsciously) become life *according to* the flesh – the dying that leads to death and life can merge into the dying that leads only to death – life in the flesh is always imperilled by life according to the flesh so long as this life lasts. It is precisely because the dividing line between the two is so difficult to draw that the believer must stand in constant dependence on the Spirit for the charisma of discernment and on his fellow Christians for the charisma of evaluation (see above §§40.5, 49).

Fourthly, we should underline the point that in all these passages Paul is talking in *experiential* terms: he actually experienced a new power of life and a dying of which his sufferings were the most obvious outward manifestation; and he experienced both the life and the dying as Christ's – he was conscious of Christ in both the life and the death – they were both somehow his. Whether this experience should be called 'mystical' or not is a fair question. The trouble is that 'mysticism' (like 'enthusiasm') means different things to different people;[172] for some indeed it is more of a stick to beat opponents with than a possible description of Christian experience.[173] The fact remains, however, that Paul was conscious both of a suffering and dying in his experience, and of Christ involved in that suffering and dying in such a way that he was able to speak of it as the experience of *Christ's* suffering and death – and that without any sense of contradicting his other statements about Christ's death and resurrection as an event of the historical past. Should we call this 'mystical' or 'pneumatic' or 'charismatic'? The name matters little so long as we are as clear as possible on the experience it describes.[174]

The rationale of Paul's thought seems to be something as follows. In his talk of sharing Christ's sufferings Paul brings together two of the basic strands of his theology – his Christology and his anthropology. We cannot do more here than sketch them in the briefest outline. (1) Jesus in his life on earth identified himself with man, was representative man, was one with man in his Adamic fallenness (Rom. 8.3; I Cor. 15.27; Phil. 2.7f.). In his suffering and death he showed man what is the only end he can expect as fallen man – suffering and death – death as the destruction of the flesh, death as the end of man as flesh (II Cor. 5.14).[175] But Jesus' suffering and death proved to be the messianic woes, since Jesus rose again beyond death, as last Adam, eschatological Adam, the beginning of a new race of men. (2) Not only is death the only end for fallen man, but death is already working in him, the forces of decay are already active. In this they are speeded forward by both the law (Rom. 8.2; I Cor. 15.56; II Cor. 3.6)[176] and the wrath of God (Rom. 1.18–32)[177] – a vicious circle of sin and sinning which only hastens the death of man as man.

When Paul brings these two strands together they provide the challenge of the gospel. For the gospel faces man (including the Christian!) with a choice: viz., he may choose *how* to die (not whether he will die or not; he has no choice in that – die he will, like it or not). On the one hand he may choose to live only on the level of the flesh (a life of self-assertion and self-indulgence); in which case when death closes its grip finally on the flesh he is destroyed – as a man of flesh he dies the death of the flesh – death has the last word (Rom. 8.6, 13; Gal. 6.8). Alternatively, he may choose to identify himself with Christ – open himself to the power of the risen Christ. This means two things: (1) he experiences the power of the Spirit as *the power of life beyond death* – a power which is therefore an alien power, alien in that it comes from beyond death and is hostile to life lived according to this world's pattern[178] – a power which is superior to the forces of corruption and death, not in the sense that it stops them, but in the sense that it lasts through them. (2) He experiences the power of the Spirit as *the power of life out of death* – a power which shapes him in his dying as well as his living – a power which enables him to put to death the attitudes and desires of life in this world, to crucify himself in his fleshness (Rom. 8.13; Gal. 5.24) even while living 'in the flesh'. In this complex experience of life experienced as a gift from beyond, and of death as the compound of his own physical and moral weakness, the sufferings inflicted on him by others and his own self mortification, Paul sees the Spirit of Christ the Crucified and Risen, and he recognizes the image of this Christ taking shape in him.[179] It is this experience which gives him the assurance that he is not simply dying his own death with nothing to look forward to beyond, but that the death he is already dying is Christ's own, or at least the very same as Christ's – so that beyond it is Christ's resurrection, the full sonship of the son. When death has done its work and the body of death is dead, then the power of the Spirit will embrace the whole man in life, the spiritual body.

In short, *if man chooses to live his own life, then he will die his own death* – and that will be that. *But if by the power of the Spirit he dies Christ's death now, then he will live Christ's life both here and hereafter.* Thus the antithesis of Paul's anthropology and his Christology find their resolution in his pneumatology. And in the experience of sharing both Christ's life and his death that resolution finds its most profound and poignant expression.

§56. CONCLUSIONS

56.1   *For Paul the religious experience of the believer is characterized by paradox and conflict – the paradox of life and death, the conflict of Spirit and flesh.* It is a religion of *Anfechtung* – of faith always assailed by question and doubt, of life always assailed by death, of Spirit always assailed by flesh (Gal. 5.16f.).[180] It is a life of tension – at times almost unbearable tension (Rom. 8.22f.; II Cor. 5.4) – the tension of belonging to two opposed worlds at the same time, of knowing the life of the Spirit but having to express it through the body of death. It is *a life-long tension*: the cry of frustration in Rom. 7.24 is the life-long cry of the Christian; all through his life the believer lives with a foot in both camps (Rom. 7.25b; 8.10); all through this life the possibility lies before him of walking according to the flesh or walking according to the Spirit – both are real possibilities, and at least to some extent actualities, till the end of this life.

It is important to realize that conversion, experience of Spirit, charismatic experience, does not raise the believer above and beyond this conflict – rather the presence and activity of the Spirit sharpens the conflict. Certainly Paul knows experiences which take him out of himself – even, it perhaps seemed at the time, out of the body (II Cor. 12.2ff.). But such experiences are the least significant for Paul; *it is the daily experience of weakness that finds him closer to God and the power of God most effective through him* (II Cor. 12.9f.; 13.4). If Paul is right, then any attempt to escape this tension and conflict is wrong-headed;[181] there is no higher experience which exempts the believer from the reality of his divided state as man of Spirit and man of flesh; so long as the believer remains in the flesh he *cannot* enjoy the full life of the Spirit. There are only two ways of escape, and both are the way of *death*: one is the way *forward* – to engage in the Spirit/flesh conflict till its end in physical death; the other is the way *backward* – to abandon the conflict, to retreat into a life lived solely on the level of the flesh, the level where death alone reigns, the way of death. In other words, *the only way of escape is death – either the death of the body, or the death of the whole man.*

In short, the Christian who takes Paul seriously should never be alarmed at the paradox and conflict of his religious experience. Nor should he be depressed at defeat, or conclude that grace has lost the struggle. On the contrary, spiritual conflict is the sign of life – a sign that the Spirit is having his say in the shaping of character. Suffering means hope (Rom. 5.3ff.). Death is part of the present experience of life (II Cor. 4.10ff.). *Since life now must be life in this body, the Spirit can only be present as paradox and conflict. It is this paradox and conflict which is the mark of healthy religious experience – not its absence.* 'The Spirit is absent when we stop fighting, not when we lose.'[182]

56.2   So far as Paul is concerned, *religious experience embraces the whole of his life*. Since the whole of this life is in some sense life in the flesh, the whole of this life becomes the arena for the conflict between Spirit and flesh. To shut the Spirit out of any part of it is to live that part of life not simply in the flesh, but according to the flesh. Since no part of life is exempt from decision and choice, every decision and choice is potentially a choice for or against God; this is why the indicatives in passages like Rom. 6 and Col. 3 are followed at once by imperatives; religious experience includes the decisions of the market place and the meal table (I Cor. 10.25–31). The believer must refuse to let himself be adapted to the pattern of the world at any point, but must rather let himself be transformed by the renewal of the Spirit at every point – so that every choice and decision is an attempt to actualize the will of God (Rom. 12.2).

Religious experience for Paul therefore is not merely a segment of a wider experience of reality. It is not something enjoyed only in periods of worship or when with other believers. It is not something peculiarly attached to sacraments or particular ministries. It does not consist in religious experiences. It is not reducible to a sequence of charismatic experiences, to the experience of individual charismata. Religious experience embraces him totally – both his worshipping and his worldliness, both his living and his dying. Dying to the world and the dying of the flesh did not mean monastic abandonment of the world for Paul. Rather it was precisely by living in the world, by extending his bodily strength to its limits (and beyond) that the death of Christ worked itself out in Paul. Or to put the same point the other way round: all experience is for Paul religious experience, for it all bears the imprint of the last Adam, both the dying of the sinful flesh and the living by the powerful Spirit, both the power of his resurrection and participation in his sufferings (Phil. 3.10). Indeed, even the believer's experiences of frustration and defeat may be seen as part of the dying that leads to life, *so long as he experiences them as frustration and defeat.*

Hopefully, enough has already been said to indicate the consequences and corollaries from all this for ethics (§§40.5, 49.2) and for later 'doctrines of sanctification' (§§53–55). To elaborate these further would go beyond the scope of this study.

56.3   The question we set ourselves in this chapter was, What was it in Paul's religious experience which authenticated it as distinctively Christian experience? The question already posed by Luke's account of early Palestinian Christianity became even sharper when we realized how ambiguous charismatic experience was (and is) – experience of inspiration, ecstasy and spiritual power are nothing exceptional in the history of religions. Fortunately Paul was well aware of this question, and the answer he gave we have summed up in the phrase '*consciousness of Christ*'. The charismatic Spirit becomes distinctive for Paul when he manifests himself also as the eschatological Spirit, that is, more precisely, as the Spirit of the Eschatological Man, Jesus Christ. The inspiration and power is distinctively Christian when it bears the marks of the new age, of the One who broke through the bounds of the old age in death and achieved the life of the age to come. *The consciousness of grace is Christian only when it is also a consciousness of Christ, that is, when it is characteristically that grace which was most fully manifested in Jesus' life, death, and resurrection.*

In the end of the day then, it is the identity of historical Jesus and Christ of faith which distinguishes Christian experience from comparable experiences of other religions. In particular, the parallels with the experiences gained in the contemporary mystery cults, of which so much was made by history of religions scholars at the turn of the century (examples in §52.2 above), break down again and again precisely at this point: the fact that Jesus' life, death and resurrection constitute a unique and central act of revelation in the past which determines the eschatological tension of Christian experience with both its already and its not yet soteriological and ethical corollaries so characteristically Christian – the fact that the experience of power and inspiration has to be defined and qualified in terms of not only Christ the life-giving Spirit but Christ the Crucified – the fact that Christian experience can and must be called to account, tested and measured against the event of Jesus Christ, against the character of the man Jesus, of his relationships and ministry, of his life and death.[183] It is by the criterion of Christ the Crucified and Risen that Paul judges religious and charismatic experience; and his verdict is clear cut and emphatic: *all religious experience, charismatic or otherwise is in the end of the day worth nothing if it is not at the same time the manifestation of love, that is, the love of Christ, the love of God in Christ.*

56.4　It is important also to stress the relationship between the more general religious experience and the more particular charismatic experience, for both are fundamental to Paul's concept of Christian faith and religion: without experience of *charis* (or Spirit or life) there is no being 'in Christ'; and without experience of *charisma* there is no community, no body of Christ. The inspiration, the concrete manifestations of Spirit in power, in revelation, in word, in service, are all necessary – for without them grace soon becomes status, gift becomes office, ministry becomes bureaucracy, body of Christ becomes institution, and *koinōnia* becomes the extension fund! But the experience of ever fresh charismata is not enough; the experience of inspiration or of spiritual power in itself is not what creates a living community of Christ or a living relation with Christ; the ἐν πνεύματι must be defined by the ἐν Χριστῷ;[184] only when charisma is expressive more of Christ's love than of inspiration, only when charismatic experience bears the mark of the paradox of death and life, of power in weakness, only when it is stamped with the hallmark of the Crucified and Risen one, is it a positive and constructive experience (cf. II Cor. 5.13ff.); *only when* charisma *expresses the distinctive* charis *of Christ is it a gift which builds.*

56.5   Finally, in the conclusion to chapter VIII we noted that in the matter of charismatic experience as such there is much similarity between Jesus and Paul (§43.9). Indeed, if we confined our investigations to charismatic phenomena Paul would appear in effect as a figure of independent religious significance in the history of religion, whose connection with Jesus was only incidental and accidental. That conclusion is still a possibility which some may wish to argue for. Windisch in particular was so impressed by the catalogue of comparisons between Jesus and Paul which he amassed in rather eclectic fashion that he did not hesitate to call Jesus 'the first Christian', or to speak of Paul in terms of 'a second Christ' and 'Saviour'.[185] But what we must now recognize is that so far as Paul is concerned, his religious experience as a whole is characterized by a dependency on Jesus as Lord: it is not merely the experience of sonship, but the experience of Jesus' sonship, made possible by the Spirit of the Son; it is not merely the experience of grace, it is the experience of the grace of Christ; it is not merely the experience of Spirit, of life and death, it is experience of the Spirit of Christ, the experience of that death which Jesus died, of that life which Jesus lives. In short, it is *experience of Jesus, consciousness of Christ*, that is, the recognition of the impress of Christ's character in Paul's experience and its outworking – a shaping of life and death which reproduces Jesus' death and life, not just in an accidental way, but as the purposeful action of divine power. Consequently, Jesus is not merely the first Christian, he is the Christ; he is not merely the typical man caught in the overlap of the ages, he is the archetypal man, the last Adam. *In the end of the day the religious experience of the Christian is not merely experience like that of Jesus, it is experience which at all characteristic and distinctive points is derived from Jesus the Lord, and which only makes sense when this derivative and dependent character is recognized.*

CONCLUSION

XI

A GLANCE ACROSS THE SECOND GENERATION OF CHRISTIANITY AND CONCLUDING REMARKS

§57. THE VISION FADES – THE LATER PAULINE CORRESPONDENCE

57.1 The task we set ourselves in this study was to investigate the religious experience of the first thirty years of Christianity, the religious experiences which shaped the first generation of one of the most significant movements of world history. To extend our researches into the years beyond, into the second generation, would be a fascinating and not unimportant pursuit. But it would extend an already long volume far beyond the bounds of most readers' patience, and much chaff would have to be winnowed for a much poorer return of grain. The problem is that if we are to come to terms with religious experience we must see it as fully as possible within the living situation which called it forth; it is only our knowledge of the Corinthian situation which enables us to gain such a well-rounded understanding of Paul's concept of charismatic community. And the fact is that we just do not have this knowledge in any readily available form for most of the other documents in the NT. Thus to push our study into the second generation of Christianity and beyond would require a most careful scrutiny of the Synoptic Gospels and of the non-Pauline correspondence. And even after much sifting of evidence our findings would only occasionally move beyond the realm of supposition and speculation.

We make only two exceptions – the later Pauline letters and the Johannine writings. I do so because Paul's vision of charismatic community is so exciting and challenging that we are bound to ask whether it actually took on flesh and blood in the concrete situations of the Pauline churches and whether it withstood the test of time. Likewise his correlation of Christology with pneumatic experience provided a dynamic synthesis which only a vital religious experience could maintain. Did it last? The later Pauline correspondence and the Johannine writings offer us the clearest answers to these questions. And it is only fitting that we should round off our study of first generation Christianity with the answers of second generation Christianity – even if we cannot enter into the many interrelated issues and must confine ourselves to sketching in the answers in broad outline.

57.2   If Paul's vision of charismatic community under the control of the Spirit of Christ was translated into reality *it was a reality which does not appear to have outlived him*. The answer is of course bound up with the question of Pauline authorship of the most disputed of the Pauline letters – Colossians, Ephesians and the Pastorals. In so far as the particular area of our investigation offers any guide, the conclusion urged upon us by the evidence is that Colossians and Ephesians take us to the very fringe of the genuine Pauline correspondence, if not beyond, and that the Pastorals belong to the next generation at least.

Of these *Colossians* has the highest claim to Pauline authorship; but the paucity of references to the Spirit (1.8; 2.5(?); πνευματικός – 1.9; 3.16) is striking, and the concept of 'church' is becoming more grandiose (1.18, though see also 4.15f.). In consequence we may have to recognize in the talk of Christ as 'the head of the body, the church' (1.18; 2.19) something of a retreat from Paul's vision. The threat to the Colossian church is much more christological in character and in order to meet it the writer has to focus attention on Christ in a way which seems to slacken the bonds between Jesus and the Spirit and between the Spirit and the community.[1] Some may feel, perhaps quite rightly, that this reads too much into the evidence, and may prefer to stress the parallels between 1.8f.; 1.29; 3.16 and the un-disputed Paulines. Others may wish to conclude that it is Paul himself beginning to qualify his hope that charismatic community will pro-vide its own safeguards against disorder and false teaching, and beginning to look for a more regulated deterrent in a more formal Christology, though not in a more regulated ministry (cf. 1.26; 2.19).[2]

The case against Pauline authorship of *Ephesians* is, from our stand-point, both stronger and weaker. On the one hand, not only is the Christology as developed as that of Colossians, but the ecclesiology is markedly advanced: ἐκκλησία is used exclusively of the universal church (1.22; 3.10, 21; 5.23–5, 27, 29, 32); and 2.20 does have the ring of a second generation veneration of first generation leaders; in which

case the listing *only* of evangelists, pastors and teachers along with
apostles and prophets as gifts (δόματα) to the church (4.11) may imply
a tendency to look to regular offices as the guarantee of unity, rather
than to the self-regulation of the charismatic community.[3] On the
other hand, the pneumatology is much more like the pneumatology
of Paul (1.13, 17; 4.23, 30; 5.18f.; 6.17f.); in particular, we should
mention the Spirit Christology implied in 3.16f., and the obvious
parallels between Eph. 4.3 and I Cor. 12.13, between Eph. 4.7 and
Rom. 12.3; I Cor. 12.11 ('to each'), and between Eph. 4.12ff. and
Rom. 12.4ff.; I Cor. 12.14–27. It is eminently arguable that these
parallels are not merely formal (note 5.18f.), but reflect the actual
parallel between the situations envisaged in Eph. 4 and that of Rom.
12, I Cor. 12 (see also Eph. 4.25; 5.30); in which case the 'gifts' of 4.11
are less likely to be offices, and we would probably be better advised
to understand them more as regular ministries, like the prophets and
teachers of I Cor. 12.28 and the 'overseers and deacons' of Phil. 1.1
(see above §48). In short, if we are handling a genuine Pauline letter,
the charismatic community remains a living reality for Paul; if we
are in a post-Pauline situation, then it looks as though charismatic
ministry is beginning to give way to a more limited, (formally?)
recognized ministry.

57.3 With the *Pastorals*, however, we move into a different world
completely. The nearest we come to authentic Pauline pneumatology
is II Tim. 1.7 (though 'timidity' and 'self-control' are not characteristically Pauline) and Titus 3.5–7 (one of the 'faithful sayings'
formally preserved by the writer). Similarly the nearest equivalents
to the life-death 'Christ-mysticism' of Paul are II Tim. 1.8 (though
'take your share of suffering' belongs solely to II Tim.), and II Tim.
2.11, again a 'faithful saying' – that is, a saying which does not
originate with the writer but is preserved and passed on by him.[4]
As for ministry, we need only note the following facts. (1) Presbyters
or elders appear for the first and only time in the Pauline corpus (I
Tim. 5.1f., 17, 19; Titus 1.5). Here we probably see the merging of
Jewish Christian church order with the more formal order which
emerged in the Pauline churches in the early catholicism of second
and third generation Christianity.[5] (2) 'Overseers' (I Tim. 3.1–7;
Titus 1.7ff.)[6] and 'deacons' (I Tim. 3.8–13) appear now as descrip-
tions of established offices (ἐπισκοπή – 'office of overseer' – I Tim. 3.1).
'Overseers' may be another name for 'presbyters' (early catholic
synonyms), otherwise the absence of any mention of presbyters in
I Tim. 3 would be rather odd (see also Titus 1.5ff.); an alternative

possibility is that overseers were appointed to a particular leadership function from among the presbyters (I Tim. 3.4f.). The functions of neither overseers nor deacons are clearly spelt out, but the presentation of I Tim. 3 suggests that deacons were subordinate officials.[7] It is also noteworthy that a recognized order of widows such as we find regularly in second-century Christianity is apparently already well established at Ephesus (I Tim. 5.3–16).[8] (3) Not least to be considered is the position of Timothy and Titus. What their precise relation is to the communities of Ephesus and Crete is not clear; but certainly they rank above the presbyters, overseers and deacons. Perhaps most striking of all is the fact that the letters are addressed solely to them, so that the primary responsibility for regulating the community's affairs seems to lie with them;[9] in particular, they envisage Timothy and Titus exercising an authority which Paul himself never exercised either directly or through his immediate co-workers (I Tim. 5.17–22; Titus 1.5f.; cf. II Tim. 2.2; contrast I Cor. 4.17; 16.15–18; Col. 4.7f.; I Thess. 5.12ff.).[10]

Most significant of all from the standpoint of our inquiry is the way in which the Pauline concept of *charisma* has been modified. Grau noted three points worthy of comment.[11] (*a*) *Charisma* no longer seems to denote a great variety of services, the particular utterances and deeds which different believers may be called upon to contribute for the benefit of all. In the Pastorals *charisma* is used only with reference to Timothy (I Tim. 4.14; II Tim. 1.6); it is a single gift once given which equips him for different responsibilities and gives him his position and authority. Exhortation and teaching (particularly I Tim. 4.13) are no longer themselves charismata, but simply part of Timothy's regular responsibilities.[12] In short, *charisma has become power of office.*[13] (*b*) In the Pastorals *charisma* has lost its dynamic character. It is no longer the individual manifestation of grace but a power or ability which Timothy *possesses*, which he *has within him* (I Tim. 4.14; II Tim. 1.6), and which he himself can stir into activity. (*c*) Charisma is no longer the wholly free gift of the Spirit, as were the charismata of the early Pauline literature. Rather it is a gift given once for all in the course of an act of ordination – 'through prophecy[14] along with the laying on of hands for ordination as an elder' (I Tim. 4.14),[15] 'through the laying on of my (Paul's) hands' (II Tim. 1.6).[16] In addition, we must note (*d*) that the finely tensed balance Paul had achieved between prophecy and teaching, that is between new revelations of the ever present eschatological Spirit and the passing on and interpretation of established tradition, seems to have gone.[17] Wholly dominant is the concern to preserve the doctrinal statements of the past – the 'sound teaching/doctrine', the 'faithful sayings', the 'sound words', 'the faith'.[18] The Spirit has become the power to guard the heritage of tradition handed on from the past (II Tim. 1.14 – φύλαξον διὰ πνεύματος ἁγίου).[19] And even Paul himself is depicted more as the keeper of tradition than as its author (II Tim. 1.12).[20]

Clearly then the vision of charismatic community has faded, ministry and authority have become the prerogative of the few, the experience of the Christ-Spirit has lost its vitality, the preservation of the past has become more important than openness to the present and future. *Spirit and charisma have become in effect subordinate to office, to ritual, to tradition* – early-Catholicism indeed! Why it should be so we cannot tell. Perhaps the enthusiasts won the day in the Pauline churches after his death,[21] and the conclusion was drawn that charismatic community is unworkable and leads inevitably to anarchy and self-destruction. Perhaps the Pastorals themselves were written in response to a resurgence of earlier enthusiastic excesses, a forerunner of the Montanism which challenged the church so profoundly later in the second century.[22] At all events, the only way the author of the Pastorals felt able to maintain Christianity was by formalization of faith and institutionalization of church. But in so doing has he not fallen into the very error he himself warns against – maintaining the outward form of piety but denying its inner power (II Tim. 3.5)? Certainly it would seem that the great distinctives in Paul's handling of religious experience have almost wholly disappeared.

Perhaps then the Pastorals are the first example of that progressive institutionalizing which seems to afflict so many movements of spiritual renewal in the second and third generations, when the flexibility of fresh religious experience begins to harden into set forms. The lesser men of the second (or third) generation, unable to live creatively out of their own experience of God, have to treat the faith of the founding era as 'the faith'. Teaching which was the living expression of the first generation's spiritual experience becomes sacred word, hallowed heritage to be preserved, guarded, handed on, but not re-interpreted. The springs of present religion are confined almost wholly to the past; the present becomes in effect only a channel whereby the religion of the past can be transmitted to the future in good order. In a word, the vitality of first generation religious experience largely disappears, and the second generation begins to attempt what is not possible – that is, to live in the present out of the religious experience of the past. This has not yet fully happened in the Pastorals, but the process is already well advanced and perhaps is already irreversible.

§58. THE JOHANNINE ALTERNATIVE

If the Pastorals testify to the loss of Pauline vitality and vision, the Johannine writings demonstrate that in the 80s and 90s of the first century there were Christians and Christian communities where the flame still burned brightly and experience of the Spirit created a fresh vision. The vitality of religious experience is demonstrated, for example, by the fact that words like 'life', 'loving', 'knowing', 'believing' all appear with great regularity in both the gospel and the epistles, indeed more frequently than in Paul, also by such passages as John 3.5–8; 3.34(?); 4.10–14; 6.63; 7.37–9; 14.17; I John 2.20, 27; 3.24; 4.13; 5.6–10.[23] If these words, particularly the vigorous metaphors, mean anything at all, they denote a living religious experience which the Johannine community could attribute only to the Spirit. A closer look at the relevant material reveals that John reaffirmed some of the key features of the Pauline vision, but also that his own conception of religious experience had its own distinctive and different features.

58.1   *The Spirit is the Spirit of Jesus* – that is, he continues the *work* of Jesus; indeed we can put it more strongly, he continues the *presence* of Jesus. John brings this out in a variety of ways. It is implied in 1.32f.: the Spirit descended on Jesus and remained on him (ἔμεινεν ἐπ' αὐτόν); that is, the union of Jesus and Spirit continued through his ministry and after his exaltation.[24] It is implied in 6.62f. and 7.37ff., where it is clear that the language of eating the body/flesh of Jesus and drinking the water from Jesus symbolizes the believing reception of the life-giving Spirit.[25] It is implied in the 'tandem' relationship or parallelism between the ministry of Jesus and that of the 'Paraclete': for example, both come forth from the Father (15.26; 16.27f.); both are given and sent by the Father (3.16f.; 14.16, 26); both teach the disciples (6.59; 7.14, 28; 8.20; 14.26); both are unrecognized by the world (14.17; 16.3).[26] It is implied in 19.30 (probably) and 20.22, where the Spirit is depicted as the spirit/breath of Jesus.[27] Above all it is indicated in the explicit description of the Spirit as the '*other* Paraclete' or Counsellor, where Jesus is clearly understood as the *first* Paraclete (I John 2.1);[28] and by the fact that the coming of the Spirit obviously fulfils the promise of Jesus to come again and dwell in his disciples (14.15–26).[29] In short, 'the Paraclete is the presence of Jesus when Jesus is absent'.[30]

Two comments must be made: first, in relating the Spirit to Jesus in this way John is doing what Paul did: *John's 'other Paraclete' is Paul's 'Spirit of Jesus'*. For John as for Paul the Spirit has ceased to be an impersonal divine power; the experience of new life alone does not sufficiently characterize the activity of the Spirit (3.5–8; 4.10–14; 6.63; 7.37ff.; 20.22). The Spirit has taken on a fuller or more precise character – the character of Jesus: *the personality of Jesus has become the personality of the Spirit*. As the Logos of revelation (and Wisdom) has been identified with the earthly Jesus and stamped with the impress of his character (1.1–18), so the Spirit of revelation has been brought into conjunction with the heavenly Jesus and bears the stamp of his personality.[31] Second, the importance of this equation is that it affords *an immediate and direct continuity between believers and Jesus*. The lengthening time gap between John and the historical Jesus, and the continuing delay of the parousia do not mean a steadily increasing distance between each generation of Christians and the Christ. On the contrary, each generation is as close to Jesus as the last – and the first – because the Paraclete is the immediate link between Jesus and his disciples in every generation. That is to say, the link and continuity is provided not by sacraments or offices or human figures, but by the Spirit.[32] The vitality of Christian experience does not cease because the historical Jesus has faded into the past and the coming of Jesus has faded into the future; it retains its vitality because the Spirit is at work here and now as the other Paraclete.

58.2   *The Spirit and the kerygmatic tradition.* It was by bringing these two into dynamic interaction that Paul achieved another control on the charismatic Spirit without sacrificing either the present to the past or the past to the present (see above pp. 284, 293f.). Whereas, in the Pastorals the balance seems to have been tipped in favour of the tradition from the past, with the Spirit almost wholly subordinated thereto, it is one of John's most positive contributions to Christianity that he does not follow suit, but rather *brings the dialectic between present Spirit and original gospel into even sharper focus*. In John's gospel this comes to clearest expression in the role attributed to the Paraclete in 14.26 and 16.12ff. Notice the balance achieved in these verses between the continuing revelatory work of the Spirit and the revelation already given. 14.26: 'he will teach you everything' – this must include teaching which Jesus had not been able to give his disciples while on earth (cf. 16.12); 'and will keep you in mind of all that I said to you' (cf. 15.15) – the new revelation has the continual check of the original revelation.[33] 16.12ff.: 'he will guide you into or in[34] all truth' (new revelation – v.12), which is balanced by, 'he will not speak on his own authority . . .' (*Jesus is the truth* – 14.6). Again, 'he will declare (ἀναγγελεῖ) to you the things that are coming', which is balanced by, 'he will glorify me, for he will take what is mine and declare it (ἀναγγελεῖ) to you'. The dialectic of the Johannine concept of revelation is summed up in that one word, ἀναγγελεῖ. For it can have the force of '*re*-announce', '*re*-proclaim'; but in 16.13 as in 4.25 it must include some idea of new information, new revelation (cf. Isa.42.9; 44.7; 46.10),[35] even if that new revelation is in effect drawn out of the old by way of reinterpretation.[36] In this word, as in these passages as a whole, both present inspiration and interpretation of the past are bound up together in *the dynamic of creative religious experience*.

What this interpretative work of the Spirit meant for John becomes clear as soon as we realize that *John would undoubtedly regard his own gospel as the product of this inspiring Spirit*;[37] his own work was a fulfilment of these very promises; indeed these promises may constitute an implicit apologia for his gospel; the way in which John handles the words and deeds of the historical Jesus is typically the way in which the Spirit interprets Jesus to a new generation, guides them into the truth of Jesus. That is to say, the teaching function of the Spirit for John is *not* limited to recalling the *ipsissima verba* of the historical Jesus. But neither does the inspiring Spirit create wholly new revelation or portray a Jesus who is not in substantial continuity with the once incarnate Jesus. There is *both freedom and control* – liberty to reinterpret and remould the original kerygma, but also the original kerygma remains as check and restraint. The more freedom we recognize in John's handling of the kerygmatic tradition, the more striking his concept of inspired reinterpretation becomes.

We should simply note that in I John a similar balance between present inspiration and the original kerygma is consistently and firmly maintained. 2.27 – 'the anointing (that is, the Spirit)[38] abides in you, and you have no need that anyone should teach you . . . his anointing teaches you about everything'. Here the teaching role of the Spirit is seen as a fulfilment of Jer.31.34. The parallel with 2.24 implies that the Spirit's teaching means in effect a continual reinterpretation of the original message of faith.[39] 4.2f., 6 – present inspiration is known and expected; but a right understanding of Jesus is always normative. Notice however, that the right confession given out here is not the original form of the kerygma. The right

confession is only arrived at in reaction to current false teaching
(docetism – late first century); this means that 'orthodoxy' is something which develops too. Hence the balance is not a static one, but a
dynamic interaction between apostolic kerygma and Spirit inspired
response to the changing present – leading to a reinterpreted kerygma.
5.6–10 – again the same dialectic between kerygma and Spirit: v. 6 –
the Spirit testifies to the truth of Jesus' humanity ('water and blood'
= baptism and death), for *the Spirit is the truth*; vv. 7f. – the Spirit
continues to bear (united) testimony along with these essential
elements of the anti-docetic kerygma; vv. 9f. – the perfect tense of
μεμαρτύρηκεν (has borne witness) implies both a past and a present
element in this testimony, that is, the kerygma about the historical
ministry of Jesus and the indwelling Spirit (see also John 6.63).[40]

We recall that Paul's understanding of the charismatic Spirit
meant preserving a balance between prophecy and teaching, where
the function of the church was to bring present inspiration and
kerygmatic tradition together in the evaluation of inspired utterance.
In both his gospel and the first epistle John is striving to express what
seems to be a similar, but rather more self-contained conception: the
Spirit as 'anointing' once given both elaborates the original kerygma
and controls the elaboration; the nature of the Spirit as other
Paraclete, as Jesus' *alter ego*, means that *his work is by definition that of
Christ-determined revelation.*

58.3   It is when we turn to *the Spirit and worship* that the distinctiveness of the Johannine understanding of religious experience begins to
become apparent. The key verse is John 4.23f. – 'God is Spirit, and
those who worship him must worship in Spirit and truth'. As most
commentators agree, the talk here (in v. 24b) is not of man's spirit,
nor is there any suggestion that worship must be a purely interior
affair.[41] Rather the worship looked for is worship in the Spirit, the
Holy Spirit, the Spirit of truth. What does John understand by this?
The clue is perhaps given by the first half of v. 24: God is Spirit.
Again, as is generally agreed, these three words are intended not as a
definition of the being of God, but as a description of his relationship
to men.[42] In other words, Spirit is God's mode of communication
with men. Consequently he looks for men to respond in the same
manner – to worship in Spirit and truth.

'In Spirit' must imply 'by inspiration of Spirit' – that is, charismatic worship – for in the immediate context worship in Spirit is set
in pointed contrast to worship through temple and sacred place. The
worship that God seeks is a worship not frozen to a sacred building

or by loyalty to a particular tradition, but a worship which is living, the ever new response to God who is Spirit as prompted and enabled by the Spirit of God. 'In truth' most probably refers again to the definitive revelation of God in Jesus as testified to in the original kerygma; this significance also is implied by the context since John has already portrayed Jesus as the one who fulfils and supercedes the role of the temple (2.21). Here then *the balance between kerygmatic tradition and Spirit of inspiration becomes determinative for worship as well*; we may refer to I John 4.1ff. as illustration of what this meant in practice in the Johannine community. In short, *true worship for John is worship in terms of Jesus – inspired by the Spirit of Jesus and according to the truth revealed in Jesus.*

So far we might infer simply that the Pauline vision of charismatic worship has been re-affirmed. But it is precisely at this point that the distinctiveness of John's appreciation of religious experience becomes apparent; for while we can talk of charismatic *worship*,[43] there is no indication that John shared Paul's vision of charismatic *community*. A sense of community, yes (John 10.1–16; 15.1–6; 17.6–26; I John 1.7; 2.19; 3.13–17 – the 'brothers'), but not of community charismatically interdependent. There is certainly the 'horizontal' responsibility laid on each to love the brethren – and this as much as in Paul is the real mark of the Christian believer (John 13.34f.; I John 3.10–18, 23f.; 4.20f.); but for John the 'vertical' relationship with God the Spirit is essentially an *individual* affair.[44] There is mutual belonging to Christ, but not a mutual interdependence in that belonging.[45] Each sheep hears the shepherd's voice for himself; each branch is rooted directly in the vine (John 10.3f., 16; 15.4ff.).[46] The talk of munching Jesus' flesh, drinking his blood, or of drinking the water from his side, is addressed more to a sequence of individuals than to a community which is itself the body of Christ (John 6.53–8; 7.37f.). The climax of the 'Gospel of Signs' (John 1–12) is the resuscitation of a single individual, symbolizing a one-to-one salvation (John 11) rather than the general resurrection of the dead.[47] The disciples to whom the Spirit is promised in John 14–16 and given in John 20.22 are not thereby appointed to special ministries *within* the community; rather they represent *all* believers in their common responsibility of mutual love and mission[48] – this is why they are simply 'the disciples' and not 'apostles' or 'the twelve', and include presumably the women.[49] So too 'the beloved disciple': whatever the historical reality underlying his presentation, John probably intends him to symbolize the individual believer (charismatic?) in the immediacy and closeness of his relationship to Jesus (John 13.23ff.; 20.2–8).[50] Similarly in I John

2.27, the anointing of the Spirit obviates the necessity of teachers – the Spirit indwelling each believer is teacher enough. In short, throughout John there is no real concept of ministry, let alone of official ministry; everything is seen in terms of the individual's immediate relationship to God through the Spirit and the word.[51]

Thus it becomes clear why John's conception of the relationship between Spirit and word is so self-contained; it has to be – where charismatic community does not provide controls the religious experience of the individual must provide its own constraints.[52] Here then the Pauline vision of charismatic community is both re-emphasized and distorted. The gain of insisting on the immediacy and vitality of personal spiritual relationship with God under the direct inspiration of the other Paraclete is counterbalanced by the loss of corporate interdependence so fundamental to Paul. Whether the gain outweighed the loss or *vice-versa* is one of these tantalizing questions which we can never answer.

58.4 The most striking difference between John and Paul in the matter of religious experience is *the virtual disappearance of the eschatological tension* which was such a key feature of Paul's understanding of religious experience. The antithesis between Spirit and flesh, life and death is certainly present; but the Pauline qualification of it in such passages as Rom. 7.25b; 8.10 and the whole power-in-weakness theme, is only hinted at in a few places – John 11.25; 12.24; I John 1.8–2.2; 3.20; 5.16f. Instead the antitheses are expressed in much sharper form, as the straight uncompromising either–or of existential decision. There is no middle ground, no both–and, it must be either Spirit or flesh, either truth or falsehood, either light or darkness, either life or death, either of God or of the world (e.g. John 3.6, 19ff.; 5.24; 8.12; 12.35, 46; 15.18f.; I John 2.4, 8–11; 3.14; 4.5f.). The dividing line does not run through the believer or the community of believers, rather it cuts believers off cleanly and sharply from non-believers. The believer is no longer of the flesh, but of the Spirit (John 3.6); he has already passed from death to life (5.24); he is no longer of the world but of God (15.18f.; I John 4.5f.).

Consequently a kind of perfectionism inevitably emerges: 'he who abides in him does not sin . . . everyone who is born of God does not commit sin . . . indeed he *cannot* sin, because he is born of God' (I John 3.6–9; 5.18; see also 2.5, 14; 4.12–18).[53] And the apostasy of some members of the community does not lead to Pauline conclusions like I Cor. 5.5; 9.27, but to the inevitable conclusion of the Johannine either-or. Their departure simply proves that they never did belong to us in the first place (I John 2.19). This is both a gain and a loss: the moral challenge is clearly and starkly posed for the hesitant or compromising believer, but we no longer sense the believer's eschatological frustration or enter into the depths of his inner contradiction. It is of course not unimportant that in this way John has been able to maintain the freshness of religious experience even when the eschatological tension is almost wholly slackened and forgotten – this indeed is one of John's chief contributions to ongoing Christianity. But at what cost? – the loss of Pauline realism about the divided state of the believer as one caught in the overlap of the ages, and a rather unyielding and unlovely self-assurance (I John 4.6). In marshalling his various 'tests of life' (indwelling Spirit, love, obedience, right confession)[54] John unfortunately did not conceive of the possibility that some might 'pass' on one while 'failing' on another. The case of an individual who, for example, displayed a Christ-like love (I John 4.7), but who made a wrong confession, is not envisaged in the Johannine either-or. How he would have responded in such a situation is another of these tantalizing historical questions whose answer would tell us much about the continuing viability of Johannine Christianity – or otherwise.[55]

58.5   To *sum up*, John's treatment and understanding of religious experience is notable for its freshness and vigour.

(1) Experience of God is experience of the Spirit, that is of the Spirit as the other Paraclete, the Spirit characterized by the personality of Jesus. As the incarnate Logos 'exegeted' ($\dot{\epsilon}\xi\eta\gamma\eta\sigma\alpha\tau o$) the Father (John 1.18), so the Spirit exegetes Jesus.

(2) Experience of the Spirit is also experience of the Spirit of truth; it involves a continual responsibility and enabling to reinterpret the truth once given in Jesus to meet the needs and challenges of each new situation. This does not of course mean that each reinterpretation becomes of lasting normative authority; the confession of I John 4.1ff. is the normative logos only in the face of the challenge of docetism. In the face of each new demand the Spirit enables a fresh reinterpretation which derives directly from the original expression of 'the truth' and not mediately through secondary tradition or official channels.

(3) John's concept of worship is individualistic. Whereas in the Pastorals there is a wholesale subordination of Spirit and individual to tradition and institution, John thinks in terms of the individualism of direct inspiration and relationship – that is, not independent of other believers, but not dependent on them either.

(4) In John's understanding of religious experience the eschatological tension has almost entirely disappeared. But the consequence is a tendency towards perfectionism and an increasing withdrawal from 'the world'. While the love of God for the world is still affirmed (John 3.16f.), in practice the love of believers is directed towards 'one another' (John 13.34; 15.12, 17; I John 2.10, 15; 3.10f., 14, 23; 4.7, 11f., 20f.; 5.2; II John 5). What this means for the 'servant church' and for mission can readily be imagined.[56]

§59. CONCLUDING REMARKS

59.1 *Summary*. What were the religious experiences of Jesus and the first Christians, and what was their distinctive character? For Jesus religious experience was distinctively experience of God as Father and experience of eschatological power and inspiration. These were the deep wells of personal experience out of which flowed his sense of mission, his authority, his gospel and his whole life-style. At several points the distinctiveness, even uniqueness of this experience came through clearly, although its self-conscious expression in the words of Jesus had not unnaturally been elaborated in the course of passing down the tradition of Jesus' words.

After Jesus' death the earliest Christian community sprang directly from a sequence of epochal experiences of two distinct sorts – experiences in which Jesus appeared to individuals and groups to be recognized as one who had already experienced the eschatological resurrection from the dead, and experiences of religious ecstasy and enthusiasm recognized as the manifestation of the eschatological Spirit. These experiences also engendered a compulsion to bear witness to these things, recognized in many cases (apostles) as a commission by the risen Lord. Luke brings out the vitality of these early days in his own fashion – particularly the sense of immediacy of divine direction through Spirit and vision, and the sense of (overwhelming) power through word and deed, though his presentation leaves many obvious questions and problems unanswered.

With Paul we have the first mature attempt within Christianity to understand and give expression to the nature and distinctive character of the experiences of believers in Christ. He recognizes that God and his Spirit may be experienced in many diverse ways, both in non-rational ecstasy and through the mind, both in experiences of dramatically effective power and in compulsion to serve, both in inspiration to pray and praise and in inspiration to preach

and teach. By describing them all as *charismata* he both demonstrates
the range of grace (*charis*) and denotes the character of genuine
charisma. All too aware of the problems which Luke ignores, he
strives to spell out this distinctive character of Christian experience
by underlining its character of eschatological tension between the
already past and the not yet future, by stressing its integral relation
both with the wider community of believers in the present and with
the revelation of Christ in the past.

With the Pastorals the creativity of religious experience in the
present has been almost wholly swallowed up by the desire to preserve the heritage of the past. Whereas with John religious experience
is still fresh and vital; but the eschatological tension is gone and the
confrontation of life and death has been simplified into the straight
either-or of faith.

59.2   *Above all, the distinctive essence of Christian experience lies in the
relation between Jesus and the Spirit.* It is this relationship which enables
us to designate the wide range of charismatic experience mentioned
above 'Christian'; it is this relationship which provides *continuity*
between the diverse experiences of different believers and those of
Jesus himself; it is this relationship which provides the dynamism of
Christian experience. Here if anywhere we are in touch with the
'essence of Christianity'. This is the relation we saw already being
forged in the distinctiveness of Jesus' own experience of sonship and
Spirit. And it is this relation which the two most profound expositions
of religious experience in the NT (those of Paul and John) take up
and elaborate as marking out the distinctive character of Christian
experience. But where Jesus experienced Spirit and sonship in a
direct and unmediated way, for both Paul and John Christian
experience is not just experience of Spirit and sonship, but of the
Spirit *of* sonship, the Spirit of the Son, the other Paraclete. Jesus'
relationship with God which we see coming to expression here and
there in the gospels therefore becomes determinative for later
Christian experience – not in the sense that Jesus appears as the first
Christian, but rather as the one whose relation with the Spirit as
God's son continued and developed through death to resurrection
life. Through that unique event Jesus attained the life-giving power
of the Spirit and the Spirit became recognizably the life-giving power
of the crucified and risen Jesus. Henceforth the Spirit reflects the
character of this Christ, of the whole Christ; so that experience of
charisma is quintessentially experience of the grace of God as manifested in Christ, and experience of eschatological tension is charac-

teristically experience of the Christ Crucified as well as Risen, of power in weakness, of life out of death.

59.3 When we look to *the corporate dimension of religious experience* within first and second generation Christianity, we are confronted in effect with at least four different models, which may perhaps serve as paradigms of the different responses to the Christ event possible to believers then (and now).

First, there is Luke with his uncritical glorying in the vitality of the charismatic and ecstatic experiences of the first generation. His presentation excites and enthuses, but because he glosses over the problems involved and all but ignores the strains and stresses that characterized the same period, his treatment provides no lasting paradigm or norm for Christian experience individual or corporate. Those who try to set up Acts in this role will soon find themselves faced with the questions which Luke avoided.

Second, there is the Pauline vision of charismatic community, that is, of a church formed and coming to be as community, as the body of Christ, through the shared experience of the Spirit and through the diverse manifestations of Spirit in occasional and regular words and acts of service – of a church whose authority lies pre-eminently in apostle and charisma, and where both can be measured by all in terms of the criteria of gospel tradition, love and the good of the church. Whether his vision was ever realized for any period of time we cannot tell. A serious, perhaps in the event, critical weakness was that Paul probably did not think in terms of more than the first (and for him last) generation; the problem of continuity beyond the generation of the apostles did not enter into his vision in any urgent way.

Third, there is the response of the Pastorals to the post-Pauline situation, where there is little place either for Lukan vitality or for the Pauline vision. Here the living voice of prophecy, ever bringing new life to the body, has been all but stifled. Everything seems to be subordinated to the preservation of the kerygmatic tradition, and there is already a great risk that the tradition will become a strait-jacket with the Spirit imprisoned within office and institution.

Fourth, there is John. Written at a time when the early Catholicism of the Pastorals and Clement was already beginning to dictate the shape of things to come, the Johannine writings can perhaps best be seen as a reaction against this tendency.[57] John seems deliberately to turn his back on the increasing institutionalization and sacramentalism of his time, maintaining the Pauline link with the past without subordinating Spirit to tradition, and resolving the problem of the slackening of eschatological tension by individualizing worship rather than institutionalizing it. Perhaps John thus represents those who hanker after the direct relationship with Jesus which is disciples enjoyed during his ministry on earth – viz., by attempting to preserve in the post-resurrection situation the horizontally unstructured relationship which characterized discipleship of the earthly Jesus – whereas for Paul and the Pastorals the concept of 'discipleship' plays no role whatsoever.

For myself I have to confess that it is the vitality and maturity of the Pauline exposition which is most attractive. Certainly the failure of the Pauline vision to outlive him does not permit us to dismiss it as merely 'a transitory stage in the Pauline constitution' in no way representing 'an authoritative ideal of the Pauline constitution'.[58] Rom. 12; I Cor. 12–14, and even Eph. 4, do not permit the conclusion that I Cor. 12 was determined solely in response to conditions at Corinth, or that Paul himself departed from his basic vision of charismatic community in response to developments within Hellenistic Christianity. It may be, of course, that the Pauline vision is unworkable in practice, so deeply does the inner contradiction within individual believers run that it prevents the sort of mutual interaction that Paul envisages as the functioning of charismatic community. But the alternatives suffer from even graver weaknesses and are exposed to more serious dangers, so that the Pauline vision retains its attractiveness.

Perhaps the biggest challenge to twentieth-century Christianity is to take the Pauline exposition seriously, and to start not from what now is by way of tradition and institution, but instead to be open to that experience of God which first launched Christianity and to let that experience, properly safeguarded as Paul insisted, create new expressions of faith, worship and mission at both individual and corporate level. One thing we may be sure of: the life of the Christian church can go forward only when each generation is able creatively to reinterpret its gospel and its common life out of its own experience of the Spirit and word which first called Christianity into existence.[59]

59.4 We began by asserting the primacy of experience in shaping the course and character of first-generation Christianity. The validity of this assertion has been repeatedly demonstrated in the intervening pages. It is clearly evident that at every stage we have been dealing with a theology and theologizing which is certainly rational, but which is no mere thinking or talking about God, far less a rationaliz-

ing of him. The theological thinking of Jesus, of the first Christians,
of Paul and John, has been at all times something dynamic, something
rooted in their experience of God, something living and growing out
of their religious experience. In particular, we have seen how the
distinctive notes of Jesus' preaching sprang at once from his own
experience – of God who is near (Father), of God's eschatological
power already in operation (Spirit). So too it has been very noticeable how much of Paul's theology we have in fact covered in our
study of his understanding of religious experience – how much of his
theology, in other words, is experience based – not merely his
soteriology, but also his theology (in the narrower sense), his Christology, ecclesiology and ethics, and even in no small measure his
eschatology. As for John we need merely remind ourselves of the
extent to which his gospel is the product of his experience of the other
Paraclete.

Of course, the theologizing that we find in the NT was not simply
the product of religious experience, conceived as an autonomous
authority. It has all in differing measures been subjected to the check
of community evaluation and to the test of kerygmatic tradition. At
the same time, Paul and John in particular, were equally wary of
allowing these checks and tests to become legal-type rules and
formulae, of allowing community evaluation to become authoritarian
church (as later Catholicism – though some may feel that John over-
reacted), of allowing kerygmatic tradition to become ecclesiastical
dogma. Their theology was produced out of the living dialectic between the religious experience of the present and the definitive
revelation of the past (the Christ event), with neither being permitted
to dictate to the other, and neither being allowed to escape from the
searching questions posed by the other – an unceasing process of
interpretation and reinterpretation.

In short, as religious experience was fundamental to and creative of
the earliest Christian community, so religious experience was fundamental to and creative of the earliest Christian theology. Ever fresh
religious experience in dynamic interaction with the original witness
to the Christ event was the living matrix of NT theology. Without the
latter, faith all too easily becomes fanaticism and burns itself out. But
without the former, without God as a living reality in religious
experience, faith never comes to life and theology remains sterile
and dead.

NOTES

Chapter I

1. H. D. Lewis, *Our Experience of God*, Allen & Unwin 1959, p.65.
2. R. Bultmann, *Jesus and the Word*, ET Fontana ²1958, pp.113f. (my italics).
3. Cf. N. Smart, *The Religious Experience of Mankind*, 1969, Fontana 1971, pp.11ff.
4. G. H. Williams, *The Radical Reformation*, Weidenfeld & Nicolson 1962, p.822.
5. E. Benz, *Swedenborg in Deutschland*, Frankfurt 1947, pp.235ff.; also *Die Vision: Erfahrungsformen und Bilderwelten*, Stuttgart 1969, p.10.
6. W. Bousset's review of Weinel (see below n.13) in *Göttingsche gelehrte Anziegen* 163, 1901, pp.763ff.
7. R. A. Knox, *Enthusiasm: A Chapter in the History of Religion*, Oxford 1950.
8. *A Treatise concerning Religious Affections*, Boston 1746, in *The Works of Jonathan Edwards*, Vol.II, ed. J. E. Smith, Yale 1959. Edwards was involved in the New England awakening of 1734-35 and in the subsequent controversies, during which he wrote *A Faithful Narrative of the Surprising Work of God*, 1736, ³1738; *The Distinguishing Marks of a Work of the Spirit of God*, 1741; and *Some Thoughts concerning the present Revival of Religion in New England*, 1742 – all in *Works* Vol.IV, ed. C. C. Goen, Yale 1972.
9. William James, *The Varieties of Religious Experience*, 1903, Fontana 1960, p.35.
10. 'Das Problem der Entstehung des Christentums', *Archiv für Religionswissenschaft* 16, 1913, pp.426f.
11. H. Gunkel, *Die Wirkungen des heiligen Geistes*, Göttingen 1888, pp.83–91 (quotation from p.86).
12. Cf. K. Barth's famous critique of the limitations of 'historical criticism', in the course of which he asserted his 'prime assumption. Paul knows of God what most of us do not know; and his Epistles enable us to know what he knew' (*The Epistle to the Romans*, ET Oxford 1933, pp.6–11).
13. I am here following the lead given by H. Weinel, *Die Wirkungen des Geistes und der Geister im nach apostolischen Zeitalter bis auf Irenäus*, Freiburg 1899, p.65, although his use of later material is very limited; his study indeed is almost wholly restricted to Christian literature – as Bousset points out in his review (above n.6).
14. Cf. the question Gunkel sets himself (p.5).
15. Those who find fewer historical and critical problems in rediscovering the 'inner life' of Jesus and the experience of primitive Christianity should skip the detailed arguments particularly of the early chapters; they will be able to omit, e.g., almost all of §§8.4 and 9.3.

Chapter II

1. See Bultmann, *Jesus* ch. IV; H. Conzelmann, *Jesus*, ET Fortress 1973, pp. 54–9.

2. I refer to the Monothelite controversy (had Jesus one will or two?). The belief in two wills (divine and human) triumphed and was adopted by the sixth Council (Constantinople 681). See A. Harnack, *History of Dogma*, ET Williams & Norgate 1898, Vol. IV pp. 252–65; H. R. Mackintosh, *The Person of Jesus Christ*, T. &. T. Clark ²1913, pp. 219ff.

3. F. D. E. Schleiermacher, *The Christian Faith*, ET T. & T. Clark 1928, p. 385.

4. A. Schweitzer, *The Quest of the Historical Jesus*, ET A. & C. Black 1910.

5. Cf. Bultmann, *Jesus*, p. 14; G. Bornkamm, *Jesus of Nazareth*, ET Hodder & Stoughton 1960, p. 13; L. E. Keck, *A Future for the Historical Jesus*, SCM Press 1971, p. 196 n. 16; W. G. Kümmel, *The Theology of the New Testament*, ET SCM Press 1974, pp. 25f.

6. G. Ebeling, *The Nature of Faith*, ET Collins 1961, Fontana 1966, ch. 4.

7. See e.g. A. Kee, *The Way of Transcendence*, Penguin 1971.

8. Mark 8.34 pars., 10.42–5 pars., 11.23 (see below p. 75)); Matt. 10.5–8; Luke's emphasis on prayer in the life of Jesus (see below n. 23); John 13.12–17; Rom. 6.17 (τύπος = Christ?); Eph. 4.20; Phil. 2.5; Col. 2.6; I Thess. 1.6; Heb. 2.10; 12.2; I Peter 2.21ff. See also below §§54, 55. But see also W. Michaelis, *TDNT* IV pp. 669–74; E. Schweizer, *Erniedrigung und Erhöhung bei Jesus und seinen Nachfolgern*, Zürich ²1962, pp. 126–44 (§11); H. D. Betz, *Nachfolge und Nachahmung Jesu Christi im Neuen Testament*, Tübingen 1967. Cf. G. N. Stanton, *Jesus of Nazareth in New Testament Preaching*, Cambridge 1974.

9. See e.g. the importance of the theme of 'witness' in Acts and John; R. Otto, *The Idea of the Holy*, ET Oxford 1923, ch. 11; Dunn, *Baptism* p. 4 n. 12; and above pp. 3ff.

10. A. Harnack, *What is Christianity?*, ET Putnam 1901, Lecture 7.

11. Conzelmann, *Jesus*: 'Jesus' self-consciousness is not comprehensible in terms of the christological titles' (p. 49).

12. A. Deissmann, *The Religion of Jesus and the Faith of Paul*, Hodder & Stoughton 1923.

13. 'The position of Jesus in the history of religion is understood when we have understood his inner life. To understand the inner life of Jesus is the chief task of research in early Christianity' (pp. 43f.).

14. I cannot forbear from referring by way of example to Robert Burns's poem, *Holy Willie's Prayer* – a magnificent satire on the prayer of religious bigotry.

15. W. G. Kümmel, *Promise and Fulfilment*, ET SCM Press 1957, p. 118.

16. F. Hahn, *The Worship of the Early Church*, ET Fortress 1973, p. 20.

17. Conzelmann, *Jesus* p. 56.

18. See particularly J. Jeremias, *The Prayers of Jesus*, ET SCM Press 1967, ch. III; see also K. G. Kuhn, *Achtzehngebet und Vaterunser und der Reim*, Tübingen 1950; E. Lohmeyer, *The Lord's Prayer*, ET Collins 1965.

19. Bultmann, *Jesus* pp. 128–34; M. Dibelius, *Jesus*, 1939 ET 1949, SCM Press 1963, pp. 110ff.; Bornkamm, *Jesus* pp. 133–7.

20. Deissmann: 'One must not assume that Jesus gave these words about prayer to his disciples merely as cold maxims. Rather a clear reflection of his own prayer life is to be seen in them . . . the ripe fruits of his own prayer-experience' (p. 63).

21. Jeremias, *Prayers* p. 75. See also A. R. George, *Communion with God in the New Testament*, Epworth 1953, pp. 31–89.

22. Hahn, *Worship* pp. 14–31, particularly nn. 20 and 31.

23. For the importance of prayer in Lukan theology see W. Ott, *Gebet und Heil: die Bedeutung der Gebetsparänese in der lukanischen Theologie*, München 1965; P. T. O'Brien, 'Prayer in Luke–Acts', *Tyndale Bulletin* 24, 1973, pp. 111–27.

24. R. Bultmann, *The History of the Synoptic Tradition*, ET Blackwell 1963, p. 155.

25. J. Weiss, *Das älteste Evangelium*, Göttingen 1903, p. 148; D. E. Nineham, *The Gospel of Saint Mark*, Penguin 1963, p. 84.

26. B. H. Streeter, *The Four Gospels*, Macmillan 1924, pp. 176f.

27. Bultmann, *Tradition* pp. 267f.

28. M. Dibelius, 'Gethsemane', *Botschaft und Geschichte* I, Tübingen 1953, pp. 258–71.

29. E.g., M. Goguel, *The Life of Jesus*, ET Allen & Unwin 1933: 'It is impossible to discuss the historicity of a scene whose only witnesses were men who were at some distance and were asleep' (p. 494).

30. For the view that Mark has combined two traditions see especially K. G. Kuhn, 'Jesus in Gethsemane', *EvTh* 12, 1952–53, pp. 263ff. But see also E. Lohse, *History of the Suffering and Death of Jesus Christ*, ET Fortress 1967, pp. 62f.; E. Linnemann, *Studien zur Passionsgeschichte*, Göttingen 1970, pp. 17–23; W. H. Kelber, 'Mark 14.32–42: Gethsemane', *ZNW* 63, 1972, pp. 169ff.

31. Cf. Linnemann p. 30 n. 47.

32. Cf. Kelber p. 175; against Lohse pp. 62f.; W. Mohn, *ZNW* 64, 1973, pp. 198f.

33. Those who think that Luke had an independent passion narrative include F. Rehkopf, *Die Lukanische Sonderquelle*, Tübingen 1959; H. Schürmann, *Traditionsgeschichtliche Untersuchungen zu den synoptischen Evangelien*, Patmos 1968, particularly pp. 193–7; G. Schneider, *Verleugnung, Verspottung und Verhör Jesu nach Lukas 22. 54–71*, Kösel 1969; D. R. Catchpole, *The Trial of Jesus*, Leiden 1971; V. Taylor, *The Passion Narrative of St. Luke*, Cambridge 1972; though see also Linnemann pp. 34–40.

34. Cf. Heb. 5.7: Jesus prayed 'to him who was able to save him from death', which also suggests the substance of Jesus' prayer.

35. Dibelius, 'Gethsemane' p. 264; Kelber pp. 171ff., 178ff.

36. R. S. Barbour, 'Gethsemane in the Passion Tradition', *NTS* 16, 1969–70, p. 235; cf. T. Boman, 'Der Gebetskampf Jesu', *NTS* 10, 1963–64, pp. 273f.; Linnemann p. 30 n. 48.

37. E. Lohmeyer, *Das Evangelium des Markus*, KEK [16]1963 = [10]1937, p. 314; cf. J. B. Lightfoot, *Philippians*, Macmillan 1868, p. 121 (on Phil. 2.26).

38. A stronger case can be made out for the dependence of Hebrews for its language on the Psalms (Dibelius, 'Gethsemane' p. 261); but even here the strength of the language overruns its Psalm allusions – particularly the phrase μετὰ κραυγῆς ἰσχυρᾶς καὶ δακρύων (with *loud* cries and *tears*) – though see O. Michel, *Die Brief an die Hebräer*, KEK [12]1966, pp. 220f.

39. V. Taylor, *The Gospel according to St Mark*, Macmillan 1952: 'Why in contrast with the martyrs who faced death with serenity, is it said that Jesus ἤρξατο ἐκθαμβεῖσθαι καὶ ἀδημονεῖν?' (p. 551).

40. Cf. J. Klausner, *Jesus of Nazareth*, Allen & Unwin 1925, pp. 330ff.

41. Cf. F. Hauck, *Das Evangelium des Markus*, THNT 1931, p. 172; J. Schniewind, *Das Evangelium nach Markus*, NTD [10]1963, p. 190.

42. Cf. W. Wrede, *The Messianic Secret*, 1901, ET James Clarke 1971, pp. 105f., 168; T. A. Burkill, *Mysterious Revelation*, Cornell 1963, pp. 238ff.; Barbour p. 235; and especially Kelber (above n. 30).

43. C. K. Barrett, *Jesus and the Gospel Tradition*, SPCK 1967, p. 47.

44. F. Hahn, *The Titles of Jesus in Christology*, ET Lutterworth 1969, p. 307. This

consensus includes the 'more sceptical' assessment of N. Perrin, *Rediscovering the Teaching of Jesus*, SCM Press 1967, pp. 40f.

45. Cf. Jeremias, *Prayers* pp. 75f.

46. Nineham pp. 83f.; J. D. G. Dunn, 'The Messianic Secret in Mark', *Tyndale Bulletin* 21, 1970, p. 103.

47. Jeremias, *Prayers* pp. 54–7; *New Testament Theology Vol. I: The Proclamation of Jesus*, ET SCM Press 1971, p. 62.

48. In view of Mark 14.36; Rom. 8.15 and Gal. 4.6, it is a reasonable assumption that an Aramaic 'Abba' underlies the Greek πάτερ.

49. So E. Schweizer, *TDNT* VIII p. 366. It is noticeable that although Perrin frames the 'criterion of dissimilarity' strictly and operates on the principle, 'When in doubt, discard', he remains confident that *abba* was 'characteristic of Jesus' (*Teaching* p. 41). Cf. Conzelmann cited in n. 60 below.

50. T. W. Manson, *The Teaching of Jesus*, Cambridge 1931, pp. 90ff. See also G. Quell, *TDNT* V pp. 971ff.; Lohmeyer, *Lord's Prayer* pp. 39ff. O. Cullmann, *The Christology of the New Testament*, ET SCM Press 1959, pp. 272–5.

51. Jeremias, *Prayers* pp. 11f.

52. Cf. Bultmann, *Theology of the New Testament* Vol. I, ET SCM Press 1952, pp. 23f. Kümmel, *Theology*, recognizes that Jesus took a 'striking and unusual' step in identifying God as 'my Father' ('quite extraordinary' – p. 40), and yet, surprisingly, hesitates to draw the obvious corollary that in this form of address we find 'a reference to Jesus' awareness of his sonship to God' (p. 75).

53. Jeremias, *Prayers* pp. 57–62; *Theology* I pp. 63–7.

54. Jeremias, *Theology* I pp. 64f., 66.

55. Cf. Schrenk, *TDNT* V p. 979 n. 209. See also Wisd. 14.3 and 3 Macc. 6.3, 8 (Schrenk p. 981; Conzelmann, *An Outline of the Theology of the New Testament*, ET SCM Press 1969, p. 104). D. Flusser, *Jesus*, New York 1969, warns against making too much of the non-appearance of *abba* in Talmudic literature in view of the scarcity of rabbinic material on charismatic prayer (n. 159), but accepts that Jesus' use of *abba* does imply consciousness of a greater closeness to God (p. 95). G. Vermes, *Jesus the Jew*, Collins 1973, maintains that 'one of the distinguishing features of ancient Hasidic piety is its habit of alluding to God precisely as "Father"' (pp. 210f.).

56. Conzelmann, *Outline* p. 103.

57. Jeremias, *Prayers* pp. 42 n. 66, 59ff.

58. G. Kittel, *TDNT* I p. 6; Jeremias, *Prayers* p. 62.

59. Contrast Luke 23.46, where the prayer in the words of Ps. 31.5 has been prefaced with πάτερ.

60. Conzelmann, *Jesus*: 'For all this, there is no doubt that Jesus possessed the consciousness of a singular bond with God' (p. 48).

61. Mark 11.25f./Matt. 6.14f.; Matt. 5.48/Luke 6.36; Matt. 6.9/Luke 11.2; Matt. 6.32/Luke 12.30; Matt. 7.11/Luke 11.13; Matt. 23.9; Luke 12.32; more doubtful are Matt. 5.16, 45; 6.1, 4, 6, 8, 18; 13.43.

62. Manson, *Teaching* pp. 89–115; Schrenk, *TDNT* V pp. 988, 990f.; H. F. D. Sparks, 'The Doctrine of Divine Fatherhood in the Gospels', *Studies in the Gospels*, ed. D. E. Nineham, Blackwell 1955, pp. 241–66; B. M. F. Iersel, '*Der Sohn*' *in den synoptischen Jesusworten*, NovTestSuppl. III, ²1964, pp. 110–3; Jeremias, *Prayers* p. 43.

63. H. W. Montefiore, 'God as Father in the Synoptic Gospels', *NTS* 3, 1956–57, pp. 31–46; Hahn, *Titles* p. 312; Conzelmann, *Outline* p. 105.

64. Bultmann, *Jesus* p. 96; *Theology* I pp. 9f.

65. Bultmann, *Jesus* pp. 30ff.; Perrin, *Teaching* pp. 142ff.

66. Schrenk: 'The message of fatherhood is part of the message of eschatological salvation . . .' (pp. 990ff.).

67. Cf. Perrin, *Teaching* pp. 148f.

68. Bornkamm, *Jesus* pp. 128f.; see also van Iersel p. 108. So earlier G. Dalman, *The Words of Jesus*, ET T. & T. Clark 1902: 'Jesus draws a sharp line of distinction between himself and his disciples in purposely setting aside the usual Jewish "our Father in heaven", where he himself is concerned, and yet prescribing its use for his disciples (Matt. 6.9)' (p. 190).

69. Conzelmann, *Outline* pp. 103, 105.

70. See e.g. E. Meyer, *Ursprung und Anfänge des Christentums* I, Stuttgart 1921, pp. 291ff., 296ff., 299; K. H. Rengstorf, *TDNT* II pp. 325f.; Taylor, *Mark* pp. 619–23; B. Rigaux, 'Die "Zwölf" in Geschichte und Kerygma', *Der historische Jesus und der Kerygmatische Christus*, hrsg. H. Ristow, V. K. Matthiae, Berlin 1961, pp. 468–86; L. Goppelt, *Apostolic and Post-Apostolic Times*, 1962, ET A. & C. Black 1970, pp. 28f.; J. Roloff, *Apostolat – Verkündigung – Kirche*, Gütersloh 1965, ch. III: F. Hahn (with A. Strobel and E. Schweizer), *The Beginnings of the Church in the New Testament*, ET St Andrew 1970, p. 31; R. P. Meye, *Jesus and the Twelve*, Eerdmans 1968, ch. 8; C. K. Barrett, *The Signs of an Apostle*, Epworth 1970, pp. 23–33; P. Stuhlmacher, 'Evangelium – Apostolat – Gemeinde', *KuD* 17, 1971, p. 31.

71. By 'distinctive' I mean both characteristic of Jesus and sufficiently unusual among his contemporaries, to mark him out, but not necessarily set him in a class apart.

72. An alternative view is that the words of Mark 1.11 originally referred only to Isa. 42.1 (υἱός being Mark's interpretation of παῖς = servant or child); so W. Bousset, *Kyrios Christos*, ²1921, ET Abingdon 1970, p. 97 n. 70; J. Jeremias, *The Servant of God*, ET SCM Press ²1965, pp. 82f.; Cullmann, *Christology* p. 66; Hahn, *Titles* p. 338; R. H. Fuller, *The Foundations of New Testament Christology*, Lutterworth 1965, pp. 169f. But see also H. Weinel, *Biblische Theologie des Neuen Testaments*, Tübingen ⁴1928: 'Mark 1.11 is in no way to be explained out of Isa. 42.1; 44.1' (p. 170); Schweizer, *TDNT* VIII p. 368; I. H. Marshall, 'Son of God or Servant of Yahweh? – A Reconsideration of Mark 1.11', *NTS* 15, 1968–69, pp. 326–36. See further below III n. 122.

73. I am inclined to the view that the Western reading of Luke 3.22 is original – so a wide range of scholarship including, Moffatt translation, F. Büchsel, *Der Geist Gottes im Neuen Testament*, Gütersloh 1926, p. 162; H. von Baer, *Der heilige Geist in den Lukasschriften*, Stuttgart 1926, p. 168; Streeter, *Gospels* pp. 143, 188; E. Klostermann, *Lukasevangelium*, HNT ²1929, p. 55; J. M. Creed, *The Gospel according to St Luke*, Macmillan 1930, p. 58; W. Manson, *The Gospel of Luke*, Moffatt 1930, p. 31; O. Procksch, *TDNT* I p. 101 n. 49; A. R. C. Leaney, *The Gospel according to St Luke*, A. & C. Black 1958, pp. 110f.; W. Grundmann, *Das Evangelium nach Lukas*, THNT 1961, p. 107; A. Feuillet, 'Le Baptême de Jésus', *RB* 71, 1964, pp. 333ff.; H. Flender, *Saint Luke: Theologian of Redemptive History*, ET SPCK 1967, p. 136 n. 6.

74. For the age of the narrative note that it takes the form of a Christian midrash; see particularly B. Gerhardsson, *The Testing of God's Son*, Lund 1966. See also Bultmann, *Tradition* pp. 254–7.

75. See particularly R. Laurentin, *Jésus au Temple*, EB 1966.

76. See also Matt. 12.18; and on Mark 12.6 (υἱὸν ἀγαπητόν) see below p. 35.

77. We ignore passages where Jesus is addressed or referred to as 'son' by others since these are usually editorial, and even if original could tell us nothing about Jesus' *own* understanding of his relationship to God – Mark 3.11; 5.7 pars.; Luke

4.41; Mark 14.61 pars.; 15.39 par.; Matt. 14.33; 16.16; 27.40, 43. Similarly Matt. 22.2; 28.19 afford us no assistance at this point.

78. A Harnack, *The Sayings of Jesus*, ET Williams & Norgate 1908, pp. 273–95, and more recently P. Winter, 'Matt. 11.27 and Luke 10.22 from the first to the fifth century', *NovTest* 1, 1956, pp. 112–48, have attempted reconstructions of the text mainly on the basis of patristic evidence. But see particularly J. Chapman, 'Dr Harnack on Luke 10.22: No Man Knoweth the Son', *JTS* 10, 1909, pp. 552–66, and M. J. Suggs, *Wisdom, Christology and Law in Matthew's Gospel*, Harvard 1970, pp. 71–7. Luke's version appears to be a hellenizing adaptation of the more primitive version which Matthew has preserved; cf. J. Bieneck, *Sohn Gottes als Christusbezeichnung der Synoptiker*, Zürich 1951, p. 84; R. H. Fuller, *The Mission and Achievement of Jesus*, SCM Press 1954, p. 92; Conzelmann, *The Theology of St Luke*, ET Faber 1960, p. 105 n. 3. Cf. Luke's treatment of Mark 4.11.

79. For bibliography see Schrenk, *TDNT* V p. 992 n. 288; P. Hoffmann, *Studien zur Theologie der Logienquelle*, Münster 1972, pp. 106–9; and H. D. Betz, 'The Logion of the Easy Yoke and of Rest (Matt. 11.28–30)', *JBL* 86, 1967, where the history of research is conveniently summarized (pp. 11–20).

80. Cf. Schrenk, *TDNT* V p. 993. See also those cited by S. Schulz, *Q: Die Spruchquelle der Evangelisten*, Zürich 1972, p. 220 n. 300.

81. Bultmann, *Tradition* p. 160. See also E. Norden, *Agnostos Theos*, Stuttgart 1913, ⁴1956, pp. 277–308; Bousset, *Kyrios Christos* pp. 85–9; M. Dibelius, *From Tradition to Gospel*, ET Nicholson & Watson 1934, pp. 279–83.

82. Kümmel, *Promise* p. 41.

83. E. Haenchen, *RGG*³ II 1654. For other proponents of this view see Hoffmann, p. 107 n. 25, Schulz, *Q* p. 221 n. 301.

84. Hahn, *Titles* p. 312.

85. Hahn, *Titles* p. 312.

86. Cf. Hoffmann pp. 124f., and those cited by him in n. 102. C. H. Dodd, *Historical Tradition in the Fourth Gospel*, Cambridge 1963, argues that the variant versions in Matthew, Luke and John 10.15 testify to the existence of some such saying which had already developed different forms in the period prior to the earliest written documents (pp. 359ff.).

87. Dalman, *Words* p. 283.

88. Jeremias, *Prayers* p. 47; *Theology* I pp. 57f. See also C. F. Burney, *The Poetry of our Lord*, Oxford 1925, pp. 171f.; T. W. Manson, *The Sayings of Jesus*, SCM Press 1949, p. 79; W. L. Knox, *Some Hellenistic Elements in Primitive Christianity*, Schweich Lectures 1942, London 1944, pp. 6f. M. Black, *An Aramaic Approach to the Gospels and Acts*, Oxford ³1967, does not comment on the verse.

89. See J. Schniewind, *Das Evangelium nach Matthäus*, NTD ¹¹1964, pp. 151f.

90. W. D. Davies, ' "Knowledge" in the Dead Sea Scrolls and Matt. 11.25–30', HTR 46, 1953, reprinted in *Christian Origins and Judaism*, Darton, Longman & Todd 1962, pp. 119–44; also *The Setting of the Sermon on the Mount*, Cambridge 1964, pp. 207f. See especially the Dead Sea Scrolls references also listed by Schweizer, *TDNT* VIII p. 373 n. 281: IQS 4.22; 9.17f., 11.3, 15–8; IQSb 4.25–8; IQH 2.13; 10.27f. Cf. also A. M. Hunter, 'Crux Criticorum – Matt. 11.25–30', *NTS* 8, 1961–62, p. 245. For a more negative assessment see H. Braun, *Qumran und das Neue Testament*, Tübingen 1966, I pp. 23ff.

91. Contrast Akhnaton's Hymn to the Sun, cited by Bultmann, *Tradition* p. 160 n. 1: 'No other knows thee save thy Son Akhnaton.
Thou hast initiated him into thy plans and thy power'.

92. F. Christ, *Jesus Sophia*, Zürich 1970, pp.81–93; Suggs pp.91ff. See also A. Feuillet, 'Jésus et la Sagesse Divine d'apres les Évangiles Synoptiques', *RB* 62, 1955, pp. 161–96. Flusser draws attention particularly to IQH 4.27–9 (p.95).

93. Hoffmann pp. 124f. Dissatisfaction with the text on this score may go some way to explaining the textual confusion we find among the second and third century authorities, a confusion which led Harnack to the conclusion that Luke (and so Q) originally lacked 'and no one (knows) who the Son is except the Father'. But see above n. 78.

94. Christ p.89 (not Job 18, as Christ and Hoffmann p. 137 n. 144).

95. Christ also draws attention to the parallels in Prov.8.1–36 and Ecclus. (Ben Sira) 24.1–22.

96. Bultmann, *Tradition* p. 159; Christ pp. 100–19 and those cited by him in p. 103 n.394; see also G. von Rad, *Wisdom in Israel*, ET SCM Press 1972, pp. 166–76.

97. Black pp. 183f.

98. See further Betz, 'Logion' pp. 19f.; also van Iersel pp. 148f. The unity of Matt. 11.25–30 in Q is however maintained by many scholars: van Iersel mentions M. Rist, W. D. Davies, and A. Feuillet (p. 147); see also e.g. Dibelius, *Tradition* p. 280; U. Wilckens, *TDNT* VII pp. 516f.

99. Suggs pp. 83ff.; Christ pp. 81–5.

100. Bultmann, *Tradition* p. 160; Manson, *Sayings* p. 79.

101. Cf. Hunter p.244; Wilckens p. 517. Bousset accepted vv.25f. as genuine words of Jesus, but thought the connection with v. 27 'wholly superficial' (p.85). So several commentators since then (see e.g. Klostermann, *Matthäusevangelium*, HNT ⁴1971, p. 102; Christ p.81 n.292). In particular, Hoffmann regards v. 27a as an interpretation of vv.25f. added by the early post-Easter community (p. 109; cf. Schulz, *Q* p.215; E. Schweizer, *Das Evangelium nach Matthäus*, NTD 1973, p. 174); but v.27 is by no means simply a development of vv. 25f., as the thought of the Son as Mediator of the revelation and particularly the idea of the unknowability of the Son makes clear (see further below).

102. πατήρ, ἀποκρύψαι, ἀποκαλύψαι, εὐδοκία corresponding to ᾧ ἐὰν βούληται.

103. Cf. Jeremias, *Prayers* p. 46; *Theology* I p. 57.

104. Jeremias, *Prayers* p.46; *Theology* I p.57. It is possible to recognize the influence of Jewish apocalyptic thought in v.27a (see particularly Schweizer, *TDNT* VIII pp.372f.; Schulz, *Q* pp.222f.), but unnecessary (see below p.31); unless one wishes to argue that the text is a combination of diverse fragments, it is more plausible to set the text against that background which influences it most.

105. See further M. Hengel, *Judaism and Hellenism*, ET SCM Press 1974, ch.III, especially vol.I pp. 202ff., 228f., 252; vol.II p. 111 n.415.

106. Cf. J. M. Robinson, 'Die Hodajot-Formel in Gebet und Hymnus des Frühchristentums', *Apophoreta: Festschrift für Ernst Haenchen*, Berlin 1964, pp. 226ff.; also 'Logoi Sophon: on the Gattung of Q', *The Future of our Religious Past: Essays in Honour of Rudolf Bultmann*, ed. J. M. Robinson, SCM Press 1971, pp. 129f.; H. Koester, 'The Structure and Criteria of Early Christian Beliefs', *Trajectories through Early Christianity*, Fortress 1971, p. 221.

107. Cf. F. Mussner, 'Wege zum Selbstbewusstsein Jesu. Ein Versuch', *BZ* 12, 1968, pp. 167ff.; Hoffmann pp. 110f.; and above n. 101. Bultmann: 'I see no compelling reason for denying it (vv.25f.) to him (Jesus)' (*Tradition* p.160). W. Grimm, 'Der Dank für die empfangene Offenbarung bei Jesus und Josephus', *BZ* 17, 1973, pp. 249–56, draws particular attention to the following parallels with Matt. 11.25–7: Enoch 39.9–11; 69.26; IQH 7.26f.; Josephus, *Bell*. III.354; Dan.

2.19–23 (the *Vorbild* of *Bell.* III.354). Catchpole, *Trial*, draws attention to the legal terminology of vv. 25f. and v. 27 as underlining the unity of vv. 25–7 and strengthening the case for the logion's authenticity as a word of Jesus (pp. 145ff.).

108. See Bultmann's collection of wisdom sayings attributed to Jesus (*Tradition* pp. 69–108). It is hard to conceive of such an extensive collection of logia being attributed to Jesus unless he already had a reputation as a teacher of wisdom.

109. E. Trocmé, *Jesus and his Contemporaries*, ET SCM Press 1973, speaks of the 'remarkable gift of expression which makes Jesus the equal of the most brilliant wisdom writers' (p. 40).

110. Those who take the passage as an authentic word of Jesus include Schlatter, Schniewind, both Mansons, Bieneck, Cullmann, Jeremias, van Iersel, I. H. Marshall, 'The Divine Sonship of Jesus', *Interpretation* 21, 1967, pp. 91–4, C. H. Dodd, *The Founder of Christianity*, Collins 1971, pp. 51f., and others cited by Hoffmann p. 109 n. 29.

111. J. Wellhausen, *Das Evangelium Matthaei*, Berlin ²1914, pp. 55f.; Klostermann, *Matt.* p. 103.

112. Jeremias, *Prayers* p. 49; *Theology* I p. 59; cf. Fuller, *Mission* p. 91; Christ p. 86. Hoffmann follows Hahn in defining the πάντα in terms of authority, since otherwise the whole statement is tautologous (p. 120). But this is simply not so: the mediating role of the Son in revelation is the main point of v. 27 and expresses a wholly new thought unheralded in vv. 25f. (see also n. 101 above).

113. Suggs p. 96; see also Hoffmann pp. 137f.; G. N. Stanton, 'On the Christology of Q', *CSNT* pp. 37f.; Schweizer, *Matthäus* p. 177. Against Christ pp. 87–93, 99, and those cited by him in p. 90 n. 336; also Schulz, *Q* pp. 224f.

114. Suggs p. 96. For Matthew's use of the Q saying see also G. Strecker, *Der Weg der Gerechtigkeit*, Göttingen 1962, pp. 172ff. See also below p. 325.

115. W. Grundmann, *Das Evangelium nach Matthäus*, THNT 1968: 'If Jesus in his prayers addresses God as Father, he speaks as son' (p. 237); also 'Sohn Gottes', *ZNW* 47, 1956, p. 128.

116. Fuller, *Foundations* p. 133 n. 20; Hahn accepts that 'the Son' derives from Jesus' use of *abba*, but in the early church (p. 313).

117. Dalman, *Words* pp. 193f.

118. Jeremias, *Prayers* pp. 47f., 50f.; *Theology* I pp. 58–60; cf. C. H. Dodd, 'A Hidden Parable in the Fourth Gospel', *More New Testament Studies*, Manchester 1968, pp. 30–40; Schweizer, *Matthäus*, p. 176.

119. Hoffmann pp. 139–42; cf. H. E. Tödt, *The Son of Man in the Synoptic Tradition*, ET SCM Press 1965, pp. 258f.

120. Jeremias, *Prayers* pp. 29–35. Cf. V. Taylor, *The Person of Christ in New Testament Teaching*, Macmillan 1958, p. 197.

121. Cf. particularly Mark 9.9; I Cor. 2.6–16; Gal. 1.12, 15f.; I Thess. 1.10.

122. Cf. Harnack's famous dictum: 'The Gospel, as Jesus proclaimed it, has to do with the Father only and not with the Son' (*What is Christianity* Lecture 8). Van Iersel's suggestion (pp. 152–7) that v. 27 comes from a context where Jesus' authority has been questioned (Matt. 13.54–6; cf. Mark 6.2f.) fails however to take into account v. 27's dependence on vv. 25f.

123. W. Eichrodt, *Theology of the Old Testament* Vol. II, ET, SCM Press 1967, p. 292; cf. Bultmann, *TDNT* I p. 698.

124. Barrett, *Jesus* pp. 25f.; cf. Schweizer, *TDNT* VIII p. 372; Kümmel, *Theology* p. 75.

125. Those who hold the saying to be an authentic word of Jesus include

Schniewind, *Markus* p.175; Lohmeyer, *Markus* p.283; Taylor, *Mark* p.522; Kümmel, *Promise* p.42; W. Grundmann, *Das Evangelium nach Markus*, THNT 1959, p.271; Marshall, 'Divine Sonship' pp.94f.; van Iersel pp.117–23, who reads the sequence, 'angels, son, Father' as an order of precedence implying a consciousness of supernatural existence (p.123).

126. See especially W. G. Kümmel, 'Das Gleichnis von den bösen Weingärtnern', *Aux sources de la tradition chrétienne, Mélanges M. Goguel*, 1950, reprinted in *Heilsgeschehen und Geschichte*, Marburg 1965, pp.207–17; also *Promise* pp.82f.

127. See further R. E. Brown, 'Parable and Allegory Reconsidered', *NovTest* V, 1962, reprinted in *New Testament Essays*, Chapman 1965, pp.254–64; C. F. D. Moule, *The Birth of the New Testament*, A. & C. Black 1962, pp.149f.; 'Mark 4.1–20 Yet Once More', *Neotestamentica et Semitica: Studies in Honour of Principal Matthew Black*, ed. E. E. Ellis & M. Wilcox, T. & T. Clark 1969, pp.95–113; J. Drury, 'The Sower, the Vineyard, and the Place of Allegory in the Interpretation of Mark's Parables', *JTS NS* 24, 1973, pp.367–79. See also n.132 below.

128. 'A Jew could not tell a story about a vineyard without embarking upon allegory (cf. Isa.5.7)' (Barrett, *Jesus* p.27).

129. Against Kümmel, 'Gleichnis' pp.213f.

130. C. H. Dodd, *The Parables of the Kingdom*, Religious Book Club 1935, pp.124–32; Jeremias, *The Parables of Jesus*, ET SCM Press, revised 1963, pp.70–7; Grundmann, *Markus* p.240; van Iersel pp.138, 141ff.; Barrett, *Jesus* pp.27f.

131. See below pp.82ff.

132. The improbable elements of the parable constitute no objection to this view (Taylor, *Mark* p.472; E. Linnemann, *Parables of Jesus*, ET SPCK 1966, pp.28f.). On the possibility that Jesus adapted a Jewish parable of a proprietor and his wicked tenants (Sifre on Deut.32.9), see Flusser pp.97f.; J. D. M. Derrett, 'Allegory and the Wicked Vinedressers', *JTS NS* 25, 1974, pp.426–32. Cf. also Schweizer, *TDNT* VIII pp.378f.; J. Blank, 'Die Sendung des Sohnes: Zur christologischen Bedeutung des Gleichnisses von den bösen Winzern Mark 12.1–12', *Neues Testament und Kirche. Für Rudolf Schnackenburg*, hrsg. J. Gnilka, Herder 1974, pp.11–41.

133. Cf. M. Hengel, 'Das Gleichnis von den Weingärtnern Mc. 12.1–12 im Lichte der Zenonpapyri und der rabbinischen Gleichnisse', *ZNW* 59, 1968, p.38.

134. E. Bammel, 'Das Ende von Q', *Verborum Veritas: Festschrift für G. Stählin*, ed. O. Böcher & K. Haacker, Wuppertal 1970, pp.39–50; Bammel cites the parallels of Test. Benj. 10.4f.; Test. Job.45.4; Test. Isaac 8.18, also John 20.22f., with 20.24ff. being regarded as the first supplement (pp.46f.); against Behm, *TDNT* II p.105.

135. Cf. Matt.4.20, 22; 8.22, 23; cf. Bornkamm in G. Bornkamm, G. Barth & H. J. Held, *Tradition and Interpretation in Matthew*, ET SCM Press 1963, pp. 54f.

136. See further Schürmann, *Jesu Abschiedsrede Lk.22.21–38*, Münster 1957, pp. 40–4; cf. Fuller, *Foundations* pp.123f. Otherwise Schulz, *Q* pp.330ff.

137. See Grundmann, *Lukas* pp.402ff. and those cited by him.

138. J. Jeremias, *The Eucharistic Words of Jesus*, ³1960, ET SCM Press 1966, pp. 207–17; Kümmel, *Promise* pp.30ff.

139. Jeremias, *Prayers* pp.30ff.

140. On Matt.16.17 see Marshall, 'Divine Sonship' pp.95ff.

141. Hahn, *Titles* p.29.

142. Cf. R. E. Brown, 'How much did Jesus Know?', *CBQ* 29, 1967: 'The way in which Jesus speaks of God as Father certainly indicates that he claimed a special relationship to God. But it remains difficult to find in the Synoptic account of the

public ministry an incontrovertible proof that he claimed a unique sonship that other men could not share' (pp. 337f.).

143. E.g. Bultmann, *Jesus* pp. 136ff.; Bornkamm, *Jesus* pp. 124ff.; and the discussion alluded to above (nn. 62, 63).

144. Cf. Manson, *Teaching* pp. 105ff.; Taylor, *Person*: 'The consciousness of Sonship was reached in experience rather than by argument and inference' (p. 174).

145. Against Taylor, *Person* pp. 172ff.

146. Against Taylor, *Person* pp. 156ff. One of course may argue that Matt. 11.27 'implies a Sonship which ultimately is one of nature and being' (p. 168); but this argument must be based on other considerations and evidence.

147. Cf. Fuller, *Mission* p. 85.

148. Cf. Dalman, *Words* p. 287; against Cullmann, *Christology* p. 288, citing A. Schweitzer; Christ p. 91; see also van Iersel p. 161.

149. Manson, *Teaching* p. 91; van Iersel p. 105.

150. Dalman, *Words* p. 272; A. A. Anderson, *The Psalms*, Oliphants 1972, p. 68; see further H. Ringgren, *Israelite Religion*, ET SPCK 1966, pp. 232f.

151. One possible exception is Ps. 45.6. But see A. R. Johnson, *Sacral Kingship in Ancient Israel*, Cardiff 1955, p. 27; J. A. Emerton, 'The Syntactical problem of Psalm 45.7, *JSS* 13, 1968, pp. 58–63. I owe these references to my colleague G. I. Davies.

152. The link between 'Son of God' and 'Son–Father' is probably more direct than Hahn allows (*Titles* p. 313) and may well be provided by the words of Mark 1.11: 'You are my son' draws in the thought of royal messianism but in fact is closer to the *abba* attitude than to the title 'Son of God'; cf. Bousset, *Kyrios Christos* p. 95; and see further below (§ 10).

153. Notably Matt. 14.33 (cf. Mark 6.51f.), Matt. 16.16 (cf. Mark 8.29), and Mark 15.39/Matt. 27.54 (cf. Luke 23.47).

154. Fuller, *Mission* p. 84.

155. Jeremias, *Prayers* p. 51; *Theology* I p. 61.

156. 'Son of God' was probably just coming into use as a messianic title in pre-Christian Judaism, or at least in the Qumran sect (Fuller, *Foundations* p. 32, referring to 4QFlor. 10–14); see also IQSa.II.11f., though the text there is uncertain (J. T. Milik, *Discoveries in the Judean Desert* Vol. I, Oxford 1955, pp. 117f.); see further E. Lohse, *TDNT* VIII pp. 361f.; and see now 4Q ps Dan A^a, the first time 'Son of God' has been found in explicit use as a title (J. A. Fitzmeyer, 'The Contribution of Qumran Aramaic to the Study of the New Testament', *NTS* 20, 1973–74, pp. 391–4). But that is beside the point here. See also Cullmann, *Christology* pp. 279ff.

157. Hahn, *Titles* pp. 148–61, 223ff.; Dunn, 'Messianic Secret' pp. 110–15.

158. For references to God as Father of Israel and Israelites, see Dalman, *Words* pp. 184ff.; Jeremias, *Prayers* pp. 11–5; e.g. Ex. 4.22f.; Deut. 32.5f.; Isa. 1.2, 4; Jer. 31.20; Hos. 11.1. Cf. the idea of the representative suffering of the righteous man and the martyr in Judaism (Schweizer, *Erniedrigung* especially pp. 24ff.; E. Lohse, *Märtyrer und Gottesknecht*, Göttingen ²1963, pp. 66–87). And note again the significance of Jesus not including himself as one of 'the twelve': Jesus' representative role is not as part of a group.

159. See I. H. Marshall, 'The Synoptic Son of Man Sayings in Recent Discussion', *NTS* 12, 1965–66, pp. 327–51; M. D. Hooker, *The Son of Man in Mark*, SPCK 1967; C. Colpe, *TDNT* VIII pp. 430–41; Jeremias, *Servant* pp. 99–106; Cullmann, *Christology* pp. 60–9; Jeremias, *Theology* I pp. 286–99. For the wider

debate see also Bultmann, *Tradition* pp. 14ff.; Taylor, *Mark* pp. 197–200; Schweizer, 'Der Menschensohn', *ZNW* 50, 1959, reprinted in *Neotestamentica*, Zürich 1963, pp. 70f.; Tödt pp. 126–30; Hahn, *Titles* ch. 1; Kümmel, *Theology* pp. 76–85, 87–90.

160. Cf. Harnack, *Sayings* p. 245 n. 2; A. E. J. Rawlinson, *The New Testament Doctrine of the Christ*, Longmans 1926, p. 251; W. Manson, *Jesus the Messiah*, Hodder & Stoughton 1943, pp. 106–9; Fuller, *Mission* p. 85; Taylor, *Person* p. 169; Marshall, 'Divine Sonship' pp. 93, 99.

161. Colpe pp. 430–3; L. S. Hay, 'The Son of Man in Mark 2.10 and 2.28', *JBL* 89, 1970, pp. 69–75; Vermes, *Jesus* ch. 7. See further below ch. IV nn. 52, 53.

Chapter III

1. J. Weiss, *Jesus' Proclamation of the Kingdom of God*, 1892, ET SCM Press 1971; A. Schweitzer, *The Mystery of the Kingdom of God*, 1901, ET Macmillan 1914; also *Quest*.

2. Harnack, *What is Christianity*, Lectures 1 and 3.

3. Since the turn of the century 'eschatological' has shifted its meaning in theological usage until in most cases it refers almost exclusively to the present, albeit in its 'future' dimension. 'Eschatological' therefore has to be supplemented by 'apocalyptic', which retains the future sense which originally characterized 'eschatological' when introduced into the debate by Weiss and particularly Schweitzer. For the beliefs to which these words allude, see below n. 30.

4. *Jesus* p. 67; see further Dunn, *Baptism* pp. 25f.

5. See e.g. N. Perrin, *The Kingdom of God in the Teaching of Jesus*, SCM Press 1963; R. Schnackenburg, *God's Rule and Kingdom*, ET Herder 1963, ch. 2; G. E. Ladd, *Jesus and the Kingdom*, SPCK 1964; Jeremias, *Theology* I ch. 3 and 4. R. H. Hiers, *The Kingdom of God in the Synoptic Tradition*, Florida 1970, appears as a rather forlorn and tendentious attempt to deny the present element in Jesus' eschatology in favour of the exclusively apocalyptic view of Weiss and Schweitzer.

6. E. Käsemann, 'The Beginnings of Christian Theology', *NTQT* p. 101.

7. K. Koch, *The Rediscovery of Apocalyptic*, ET SCM Press 1972 p. 78. For the 'criterion of dissimilarity' see particularly Perrin, *Teaching* pp. 39–43.

8. E. Käsemann, 'The Problem of the Historical Jesus', *ENTT* p. 40.

9. *Tradition* pp. 134ff.; see also p. 91; and G. Barth in Bornkamm–Barth–Held p. 93.

10. Suggs pp. 109ff., and in more recent discussion.

11. Davies, *Sermon* pp. 387f.

12. Jeremias, *Theology* I pp. 250–5.

13. Jeremias, *Prayers* pp. 112–5; *Theology* I pp. 35f.; Käsemann, *ENTT* pp. 41f.; Schürmann, *Untersuchungen* pp. 96ff.; Perrin, *Teaching* p. 38; though see also below n. 46.

14. E. Fuchs, *Studies of the Historical Jesus*, ET SCM Press 1964, pp. 20ff.; Perrin, *Teaching* p. 46; Käsemann, *Jesus Means Freedom*, ET SCM Press 1969, p. 31; Jeremias, *Theology* I §12; Stanton, *Jesus* pp. 138–46.

15. D. F. Strauss, *The Life of Jesus*, ET 1846, reprinted 1892, SCM Press 1973, §§92 and 93.

16. See e.g. Bultmann, *Jesus* p. 124; Dibelius, *Jesus* pp. 71ff.; J. M. Robinson, *A*

New Quest of the Historical Jesus, SCM Press 1959, p. 121; Hahn, *Titles* p.292; Perrin, *Teaching* p.65; Jeremias, *Theology* I pp.86–92.

17. Cf. Bultmann, *Tradition* pp.13f.; C. K. Barrett, *The Holy Spirit and lhe Gospel Tradition*, SPCK 1947, pp.59–63; Hahn, *Titles* p.322 n.80.

18. See Käsemann, *ENTT* p. 39; Perrin, *Teaching* p.64; and the others cited above in n.16.

19. Cf. e.g. B. W. Bacon, *Studies in Matthew*, Constable 1930, pp.8off.; J. Jeremias, *TDNT* IV pp.87of.; K. Stendahl, *The School of St Matthew*, Lund 1954, pp.24ff.; H. M. Teeple, *The Mosaic Eschatological Prophet*, *JBL* Monograph Series Vol.X, 1957, pp.74–83; F. V. Filson, *The Gospel according to St Matthew*, A. & C. Black 1960, pp.28f.; G. Barth in Bornkamm–Barth–Held pp.157ff.; Davies, *Sermon* ch.II.

20. See particularly E. Lövestam, *Spiritus Blasphemia: Eine Studie zu Mk 32.8f. par. Mt.12.31f., Lk 12.10*, Lund 1968, pp.9ff.

21. A. Fridrichsen, *The Problem of Miracle in Primitive Christianity*, 1925, ET Augsburg 1972, pp.147–52; Käsemann, *NTQT* pp.83f.; G. Barth in Bornkamm–Barth–Held pp.159–64. This passage should however not be taken to imply that Matthew was anti-charismatic; see E. Schweizer, 'Observance of the Law and Charismatic Activity in Matthew', *NTS* 16, 1969–70, pp.213–30.

22. Cf. 7.22 – τῷ σῷ ὀνόματι δαιμόνια ἐξεβάλομεν;
12.28 – ἐν πνεύματι θεοῦ ἐγὼ ἐκβάλλω τὰ δαιμόνια.

23. Luke 1.67ff., 2.30 (cf. Isa.52.10), 2.38 (cf. Isa.52.9), 12.32 ('little flock' – cf. Ps. 77.20; 78.52); and particularly Luke 9.31 ἔξοδον; also the thesis of C. F. Evans, 'The Central Section of Luke's Gospel', *Studies in the Gospels*, ed. D. E. Nineham, Blackwell 1955, pp.37–53, that Luke 9.51–18.14 is modelled on Deuteronomy. See further J. Mánek, 'The New Exodus in the Books of Luke', *NovTest* II, 1958, pp. 8ff.; R. E. Nixon, *The Exodus in the New Testament*, Tyndale 1963, pp.12–19; A. Denaux in *L'Évangile de Luc*, par F. Neirynck, Gembloux 1973, pp.278ff.

24. Dunn, *Baptism* pp.4off.; also, 'Spirit and Kingdom', *ExpT* 82, 1970–71, pp. 38f. This is an elaboration of the original suggestion of von Baer, developed by Conzelmann, *Luke* pp.103 n.1, 150, 179.

25. This could also account for Luke's dropping of the ἐγώ in 11.20; the point is textually uncertain, but the most likely original lacks the ἐγώ.

26. Cf. C. S. Rodd, 'Spirit or Finger', *ExpT* 72, 1960–61, pp. 157f.; J. E. Yates, 'Luke's Pneumatology and Luke 11.20', *Studia Evangelica* II Part I, 1964, pp.295–9; R. G. Hamerton-Kelly, 'A Note on Matthew 12.28 par. Luke 11.20', *NTS* 11, 1964–65, pp.167ff.

27. Lövestam pp.36f. H. Windisch, 'Jesus und der Geist nach synoptischer Über-lieferung', *Studies in Early Christianity*, ed. S. J. Case, New York 1928, p.229, points out that Moses was regarded as Pneumatiker anyway (cf. Ass.Mos. 11.16; Philo, *Vit.Mos.* II 37ff.). A more pertinent Philo reference would be *Mut.Nom.* 120.

28. Barrett, *Holy Spirit* p.63; Hamerton-Kelly pp.168f.; G. R. Beasley-Murray, 'Jesus and the Spirit', *Mélanges Bibliques en hommage au R. P. Béda Rigaux*, ed. A. Descamps & A. de Halleux, Gembloux 1970, pp.469f.

29. For the ancient belief in demons and exorcistic practices see W. Foerster, *TDNT* II pp.1–19; E. Langton, *Essentials of Demonology: A Study of Jewish and Christian Doctrine. Its Origin and Development*, Epworth 1949; H. van der Loos, *The Miracles of Jesus*, NovTestSuppl VIIII, 1965, pp.339–61; O. Böcher, *Dämonenfurcht und Dämonenabwehr*, Köhlhammer 1970.

30. See particularly W. Bousset & H. Gressmann, *Die Religion des Judentums im späthellenistischen Zeitalter*, Tübingen ⁴1966, chs. XII and XIII; G. von Rad, K. G.

Kuhn & K. L. Schmidt, *TDNT* I pp. 565–89. See also Ladd and Schnackenburg cited above (n.5).

31. See particularly F. Baumgärtel, W. Bieder, E. Sjoberg, *TDNT* VI, pp. 365ff., 370, 381ff. The recognition that 'Spirit' = power, has been familiar since Gunkel, particularly p.47; see also e.g. H. Bertrams, *Das Wesen des Geistes nach der Anschauung des Apostels Paulus*, Münster 1913, ch.II particularly pp.28ff.; H. W. Robinson, *The Christian Experience of the Holy Spirit*, Nisbet 1928, p.128; W. Grundmann, *Der Begriff der Kraft in der neutestamentlicher Gedankenwelt*, Stuttgart 1932, p.47; Baumgärtel, *TDNT* VI pp. 362f.; Käsemann, *RGG*[3] II 1272f.

32. On the meaning of ἔφθασεν see particularly Kümmel, *Promise* pp. 106ff.

33. Jesus 'is the only Jew of ancient times known to us, who preached not only that men were on the threshold of the end of time, but that the new age of salvation had already begun' (Flusser p.90); cf. H. Baltensweiler, 'Wunder und Glaube im Neuen Testament', *TZ* 23, 1967, pp. 243–8.

34. See Bultmann, *Theology* I pp.4f., 22; Kümmel, *Promise*, particularly pp. 54–64; G. R. Beasley-Murray, *Jesus and the Future*, Macmillan 1954, particularly pp. 183–7; Barrett, *Jesus* pp. 76–86; Jeremias, *Theology* I §§ 13 and 21. See also above n.30.

35. So e.g. E. Percy, *Die Botschaft Jesu*, Lund 1953, pp. 179f.; Grundmann, *Matthäus* p.329. The usual objection, that an original connection makes the activity of the Jewish exorcists also a manifestation of the kingdom (Kümmel, *Promise* pp. 105f.; Perrin, *Teaching* p.63), misses the emphasis given to 'Spirit/finger of God' in v.28.

36. The δέ ('but') at the beginning of v. 28 is adversative.

37. Πνεύματι/δακτύλῳ θεοῦ has a position of emphasis in the sentence. The rabbis do not mention the Spirit of God as one of the many means of driving out demons (Strack-Billerbeck IV pp. 532–5).

38. The authenticity of the saying as a word of Jesus is little disputed; see e.g. Bultmann, *Tradition* p.105; Taylor, *Mark* pp.240f.; Kümmel, *Promise* pp.108f.; Bornkamm, *Jesus* p.68.

39. Isa.24.21f.; I Enoch 10.4ff., 11ff.; 54.4ff.; Test.Sim.6.6; Test.Levi 18.12; 1QS 4.18. See also Bousset-Gressmann pp.251–4.

40. Cf. R. Leivestad, *Christ the Conqueror*, SPCK 1954, pp.46f. See also J. M. Robinson, *The Problem of History in Mark*, SCM Press 1957, ch.III; J. Kallas, *The Significance of the Synoptic Miracles*, SPCK 1961; H. C. Kee, 'The Terminology of Mark's Exorcism Stories', *NTS* 14, 1967–68, pp.232–46.

41. Cf. R. Otto, *The Kingdom of God and the Son of Man*, ET Lutterworth 1938, p. 104; Hoffmann, 'It is not the messenger who makes the kingdom, but the kingdom that makes him' (p.204). Contrast Keck's formulation (*Jesus* pp.217, 223).

42. Cf. Dunn, 'Spirit and Kingdom' pp.38f.

43. Von Baer suggests that the Markan and Q forms were originally two independent sayings (pp.139f.).

44. See particularly J. Wellhausen, *Einleitung in die drei ersten Evangelien*, Berlin [2]1911, pp.66f.; also *Matthaei* pp. 6of.; R. Schippers, 'The Son of Man in Matt. 12.32 = Luke 12.10 compared with Mark 3.28', *Studia Evangelica* IV, 1968, pp. 233f.; C. Colpe, *TDNT* VIII pp.442f.; also 'Der Spruch von der Lästerung des Geistes', *Der Ruf Jesu und die Antwort der Gemeinde: Festschrift für J. Jeremias*, Göttingen 1970, pp.65ff. See also Bultmann, *Tradition* p.131; Klostermann, *Das Markusevangelium*, HNT [5]1971, p.38; Taylor, *Mark* p.242; Bornkamm in Bornkamm–Barth–Held p.34; Hahn, *Titles* p.323 n.88, Schweizer, *Matthäus* p.185.

45. Tödt pp.312–8; see also Lohmeyer, *Markus* p.79; Percy, *Botschaft* pp.253–6;

A. J. B. Higgins, *Jesus and the Son of Man*, Lutterworth 1964, pp. 127–32; Lövestam pp. 71f.; Hoffmann p. 150; Schulz, Q p. 247.

46. Against K. Berger, *Die Amen-Worte Jesu*, Berlin 1970, pp. 36–41.

47. The sole parallel in the NT documents is Eph. 3.5.

48. Hahn, *Titles* p. 323 n. 88.

49. Tödt pp. 315f.

50. The semitic form 'the sons of men' makes this impossible.

51. Cf. Black p. 195; Colpe, *TDNT* VIII p. 443 n. 304.

52. Bousset, *Kyrios Christos* p. 39; A. Fridrichsen, 'Le péché contre le St. Esprit', *RHPR* 3, 1923, pp. 367–72; Käsemann, *NTQT* p. 99; E. Schweizer, *TDNT* VI p. 397; *Das Evangelium nach Markus*, NTD 1967, pp. 46ff.; Tödt p. 119; Hahn, *Titles* p. 324 n. 88; R. Scroggs, 'The Exaltation of the Spirit by Some Early Christians', *JBL* 84, 1965, pp. 360–5; Hoffmann pp. 150ff.; Schulz, Q pp. 247ff.

53. Von Baer pp. 75f., 137f.; O. Procksch, *TDNT* I p. 104; cf. B. H. Branscomb, *The Gospel of Mark*, Moffatt 1937, pp. 74f.; Barrett, *Holy Spirit* pp. 106f. M. E. Boring, 'How May We Identify Oracles of Christian Prophets in the Synoptic Tradition? Mark 3.28–29 as a Test Case', *JBL* 91, 1972, suggests that Mark 3.28f. 'was formed as something of a pesher on Isaiah 63.3–11' (pp. 517f.), though Isa. 63.10f. is hardly close enough to explain Mark 3.28f.

54. See also Frövig pp. 174ff. Bousset took the contrast as between the presently exalted Son of Man (but remote in his sojourn in heaven) and the Spirit active in the community: blasphemy against the exalted, transcendent Son of Man was quite permissible (*Kyrios Christos* p. 39; cf. Scroggs pp. 364f.)! Is this credible?

55. 'He who blasphemes against the Father will be forgiven, and he who blasphemes against the Son will be forgiven; but he who blasphemes against the Holy Spirit will not be forgiven, either on earth or in heaven'.

56. 'Only as a word of Jesus himself is a statement like Matt. 12.32 = Luke 12.10 in fact intelligible' (Frövig p. 182).

57. Bornkamm in Bornkamm–Barth–Held p. 34. The Talmud's statement that Jesus of Nazareth 'practised sorcery and led the people astray' (Sanhedrin 43a) is a clear echo of this controversy. See further Klausner pp. 18–47; van der Loos pp. 156–75.

58. Tödt pp. 118f.

59. Cf. Schippers p. 235.

60. Jeremias, *Theology* I pp. 81f.; though see below ch. IV n. 81.

61. Cf. Frövig pp. 184ff.

62. Cf. Lövestam p. 46; also Gospel of Thomas 44.

63. Strack-Billerbeck I pp. 637f.

64. Cf. H. Sasse, 'Jesus Christ the Lord', *Mysterium Christi*, ed. G. K. A. Bell & A. Deissmann, Longmans 1930: 'How can this conflict be understood unless there is seen behind it a consciousness so overpowering of the reality of the Holy Spirit that in comparison with it all that "pneumatics" have experienced, both before and since, fades away into nothing' (pp. 115f.).

65. See e.g. Schürmann, *Das Lukasevangelium* I, Herder 1969, p. 242 and those cited there in n. 162.

66. 'Zur Traditionsgeschichte der Nazareth-Perikope Lk 4.16–30', *Mélanges Bibliques* (Rigaux Festschrift) pp. 187–205.

67. 'Zur Nazareth-Perikope' pp. 190, 203f.

68. See further Stanton, *CSNT* p. 33; Hoffmann and Schulz ignore Luke 4.16–30 entirely in their reconstruction of Q.

69. Cf. the function of Acts 1.8 in the construction of Acts.

70. 'Kingdom of heaven' occurs more than thirty times in Matthew and nowhere else in the Synoptics. 'Righteousness' occurs seven times in Matthew and only once elsewhere in the Synoptics.

71. Cf. E. Schweizer, 'Formgeschichtliches zu den Seligpreisungen Jesu', *NTS* 19, 1972–73, p.122 n.4.

72. See particularly A. Finkel, *The Pharisees and the Teacher of Righteousness*, Leiden 1964, pp.155–8; also 'Jesus' Sermon at Nazareth', *Abraham unser Vater, Festschrift für O. Michel*, hrsg. O. Betz, M. Hengel, P. Schmidt, Leiden 1963, pp.113f.; J. Dupont, *Les Béatitudes* II, EB 1970, pp.92–9; Schürmann, *Lukasevangelium* p.327. See also Black p.158 n.2. H. Frankemölle, 'Die Makarismen (Mt 5.1–12, Lk. 6.20–23)', *BZ* 15, 1971, 59f., 68f., agrees that Matthew draws on Isa.61.1ff., but disputes that Q and Luke do so – the reference to Isa.61.1ff. is due to Matthean redaction. But if Luke 7.18–23 is Q and it contains a reference to Isa.61.1, as Frankemölle agrees (see further below §9.3), then that makes a Q reference to Isa.61.1 in Luke 6.20 more probable. It is more likely that Luke 4.18f. is derived from this Q tradition than that 6.20 is 'merely a (Lukan) reminiscence of Luke 4.18f.' (p.60). That Matthew strengthens the allusion to Isa.61.1ff. (πενθοῦντες/παρακληθήσονται – 5.4) and adds τῷ πνεύματι in 5.3 does not demonstrate the redactional nature of the Isa.61.1 allusion in 5.3.

73. See further Jeremias, *Theology* I §12.

74. Strauss pp.219ff. The Baptist's recognition of Jesus' Messiahship at Jordan would then be a *further* development in the tradition of Jesus' relation to the Baptist (§46). See also Schürmann, *Lukasevangelium* I p.414.

75. C. H. Kraeling, *John the Baptist*, New York 1951, p.129. See also M. Goguel, *Jean Baptiste*, Paris 1928, pp.63ff.; *Life of Jesus* pp.278ff.; E. Lohmeyer, *Johannes der Täufer*, Göttingen 1932, p.18; Bornkamm, *Jesus* p.49; Hoffmann, p.201; Schweizer, *Matthäus* pp.165f.

76. Kümmel, *Promise* p.110.

77. Hoffmann pp.23–7, 199f.; cf. Schulz, Q p.194.

78. M. Dibelius, *Die urchristliche Überlieferung von Johannes dem Täufer*, Göttingen 1911, p.37; so Kümmel, *Promise* p.110.

79. See above n.74, and further below.

80. Hoffmann p.201.

81. Kümmel, *Promise* p.111.

82. Fridrichsen, *Miracle* pp.97f.; Bultmann, *Tradition* pp.23f.; Klostermann, *Matthäusevangelium* pp.94f.; Grundmann, *Lukas* p.163; Fuller, *Foundations* pp.128f., 171; P. Stuhlmacher, *Das paulinische Evangelium I. Vorgeschichte*, Göttingen 1968, pp.219f.; Schulz, Q pp.193, 203.

83. Kraeling pp.129f.; Hoffmann pp.214f.

84. Hoffmann p.215.

85. Fridrichsen, *Miracle* p.100.

86. But see Stanton, *CSNT* pp.31f.

87. Hahn, *Titles* p.380; E. Lohse, *RGG*³ VI 1834; Stuhlmacher p.218.

88. Stuhlmacher refers to O. Michel, F. Hahn and R. Meyer (p.219 n.1).

89. Stuhlmacher pp.142ff., 150; J. A. Fitzmeyer, 'Further Light on Melchizedek from Qumran Cave 11', *JBL* 86, 1967, reprinted in *Essays on the Semitic Background of the New Testament*, Chapman 1971, pp.245–67; M. P. Miller, 'The Function of Isa.61.1–2 in 11Q Melchizedek', *JBL* 88, 1969, pp.467–9; Stanton, *CSNT* pp.30f.

90. Stuhlmacher p.220; so Schulz, Q p.195.

91. R. Meyer, *TDNT* VI pp. 826f. See further Hoffmann pp. 206ff.

92. Cf. Hoffmann pp. 213f.

93. Tödt pp. 269–74.

94. Schulz, *Q* pp. 195ff.

95. Against Bultmann, *Tradition* p. 23; cf. Wellhausen, *Matthaei* p. 51; Schulz, *Q* p. 198.

96. Hoffmann p. 210.

97. Bultmann, *Tradition* p. 110.

98. Stanton, *CSNT* p. 30; and see above §9.2.

99. Hoffmann p. 210.

100. J. Jeremias, *Jesus' Promise to the Nations*, ET SCM Press 1958, p. 46.

101. Bultmann, *Tradition* p. 126 (my italics).

102. See e.g. Grundmann, *Matthäus* p. 305; Schürmann, *Lukasevangelium* I p. 411; Hoffmann p. 205; Schulz, *Q* p. 199 n. 173.

103. Perrin, *Teaching* pp. 103–8; Jeremias, *Theology* I §12.

104. Bultmann, *Tradition* p. 128. See also his 'The Primitive Christian Kerygma and the Historical Jesus', *The Historical Jesus and the Kerygmatic Christ*, ed. C. E. Braaten & R. A. Harrisville, Abingdon 1964, p. 23.

105. Cf. Windisch, 'Jesus und der Geist' pp. 229f.; Otto, *Kingdom* pp. 380f.

106. Jeremias, *Theology* I pp. 51ff.

107. See above p. 27 with nn. 72, 73 and below n. 122.

108. Dibelius, *Tradition* p. 274.

109. The lack of overlap is also implied (deliberately?) by Mark 6.14. See further Dunn, *Baptism* p. 25 and n. 8.

110. A. Schweitzer, *The Mysticism of St Paul*, ET A. & C. Black 1931, p. 234; G. R. Beasley-Murray, *Baptism in the New Testament*, Macmillan 1963, p. 64; cf. Dunn, *Baptism* pp. 36, 99.

111. Kümmel, *Theology*: 'It is also probable that at this baptism he had an experience that was crucial for his activity, since the shifting of such an experience to the baptismal event is not obvious from the content in meaning of this action' (p. 74).

112. Jeremias, *Theology* I p. 56.

113. Cf. W. Manson, *Jesus* p. 40. See further below p. 77 and n. 49.

114. Strauss §§71, 101, 104; Bultmann, *Tradition* pp. 230f.

115. The fact that these accounts (Isa. 6, Jer. 1, Ezek. 1ff.) are in the first person underlines the force of Dibelius's point.

116. See further J. Lindblom, *Prophecy in Ancient Israel*, Blackwell 1962, pp. 12–21, 31f., 46; see also below ch. IV n. 103.

117. Bultmann, *Tradition* pp. 247f. The influences which may have determined Mark's presentation of the episode are discussed e.g. by Bultmann, *Tradition* pp. 248–53, and Barrett, *Holy Spirit* pp. 35–45.

118. Dunn, *Baptism* pp. 10–14; also 'Spirit-and-fire Baptism', *NovTest* XIV, 1972, pp. 81–92.

119. Dunn, *Baptism* p. 27 nn. 12, 13.

120. 'Echoing voices were not an uncommon phenomenon among the Jews of these days, and frequently these voices were heard to utter verses of scripture. Endowment with the Holy Spirit, accompanied by an ecstatic experience, was apparently no unique experience among those who were baptized in John's presence in the Jordan' (Flusser p. 29; although he goes on to note that if the heavenly message came to Jesus in the words of Isa. 42.1 (or Ps. 2.7) they would have possessed 'unique significance' for Jesus). See also Vermes, *Jesus* pp. 92, 206f.

121. See above II n. 73.

122. Despite the weight of scholarship favouring an original reference only to Isa. 42.1 (υἱός being derived from παῖς – see above ch. II n.72), it seems to me more probable that 'son' is original: there is in fact no clear instance of παῖς being replaced by υἱός; Q (Matt.4.3, 6/Luke 4.3, 9) presupposes υἱός; Servant categories seem to have played little role in the Christology of the earliest communities (cf. Schweizer, TDNT VIII p.368); and Jesus' sense of sonship seems to have been more basic than the idea of Servant in Jesus' self-understanding and missionary compulsion. Fuller discussion may be found in Marshall, 'Son of God' pp.326–36.

In the Gospel of the Hebrews it is the Spirit himself who addresses Jesus as Son: 'And it came to pass when the Lord was come up out of the water, the whole fount of the Holy Spirit descended upon him and rested on him and said to him: My Son, in all the prophets was I waiting for thee . . . thou art my first-begotten Son that reignest for ever' (Hennecke, Apocrypha I pp. 163f.).

123. I have demonstrated in Baptism how consistently the rite of baptism is understood in the NT as the expression of repentance and faith.

124. Cf. Bultmann, Tradition p.255.

125. According to Flusser, three miracle workers belonging to the period of the second temple were described as sons in their relationship with God (pp.93f.). Cf. Otto, Kingdom p.345. So now Vermes, Jesus: 'There is no reason to contest the possibility, and even the great probability, that already during his life Jesus was spoken of and addressed by admiring believers (sic!) as son of God' (p.209). This suggests that there may be more historical ground for the cries of the demoniacs than the 'messianic secret' thesis would allow.

Chapter IV

1. See particularly Büchsel, Geist ch.8 and pp.215–27; Weinel, Theologie pp.132ff.; Windisch, 'Jesus und der Geist' pp.209–36; Otto, Kingdom pp.344ff.; Barrett, Holy Spirit pp.57, 68, 75ff., 113–21.

2. See particularly L. Newbigin, The Household of God, SCM Press 1953, ch.IV; W. Hollenweger, The Pentecostals, SCM Press 1972. See also below p.272 and n.72.

3. To avoid possible confusion I should perhaps note that I am using 'miracle' in the sense defined by R. Swinburne, The Concept of Miracle, Macmillan 1970: 'Miracle is an event of an extraordinary kind, brought about by a god, and of religious significance' (p.1).

4. See e.g. S. Schulz, Die Stunde der Botschaft, Hamburg/Zürich 1967, pp.64–79; H. D. Betz, 'Jesus as Divine Man', Jesus and the Historian: In Honour of E. C. Colwell, ed. F. T. Trotter, Westminster 1968, pp.114–33; M. Smith, 'Prolegomena to a Discussion of Aretologies, Divine Men, the Gospels and Jesus', JBL 90, 1971, pp. 174–99; P. J. Achtemeier, 'Gospel Miracle Tradition and the Divine Man', Interpretation 26, 1972, pp.179–97.

5. See especially D. Georgi, Die Gegner des Paulus im 2 Korintherbrief Neukirchen 1964. But see also below p.307 and n.34.

6. Georgi, Gegner pp.213–6; L. E. Keck, 'Mark 3.7–12 and Mark's Christology', JBL 84, 1965, pp.341–58. The thesis is maintained in a forced and extreme form by T. J. Weeden, Mark – Traditions in Conflict, Fortress 1971; and in a more

moderate form by R. P. Martin, *Mark: Evangelist and Theologian*, Paternoster 1972.

7. Dibelius, *Tradition* pp. 79ff.; Bultmann, *Tradition* p. 241.

8. See particularly O. Betz, 'The Concept of the So-called "Divine Man" in Mark's Christology', *Studies in New Testament and Early Christian Literature*, ed. D. E. Aune, Leiden 1972, pp. 229–34; D. L. Tiede, *The Charismatic Figure as Miracle Worker*, SBL Dissertation Series 1, 1972. Cf. W. v. Martitz, *TDNT* VIII, pp. 338f.

9. Achtemeier p. 196.

10. Cf. Trocmé, *Jesus* pp. 101ff.

11. See below §39; but see also Paul's response to what he regards as an over-evaluation of *dunameis*, ch. X, particularly §55.

12. W. Manson, *Jesus* pp. 33f. E. Käsemann suggests that old confessional formulae have been incorporated in 2.22 and 10.38 (*RGG*³ VI 1835).

13. Jeremias, *Theology* I p. 91.

14. Bultmann, *Tradition* p. 112; E. Haenchen, *Der Weg Jesu*, Berlin 1966, p. 226.

15. See also Percy, *Botschaft* pp. 112f.; F. Mussner, *The Miracles of Jesus*, ET Ecclesia 1970, pp. 19–22: 'If there is one pre-Easter logion, then it is the lament of Jesus over these three cities of his native Galilee' (p. 21). Cf. F. Hahn, *Mission in the New Testament*, ET SCM Press 1965, p. 34; Grundmann, *Matthäus* p. 313.

16. Vermes, *Jesus*, concludes: 'the person of Jesus is to be seen as part of first-century charismatic Judaism and as the paramount example of the early Hasidim or Devout' (p. 79).

17. On Mark 1.40–5 cf. Mussner, *Miracles* pp. 28–37.

18. Otto, *Kingdom* p. 347; Jeremias, *Theology* I p. 92 n. 5; cf. van der Loos pp. 466f.

19. Luke 22.51b is most probably a development in the tradition. The redaction is of a piece with Luke's less cautious and more materialistic presentation of the miraculous (see below pp. 121f. and 190); and Mark would hardly have omitted noting that Jesus healed the severed ear if a description of such a healing had belonged to the tradition (14.47). We may, however, note that there are not a few claims to healings today which involve a quite perceptible physical change – particularly to lengthening of short limbs (see e.g. S. Durasoff, *Bright Wind of the Spirit*, Hodder & Stoughton 1973, p. 52; T. L. Osborn, *Faith Digest*, June 1965; I have such a personal testimony in my files). Cf. the phenomenon of 'bodily elongation' – H. Thurston, *The Physical Phenomena of Mysticism*, Burns & Oates 1952, ch. VII.

20. F. Fenner, *Die Krankheit im Neuen Testament*, Leipzig 1930, argued that the illnesses of the gospels and Acts, including Paul's, were all with few exceptions, basically forms of hysteria (pp. 30–78) and that psychotherapy was the chief method of healing in the NT (pp. 96–106); cf. T. A. Burkill, 'The Notion of Miracle with special reference to St Mark's Gospel', *ZNW* 50, 1959, pp. 47f.

21. See e.g. D. Kerin, *The Living Touch*, 1914, Hodder & Stoughton [22]1961; E. G. Neal, *A Reporter Finds God through Spiritual Healing*, Longmans 1956; J. C. Peddie, *The Forgotten Talent*, Oldbourne 1961; K. Kuhlman, *I believe in Miracles*, Prentice-Hall 1963; F. MacNutt, *Healing*, Notre Dame 1974; cf. L. D. Weatherhead, *Psychology, Religion and Healing*, Hodder & Stoughton 1951. We should also recall the seventy or so miraculous cures at Lourdes proclaimed since 1858 – 'To be accepted, a cure has to be instantaneous, permanent and scientifically inexplicable. Only organic cures are considered . . . cures of psycho-somatic or hysterical ailments are not entertained' (*Observer*, 22.7.73). See further below §30.

22. C. Wilson, *The Occult*, Hodder & Stoughton 1971, p. 63.

23. I do not mention the stories of the miraculous catch of fishes (Luke 5.1–11) and of the coin in the fish's mouth (Matt. 17.24–7) which are more vulnerable to

the charges of legendary development than most other traditions about Jesus.

24. E.g. A. E. J. Rawlinson, *The Gospel according to St Mark*, Methuen 1925; Taylor, *Mark*; J. Schmid, *The Gospel according to Mark* (ET Mercier 1968).

25. For authenticity see Perrin, *Teaching* pp. 137f.; see further below p. 75.

26. Otto, *Kingdom* pp. 347f.; see also Thurston ch. XVII; van der Loos pp. 625ff. From Indonesia, where Pentecostal Christianity is growing, comes the claim of a feeding miracle very like that attributed to Jesus – Mel Tari, *Like a Mighty Wind*, Coverdale 1973, pp. 47ff.

27. The most famous cases in Christian history are Joseph of Copertino and St Teresa, and outside Christian circles, Daniel Dunglas Home; see Thurston ch. I; Wilson, *Occult* p. 462–74. Benz refers particularly to Filippo Neri (*Vision* pp. 218ff.). G. Widengren, *Literary and Psychological Aspects of the Hebrew Prophets*, Uppsala 1948, argues that Ezekiel experienced levitation (p. 110). Levitation is apparently familiar to the Yogis: according to Patanjali, 'By making samyama on the relation between the body and the ether or by acquiring through meditation the lightness of cotton fiber, the yogi can fly through the air' (Swami Prabhavananda & C. Isherwood, *How to Know God: the Yogi Aphorisms of Patanjali*, Signet 1969, p. 133; I am grateful to my colleague D. Hay for this reference). Mel Tari claims that one of the Indonesian mission teams walked across a flooded river thirty feet deep in places, with the water never coming higher than their knees (pp. 45ff.)!

28. Wilson cites several examples in *Occult* pp. 54f., 100f., 104; also Benz, *Vision* pp. 210ff.

29. Otto, *Kingdom* pp. 350, 368–74.

30. So e.g. more conservative scholars like Jeremias, *Theology* I §10 and O. Betz, 'So-called "Divine Man"' pp. 234–9.

31. Cf. Harnack, 'Jesus himself did not assign that critical importance to his miraculous deeds which even the evangelist Mark and the others all attributed to him' (*What is Christianity* Lecture 2).

32. Cf. Sir Alister Hardy, *The Living Stream*, Gifford Lectures, Collins 1965, pp. 284f., cited by J. V. Taylor, *The Go-Between God*, SCM Press 1972, p. 67. For further literature see J. D. Pearce-Higgins & G. S. Whitby, *Life, Death and Psychical Research*, Rider 1973.

33. Mark 2.5 pars.; 4.40 pars.; 5.34 pars.; 5.36 par.; 6.6 par.; 9.19 pars.; 9.23f.; 10.52 pars.; 11.22ff. par.; Matt. 8.10/Luke 7.9; Matt. 8.13; 9.28; 14.31; 15.28; 16.8; 17.20; Luke 17.5f.; 17.19; cf. Mark 13.21 par.; 15.32 par.; Matt. 6.30. Bornkamm's observation that 'in the tradition of Jesus' sayings faith is always linked with power and miracle' (*Jesus* p. 130) is not quite accurate. See Mark 9.42 par.; 11.31 pars.; Matt. 21.32; Luke 7.50; 8.12f.; 18.8.

34. Whereas Mark opposes the tendency to present Jesus simply as a miracle-worker or 'divine man'. See above n. 6 and below n. 36.

35. See the fuller treatment of J. Roloff, *Das Kerygma und der irdische Jesus*, Göttingen 1970, pp. 152–73.

36. See especially Perrin, *Teaching* pp. 130–6; also van der Loos p. 269; Jeremias, *Theology* I pp. 162f. See also Baltensweiler cited in ch. III n. 33.

37. Cf. Grundmann, *Kraft* pp. 64–71; also *TDNT* II p. 302; Otto, *Kingdom* pp. 340ff. The counter evidence – that Jesus used magical techniques – is scanty (Mark 7.33, 35; 8.23 – see J. M. Hull, *Hellenistic Magic and the Synoptic Tradition*, SCM Press 1974, pp. 76ff., 83ff.) and can hardly overthrow the weightier evidence cited above. Within the context of Jesus' ministry these actions have more charismatic than magical significance; see also Hull pp. 101 n. 29, 142ff.; against M. Smith,

Clement of Alexandria and a Secret Gospel of Mark, Harvard 1973, pp. 220–37, who does not take sufficient cognizance of these points.

38. G. Ebeling, *Word and Faith*, ET Fortress 1963, pp. 227ff.; Perrin, *Teaching* pp. 137f.

39. Roloff, *Kerygma* pp. 166ff., 172f.; cf. van der Loos pp. 188f., 265.

40. Ebeling, *Nature* p. 56; so also *Word* p. 234; Fuchs, 'Jesus and Faith', *Studies* pp. 6off.

41. Cf. Bultmann, *Theology* I p. 9; Roloff, *Kerygma* pp. 154ff., 169f., 173; Kümmel, *Theology* pp. 63ff.; against van der Loos p. 270; E. D. O'Connor, *Faith in the Synoptic Gospels*, Notre Dame 1961, ch. III, fails to exercise proper historical discrimination.

42. Mark 1.22/Luke 4.32; Mark 6.2/Matt. 13.54/Luke 4.22; Mark 10.26/Matt. 19.25; Mark 11.18/(Luke 19.48); Matt. 7.28f.; 22.33; cf. Mark 12.34/Matt. 22.46/Luke 20.40.

43. Perhaps, as has often been suggested, it is the authority of Jesus' presence which underlies the account of the stilling of the storm.

44. Cf. Wrede pp. 96f. and Appendix 5.

45. Black pp. 158f.

46. Bultmann, *Tradition* p. 41.

47. Jeremias, *Promise* p. 30 n. 4.

48. Cf. Dodd, *Founder* p. 50.

49. See e.g. Dibelius, *Täufer* pp. 21f.; Grundmann, *Markus* p. 236; Bornkamm, *Jesus* pp. 49f.; G. S. Shae, 'The Question on the Authority of Jesus', *NovTest* XVI, 1974, pp. 1–29. It is most unlikely that the early church would base its defence of Jesus' authority on his baptism by John (Lohmeyer, *Markus* p. 243).

50. Nineham, *Mark* p. 306.

51. Jeremias, *Theology* I pp. 114f.

52. Cf. C. P. Ceroke, 'Is Mark 2.10 a Saying of Jesus?', *CBQ* 22, 1960, pp. 369–90.

53. Cf. Hooker, *Son of Man* pp. 81–93; Colpe, *TDNT* VIII pp. 420f.; Jeremias, *Theology* I p. 262; Kümmel, *Theology* pp. 81f. See also above ch. II nn. 159, 161.

54. Bultmann, *Tradition* p. 158.

55. Hahn, *Mission* pp. 40–6; M. Hengel, *Nachfolge und Charisma*, Berlin 1968, pp. 82–9; Jeremias, *Theology* I pp. 234–9. See further below §13.4.

56. U. Wilckens comments on Mark 6.2: 'In the traditional image of the Jewish teacher of the Law Jesus is for him (Mark) the prototype of all Church charismatics' (*TDNT* VII p. 515).

57. The Fourth Gospel brings this out in masterly fashion by developing the theme of κρίσις (judgment, separation) and by sharpening the antitheses: life/death, light/darkness, sight/blindness, etc. See also below §58.4.

58. See Windisch, 'Jesus und der Geist' p. 226; Käsemann, *ENTT* pp. 41f. Jesus 'was regarded as a *charismatic* rather than as a professional theologian' (Jeremias, *Theology* I p. 77).

59. K. H. Rengstorf, *TDNT* II p. 156; Manson, *Teaching* p. 106; Hengel, *Nachfolge* pp. 70f., 76ff.

60. For authenticity see Kümmel, *Promise* p. 91.

61. 'Again and again the only discernible backing for his words and actions is himself and his own decision; and for this there seems to be no appropriate name nor standard of comparison' (H. von Campenhausen, *Ecclesiastical Authority and Spiritual Power in the Church of the First Three Centuries*, ET A. & C. Black 1969, p. 4). See also ch. III n. 64.

62. Conzelmann, *Jesus*: 'In the relationship of Jesus to his disciples what is specific in his self-understanding is documented' (p. 35).

63. Bornkamm in Bornkamm-Barth-Held pp. 52–7.

64. See particularly Mark 9.17 par.; 9.38; 10.17 pars.; 10.35; 12.14 pars.; 12.19 pars.; 12.32; 13.1; Matt. 8.19; 12.38; Luke 7.40; 10.25; 12.13; 19.39. The Aramaic 'Rabbi' is preserved four times in the Markan tradition in address to Jesus – Mark 9.5; 10.51; 11.21; 14.45.

65. Mark 1.17–20 par.; 2.14 pars.; 8.34 pars.; 10.21 pars.; Matt. 8.21f./Luke 9.59f.; Matt. 10.37f./Luke 14.26f.

66. See e.g. Rengstorf, *TDNT* II pp. 153ff.; C. H. Dodd, 'Jesus as Teacher and Prophet', *Mysterium Christi*, ed. G. K. A. Bell & A. Deissmann, Longmans 1930, pp. 53ff.; A. Schulz, *Nachfolgen und Nachahmen*, Kösel 1962.

67. Hengel, *Nachfolge* pp. 46–63 : 'Jesus was no rabbi . . . Following and discipleship are not to be explained on the rabbinic model'; against A. Schulz, *Nachfolgen*. See also Hengel's strictures (pp. 94ff.) on H. D. Betz, *Nachfolge*.

68. Hengel, *Nachfolge* pp. 63–7.

69. Jeremias, *Theology* I §17.

70. See also e.g. Mark 2.15; 5.18ff. par.; 9.40 par., and the undiscriminating use of ἀκολουθεῖν (follow) at this point. See further W. G. Kümmel, *Kirchenbegriff und Geschichtsbewusstsein in der Urgemeinde und bei Jesus*, Göttingen ²1968, pp. 28ff.; also *Theology* pp. 37f.

71. N. A. Dahl, *Das Volk Gottes*, Darmstadt ²1963, p. 159.

72. See above ch. II n. 70, particularly Meye, *Jesus and the Twelve*.

73. The only two references to ἐκκλησία (church, assembly) in the gospels (Matt. 16.18; 18.17) are generally regarded as due to later editing or as the work of the early church; but see further ch. V n. 126.

74. Cf. Schweizer, *Erniedrigung* §1m.

75. See Bornkamm, *Jesus* pp. 148f.

76. See above n. 55.

77. See Jeremias, *Theology* I p. 242.

78. Hahn, *Beginnings* p. 21.

79. H. Koester, 'One Jesus and Four Primitive Gospels', *Trajectories* p. 168.

80. See the bibliography in G. Friedrich, *TDNT* VI pp. 781f.; É. Cothenet, 'Prophétisme dans le nouveau testament', *DBS* 8, 1972, 1268f.; Hahn, *Titles* pp. 352–406; Fuller, *Foundations* pp. 125–9; Jeremias, *Theology* I pp. 76–80; Vermes, *Jesus* ch. 4; K. H. Schelkle, 'Jesus – Lehrer und Prophet', *Orientierung an Jesus. Zur Theologie der Synoptiker. Für J. Schmid*, hrsg. P. Hoffmann, Herder 1973, pp. 300–8.

81. Rabbinic references in Strack-Billerbeck I.63, 127, II.133; P. Schäfer, *Die Vorstellung vom heiligen Geist in der rabbinischen Literatur*, München 1972, pp. 89–115, 143–6; see also R. Leivestad, 'Das Dogma von der prophetenlosen Zeit', *NTS* 19, 1972–73, pp. 288–99. We should however beware of assuming that this rabbinic dogma was the only possible opinion on the matter; see P. Volz, *Der Geist Gottes*, Tübingen 1910, pp. 116f.; R. Meyer, *TDNT* VI pp. 812–28; Hengel, *Nachfolge* pp. 20–7; Schäfer pp. 116–34, 147ff.; cf. W. D. Davies, *Paul and Rabbinic Judaism*, SPCK 1948, pp. 208–16.

82. Cullmann, *Christology* pp. 23–37.

83. Cf. Jeremias, *Theology* I pp. 8off.

84. Jeremias, *Theology* I p. 78. See also Strack-Billerbeck II.127–38; G. F. Moore, *Judaism in the First Three Centuries of the Christian Era*, Cambridge 1946–48, 'The holy spirit is the spirit of prophecy' (I.237); Schäfer pp. 21–6.

85. E. Fascher, *ΠΡΟΦΗΤΗΣ*, Giessen 1927, p. 178; R. Meyer, *Der Prophet aus Galiläa*, Darmstadt ²1970, p. 121. Barrett, *Holy Spirit* pp. 97f., is more cautious.

86. Frövig pp. 133ff.; Barrett, *Holy Spirit* p.95; Jeremias, *Promise* pp.26ff.; Fuller, *Foundations* pp.127ff.; against Bultmann, *Tradition* pp.152-6. Cf. O. Michel, '"Ich Komme" (Jos. Bell. III, 400)', *TZ* 24, 1968, pp.123f. The fourth evangelist has greatly extended the motif, but this is one of the instances where we can detect the core of authentic tradition round which he builds. See also Weinel, *Theologie* pp.163-6.

87. Cf. N. Q. Hamilton, 'Temple Cleansing and Temple Bank', *JBL* 83, 1964, pp. 365-72; Roloff, *Kerygma*, pp.95f.

88. Cf. Dodd, 'Prophet' pp.59f.

89. Cf. Fuller, *Foundations* pp.128f.

90. Bultmann, *Tradition* pp.109-18; Meyer, *Prophet* pp.13-17.

91. Dodd, 'Prophet' pp.6of.

92. Cf. Fuller, *Foundations* p.128.

93. Mark 2.5 pars.; 2.8 pars.; 3.4 pars.; 3.16 pars.; 9.33ff., 10.21 pars.; 12.15 pars.; 12.43f. par.; 14.18, 20 pars.; Matt. 12.15/Luke 11.17; Luke 7.39ff.; 19.5; John 1.47f.; 2.24f.; 4.17ff. See also Meyer, *Prophet* pp.11f.; Bornkamm, *Jesus* p.60. For religious historical parallels see R. Bultmann, *The Gospel of John*, KEK, ET Blackwell 1971, p.102 n.1; Benz, *Vision* pp.185-207; Wilson, *Occult* pp.92, 103f.; A. Bittlinger, *Gifts and Ministries*, ET Eerdmans 1973, refers particularly to the role of the stareta in Eastern Christianity (pp.58f.).

94. See below n.122; cf. *Martyr. Polyc.* 5; *Martyr. Perp. et Fel.* I.3, IV.

95. See especially Jeremias, *Theology* I pp.277-86.

96. Cf. Jeremias, *Theology* I pp.241ff. For belief in the 'messianic woes' see Strack-Billerbeck IV 977-86.

97. Mark 11.2f.; 14.13ff. are presented as prophetic foretellings, but appear to be more contrived, whether historically or by the tradition.

98. For modern parallels see A. Guillaume, *Prophecy and Divination*, Hodder & Stoughton 1938, p.116; Wilson, *Occult* pp.43f., 47, 101ff.; R. Montgomery, *A Gift of Prophecy: The Phenomenal Jeane Dixon*, New York 1965 – Jeane Dixon is best known for her prediction of President John F. Kennedy's assassination. For the famous rhyming quatrains of Nostradamus (1503-66) see E. Cheetham, *The Prophecies of Nostradamus*, Spearman 1973.

99. Friedrich, *TDNT* VI pp.838f.

100. Dodd, 'Prophet' p.63; cf. Schürmann, *Untersuchungen* pp.89f.

101. O. Holtzmann, *War Jesus Ekstatiker?*, Tübingen 1903, pp.50-71, 73, 105. For criticism see A. Oepke, *TDNT* II pp.456f.

102. Cf. Frövig pp.92f. Leivestad suggests that the words are better understood 'symbolically, as a dramatic, illustrative way of expressing the certainty of the ruin of Satan' (*Christ* p.49).

103. See above §10.1. For history of religion parallels see Benz, *Vision* pp.253-66.

104. Schweizer, *TDNT* VI p.400.

105. 'An ecstatic condition' (B. S. Easton cited in Barrett, *Holy Spirit* p.49). Taylor, *Go-Between God*, cites the parallel of 'the primitive prophets of Ghana, who almost invariably begin a career of divination by running off in a state of possession into the bush where they remain lost for weeks or even months' (p.92).

106. Though some have interpreted it as an experience of Jesus (see Taylor, *Mark* pp.386f.). M. Smith uses this episode as possibly the strongest section of a sequence of flimsy evidence to support the thesis that Jesus practised a technique (magical ecstatic) for ascent to the heavens (*Clement* pp.240-8).

107. I. M. Lewis, *Ecstatic Religion*, Penguin 1971, pp.39, 52f.

108. Luke recognizes Jesus' utterance 'as similar in character to these ecstatic outbursts with which he was familiar in the church of his own day. Like the Christian prophets Jesus was suddenly overmastered by the Spirit and expressed himself in rhapsody' (E. F. Scott, *The Spirit in the New Testament*, Hodder & Stoughton 1923, p.69). But see also von Baer pp.73f.

109. Jeremias, *Theology* I pp.239–44. On 14.38 cf. Schweizer, *Markus*, p.181.

110. Windisch, 'Jesus und der Geist' p.230.

111. Cf. A. Bittlinger, *Gifts and Graces*, ET Hodder & Stoughton 1967, pp.49f.

112. See Arndt & Gingrich, ἐμβριμάομαι.

113. Bultmann, *Tradition*, pp.222f. In the modern charismatic movement the one who exercises 'the gift of healing' will often speak in tongues when he lays hands on the person who seeks healing.

114. A. Schweitzer, *The Psychiatric Study of Jesus*, 1913, ET Boston 1948.

115. H. Wansbrough suggests the translation: 'When they heard it, his followers went out to calm it (the crowd) down, for they said that it was out of control with enthusiasm' – 'Mark 3.21, Was Jesus out of his Mind?', *NTS* 18, 1971–72, pp. 233ff.; but the exegesis breaks down on κρατῆσαι (to seize) which can hardly be translated 'calm down'. Cf. D. Wenham, *NTS* 21, 1974–75, pp.295–300.

116. As e.g. by Scott, *Spirit* pp.77–80. He goes so far as to affirm that 'the idea of the Spirit' was 'an alien element' in Jesus' religion (p.245).

117. Cf. Beasley-Murray, *Rigaux Festschrift* pp.475f.

118. Windisch, 'Jesus und der Geist' pp.231ff.

119. Schweizer, *TDNT* VI pp.402f.; also 'The Spirit of Power', *Interpretation 6*, 1952, p.264.

120. These should not be sharply distinguished; see above p.76.

121. Kümmel, *Promise*, pp.20f.; cf. W. Manson, *Jesus* p.50; Bultmann, *Theology* I pp.22f. See also above ch.III n.34.

122. W. Pannenberg, *Jesus God and Man*, ET SCM Press 1968, pp.58–66.

123. P. Althaus, *Die christliche Wahrheit*, Gütersloh 1962, p.440.

124. Cf. Ebeling, *Word* pp.205, 289; Käsemann, 'Blind Alleys in the "Jesus of History"'. Controversy', *NTQT*, pp.43–50.

125. Cf. G. W. H. Lampe, 'The Holy Spirit and the Person of Christ', *Christ, Faith and History*, ed. S. W. Sykes & J. P. Clayton, Cambridge 1972, pp.111–30.

Chapter V

1. Cf. the revolutionary slogan of the late 1960s – 'Che lives!'

2. Most recently in effect by W. Marxsen, *The Resurrection of Jesus of Nazareth*, ET SCM Press 1970 – 'Jesus is risen' reduces to 'the cause of Jesus continues' (p.141); H. M. Teeple, 'The Historical Beginnings of the Resurrection Faith', *Studies in New Testament and Early Christian Literature*, ed. D. E. Aune, Leiden 1972, pp.107–20.

3. A. Seeberg, *Der Katechismus der Urchristenheit*, Leipzig 1903, pp.43–58; A. M. Hunter, *Paul and his Predecessors*, SCM Press 1940, ²1961, pp.15–18.

4. ἐπίσημοι ἐν τοῖς ἀποστόλοις could be translated 'highly regarded among (= by) the apostles'; but much the more natural sense is 'outstanding among (= within the circle of) the apostles' – so the great majority of commentators. Instead of Junias we could well translate Junia (feminine – some versions, including the important p[46] read Julia): one of the apostles may have been a woman!

5. W. Schmithals, *The Office of Apostle in the Early Church*, ET SPCK 1971, pp.63f.; citing also J. B. Lightfoot, Kümmel, Rengstorf, Lietzmann and Munck. On Silvanus see Schmithals pp.65ff.; Roloff, *Apostolat*, rejects Schmithal's argument (p.61), but fails to consider I Thess.2.7. On Apollos see J. Héring, *The Second Epistle of Saint Paul to the Corinthians*, ET Epworth 1967, p.110. We must of course give up the old equation of 'all the apostles' with 'the twelve', as the list itself and these other uses of 'apostle' make clear; against, most recently, P. Winter, 'I Corinthians 15.3b–7', *Nov.Test* II, 1958, pp.145f. See further below p.143 and n.36.

6. The dominant view is that the formula handed down to Paul stopped at v.5; see especially Kümmel, *Kirchenbegriff* pp.3–5; Jeremias, *Eucharistic Words* pp.101ff.; K. Wegenast, *Das Verständnis der Tradition bei Paulus und in den Deuteropaulinen*, Neukirchen 1962, pp.54f.; Conzelmann, *Der erste Brief an die Korinther*, KEK 1969, pp.296–300.

7. U. Wilckens, 'Der Ursprung der Überlieferung der Erscheinungen des Auferstandenen', *Dogma und Denkstrukturen*, E. Schlink Festschrift, hrsg. W. Joest & W. Pannenberg, Göttingen 1963, pp.73–81, and R. H. Fuller, *The Formation of the Resurrection Narratives*, SPCK 1972, pp.11–30, argue that a plurality of traditions lie behind these verses: three different traditions in vv.3–4, and a further three separate traditions grouped under the fourth ὅτι in vv.5ff.!

8. See e.g. G. Bornkamm, *Paul*, ET Hodder & Stoughton 1969, pp.18ff., 64f., 75ff.

9. Marxsen, *Resurrection* pp.101–5.

10. See e.g. M. Goguel, *The Primitive Church*, ET Allen & Unwin 1964, pp.98–115; Conzelmann, *Theology of Luke* p.216 n.1; E. Haenchen, *The Acts of the Apostles*, KEK, ET Blackwell 1971, pp.114f.; Goppelt, *Apostolic Times* p.181; M. M. Bourke, 'Reflections on Church Order in the New Testament', *CBQ* 30, 1968, pp.496ff.; C. K. Barrett, *New Testament Essays*, SPCK 1972, pp.78–82; Fuller, *Resurrection* pp.45f.

11. Lindblom, *Gesichte* pp.41–58, 105–11 (quotation from p.111 n.45). It is highly improbable that II Cor.12.1–10 is Paul's own description of his Damascus road experience (cf. Weinel, *Theologie* pp.193, 332; E. Benz, *Paulus als Visionär*, Wiesbaden 1952, pp.31f.). Such an equation would make it virtually impossible to correlate the 'fourteen years' of Gal.2.1 and the 'fourteen years' of II Cor.12.2; and the quite different attitudes reflected in I Cor.9.1f. and II Cor.12.1ff. can only be fully explained if they allude to quite different events.

12. Roloff, *Apostolat* p.55; Schmithals, *Apostle* pp.60, 75–9. The πᾶσιν of v.7b does not of course imply that Paul *excluded* himself from the ranks of the apostles; the phrase 'all the apostles' is hardly of Paul's own choosing and must therefore belong to the tradition from which Paul here quotes (Kümmel, *Kirchenbegriff* pp.6f.).

13. See e.g. W. Michaelis, *Die Erscheinungen des Auferstandenen*, Basel 1944, pp.23ff.; E. Bammel, 'Herkunft und Funktion der Traditions-elemente in I Kor. 15.1–11', *TZ* 11, 1955, p.414; H. W. Bartsch, 'Die Argumentation des Paulus in I Kor. 15.3–11', *ZNW* 55, 1964, p.264 n.10. The case can be best argued in terms of Harnack's original suggestion that Paul has brought together different (and competing) lists of appearances; see U. Wilckens, *Die Missionsreden der Apostelgeschichte*, Neukirchen 1963, p.75 n.1, and those cited there.

14. Kümmel, *Kirchenbegriff* p.45 n.12; H. Lietzmann–W. G. Kümmel, *An die Korinther*, HNT 1949, pp.77, 191; H. von Campenhausen, 'The Events of Easter and the Empty Tomb', *Tradition and Life in the Church*, ET Collins 1968, p.45; H. Grass, *Ostergeschehen und Osterberichte*, Göttingen ²1962, pp.96f.; Schmithals, *Apostle* p.73; Fuller, *Resurrection* pp.42f.

15. Roloff, *Apostolat* p. 49; Conzelmann, *I Kor.* pp. 304f.

16. See T. C. Edwards, *The First Epistle to the Corinthians*, Hodder & Stoughton 1885, pp. 298f.

17. Cf. von Campenhausen, 'Empty Tomb' p. 54 n. 50. Cf. also J. Blank, *Paulus und Jesus*, München 1968, pp. 187ff.

18. See e.g. J. Schneider, *TDNT* II p. 466; J. Héring, *The First Epistle of Saint Paul to the Corinthians*, ET Epworth 1962, p. 162.

19. E.g. A. Robertson & A. Plummer, *I Corinthians*, ICC ²1914, p. 339; Schneider, *TDNT* II p. 466; Héring, *I Cor.* p. 162.

20. J. Munck, 'Paulus Tanquam Abortivus (I Cor. 15.8)', *New Testament Essays in Memory of T. W. Manson*, Manchester 1959, pp. 182–7.

21. G. Björck, 'Nochmals Paulus abortivus', *Coniectanea Neotestamentica* III, 1938, pp. 3–8; Kümmel in Lietzmann-Kümmel, *Kor.* p. 192; T. Boman, 'Paulus abortivus (I Kor. 15.8)', *StTh* 18, 1964, p. 50; C. K. Barrett, *The First Epistle to the Corinthians*, A. & C. Black 1968, p. 344; F. F. Bruce, *I & II Corinthians*, Oliphants 1971, p. 142; Fuller, *Resurrection* p. 43.

22. Barrett, *I Cor.* p. 344.

23. Munck, 'Paulus' pp. 190f.

24. Against Fuller, *Resurrection* p. 43.

25. Cf. Lietzmann in Lietzmann-Kümmel, *Kor.*: '. . . . the unripeness of the one born in comparison with the other sons' (p. 78). Hence, presumably, the need for the time in 'Arabia' (Gal. 1.17) – a readjustment(?) period without parallel among the earliest disciples and apostles, so far as we know.

26. Cf. Barrett, *I Cor.* p. 344.

27. This is the understanding of resurrection appearance and apostleship at the time Paul wrote I Cor. It is unlikely that resurrection appearances were thought to be ended or the circle of apostles closed *at the time of Paul's conversion*; otherwise *his* claim would never have been accepted. Against Wilckens, 'Ursprung' pp. 64f. See further below p. 108 and ch. VI nn. 35, 36.

28. Roloff, *Apostolat* p. 55.

29. E.g. Fuller, *Resurrection* p. 32.

30. Cf. M. Goguel, *The Birth of Christianity*, ET Allen & Unwin 1953, p. 80; Wegenast, *Tradition* pp. 62f. See also below pp. 275, 323.

31. Cf. the three types of revelation distinguished by the mediaeval theologians – corporeal, imaginative and intellectual; Lindblom, *Prophecy* p. 36.

32. Michaelis, *Erscheinungen* pp. 104–9, 117–21; *TDNT* V pp. 326f., 356–61 (quotation from pp. 358f.).

33. K. H. Rengstorf, *Die Auferstehung Jesu*, Witten/Ruhr ⁴1960, pp. 56ff., 117–27; Lindblom, *Gesichte* pp. 86–9.

34. See e.g., theophany – Gen. 16.13; Ex. 3.2; 16.10; 24.11; Lev. 9.6, 23; 16.2; Num. 14.10; Judg. 6.12; Ps. 102.16; Isa. 60.2; dream – Gen. 26.24; I Kings 3.5; II Chron. 1.17; 7.12. NT: physical appearance – Acts 7.26; transfiguration – Mark 9.4 pars.; angel – Luke 1.11; Acts 7.30, 35; dream – Acts 16.9; vision – Rev. 11.19; 12.1, 3.

35. J. Weiss, *Earliest Christianity*, ET 1937, Harper 1959: 'There is no doubt of what he means: I have actually and really seen him; but there is no doubt, either, that he means: I have seen him as the heavenly, exalted Lord, in the lustre of the divine glory (II Cor. 4.6)' (p. 26); cf. Fuller, *Resurrection* pp. 30–4. Michaelis unjustifiably dismisses I Cor. 9.1: It gives no information about the kind of seeing and signifies no more than an encounter with the Risen One in his 'revelation-presence'

(Offenbarungsgegenwart) (*Erscheinungen* pp. 100ff., 108). Equally unconvincing is his treatment of angelophanies (pp. 111f., 116f.). As to Marxsen: it would be wrong to assume that Paul is free-er to use the language of his choice in Gal. 1 simply because Gal. 1 was written before I Cor. 15; in *both* cases the language may already have been determined for him whether by tradition or the opponents confronting him (cf. K. Kertelge, 'Apokalypsis Jesou Christou (Gal. 1.12)' *Neues Testament und Kirche*, Schnackenburg Festschrift, pp. 275f., 279f.). The point remains that Paul found no difficulty in using both revelation *and* appearance language for his conversion experience.

36. Rengstorf, *Auferstehung* pp. 58–62 (quotation from p. 58).

37. Cf. Rengstorf, *Auferstehung* pp. 85f.; Bruce, *Cor.*: 'If Paul uses the same language . . . it is to suggest not that their experience was as "visionary" as his but that his was as objective as theirs' (p. 142); D. P. Fuller, *Easter Faith and History*, Tyndale 1968, argues that Paul got the idea of the 'spiritual body' of the resurrection 'from the tradition by which he learned of the appearances of Jesus to the apostles' (p. 171).

38. Blass–Debrunner–Funk §220.1; Arndt-Gingrich, ἐν IV.4; RSV; NEB – 'to me and through me'.

39. Cf. H. Lietzmann, *Galaterbrief*, HNT 1910, ⁴1971, p. 8; E. D. Burton, *Galatians*, ICC 1921, pp. 50f.; G. S. Duncan, *The Epistle to the Galatians*, Moffatt 1934, pp. 27f.; H. Schlier, *Der Brief an die Galater*, KEK 1949, ⁴1965, p. 55; A. Wikenhauser, *Pauline Mysticism*, ET Herder/Nelson 1960, pp. 135f.

40. D. Lührmann, *Das Offenbarungsverständnis bei Paulus und in paulinischen Gemeinden*, Neukirchen 1965, pp. 40f., 73ff.; cf. Michaelis, *Erscheinungen* pp. 114ff.

41. Pannenberg, *Jesus* p. 93, taking up the point of Grass p. 229; see also Lindblom, *Gesichte* (see above n. 11).

42. So most commentators; e.g. see A. Plummer, *II Corinthians*, ICC 1915, p. 121; M. Dibelius & W. G. Kümmel, *Paul*, ET Longmans 1953, p. 60; D. M. Stanley, *Christ's Resurrection in Pauline Soteriology*, Rome 1961, p. 48; P. Seidensticker, *Die Auferstehung Jesu in der Botschaft der Evangelisten*, Stuttgart 1967, pp. 35f.; Bruce, *Cor.* p. 196; Kümmel, *Theology* p. 222; M. E. Thrall, 'Christ Crucified or Second Adam', *CSNT* p. 148.

43. See Wegenast, *Tradition* pp. 61f., and those cited in J. D. G. Dunn, 'I Corinthians 15.45: Last Adam – Life-giving Spirit', *CSNT* p. 128 n. 2; also below p. 219. For the debate on this point see B. Spörlein, *Die Leugnung der Auferstehung*, Regensburg 1971.

44. Cf. Schmithals, *Gnosticism in Corinth*, ET Abingdon 1971, p. 210; also *Apostle* pp. 26f., 32ff.

45. Cf. Fuller, *Resurrection* p. 47. The primary reference of the plural pronouns in these verses (we, us, our) is Paul's (and his companions') apostolic ministry (as 3.1ff., 4.5, 12ff. indicate). Paul's own experience shapes his more general statements. See also below p. 213 and n. 74.

46. C. G. Jung, *Contributions to Analytical Psychology*, ET 1945, p. 257, cited by C. S. C. Williams, *Acts*, A. & C. Black 1957, p. 123; cf. Goguel, *Birth* pp. 81–6.

47. Cf. Pannenberg, *Jesus*: 'In our context the term "vision" can only express something about the subjective mode of experience, not something about the reality of an event experienced in this form' (p. 95); so Kümmel, *Theology* p. 102. Cf. also N. Smart, *The Phenomenon of Religion*, Macmillan 1973, pp. 132–6.

48. U. Wilckens, 'The Tradition-History of the Resurrection of Jesus', in *The Significance of the Message of the Resurrection for Faith in Jesus Christ*, ed. C. F. D.

Moule, ET SCM Press 1968, p. 67; see also Roloff, *Apostolat* pp. 48f.; Blank pp. 157ff.; G. O'Collins, *The Easter Jesus*, Darton, Longman & Todd 1973, pp. 7f.

49. See further Lührmann, *Offenbarung* pp. 75–80.

50. It is questionable whether 'objective vision' is the best summary formula to describe this seeing/appearance; see J. Kremer, *Das älteste Zeugnis von der Auferstehung Christi*, Stuttgart [3]1970, pp. 61ff.

51. Cf. Kümmel, *Kirchenbegriff* p. 9.

52. C. F. D. Moule, *The Epistle to the Colossians and to Philemon* Cambridge 1957, pp. 104ff.

53. See particularly E. Lohse, *Colossians and Philemon*, KEK, ET Fortress 1971, pp. 119ff., and literature cited there.

54. Lohse, *Colossians* pp. 119f. and n. 47.

55. Alternatively we may link the phrase more closely with what follows: 'puffed up without reason by what he saw when he was initiated' (Fridrichen in Arndt-Gingrich ἐμβατεύω); so also N. Turner, *A Grammar of New Testament Greek* Vol. III, T. & T. Clark 1963, p. 246.

56. W. L. Knox suggested that the thought of v. 18 was very closely connected: 'Nor must they let themselves be impressed by those who sought to impose on them higher standards of special fasts, enjoined as a means of propitiating the angels, whose appearance to them in vision would mark the stages of their progress to higher things' (*St Paul and the Church of the Gentiles*, Cambridge 1939, p. 170).

57. Cf. Lucius's experience of initiation into the mystery of Isis, cited below §52.2; see also Lohse, *Colossians* pp. 120ff.

58. J. Knox, *Chapters in a Life of Paul*, A. & C. Black 1954, p. 117; U. Wilckens, 'Die Bekehrung des Paulus als religionsgeschichtliche Problem', *ZTK* 56, 1959, pp. 273ff.

59. Cf. K. H. Rengstorf, *TDNT* I pp. 430f.; also *Apostelamt und Predigtamt*, Stuttgart [2]1954, pp. 28f.; Kümmel, *Kirchenbegriff* p. 7; Roloff, *Apostolat* pp. 44f.; Schmithals, *Apostle* pp. 30f.

60. This is not to deny the important role which Paul gives to kerygmatic tradition in regulating his own life and worship and that of his churches – see below §§47.3, 49.2.

61. It is possible that the snatch of dialogue which remains constant in all three Acts accounts of Paul's conversation and which is the heart of these narratives ('Saul, Saul, why do you persecute me?' 'Who are you, Lord?' 'I am Jesus . . .') goes back to Paul himself. Cf. the dialogue element in the prophetic vision and commissioning of Isaiah and Jeremiah.

62. Dunn, *Baptism* ch. 6.

63. Cf. Lindblom, *Prophecy*: 'It was to Jeremiah (as well as to Ezekiel) as though the sum-total of his preaching was given him in a single moment, at the time of the call' (p. 189).

64. Cf. H. A. A. Kennedy, *St Paul's Conception of the Last Things*, Hodder & Stoughton 1904, pp. 91ff. For Jewish thought about the glory of the age to come see e.g. Isa. 58.8; Ezek. 39.21; Hab. 2.14; Ps. Sol. 3.16.

65. O. Cullmann, 'Le caractère eschatologique du devoir missionnaire et de la conscience apostolique de S. Paul. Étude sur le κατέχον (-ων) de II Thess. 2.6–7', *RHPR* 16, 1936, pp. 210–45; A. Fridrichsen, *The Apostle and his Message*, Uppsala 1947.

66. See also Cullmann, *Christ and Time*, ET SCM Press [3]1962, pp. 164ff.; J. Munck, *Paul and the Salvation of Mankind*, ET SCM Press 1959, pp. 36–42.

67. See B. Rigaux, *Les Épîtres aux Thessaloniciens*, EB 1956, p.277; E. Best, *The First and Second Epistles to the Thessalonians*, A. & C. Black 1972, pp.297f.

68. See Roloff, *Apostolat* pp.25f.; J. Knox, 'Romans 15.14–33 and Paul's Conception of his Apostolic Mission', *JBL* 83, 1964, pp.3–8.

69. See further Munck, *Paul* pp.42–68, though Munck presses his case too far; cf. L. Cerfaux, *The Christian in the Theology of St Paul*, ET Chapman 1967, pp.97ff.

70. Rom.15.20ff. (=Isa.52.15); II Cor.6.1f. (=Isa.49.8); also Gal.1.15 (cf. Isa. 49.1–6); Phil.2.16 (cf. Isa.49.4).

71. Acts 13.47 (=Isa.49.6); 26.16ff. (cf. Isa.42.7); also Acts 18.9f. (cf. Isa.41.10, 43.5).

72. See Jeremias, *Servant* pp.88f.; Cullmann, *Christology* pp.75ff.

73. Cf. H. Windisch, *Paulus und Christus*, Leipzig 1934, pp.137f., 147–50; D. M. Stanley, 'The Theme of the Servant of Yahweh in Primitive Christian Soteriology and its Transformation by St Paul', *CBQ* 16, 1954, pp.415ff.; Cerfaux, *Christian* pp.84–88.

74. C. K. Barrett, 'The Apostles in and after the New Testament', *SEA* 21, 1956, pp.42f.; also *Signs* pp.42f. See further below §55.

75. Cf. Wilckens, 'Ursprung' pp.83–93; Lührmann, *Offenbarung* pp.75–80.

76. Cf. Goguel, *Birth*: 'One difference between the appearances of Christ and visions is what we may call functional; appearances of Christ created a faith in the resurrection, while ecstatic visions, even though they enriched those who received them, did not fundamentally modify their religious attitude' (p.45).

77. 'The apostles are witnesses of the resurrection, though not all witnesses of the resurrection are apostles' (Rengstorf, *TDNT* I p.430).

78. ὅτι ὤφθη . . .
  ἔπειτα ὤφθη . . .
  ἔπειτα ὤφθη . . .
  ἔσχατον δὲ πάντων . . . ὤφθη . . .

79. Probably from συναλίζεσθαι = literally 'to eat salt with', so 'to eat or have a meal with someone' (see e.g. Haenchen, *Acts* p.141 n.3; F. F. Bruce, *The Book of the Acts*, Marshall, Morgan & Scott 1954, p.36; Grass p.89).

80. E. Käsemann, 'Is the Gospel Objective?', *ENTT* p.49

81. See e.g. Bultmann, *Theology* I p.45; Grass pp.89f.; Fuller, *Resurrection* pp.66f., 77ff.

82. Fuller, *Resurrection* p.115.

83. Lindblom, *Gesichte* pp.104f., 108f., 111f.

84. W. Grundmann, 'Die Apostel zwischen Jerusalem und Antiochia', *ZNW* 39, 1940, pp.111ff.

85. I tend to the view that Mark intended to end his gospel at 16.8 – a view which commends itself increasingly in modern scholarship; see W. G. Kümmel, *Introduction to the New Testament*, ET SCM Press 1966, pp.71f.

86. Hennecke, *Apocrypha* I p.165, 185f., 195ff.

87. E. Haenchen, 'Auferstehung im Alten Testament', *Die Bibel und Wir*, Tübingen 1968, traces its roots much deeper into the OT (pp.73–90).

88. The reference to resurrection here is a subject of dispute. Some scholars would interpret it not of resurrection of the dead but of restoration of the nation, as in the vision of Ezek.37. E.g., D. S. Russell, *The Method and Message of Jewish Apocalyptic*, SCM Press 1964, refers it to resurrection of the dead (pp.367f.); U. Wilckens, *Auferstehung: das biblische Auferstehungszeugnis historisch untersucht und erklärt*, Stuttgart 1970, refers it to restoration of the nation (pp.116f.).

89. Cf. Russell, *Apocalyptic* pp. 377f.; Hengel, *Judaism* I pp. 196ff.

90. Cf. K. Schubert, 'Die Entwicklung der Aufterstehungslehre von der nachexilischen bis zur frührabbinischen Zeit', *BZ* 6, 1962, pp. 198ff.; Hengel, I. p. 200.

91. G. Stemberger, *Der Leib der Auferstehung*, Rome 1972, pp. 16–20, overemphasizes the parallel with the creation in 7.28 ('out of nothing') and does not give enough weight to the πάλιν in these three verses, particularly in its conjunction with ἀποδίδωμι in 7.23; 14.46.

92. Russell, *Apocalyptic* pp. 376f. Stemberger does not discuss the Sib. Or. passages.

93. Cf. Enoch 46.6; 51.1f., 4f.; 58.3; 61.5; Test. Jud. 25; Test. Zeb. 10.1–3; Test. Ben. 10.6–8; IQH 11.10ff.; and particularly the controversy between Hillel and Shammai in *Genesis Rabbah* 14.5.

94. K. Lake, *The Historical Evidence for the Resurrection of Jesus Christ*, Williams & Norgate 1907, pp. 24ff.; cf. Stemberger pp. 87ff. See also S. H. Hooke, *The Resurrection of Christ*, Darton, Longman & Todd 1967, pp. 18–22; Wilckens, *Auferstehung* pp. 124–7. Fuller's review of the evidence is too brief and one-sided (*Resurrection* pp. 17f.).

95. See particularly Jeremias, *Theology* I pp. 309f.; see further below p. 159.

96. Cf. Fuller, *Resurrection* p. 17.

97. For parallels see R. E. Brown, *The Gospel according to John*, Anchor Bible 29, Chapman 1966, pp. 423, 437.

98. Cf. B. Lindars, *The Gospel of John*, Oliphants 1972, pp. 382–6.

99. See especially U. Wilckens, *Missionsreden*; but also F. F. Bruce, 'The Speeches in Acts – Thirty Years After', *Reconciliation and Hope*, L. L. Morris Festschrift, ed. R. J. Banks, Paternoster 1974, pp. 53–68.

100. H. Conzelmann, *Die Apostelgeschichte*, HNT 1963, p. 29; Haenchen, *Acts* p. 182 n. 1. Note particularly the ἐπ' ἐλπίδι in v. 16 and διαφθοράν in v. 17.

101. Strack-Billerbeck II p. 618. See also A. Schmitt, 'Ps. 16.8–11 als Zeugnis der Auferstehung in der Apostelgeschichte', *BZ* 17, 1973, pp. 245f.

102. See also W. L. Knox, *The Acts of the Apostles*, Cambridge 1948, p. 86; J. V. Doeve, *Jewish Hermeneutics in the Synoptic Gospels and Acts*, Assen 1953, ch. VI; B. Lindars, *New Testament Apologetic*, SCM Press 1961, pp. 40ff.; J. W. Bowker, 'Speeches in Acts: A Study in Proem and Yelammedenu form', *NTS* 14, 1967–68, pp. 96–106.

103. The physical nature of the resurrection body of Jesus is emphasized by the insertion of 'his flesh' into the interpretation of the LXX passage in v. 31 – 'nor did *his flesh* see corruption'; but this is a natural interpretation in view of Ps. 16.8 ('my flesh will dwell in hope' – Hebrew, 'in safety'), and cannot be so easily dismissed as the product of Luke's 'hellenizing-early catholic interest in the incorruptability of Christ's flesh' (against Wilckens, *Missionsreden* pp. 141 n. 2, 150). In view of the other evidence it is likely that Luke's materialistic view of Jesus' resurrection body is prompted as much by the primitive traditions of which he became aware as by his own interests (see further below §21.3).

104. On the historicity of the empty tomb tradition see e.g. von Campenhausen, 'Empty Tomb', pp. 42–89; W. Nauck, 'Die Bedeutung des leeren Grabes für den Glauben an den Auferstandenen', *ZNW* 47, 1956, pp. 243–67; Pannenberg, *Jesus* pp. 100–6; M. Hengel, 'Maria Magdalena und die Frauen als Zeugen', *Abraham unser Vater: Festschrift für O. Michel*, hrsg. O. Betz, M. Hengel & P. Schmidt, Leiden 1963, pp. 253ff.; Jeremias, *Theology* I pp. 300–5; Wilckens, *Auferstehung* pp. 55–64, 149ff.; Fuller, *Resurrection* ch. 3; E. L. Bode, *The First Easter Morning: the Gospel Accounts of the Women's Visit to the Tomb of Jesus*, Rome 1970; Vermes, *Jesus*

pp. 39ff. For arguments in favour of the lateness of the tradition see especially Grass pp. 138–86. For a discussion of the burial narratives, particularly Mark 15.42–6, see I. Broer, *Die Urgemeinde und das Grab Jesu*, München 1972.

105. For Judaism in particular I need refer only to the documentation of J. Jeremias, *Heiligengräber in Jesu Umwelt*, Göttingen 1958; also 'Drei weitere spätjudische Heiligengräber', *ZNW* 52, 1961, pp. 95–101.

106. L. Schenke, *Auferstehungsverkündigung und leeres Grab*, Stuttgart 1968, argues that the original form of Mark 16.1–8 emerged as an aetiological legend out of a cultic celebration which took place at the tomb each Easter morning (followed by O'Collins, *Jesus* pp. 41f.). The thesis presupposes the prior judgment that Mark 16.1–8 has no historical foundation (in the events of the first Easter at any rate) and otherwise is wholly speculative. Besides which it does not adequately answer the questions, Why should such an important role as guarantors or within the cult be given to women? (cf. n. 131 below). G. Schille, 'Die Himmelfahrt', *ZNW* 57, 1966, pp. 183–99, offers a similar thesis with respect to Acts 1.9–11; but see S. G. Wilson, 'The Ascension: A Critique and an Interpretation', *ZNW* 59, 1968, pp. 269–74.

107. See e.g. Acts 2.32f.; 13.33; Rom. 1.3f.; 10.9; Phil. 2.8ff.; Col. 1.18; Heb. 1.3–5.

108. Cf. J. Weiss, *Der erste Korintherbrief*, KEK 1910, pp. 345, 377. I Cor. 15.50a may apply to those still living at the parousia (J. Jeremias, '"Flesh and Blood Cannot Inherit the Kingdom of God" (I Cor. 15.50)', *NTS* 2, 1955–56, pp. 151–9; Barrett, *I Cor.* p. 379; though see also E. Schweizer, *TDNT* VII pp. 128.f; Conzelmann, *I Kor.* pp. 345f.). But even so it certainly also serves to rule out a reconstitution of the physical body understanding of the resurrection.

109. O. Cullmann, *Immortality of the Soul or Resurrection of the Dead?*, ET Epworth 1958.

110. J. A. T. Robinson, *The Body*, SCM Press 1952, pp. 11f.; Schweizer, *TDNT* VII p. 1047.

111. Cf. Schweizer, *TDNT* VII pp. 1055f. See also B. A. Pearson, *The Pneumatikos-psychikos Terminology in I Corinthians*, SBL Dissertation 12, 1973, ch. 3, who describes Paul's argument with his opponents appropriately as 'a conflict of dualisms' – Paul's *eschatological* dualism set against their *anthropological* dualism (p. 26).

112. See further Dunn, *CSNT* pp. 128ff. Spörlein's exposition here lacks penetration.

113. Mark's account of the empty tomb is possibly a further variation on the theme – a 'translation' rather than a 'resurrection' account; see E. Bickermann, 'Das leere Grab', *ZNW* 23, 1924, pp. 281–92; M. Goguel, *La foi à la résurrection de Jésus dans la christianisme primitif*, Paris 1933, pp. 213–33; N. Q. Hamilton, 'Resurrection Tradition and the Composition of Mark', *JBL* 84, 1965, pp. 415–21; also *Jesus for a No-God World*, Westminster 1969, pp. 6off.; Weeden, *Mark* pp. 106ff.

114. See also G. Lohfink, *Die Himmelfahrt Jesu*, München 1971, particularly pp. 251ff.

115. J. Denney, *Jesus and the Gospel*, Hodder & Stoughton [4]1913, p. 146.

116. διαγρηγορήσαντες δὲ εἶδαν τὴν δόξαν αὐτοῦ – either 'they kept awake and saw his glory . . .', or 'when they were fully awake they saw his glory . . .'.

117. Luke 1.11ff., 26ff.; 2.9ff.; 22.43f.(?); 24.4ff. (*two* men); Acts 1.10f.; 5.19; 8.26; 10.3ff. ('clearly'); 12.7ff. ('real', not a 'vision'); 27.23. See Hull, *Hellenistic Magic* pp. 88ff. – 'a quite phenomenal outburst of angelic activity, mostly in the form of direct intervention . . . In Luke the visits of the angels are regarded as literal events'.

118. See particularly C. H. Talbert, *Luke and the Gnostics*, Abingdon 1966, pp. 14, 30ff., and those cited by him.

119. Grass p. 71; Fuller, *Resurrection* pp. 144f.

120. Visionary experiences can include sensations of taste, smell and physical contact: Isaiah felt his lips touched (Isa. 6.7); Jeremiah felt Yahweh's hand touch his mouth (Jer. 1.9); Ezekiel experienced a sweet taste in his mouth (Ezek. 3.3). In the OT theophany to Abraham the angel of the Lord ate actual food (Gen. 18.8). It is interesting to note that within Jewish tradition this eating was being interpreted as mere appearance at the time of the NT (Tob. 12.19; Philo, *Abr.* 118; Josephus, *Ant.* I. xi.2 (197); cf. Philo, *Sac.* 59; Justin, *Dial.* 34). See also Weinel, *Wirkungen* pp. 196ff.

121. Cf. Hopwood p. 129.

122. C. H. Dodd, 'The Appearances of the Risen Christ: An Essay in Form-Criticism of the Gospels', *Studies in the Gospels: Essays in Memory of R. H. Lightfoot*, ed. D. E. Nineham, Blackwell 1955, pp. 10ff., 33; cf. R. R. Bater, 'Towards a More Biblical View of the Resurrection', *Interpretation* 23, 1969, pp. 58ff.

123. Alternatively, scriptural proof serves the apologetic purpose of helping to lift the veil of non-recognition (Luke 24.11, 16, 25ff., 31f., 44ff.; cf. I Cor. 15.4, 'according to the scriptures').

124. Cf. Klostermann, *Matthäusevangelium* p. 231; Goguel, *Birth* p. 47; Fuller, *Resurrection* pp. 81f.; Schweizer, *Matthäus* p. 346; against O. Michel, 'Der Abschluss des Mätthäusevangelium', *EvTh* 10, 1950–51, pp. 16ff.; G. Barth in Bornkamm-Barth-Held pp. 132f.; Bornkamm, 'The Risen Lord and the Earthly Jesus: Matthew 28.16–20', *The Future of our Religious Past: Essays in Honour of R. Bultmann*, ed. J. M. Robinson, SCM Press 1971, pp. 204f. Cf. Grass pp. 29f.

125. See also John 20.3–10: 'This story of the disciples' race is undoubtedly designed to bring out the priority of Peter in some form or other' (Marxsen, *Resurrection* pp. 58f.; also Fuller, *Resurrection* pp. 135f.). True, but Marxsen presses his argument beyond the limits that the evidence will allow.

126. Matt. 16.17–19 is one of the more plausible suggestions of post-Easter material being set within the pre-Easter life of Jesus; see e.g. Bultmann, *Tradition* pp. 258f.; von Campenhausen, *Authority* p. 129; Bornkamm in Bornkamm-Barth-Held pp. 44ff.; Grundmann, *Matthäus* p. 385; Fuller, *Resurrection* pp. 166ff., 203 n. 52. But see also O. Cullmann, *Peter: Disciple, Apostle, Martyr*, ET SCM Press ²1962, pp. 164–217; Jeremias, *Theology* I pp. 167f., 245; Trocmé, *Jesus* p. 59.

127. Mark 6.45–52, Luke 5.3–11 and John 21.1–14 have been suggested as accounts of the resurrection appearance to Peter 'in maskierter Gestalt' (Hirsch); also the transfiguration (Mark 9.2–8) – so well 'masked' as to be unrecognizable as a resurrection appearance to Peter alone! See also Fuller, *Resurrection* pp. 160–6. John 21.15–17 has the best claim at this point, but that it owes any of its present form to Peter himself must be regarded as highly doubtful.

128. Presumably the same applies to the appearance to James, brother of Jesus, as well.

129. So particularly Grass pp. 27f.; 86f.

130. Fuller, *Resurrection* pp. 78f., 137.

131. J. Jeremias, *Jerusalem in the Time of Jesus*, ET SCM Press 1969, pp. 374f.; this would be reason enough for Paul and the tradition he quotes to omit the women from the list of witnesses in I Cor. 15. On I Cor. 15.5ff. as a 'list of witnesses' see Bammel, 'Herkunft' pp. 401–19.

132. Cf. Hengel, 'Maria Magdalena' pp. 250ff.

133. There are some tradition–history grounds for separating the account of the visit to the empty tomb from that of the appearance to the women (Hengel, 'Maria Magdalena' pp. 253ff.); but see below.

134. Cf. Hopwood p. 130. Visions were not uncommon among the classical prophets; see Lindblom, *Prophecy* pp. 122–37, 144f., 147. In the NT period we need refer only to II Cor. 12.1ff. and the book of Revelation. Within Christianity see e.g. E. Underhill, *Mysticism*, Methuen ¹²1930, reprinted 1967, pp. 266–97 and index; K. E. Kirk, *The Vision of God*, Longmans 1931, index 'visions'; Lindblom, *Gesichte* pp. 13–26; M. Kelsey, *Dreams: The Dark Speeck of the Spirit*, Doubleday 1968; and particularly Benz, *Vision*. William James in describing those 'for whom religion exists not as a dull habit, but as an acute fever rather', notes that 'frequently they have fallen into trances, heard voices, seen visions . . .' (*Varieties* p. 29).

135. *Holy* chs. 4–6. Otto did not actually use the complete Latin phrase as such.

136. Lindblom, *Gesichte* pp. 94f.

137. Cf. Lake, *Resurrection* pp. 186ff. Cf. also the ambivalence of the OT theophanies – the figure in the appearance being described alternatively as 'the angel of the Lord/God' and 'the Lord/God' (Gen. 16.7–13; 21.17–19; 22.11–18; Ex. 3.2ff.; Judg. 6.11ff.; 13.19–22). Cf. also Dan. 7.13 ('one like a son of man') with Dan. 8.15f. ('one having the appearance of a man' = Gabriel). It is not without relevance to our study to note that within the OT tradition the temporary, more physically conceived manifestations of the divine presence gradually gave way to the conviction that God's presence was manifested by the Shekinah – the visible, radiant glory of God in the midst of his people in a *formless* brightness of cloud or fire (cf. e.g. Ex. 13.21f.; 19.16, 18; 24.16f.; 33.10f.; 40.34f.; Num. 9.15f.; I Kings 8.10f.). See also n. 120 above.

138. Cf. Grass p. 253.

139. Weiss, *Earliest Christianity* pp. 14–18; Lohmeyer, *Markus* pp. 355f.; W. Marxsen, *Mark the Evangelist*, ET Abingdon 1969, pp. 85ff.; N. Perrin, *Christology and a Modern Pilgrimage*, ed. H. D. Betz, California 1971, pp. 37–44; Weeden pp. 111–17; cf. Nineham, *Mark* p. 446; see also B. Steinseifer, 'Der Ort der Erscheinungen des Auferstandenen', *ZNW* 62, 1971, pp. 232–65.

140. See e.g. Lake, *Resurrection* pp. 206–13; Taylor, *Mark* p. 608; Grass pp. 113–27; T. Lorenzen, 'Ist der Auferstandene in Galiläa erschienen?', *ZNW* 64, 1973, pp. 209–21. R. H. Stein, 'A Short Note on Mark 14.28 and 16.7', *NTS* 20, 1973–74, pp. 445–52; and those cited by Weeden p. 111 n. 13. Cf. Michaelis's vigorous discussion with Hirsch (*Erscheinungen* pp. 41–72). See also below n. 143.

141. Dodd, 'Appearances' p. 33.

142. Cf. Roloff, *Apostolat* pp. 52ff. Note also Wilckens' view that I Cor. 15.5 and 7 served originally as 'legitimation formulae' ('Ursprung' pp. 67ff., 75ff.).

143. The case for the view that Luke has altered the tradition to exclude Galilee appearances is much stronger than its opposite, that the Galilee appearance tradition is a later development. See below p. 137 and above n. 140.

144. Cf. Grass p. 254.

145. Against Marxsen, *Resurrection* pp. 89–96.

146. See C. F. D. Moule, *The Phenomenon of the New Testament*, SCM Press 1967, especially ch. 2.

147. Note the lack of satisfactory parallels in the history of religions which could explain the rise of the Easter faith. S. G. F. Brandon speaks of the resurrection of Jesus as 'a unique instance', though it has some phenomenological parallels with the resurrection of Osiris (*A Dictionary of Comparative Religion*, art. 'resurrection', ed. S. G. F. Brandon, Weidenfeld & Nicolson 1970, pp. 536f.). We should perhaps also note here Paramhansa Yogananda's account of a two-hour appearance after

death of his guru Sri Yukteswar in a Bombay hotel room in 1936, during which the resurrected sage instructed him on the nature of cosmic reality (*Autobiography of a Yogi*, Rider 1950, ch. XLIII). There are some similarities to the resurrection appearances of the gospels, but the much closer parallels are to be found in the fanciful works which emerged from gnosticism or the confrontation with gnosticism from the second century onwards – particularly *Epistula Apostolorum* and *Pistis Sophia*.

148. Pannenberg, *Jesus* p. 74; Marxsen, 'The Resurrection of Jesus as a Historical and Theological Problem', *The Significance of the Message of the Resurrection for Faith in Jesus Christ*, ed. C. F. D. Moule, ET SCM Press 1968, p. 31.

149. Bultmann, 'The Primitive Christian Kerygma and the Historical Jesus', p. 42; Marxsen, *Resurrection* p. 126.

150. The conversion of Sadhu Sundar Singh has some very striking parallels to the conversion of Paul, particularly vision – 'the form of the Lord Jesus Christ' in light; and audition – words in Hindustani, beginning 'How long will you persecute me?' (B. H. Streeter & A. J. Appasamy, *The Sadhu*, Macmillan 1921, pp. 6ff.). The note of eschatological urgency has been a regular feature of the sects in Christian history (see N. Cohn, *The Pursuit of the Millenium*, Secker & Warburg 1957) and is a prominent feature of modern Pentecostalism (Hollenweger, *Pentecostals* ch. 29).

Chapter VI

1. See Scott, *Spirit* pp. 85ff.; Schweizer, *TDNT* VI p. 404 n. 462; H. Conzelmann, *History of Primitive Christianity*, ET Darton, Longman & Todd 1973, p. 49; against Goguel, *Birth* pp. 95ff.; cf. also above ch. I n. 6, ch. IV nn. 4–6.

2. Haenchen, *Acts* pp. 172–5.

3. E.g. the settlement of Canaan by the tribes of Israel is now recognized to have been a much more complex process than the biblical tradition suggests (M. Noth, *The History of Israel*, ET A. & C. Black 1958, pp. 71ff.; J. Bright, *A History of Israel*, SCM Press 1960, pp. 120–7). A closer parallel is the tendency among Pentecostals and those caught up in the current 'charismatic revival' to root Pentecostalism in a single source; viz., a series of meetings held in an old stable in Los Angeles. Thus e.g. M. Harper, *As at the Beginning: the Twentieth Century Pentecostal Revival*, Hodder & Stoughton 1965: 'The Pentecostal Movement was born in a stable' (p. 23). Whereas closer scrutiny reveals that Pentecostalism is a diverse phenomenon deriving from different and independent sources (see e.g. Hollenweger, *Pentecostals* pp. 47ff., 116ff.).

4. E. Lohmeyer, *Galiläa und Jerusalem*, Göttingen 1936; see also R. H. Lightfoot, *Locality and Doctrine in the Gospels*, Hodder & Stoughton 1938, p. 72; L. E. Elliot-Binns, *Galilean Christianity*, SCM Press 1956, pp. 43ff.; W. Schmithals, *Paul and James*, ET SCM Press 1965: 'Not Jerusalem, but Galilee is the home of Christianity' (p. 33); G. Schille, *Anfänge der Kirche*, München 1966, pp. 175–87; Conzelmann, *History* p. 33.

5. Such groups may have been responsible for the preservation of many of Jesus' sayings and of stories about his healing activities (cf. particularly Trocmé, *Jesus*).

6. As most commentators recognize – see e.g. Leaney, *Luke* p. 292; Fuller, *Resurrection* pp. 97f.; O'Collins, *Jesus* p. 23; cf. I. H. Marshall, *Luke, Historian and Theologian*, Paternoster 1970, pp. 155f.

7. Though see also below – n. 28.

8. Lohmeyer, *Galiläa* pp. 53ff.; Elliot-Binns pp. 43f.; Schmithals, *Paul* p. 34.

9. See Dunn, *Baptism* p. 88.

10. Cf. Dunn, *Baptism* p. 85.

11. Cf. K. Holl, 'Der Kirchenbegriff des Paulus in seinem Verhältnis zu dem der Urgemeinde', *Gesammelte Aufsätze zur Kirchengeschichte* II, Tübingen 1928, pp. 57ff.; Bultmann, *Theology* I p. 52.

12. Weiss, *Earliest Christianity*: 'The language is obviously a survival from a time when the community was concentrated in Jerusalem . . .' (p. 45).

13. On ἐν τῷ συμπληροῦσθαι see particularly K. L. Schmidt, *Die Pfingsterzählung und das Pfingstereignis*, Leipzig 1919, pp. 8ff.; K. Lake & H. J. Cadbury, *The Beginnings of Christianity Part I: The Acts of the Apostles* Vol. IV, Macmillan 1933, pp. 16f.; N. Adler, *Das erste christliche Pfingstfest*, Münster 1938, pp. 118–21.

14. Von Baer pp. 77–85; Dunn, *Baptism* ch. IV.

15. So Haenchen, *Acts* p. 174.

16. H. Braun, *RGG*³ I 1693f.; G. Ogg, *The Chronology of the Life of Paul*, Epworth 1968, ch. 5.

17. See Dunn, *Baptism* pp. 48f.

18. Philo, *Decal.* 32–5, 44, 46f., cf. *Spec. Leg.* II 189; *Exodus Rabbah* 28.6; *Tanḥuma* on Ex. 4.27. See e.g. Lake, *Beginnings* V pp. 114ff.; J. Kremer, *Pfingstbericht und Pfingstgeschehen*, Stuttgarter Bible Studien 63/64, 1973, pp. 238–53.

19. See particularly E. Lohse, 'Die Bedeutung des Pfingstberichtes im Rahmen des lukanischen Geschichtswerkes', *EvTh* 13, 1953, pp. 420–4.

20. Haenchen, *Acts* p. 174; cf. Schweizer, *TDNT* VI pp. 410f.

21. Luke's picture of 'every nation under heaven' being represented at Pentecost is determined more by his concept of the universality of the gospel (Acts 1.8) than by the later portrayal of the Ten Commandments being given in the *seventy* languages of the peoples of the world.

22. Philo: 'Then from the midst of the fire that streamed from heaven there sounded forth to their utter amazement a voice, for the flame became articulate speech in the language familiar to the audience . . .' (*Decal.* 46, Loeb edition Vol. VII). There is nothing about *tongues as of* fire, or a miracle of *many* languages spoken *by* men. Philo indeed explicitly denies that the heavenly voice required the use of human speech organs (*Decal.* 32f.).

23. See also Schmidt, *Pfingsterzählung* p. 27; Adler, *Pfingstfest* pp. 46–58.

24. Haenchen, *Acts* p. 174; Conzelmann, *Apg.* p. 25.

25. Wilson, 'Ascension' pp. 270ff.; cf. Lohfink pp. 176–86.

26. Dunn, *Baptism* ch. XIV.

27. Against A. Richardson, *An Introduction to the Theology of the New Testament*, SCM Press 1958, pp. 116f.

28. Cf. C. F. D. Moule, 'The Post-resurrection Appearances in the Light of Festival Pilgrimages', *NTS* 4, 1957–58, pp. 58–61; Goppelt, *Apostolic Times* p. 21.

29. Lohse, *TDNT* VI pp. 45–8.

30. Von Baer p. 90 n. 3.

31. The best example in recent religious history is the key role filled by the phrase 'baptism in the Spirit' in the development of Pentecostalism (see J. D. G. Dunn, 'Spirit-baptism and Pentecostalism', *SJT* 23, 1970, pp. 397–407).

32. The possibility of a different tradition (Acts 4.31 – date unspecified) has never gained much support; see J. Dupont, *The Sources of Acts*, ET Darton, Longman & Todd 1964, particularly ch. II.

33. So also Lohse, 'Bedeutung' p. 436; B. Reicke, *Glaube und Leben der Urgemeinde*, Zürich 1957, p.28; Kremer, *Pfingstbericht* pp.126, 213, 259f.; as well as those mentioned above in nn.23 and 28, and most English speaking commentators; cf. Kümmel, *Theology* pp.130f.

34. See above pp.121f. and n.114. A literal ascension is the logical and inevitable corollary of Luke's very physical conception of Jesus' resurrection body/appearances. Cf. J. G. Davies, *He Ascended into Heaven*, Lutterworth 1958, pp.47–56. It should perhaps be noted that whereas the NT writers (apart from Luke in Acts) generally regard 'resurrection' and 'ascension' more or less as synonymous (Paul, Hebrews), or at least as following in close chronological sequence (Matthew, Luke, John), various gnostic sects outdid Luke by having the risen Jesus dwelling with his disciples for eighteen months or even twelve years (see Hennecke, *Apocrypha* II p.45).

35. Kümmel, *Kirchenbegriff* p.9. Holl's view that the early community considered the resurrection appearances closed with the appearance to the apostles hangs together with his thesis that 'the apostles' = 'the twelve' plus James ('Kirchenbegriff' p.50). But see below n.36.

36. See e.g. Kümmel, *Kirchenbegriff* pp.5–7; von Campenhausen, 'Der urchristliche Apostelbegriff', *StTh* I, 1947, pp.96–130; also *Authority* p.21; Barrett, *I Cor.* p.343; and above ch. V nn.4, 5. Schmithals argues for a complete dichotomy between 'the twelve' and 'all the apostles' (*Apostle* p.77) – forcing the evidence to an unnatural extent. Paul possibly groups together here a number of different resurrection appearances: every missionary of the earliest community was acknowledged as such by virtue of his direct appointment by the risen Lord (Schmithals p.77; otherwise Wilckens, 'Ursprung' p.65 n.21). The treatments of Richardson, *Theology* pp.319ff. and of Cerfaux, *Christian* ch.3, are strained and unsatisfactory. On Matt. 28.18ff. see below p.153.

37. Note that all the apostles mentioned above (p.98) were active in the Gentile mission. R. Schnackenburg, 'Apostles Before and During Paul's Time', *Apostolic History and the Gospel*, F. F. Bruce Festschrift, ed. W. W. Gasque & R. P. Martin, Paternoster 1970, pp.287–303, argues that Luke's time limitation of resurrection appearances is to be accepted and that Andronicus and Junias *et al.* were apostles who could lay no claim to an appearance of the risen Jesus (pp.293ff.; cf. F. Hahn, 'Der Apostolät im Urchristentum', *KuD* 20, 1974. pp.74–7). This is most unlikely in view of I Cor.15.7 ('all the apostles') and since Andronicus and Junias 'were in Christ' before Paul (Rom.16.7). Was there ever a recognized apostleship in constituting which a resurrection appearance had no place? The clearest evidence (I Cor.9.1; 15.7ff.) leaves little room for anything other than a negative answer – both from Paul and from his opponents! 'Apostles (= delegates) of the churches' (II Cor.8.23; Phil.2.25) are not relevant here, and II Cor. 10–13 can be used only with the greatest circumspection (see further below §47.2).

38. If the appearance to James took place in Galilee, as seems likely (cf. Holl, 'Kirchenbegriff' p.49), then his apparently immediate move to Jerusalem is significant in relation to the discussion above (pp.138f.). The reference to Jesus' brothers in Acts 1.14 is made possible by Luke's squeezing all resurrection appearances (including that to James presumably), concertina-fashion, into the preceding forty day period centred on Jerusalem.

39. E. von Dobschütz, *Ostern und Pfingsten*, Leipzig 1903, pp.31–43. It did not originate with Dobschütz; Adler mentions C. H. Weisse (1838) and Pfleiderer as proponents of the thesis before von Dobschütz (*Pfingstfest* p.146 n.50); but the latter was the first to attempt an adequate justification of it.

40. Those who have accepted von Dobschütz's thesis with greater or less confidence include Bousset, Holl, E. Meyer, Harnack, Burkitt, Goguel, Lietzmann, Hirsch, Grundmann, and more recently S. M. Gilmour, 'Easter and Pentecost', *JBL* 81, 1962, pp.62–6; Jeremias, *Theology* I pp.307f.

41. Notice also the tradition found in the Syrian and Palestinian churches as early as the third(?) and fourth centuries, in which ascension and Pentecost fall on the same day (fifty days after Easter) – G. Kretschmar, 'Himmelfahrt und Pfingsten', *Zeitschrift für Kirchengeschichte* LXVI, 1954–55, pp.209–12. See also P. A. van Stempvoort, 'The Interpretation of the Ascension in Luke and Acts', *NTS* 5, 1958–59, pp.30f.

42. Dobschütz, *Ostern* p.39.

43. Holl, 'Kirchenbegriff' p.47 n.1.

44. Lohse, 'Bedeuting' pp.435f.; see also Kremer, *Pfingstbericht* pp.235ff.

45. Conzelmann, *History*: 'For the appearances it is characteristic that they appear to have no recognizable ecstatic character' (p.40).

46. Kümmel's argument that 'the oldest community's church consciousness is connected with its consciousness of being bearer of the resurrection tradition' (*Kirchenbegriff* pp.8f.; cf. Rengstorf, *Auferstehung* pp.43–8, 155–9) is not entirely convincing. We do not know enough about the origin and function of the formulae in I Cor.15.3ff. (cf. ch.V nn.7, 142 above). Anyway, the issue does not affect my point, since the 'consciousness of being bearer of the resurrection *tradition*' would itself come about only with the passage of time.

47. See Dunn, *Baptism* pp.45f.; see further below §§29, 33; also §45.1 (Paul), cf. §58.3 (John).

48. Kremer, *Pfingstbericht*.

49. According to Sanhedrin I.6, 120 men were necessary before a local Sanhedrin could be constituted; but Luke's figure includes women. The 'all' of Acts 2.1 almost certainly refers to the 120 and not just the twelve (Dunn, *Baptism* p.40; against Kremer, *Pfingstbericht* p.96).

50. Haenchen, *Acts* p.168 n.1; for those who took οἶκος = temple, see e.g. Adler, *Pfingstfest* p.128. Examples of οἶκος = temple include Isa.6.4; Acts 7.47; Josephus *Ant*.VIII.65f. The temple was of course frequently called 'God's house', 'the house of the Lord' etc. in the OT (see particularly I Kings 5–7; Ezek.40f.; Hag.1–2).

51. Cf. further Adler, *Pfingstfest* pp.126–32; Bruce, *Book of Acts* pp.55f.

52. See above ch.V n.134.

53. Lindblom, *Gesichte* p.109 n.44. Donald Gee records a striking vision in Llanelly, South Wales, two weeks before the first World War: first appeared a lamb's face which after about fifteen minutes 'was transformed into the face of our Lord. The face was of singular beauty, sorrowful in expression and yet shrouded with glory . . . The vision remained on the wall for many hours and was seen by hundreds of people, who flocked to see such an amazing sight' (*The Pentecostal Movement*, Elim, revised 1949, p.92).

54. Cf. Lindblom, *Prophecy* p.134.

55. See also Schweizer, *TDNT* VI pp.406f.; Kremer, *Pfingstbericht* pp.108, 216; Hull, *Hellenistic Magic* pp.87–96.

56. Kremer, *Pfingstbericht* pp.102, 113f.; wind – I Kings 19.11; Isa. 66.15; 4 Ezra 13.10; fire – Ex.3.2ff.; 13.21; 14.24; 19.18; 24.17; Num.14.14; Judg.6.21; I Kings 18.38; Isa.6.6; Ezek.1.13, 27; Dan.7.9f. For rabbinic parallels see J. Abelson, *The Immanence of God in Rabbinical Literature*, Macmillan 1912, pp.213–19.

57. πνεῦμα (*pneuma*) means both 'wind', 'breath' and 'spirit'.

58. Haenchen, *Acts* p. 174.

59. Cf. Schweizer, *TDNT* VI p. 411.

60. Cf. Dunn, *Baptism* pp. 41ff. Unfortunately these words attributed to the risen Jesus are too deeply embedded in Luke's schematization and theological representation of the resurrection appearances to allow us to use them as evidence of the disciples' pre-Pentecost expectation. The more certain promise of the Spirit by the historical Jesus (Mark 13.11 pars.; 14.38) is a promise of inspiration when on trial during (the final) persecution (see above p. 86).

61. Cf. Hopwood pp. 145f.

62. Against K. Haacker, 'Das Pfingstwunder als exegetisches Problem', *Verborum Veritas: Festschrift für G. Stählin*, hrsg. O. Böcher & K. Haacker, Wuppertal 1970, pp. 127f.

63. This question was first posed by Gregory of Nazianzus (Adler, *Pfingstfest* p. 3).

64. E.g. Adler, *Pfingstfest* pp. 93–118, and many Catholic and conservative commentators.

65. Schmidt, *Pfingsterzählung* pp. 17–23. To insist however that there is a contradiction between 'Judea' (v. 10) and foreign languages ('our own tongues' – v. 11) is exegesis of the pedant.

66. Adler, *Pfingstfest* p. 14. More or less the same view has more recently been proposed afresh by G. J. Sirks, 'The Cinderella of Theology: the Doctrine of the Holy Spirit', *HTR* 50, 1957, pp. 77–89, and adopted by C. S. Mann in J. Munck, *The Acts of the Apostles*, Anchor Bible 31, Doubleday 1967, p. 275.

67. Mann pp. 275, 272.

68. See e.g. H. E. Edwards, 'The Tongues at Pentecost: A Suggestion', *Theology* 16, 1928, pp. 248–52; F. F. Bruce, *The Acts of the Apostles*, Tyndale 1951, p. 82; in the nineteenth century cf. Wieseler cited by Zeller (as below n. 70) pp. 192f.

69. See H. A. W. Meyer, *The Acts of the Apostles*, ET T. & T. Clark 1877, pp. 67ff.

70. E. Zeller, *The Contents and Origin of the Acts of the Apostles Critically Investigated*, 1854, ET Williams & Norgate 1875, pp. 202ff. Strauss had already dismissed the Lukan account of the Pentecostal glossolalia = languages as 'a mythical modification' (*Life* §141).

71. The reappearance of glossolalia among the Irvingites in the 1830s had brought the subject into topical prominence; and the sustained outbreak of ecstatic prophecy among the Camisards at the end of the seventeenth and beginning of the eighteenth centuries was well remembered in Europe.

72. E. Trocmé, *Le 'Livre des Actes' et L'Histoire*, Paris 1957, p. 204; see also e.g. J. G. Davies, 'Pentecost and Glossolalia', *JTS NS* 3, 1952, pp. 228f.

73. A. Loisy, *Les Actes des Apôtres*, Paris 1920, pp. 184–95.

74. Besides, the distinction between Corinthian glossolalia and the glossolalia of Acts 2 is not at all clear. It is very probable that Paul thought γλῶσσαι meant 'languages'; see Davies, 'Pentecost' pp. 229–31; so Haacker p. 128; see further below §41.7.

75. Adler, *Pfingstfest* pp. 32–46; Lohse, 'Bedeutung' pp. 426f.

76. E.g. Lake, *Beginnings* V, note X. O. Betz, 'Zungenreden und süsser Wein', *Bibel und Qumran*, Festschrift für H. Bardtke, Berlin 1968, argues that 'the report of Acts 2 betrays the influence of an early Christian tradition based on Isa. 28' (pp. 29ff.); but the suggested indications are at best allusive.

77. E. Lombard, *De la glossolalie chez les premiers chrétiens et des phénomènes similaires*, Lausanne 1910; E. Mosiman, *Das Zungenreden*, Tübingen 1911. See also C.

Clemens, 'The "Speaking with Tongues" of the Early Christians', *ExpT* 10, 1898–99, pp. 344–52.

78. Schmidt, *Pfingsterzählung* pp. 28–32.

79. C. A. A. Scott, 'What Happened at Pentecost', *The Spirit*, ed. B. H. Streeter, Macmillan 1919, pp. 128f.; see also C. E. Raven, *The Creator Spirit*, Hopkinson 1927, p. 240.

80. Hopwood p. 160.

81. Williams, *Acts* p. 63; cf. J. B. Pratt, *The Religious Consciousness*, New York 1921, p. 183; A. L. Humphries, *The Holy Spirit in Faith and Experience*, SCM Press 1917, pp. 179f.; L. Dewer, 'The Problem of Pentecost', *Theology* 9, 1924, pp. 250–4. Notice also the comments of the linguist W. J. Samarin, *Tongues of Men and Angels*, Macmillan 1972, pp. 109–15.

82. G. B. Cutten, *Speaking with Tongues: Historically and Psychologically Considered*, Yale 1927, pp. 176ff.; see also Humphries pp. 178f. The case of Hélène Smith was well known at the turn of the century. Her automatic speech included snatches of several languages, including Sanskrit (see Cutten pp. 136–48).

83. See e.g. S. H. Frodsham, *With Signs Following*, Springfield 1946, ch. XXII; M. T. Kelsey, *Speaking with Tongues*, Epworth 1965, pp. 152–7, 162f.; J. L. Sherrill, *They Speak with Other Tongues*, Hodder & Stoughton 1965, pp. 13ff. D. and R. Bennett claim to know people who have spoken in tongues in Latin, Spanish, French, Hebrew, Old Basque, Japanese, Aramaic, Mandarin Chinese, German, Indonesian, Chinese Foochow dialect, NT Greek, English (non-English speaker) and Polish (*The Holy Spirit and You*, Logos 1971, pp. 91f.).

84. J. P. Kildahl, *The Psychology of Speaking in Tongues*, Hodder & Stoughton 1972: 'In the history of tongue-speaking there are no scientifically confirmed recordings of anyone speaking in a foreign language which he had never learned' (p. 39); Samarin: 'It is extremely doubtful that the alleged cases of xenoglossia among charismatics are real' (p. 112). So also Mosiman pp. 118ff.

85. Cf. Kremer, *Pfingstbericht*, who concludes that the tradition of foreign speech on the day of Pentecost was already in existence before Luke took it up (pp. 165f.).

86. So Schmidt, *Pfingsterzählung* pp. 27, 32 ('a grandiose mass ecstacy'); Behm, *TDNT* I p. 725; Lohse, 'Bedeutung' p. 436; Goppelt, *Apostolic Times* p. 22; cf. M. Dibelius, *Studies in the Acts of the Apostles*, ET SCM Press 1956, p. 106.

87. Adler, *Pfingstfest* pp. 65ff.

88. Dunn, *Baptism* pp. 91ff.

89. Cf. A. H. McNeile, *The Gospel according to St. Matthew*. Macmillan 1915, p. 435; Bornkamm, 'Matt. 28.16–20' pp. 203–29; U. Luck, 'Herrenwort und Geschichte in Matt. 28.16–20', *EvTh* 27, 1967, pp. 494–508; Schweizer, *Matthäus* p. 347. See also H. R. Boer, *Pentecost and Missions*, Lutterworth 1961, ch. 2.

90. See below pp. 170f. and §41.1

91. Modern Pentecostalism again provides us with one of the closest parallels. For example, according to one Pentecostal historian in reference to the events in Los Angeles in 1906: 'The baptism in the Holy Spirit made every one of them a preacher, a testifier to his own wondrous experience, a teller of the message' (C. Brumback, *Suddenly . . . from Heaven*, Springfield 1961, p. 64).

92. Cf. Dunn, *Baptism* pp. 60ff.

93. Cf. Dibelius, *Studies* pp. 109–22; Hahn, *Mission* p. 52; against Haenchen, *Acts* pp. 355–63.

94. Cf. Goppelt, *Apostolic Times* p. 70.

Chapter VII

1. Cf. Knox, *Enthusiasm* pp. 1–4.
2. See e.g. Conzelmann, *Luke* Part 2; Haenchen, *Acts* pp. 95–8; R. P. C. Hanson, *The Acts*, Oxford 1967, p. 45.
3. On the subject as a whole see also A. L. Moore, *The Parousia in the New Testament*, NovTestSuppl XIII, 1966, particularly chs. VII–XI.
4. See the discussion of the phrase in Hahn, *Titles* pp. 93–103. C. F. D. Moule, 'A Reconsideration of the Context of *Maranatha*', *NTS* 6, 1959–60, pp. 307–10, has demonstrated that it is unnecessary to confine the use of the phrase to a eucharistic context. See also C. J. Roetzel, *Judgment in the Community*, Leiden 1972, pp. 142–62.
5. Cf. Dunn, 'Jesus – Flesh and Spirit', *JTS NS* 24, 1973, p. 56. See also Matt. 27.51b–53 (above p. 118); and cf. Acts 4.2; 23.6.
6. See particularly Tödt pp. 269–74; D. Lührmann, *Die Redaktion der Logionquelle*, Neukirchen 1969, pp. 96f.; Hoffmann, *Logionquelle*, Erster Teil: Die Naherwartung; Schulz, *Q* pp. 57–76. See also E. Käsemann, 'The Beginnings of Christian Theology', *NTQT* pp. 82–107, with its provocative thesis that 'Apocalyptic was the mother of all Christian theology' (p. 102); and his reply in the subsequent debate, 'On the Subject of Primitive Christian Apocalyptic', *NTQT* pp. 110–37.
7. Luke 12.8f./(Matt. 10.32f.); Luke 11.30/(Matt. 12.40); Matt. 24.27/Luke 17.24; Matt. 24.37/Luke 17.26; Luke 17.30/(Matt. 24.39); Matt. 24.44/Luke 12.40. See also Mark 8.38 par.
8. Conzelmann, *Jesus* pp. 43–6; Perrin, *Teaching* pp. 164–202.
9. Bultmann, *Theology* I pp. 29f.; Bornkamm, *Jesus* pp. 175ff.; Hahn, *Titles* pp. 21–34; Fuller, *Foundations* pp. 119–25; Higgins, *Son of Man* pp. 200–3; cf. Jeremias, *Theology* I §23. See also n. 6 above.
10. See also above p. 142. Haenchen recognizes the eschatological significance of the ἐν ταῖς ἐσχάταις ἡμέραις and therefore prefers the otherwise weakly attested B reading, μετὰ ταῦτα, as the original text of 2.17: 'in Lucan theology the last days do not begin as soon as the Spirit has been outpoured!' (*Acts* p. 179). The reasoning here is up-side down. Μετὰ ταῦτα is certainly a correction of the longer phrase to bring it into line with the LXX. Had it been original the alteration to ἐν ταῖς ἐσχάταις ἡμέραις becomes incomprehensible.
11. See Wilckens, *Missionsreden* pp. 153f.; Hahn, *Titles* pp. 164f.; Kümmel, *Theology* p. 107; Bruce, 'Speeches' pp. 66ff.; cf. J. A. T. Robinson, 'The Most Primitive Christology of All?' *JTS NS* 7, 1956, pp. 177–89, reprinted in *Twelve New Testament Studies*, SCM Press 1962, pp. 139–52; against Haenchen, *Acts* p. 208; Conzelmann, *Apg.* pp. 34f.
12. On 11.17 see above p. 16 and n. 15; on 14.58 see below p. 186.
13. Bultmann, *Tradition* pp. 158; Tödt pp. 62ff.; cf. Goppelt, *Apostolic Times* p. 29.
14. For the debate on the origin and character of the Lord's Supper see particularly E. Schweizer, 'Abendmahl', *RGG*[3] I, revised as *The Lord's Supper according to the New Testament*, ET Fortress 1967; see also further below §33.1.
15. Kümmel, *Kirchenbegriff* pp. 19–25; also *Theology* pp. 128ff.; Bultmann, *Theology* I pp. 37f.; Jeremias, *Theology* I pp. 167f.
16. See Goppelt, *Apostolic Times* pp. 34f.; Hahn, *Mission* pp. 54ff.
17. Note the tense of 2.44f. – imperfect, '*used* to sell' – that is, not just one great sale, but rather 'they sold things as they had need of more money. They followed a policy of selling possessions' (Cadbury & Lake *Beginnings* IV p. 29).

18. Against Haenchen, *Acts* p.233.

19. A. Ehrhardt, *The Acts of the Apostles*, Manchester 1969, pp.20f.

20. Goppelt, *Apostolic Times* pp.49f.

21. IQSa 1.1; 4QpIs^c 10; 4QFlor.1.2, 15; see A. Dupont-Sommer, *The Essene Writings from Qumran*, ET Blackwell 1961, pp.264 n.6, 311 n.2; F. M. Cross Jnr, *The Ancient Library of Qumran*, Duckworth 1958, pp.82f.; and particularly H. W. Kuhn, *Enderwartung und gegenwärtiges Heil: Untersuchungen zu den Gemeindeliedern von Qumran*, Göttingen 1966.

22. IQpHab.2.5, 9.6; 4QpIs^a A.8; 4QpIs^b 2.1; 4QpHos^b 1.11(?); 4QFlor. 1.19.

23. CD 6.11; 4QFlor 1.11f.; 4QpIs^a D.1(?).

24. Cf. the essays by O. Cullmann and S. E. Johnson in K. Stendahl, *The Scrolls and the New Testament*, SCM Press 1958, pp.21, 131ff.; also M. H. Scharlemann, *Qumran and Corinth*, New York 1962; J. A. Fitzmeyer, 'Jewish Christianity in Acts in the Light of the Qumran Scrolls', *Studies in Luke Acts*, ed. L. E. Keck & J. L. Martyn, Abingdon 1966, pp.242ff.

25. Σημεῖα has been added to the Joel text by Luke or his source.

26. K. H. Rengstorf, *TDNT* VII pp.216, 221, 241.

27. We need not include the death of Herod (12.23) since it is not attributed to the Christian community. Luke takes up a Jewish or Christian tradition which interprets the death of Herod as an act of divine judgment. Cf. the variant tradition in Josephus, *Ant.* XIX.8.2 (344–50).

28. Luke probably thinks of Philip's removal in 8.39 as a miraculous transportation (cf. Haenchen, *Acts* p.313; Schweizer, *TDNT* VI p.409). But we should note Lindblom's remark: 'When in ecstasy a prophet suddenly disappears and departs to another place, it is said that he is taken away by the Spirit of Yahweh (I Kings 18.12)' (*Prophecy* p.57).

29. M. Bloch, *Les Rois Thaumaturges*, Paris 1924, describes the cures attributed particularly to the kings of England and France.

30. L. Rose, *Faith Healing*, Penguin 1971, offers a brief history. See also M. Kelsey, *Healing and Christianity*, SCM Press 1973. For details of the Pentecostals mentioned see Hollenweger, *Pentecostals* index. For another view on the subject reference may be made to B. B. Warfield, *Counterfeit Miracles*, Scribner 1918 – a classic of theological scepticism on the subject.

31. See e.g. Hopwood pp.165–70; Knox, *Enthusiasm*, index 'miraculous powers'; and above ch.IV nn.19, 21. For the second century see Weinel, *Wirkungen* pp. 111–15.

32. H. Bietenhard, *TDNT* V pp.243, 253ff.

33. Cf. W. Heitmüller, '*Im Namen Jesu*', Göttingen 1903, Zweiter Teil, especially pp.232–43.

34. The equivalence between the name of Jesus and Jesus himself is clear from such uses as 9.14, 16; 15.26; 19.17; 26.9; cf. particularly 8.12 and 8.35; 4.10 with 9.34.

35. Bietenhard p.277.

36. This sort of experience is fairly common in cases of faith or spiritual healing. E.g. Peddie, *Forgotten Talent*: 'The person ministering is always conscious of the power passing through (provided he has developed sufficient spiritual sensitivity) and the patient is aware of its presence from the strange heat or coldness that develops' (p.123). C. Wilson instances the case of Harry Edwards, the spiritualist healer, who 'describes the feeling of a power – a kind of fluid flowing down his arm and through his fingertips when he touches an affected part of the patient's body' (*Occult* p.180).

37. Cf. Cadbury & Lake, *Beginnings* IV p. 111.

38. Dibelius, *Studies* draws attention to 'the abundance of personal details' (pp. 12f.).

39. Cf. Cadbury & Lake, *Beginnings* IV pp. 256.; Dibelius, *Studies* p. 18.

40. See e.g. Fridrichsen, *Miracle* pp. 61f.; Haenchen, *Acts*: in 5.15 the 'idea of the Apostle is so heightened as to be fantastic' (p. 246); 19.11f. – 'Paul, already transfigured by legend' (p. 563).

41. Cf. above §12.3.

42. See Goguel, *Church* pp. 232–5; cf. the anathema of I Cor. 16.22 (above n. 4).

43. A. D. Nock in Lake & Cadbury, *Beginnings* V pp. 186ff.: 'So lame a story would not readily have been invented in Luke's time' (p. 188).

44. But see Cadbury & Lake, *Beginnings* IV p. 135 and the points made there in reference to literary parallels. Other references in Conzelmann, *Apg.* pp. 70f.

45. See above pp. 121f. and below §34.

46. Nine times in Acts; it appears no more than once in any other NT document.

47. On II Cor. 12.12 see below pp. 329f. Note too that Mark was probably written to correct a 'divine man' portrayal of Jesus (see above §12.1).

48. Cf. Schweizer, *TDNT* VI p. 407; also 'Spirit of Power' p. 266.

49. For the OT use of the phrase 'signs and wonders' see J. V. McCasland, 'Signs and Wonders', *JBL* 76, 1957, pp. 149–52.

50. See M. Whittaker, '"Signs and Wonders": the Pagan Background', *Studia Evangelica* V pp. 155f.; see further below §52.1.

51. Roloff, *Kerygma* pp. 190f.

52. Fridrichsen, *Miracle* p. 61; Hennecke, *Apocrypha* II pp. 173f. See also G. W. H. Lampe, 'Miracles in the Acts of the Apostles', *Miracles*, ed. C. F. D. Moule, Mowbray 1965, pp. 166f., 170ff.; Roloff, *Kerygma* pp. 193–200. The Lukan addition to the Q passage Matt. 11.2–6/Luke 7.18–23 serves the same purpose: the cures of v. 21 demonstrate (and validate?) the word of Matt. 11.5/Luke 7.22.

53. Nock, *Beginnings* V p. 188.

54. Haenchen, *Acts* pp. 432ff.; though contrast Acts 28.1–6 – 'The Malta episode (Acts 28.1–6) paints Paul in the colours of a θεῖος ἀνήρ (v. 6!)' (Roloff, *Kerygma* p. 192).

55. Contrast *The Acts of Peter* 23–32 in Hennecke, *Apocrypha* II pp. 306–16.

56. Cf. Fridrichsen, *Miracle*: 'the supernatural irresistibly imposed itself on the disciples and produced a state of mind which revelled in miracle' (p. 58).

57. See e.g. J. B. Phillips's preface to his translation of Acts, *The Young Church in Action*, Bles 1955.

58. Schweizer, *TDNT* VI pp. 407ff.: 'προφητεύειν is for Luke quite central as *the* work of the Spirit' (p. 408); cf. D. Hill, *Greek Words and Hebrew Meanings*, Cambridge 1967, pp. 260ff.

59. 'If the words (2.38c) were used in the Jewish sense this would mean "become prophets"' (Cadbury & Lake, *Beginnings* IV p. 26). G. Dix, *Confirmation or the Laying on of Hands*, *Theology* Occasional Papers 5, 1936, interpreted the laying on of hands in Acts 8.17 etc. as the ordination of prophets (p. 18).

60. *Numbers Rabbah* on Num. 11.17 – 'In this world few have prophesied, but in the world to come all Israelites will be prophets'. See I. Abrahams, *Studies in Pharisaism and the Gospels*, Second Series, Cambridge 1924, p. 127; Strack-Billerbeck II p. 134.

61. Cf. H. B. Swete, *The Holy Spirit in the New Testament*, Macmillan 1910, p. 377; Lindblom, *Gesichte* p. 179; E. E. Ellis, 'The Role of the Christian Prophet in Acts',

Apostolic History and the Gospel, F. F. Bruce Festschrift, ed. W. W. Gasque & R. P. Martin, Paternoster 1970, pp. 55f., 62f.

62. The tense of προφητεύουσαι (present, not aorist) indicates that the four daughters of Philip exercised the gift of prophecy regularly, not that they uttered a particular prophecy on that one occasion.

63. Cf. here too the early prophets of ancient Israel (Lindblom, *Prophecy* pp. 82f.) and *Didache* 11.7–13.1. See further below §48.1.

64. G. Friedrich, *TDNT* VI p. 849 n. 426.

65. Cf. Cothenet, *DBS* 8, 1972, 1280f., who considers also Stephen and Philip under the heading of 'prophets of the primitive community' (1281ff.).

66. See particularly Lindblom, *Prophecy*. Cf. Dunn, 'New Wine in Old Wine Skins: Prophet', *ExpT* 85, 1973–74, pp. 4–8; also above §14 and below §§41.2, 52.3.

67. Cf. Enoch 91.1; Josephus, *Ant.* XIII. 10.7.

68. Lindblom, *Gesichte* pp. 185f.

69. For a modern parallel I may refer to the word of prophecy which sent Ivan Veronaev (the apostle of Pentecostalism in Russia) back to Russia (Durasoff p. 222), or the vision and prophecy which sent evangelist Tommy Hicks to Argentina (P. Wagner, *Look Out! The Pentecostals are Coming*, Coverdale 1974, pp. 19–22).

70. See further Ellis, 'Prophet' pp. 56ff.

71. Cf. E. G. Selwyn, *The First Epistle of St Peter*, Macmillan 1946, pp. 259–68; and below.

72. καὶ τοῦ εὐαγγελίου being a Markan addition.

73. I am indebted for this suggestion to A. R. Bates, *Some Aspects of Prophecy in the New Testament and in the Early Church*, Manchester University M.A. thesis, 1971. Cf. particularly Rev. 11.2 and Wellhausen's suggestion that Rev. 11.1–2 originated as a Zealot prophecy (see R. H. Charles, *The Revelation of St John*, ICC 1920, I p. 270).

74. Cf. F. Hahn, 'Die Sendschreiben der Johannesapokalypse', *Tradition und Glaube*, Festgabe für K. G. Kuhn, Göttingen 1971, pp. 377ff. On the relation between prophecy and teaching see below pp. 186f.

75. Within Christian history see e.g. Weinel, *Wirkungen* pp. 83ff. In Polynesia the evocative term 'god-box' is used in describing the role of the shaman (Lewis, *Ecstatic Religion* p. 56). See also below p. 305.

76. Cf. D. Hill, 'Prophecy and Prophets in the Revelation of St John', *NTS* 18, 1971–72, pp. 403f.

77. G. Stählin, 'Τὸ πνεῦμα ᾿Ιησοῦ (Apostelgeschichte 16.7)', *CSNT* pp. 250f.

78. Cf. Wellhausen, *Matthaei* p. 44; Hahn, *Mission* pp. 54ff.

79. See e.g. Bultmann, *Tradition* p. 149; Manson, *Sayings* p. 211; Grundmann, *Matthäus* pp. 420f.

80. Cf. E. E. Ellis, 'Luke 11.49–51: An Oracle of a Christian Prophet?', *ExpT* 74, 1962–63, pp. 157f.; also *The Gospel of Luke*, Oliphants 1966, pp. 170f.

81. The most widely accepted suggestion has been that of E. Käsemann, 'Sentences of Holy Law in the New Testament', *NTQT* pp. 66–81. But see also K. Berger, 'Zu den sogennanten Sätzen heiligen Rechts', *NTS* 17, 1970–71, pp. 10–40.

82. I hope to take up this subject in a future study.

83. So Bultmann, *Tradition* pp. 127f., 150–63; Käsemann (n. 81); F. W. Beare, 'Sayings of the Risen Jesus in the Synoptic Tradition: an Inquiry into their Origin and Significance', *Christian History and Interpretation: Studies presented to John Knox*, ed. W. R. Farmer, C. F. D. Moule & R. R. Niebuhr, Cambridge 1967, pp. 161–81; Perrin, *Teaching* p. 15; H. M. Teeple, 'The Oral Tradition that Never Existed', *JBL* 89, 1970, pp. 56–68; Schulz, Q pp. 57ff.

84. See also F. Neugebauer, 'Geistsprüche und Jesuslogien', *ZNW* 53, 1962, pp. 218–28; Cothenet, *DBS* 8, 1972, 1285ff.; D. Hill, 'On the Evidence for the Creative Role of Christian Prophets', *NTS* 20, 1973–74, pp. 262–74; J. D. G. Dunn, 'Prophetic "I"-sayings and the Jesus Tradition: the Importance of Testing Prophetic Utterances within Early Christianity', forthcoming in *NTS*.

85. Lindblom, *Prophecy* pp. 122–37.

86. Cf. H. A. Guy, *New Testament Prophecy: its Origin and Significance*, Epworth 1947, p. 91.

87. See A. Oepke, *TDNT* III p. 575; J. L. Crenshaw, *Prophetic Conflict*, Berlin 1971.

88. In 20.29 the 'wolves' are all thought of as coming from outside.

89. Cf. Lindblom, *Gesichte* pp. 158f.

90. If the direction came in a voice speaking directly in his inner consciousness or in a prophecy it would have been attributed to the Spirit rather than to 'an angel' (cf. 16.6f.). Cf. also below ch. VIII n. 170.

91. For discussion of the significance of this vision for Luke see O. Betz, 'Die Vision des Paulus im Tempel von Jerusalem', *Verborum Veritas*, Stählin Festschrift, pp. 113–23.

92. The angel of 12.7–11 is more real and tangible (ἀληθές) to Peter than the risen Jesus is to Paul (12.9; 26.19)!

93. See Hopwood pp. 173–7, and above ch. V n. 134. Benz's survey includes accounts of visions of heavenly men and of Christ (also of the Trinity and of the Holy Spirit!) – *Vision* ch. VIII.

94. Cf. Benz, *Paulus als Visionär* pp. 11f.

95. Cf. e.g. Oepke, *TDNT* V pp. 230f. The problem of an authority which is rooted in visions is classically illustrated by Montanism: the belief that Pepuza would be the site of the heavenly Jerusalem originated in a vision (see Hennecke, *Apocrypha* II p. 687). Donald Gee records that at the International Pentecostal Convention, at Amsterdam in 1921, a new teaching sponsored by German preachers 'was reinforced by frequent visions of an extremely personal nature for those present and by prophecies' (*Pentecostal Movement* p. 12).

96. Cf. Stählin, *CSNT* pp. 229–51.

97. Gunkel p. 23.

98. Von Baer p. 42; but see above n. 90.

99. For the debate initiated by R. Sohm and A. Harnack see below §47.1.

100. Thus A. M. Farrer, 'The Ministry in the New Testament', *The Apostolic Ministry*, ed. K. E. Kirk, Hodder & Stoughton 1946, pp. 133–42; cf. R. C. Moberly, *Ministerial Priesthood*, John Murray ²1910, ch. V; A. Ehrhardt, *The Apostolic Ministry*, *SJT* Occasional Papers No. 7, 1958, pp. 21–8.

101. Cf. Bultmann, *Theology* I pp. 37, 58f.

102. E. Lohse, 'Ursprung und Prägung des christlichen Apostolates', *TZ* 9, 1953, pp. 265f.

103. Cf. S. G. F. Brandon, *The Fall of Jerusalem and the Christian Church*, SPCK 1951, pp. 48ff.

104. See e.g. W. L. Knox, *St Paul and the Church of Jerusalem*, Cambridge 1925, pp. 48f.; Haenchen, *Acts* pp. 264–9; Goppelt, *Apostolic Times* pp. 53ff.

105. D. Daube, *The New Testament and Rabbinic Judaism*, London 1956, pp. 237ff.

106. See also above §27. Elsewhere in Acts laying on of hands is the expression of charismatic authority rather than of any formal authority (8.17f.; 9.12, 17; 13.3; 19.6; 28.8).

107. Why does Luke tell us absolutely nothing about James's conversion and rise to leadership? Here is one of Luke's most tantalizing silences.

108. Meyer, *Ursprung* III pp. 224ff.; B. H. Streeter, *The Primitive Church*, Macmillan 1930, pp. 38ff.; cf. Goguel, *Birth* pp. 110–8.

109. G. Bornkamm, *TDNT* VI pp. 66of. On the question of possible influence from Qumran on the early community's organization see Fitzmeyer, 'Jewish Christianity' pp. 244–50.

110. Cf. A. Schlatter: 'For the "pneumatic" there was no room in the Palestine synagogue' (cited by R. B. Hoyle, *The Holy Spirit in St Paul*, Hodder & Stoughton 1927, p. 208). The 'false apostles' of II Cor. 10–13 (from Jerusalem) certainly displayed charismatic gifts, but they had probably adapted themselves to the situation at Corinth in order to commend themselves to the Corinthians (see below ch. IX n. 39).

111. See e.g. von Campenhausen, *Authority* p. 77; Bornkamm, *TDNT* VI pp. 664f; Haenchen, *Acts* p. 436; Goppelt, *Apostolic Times* pp. 186f.; H. Küng, *The Church*, ET Burns & Oates 1968, p. 405; Stühlmacher, *KuD* 17, 1971, p. 35; K. Kertelge, *Gemeinde und Amt im Neuen Testament*, München 1972, p. 99.

112. Cf. Scott's too strong assertion: 'The disciples rejected the very idea of organisation' (*Spirit* p. 109).

113. Early Pentecostalism was notable for its distrust of forms and unwillingness to organize itself (Brumback, *Suddenly* ch. 11).

114. The breakdown of the equation, 'the twelve' = 'the apostles', undermines the otherwise neatly argued distinction of J. L. Leuba, *L'institution et l'evénement*, Neuchatel 1950, Part II, between the 'institutional' apostleship of the twelve and the 'charismatic' apostleship of Paul.

115. Cf. Hahn, *Worship* p. 35.

116. Cf. C. F. D. Moule, *Worship in the New Testament*, Lutterworth 1961, pp. 18f.

117. Beasley-Murray, *Baptism* pp. 93–9.

118. Cf. Bultmann, *Theology* I p. 39.

119. See further Dunn, *Baptism* pp. 96–101.

120. Cf. Munck, *Paul* p. 18 n. 1.

121. Jeremias, *Eucharistic Words* pp. 207–17; *Theology* I p. 137, 289f. That fasting played a role in the early Christian communities is implied by Mark 2.20 – but how important a role and how eschatological in significance, we cannot say.

122. See above pp. 158f.; but see also n. 4.

123. Jeremias, *Eucharistic Words*; *Theology* I pp. 288ff.; Schweizer, *Supper*, pp. 10–17.

124. The thesis that Paul's language denotes a word received from the Lord by direct revelation has rightly received little support. See e.g. Jeremias, *Eucharistic Words* pp. 101ff.; O. Cullmann, *The Early Church* ET SCM Press 1956, pp. 6off.; G. Bornkamm, 'Lord's Supper and Church in Paul', *Early Christian Experience*, ET SCM Press 1969, pp. 130ff.

125. Cf. O. Cullmann, *Early Christian Worship*, ET SCM Press 1953, pp. 15–19.

126. Too much significance should not be read into the words of Jesus in the encounter with Paul on the Damascus road: 'Why do you persecute *me*?'; against Robinson, *Body* p. 58; see also D. E. H. Whiteley, *The Theology of St Paul*, Blackwell 1964, pp. 193f.

127. Isa. 53, where alluded to, is used for its suffering-vindication pattern rather than for what it says about the suffering as vicarious; cf. Conzelmann, *Luke* p. 230 n. 1; otherwise Bruce, 'Speeches' pp. 6off.

128. There are no grounds for describing the 'breaking of the bread' in Acts 2.46

as 'a fixed designation in the Church's language for a sacramental meal'. Nor is that phrase as such intended as a parallel to the attendance at the temple observances (Goppelt, *Apostolic Times* p.'45). The 'breaking of the bread' means simply a *shared* meal (2.46c), *not* a *sacramental* meal as such. Thus rightly Cadbury & Lake on 27.35: 'It would be absurd to see in this passage any reference to the Eucharist' (*Beginnings* IV p.336; cf. Bultmann, *Theology* I pp.57f.; Haenchen, *Acts* p.707 n.3; against J. Dupont in J. Delorme *et. al.*, *The Eucharist in the New Testament*, ET Chapman 1965, pp.117ff.).

129. H. Lietzmann, *Mass and Lord's Supper: A Study in the History of the Liturgy*, ET Leiden 1953–) pp.204–8; W. Marxsen, *The Lord's Supper as a Christological Problem*, ET Fortress 1970.

130. Moule is more confident of the meal's original *sacramental* significance (*Worship* pp.20ff.).

131. On the role of the scribes within Judaism at the time of Jesus see Jeremias, *Jerusalem* pp.233–45.

132. Rengstorf, *TDNT* II p.157. There is however no direct evidence that readings from the OT were part of the early Christian worship (G. Delling, *Worship in the New Testament*, ET Darton, Longman & Todd 1962, pp.92ff.); though see also A. Schlatter, *The Church in the New Testament Period*, ET SPCK 1955, pp.63–8.

133. Cf. the Qumran sect's concern to understand the OT appropriately, as evidenced particularly by their commentaries.

134. Against particularly B. Gerhardsson, *Memory and Manuscript*, Uppsala 1961, Part II. 'The teaching of the *apostles*' is an anachronism arising from Luke's equation of 'the twelve' with 'the apostles' whereby he gives 'the twelve' more of a leadership role than they seem actually to have exercised. Bultmann however is sufficiently certain of their role to describe them as 'proclaimers of the word and guardians of the tradition' (*Theology* I p.59).

135. See also Goppelt, *Apostolic Times* pp.43f.; and below §41.4.

136. See Kümmel, *Introduction* pp.287f.

137. See particularly Hahn, *Mission* p.37 n.1. The life-setting of the saying is fully discussed by L. Gaston, *No Stone on Another*, NovTestSuppl XXIII, 1970, who reaches somewhat different conclusions (ch.3).

138. Cf. Hahn, *Worship* p.49.

139. For the equivalence of the terms 'interpreter' and 'prophet' in Philo see E. R. Goodenough, *By Light, Light*, New Haven 1935, p.193 n.70; H. A. Wolfson, *Philo*, Harvard 1947, II pp.40–3. See e.g. Philo's account of the translation of the Law into Greek (LXX) particularly *Vit.Mos.*II.31, 34 with II.37. See also Georgi, *Gegner* pp.127ff.; Ellis, 'Prophet' pp.58–64.

140. Cf. the *pesher* form at Qumran as evidenced most clearly in the Habakkuk commentary.

141. See below §§41.2; 47.3; 48.1, 2; 49.2.

142. See Hahn, *Worship* p.47 n.26; cf. A. B. Macdonald, *Christian Worship in the Primitive Church*, T. & T. Clark 1934, pp.33f.; Delling, *Worship* pp.61–70.

143. H. Greeven, *TDNT* II p.803.

144. See further Delling, *Worship* pp.117ff. Even in Paul, prayer, praise and adoration is regularly to God *through* or *in the name of* Jesus, not *to* Jesus (cf. Moule, *Worship* p.71). See also Greeven, *TDNT* II p.806.

145. D. R. Jones, 'The Background and Character of the Lukan Psalms', *JTS NS* 19, 1968, p.48. Other references in Hahn, *Worship* p.48 n.28.

146. Jeremias, *Eucharistic Words* p.120; so B. Reicke, 'Some Reflections on Worship

in the New Testament', *New Testament Essays: Studies in Memory of T. W. Manson*, Manchester 1959, pp. 204f.

147. Cf. Haenchen, *Acts* p. 191; F. Mussner, 'Die Una Sancta nach Apg. 2.42', *Praesentia Salutis: Gesammelte Studien zu Fragen und Themen des Neuen Testamentes*, Patmos 1967, pp. 212–22.

148. Hahn, *Worship*: 'The "unified worship" repeatedly assumed to have existed throughout primitive Christianity is not very likely. The separate existence of a worship service consisting of word of God and prayer can hardly be disputed' (p. 72); cf. Macdonald, *Worship* p. 47; Reicke, 'Worship' p. 206; against Cullmann, *Worship* pp. 26–32.

149. Cf. Delling, *Worship* p. 24. 'The word characterizes the consciousness of the community that it is the community of the last time . . .' (Bultmann, *TDNT* I p. 20). 'Unless one can understand this constant mood of victorious, jubilant happiness and confidence, he simply will not understand primitive Christianity' (Weiss, *Earliest Christianity* p. 41). Hopwood appositely cites James: 'The most characteristic of all the elements of the conversion crisis . . . is the ecstasy of happiness produced' – with examples (pp. 191f.).

150. The description of the building where they were gathered being shaken in response to their prayer (4.31) should not be dismissed as a literary convention; cf. Isa. 6.4. A striking parallel occurs in Duncan Campbell's description of *The Lewis Awakening (1949–53)*: 'There are those in Arnol today who will bear witness to the fact that, while a brother prayed, the very house shook. I could only stand in silence as wave after wave of Divine power swept through the house, and in a matter of minutes following this heaven-sent visitation, men and women were on their faces in distress of soul' (*God's Answer*, Edinburgh 1960, p. 78). See also the passages from George Fox's *Journal* in Hopwood p. 156.

151. Or, if an answer in terms of experience be eschewed, in various forms of ecclesiasticism or biblicism. See also below ch. X n. 181.

152. Brumback, *Suddenly* p. 23, quoting J. R. Flower, a leading figure in the American Assemblies of God from 1914 to 1959. In Pentecostal and neo-Pentecostal literature see e.g. Brumback, *What Meaneth This?*, Springfield 1947, chs. 10–19; R. M. Riggs, *The Spirit Himself*, Springfield 1949, ch. 11; M. C. Harper, *Power for the Body of Christ*, Fountain Trust 1964, pp. 32ff.; L. Christenson, *Speaking in Tongues and its Significance for the Church*, Fountain Trust 1968, pp. 52ff.

153. Cf. Adler, *Pfingstfest* p. 111.

154. It is not actually described in 2.38ff. or 9.17ff.; 4.8, 31 and 13.9 describe *further* 'fillings'.

155. Cf. e.g. Meyer, *Ursprung*: 'The characteristic manifestation (of the "Holy Spirit" in the primitive community) is the utterance of unintelligible sounds, the "speaking in tongues"' (III p. 221).

156. 9.31 and 13.52 are only formal exceptions. 'In Luke's view, *the* gift of the Spirit is the power for missionary enterprise, not church cohesion or a quality of Christian living' (Hill, *Greek Words* p. 265); cf. Schweizer, *TDNT* VI p. 408.

157. Cf. Dunn, *Baptism* pp. 70ff.

158. J. H. E. Hull, *The Holy Spirit in the Acts of the Apostles*, Lutterworth 1967, p. 107; see also Schweizer, *TDNT* VI pp. 407ff.

159. E.g. Spiritualism, Mormonism. Cf. F. C. Goodman, 'Speaking in Tongues', *New Society* 7, 1972, pp. 565f. Though note Samarin's hypothesis – *Tongues* p. 222.

160. Cf. Gunkel pp. 6–20.

161. I have witnessed such counselling.

162. F. M. Davenport, *Primitive Traits in Religious Revivals*, Macmillan 1905.

163. Examples from Wesley's *Journal* in Hopwood pp. 184f.

164. W. Gibson, *The Year of Grace: A History of the Ulster Revival of 1859*, Edinburgh 1860.

165. M. Warren, *Revival: An Enquiry*, SCM Press 1954, pp. 63ff.

166. W. Sargent, *Battle for the Mind*, Pan Books 1959, notes that an individual undergoing Freudian analysis may well have dreams of a Freudian type; while the same type of person, or even the same patient, who (then) attends a Jungian analyst will often dream Jungian 'collective subconscious' dreams (p. 67).

167. 'In London alone I found 652 members of our Society who were exceeding clear in their experience, and whose testimony I could see no reason to doubt. And every one of these (without a single exception) has declared that his deliverance from sin was instantaneous; that the change was wrought in a moment. Had half of these, or one third, or one in twenty, declared that it was *gradually* wrought in *them*, I should have believed this, with regard to *them*, and thought that *some* were gradually sanctified and some instantaneously. But as I have not found, in so long a space of time, a single person speaking thus, I cannot but believe that sanctification is commonly, if not always, an instantaneous work' (Tyerman's *Life of Wesley* I p. 463, quoted by James, *Varieties* p. 229).

168. Brumback, *Suddenly* pp. 216ff.

169. Knox, *Enthusiasm* chs. 15 and 16.

170. The chronicler of the 1742 Cambuslang revival (near Glasgow) attempts to give these scriptural justification and precedent by referring to Zech. 12.10 and the conversions of the day of Pentecost (Acts 2): 'It is true we are not told of bodily agitations; but this was not to be expected in so brief a history, nor was it necessary, as these are merely the natural effects of such feelings as are here expressed' (D. Macfarlan, *The Revivals of the Eighteenth Century particularly at Cambuslang*, John Johnstone, p. 67).

171. B. G. M. Sundkler, *Bantu Prophets in South Africa*, Oxford ²1961, pp. 267ff.: 'To be converted, one must see visions' (p. 267).

172. Contrast his handling of the earliest Christians' belief in an imminent parousia (§29 above), the way he gives expression to his concept of apostleship (see above pp. 99f., 143), and his attempts to disguise the divisions and diversity within earliest Christianity (see above pp. 181f.).

173. For the authenticity of the Baptist's prediction see above ch. III n. 118.

174. Not to mention the other matters indicated above in n. 172.

Chapter VIII

1. See e.g. C. H. Dodd, 'The Mind of Paul', *New Testament Studies*, Manchester 1953, pp. 67–128; but see also C. F. D. Moule, 'The Influence of Circumstances on the Use of Eschatological Terms, *JTS NS* 15, 1964, pp. 1–15.

2. A. Deissmann, *Religion*, pp. 153ff.; *Paul: A Study in Social and Religious History*, ²1925, ET 1927, Harper 1957, pp. 135f. Cf. Gardner, *Paul*, p. 175; Bousset, *Kyrios Christos* pp. 153–63; Weiss, *Earliest Christianity* p. 441; Hoyle pp. 277, 291; Weinel, *Theologie* p. 286. See also above pp. 4f.

3. Otto, *Holy* p. 91. It is worth extending the quotation: 'The recipient of divine

grace feels and knows ever more and more surely, as he looks back on his past, that he has not grown into his present self through any achievement or effort of his own, and that, apart from his own will or power, grace was imparted to him, grasped him, impelled, and led him. And even the resolves and decisions that were most his own and most free become to him, without losing the element of freedom, something that he *experienced* rather than *did*'.

4. Gunkel p.82.

5. *Baptism* Part III.

6. See J. Behm, *TDNT* III pp.611ff.; Bultmann, *Theology* I pp.220–7; W. D. Stacey, *The Pauline View of Man*, Macmillan 1956, pp.194–7; R. Jewett, *Paul's Anthropological Terms*, Leiden 1971, ch.VI.

7. Schweizer, *TDNT* VI p.423. Paul speaks (Gal.3.2ff.) 'as if the reception of the Spirit was something as definite and observable as, for example, an attack of influenza' (Streeter, *Church* p.69). Cf. O. Kuss, *Der Römerbrief*, Regensburg 1957, 1959, p.551.

8. See Dunn, *Baptism* pp.129ff., 133f., 149 *et passim* for fuller exposition of these passages.

9. H. Conzelmann, *TDNT* IX p.393; see also J. Moffatt, *Grace in the New Testament*, Hodder & Stoughton 1931, pp.131–296; P. Bonnetain appropriately describes Paul's theology as 'charitocentric' (*DBS* III 1002). The Pauline letters use χάρις 100 times as against 55 for the rest of the NT (not at all in Matthew and Mark, and in the Fourth Gospel only in the prologue).

10. Bultmann, *Theology* I p.289. For analysis of χάρις see and cf. particularly G. P. Wetter, *Charis*, Leipzig 1913.

11. See Wetter, *Charis*, e.g. pp.40f., 71f., 96f., 104f.; cf. Bultmann, *Theology* I pp.290f.; G. Stählin, *RGG*[3] II 1635f.

12. Note the parallelism between 'grace' and 'power' in this verse.

13. Moffatt, *Grace* p.179. J. Wobbe, *Der Charis-Gedanke bei Paulus*, Münster 1932, justifiably draws attention to the close connection between charis and chara (χαρά – joy) implied in several Pauline passages (pp.14f.).

14. Moffatt, *Grace* pp.136–43.

15. Cf. Wetter, *Charis* pp.97f.; cf. also Wobbe pp.50–7.

16. Rom.12.6–8 is slightly obscure since it is a sentence without a finite verb; see e.g. C. K. Barrett, *The Epistle to the Romans*, A. & C. Black 1957, p.237.

17. Χάρις here probably means 'inspired liberality'. NEB translates 'the grace of generosity'; see also Wobbe p.58.

18. Wetter, *Charis* pp.26f.; Wobbe pp.40–6; cf. Bultmann, *Theology* I pp.290f.

19. Cf. Conzelmann, *Outline* p.213 (though the point is expressed misleadingly).

20. Wetter, *Charis* pp.14, 21ff.; cf. Wobbe pp.18ff.

21. Does Paul speak of 'my grace' in Phil.1.7 (συνκοινωνούς μου τῆς χάριτος)? The answer is uncertain. The phrase could be rendered either 'partakers with me of grace' (RSV), or 'share in the privilege that is mine' (NEB). For contrasting views see M. R. Vincent, *Philippians and Philemon*, ICC 1897, p.10, and E. Lohmeyer, *Die Briefe an die Philipper, Kolosser und an Philemon*, KEK [13]1964 = [8]1930, p.25 n.2. In either case 'grace' denotes Paul's ministry recognized in all its aspects (including his time in prison) as an outworking of God's grace.

22. Wetter, *Charis* p.99.

23. Ecclus.7.33; 38.30; Theodotian also uses it once, in his translation of Ps.30.22, where LXX translates with ἔλεος, See F. Grau, *Der neutestamentliche Begriff χάρισμα*, Tübingen dissertation 1946, pp.13–21.

24. Hasenhüttl pp. 105f.
25. Philo, *Leg.All.* III.78.
26. Moffatt, *Grace* pp. 114f.
27. Arndt & Gingrich, χάρισμα; Conzelmann, *TDNT* IX pp. 402f.
28. Grau §§8, 9; E. Schweizer, *Church Order in the New Testament*, ET SCM Press 1961, nn. 377, 519.
29. Cf. Wetter, *Charis* pp. 174ff.
30. Conzelmann, *TDNT* IX p. 404 and n. 18; NEB translates 'God's act of grace'. Cf. Grau p. 75.
31. So most; against Conzelmann, *TDNT* IX p. 404 and n. 16: to argue that the meaning 'gracious intervention is nowhere else attested' is to beg the question on the basis of a very small sample.
32. Grau's interpretation here is somewhat strained (pp. 72f.).
33. See especially Grau pp. 64–9.
34. E.g. Wobbe p. 66; Käsemann, *ENTT* pp. 69f.; Bruce, *Cor.* p. 68; J. Ruef, *Paul's First Letter to Corinth*, Penguin 1971, p. 55.
35. Lietzmann in Lietzmann-Kümmel, *Kor.* p. 30; Grau pp. 67f.; Barrett, *I Cor.* pp. 158f. For history of religion parallels to the belief that continence is a divine gift see Weiss, *I Kor.* p. 176 n. 1; Kirk, *Vision* index 'celibacy', 'continence'.
36. Cf. Barrett, *Romans* p. 225.
37. Delling thinks the gift 'is undoubtedly primarily teaching' (*Worship* p. 154), without giving adequate justification.
38. Since the 12.8–10 kind of charismata are so clearly in mind (cf. 1.5 with 12.8), ὑστερεῖσθαι is better translated as 'lack' rather than 'fall short of' (cf. Conzelmann, *I Kor.* pp. 41f.; against Barrett, *I Cor.* p. 38). For fuller treatment of the passages see particularly Grau pp. 58–64.
39. R. Reitzenstein, *Die hellenistischen Mysterienreligionen*, Leipzig ³1927, pp. 70ff., 311, 319.
40. See further below §40.4 particularly p. 219.
41. See Dunn, *CSNT* pp. 127ff.
42. Cf. H. Schlier, *Die Brief an die Epheser*, Patmos 1957, p. 44.
43. Cf. Wetter, *Charis* p. 169.
44. The threefold use of *pneumatikos* is I Cor. 10.3f. is slightly different, having more the sense of 'allegorical' (cf. Rev. 11.8 – πνευματικῶς). The events of the Exodus and of the wilderness wanderings can be taken as representative of the realities of life in the Spirit, depicting the spiritual sustenance received from Christ the life-giving Spirit (see also Dunn, *Baptism* pp. 125ff.). Cf. I Peter 2.5; Ignatius, *Eph.* 11.2; *Magn.* 13.1.
45. E. E. Ellis, 'Christ and Spirit in I Corinthians', *CSNT* p. 274; also, '"Spiritual" Gifts in the Pauline Community', *NTS* 20, 1973–74, pp. 128ff., argues that πνεῦμα and πνευματικά are used in I Cor. 12.1ff., 14, in a more restricted sense of 'spirit of prophecy' and 'gifts of inspired utterance or discernment'. This is possible; but would Paul withhold the title *pneumatika* from Spirit-inspired acts (12.9f., 28) or the title *pneumatikos* from those whose charismata were acts of service?; and note the further parallel τὰ χαρισθέντα = πνευματικά (I Cor. 2.12f.). See further below ch. IX n. 142.
46. Τῶν πνευματικῶν in 12.1 could refer to either spiritual men (masculine – οἱ πνευματικοί) or spiritual gifts (neuter – τὰ πνευματικά). In view of the subsequent discussion and particularly 14.1, the neuter sense is to be preferred. Paul probably takes up a question from (some of) the Corinthians about the role (and abuse) of

the *pneumatika*. So most commentators; otherwise Weiss, *I Kor.* pp. 294, 321 n. 3; Schmithals, *Gnosticism* pp. 171f.; J. C. Hurd, *The Origin of I Corinthians*, SPCK 1965, p. 194. In the event there is little difference in the sense (Barrett, *I Cor.* p. 278).

47. Conzelmann, *I Kor.* p. 241. The thesis that Paul is critical of Corinthian use of the word πνευματικά (D. J. Doughty, 'The Priority of ΧΑΡΙΣ', *NTS* 19, 1972–73, p. 178) could be sustained only if 14.1 is seen as the reworking of an editor who inserted I Cor. 13 (cf. Héring, *I Cor.* p. 145). But see below ch. IX n. 37.

48. E. Käsemann, *An die Römer*, HNT 1974: 'χάρισμα is the πνευματικόν taken into Christ's service' (p. 318).

49. The other Pauline use of τὰ πνευματικά (Eph. 6.12 – pertaining to evil spirits – Arndt & Gingrich, πνευματικός) confirms that πνευματικός has a more ambiguous meaning in Paul's mind.

50. In view of 12.11 the primary meaning of διαιρέσεις is probably 'distributions' (see particularly Robertson-Plummer, *I Cor.* pp. 262f.); but in view of 12.8–10 and the parallel Rom. 12.6–8 it is hard to exclude the sense 'varieties'.

51. The association of charismata with the Spirit, of services with Jesus the Lord, and of action with God in vv. 4–6, is perhaps deliberate (the Spirit who gives, the Lord who serves, the God who acts; cf. Weiss, *I Kor.* p. 297; I. Hermann, *Kyrios und Pneuma*, München 1961, pp. 72ff.), though whether the verses are arranged to form a climax is not so clear (cf. Conzelmann, *TDNT* IX p. 405).

52. G. Bertram, *TDNT* II pp. 652ff. In Paul see particularly: divine – I Cor. 12.6, 11; Gal. 2.8; 3.5; Eph. 1.11, 19f.; 3.7, 20; Phil. 2.13; 3.21; Col. 1.29; 2.12; I Thess. 2.13; demonic – Eph. 2.2; II Thess. 2.7, 9 – though note also II Thess. 2.11.

53. Similarly ἐνέργεια and ἐνεργέω in Gal. 2.8; 3.5; 5.6; Eph. 1.19; 3.7, 20; 4.16; Col. 1.29; I Thess. 2.13.

54. The same is true of διακονία, φανέρωσις and faith; see below §§ 39.4, 40.1, and 42.

55. For definition of 'miracle' see above ch. IV n. 3.

56. In view of Paul's disparagement of 'signs and wonders' in II Cor. 12.12 (see below § 55) some have argued that Paul could have performed no miracles during his ministry – the 'signs and wonders' of Rom. 15.19 referring only to 'the wonder of the proclamation of the gospel' (H. D. Betz, *Der Apostel Paulus und die sokratische Tradition: Eine exegetische Untersuchung zu seiner 'Apologie' II Korinther* 10–13, Tübingen 1972, p. 71; cf. Haenchen, *Acts* pp. 113f., 563). But Paul clearly does claim to have performed *dunameis* in both Rom. 15.19 and II Cor. 12.12, even though he puts no weight on them as proof of divine approval or the like.

57. See above p. 72.

58. Weiss, *I Kor.* p. 301; Grundmann, *TDNT* II p. 315; Héring, *I Cor.* p. 126; Grau p. 221; Hasenhüttl p. 146 n. 37.

59. Barrett, *I Cor.* p. 286.

60. Cf. Peddie, *Forgotten Talent*: 'During a service with the laying on of hands, the volume of power is modified in various ways, gradually increasing in strength and when enough has been ministered gradually decreasing until it is completely withdrawn. This is the time when the hand should be lifted and placed on another part if necessary. Then if needed the power will return . . . When the power expresses itself in coldness (see above ch. VII n. 36), it is nerve treatment that is being given . . .' (pp. 122ff.).

61. So too probably 'faith' in II Cor. 8.7 = charismatic faith (cf. Acts 6.5). However, we should not draw too sharp a line between charismatic faith and 'justifying faith', since Paul thinks of 'faith' in general as something that can wax and wane (cf. Rom. 1.17; 4.20; 14.1; II Cor. 10.15; I Thess. 3.10; II Thess. 1.3); cf. A.

Schlatter, *Der Glaube im Neuen Testament*, Stuttgart [5]1963, p.383; also *Paulus der Bote Jesu*, Stuttgart 1934, p.341; Büchsel, *Geist* pp.308–11; Grau pp.218f.; H. D. Wendland, *Die Briefe an die Korinther*, NTD [10]1964, p.94; Hasenhüttl p.145.

62. Against Schmithals, *Gnosticism* pp.172f.

63. F. Prat, *The Theology of St Paul* I, ET Burns & Oates 1945: 'an invincible confidence, founded on theological faith and assured by a supernatural instinct, that God, in a given case, will manifest his power, his justice, or his mercy' (p.426).

64. Some striking examples are claimed for the ministry of the Pentecostalist William Branham; see G. Lindsay, *William Branham, a Man sent from God*, Jeffersonville 1950. But note also Oral Roberts' candid admission that many of his prayers of faith had failed to produce any healing. 'Incomprehensible were the apparent failures after he prayed with great confidence and the supernatural healings which occurred following his barren prayers. . . . More people had been prayed for by him who were not healed than by any man in the world' (Durasoff pp.129f.).

65. Just as 'services', 'workings' and 'manifestation' (I Cor.12.5ff.) cover all charismata as well as having special reference to particular charismata; see above n.54.

66. 'Measure' (μέτρον) certainly denotes that Paul is thinking of charismatic faith rather than justifying faith – and of the diversity of such gifts of faith (ἐμέρισεν ἑκάστῳ). In fact the gift of faith in this context is almost synonymous with the gift of grace (cf. 12.6a with 6b and Eph.4.7), both implying a consciousness of enabling in a particular instance (cf. K. Deissner, *TDNT* IV p.634; H. Lietzmann, *An die Römer*, HNT [5]1971, p.109; Barrett, *Romans* pp.235, 238; H. W. Schmidt, *Der Brief an die Römer*, THNT 1963, pp.209f.). Note also the comment of O. Michel, *Der Brief an die Römer*, KEK [12]1963: 'In this allocation lies an act of grace but also a particular commission' (p.296). For other ways of taking the phrase 'measure of faith' see C. E. B. Cranfield, '*Μέτρον πίστεως* in Romans 12.3', *NTS* 8, 1961–62, pp. 345–51; also *A Commentary on Romans* 12–13, *SJT* Occasional Papers No. 12, 1965, pp.23–7.

67. Cranfield's objection to this interpretation of 'measure of faith' misses the point: 'the implication would be that a Christian is to think of himself more highly than he thinks of his fellow Christian who has a smaller quantity of faith' (*Commentary* p.24). The 'sober estimate' involves the recognition of the diversity (not superiority; cf. I Cor.12.14–26) of the charismata and the corresponding faith, and the conscious acknowledgment that both charisma and faith to exercise it are given by God.

68. F. J. Leenhardt, *The Epistle to the Romans*, ET Lutterworth 1961: 'The expression should neither fall short of nor exceed the controlling inspiration' (p.310). Cf. G. Kittel, *TDNT* I pp.347f.; E. Gaugler, *Der Brief and die Römer*, Zürich 1952, II pp. 243f.; Delling, *Worship* p.31. The earlier view that Rom. 12.6b referred to 'the standard of the faith' – 'the faith' being the body of truth to be believed – cannot stand in view of 12.3 (see above n.66), although it is still found in M. J. Lagrange, *Épitre aux Romains*, EB 1950, p.299; cf. Bultmann, *TDNT* VI p.213. See also A. Schlatter, *Gottes Gerechtigkeit*, Stuttgart 1935, pp.339f.

69. Cf. Weiss, *I Kor.* p.298; Schlatter, *Bote* p.338; Lührmann, *Offenbarung.* p.28; R. Bultmann/D. Lührmann, *TDNT* IX p.6.

70. These verses show that φανερόω, ἀποκαλύπτω and γνωρίζω (make known) are all synonymous at this point. See also Rom.3.21; Col.3.4 (φανερόω); Rom.1.17; 8.18; Gal.3.23 (ἀποκαλύπτω); Rom. 2.5; 8.19; I Cor.1.7; II Thess. 1.7 (ἀποκάλυψις); Eph.

1.9; 6.19 (γνωρίζω); also φωτίζω (enlighten) – I Cor.4.5; Eph.3.9; and particularly μυστήριον (mystery) – Rom.11.25; I Cor.2.7; 4.1; Eph.1.9; 3.9; 6.19; Col.2.2; 4.3. For Jewish background and parallels to Paul's concept of 'mystery' see R. E. Brown, *The Semitic Background of the Term "Mystery" in the New Testament*, Fortress 1968; J. Coppens, '"Mystery" in the Theology of Saint Paul and its Parallels at Qumran', *Paul and Qumran*, ed. J. Murphy-O'Connor, Chapman 1968, pp.132–56.

71. Emphasized in Col.1.26f.; 2.2; 4.3; Eph.1.9; 3.4; but already implicit in the equation, Christ = wisdom – I Cor.1.30; 2.1 (p46א* etc.); 2.7.

72. Cf. G. Bornkamm, *TDNT* IV pp.819ff.; A. Oepke, *TDNT* III pp.584f.

73. Cf. R. Bultmann, 'Revelation in the New Testament', *Existence and Faith*, ET Fontana 1964, pp.82–93: 'The preaching is itself revelation and does not merely speak about it' (p.91).

74. Notice particularly the 'our' rather than 'my' in II Cor.4.6. See also above ch. V nn.42 and 45.

75. Contrast the phrase, 'the Word of God', according to Kittel, *TDNT* IV p.113 – though note I Thess.4.15 (see below p.230).

76. H. Windisch, *Der zweite Korintherbrief*, KEK ⁹1924, p.368; C. K. Barrett, *The Second Epistle to the Corinthians*, A. & C. Black 1973, p.307.

77. Lindblom, *Gesichte* pp.43f. Betz describes II Cor.12.2–4 as 'the parody of an account of a heavenly journey' (*Paulus und sokratische Tradition* pp.84ff.). But this was undoubtedly an actual experience of which Paul could boast had he wanted to, not merely a literary parody; see also below n.82.

78. It is likely that 'third heaven' and 'paradise' describe the same experience, rather than different experiences or different stages in the one experience (Windisch, *II Kor.* pp.371f.; H. Bietenhard, *Die himmlische Welt im Urchristentum und Spätjudentum*, Tübingen 1951, pp.164f.; Lührmann, *Offenbarung.* p.57; Barrett, *II Cor.* p.310; otherwise Plummer, *II Cor.* p.344). Jewish tradition spoke frequently of seven heavens, but the tradition with which Paul was familiar probably thought in terms of only three (see Strack-Billerbeck III pp.431ff.; Windisch, *II Kor.* pp. 371ff.; H. Traub, *TDNT* V pp.511f., 534f.).

79. Cf. Windisch, *II Kor.* p.377.

80. See further Strack-Billerbeck III pp.533f., IV.2 pp.1130–65; Bousset-Gressmann pp.282–5; Bietenhard, *himmlische Welt*. As we would expect, the content of the vision would be largely conditioned by Paul's presuppositions regarding paradise; but it does not necessarily follow that the vision was nothing more than the projection of his fantasies or beliefs. Paul certainly regarded it as a 'revelation', particularly the 'unutterable utterance'. For the imagery of visions in religious history see particularly Benz, *Vision* ch. V.

81. See Underhill, *Mysticism*, particularly the vision of Suso described on p.187; Lindblom, *Gesichte* p.44 n.17; Benz, *Vision* pp.267–77; Wilson, *Occult* pp.542–7; and particularly C. Green, *Out-of-the-Body Experiences*, Hamilton 1968; M. Eliade, *Shamanism: Archaic Techniques of Ecstasy*, Princeton 1970: 'the shaman specializes in a trance during which his soul is believed to leave his body and ascend to the sky or descend to the underworld' (pp.4f.).

82. Windisch, *II Kor.* pp.369f. – though he agrees that 'the double consciousness of the pneumatic and the possessed may play a secondary role'. There is no question that Paul is speaking about *his own* experience, as v.7 makes clear, and almost all commentators agree.

83. Cf. Schmithals, *Gnosticism* pp.212f.; Lührmann, *Offenbarung.* p.58.

84. Lindblom, *Gesichte* p.45; cf. Weinel, *Wirkungen* pp.164ff.

85. See particularly Windisch, *II Kor.* pp. 377f.; Jeremias, *Eucharistic Words* pp. 125–32.

86. Windisch, *II Kor.* p. 379; cf. n. 99 below.

87. Lindblom, *Gesichte* p. 44; cf. Weinel, *Wirkungen* pp. 162ff.

88. Arndt & Gingrich, ὑπερβολή. The genitive in 12.1 – 'visions and revelations of the Lord' – may be deliberately ambiguous to include both the thought that the Lord was the author of the experience and the implication that Paul saw the Lord in some of his visions (cf. Acts 18.9; 22.17; 23.11; 26.16).

89. Barrett, *II Cor.* pp. 34, 308, 310.

90. Georgi, *Gegner* pp. 296f.

91. Schmithals, *Gnosticism* pp. 190f.

92. Lührmann, *Offenbarung*. pp. 56f.; cf. F. Dumermuth, 'Moses strahlendes Gericht', *TZ* 17, 1961, pp. 241–8.

93. Cf. H. A. A. Kennedy, *St Paul and the Mystery Religions*, Hodder & Stoughton 1913, pp. 180–98; J. Behm, *TDNT* IV pp. 736–9; cf. J. F. Collange, *Enigmes de la Deuxieme Epitre de Paul aux Corinthiens*, Cambridge 1972, p. 119. See further below pp. 320f., 333f.

94. J. Bowker, '"Merkabah" Visions and the Visions of Paul', *JSS* 16, 1971, pp. 157–73, suggests that Paul may have 'practised *merkabah* contemplation as an ordinary consequence of his highly extended rabbinic training', and that his visions (including the one outside Damascus) may have arisen out of such contemplation.

95. See Schmithals, *Gnosticism* pp. 141–55; C. K. Barrett, 'Christianity at Corinth' *BJRL* 46, 1963–64, pp. 275–86; and those mentioned below in n. 105. On the wider questions of whether we should speak of 'opponents' at all, of 'faction' or 'factions', of 'gnostics' or 'Gnostics' or not use the term at all, see Munck, *Paul* ch. 5; Hurd pp. 96–107; N. A. Dahl, 'Paul and the Church at Corinth according to I Corinthians 1.10–4.21', *Christian History and Interpretation*, Knox Festschrift, ch. 15; R. McL. Wilson, 'How Gnostic were the Corinthians?', *NTS* 19, 1972–73, pp. 65–74; S. Arai, 'Die Gegner des Paulus im I Korintherbrief und das Problem der Gnosis', *NTS* 19, 1972–73, pp. 430–7. Against the view that 'Gnostics' are in view see J. Dupont, *Gnosis: La Connaissance Religieuse dans les Épitres de Saint Paul*, Paris ²1960, pp. 261ff.; and Pearson, *Pneumatikos-Psychikos*, with his concern for more precise definitions.

96. γνῶσις: 16 times in I & II Cor.
       7 times elsewhere in Pauline literature
       6 times elsewhere in the NT
σοφία: 17 times in I Cor. (16 in I Cor. 1–3)
       once in II Cor., once in Rom., 3 times in Eph., 6 times in Col.
σοφός: 11 times in I Cor. (10 in I Cor. 1–3)
       5 times elsewhere in Paul.

97. That Paul is quoting the Corinthians themselves in 8.1, 4 is generally recognized – RSV, NEB, JB; Hurd pp. 68, 120ff. J. Weiss draws attention to the absence of the article before γνῶσιν in 8.1: 'it is not merely particular knowledge with respect to the εἴδωλα that is meant, but something general; they feel themselves to be people for whom "knowledge" is characteristic, that whereby they distinguish themselves from their surroundings' (*I Kor.* p. 214).

98. Εἴδωλον probably should be taken as 'idol', rather than 'supernatural beings' (Weiss, *I Kor.* p. 219) or as 'a false god' (NEB), since Paul recognized the activity of spiritual beings other than God operating behind the outward trappings and the functions of the various cults (8.5, 7, 10; 10.19ff., and particularly 12.2), as perhaps

also through the actions of the civil authorities (I Cor. 2.6; Rom. 13.1–6).

99. On the question of how much later gnostic speculation can be presupposed within the situations addressed by the NT writers, see particularly R. McL. Wilson, *Gnosis and the New Testament*, Blackwell 1968, particularly ch.2; E. Yamauchi, *Pre-Christian Gnosticism*, Tyndale 1973; also Wilson, Arai and Pearson as in n.95 above. That the Corinthian experience of *gnosis* already included mystical vision of God and the sense of deification is unlikely (cf. Weiss, *I Kor.* p.300; Bultmann, *TDNT* I pp.694ff.) – although their experience may have been ecstatic (cf. above §40.3; and I Cor.2.9 if it takes up a Corinthian citation, as Pearson suggests – pp.34f.), and certainly led to highly inflated ideas of their own superiority (I Cor.4.8; 8.1).

100. Cf. Bultmann, *TDNT* I pp.697, 706.

101. 'Both for the opponents and for Paul, γνῶσις is Christian insight into the realities of Christian existence here and now and its practical consequences' (Pearson p.42).

102. Cf. Bultmann, *TDNT* I pp.707–11. Kennedy holds that Paul's thought shows influences of both OT and current usage in the Mysteries (*Paul* pp.162–72).

103. Bultmann, *TDNT* I pp.706, 710: γνῶσις is regarded as a gift of grace which marks the life of the Christian by determining its expression (I Cor.1.5; 12.8; II Cor.8.7; I Clem.1.2)' (pp.707f.). See also Dupont, *Gnosis* pp.231ff. and above p.34.

104. Barrett, 'Christianity at Corinth' pp.277ff.; also *I Cor.* pp.53f., 67f.

105. On I Cor.15 and the Corinthian view(s) of the resurrection see above ch.V n.43. U. Wilckens, *Weisheit und Torheit*, Tübingen 1959, particularly pp.205–13, also *TDNT* VII pp.519ff., and Lührmann, *Offenbarung*. ch.9, propose more elaborate understandings of Corinthian *sophia*. But see also Schmithals, *Gnosticism* pp.138ff.; Conzelmann, 'Paulus und die Weisheit', *NTS* 12, 1965–66, pp.231–44; also *I Kor.* pp.75ff.; R. Scroggs, 'Paul: Σοφός and Πνευματικός', *NTS* 14, 1967–68, pp.33–55. That the Corinthian faction identified Wisdom with the Spirit hardly follows from I Cor.2.13 (against Pearson pp.35ff.).

106. Cf. Grau p.58.

107. As many commentators think: e.g. Bultmann, *TDNT* I p.708 n.73; J. Moffatt, *The First Epistle of Paul to the Corinthians*, Moffatt 1938, p.181; Lietzmann in Lietzmann-Kümmel, *Kor.* p.61; Conzelmann, *I Kor.* p.246. That γνῶσις and σοφία are to so large an extent twin concepts is indicated by Rom.11.33; Col.2.3 and I Cor.2 (where σοφία occurs 7 times and γινώσκειν 5 times). Weiss associates 'word of knowledge' with prophecy and 'word of wisdom' with teaching (*I Kor.* p.300). Pentecostal expositions often take 'word of knowledge' as a sort of pastoral insight into the needs or problems of others. This does not accord with Paul's use of γνῶσις elsewhere, and is more a feature of prophecy (I Cor.14.24f.; see below §41.2). But we should not strive for pedantic precision in these distinctions (cf. Rom.12.6–8, where the charismata listed include both prophecy and exhortation, despite I Cor.14.3; see further below §43.6).

108. Cf. Schlatter, *Bote* p.339; Hasenhüttl p.143.

109. A baptismal reference as such is neither explicit nor implicit (Dunn, *Baptism* p.210 and n.14).

110. Despite the uncertainty of commentators, πνεῦμα here probably means 'Spirit of God'; the closest verbal parallel in Paul is Rom.8.15 ('a spirit of adoption'); and the closest contextual parallel is I Cor.2.6–16; cf. Isa.11.2; Zech.12.10; other parallels in Schlier, *Epheser* p.78 n.1.

111. 'Εν is ambiguous; cf. Schlier, *Epheser* p.79. For the sense of ἐπίγνωσις cf. Rom.

3.20; I Cor. 13.12; cf. Moule, *Colossians* pp. 159–64. 'The "knowledge" is an experience of faith and love' (Schlier, *Epheser* p. 79); cf. also K. Sullivan, 'Epignosis in the Epistles of St Paul', *Studiorum Paulinorum Congressus Internationalis Catholicus 1961, Rome 1963*, pp. 405–16.

112. Οἶδα includes both senses: rational cognizance (τίς . . . τίς . . . τί) and existential experience (cf. ἐπίγνωσις and ἐνέργεια – Eph. 1.19; 3.7, 20; 4.16; Col. 1.29).

113. The overlap is most clearly visible in Col. 1.9f.; see below p. 224.

114. Schlier, *Galater* p. 66.

115. Cf. R. P. Martin, *The Epistle of Paul to the Philippians*, Tyndale 1959: 'So confident is he that the truth has been stated that he invokes the aid of God to illuminate the minds and correct the behaviour of those who do not share his conviction (cf. Gal. 5.10)' (p. 156).

116. See V. P. Furnish, *Theology and Ethics in Paul*, Abingdon 1968 – the most recent full scale treatment which includes a useful Appendix surveying nineteenth- and twentieth-century interpretations of Paul's ethics.

117. The language stems from 'enthusiastic speech' (Käsemann, *Römer* p. 216).

118. Cf. C. F. D. Moule, 'Obligation in the Ethic of Paul', *Christian History and Interpretation*, Knox Festschrift: 'Gal. 5.25, "If we live by the Spirit" – that is, if we owe our very "existence" as Christians, to the Spirit – "let us also walk by the Spirit" – that is, let our conduct conform to this' (p. 401).

119. See further Dunn, *Baptism* pp. 135, 146f., 156.

120. Cf. Gunkel pp. 79ff.; Weiss, *Earliest Christianity* p. 557.

121. 'Faith' here should not be confused with 'conscience' as used in I Cor. 8.7–13 (so rightly Käsemann, *Römer* p. 363); faith as conviction on a particular issue is something positive and directive, whereas conscience is primarily something more negative and regulative (post eventum) (see C. A. Pierce, *Conscience in the New Testament*, SCM Press 1955).

122. Barrett, *Romans* p. 104.

123. Cf. J. Behm, *TDNT* IV p. 958.

124. That Paul has the Spirit in mind at this point is implied by (a) ἀνακαίνωσις: the only other time the word is used in Pauline literature (Titus 3.5, but a more traditional Pauline formula) it is attributed explicitly to the Spirit; note also Rom. 7.6 – ἐν καινότητι πνεύματος; (b) the Spirit is typically understood as the beginning, first fruits and guarantee of the whole process of metamorphosis and new creation (Rom. 8.23; II Cor. 3.18; 5.5); (c) the specifically charismatic context of Rom. 12.1–8; note also the revelation context of Eph. 5.8–14.

125. Furnish, *Ethics*, unjustifiably takes δοκιμάζειν here in the sense of 'seek out' (pp. 104, 188f., 230).

126. Cullmann, *Christ* p. 228. Cf. W. Grundmann, *TDNT* II p. 260 n. 19: 'By the endowment of the Spirit the Christian can have direct knowledge of the will of God'; Michel, *Römer* p. 294 n. 2. On Rom. 12.1–2 as a whole see particularly Leenhardt, *Romans* pp. 301–7.

127. Against Furnish, *Ethics* pp. 227–37. To speak of the 'command to "abound in love"' (p. 235) is a distortion of the evidence. Of the passages referred to, I Thess. 3.12 and Phil. 1.9 are both prayers; in I Thess. 4.10 the governing word is φιλαδελφία, not ἀγάπη; and in II Cor. 8.7 it is a statement, not a command in which Paul thinks of love (ἀγάπη) as a charisma. For Paul overflowing love is a divine gift, not something that can be commanded or insisted on (see also below pp. 294f.).

128. Cf. Conzelmann, *Outline* p. 278; also Lohmeyer, *Philipper* pp. 32f.

129. Käsemann, 'Principles of the Interpretation of Romans 13', *NTQT*, translates αἴσθησις, 'the feeling for the actual situation at the time' (p. 214); cf. Arndt & Gingrich, αἴσθησις; and note the use of the phrase πνευματικὴ αἴσθησις in the papyri (cited by Reitzenstein, *Mysterien*. p. 311).

130. See M. Dibelius, *An die Kolosser, Epheser an Philemon*, HNT ³1953, p. 7; cf. Schweizer, *TDNT* VI p. 437 n. 704; Lohse, *Colossians* pp. 26f.; R. P. Martin, *Colossians and Philemon*, Oliphants 1974, p. 51. Cf. also Philemon 6, where the 'all good' may refer to Christian conduct (Lohse, *Colossians* p. 194).

131. See particularly W. Schrage, *Die konkreten Einzelgebote in der paulinischen Paränese*, Gütersloh 1961, especially pp. 71–93.

132. See particularly R. N. Longenecker, *Paul, Apostle of Liberty*, Harper & Row 1964, pp. 181–96.

133. Conzelmann, *Outline* pp. 91ff.

134. See also W. Pfister, *Das Leben im Geist nach Paulus*, Freiburg 1963; 'The whole Christian ethic according to Paul can be summed up in the one sentence: "Walk in the Spirit" . . . Pneuma is both the *power* and the *norm* of the Christian life' (p. 91); S. Lyonnet, Liberté chrétienne et loi de l'Esprit selon saint Paul', in I. de la Potterie & S. Lyonnet, *La vie selon l'Esprit*, Paris 1965, ch. VI.

135. Most Christians today seem to understand such exhortations as little as they are able to answer the question, 'Did you receive the Spirit when you believed?' (Acts 19.2; cf. Gal. 3.2). Those who could answer the latter affirmatively would presumably have had as little difficulty in understanding the former.

136. See A. Oepke, *TDNT* III pp. 577f.

137. H. Berkhof, *The Doctrine of the Holy Spirit*, Epworth 1965, p. 36; so G. Friedrich, 'Geist und Amt', *Wort und Dienst* NF 3, 1952, p. 68; cf. Grau p. 265; Schniewind, 'All charismata are charismata of the Word (Wortcharismen)' (cited by Friedrich p. 81); Bultmann, *Theology* II p. 97. G Eichholz, *Was heisst charismatische Gemeinde?*, TheolEx 77, München 1960, conversely argues that charismata are functions for which believers are empowered through the proclaimed word – with reference to I Cor. 1.5–7a (p. 18). I Peter 4.10f. speaks of only two charismata: 'he who speaks' and 'he who serves'.

138. πληροφορία is best taken as a reference to the hearers' full conviction rather than to Paul's assurance. As in I Cor. 2.4f., so here, Paul is thinking of the impact of his message rather than of his own experience in preaching. Cf. C. Masson, *Les deux Épitres de Saint Paul aux Thessaloniciens*, Neuchatel 1957, p. 20.

139. Weiss, *I Kor.* p. 50; Robertson-Plummer, *I Cor.* p. 33; Moffatt, *I Cor.* p. 24; L. Hartman, 'Some Remarks on I Cor. 2.1–5', *SEA* 39, 1974, pp. 109–20.

140. See Weiss, *I Kor.* pp. 50f.; cf. Barrett, *I Cor.* p. 65.

141. Cf. Conzelmann, *I Kor.* p. 72. See further below §55.

142. 'Ρῆμα denotes spoken word, so here, in effect, inspired utterance, inspired preaching. See further Dunn, *Baptism* pp. 164f.

143. See also G. Friedrich, *TDNT* II pp. 731ff.; G. Kittel, *TDNT* IV p. 118. Kittel also rightly draws attention to 'the genuine and all-pervasive NT dialectic of grasping and being grasped . . . The Word must be received . . .' (pp. 118f.). On I Cor. 14.24f. see below pp. 232f.

144. H. Schlier, *TDNT* V p. 883.

145. The passages are set out in synoptic fashion most fully by H. Schürmann, 'Die geistlichen Gnadengaben in den paulinischen Gemeinden', *Ursprung und Gestalt*, Patmos 1970, pp. 250f.

146. Plato, *Timaeus* 71e–72b; *Phaedrus* 244a–d. See also Fascher, *ΠΡΟΦΗΤΗΣ* pp.

66–70; Friedrich, *TDNT* VI pp. 787f.

147. Calvin on I Thess. 5.20 understands 'prophesying to mean the interpretation of Scripture applied to present need'. Cf. e.g. H. Leisegang, *Pneuma Hagion*, Leipzig 1922, pp. 119ff.; Knox, *Gentiles*, p. 121; Bornkamm, 'Faith and Reason in Paul', *Early Christian Experience*, ET SCM Press 1969, p. 39; Kertelge, *Gemeinde* p. 120. See also above pp. 186f.

148. In Hermas, *Mand.* XI. 1–9, a proof of the false prophet is that he divines on request. So too Irenaeus: 'The gift of prophecy is not conferred on men by Marcus the magician, but only those to whom God sends his grace from above possess the divinely-bestowed power of prophesying; and then they speak where and when God pleases, and not when Marcus orders them to do so' (*Adv. Haer.* I.13.4). See also Weinel, *Wirkungen* pp. 87–96; J. Reiling, *Hermas and Christian Prophecy: A Study of the Eleventh Mandate*, NovTestSuppl XXXVII, 1973, ch. 5.

149. Friedrich, *TDNT* VI: 'The prophet does not declare what he has taken from tradition or what he has thought up himself. He declares what has been revealed to him' (p. 853). See also Hasenhüttl p. 189.

150. Cf. Bultmann, *Theology* I pp. 159f.; Conzelmann, *I Kor.* p. 286 and n. 29. Lindblom, *Prophecy*: 'The prophet knows that his thoughts and words never come from himself; they are given him . . . Few things are so characteristic of the prophets, wherever we meet them in the world of religion, as the feeling of being under a superhuman and supernatural constraint' (p. 2); also *Gesichte* pp. 162f. Similarly I Thess. 5.20; see Best, *Thess.* p. 239. Cf. II Peter 1.21; Athenagoras, *Legatio* 7, 9.

151. Barrett, *I Cor.* p. 322; against Weinel, *Wirkungen* p. 78; Bornkamm, 'Faith' p. 39; cf. his *Paul* p. 181. See also W. Bieder, 'Gebetswirklichkeit und Gebetsmöglichkeit bei Paulus', *TZ* 4, 1948, pp. 34f.

152. Παράκλησις – e.g. Rom. 12.1; II Cor. 1.3–7 (quite frequent in Paul); παραμυθία – I Thess. 2.12; 5.14. Notice again that Rom. 12.6–8 lists προφητεία and παρακαλῶν as separate charismata. See also Cothenet, *DBS* 8, 1972, 1299ff.

153. Cf. also Schürmann, 'Gnadengaben' pp. 255f.

154. See particularly J. G. Davies, 'The Genesis of Belief in an Imminent Parousia', *JTS NS* 14, 1963, pp. 104–7; B. Henneken, *Verkündigung und Prophetie im I. Thessalonischerbrief*, Stuttgarter Bible Studien 29, 1969, pp. 73–98, especially pp. 85–91; Best, *Thess.* pp. 189–93. It is possible, but less likely, that the 'word' is a saying of the earthly Jesus (against especially J. Jeremias, *Unknown Sayings of Jesus*, ET SPCK ²1964, pp. 80–3). By far the most probable life-setting for the saying is the concern which arose some years after the resurrection over the relation between the Lord (the exalted Jesus) and those who had in the meantime died.

155. See especially J. P. M. Sweet, 'A Sign for Unbelievers: Paul's Attitude to Glossolalia', *NTS* 13, 1966–67, pp. 240–6.

156. Cf. K. H. Rengstorf, *TDNT* VII p. 259.

157. 'He does not say that they *are* a sign, but that they are intended to *serve* as such – εἰς σημεῖον: Gen. 9.13; Num. 16.38; 17.10; Deut. 6.8; 11.18; etc.' (Robertson-Plummer, *I Cor.* p. 317).

158. The 'all speak in tongues' (v. 23) is not intended as a caricature (the whole place in ecstatic uproar), as the parallel 'all prophesy' (v. 24) surely indicates (cf. Robertson-Plummer, *I Cor.* p. 317).

159. We must add 'a sign' in v. 22b even though it is lacking in the Greek, since the balance of the sentence requires this (Barrett, *I Cor.* pp. 323f.; against Weiss, *I Kor.* p. 324), and since in vv. 24f. prophecy can quite justifiably be described as 'for

unbelievers' since it serves as a word of revelation to them.

160. Against Barrett, *I Cor.* p.324.

161. 14.25 – 'God is ἐν ὑμῖν' must be translated, 'God is in you as an assembly, that is, among you'; *not* 'God is in you as individual speakers'. As the OT passage on which 14.25 is modelled (Isa.45.14) makes clear, what is being confessed is not the inspiration of the speakers but the presence of God. So most commentators. The idea of God-possession is more appropriate to ecstatic speech than to prophecy; in Greek thought at this point ἐνθουσιασμός (God-possession) and μανία (divine madness; cf. I Cor.14.23) are near synonyms. See below §52.3; and also G. Schrenk, 'Geist und Enthusiasmus', *Studien zu Paulus*, Zürich 1954, pp. 107–13.

162. So e.g. in Montanism – N. Bonwetsch, *Die Geschichte des Montanismus*, Erlangen 1881, p.58.

163. For later parallels see Weinel, *Wirkungen* pp.183–90, and above ch.IV n.93. Weinel defines the charisma too precisely as 'thought reading'; so Héring, *I Cor.* p.152. But one should not object to this too strongly (as Weiss, *I Kor.* p.333; Barrett, *I Cor.* p.326), since 'thought reading' as such is only a particular example of the more general gift of charismatic insight, and a prophetic word, a quite unspecific utterance so far as the speaker is concerned, can seem like thought or 'heart-reading' to the person thereby exposed to himself and convicted before God (cf. Lietzmann in Lietzmann-Kümmel, *Kor.* p.73). See also below p.305.

164. Käsemann, *NTQT* pp.66–81.

165. Cf. Hasenhüttl pp.191f.

166. Cf. Moffatt, *I Cor.* p.224. On the significance of προσκυνέω (worship) – the only time the word is used by Paul! – see H. Greeven, *TDNT* VI p.765.

167. Cf. Bornkamm, 'Faith' pp.39f.

168. A mistake made in the standard Pentecostal expositions of I Cor.12.8–10; so H. Horton, *The Gifts of the Spirit*, Assemblies of God [7]1962; Riggs, *Spirit*; J. Rea, *Layman's Commentary on the Holy Spirit*, Logos 1972, pp.62f.; cf. D. Gee, *Concerning Spiritual Gifts*, Springfield, revised, no date.

169. Cf. Schlatter, *Bote* p.343; and see further below §41.8.

170. M. Dibelius, *Die Geisterwelt im Glauben des Paulus*, Göttingen 1909, pp.73–6; Weiss, *I Kor.* pp.326f. K. Lake, *The Earlier Epistles of St Paul*, Rivingtons 1911: 'One of the main reasons for which the ordinary man took part in religious ceremonies was to avoid obsession by evil demons and to secure obsession or inspiration by good spirits' (p.192). Less likely is the suggestion that πνεύματα = angelic beings (cf. Heb.1.7, 14 – revived by Ellis, *CSNT* pp.275ff.; '"Spiritual" Gifts' pp.134ff.). Paul nowhere speaks of angelic mediation (except in unequivocally negative tones – Rom.8.38; II Cor.11.14; 12.7; Gal.1.8; Col.2.18), now that the Spirit has been given in eschatological fullness (cf. Dibelius, *Geisterwelt* pp.74f.).

171. So e.g. Moffatt, *I Cor.* p.219; Conzelmann, *I Kor.* p.279; Barrett's exposition is particularly helpful (*I Cor.* p.320).

172. The plural ('discernings') presumably means 'the gift of discerning in various cases' (Robertson-Plummer, *I Cor.* p.267).

173. G. Dautzenberg, 'Zum religionsgeschichtlichen Hintergrund der διάκρισις πνευμάτων (I Kor.12.10)', *BZ* 15, 1971, pp.93–104. See particularly Gen.40.8 (Symmachus revision) and references to Gen.40f. in Philo (Dautzenberg p.99); see also the references above to Plato's distinction between prophecy of inspiration and prophecy of interpretation; and p.186 above.

174. It is the principal weakness of Dautzenberg's thesis that he pays too little heed to this issue.

175. See e.g. Weiss, *I Kor.* pp. 294, 333; Barrett, *I Cor.* pp. 278f.; L. Cerfaux, *The Church in the Theology of St Paul*, ET Herder 1959, p. 202. See also below §52.2, 3.

176. To argue that Paul is merely presenting a hypothetical case (see Wendland, *Kor.* p. 93; Hurd pp. 193f.; K. Maly, 'I Kor. 12.1–3, eine Regel zur Unterscheidung der Geister?', *BZ* 10, 1966, pp. 82–95), or that in 12.3a he is referring to the Corinthians' previous experience of heathen ecstasy (so Lührmann, *Offenbarung.* p. 29; Pearson pp. 47–50 in effect) trivializes one of Paul's most emphatic and didactic utterances. The context indicates a situation of Christian worship; and the seriousness with which Paul speaks strongly suggests that he is answering a query put to him (cf. n. 178 below). More weighty is Allo's suggestion that Paul is referring to the cries of Christian ecstatics when they attempted to resist the trance or ecstasy they felt coming upon them 'in the manner of the Sibyl who foamed as she resisted the inspiration that was taking possession of her, or of Cassandra, who curses Apollo in Aeschylus's *Agamemnon*' (*Première Épitre aux Corinthiens*, EB 1934, pp. 321f., followed by Barrett, *I Cor.* p. 280); but would the Corinthians not have recognized the nature of such cries? Whence then the problem they have posed to Paul? Other explanations are less coherent.

177. See particularly Schmithals, *Gnosticism* pp. 124–30; also J. Schniewind, 'Das Seufzen des Geistes', *Nachgelassene Reden und Aufsätze*, Berlin 1952, p. 115; Eichholz, *Gemeinde* pp. 12f.; E. Güttgemanns, *Der leidende Apostel und sein Herr*, Göttingen 1966, pp. 62ff.; Bittlinger, *Graces* pp. 16ff.; N. Brox, '*ΑΝΑΘΕΜΑ ΙΗΣΟΥΣ* (I Kor. 12.3)', *BZ* 12, 1968, pp. 103–11. To be sure, the Christology of Corinthian gnosticism does not seem to be much developed (though cf. I Cor. 15.44ff.). But perhaps the significance of 12.3a (and hence the question about it to Paul) is that it marks the *beginning* of that development to the full-blown systems of Cerinthus etc. attacked in I John 4.1ff.

178. It is generally recognized that in 12.1ff. Paul is taking up a question or questions put to him by the Corinthians – see Hurd pp. 63f., 71ff., 186ff.

179. As Weiss and Barrett point out, the question of the sincerity of the speaker is not an issue here; it is not the individual who speaks but the Spirit, the source of inspiration being demonstrated by the actual words uttered (Weiss, *I Kor.* pp. 295f.; Barrett, *I Cor.* p. 281). Paul does not say anything about the spiritual status of the speakers beyond this particular utterance; nor does the test in question extend beyond the moment of inspiration to the wider faith and life of the speaker (against T. Holtz, 'Das Kennzeichen des Geistes (I Kor. 12.1–3)', *NTS* 18, 1971–72, pp. 365–7).

180. Cf. Scroggs, 'Exaltation of the Spirit' pp. 365f. There are various historical parallels. For example, Abiezer Coppe, one of 'the vulgar prophets' in the Puritan era defended his habit of 'base hellish swearing, and cursing' (O. C. Watkins, *The Puritan Experience*, Routledge & Kegan Paul 1972, pp. 145f.). Clemen noted as a parallel the so-called 'sermon-sickness' in Sweden in the 1840's: 'in many of those who were attacked, the sermon-sickness expressed itself at first in horrible oaths' (*ExpT* X, 1898–99, p. 350). Claims to hearing similar cries ('Jesus be cursed') within modern Pentecostalism have been made from time to time, although it must be said that none of these is well attested. When questioned about this in private conversation (in the mid-1960s) David du Plessis suggested that if these claims were in fact true the best explanation may be that such cries had a cathartic effect, the Spirit presumably drawing out and cleansing the speaker of his unbelief. Cf. H. Weinel, *St Paul, the Man and his Work*, ET Williams & Norgate 1906, p. 251.

181. Cf. K. Berger, 'Die sog. "Sätze heiligen Rechts" im N.T. Ihre Funktion und ihr Sitz im Leben', *TZ* 28, 1972, pp. 321ff., who suggests that conditional sentences

with present apodosis provide us with the form for such tests – with particular reference to I John 4.2f.; Polycarp, *Phil.* 7.1f.

182. Arndt & Gingrich, συγκρίνω; Reitzenstein, *Mysterien.* p. 336; Lietzmann in Lietzmann-Kümmel, *Kor.* p. 14. II Cor. 10.12 contains the only other occurrence of συγκρίνω in Paul.

183. Dibelius, *Geisterwelt* p. 91 n. 4; Barrett, *I Cor.* p. 76; cf. Conzelmann, *I Kor.* p. 86.

184. F. Büchsel, *TDNT* III p. 954; Dupont, *Gnosis* p. 152 n. 3; cf. Schweizer, *TDNT* VI p. 437 n. 704.

185. Wilckens, *Weisheit* pp. 84ff. Pearson's attribution of the phrase to Paul's opponents on the grounds that 'the idea expressed in I Cor. 2.13 is nowhere else attested in his writings' (p. 38) ignores the emphasis Paul places elsewhere on the evaluation of *pneumatika*.

186. Note the variant reading in 2.13, πνευματικῶς (B 33) an adverb, instead of πνευματικοῖς, the superior reading. This would make the parallel with 2.14 more precise – πνευματικῶς ἀνακρίνεται.

187. Rom. 14.1 is Paul's only other use of διάκρισις.

188. For δοκιμάζειν = 'test' in the Pauline corpus, cf. I Cor. 11.28; 16.3; II Cor. 8.8, 22(?); 13.5; Gal. 6.4 (I Tim. 3.10). See also G. Therrien, *Le Discernement dans les Ecrits Pauliniens*, EB 1973, particularly pp. 56f., 75f.

189. Jeremias, *Unknown Sayings*, pp. 102ff.

190. See e.g. J. E. Frame, *Thessalonians*, ICC 1912, pp. 208f.; W. Schmithals; *Paul and the Gnostics*, ET Abingdon 1972, p. 173 n. 192.

191. The parallel with the I Cor. passages is all the closer if, as is very likely, there was a somewhat similar abuse of charismata in Thessalonica as in Corinth. See below §46.1, 3.

192. It is not really possible to draw a hard and fast line between the different items listed here; so Lietzmann in Lietzmann–Kümmel, *Kor.* p. 71; Barrett, *I Cor.* p. 317. Interesting, but with little to commend them, are the suggestions of Reitzenstein that the list of v. 6 is ordered according to intelligibility and (inversely) height of ecstasy (*Mysterien.* p. 67), and of Robertson-Plummer that 'ἀποκάλυψις and γνῶσις are the internal gifts of which προφητεία and διδαχή are the external manifestation' p. 308).

193. 'By διδαχή must be understood a particular teaching on a particular subject; for example a "pneumatic" interpretation of Scripture' (Weiss, *I Kor.* pp. 334f.).

194. In II Cor. 3.14ff. the veil which obscures the meaning and significance of the old covenant, the law of Moses, is removed only when one turns to the Lord, that is the Spirit. That is, the significance of the law is given charismatically, as revelation, to believers. Cf. also Käsemann, 'The Spirit and the Letter', *Perspectives* ch. VII. More generally see E. E. Ellis, *Paul's Use of the Old Testament*, Eerdmans 1957.

195. Cf. H. Greeven 'Propheten, Lehrer, Vorsteher bei Paulus', *ZNW* 44, 1952, pp. 17f. Bittlinger cites the fifteenth-century monk Johannes Ruysbroek as an example (*Ministries* pp. 68f.).

196. Notice how Paul interprets the dominical word in I Cor. 9.14ff., and presumably II Thess. 3.6ff. – as a right which he foregoes! (see below §47.3).

197. Cf. Lindblom, *Gesichte* p. 131.

198. See above p. 186.

199. One of the most beautiful features of the current charismatic movement are those occasions when (almost) a whole gathering sing in tongues. On those occasions when I have been present it has sounded as a common chord held almost in drone-like fashion (not loudly), with different individual voices elaborating the chord with more complex harmonies.

200. See above pp.228f.

201. 'There is no thought here of liturgical music; it is the individual spontaneously using a special gift in the congregation' (Robertson-Plummer, *I Cor.* p.312).

202. 'At Corinth it is significant that the first contribution mentioned is praise, the glad and grateful sense of God finding expression in rapt rhythms or doxologies' (Moffatt, *I Cor.* p.227).

203. Cf. Wetter, *Charis* pp.77f.; Lohmeyer, *Kolosser* pp.150f.; E. F. Scott, *The Epistle of Paul to the Colossians, to Philemon and to the Ephesians*, Moffatt 1930, pp.74ff.; Dibelius-Greeven, *Kolosser* pp.44f.; Lohse, *Colossians* pp.150f. See also above p.237.

204. Schlier, *Epheser* p.247; cf. Martin, *Colossians* p.115.

205. G. Delling, *TDNT* VIII p.499; Lohse, *Colossians* p.151.

206. Delling, *Worship* pp.86f.; Schlier, *Epheser* p.247 n.2; Lohse, *Colossians* p.151 n.151; Martin, *Colossians* pp.115f. The gender of 'spiritual' is naturally attracted to that of the nearest member of the triad.

207. F. F. Bruce, *The Epistle to the Colossians*, Marshall, Morgan & Scott 1957, p. 284, appositely cites Tertullian's description of the Christian love-feast at which, 'after water for the hands and lights have been brought in, each is invited to sing to God in the presence of others from what he knows of the holy scriptures or from his own heart' (*Apology* 39). Cf. Philo's description of the meetings of the Therapeutae (*Vit.Cont.* 80, 83–9 conveniently summarized in Delling, *Worship* pp.85f.). For later parallels see Weinel, *Wirkungen* pp.80f. Most religious awakenings find some sort of expression in more spontaneous forms of praise and worship closer to the idiom of the people involved than more traditional hymnody. The present charismatic movement is a good example.

208. See particularly R. Deichgräber, *Gotteshymnus und Christushymnus in der frühen Christenheit*, Göttingen 1967; K. Wengst, *Christologische Formeln und Lieder des Urchristentums*, Gütersloh 1972, pp.144–208.

209. G. Friedrich, *TDNT* VI p.853. Perhaps surprising too is the absence of prayers of confession (Delling, *Worship* p.125). Prayers of confession are first mentioned in *Didache* 14.1.

210. Προσευχή – Rom. 1.10; 15.30; Eph. 1.16; Col. 4.12; I Thess. 1.2; Philemon 4, 22; προσεύχομαι – Phil. 1.9; Col. 1.3, 9; 4.3; I Thess. 5.25; δέησις – Rom. 10.1; II Cor. 1.11; 9.14; Eph. 6.18; Phil. 1.4, 19;4.6; δέομαι – Rom. 1.10; I Thess. 3.10; εὐχαριστία. – II Cor.9.11f.; Phil.4.6; I Thess.3.9; εὐχαριστέω – Eph. 5.20. I include only those references where there is some clear indication of the content of the prayer. Delling, *Worship* pp.110f. suggests that the congregations sometimes spent whole nights in prayer (cf. I Thess.3.10; Col.4.2; Eph.6.18f.).

211. Schlier, *Epheser* p.301. A classic example would be Polycarp of Smyrna, who on being arrested (155 or 156 AD) was given leave to pray: 'And when they consented, he stood and prayed – being so filled with the grace of God that for two hours he could not hold his peace, to the amazement of those who heard' (*Martyrdom of Polycarp* 7.2).

212. Seeberg, *Katechismus* p.242; G. Kittel, *TDNT* I p.6; Lietzmann, *Römer* pp. 83f.; Leenhardt, *Romans* p.214; Barrett, *Romans* p.164; H. Paulsen, *Überlieferung und Auslegung in Röm.8*, Inaugural-Dissertation, Mainz 1972, pp.172–85.

213. 'Absolutely excluded' (Käsemann, *Römer* p.217).

214. See Dunn, *Baptism* pp.113f. and those cited there in n.33.

215. 'An overwhelming sense of sonship' (C. A. A. Scott, *Christianity according to St Paul*, Cambridge 1927, p.170); 'With prophetic immediacy' (P. Althaus, *Der Brief an die Römer*, NTD 101966, p.91).

216. Cf. Bultmann, *Theology* I pp. 243f.

217. 'A Spirit of sonship' denotes 'a Spirit who makes us sons', not merely makes us conscious of being sons; but it is the latter aspect on which I wish to focus attention here; cf. Cerfaux, *Christian* p. 300.

218. See Arndt & Gingrich, κράζω. The formal parallel with rabbinic usage(' the Holy Spirit cries and says' – see Grundmann, *TDNT* III p. 900) is only formal, since it always introduces scriptural quotations; whereas Paul's concept of Spirit is very far from formal.

219. Bieder, 'Gebetswirklichkeit' pp. 25f.; M. Dibelius, 'Paulus und die Mystik', *Botschaft und Geschichte* II, Tübingen 1956, pp. 148f.; Delling, *Worship* p. 71; A. Oepke, *Der Brief des Paulus an die Galater*, THNT 1957, pp. 97f.; Schlier, *Galater* p. 198 n. 2; Michel, *Römer* p. 198 (though the present tense rules out a baptismal reference); Kuss, *Römerbrief* pp. 602ff.; Paulsen pp. 192f.; Käsemann, *Römer* pp. 217f.; and see particularly C. H. Dodd, *The Epistle to the Romans*, Moffatt 1932, pp. 129f. – 'the cry Abba! uttered by Christians under obvious spiritual stress' (p. 129).

220. On συμμαρτυρεῖν see H. Strathmann, *TDNT* IV p. 509; Kuss, *Römerbrief* pp. 604ff. Though the Greek allows us to take the witness bearing of the Spirit as something independent of and additional to the *abba*-prayer (so e.g. Althaus, *Römer* p. 91), it is better to take v. 16 as a direct continuation of the flow of thought in v. 15 (RSV, NEB).

221. J. Schneider, *TDNT* VII p. 602; Michel, *Römer* p. 208.

222. I do not understand Schneider therefore when he says, 'the reference is not to something which takes place in us.'

223. Lietzmann, *Römer* p. 86 – that is, glossolalia understood as a jumble of formless sounds. So Althaus, *Römer* p. 94; see also Cutten pp. 170ff. N. Q. Hamilton, *The Holy Spirit and Eschatology in Paul*, *SJT* Occasional Papers No. 6, 1957, in effect takes ἀλαλήτοις as 'impossible-to-understand' – an inadmissable interpretation.

224. See particularly Käsemann, 'The Cry for Liberty in the Worship of the Church', *Perspectives* pp. 122–37 (here p. 130); also *Römer* pp. 230f.

225. Cf. Schniewind, 'Seufzen' pp. 82ff.; Barrett, *Romans* p. 168. However Michel, *Römer* p. 208, Leenhardt, *Romans* p. 231, Gaugler, *Römer* pp. 322f. and K. Niederwimmer, 'Das Gebet des Geistes, Röm. 8.26f.', *TZ* 20, 1964, pp. 263f., all reject a reference to glossolalia outright. Nothing in the text compels us to confine Paul's reference here to the assembly (Delling, *Worship* p. 23 n. 4, Michel, *Römer* p. 208; against Käsemann, *Perspectives* pp. 129f.). Rather the reverse: Paul strongly discourages glossolalia in the Corinthian assembly, viewing it very negatively; whereas Rom. 8.26f. is a very positive appreciation of charismatic prayer.

226. Cf. Bieder, 'Gebetswirklichkeit' pp. 29f.; Niederwimmer pp. 254ff.; see further below §55.

227. For 'Spirit' as the subject (understood) of συνεργεῖ (rather than 'all things' or 'God') see M. Black, 'The Interpretation of Romans 8.28', *Neotestamentica et Patristica: Freundesgabe O. Cullmann*, NovTestSuppl VI, 1962, pp. 166–72; also *Romans*, Oliphants 1973, p. 124; cf. F. F. Bruce, *Romans*, Tyndale 1963, pp. 175f.

228. Arndt & Gingrich, γλῶσσα; 'unintelligible ecstatic utterance' (Behm, *TDNT* I p. 722); see also Moffatt, *I Cor.* pp. 208–17.

229. Weiss, *I Kor.* pp. 337f.; Wendland, *Kor.* p. 119; Barrett, *I Cor.* pp. 299f.

230. R. H. Gundry, '"Ecstatic Utterance" (NEB)', *JTS NS* 17, 1966, pp. 299–307 (here p. 299); earlier J. G. Davies, 'Pentecost' pp. 229ff.; so the standard

Pentecostal interpretation; for modern examples claimed by Pentecostals see above ch. VI n.83.

231. Conzelmann, *I. Kor* p. 295; Bultmann, *Theology* I p. 161.

232. See below §52.3; also Pearson pp.45ff. The attempts of Schlatter, *Bote* pp. 372f., Dupont, *Gnosis* pp.171, 204–12, Delling, *Worship* pp.38f., and of T. W. Manson, *Studies in the Gospels and Epistles*, Manchester 1962, pp.203f., to minimize Hellenistic influence and maximize Palestinian influence on Corinthian glossolalia makes shipwreck on the reef running between 12.2 and 14.12. See above p.234. This is not to deny that glossolalia was well known in the Palestinian churches (see above ch. VI n.1 and §26.3 and below p.246); indeed it is possible that Paul's use of Isa.28.11f. reflects the earlier use of this passage in the early communities as justification for glossolalia (Betz, 'Zungenreden' p.26).

233. If the use of κατηχέω in I Cor.14.19 implies formal instruction rather than charismatic teaching (see below pp.282f.), then it would heighten Paul's antithesis considerably: five 'uninspired' words of teaching better than ten thousand inspired but unintelligible ones.

234. Hurd suggests that on his first visit to Corinth Paul had been less reserved in his attitude to glossolalia and had encouraged its practice (p.281).

235. Hollenweger, *Pentecostals*: 'Since the uninformed view that speaking in tongues is of its nature ecstatic appears ineradicable, it must be explicitly stated here that this is not so. There exists not only "hot" speaking in tongues (which can be described as ecstatic, although the person speaking in tongues is never "outside himself"), but also "cool" speaking in tongues, sometimes mystical, and sometimes sounding like an incomprehensible foreign language . . .' (p.344). See also Samarin, *Tongues* chs. 2 and 11, and n.245 below.

236. Gundry, 'Ecstatic Utterance' p.299. We also regularly and appropriately use such phrases as 'mother tongue', 'foreign tongues'; so Rev.5.9; 7.9; 10.11, etc.

237. Weiss, *I Kor.* pp.337f.; Héring, *I Cor.* p.128.

238. Davies, 'Pentecost' pp.229f.

239. Against Barrett, *1 Cor.* p.299.

240. G. Bornkamm, *TDNT* IV p.822. In 14.2 it may not be reduced to the sense of 'riddles with no solution' (against Bruce, *Cor.* p.130).

241. For parallels see below §52.3.

242. Against Gundry, 'Ecstatic Utterance' p.306.

243. Weiss, *I Kor.* p.336. That Paul intends 'different human languages' as an analogy with and not a definition of glossolalia is indicated by the different word he uses – φωνή instead of γλῶσσα. In 14.21f. the point of comparison is the same.

244. Schlatter, *Bote* p.371. Note the reading of 14.2 in G and a few Latin manuscripts – 'the Spirit (πνεῦμα, not πνεύματι) speaks mysteries'. On the meaning of tongues as 'a sign for unbelievers' see above pp.230f.

245. For positive assessments of modern glossolalia along these lines see L. M. Vivier, *Glossolalia*, University of Witwatersrand M.D. thesis, Johannesburg 1960 (kindly lent me by the late Donald Gee); Kelsey, *Tongues* ch. VIII; Christenson, *Tongues* pp.72–81; J. M. Ford, 'Towards a Theology of "Speaking in Tongues"', *ThStud* 32, 1971, pp.23ff.

246. See above §41.6. Dibelius-Greeven, *Epheser* p.99 and Schlier, *Epheser* p.301, deny that Eph.6.18 includes a reference to glossolalia.

247. See above §41.5.

248. Bittlinger, *Graces* p.50.

249. It should be pointed out that the classic Calvinist view of I Cor.13.8ff. – that

glossolalia and prophecy (and knowledge) belonged only to the apostolic, or pre-canonical age, is quite foreign to Paul's thought (so recently, J. F. Walvoord, *The Holy Spirit*, Dunham reprinted 1965, pp. 179, 186; M. F. Unger, *New Testament Teaching on Tongues*, Kregel 1971, ch. XI). The charismata are all temporary enough in Paul's view, to be sure, because 'the perfect', that is the parousia, is imminent; but he does not envisage them ceasing or passing away before the 'face to face' knowledge of the parousia (correctly recognized by A. A. Hoekema, *What about Tongue-speaking?*, Paternoster 1966, p. 106 n. 8; D. Bridge & D. Phypers, *Spiritual Gifts and the Church*, IVF 1973, pp. 26–31).

250. Cf. E. M. B. Green, *II Peter and Jude*, Tyndale 1968, pp. 183f.

251. The miracle of drinking deadly poison without harm is attributed to Justus Barsabbas (Acts 1.23) by Papias, *c.*130 AD (Eusebius, *Eccles.Hist.* III.39.9).

252. Cf. Irenaeus, *Adv.Haer.* V.6.1; Tertullian, *Adv.Marc.* V.8; Origen, *Contra Cels.* VII.8. See also Weinel, *Wirkungen* pp. 72–8. For lesser known references to glossolalia or similar experiences in later Christian literature see K. Richstaetter, 'Die Glossolalie im Licht der Mystik', *Scholastik* II, 1936, pp. 321–45; S. Lyonnet, 'De glossolalia Pentecostes euisque significatione', *Verbum Domini* 24, 1944, pp. 65–75; S. Tugwell, *Did You Receive the Spirit?*, Darton, Longman & Todd 1972, chs. 6 and 8.

253. See further J. Behm, *TDNT* II pp. 661–5.

254. Hollenweger however, draws attention to the therapeutic value of speaking in tongues in twentieth-century Pentecostal assemblies: 'The Elim member, afraid to express himself in public, experiences a feeling of dramatic tension which is resolved when the psychological blockage is overcome in speaking in tongues – which is analogous to the practice of free association in the group-dynamic process. The Elim congregation is carrying out an unconscious psycho-therapeutic function, helps to overcome loneliness, anxiety and fear, releases emotional blockages in cathartic sessions and makes it possible for the individual to integrate himself into a community by passing through and leaving behind him a shared experience of guilt for the past (loneliness, misfortune, remorse, and everything else associated with sin)' (*Pentecostals* p. 203); see also p. 13 ('a kind of sacramentalism of speaking with tongues'), p. 459 ('the function of the Pentecostal movement is to restore the power of expression to people without identity and powers of speech, and to heal them from the terror of the loss of speech'). See also Samarin, *Tongues* chs. 10 and 12: 'glossolalia is a linguistic symbol of the sacred' (p. 231); Christenson: 'it lends a distinct note of the supernatural to the meeting' (p. 122).

255. In the twentieth-century Pentecostal and charismatic movements the interpretation of a tongue has often sounded more like a prophecy than the interpretation of a prayer; cf. e.g. Bennett, *Spirit* p. 89. Worth noting also are Samarin's comments on interpretation of tongues (pp. 162–72).

256. Gee, *Concerning Spiritual Gifts* p. 62.

257. Delling, *Worship* p. 33.

258. Moffatt, *I Cor.* p. 213. See also above n. 163.

259. H. Greeven, 'Die Geistesgaben bei Paulus', *Wort und Dienst* 6, 1959, p. 112; J. Hainz, *Ekklesia: Strukturen paulinischer Gemeinde-Theologie und Gemeinde-Ordnung*, Regensburg 1972, pp. 186–93; cf. Grau p. 47.

260. J. N. D. Kelly, *The Pastoral Epistles*, A. & C. Black 1963, p. 214.

261. On Col. 4.17 see below p. 289.

262. See Barrett, *I Cor.* pp. 393f.; cf. also Moffatt, *I Cor.* p. 278.

263. Cf. Eph. 4.28 and Paul's collection, particularly II Cor. 9.13 – ἁπλότητι τῆς κοινωνίας. On κοινωνία see below §45.1.

264. The sense of ἁπλότης is best illustrated by *Test.Issachar* 3 and 4. Other references in Arndt & Gingrich, ἁπλότης;see also Strack-Billerbeck III p. 296.

265. We should probably read κανθήσομαι rather than καυχήσωμαι despite the latter's superior attestation (RSV, NEB, JB; Weiss, *I Kor.* p. 314 n. 1; Barrett, *I Cor.* p. 302; J. K. Elliot, 'In Favour of κανθήσομαι at I Corinthians 13.3', *ZNW* 62, 1971, pp. 297f.; against Héring, *I Cor.* pp. 137f.; also Moffatt, *I Cor.* pp. 193f.). Examples of martyrdom by fire and self-burning, 'reckoned a particularly glorious act in the Graeco-Roman world', are given by K. L. Schmidt, *TDNT* III pp. 465ff. See also references in Conzelmann, *I Kor.* pp. 263f. For the dramatic and deeply moving effect that such self immolation by fire can have when not prompted by motives of mere exhibitionism we need only think of the self-burning of Buddhist priests in Vietnam and of Jan Palach in Czechoslovakia in the 1960s.

266. On the question of 'Early Christian Asceticism' see von Campenhausen, *Tradition and Life* ch. 4.

267. Bultmann, *TDNT* II p. 483; RSV, NEB; Cranfield, 'tend the sick, relieve the poor, or care for the aged and disabled' (*Commentary* p. 36).

268. Michel, *Römer* p. 300.

269. On the importance of almsgiving for Judaism see Strack-Billerbeck II pp. 188f. Bousset-Gressmann pp. 180f. See Tobit 4.7–11; Matt. 6.2–4. Judaism usually spoke of 'making alms' (= ποιεῖν ἐλεημοσύνην), but *Leviticus Rabbah* 34 uses an expression equivalent to Paul's ὁ ἐλεῶν in the same sense (Strack-Billerbeck III p. 296).

270. Μεταδιδούς and ἐλεῶν thus obviously overlap, but in the former Paul probably thinks chiefly of shared food and possessions, particularly clothing, and in the latter chiefly of the giving of financial aid.

271. See particularly Rom. 11.30ff.; 15.9; I Cor. 7.25; II Cor. 4.1; Eph. 2.4; Phil. 2.27; (I Tim. 1.13, 16; Titus 3.5).

272. Hasenhüttl p. 150.

273. See B. Reicke, *TDNT* VI pp. 700f.; Moulton & Milligan, προΐστημι. The third meaning occurs in Titus 3.8, 14.

274. So W. Sanday & A. C. Headlam, *The Epistle to the Romans*, ICC ⁵1902, p. 358; Lietzmann, *Römer* pp. 109f.; Prat, *Theology* I p. 426; Goguel, *Church* p. 120; Barrett, *Romans* p. 239. But 'officials' (JB) is an unwarranted or at least very anachronistic translation; see further below §48.3.

275. Michel, *Römer* p. 300; Cranfield, *Commentary* pp. 35f.; references in Reicke and Moulton & Milligan (as n. 273 above).

276. Note the use of ἐπιμελέομαι, 'care for, take care of', as parallel in meaning to προΐστημι in I Tim. 3.5.

277. Lagrange, *Romains* p. 300; Reicke, *TDNT* VI p. 701; J. Brosch, *Charismen und Ämter in der Urkirche*, Bonn 1951, p. 120; Friedrich, 'Geist und Amt' p. 80 n. 65; see also above n. 275 and below pp. 285ff.

278. E. von Dobschütz, *Die Thessalonischer Briefe*, KEK ⁷1909, pp. 215f.; M. Dibelius, *Thessalonischer I/II und Philipper*, HNT 1911, p. 23; Best, *Thess.* pp. 224f.

279. Leenhardt sees a much closer relation in administrative terms between the three words (*Romans* p. 312).

280. 'What is meant is the "holy zeal" which demands full dedication to serving the community' (G. Harder, *TDNT* VII p. 566); cf. II Cor. 8.17, 22 (σπουδαῖος); Gal. 2.10; Eph. 4.3; I Thess. 2.17; (II Tim. 2.15) (σπουδάζω). Note also that in II Cor. 8.7 σπουδή is reckoned as itself a charisma.

281. Hainz pp. 188f.; 'There could hardly be an order of "givers"!' (Richardson, *Theology* p. 334).

282. Hasenhüttl p. 149 n. 45.

283. A. Deissmann, *Bible Studies*, ET T. & T. Clark 1901, p. 92; Moulton & Milligan p. 48.

284. H. W. Beyer, *TDNT* III pp. 1033f.

285. Fenner, *Krankheit* suggests that ἀντιλήμψεις includes nursing the sick (p. 85).

286. Cf. NEB: 'those who have power to guide others'.

287. Lietzmann in Lietzmann-Kümmel, *Kor.* p. 63; Schlatter, *Bote* p. 351; Barrett, *I Cor.* pp. 295f.; Hasenhüttl p. 225; cf. Beyer, *TDNT* III p. 1036. Goppelt, *Apostolic Times* has no justification for singling out these two of the I Cor. 12.28 list as 'the two most important functions' (p. 183).

288. RSV and NEB do not bring out this change in the character of the list. See S. S. Smalley, 'Spiritual Gifts and I Corinthians 12.16', *JBL* 87, 1968, pp. 429f.

289. Hainz pp. 86f.; cf. Schürmann, 'Gnadengaben' p. 252.

290. Greeven, 'Geistesgaben' p. 113.

291. See also below ch. IX nn., 116, 117.

292. Greeven, 'Geistesgaben' pp. 114ff.; see also pp. 119f.

293. Käsemann, 'Ministry' p. 65; see also Grau p. 12.

294. Cf. F. J. A. Hort, *The Christian Ecclesia*, Macmillan 1897, pp. 155f; Conzelmann, *TDNT* IX p. 405 n. 25.

295. Bittlinger, *Graces* p. 63.

296. Käsemann: 'There is no divine gift which does not bring with it a task, there is no grace which does not move to action. Service is not merely the consequence but the outward form and the realization of grace' ('Ministry' p. 65).

297. Contrast the rabbinic view of prophecy in Abelson, *Immanence* ch. 18; Schäfer, *Geist* pp. 131f. Classic Pentecostalism also fell into this error, as F. D. Bruner demonstrates in *A Theology of the Holy Spirit*, Eerdmans 1970, pp. 87–117, 225–67; although Bruner's criticism is too sweeping, since Pentecostalism itself was aware of the danger; see e.g. Brumback, *Suddenly* ch. 9; J. E. Stiles, *The Gift of the Holy Spirit*, California, no date.

298. See Hasenhüttl pp. 121f.; G. Murphy, *Charisma and Church Renewal*, Rome 1965, pp. 69–78, particularly p. 77, against K. Rahner, *The Dynamic Element in the Church*, ET New York 1964, p. 55.

299. Prat, *Theology* I p. 128; cf. Bittlinger, *Graces* pp. 25f.

300. Cf. Brosch, *Charismen* pp. 33f.; Eichholz, *Gemeinde* pp. 16ff.; Schmidt, *Römer* p. 210; Hasenhüttl pp. 114ff.

301. Gunkel pp. 82f.; Wetter as above n. 11; see also Bultmann, *Theology* I pp. 153f. According to Baur, 'The charisma are originally nothing but the gifts and qualities which each man brings with him to Christianity; and these gifts and qualities are exalted into charisms because the Christian consciousness and life are found on them, and reared on the materials which they bring, and moulded by the operation of the spirit into their different individual forms' (*Paul*, Vol. II, ET Williams & Norgate 1875, p. 172). Cf. Philo (above pp. 204, 206).

302. As e.g. Bittlinger, *Graces* pp. 70ff., citing Hollenweger. But see also Bittlinger's definition in *Ministries* p. 18.

303. Against Conzelmann, *Outline*: 'All Christians are pneumatics to the degree that they serve the community' (p. 260).

304. See also Grau pp. 166ff.

305. A regular mistake in Pentecostal expositions.

306. Cf. Käsemann, 'Ministry' pp. 71f., although he overstates his case; also *Römer* pp. 314, 319.

307. Käsemann, 'Worship and Everyday Life', *NTQT* pp. 188–95; E. Schweizer, 'The Service of Worship', *Interpretation* 13, 1959, p. 400.

308. Macdonald, *Worship* p. 18.

309. Dunn, *Baptism* Part III. Paul never actually speaks of 'grace' in a 'baptismal context' or with reference to the Lord's Supper.

310. 10.20 shows that the thought is of eating in partnership with the Lord of the meal rather than of eating the Lord! (see especially Kümmel in Lietzmann-Kümmel, *Kor.* pp. 181f.). Käsemann argues that by 'spiritual (πνευματικόν) food and drink' (10.3f.) Paul means 'food and drink which conveys πνεῦμα ('The Pauline Doctrine of of the Lord's Supper', *ENTT* p. 113). But he ignores the fact that 10.1–4 is an allegory; see above n. 44; cf. P. Neuenzeit, *Das Herrenmahl*, München 1960, p. 185.

311. Cf. W. Manson, *The Doctrine of Grace*, ed. W. T. Whitley, SCM Press 1932, p. 60. T. F. Torrance, *Royal Priesthood*, *SJT* Occasional Papers No. 3, 1955: 'It is made clear in the twelfth chapter that the Lord's Supper and the χαρίσματα belong inseparably together' (p. 65). This statement has no foundation in the text.

Chapter IX

1. Though see Grau pp. 72f.

2. Grau defines exclusively in community terms as follows: 'The charismata are possibilities (Moglichkeiten) of Christian action given by the Holy Spirit through the unmerited grace of God which come to concrete expression in acts of service and offices for the building up of the community' (pp. 79f.).

3. For fuller treatment of these passages see Dunn, *Baptism*.

4. See J. Y. Campbell, '*KOINΩNIA* and its Cognates in the New Testament', *JBL* 51, 1932, reprinted in *Three New Testament Studies*, Leiden 1965, pp. 1–28 – see especially pp. 25ff.; F. Hauck, *TDNT* III p. 807; Barrett, *II Cor.* pp. 344f.

5. NEB translates, 'If then our common life in Christ yields anything to stir the heart, any loving consolation, any sharing of the Spirit, any warmth, or affection or compassion . . .'.

6. E.g. Weiss, *Earliest Christianity* p. 637; Lietzmann in Lietzmann-Kümmel, *Kor.* p. 63; J. J. Meuzelaar, *Der Leib des Messias*, Assen 1961, p. 87; Barrett, *I Cor.* p. 288.

7. See e.g. E. Percy, *Der Leib Christi*, Lund 1942, pp. 15ff.; Kümmel in Lietzmann-Kümmel, *Kor.* p. 187; Bultmann, *Theology* I p. 310; Robinson, *Body* pp. 49–67; Schweizer, *TDNT* VII pp. 1070f.; Käsemann, *Perspectives* pp. 104, 112; Conzelmann, *I Kor.* pp. 249f.

8. P. S. Minear, *Images of the Church in the New Testament*, Westminster 1960: 'Observe how the pneumatological note dominated the Christological' (p. 191). Cf. Hermann p. 83, and see further below ch. X.

9. Barrett, *I Cor.* pp. 288f.; Conzelmann, *I Kor.* p. 250; E. Dinkler, 'Die Taufaussagen des Neuen Testaments', *Zu Karl Barths Lehre von der Taufe*, hrsg K. Viering, Gütersloh 1971, pp. 87f.

10. Dunn, *Baptism* pp. 109–13, 129ff.

11. Cf. Scott, *Ephesians* p. 203; Schlier, *Epheser* p. 184; Kuss, *Römerbrief* p. 567.

12. Cf. H. Riesenfeld, *TDNT* VIII p. 143.

13. See the discussion in Meuzelaar, *Leib*.

14. Käsemann, *Perspectives* p.103; *Römer* p.321. See e.g., Epictetus, *Encheiridion* II.10.4; Seneca, *Epp.*95.52; Marcus Aurelius II.1. Most famous of all is the allegory attributed to Menenius Agrippa by Livy II.32. Other references in Weiss, *I. Kor.* p.302 n.2; Lietzmann in Lietzmann-Kümmel, *Kor.* p.62; Robinson, *Body* p.59 n.1.

15. 'Only in this context of the effects and gifts of grace does the apostle utilize the ancient world's figure of the one body and the variety of its members' (Bornkamm, *Paul* p.195). Percy does not give enough weight to this fact in his discussion of the relation between 'body of Christ', 'in Christ' and 'in Spirit' (*Leib* pp.18–43).

16. Hainz, *Ekklesia* pp.84 and n.4; 235f.; cf. K. L. Schmidt, *TDNT* III p.506; R. Schnackenburg, *The Church in the New Testament*, ET Burns & Oates 1965, p.167.

17. Arndt & Gingrich, ἐκκλησία; Hort, *Ecclesia* pp.116ff., 164, 168; Cerfaux, *Church* pp.192ff.; Hainz, pp.229–39, 250–5. Note also the use of ἐκκλησία in reference to local house groups/churches – Rom. 16.5; I Cor. 16.19; Col.4.15; Philemon 2. I Cor. 12.28 is frequently taken as an exception (Richardson, *Theology* p.287 – 'St Paul cannot be saying that God has "set" apostles in the local congregation'); but see Hainz pp.252ff. and below §47.2.

18. Weiss, *I Kor.* p.304; Conzelmann, *I Kor.* p.250.

19. Notice how much coming and going and communication there was between communities (cf. Rom. 16; I Cor. 16.17; Col.4.9–16; and see Kertelge, *Gemeinde* p.76). Consider also the complementary images of the risen Jesus as the last Adam, and of Christians as together constituting the eschatological people of God (see particularly Dahl, *Volk* pp.212ff., 225ff.; Schweizer, *Church Order* §7). But when we bring all these ways of speaking together (body, Adam, Israel), what emerges is the mutual, but immediate dependence of each community directly on the risen Lord, not on Jerusalem. Despite similarities to the Jewish temple tax, the collection 'for the poor among the saints at Jerusalem' (Rom. 15.25f.) does not denote the subordination and dependence of the Pauline churches on Jerusalem, but simply the common concern of Christians one for another (cf. Rom. 12.8; I Cor. 12.25f.), and in this particular case, the gratitude of the younger churches for the spiritual blessings which came through Judaism and Jerusalem (Rom. 15.27); cf. K. F. Nickle, *The Collection*, SCM Press 1966, ch.III; Hainz pp.232–6, 239–50. As we shall see below, pp.274f.), II Cor. 10–13 shows Paul's attitude to a Jerusalem which tried to assert primacy and authority over the churches of the Hellenistic mission.

20. Harnack in his debate with Sohm; Cf. Harnack, *The Constitution and Law of the Church*, ET Williams & Norgate 1910, pp.45ff., 234ff.

21. Cf. Schweizer, *Church Order* n.358: 'the body of Christ assumes form in the divine service of the primitive Church' – with acknowledgment to Cullmann, *Worship* pp.26, 33f.

22. On the range of diversity see above §43.6.

23. Grau p.55.

24. Käsemann, *ENTT* p.76; also *RGG*³ II 1276; G. Eichholz, *Die Theologie des Paulus im Umriss*, Neukirchen 1972, p.275; so also among Catholic commentators, Küng, *Church* p.189; Hasenhüttl p.234; Schürmann, 'Gnadengaben' pp.248f.; J. Gnilka, 'Geistliches Amt und Gemeinde nach Paulus', *Foi et Salut selon S.Paul*, Rome 1970, p.238.

25. Friedrich, 'Geist' p.77; Schweizer, *TDNT* VI p.432; Conzelmann, *I Kor.* p.252; Käsemann, *Römer* p.319.

26. Cf. Käsemann, *ENTT* p.73; 'In such a context all the baptized are "office-bearers"' (p.80). See also Bittlinger, *Graces* p.58.

27. The metaphor of the body illustrates Paul's theology; it must not be allowed to dictate it.

28. J. Horst, *TDNT* IV p. 563; see also n. 173 below.

29. Cf. Horst, *TDNT* IV p. 564; Conzelmann, *I Kor.* p. 252.

30. E. Schweizer, *The Church as the Body of Christ*, ET SPCK 1965, p. 63; see also *TDNT* VII p. 1070; Conzelmann, *Outline* p. 261.

31. Hence Paul's attitude to glossolalia in the assembly and the 'unresolved tension' in his appreciation of glossolalia which results (see above pp. 247f.).

32. Küng's definition of 'charisma' manages to catch something of the dynamic nature as event and of the diversity and community orientation of Paul's concept: 'in its widest sense it signifies the call of God, addressed to an individual, to a particular ministry in the community, which brings with it the ability to fulfil that ministry' (*Church* p. 188).

33. Hence the manner in which Paul frames the lists in Rom. 12.6–8 and I Cor. 12.8–10, where it is the gift, the activity, the service which is in view and not the individual who exercises it, see above ch. VIII pp. 210, 212, *et passim*.

34. Rom. 12 shows that the vision of I Cor. 12.12–30 applies to all Pauline communities, not simply to Corinth. E. von Dobschütz, *Christian Life in the Primitive Church*, ET Williams & Norgate 1904, suggests that Rom. 12–16 is 'precipitate of the experience which he (Paul) had gained in his Greek–Asia Minor communities' (p. 132).

35. Eichhloz, *Gemeinde* p. 5.

36. Käsemann, *ENTT* pp. 70, 81.

37. Hence the difficulty of regarding the chapter as an interpolation – against Weiss, *I Kor.*, Héring, *I Cor.* J. T. Sanders, 'First Corinthians 13: Its Interpretation since the First World War', *Interpretation* 20, 1966, also maintains that I Cor. 13 did not originally belong in its present position, but rightly recognizes that 'it must be understood in connection with chapters 12 and 14', as most commentators now agree (pp. 181ff.).

It is quite likely that Paul intends ζηλοῦτε in 12.31a as an indicative (rather than imperative) and thus as a rebuke: 'You desire the higher gifts (that is, in Corinthian terms, the gifts of highest inspiration); very well then, I will show you the most extreme way there is – this is the way to "go to the limit"' (Ruef). See G. Iber, 'Zum Verständnis von I Kor. 12.31', *ZNW* 54, 1963, pp. 43–52; followed by Bittlinger, *Graces* pp. 73f.; Ruef, *I Cor.* pp. 140f. On καθ' ὑπερβολήν see Arndt & Gingrich, ὑπερβολή.

38. Cf. G. Bornkamm, 'The More Excellent Way: I Corinthians 13', *Early Christian Experience* pp. 182f.; I. J. Martin, 'I Corinthians 13 Interpreted in its Context', *Journal of Bible and Religion* 18, 1950, pp. 101–5; also N. Johansson, 'I Cor. 13 and I Cor. 14', *NTS* 10, 1963–64, pp. 383–92; other references in Hurd p. 112.

39. E. Käsemann, *Die Legitimität des Apostels*, Darmstadt 1956, reprint of *ZNW* 41, 1942, pp. 33–71; C. K. Barrett, 'Christianity at Corinth' pp. 286–97; also 'ΨΕΥΔΑΠΟΣΤΟΛΟΙ (II Cor. 11.13)', *Melanges Bibliques*, Rigaux Festschrift, pp. 377–96; also *Signs* pp. 36ff.; also 'Paul's Opponents in II Corinthians', *NTS* 17, 1970–71, pp. 233–54; also *II Cor.* pp. 5–10, 28–32, 277f. Though I am less certain that Paul's reference to 'super apostles' (11.5, 12.11) extends beyond his opponents in Corinth; the immediate context in both cases hardly demands it. See further below §47.2. For contemporary parallels to the points at issue between Paul and the false apostles see Betz, *Paulus und sokratische Tradition*.

40. See also J. Rohde, 'Häresie und Schisma bei Clemens und Ignatius', *NovTest* X, 1968, pp. 218–26.

41. As parallels from the history of Christianity we might cite, for example, the 'Spiritual Franciscans' who emerged as a distinct party after Francis' death (see e.g. R. M. Jones, *Studies in Mystical Religion*, Macmillan 1909, ch.9); the Holiness Movement of the nineteenth century which was the true heir of early Methodist piety and feeling after sanctification (Raymond Brown, *Evangelical Ideas of Perfection: A Comparative Study of the Spirituality of Men and Movements in Nineteenth Century England*, Cambridge Ph.D. Dissertation 1965); and the emergence within classic Pentecostalism of the Latter Rain Movement as a protest against the decline of enthusiasm in the older Pentecostal churches (see e.g. Brumback, *Suddenly* pp. 330–3; Hollenweger, *Pentecostals* ch.11).

42. On Eph.4.7–16 see below §57.2.

43. P. S. Minear, *The Obedience of Faith*, SCM Press 1971; H. W. Bartsch, 'Die Empfänger des Römerbriefes', *StTh* 25, 1971, pp.81–9. The thesis is disputed by R. J. Karris, 'Rom. 14.1–15.13 and the Occasion of Romans', *CBQ* 35, 1973, pp. 155–78, with some effect. See also n.34 above.

44. Cf. Schmithals, *Paul and Gnostics* pp.219–38; although Schmithals sides with a number of scholars who think that Rom.16 was originally independent of Rom. 1–15 and directed to Ephesus. For the discussion and the contrary view see Kümmel, *Introduction* pp.222–6.

45. See Dunn, *Baptism* pp.143f. and those cited there.

46. Käsemann, *NTQT* pp.132ff. On I Cor.15.12 see above V n.43 and p.219.

47. Cf. Bieder, 'Gebetswirklichkeit' pp.32f.; Käsemann, *Perspectives* p.132; *Römer* pp.217f., 230f.

48. Minear, *Obedience* ch.6.

49. Cf. Althaus, *Römer* p.126; Käsemann, *Römer* p.317.

50. See particularly W. Lütgert, *Die Vollkommenen im Philipperbrief und die Enthusiasten im Thessalonisch*, Gütersloh 1909; R. Jewett, 'Enthusiastic Radicalism and the Thessalonian Correspondence', *Proceedings of the Society of Biblical Literature* 1972, Vol. I pp.181–232; see also Schmithals, *Paul and Gnostics* pp.123–218.

51. Cf. Schmithals, *Paul and Gnostics* pp.139–55.

52. Cf. Henneken, *Verkündigung* pp.103–11.

53. Best, *Thess.* p.239.

54. Cf. Best, *Thess.* p.279.

55. Cf. Masson, *Thess.* pp.93f.; Kuss, *Römerbrief* pp.552f.; C. H. Giblin, *The Threat to Faith*, Rome 1967, pp.148ff., who interprets τὸ κατέχον (v.6) as 'a demonic pseudocharismatic force'.

56. See particularly W. Lütgert, *Gesetz und Geist*, Gütersloh 1919; J. H. Ropes, *The Singular Problem of the Epistle to the Galatians*, Harvard Theological Studies 14, 1929; Schmithals, *Paul and Gnostics* pp.13–64.

57. See also R. McL. Wilson, 'Gnostics in Galatia?', *Studia Evangelica* IV, 1968, pp. 358–67; J. Eckert, *Die urchristliche Verkündigung im Streit zwischen Paulus und seinen Gegnern nach dem Galaterbrief*, Regensburg 1971; F. Mussner, *Der Galaterbrief*, Herder 1974, pp.11–29. But H. D. Betz, 'Geist, Freiheit und Gesetz', *ZTK* 71, 1974, pp.78–93, goes too far in the other direction when he concludes that in Galatians Paul 'speaks as a gnostic' (p.92).

The situation at Philippi seems to have been rather more complicated; I will simply refer to the discussion of R. Jewett, 'Conflicting Movements in the Early Church as Reflected in Philippians', *NovTest* XII, 1970, pp.362–90, for the various hypotheses and Jewett's own attempted synthesis. See also below ch.X n.164.

58. Note the parallel with the law in Rom.7.17–14, described in 7.14 as *pneumatikos*.

59. Cf. Cerfaux, *Christian* p. 261; Bittlinger, *Graces* p. 81. In Matt. 7.15–23 the false prophets pass the test of I Cor. 12.3 (they call Jesus 'Lord'); in addition they prophesy and perform exorcisms and *dunameis* 'in the name of Jesus'; yet their rejection is unqualified.

60. R. Sohm, *Kirchenrecht* I, Leipzig 1892.

61. O. Linton, *Das Problem der Urkirche in der neueren Forschung*, Uppsala 1932, p. 211. Unfortunately he neglected the not unimportant work of T. M. Lindsay, *The Church and the Ministry in the Early Centuries*, Hodder & Stoughton 1902, and paid too little attention to Streeter, *Church*. For other issues in more recent debates see M. Barth, 'A Chapter on the Church – The Body of Christ', *Interpretation* 12, 1958, pp. 131–56.

62. Harnack, *Constitution* §§ 5 and 14.

63. See particularly Farrer, 'Ministry' pp. 145ff., who scathingly dismisses what he calls 'Harnack's heresy' (p. 145 n. 1), but without supporting exegesis; Brosch, *Charismen* pp. 46ff., 94ff.

64. See e.g. O. Michel, 'Gnadengabe und Amt', *Deutsche Theologie*, 1942, p. 135; Friedrich, 'Geist' pp. 73f., 76f., 81–5. See also Bultmann, *Theology* II pp. 95–100.

65. In a series of studies culminating in *Church Order*; also *Beiträge zur Theologie des Neuen Testaments*, Zürich 1970, ch. 15 and pp. 274ff. See also from the same 'stable', E. Brunner, *The Misunderstanding of the Church*, ET Lutterworth 1952.

66. Particularly his essay on 'Ministry and Community' in *ENTT*. For a discussion of Käsemann's views see D. J. Harrington, 'Ernst Käsemann on the Church in the New Testament', *The Heythrop Journal* XII, 1971, pp. 246–57, 365–76.

67. We should mention also here F. Grau's Tübingen dissertation, unfortunately never published, and H. von Campenhausen, *Ecclesiastical Authority*.

68. *Church Order* 21g.

69. *ENTT* p. 83.

70. *The Church* pp. 179ff.

71. See particularly pp. 102ff. The Catholic apologetic comes to clearest expression in pp. 223–32, where the discussion soon leaves the Pauline material behind. See also Schürmann, 'Gnadengaben' pp. 264ff.; Kertelge, *Gemeinde* pp. 109–15. So J. L. Mackenzie, 'Authority and Power in the New Testament', *CBQ* 26, 1964: 'Authority in the Church must be charismatic . . .' (p. 419).

72. K. & D. Ranaghan, *Catholic Pentecostals*, Paulist Press 1969; E. D. O'Connor, *The Pentecostal Movement in the Catholic Church*, Notre Dame 1971; D. L. Gelpi, *Pentecostalism, A Theological Viewpoint*, Paulist Press 1971; F. A. Sullivan, 'The Pentecostal Movement', *Gregorianum* 53, 1972, pp. 237–65; E. Sullivan, *Can the Pentecostal Movement Renew the Churches?*, British Council of Churches 1972; several articles in *One Body in Christ* 7, 1971, no. 4, and 9, 1973, no. 1. See also IV n. 2 above.

73. It is quite likely that we owe the distinctively Christian sense of 'apostle', as apostle of Jesus Christ, to Paul; see particularly, J. Munck, 'Paul, the Apostles, and the Twelve', *St Th* III, 1949, pp. 96–110; Lohse, 'Ursprung' pp. 259–75. For the debate see Roloff, *Apostolat* ch. 1.

74. Paul does not recognize other ways for apostles to be called; see above §§ 18–20, and on II Cor. 10–13 below; against Schnackenburg, 'Apostles', followed by Kertelge, *Gemeinde* p. 90 (see above ch. VI n. 37); both also unjustifiably call Timothy an apostle (Schnackenburg pp. 290, 295; Kertelge pp. 83f., 95).

75. Schmithals, *Apostle* pp. 64f.; cf. Lindsay p. 81; Schnackenburg, 'Apostles' pp. 290f.

76. Conzelmann, *I Kor.* p. 108.

77. See also Hainz pp.85f. Against Brosch, who arbitrarily distinguishes between the 'charismatic' apostle, and apostle 'in the highest sense of the word' (pp.44, 101ff.) – a suggestion rightly rejected by Kertelge, *Gemeinde* p.111 n.60.

78. Perhaps a visit from Peter to Corinth (? – cf. I Cor. 1.12; Barrett, 'Cephas and Corinth', *Abraham unser Vater*, Michel Festschrift, pp.1–12) had blurred the border between the spheres of operation of the Jewish and Gentile missions (Gal.2.9).

79. See Käsemann and Barrett (above n.39); so also Héring, *II Cor.* p.79; Goppelt, *Apostolic Times* p.179. Others would deny that the 'super apostles' are to be distinguished from the 'false apostles' (11.13); so Roloff, *Apostolat* pp.78f. and those cited by him there – Kümmel, Bornkamm, Bultmann, Klein and Munck (n 129).

80. See especially K. H. Rengstorf, *Apostolat*; also *TDNT* I pp.414ff.; T. W. Manson, *The Church's Ministry*, Hodder & Stoughton 1948, pp.35–44. Note the talk of 'letters of accreditation' in II Cor.3.1, and cf. Rengstorf, *TDNT* I p.417.

81. See especially Barrett, *II Cor.* on these verses.

82. Paul's use of ἀποστέλλειν is deliberate and significant, as in its only other two occurrences in the undisputed Paulines (Rom. 10.15; I Cor. 1.17); cf. Barrett, *I Cor.* p.293.

83. G. Bornkamm, *Die Vorgeschichte des sogenannten Zweiten Korintherbriefes*, 1961, reprinted in *Geschichte und Glaube* II, München 1971, pp.166f.; Georgi, *Gegner* p.39; Roloff, *Apostolat* pp.76f., who rightly notes that this does not however weaken Käsemann's case for seeing the Corinthian 'false apostles' against a Palestinian Jewish Christian background (p.79). For an alternative view of 10.7 see Barrett, *II Cor.* pp.256f.

84. Cf. H. W. Beyer, *TDNT* III p.599, followed by Käsemann, *Legitimität* pp.48 (*ZNW* pp.59f.), Kümmel in Lietzmann-Kümmel, p.209, Georgi, *Gegner* p.231, and Hainz pp.164ff., 311ff. – that is, Paul's 'canon' is the mission God gave him and its success.

85. Plummer, *II Cor.* pp.287f.; Windisch, *II Kor.* p.310; Barrett, *II Cor.* pp.265f.

86. Cf. Roloff, *Apostolat* pp.80f.; and see above pp.103, 108f.

87. Possibly also Silvanus (cf. Acts 18.5; I Thess. 2.6/7) and even Apollos (I Cor. 4.9); see above ch. V n.5. Clement explicitly excluded the latter from apostleship (I Clem.47.3f.); but that may not be decisive in view of Clement's early-Catholicism.

88. That was the function of the 'apostles of the churches' (II Cor.8.23).

89. Von Campenhausen goes so far as to describe Paul as 'the true founder and discoverer of the Christian concept of authority' (*Authority* p.47).

90. See further von Campenhausen, *Authority* pp.44f.; Schweizer, *Church Order* 7h; and see also P. Gutierrez, *La Paternité Spirituelle selon Saint Paul*, EB 1968.

91. Schmithals, *Apostle* p.40. See also Roloff, *Apostolat* pp.83f.; Kertelge, 'Das Apostelamt des Paulus, sein Ursprung und seine Bedeutung', *BZ* 14, 1970, pp. 169ff., 177; also *Gemeinde* p.84. Cf. the primacy Paul accords to charismata of the Word (Stuhlmacher, *KuD* 17, 1971, p.36; see also above ch.VIII n.137).

92. Von Campenhausen, *Authority* pp.37f.

93. See Wegenast, *Tradition* pp.93–120; on I Cor.7.10; 9.14 see particularly D. L. Dungan, *The Sayings of Jesus in the Churches of Paul*, Blackwell 1971; on I Thess.4.1; II Thess.3.6ff. see above p.237; and on I Thess.4.15 see above p.230.

94. See above pp.224f. and §§41.2, 4. I refer particularly to the distinction suggested between the 'mind of Christ' and the 'law of Christ'.

95. F. Büchsel. *TDNT* II p.172. See particularly L. Goppelt, 'Tradition nach Paulus', *KuD* 4, 1958, pp.213–33, also *Apostolic Times* pp.152ff., who rightly emphasizes the pneumatic and kerygmatic character of tradition for Paul; Roloff, *Apostolat* pp.84–98; K. Wengst, 'Der Apostel und die Tradition', *ZTK* 69, 1972,

pp. 145–62, who emphasizes that for Paul tradition is interpreted tradition. To speak of tradition as 'a logos fixed by the college of Apostles in Jerusalem' (Gerhardsson, *Memory* p. 297) goes beyond the evidence.

96. Michaelis, *TDNT* IV p. 669; cf. W. P. de Boer, *The Imitation of Paul*, Kampen 1962, pp. 207f.

97. παραγγέλλω (7 – 4 in II Thess. 3), νουθετέω (2), διατάσσω (3).

98. ἐπιταγή – the command of a superior to a subordinate (cf. Delling, *TDNT* VIII pp. 36f.).

99. C. J. Bjerkelund, *Parakalō*, Oslo 1967, concludes that Paul uses παρακαλέω 'when the question of his authority presents no problem' (p. 188). Particularly noticeable is its absence from Gal. But note also I Cor. 1.10; II Cor. 10.1 (solely stylistic?).

100. *Authority* pp. 46–50.

101. *Authority* p. 47; see also Lindsay p. 49; Hasenhüttl pp. 77–83.

102. Contrast the 'false apostles' of II Cor. 10–13.

103. *Authority* p. 50; cf. Barrett, *Signs* pp. 41f.; Hainz pp. 54–7, 293f. Notice the παρὼν δὲ τῷ πνεύματι,, ὡς παρών,, of I Cor. 5.3. Paul evidently feels it inappropriate for him to exercise his authority at a distance; it can only properly be exercised from *within* the community (where it can be validated and confirmed by the community).

104. Wobbe pp. 73f.; von Campenhausen, *Authority* pp. 33 n. 12, 295; Hasenhüttl p. 77 n. 1. Against Büchsel, *Geist* p. 335; Käsemann, *ENTT* p. 81; Schnackenburg, 'Apostles' p. 300; Kertelge, *Gemeinde* p. 105; Hainz p. 339 n. 1. Schürmann calls apostleship the 'essence and peak (Inbegriff und Spitze) of all "offices" and "charismata"' ('Gnadengaben' pp. 245f.); 'Spitze' is arguable, 'Inbegriff' is not.

105. On the significance of the distinction see A. Satake, 'Apostolat und Gnade bei Paulus', *NTS* 15, 1968–69, pp. 96–107.

106. See Goppelt, 'Tradition' p. 224; *Apostolic Times* p. 154. Roloff notes that there are 'three different grades of authority' in the instructions given in I Cor. 7: 7.10; 7.12 and 7.25 (*Apostolat* p. 97). Contrast Lindblom, *Gesichte* pp. 160f.

107. See particularly Greeven, 'Propheten' pp. 4–8; otherwise Hainz pp. 87f.

108. A. Harnack, *Expansion of Christianity*, ET Williams & Norgate 1904, I pp. 417–44, who unjustifiably took *Didache* as the norm.

109. Reiling suggests that the three forms of prophecy (congregational occasional prophecy, local prophets, itinerant prophets) continued to feature within Christianity, probably until the Montanists (*Hermas* pp. 7–12, 122–54, 175).

110. So Greeven, 'Propheten' p. 7; G. G. Blum, 'Des Amt der Frau im Neuen Testament', *NovTest* VII, 1964–65, pp. 148f.; Kertelge, *Gemeinde* p. 121. Note however, the prominence of Prisca (I Cor. 16.19; Rom. 16.3; Acts 18.2, 18, 26), and particularly her precedence over her husband Aquila in Rom. 16.3; Acts 18.18, 26. On I Cor. 14.33b–36 see below n. 115. That I Cor. 11.1–16 refers only to worship in private rather than the worship of the assembly is unlikely (against J. Leipoldt, *Die Frau in der antiken Welt und im Urchristentum*, Gütersloh 1962, p. 114).

111. Robertson-Plummer, *I Cor.*: 'The Apostle does not say σιγησάτω, "let him *at once* be silent", but σιγάτω, which need not mean that' (p. 322).

112. Greeven, 'Propheten', thinks that two different prophets are in view in 14.32 (pp. 12f.). But most commentators take Paul to be speaking of each prophet's ability to control his own inspiration (cf. 14.30).

113. Weiss, *I Kor.* p. 340; Büchsel, *TDNT* III p. 947 n. 8; Greeven, 'Propheten' pp. 5f.; Delling, *Worship* p. 31; Bittlinger, *Graces* pp. 108ff; Hainz p. 94. This is the most natural sense of οἱ ἄλλοι in the immediate context. A reference to another

THE BODY OF CHRIST

group, other than the prophets, whose regular ministry was exercising the gift of 'discernment' would almost certainly be more explicit (against Allo, *I Cor.* p. 370).

Similarly unfounded is the view that Paul envisaged a recognized group of 'interpreters' whose charisma was 'a permanent possession', or that I Cor. 14.27f. directed the assembly to ascertain whether one of these 'interpreters' was present before beginning the worship (against Delling, *Worship* pp. 33f.; so Prat, *Theology* I p. 132). Paul probably means that if an initial contribution in tongues was not interpreted, no further utterance in tongues should be permitted.

114. Wendland, *Kor.* p. 114; Barrett, *I Cor.* p. 328; K. Wengst, 'Das Zusammenkommen der Gemeinde und ihr "Gottesdienst" nach Paulus', *EvTh* 33, 1973, pp. 552f.

115. Many commentators think that 14.33b–36 is in interpolation, in whole or in part – e.g. Weiss, Barrett, Conzelmann, Leipoldt pp. 125f., Schweizer, *Church Order* n. 783, Bittlinger, *Graces* pp. 110f.; Hahn, *Worship* p. 76. But see also Héring, *I Cor.* pp. 154f.; K. Stendahl, *The Bible and the Role of Women*, ET Fortress 1966, pp. 29f.; M. E. Thrall, *The Ordination of Women to the Priesthood*, SCM Press 1958, pp. 77ff.; Blum pp. 149ff.; A Feuillet, 'La dignité et le rôle de la femme d'après quelques textes pauliniens', *NTS* 21, 1974–75, pp. 162–8. Either way the implication is that women were disturbing the process of evaluation by asking unnecessary questions (v. 35).

116. Schweizer, *Church Order*: 'Their service is everywhere regarded as a direct gift of the Spirit; and the Church no more chooses prophets than it chooses apostles' (24c; see also 7m). Cf. the more general definition of 'minister', in Bittlinger, *Ministries* p. 24, though his subsequent discussion does not allow for the diversity and development in 'church order' during the first two or three generations of Christianity (see §§32.3, 57).

117. Greeven, 'Propheten' pp. 4–8; Goppelt, *Apostolic Times* p. 183; Hainz pp. 87f.; cf. Barrett, *I Cor.* p. 329; against Richardson, *Theology* p. 111; Bourke p. 499.

118. Greeven, 'Propheten' pp. 16f.; against Brosch, *Charismen* pp. 112ff.

119. See also Greeven, 'Propheten' pp. 18–24; Kertelge, *Gemeinde* pp. 122f. A firm distinction between 'kerygma' and 'didache', between matters of belief (faith) and matters of conduct (ethics), cannot be made here (cf. 'revelation' above – §40).

120. Rengstorf, *TDNT* II p. 157; Greeven, 'Propheten' pp. 24ff.

121. Beyer, *TDNT* III p. 639.

122. See above p. 185f. Cf. particularly Justin Martyr's *Dialogue*.

123. For the esteem in which pupils held their teachers within Judaism see Harnack, *Expansion* I pp. 416f.; Jeremias, *Jerusalem* pp. 243ff.

124. Although in Corinth the thought was possibly more in terms of a mystical relationship founded at initiation between baptizer and baptized; e.g. Lietzmann in Lietzmann–Kümmel, p. 8; Héring, *I Cor.* p. 7; Conzelmann, *I Kor.* pp. 49f.

125. Cf. Hasenhüttl p. 203.

126. Cf. Lindsay p. 104. Rengstorf's description of teachers simply as 'non-pneumatics' (*TDNT* II p. 158) is therefore misleading and unjustified.

127. Cf. I Clem. 48.5: 'Let a man be faithful, capable of uttering knowledge (γνῶσις), let him be discriminating in the evaluation of what is said (σοφὸς ἐν διακρίσει λόγων) . . .'; note how Clement associates utterance of knowledge (teaching?) with the gift (or ability?) to evaluate utterances – an association which strengthens the case for recognizing an allusion to I Cor. 12.8ff. at this point.

128. Greeven, 'Propheten' p. 29.

129. See also Dunn, 'Prophet' pp. 4–8, and above pp. 232f.

130. Nor does the Mebaqqer of Qumran (see P. von der Osten-Sacken, 'Bemerkungen zur Stellung des Mebaqqer in der Sektenschrift', *ZNW* 55, 1964, pp. 18–26) provide any pattern, even for the overseers (plural) at Philippi (see particularly J. Gnilka, *Der Philipperbrief*, Herder 1968, pp. 36f.; against Goppelt, *Apostolic Times* pp. 188f.).

131. For secular parallels see Arndt & Gingrich, ὑπηρέτης; Rengstorf, *TDNT* VIII pp. 530ff., 542.

132. See also Greeven, 'Propheten' pp. 40f.; Schweizer, *Church Order* 7i; and those cited above in ch. VII n. 111.

133. See Schweizer, *Church Order* 21a; Käsemann, *ENTT* p. 63. The other verse is Rom. 13.6, which refers to the service rendered by the Roman authorities. Cf. Lightfoot, 'The Christian Ministry', *Philippians*: '. . . . for the most exalted office in the Church, the highest gift of the Spirit, conveyed no sacerdotal right which was not enjoyed by the humblest member of the Christian community' (p. 184; also pp. 243ff.). See also Hahn, *Worship* pp. 36ff.

134. Von Campenhausen, *Authority* p. 63; Gnilka, 'Geistliches Amt' p. 239; against Farrer, 'Ministry' pp. 154f. On Gal. 6.1 and I Thess. 5.12f. see below pp. 286ff.

135. Cf. Greeven, 'Propheten' pp. 35f.; von Campenhausen, *Authority* p. 66; against Allo, *I Cor.* p. 338.

136. Against Beyer, *TDNT* II p. 92; Bourke, 'Church Order' p. 502, who wants to give more historical weight to Acts 14.23 (but see above §32.3).

137. Against Clement: 'They preached in country and city, and appointed their first converts (τὰς ἀπαρχὰς αὐτῶν), after testing them by the Spirit, to be the bishops and deacons of future believers' (I Clem. 42.4); so also Farrer, 'Ministry' pp. 147f.; cf. Schnackenburg, *Church* pp. 29f. But see Robertson-Plummer, *I Cor.* p. 395, and those cited in ch. VIII n. 262 above. We might note also that I Cor. 16.15f. is itself more an exhortation than a command.

138. Cf. Conzelmann, *I Kor.* pp. 357f.

139. Ἐπιγινώσκετε οὖν τοὺς τοιούτους (16.17f.) means, 'Recognize the charismatic function and authority of which they have already given so much evidence'.

140. Cf. Masson, *Thess.* p. 72.

141. Dibelius, *Thess.* p. 23; Dobschütz, *Thess.* pp. 218f.; Lohse, *Colossians* pp. 150–51; Campenhausen, *Authority* pp. 49ff.; Schweizer, *Church Order* n. 394 and 24e; cf. Best, *Thess.* pp. 226f.; Hainz pp. 37–47. Against Farrer, 'Ministry', who offers the extraordinary eisegesis that the 'brothers' of v. 12 = the community, whereas the 'brothers' of v. 14 = 'the ruling men' (p. 146, 154); F. Hauck, *TDNT* III p. 829; Rigaux, *Thess.* pp. 576f.; E. E. Ellis, 'Paul and his Co-workers', *NTS* 17, 1970–71, p. 441. For κοπιάω cf. particularly I Cor. 16.16; and for προϊστάμενος see above §42.2.

142. See Dunn, *Baptism* p. 120; so commentators generally; against A. Schlatter, *Die Theologie der Apostel*, Stuttgart ²1922, who equates 'die Pneumatiker' with 'the prophets' (pp. 506ff.; cf. Ellis, 'Spiritual Gifts' p. 132).

143. See R. Schnackenburg, 'Christian Adulthood according to the Apostle Paul', *CBQ* 25, 1963, pp. 357ff.; cf. Wilckens, *Weisheit* pp. 87–93; Conzelmann, *I Kor.* pp. 87f. On the distinction between ψυχικός and σαρκικός (I Cor. 2.14; 3.3) see Schweizer, *TDNT* IX p. 663.

144. J. B. Lightfoot, *Epistle to the Galatians*, Macmillan ¹⁰1890, p. 215; Burton, *Galatians* p. 327; Schlier, *Galater* p. 270; J. Bligh, *Galatians*, St Paul 1969, p. 471; Mussner, *Galater* p. 398; others in Eckert p. 144 n. 4. Against Lütgert, *Gesetz* pp. 12f.; Lietzmann, *Galater* p. 41; Schmithals, *Paul and Gnostics* p. 46.

145. Von Campenhausen, *Authority* p. 63 n. 50; against Farrer, 'Ministry' p. 154.

146. Eckert p. 144; Pearson p. 5; Mussner, *Galater* p. 398.

147. So J. H. Elliott, 'Ministry and Church Order in the NT: A Tradition-Historical Analysis (I Peter 5.1–5 and plls)', *CBQ* 32, 1970, p. 381.

148. Cf. G. Bertram, *TDNT* VII p. 874 and n. 21. Against Ellis, 'Co-workers' pp. 440f. Hainz also tends to overstructure the role of the co-worker (pp. 295–310).

149. Against Ellis, 'Co-workers' pp. 445–51. In I Cor. 16.19f. and Phil. 4.21f. 'the brothers' are *not* 'a more restricted group than "the Christians"'; in the former the phrase is '*all* the brothers' ('all' probably emphatic, gathering up all the previous greetings); and in the latter 'the brothers' are specified as 'the brothers, that is, Christians *with me*'.

150. Richardson, *Theology* p. 333; Hainz p. 194.

151. Paul's Corinthian opponents call themselves *diakonoi* of Christ (II Cor. 11.23) – obviously a *self*-designation (Georgi, *Gegner* pp. 31f.). Note also the use of *diakonos* in reference to Christ in Rom. 15.8; Gal. 2.17.

152. Against Ellis, 'Co-workers' pp. 441ff., who unjustifiably equates *diakonos* with the teacher of Gal. 6.6, and concludes from that that the *diakonoi* constituted a professional 'class' (pp. 443f.). Beyer however, recognizes in the case of Phoebe (Rom. 16.1) that he has to leave the question open as to whether Paul 'is referring to a fixed office or simply to her services on behalf of the community' (*TDNT* II p. 93). See also Delling, *Worship* pp. 157f., and above §42.1.

153. Beyer, *TDNT* II p. 616; von Campenhausen, *Authority* p. 68; E. Best, 'Bishops and Deacons: Philippians 1.1', *Studia Evangelica* IV pp. 371–6.

154. See Arndt & Gingrich, ἐπίσκοπος; Beyer, *TDNT* II pp. 608–17; Goguel, *Church* pp. 124f.; B. S. Easton, *The Pastoral Epistles*, SCM Press 1948, pp. 221–8: 'Nowhere is there any evidence of any accepted technical significance in the word' (p. 222).

155. Against Hasenhüttl p. 223.

156. Easton, *Pastorals* p. 224. The 'elder' nowhere appears in the Pauline churches at or before this time (see above n. 132).

157. Georgi, *Gegner* pp. 32–8; Gnilka, *Philipperbrief* p. 39; Ellis, 'Co-workers' pp. 442f. But see also J. N. Collins, 'Georgi's "Envoys" in II Cor. 11.23', *JBL* 93, 1974, pp. 88–96.

158. The sense of 'messengers' which Collins finds better attested than Georgi's 'envoys' is hardly appropriate for Phil. 1.1.

159. There is still much to be said for the view, originating with Chrysostom, that Paul particularly singles out the 'overseers and deacons' because they had had the special responsibility for raising and transmitting the Philippians' financial gift to Paul (Phil. 4.10–18); so e.g. Harnack, *Constitution* p. 58; Beyer, *TDNT* II p. 90; Goguel, *Church* p. 129; though the case is perhaps weakened by the absence of any allusion to the 'overseers and deacons' in 4. 10–18.

160. Cf. W. Michaelis, *Der Brief des Paulus an die Philipper*, THNT 1935, pp. 11f.; Gnilka, 'Geistliches Amt' pp. 240–5; Bornkamm, *Paul* p. 183. The plurals (overseers and deacons) and lack of a definite article are particularly noteworthy on this point. Best notes that Paul designates himself solely as 'slave' and not as 'apostle' (his usual self-designation in epistolary greeting), and suggests that in this address (1.1) Paul is correcting 'the first case of the desire for ecclesiastical position . . . with a little mild irony' (*Studia Evangelica* IV p. 376).

161. Cf. Goguel, *Church* pp. 129, 382; C. Masson, *L'Épitre de Saint Paul aux Colossiens*, Neuchatel 1950, p. 157.

162. Against Farrer, 'Ministry' pp. 148f.

163. So e.g. Scott, *Ephesians* p. 210; Schlier, *Epheser* p. 196. Philip is described as

'the evangelist' in Acts 21.8. D. Y. Hadidian revives the old suggestion (Oecumenius, Chrysostom) that the word refers to 'the "office" of gospel writer', but is able to cite only scattered and inconsequential evidence (*'tous de euangelistas* in Eph. 4.11', *CBQ* 28, 1966, pp.317–21).

164. Cf. Schweizer, *Church Order* 24h; Goppelt, *Apostolic Times* p.191; J. Gnilka, *Der Epheserbrief*, Herder 1971, pp.211f.

165. I Peter 2.25 associates the words pastor and overseer in a description of Christ.

166. R. Schnackenburg, 'Christus, Geist und Gemeinde (Eph.4.1–16)', *CSNT* pp. 292ff. For the other issues involved in determining the authorship of Ephesians see Kümmel, *Introduction* pp.251–6.

167. Friedrich, *TDNT* II p.737; Jeremias, *TDNT* VI pp.497f.

168. As Gnilka recognizes, 'Das Kirchenmodell des Epheserbriefes', *BZ* 15, 1971, pp.180ff.

169. Greeven, 'Propheten', argues that prophets and teachers were the only authorities within the Pauline communities (p.42).

170. ἀντιλήμψεις, διακονία, ἐλεέω, κοπιάω, κυβερνήσεις, μεταδίδωμι, νουθετέω, παρακαλέω, παραμυθέομαι, προΐστημι, συνεργέω.

171. Schweizer, *Church Order*: 'Speaking generally, the Church emphasized its different nature with surprising freedom by creating new ministries and transforming old ones' (24i).

172. Schweizer, *Church Order* 24k.

173. Schweizer, *Church Order*: 'The Church becomes a church, not by tradition itself, but by repeated action of the Spirit' (7i). See also von Campenhausen, *Authority* pp.68ff.; and above §45.2.

174. H. Küng, *Why Priests?*, ET Fontana 1972: 'Ecclesial "office" is not a New Testament notion, but a problematical concept which emerged from later reflections' (p.26).

175. Käsemann, *ENTT* p.78.

176. Lindsay pp.32f., 58f.

177. Against Greeven, 'Propheten' pp.35f.

178. On judgment cf. Roetzel pp.112–36.

179. Without forgetting the qualification outlined above (p.287). Note also I Cor. 2.6 – 'we speak wisdom *among* (not to) mature Christians' – that is, Paul envisages a discussion rather than a monologue – all may speak (Barrett, *I Cor.* p.69).

180. Lindsay pp.99f.; Henneken, *Verkündigung* pp.106f. In Hermas, *Mand.* XI.14, the false prophet is exposed by the prayer of the assembly as a whole (Reiling, *Hermas* pp.15f., 73). Cf. the importance and manner of 'discerning the spirits' of members of the Qumran community (IQS 5.20b–24; cf. 6.14ff.).

181. Cf. Schweizer, *Church Order* 7k.

182. Barrett, *I Cor.* p.321.

183. Cf. Windisch, *II Cor.* p.87; Blass-Debrunner-Funk §244.3. Wengst, 'Zusammenkommen' pp.547–54, justifiably understands the latter passages in terms of activities undertaken by the community when gathered together.

184. Paul does not use the test of fulfilled prediction (cf. Deut.18.21f.; Jer.28.9); though note II Thess.2.1ff. This does not mean that there was no predictive prophecy in the Pauline congregations, although it may mean that any such prophecy was primarily eschatological (cf. I Thess.4.15).

185. Cf. C. H. Dodd, *History and the Gospel* pp.56ff.; von Campenhausen, *Authority* p.294. W. C. van Unnik's attempt to equate the ἀνάθεμα of I Cor.12.3 with the κατάρα of Gal.3.13 must be judged a failure since in that case Paul could never

condemn the ᾽Ανάθεμα ᾽Ιησοῦς so unequivocally ('Jesus: Anathema or Kyrios (1 Cor. 12.3)', *CSNT* pp. 113–26).

186. If 'the faith' in Rom. 12.6 meant the kerygma or the 'believing hearing' of conversion (cf. Gal. 3.2; Rom. 10.17) it would add weight to this point – κατὰ τὴν ἀναλογίαν τῆς πίστεως would then stand in the same relation to 'prophecy' (Rom. 12.6) as does 'evaluation of spiritual utterances' to 'prophecy' in I Cor. 12.10 (cf. Käsemann, *Römer* p. 326). But see above §39.4.

187. See also Schürmann, 'Gnadengaben' pp. 261ff.

188. The 'noisy gong' and 'clanging cymbal' may be a reference to practices of pagan worship; cf. K. L. Schmidt, *TDNT* III pp. 1037ff.; Conzelmann, *I Kor.* p. 262. On glossolalia see above §41.7.

189. Strack-Billerbeck I p. 759: '"To uproot" or "to tear out mountains" is a proverbial expression which means in effect "to make possible what seems impossible"'. On faith, knowledge and prophecy see above §§39.4, 40.4, 41.2.

190. On v. 3 see above p. 250.

191. Note the distinction, perhaps antithesis (see n. 37 above) between gift and love in 12.31 and 14.1. '*Agapē* is qualitatively different from these other "possibilities" discussed in chapter 12. Even prophecy may be "strived for" (14.1), but in 13.1–3 "love is distinctly enough set apart from all other gifts, even the highest"' (Sanders, 'I Cor. 13' p. 173, citing K. Barth).

192. Cf. Fridrichsen, *Miracle* pp. 145f.

193. ᾽Ανυπόκριτος is only used with reference to love in the undisputed Paulines. See also Wilckens, *TDNT* VIII pp. 570f.

194. The chapters are dominated by the word καυχάομαι – 14 times; also καύχησις – twice.

195. The singular 'fruit', not 'fruits', indicates the single source of character transformation and the mutual coherence of these characteristics in the man of the Spirit: Paul may also imply that the other characteristics (joy, peace, etc.) are an outworking of love. See also Schlier, *Galater* pp. 256f. For fuller exposition see commentaries; also Kuss, *Römerbrief* pp. 568ff.; W. Barclay, *Flesh and Spirit*, SCM Press 1962, ch. III.

196. The parallel between 5.14 and 6.1f. makes it clear that for Paul the 'spiritual man' is to be defined as the man who 'loves his neighbour as himself'. See also above pp. 287f.

197. Cf. Bertrams, *Wesen* pp. 46–70.

198. Wengst, 'Zusammenkommen' pp. 555ff.

199. The use of the verb in 8.10 perhaps indicates that the Corinthian gnostics claimed that the free exercise of individual liberty was the best way to build up the weak consciences of the 'weak': 'Knowledge builds up' (see e.g. Moffatt, *I Cor.* pp. 110f.; Allo, *I Cor.* p. 205; Michel, *TDNT* V p. 141). Paul's reply is to the effect that the spiritual anguish caused to the 'weak' by the conduct of the gnostic is destructive rather than constructive (cf. II Cor. 10.8; 13.10). But see also M. E. Thrall, 'The Meaning of οἰκοδομέω in relation to the Concept of συνείδησις (I Cor. 8.10)', *Studia Evangelica* IV pp. 468–72.

200. See P. Vielhauer, *Oikodome*, Heidelberg 1939, pp. 9off.

201. Cf. Bornkamm, *Experience* pp. 163f.; Schweizer, *Church Order* 7f.

202. Michel rightly points to the 'charismatic character of the process of growth' (*TDNT* V p. 141).

203. Cf. Gunkel pp. 73ff. The tests of false prophecy in *Didache* 11.5f., 9f.; 12 and Hermas, *Mand.* XI.7–16, are simply extensions and applications of Paul's criterion

of *oikodomē*. Gunkel makes the interesting comment: 'The sentence – "the gifts of the Spirit serve the mutual upbuilding of the community' – is not a judgment gained from experience, but a requirement laid upon the Pneumatiker' (p. 74).

204. Cf. Bornkamm, *Paul* pp. 183ff.

205. Thus the test of I John 4.2f. is not the kerygma in its original form, but the kerygma as developed to counter the threat of docetism (see below' §58.2). Similarly the traditions which included ethical directions (Goppelt, 'Tradition' pp. 227f.). Cf. Schweizer, 'Service of Worship': 'A mere taking over of doctrines or of ethical commands which does not include a real understanding which enables the hearer to live really by grace is useless' (p. 406).

206. Von Campenhausen, *Authority* pp. 70f.

207. For elaboration of the metaphor see W. C. van Unnik, '"Den Geist Löschet nich aus" (I Thess. 5.19)', *NovTest* X, 1968, pp. 255–69. Cf. also O. Kuss, 'Enthusiasmus und Realismus bei Paulus', *Auslegung und Verkündigung* I, Regensburg 1963, pp. 260–70.

208. Cf. Michel, *Römer* p. 297.

209. Cf. the Johannine concept of church (see below §58.3).

210. Käsemann, *ENTT* p. 78.

211. Apostleship as Paul conceives it is *sui generis* (see above §§18–20, 47.2).

212. So Torrance, *Priesthood* p. 69.

213. Cf. Hainz – 'Each χάρισμα is subject to its own μέτρον τοῦ κανόνος' (p. 339).

214. If a modern attempt to achieve charismatic community on the Pauline pattern asks about apostolic authority, the best answer would probably be this: outside the completely new missionary situation the same authority, stemming from the decisive events of the past, now lies to hand in the apostolic gospel(s) and the traditions of Jesus' sayings in the New Testament. A completely new missionary situation might require a more personal apostolic-type authority in the church-founding missionary. At all events, continuity with the apostolic churches lies in the kerygmatic tradition and not in office; cf. W. Marxsen, 'Die Nachfolge der Apostel', *Der Exeget als Theologe*, Gütersloh 1968, pp. 75–90.

Chapter X

1. See further Volz, *Geist* pp. 116f.; P. Fiebig, *Rabbinische Wundergeschichten des neutestamentlichen Zeitalters*, Berlin ²1933; Vermes, *Jesus* pp. 69–78.

2. O. Weinreich, *Antike Heilungswunder*, Giessen 1909; P. Fiebig, *Antike Wundergeschichten zum Studium der Wunder des Neuen Testaments*, Bonn 1921; S. Angus, *The Religious Quests of the Graeco-Roman World*, Murray 1929, ch. XXII; A. Oepke, *TDNT* III pp. 196–9; M. P. Nilsson, *Geschichte der griechischen Religion* II, München 1950, pp. 211–14; G. Delling, *Antike Wundertexte*, Berlin 1960; Hull, *Hellenistic Magic* ch. IV.

3. Most easily accessible as part of the last volume of Livy in the Loeb edition.

4. A. Giannini, *Paradoxographorum Graecorum Reliquiae*, Milano 1967. I am grateful to Prof. E. A. Judge of Macquarie University, New South Wales, for reference to this work. Other references in R. M. Grant, *Miracle and Natural Law in Graeco-Roman and Early Christian Thought*, Amsterdam 1952, ch. 5.

5. Lucian, *Philopseudes* 13. For other ancient accounts of walking on water miracles

see van der Loos pp. 655ff.

6. Dio Cassius 56.46.2.

7. See further Guillaume ch. V; Oepke, *TDNT* V pp. 221–34; E. R. Dodds, *The Greeks and the Irrational*, California 1951, ch. 4; Nilsson, *Geschichte* pp. 214ff.; W. Richter, 'Traum und Traumdeutung im AT', *BZ* 7, 1963, pp. 202–20; A. D. Nock, *Essays on Religion and the Ancient World*, Oxford 1972, pp. 46, 629ff., 866.

8. W. Bousset, *Die Himmelreise der Seele*, 1901, reprinted Darmstadt 1971; Volz, *Geist* pp. 118, 121–6; Windisch, *II Kor.* pp. 374ff.; Angus ch. XVII; G. G. Scholem, *Jewish Gnosticism, Merkabah Mysticism and Talmudic Tradition*, New York 1960, ch. 3; Schweizer, *TDNT* VII p. 1043 n. 245; Lohfink, *Himmelfahrt* ch. I; Smith, *Clement* pp. 238ff.; Barrett, *II Cor.* pp. 308ff.

9. Probably second-century Christian, but with Gnostic influences, most marked in this section; see A. K. Helmbold, 'Gnostic Elements in the "Ascension of Isaiah"', *NTS* 18, 1971–72, pp. 222–6.

10. Translation in Hennecke, *Apocrypha* II pp. 651ff.

11. Following the English translation in R. M. Grant, *Gnosticism, An Anthology*, Collins 1961, pp. 217f. See further Reitzenstein, *Poimandres*, Leipzig 1904, pp. 9ff., 158f.; *Mysterienreligionen* pp. 284ff.; Nock, *Essays* p. 87.

12. Apuleius, *Metamorphoses* XI.23 (translation by R. Graves, *The Golden Ass*, Penguin 1950). See also Reitzenstein, *Mysterien.* pp. 220ff., 242ff., 262ff.; Angus pp. 88ff.; Nock, 'A Vision of Mandulis Aion', *Essays* ch. 19.

13. There is of course no clear dividing line between the experiences indicated in §52.2 and those of §52.3.

14. *TDNT* VI p. 821; see the whole section, pp. 819–28. Cf. Volz, *Geist* pp. 103, 130–3; Guillaume ch. VII.

15. Philo, *Mig. Abr.* 35, *Spec. Leg.* III.1f.

16. Loeb edition, Vol. IV. See also *Quis Her.* 69f.; *Vit. Mos.* I.277, 283, II.188; *Spec. Leg.* I.65, IV.49. Contrast however Paul's understanding of prophetic inspiration (I Cor. 14.15 – 'with the Spirit and with the mind also'); see above §41.2.

17. Georgi, *Gegner* pp. 114–30.

18. Strack-Billerbeck III p. 449.

19. See e.g. S. D. Currie, '"Speaking in Tongues"; Early Evidence outside the New Testament Bearing on "Glossais Lalein"', *Interpretation* XIX, 1965, pp. 282ff. See also *The Apocalypse of Abraham* 17, where Abraham is taught a song by an angel; *Ascension of Isaiah* 8.17, where in the sixth heaven Isaiah sings praises with the angels 'and our praise was like theirs'; cf. Enoch 71.11. For other examples of glossolalia and charismatic praise within the OT and Judaism, see Volz, *Geist* pp. 8f., 136f. As Qumran parallels to Paul's experience of 'praying in the Spirit' A. Dietzel, 'Beten im Geist', *TZ* 13, 1957, pp. 24ff., cites IQH 3.22f.; 16.11; 17.17; see also Jubilees 25.10–23. Dupont-Sommer, *Qumran*, finds a reference to speaking in tongues in CD 14.10 (p. 159).

20. Plato, *Phaedrus* 244a–245a, 265a–b, following Dodd's summary (p. 64).

21. See H. W. Parke and D. E. W. Wormell, *The Delphic Oracle: Vol. II The Oracular Responses*, Blackwell 1956 – a collection of more than 600.

22. See Fascher ch. 1; Dodds, *Irrational* pp. 65–75; H. Krämer, *TDNT* VI pp. 784–96. For those called 'prophet' in the ancient world see *Paulys Realencyclopedie der classischen Altertumswissenschaft* XXIII.1, Stuttgart 1957, 'Prophetes'.

23. Origen, *Contra Celsum* VII.9; on glossolalia in particular see further Reitzenstein, *Poimandres* pp. 55ff.; Behm, *TDNT* I pp. 722f.; Lietzmann in Lietzmann-Kümmel, *Kor.* pp. 68ff.

24. E. Rohde, *Psyche*, ET Kegan Paul 1925, pp. 255–60 and ch. IX. See also Reitzenstein, *Poimandres* pp. 200ff.; Oepke, *TDNT* II pp. 451–4; Dodds, *Irrational* pp. 75–80.

25. See E. R. Dodds, 'Supernatural Phenomena in Classical Antiquity', *The Ancient Concept of Progress*, Oxford 1973, ch. X.

26. Plato, *Symposium* 215–16.

27. *Encheiridion* III.23.1, following Moffatt's translation (*I Cor.* p. 224).

28. The text consulted was that of F. C. Conybeare in the Loeb Classical Library. On questions of sources used by Philostratus and their tradition history see especially G. Petzke, *Die Traditionen über Apollonius von Tyana und das Neue Testament*, Leiden 1970. See also the introduction by G. W. Bowersock to the Penguin edition (abbreviated 1970).

29. Grant, *Miracle* p. 41; see further chs. 4 and 5; Dodds, *Irrational* ch. 6; G. Delling, 'Zur Beurteilung des Wunders durch die Antike', *Studien zum Neuen Testament und zum hellenistischen Judentum*, Göttingen 1970, pp. 53–71; Nock, *Essays* p. 327.

30. Dodds, *Irrational* pp. 116–18.

31. *Alexander the False Prophet*. Alexander of Abonoteichus was a prophet of Asclepius who had widespread influence from about 150–170 AD. See also H. D. Betz, *Lukian von Samosata und das Neue Testament*, Berlin 1961.

32. *The Pumpkinification of Claudius* (available as an appendix to R. Graves, *Claudius the God*, 1934, Penguin 1954). See also Lucian, *de Morte Peregrini* 39–40.

33. See Tiede, *The Charismatic Figure as Miracle Worker*.

34. Tiede's findings put a question mark against Georgi's thesis that Paul's opponents in Corinth presented Christ and themselves as 'divine men' in terms of 'signs and wonders'.

35. Cf. the attack of Celsus on Christianity in the second century, an example of which is given above (§52.3). On the other hand we should recall the vigorous and crude heightening of the miraculous in the apocryphal gospels and Acts of the second and third centuries – see Hennecke, *Apocrypha* I & II; also the essays by G. W. H. Lampe and M. F. Wiles in Moule, *Miracles* chs. 13 and 14.

36. This aspect of Paul's theology has been developed most helpfully by Cullmann, *Christ and Time*; also *Salvation in History*, ET SCM Press 1967, pp. 248–68: 'It is characteristic of all NT salvation history that between Christ's resurrection and his return there is an interval the essence of which is determined by this tension' (p. 202). See earlier W. Wrede, *Paul*, ET London 1907, pp. 102–11; G. Vos, *The Pauline Eschatology*, 1930, reprinted Eerdmans 1961, pp. 51f. It was A. Schweitzer, *Paul and his Interpreters*, ET A. & C. Black 1912, who most effectively drew our attention to the need to approach Paul from the perspective of eschatology instead of reducing the subject to an ill-fitting last chapter inadequately related to the 'system of doctrine' already neatly set out and tied up in the preceding chapters (pp. 53f.).

37. For what the 'End' meant for Paul see e.g. Kennedy, *Last Things*. The importance of this belief for Paul is indicated in such passages as II Thess. 2.1–12; I Cor. 15; II Cor. 5.1–10; Rom. 8.18–25; 11. See also above §20.2 and cf. ch. III nn. 30, 34 above.

38. A full list would be tedious; I will give only one or two examples in each case. Justification and redemption, salvation and putting on (see below p. 309f.); reconciliation (II Cor. 5.18–20); waking up (Eph. 5.14); invitation (I Cor. 7.17–24); Gal. 1.15; II Thess. 2.14); sowing (I Cor. 3.6–8); watering (I Cor. 12.13c); grafting (Rom. 11.17–24); harvest (Rom. 8.23); seal and down payment (II Cor. 1.22); accounting (Rom. 4.3–12, 22ff.); refining (Rom. 16.10); building (I Cor. 3.10–14); circumcision (Phil. 3.3); baptism (I Cor. 12.13a); purification and consecration

(I Cor.6.11); anointing (II Cor.1.21); creation (II Cor.5.17; Gal.6.15); birth (I Cor.4.15); adoption (Gal.4.4f. and below); marriage (Rom.7.1–6 and below); death (Gal.2.19; Col.3.3); resurrection (see below p.310).

39. Cf. Windisch, *II Kor.* pp.189f.; Barrett, *II Cor.* pp.173ff.

40. Though this difference in perspective may indicate post-Pauline authorship; see also below §57.2.

41. Cf. Schweizer, *TDNT* VIII p.399.

42. Cf. R. A. Batey, *New Testament Nuptial Imagery*, Leiden 1971, p.29.

43. See also Dunn, 'Spirit and Kingdom' pp.36f.; on Rom.6.5 as a reference to future resurrection, see Dunn, *Baptism* pp.143f.

44. The best treatments of this theme are H. D. Wendland, 'Das Wirken des Heiligen Geistes in den Gläubigen nach Paulus', *TLZ* 77, 1952, 457–70, and Hamilton, *The Holy Spirit and Eschatology in Paul*, especially pp.19–25, 31–7. Still valuable is the earlier essay of G. Vos, 'The Eschatological Aspect of the Pauline Concept of the Spirit', in *Biblical and Theological Studies*, Princeton Theological Seminary, Scribner 1912, pp.211–59. See also R. Koch, 'L'Aspect Eschatologique de l'Esprit du Seigneur d'après Saint Paul', *Studiorum Paulinorum Congressus Internationalis Catholicus 1961*, Rome 1963, pp.131–41; B. Rigaux, 'L'anticipation du salut eschatologique par l'Esprit', *Foi et Salut selon S.Paul*, Rome 1970, pp.101–30.

45. See also Dunn, 'Spirit and Kingdom' pp.36–40.

46. See further Gunkel pp.69ff.; W. Michaelis, *Reich Gottes und Geist Gottes nach dem Neuen Testament*, Basel 1931, p.24; J. D. Hester, *Paul's Concept of Inheritance*, *SJT* Occasional Papers No. 14, 1968, pp.96–103.

47. Lev.23.9–14; for fuller background details see R. de Vaux, *Ancient Israel*, ET Darton, Longman & Todd ²1965, pp.490f.

48. J. Behm, *TDNT* I p.475. Moulton & Milligan point out that in modern Greek ἡ ἀρραβῶνα is used for 'the engagement ring'.

49. The genitives ἀπαρχὴ πνεύματος and ἀρραβὼν πνεύματος are generally and correctly taken as genitives of apposition: the first instalment which *is* the Spirit. There is no thought of an initial gift of the Spirit to be followed by a complete outpouring later (at parousia/resurrection); so rightly, Michel, *Römer* p.205 n.3. The forward looking emphasis in both metaphors does not imply further givings of the Spirit, simply the increasing control of the believer by the one Spirit already given. Hamilton tries to safeguard this emphasis by translating 'the firstfruits of what the Spirit has to give' (*Spirit* p.32 n.2). But this is unnecessary and misleading since it suggests that the ἀπαρχή is something other than the Spirit.

50. Cf. Cullmann: 'If the later Church has lost so much in vitality, if the workings of the Spirit, measured by those of the Primitive Church, are so very few, this is connected with the fact that this consciousness of standing as a Church in redemptive history's quite definite plan, and of being on the way from the resurrection to the Parousia, has been lost or in any case greatly weakened' (*Christ and Time* p.144).

51. See further Dunn, *CSNT* pp.132ff.; and below §54.2.

52. Scott: 'He remained ἐν σαρκί even though he was ἐν Χριστῷ (Phm.16; cf. Rom. 8.10)' (*Paul* p.148). See also below p.336. For a fuller study of σάρξ, though from a somewhat different angle, see Dunn, 'Jesus – Flesh and Spirit', pp.44–9.

53. On ἐπιθυμία see Büchsel, *TDNT* III p.171: 'The essential point in ἐπιθυμία is that it is desire as impulse, as a motion of the will'. See also Bultmann, *Theology* I p.241. On 'walking by the Spirit' see above §40.5.

54. Burton, *Galatians* pp.301f.; Schlier, *Galater* p.249; Mussner, *Galater* p.377.

55. Lightfoot, *Galatians* p.210; M. J. Lagrange, *Épitre aux Galates*, EB 1950, pp. 147f.; P. Bonnard, *L'Épitre de Saint Paul aux Galates*, Neuchatel 1953, p.113; Oepke, *Galater* pp.135f.; C. F. D. Moule, *An Idiom Book of New Testament Greek*, Cambridge ²1959, p.142; Eckert p.137 and n.1.

56. See particularly W. G. Kümmel, *Römer 7 und die Bekehrung des Paulus*, Leipzig 1929; R. Bultmann, 'Romans 7 and the Anthropology of Paul', *Existence and Faith*, ET 1961, Fontana 1964, pp.173–85.

57. See more fully J. D. G. Dunn, 'Romans 7.14–25 in the Theology of Paul', forthcoming in *TZ* 31, 1975. Others who follow the exegesis of Augustine, Luther and Calvin in more recent times include A. Nygren, *Commentary on Romans*, ET SCM Press 1952; J. Knox, *Interpreters Bible* 9, 1954; J. Murray, *The Epistle of Paul to the Romans*, Marshall, Morgan & Scott 1960; K. Stalder, *Das Werk des Geistes in der Heilungg bei Paulus*, Zürich 1962, pp.291–307; F. F. Bruce, *The Epistle of Paul to the Romans*, Tyndale 1963; J. I. Packer, 'The "Wretched Man" of Romans 7', *Studia Evangelica* II, 1964, pp.621–7.

58. Kümmel, *Römer 7* pp.10ff., *et passim.*

59. Cf. particularly Nygren, *Romans* pp.284–97.

60. Cf. II Baruch 54.19; Barrett, *Romans* pp.143f.; Leenhardt, *Romans* pp.186ff.; E. Brandenburger, *Adam und Christus*, Neukirchen 1962, pp.215f.

61. Dodd, *Romans* pp.106f.; against Kümmel, *Römer 7* pp.118–32; E. Stauffer, *TDNT* II pp.358ff.; G. Bornkamm, 'Sin, Law and Death', *Early Christian Experience* pp.92ff.

62. Rom.8.1 does not provide a conclusion to Rom.7, but gathers up the whole of the preceding section, Rom.5–7 – as Kümmel recognizes (*Römer 7* p.69).

63. Rom.7.25b is regarded as an interpolated gloss by Bultmann, 'Glossen im Römerbrief', *TLZ* 72, 1947, 198f.; G. Zuntz, *The Text of the Epistles*, Schweich Lectures 1946, London 1953, p.16; Kuss, *Römerbrief* p.461; U. Luz, *Das Geschichtsverständnis des Paulus*, München 1968, p.160; Paulsen pp.44–50; cf. Bornkamm, 'Sin' p.99; Leenhardt, *Romans* p.195; Schweizer, *TDNT* VII p.133 n.276; Käsemann, *Römer* pp.201f. Others, including Moffatt translation, Dodd, *Romans* pp.114f.; Michel, *Römer* p.179; and Eichholz, *Theologie* p.257, think 7.25b originally came between 7.23 and 7.24. There is no textual support for either hypothesis.

64. A difficulty recognized by Kümmel, *Römer 7* pp.27ff.

65. Barrett, *Romans* p.150. Kümmel (*Römer 7* pp.59ff.) and Käsemann (*Römer* pp.196f.) recognize the sharpness of the problem posed by this phrase for their interpretations of Rom.7, without achieving a satisfactory resolution of it.

66. To read 7.25b as a summary of the pre-Christian experience of 7.7–24, following after v.25a! (Sanday & Headlam, *Romans* p.184; Kümmel, *Römer 7* pp.65f.; Gaugler, *Römer* p.282) makes too light of v.25a and leaves 7.25b as a pathetic anticlimax.

67. Cf. Calvin on 7.15: 'It has been well said that the carnal man plunges into sin with the consent and concurrence of his whole soul, but that a division at once begins as soon as he is called by the Lord and renewed by the Spirit' (Torrance edition).

68. In 8.9 note the εἴπερ; see Dunn, *Baptism* p.148.

69. RSV is wrong in translating σῶμα and πνεῦμα as the plurals, 'bodies' and 'spirits'. Most modern commentators recognize that in the context πνεῦμα almost certainly means (Holy) Spirit.

70. Cf. W. Grundmann, *TDNT* I p.313; Dibelius, 'Paulus und die Mystik' p.150; Pfister, *Leben* p.46.

71. Cf. Bultmann, 'Romans 7' pp. 177ff.; Bornkamm, 'Sin' pp. 96ff.; Kuss, *Römerbrief* p. 563.

72. On τελείωσις see Weiss, *I Kor.* pp. 73ff.; Reitzenstein, *Mysterien.* pp. 338f.; Wilckens, *Weisheit* pp. 53–60. Unfortunately I was unable to consult P. J. du Plessis, *Teleios: the Idea of Perfection in the New Testament*, Kampen 1959.

73. Bousset, *Kyrios Christos* pp. 170, 174; so also Bousset, *Jesus der Herr*, Göttingen 1916, pp. 47ff.; cf. Reitzenstein, *Mysterien.* pp. 340ff.; Windisch, 'Das Problem des paulinischen Imperativs', *ZNW* 23, 1924, pp. 265–71; also *Paulus und Christus* pp. 269–72.

74. Schweitzer, *Mysticism* p. 167; cf. p. 220.

75. Wendland, 'Wirken' 461.

76. See also Dunn, *CSNT* pp. 137f. For a broader critique of the view that Paul's concept of the Christian as πνευματικός is derived from Hellenistic mysticism, see Kennedy, *Paul* pp. 130–59; Davies, *Paul* pp. 191–200. E. W. Smith offers some formal parallels to Rom. 7.24–25a from Hellenistic religious and philosophical literature ('The Form and Religious Background of Romans 7.24–25a', *NovTest* 13, 1971, pp. 127–35), but none of them maintain the eschatological tension so characteristic of Paul.

77. I follow here the translation of Dupont-Sommer, *Qumran* pp. 78ff. Cf. also IQS 11.9–15; IQH 4.29–31.

78. That is, the last judgment.

79. Cf. K. G. Kuhn, 'New Light on Temptation, Sin and Flesh in the New Testament', *The Scrolls and the New Testament*, ed. K. Stendahl, SCM Press 1958, pp. 103f.; W. Nauck, *Die Tradition und der Charakter des ersten Johannesbriefes*, Tübingen 1957, pp. 104ff., 117ff.; O. J. F. Seitz, 'Two Spirits in Man: An Essay in Biblical Exegesis', *NTS* 6, 1959–60, pp. 82–95; A. A. Anderson, 'The Use of "Ruah" in IQS, IQH and IQM', *JSS* 7, 1962, pp. 298–301; A. R. C. Leaney, *The Rule of Qumran and Its Meaning*, SCM Press 1966 p. 149; cf. D. E. Aune, *The Cultic Setting of Realized Eschatology in Early Christianity*, Leiden 1972, p. 43. Less impressed by the parallel in Mussner, *Galater* pp. 392–5. The parallel in rabbinic teaching (the tension between the 'good impulse' and the 'bad impulse' – see e.g. Davies, *Paul* pp. 17–35) lacks the eschatological character which belongs to both the Qumran and Pauline teaching. Cf. Hermas, *Mand.* VI.2.

80. See H. Braun, 'Römer 7.7–25 und das Selbstverständnis des Qumran-Frommen', *ZTK* 56, 1959, pp. 1–18; also *Qumran* I pp. 177f. See also n. 176 below.

81. On these passages see Dunn, *Baptism* pp. 105f., 133, 135, 139.

82. Cf. Acts 16.7 – see above p. 180; and on John see below §58.1.

83. Cf. Schrenk, 'Geist' pp. 116f.; Hermann p. 71.

84. Cf. Michel on 8.14: 'The concept of "sonship" was a bone of contention between Judaism and early Christianity (Deut. 14.1). Our verse sounds like a means of determining this sonship gained in the confrontation with Judaism' (*Römer* p. 196). See also Lietzmann, *Römer* p. 93.

85. Michel: 'The "leading" and "witness" of the Spirit shows how Paul will have understood the "indwelling" of the Spirit' (*Römer* p. 197 n. 2).

86. On the tradition history of the *abba*-prayer, see particularly Paulsen pp. 174–89; though to confine its life-setting to baptism is unnecessarily restrictive. Charismatic worship was not confined to baptismal occasions! Strack–Billerbeck point out that nowhere in rabbinic literature is the Holy Spirit connected with the praying of an Israelite (III p. 243).

87. See particularly Georgi, *Gegner* pp. 246–82; though it is unlikely that in vv.

7–18 Paul takes over an already existing midrash of Ex. 34 used by his opponents (Collange pp. 67f., 72f.). See also above n. 34. The question of the relation between this section of II Cor. and II Cor. 10–13 and of the opponents attacked in each section (the same or different?) is too complex to go into here. See above §47.2.

88. See J. D. G. Dunn, 'II Cor. 3.17 – "The Lord is the Spirit"', *JTS NS* 21, 1970, pp. 309–20; C. F. D. Moule, 'II Cor. 3.18b, "καθάπερ ἀπὸ κυρίου πνεύματος"', *Neues Testament und Geschichte: historisches Geschehen und Deutung im Neuen Testament. Oscar Cullmann zum 70 Geburtstag*, hrsg. H. Baltensweiler & B. Reicke, Zürich 1972, pp. 231–7; Barrett, *II Cor.* pp. 122f. 3.17 means that 'the Lord' of Ex. 34.34 (v. 16) is to be understood in terms of the Spirit of II Cor. 3.6; so in 3.18, 'the Lord', the source of glory, as in the Ex. 34 passage, is Yahweh experienced by Paul as Spirit.

89. The πάντες makes it clear that in 3.18 Paul is no longer thinking solely of his own ministry, but of the Spirit as experienced by all believers.

90. Though cf. also Collange p. 123. See also above p. 216.

91. See further R. Scroggs, *The Last Adam*, Fortress 1966, pp. 97ff.

92. Hermann rightly emphasizes that Paul is talking in existential terms, of an *experienced* relationship (pp. 29ff., 49ff.).

93. Cf. II Thess. 2.13f. – the end of 'sanctification by the Spirit' is 'that you might possess for your own the glory of our Lord Jesus Christ'.

94. For 'Spirit' as the subject of συνεργεῖ in 8.28 see ch. VIII n. 227 above.

95. See Dunn, *Baptism* pp. 110f.

96. Cf. Lietzmann, *Galater* p. 29; Wikenhauser, *Mysticism* pp. 43f. There is no explicit reference to the Spirit here. On the possible use of terminology typical of the mysteries see Oepke, *Galater* p. 108; Güttgemanns pp. 187f. See further below pp. 328f.

97. Cf. H. Schürmann, '"Das Gesetz des Christus" (Gal. 6.2)', *Neues Testament und Kirche*, Schnackenburg Festschrift, pp. 282–94.

98. In what follows I draw on my study of this verse in *CSNT* pp. 127–41, where the verse is expounded against its context and where other issues are discussed more fully. I may add a reference to Vos, 'Eschatology and the Spirit' pp. 231ff., 242ff., 255ff., which I have been able to consult since then. On the use and importance of Gen. 2.7 in the theology of Paul's opponents and in later Gnosticism, see Pearson's dissertation.

99. Dunn, *CSNT* pp. 140f. and those cited there in n. 37.

100. Dunn, *CSNT* pp. 131f.

101. Cf. Vos, 'Eschatology and the Spirit': 'The pneumatic life of the Christian is a product and a reflex of the pneumatic life of the Christ' (pp. 241ff.).

102. See Wikenhauser, *Mysticism* pp. 83ff., though I do not agree at every point. Cf. Hermann pp. 61ff., but more strongly than the passage (I Cor. 15.45) permits.

103. In II Cor. 3.17 Paul does not equate Christ and the Spirit: 'the Lord' is Yahweh of Ex. 34.34. See above n. 88, against particularly Hermann.

104. Cf. Hamilton, *Spirit* pp. 10f.; Hermann pp. 65f. See also Wikenhauser, *Mysticism* pp. 40–9.

105. For the spectrum of meaning of σάρξ see Dunn, 'Jesus – Flesh and Spirit' pp. 44f.

106. See also Hermann pp. 63ff. Schweitzer wholly distorts the contrast clearly intended between 'flesh' and 'Spirit' in vv. 16f. when he uses the passage as proof that Paul's mysticism involved the idea of 'an actual physical union between Christ and the Elect' (*Mysticism* p. 127).

107. Cf. also 12.4–6 with vv. 7 and 11: 'The Spirit is nothing other than the mani-

festation of the Lord, who for his part is the salvation of God' (Conzelmann, *I Kor.* p. 245 n. 9).

108. See the bibliography in Conzelmann, *Outline* p. 208.

109. F. Neugebauer, *In Christus*, Göttingen 1961; W. Kramer, *Christ, Lord, Son of God*, ET SCM Press 1966, pp. 141–6; Conzelmann, *Outline* p. 210.

110. E. Käsemann, *Leib und Leib Christi*, Tübingen 1933, p. 183.

111. E. Best, *One Body in Christ*, SPCK 1955, ch. I.

112. A. Deissmann, *Die neutestamentliche Formel 'in Christo Jesu'*, Marburg 1892; also *Paul* p. 140.

113. I am thinking particularly of Rom. 12.5; I Cor. 4.15b; II Cor. 2.17; 5.17; 12.19; Gal. 3.26; 5.10; Eph. 3.12; 6.10, 20; Phil. 1.14; 2.19, 24; 4.13; Col. 2.6; 4.17; I Thess. 4.1; 5.12; II Thess. 3.4, 12; Philemon 8. Cf. Wikenhauser, *Mysticism* pp. 25–31; Dibelius, *Glaube und Mystik* p. 696: 'Evidently being a Christian entailed being aware that one was in Christ' (cited by Wikenhauser p. 30 n. 19); Lindblom, *Gesichte* ch. 7. Wikenhauser refers also to II Cor. 5.14 – 'the love of Christ constrains us' (pp. 35f.). See also p. 237 above and n. 148 below.

114. The old debate about whether the basis and fulcrum of Paul's religion and theology is to be found in his Christ-mysticism (Bousset, Schweitzer) or in his doctrine of justification (the dominant Lutheran tradition) has been to some extent resolved by the recognition of Käsemann that divine righteousness is a gift which has 'the character of power'; cf. 'grace' and 'Spirit' ('"The Righteousness of God" in Paul', *NTQT* pp. 170ff.; cf. P. Stuhlmacher, *Gerechtigkeit Gottes bei Paulus*, Göttingen 1966, pp. 238ff.). In other words, the synthesis and coherence of Paul's thought here lies not in an externally or formally conceived relationship or forensic act of God *extra nos*, nor yet in an enthusiastic, mystical piety, but in the experience of grace, of grace as the grace of Christ. Note particularly Gal. 3.6–14. Cf. Büchsel: 'There is no justification without Spirit-possession. Justification is in this sense something pneumatic' (*Geist* p. 307); similarly Wendland, 'Wirken' 460.

115. The definition of the Spirit as 'the total impact of the Christ event' (Hill, *Greek Words* pp. 275, 281) is on the right lines, but hardly adequate.

116. Κατὰ πνεῦμα in Rom. 1.4 certainly refers primarily to Jesus' post-resurrection state. But since the κατὰ σάρκα/κατὰ πνεῦμα antithesis is so distinctive of the *Christian's pre-resurrection* experience, it is probable that Paul understood κατὰ πνεῦμα in Rom. 1.4 more loosely, 'in terms of the Spirit', and referred it to Jesus' pre-resurrection experience as well as his post resurrection state. This is the thesis argued in Dunn, 'Jesus – Flesh and Spirit'.

117. In 'Jesus – Flesh and Spirit' I point out that Paul fights shy of actually saying that Jesus was raised by the Spirit (although it is the logical corollary of Rom. 8.11; I Cor. 15.20, 44f.). The reason is that it was precisely *in and by the resurrection* that the relationship between Jesus and Spirit was reversed – instead of 'Jesus and the Spirit' we have 'the Spirit of Jesus' (pp. 67f.).

118. It will have been evident from the way I have used this phrase that by 'character of Jesus' I do not mean his 'inner life', but the character of his life and relationships.

119. B. H. Streeter, *The Spirit*, Macmillan 1919: 'What is this Holy Spirit? It is no other than the spirit manifested in the life of Christ. If Christ is our portrait of the Father, He is no less our portrait of the Holy Ghost' (p. 371). Cf. Scott, *Paul* p. 173; Hunter, *Paul* p. 96; G. S. Hendry, *The Holy Spirit in Christian Theology*, SCM Press ²1965, pp. 26, 29, 41, 89. It is not the case that the personality of Christ is dissolved by equating Christ with the impersonal Spirit (so Weiss, *I Kor.* p. 303;

also 'Die Bedeutung des Paulus für den modernen Christen', *ZNW* 19, 1919–20, pp. 139f.; cf. Bousset, *Kyrios Christos* p. 155). Precisely the reverse! See also Hermann, Zweiter Teil, particularly pp. 140f.

120. Cf. Dodd, *Romans* p. 124; Hendry, *Holy Spirit* pp. 68f.; M. Bouttier, *Christianity according to Paul*, ET SCM Press 1966, pp. 45f.; Käsemann, *NTQT* pp. 50, 62ff.

121. Cf. Dunn, *CSNT* p. 139: 'A theology which reckons seriously with the ἐγένετο of John 1.14 must reckon just as seriously with the ἐγένετο implied in I Cor. 15.45b'.

122. See also Dunn, 'Rediscovering the Spirit', *ExpT* 84, 1972–73, p. 12.

123. Cf. Schweitzer's observation that 'Paul is the only Christian thinker who knows only Christ-mysticism, unaccompanied by God-mysticism' (*Mysticism* p. 5).

124. J. Schneider, *Die Passionsmystik des Paulus*, Leipzig 1929, p. 14. 'There is no doubt that Paul was one of the greatest martyrs who ever lived' (p. 14).

125. I need only mention such passages as Rom. 8.35f.; I Cor. 4.9–13; 15.30ff.; II Cor. 1.4–10; 4.8–12, 16f.; 6.4–10; 7.4f.; 11.23–9; 12.7–10; Gal. 4.13ff.; 5.11; Eph. 3.13; Col. 1.24; I Thess. 3.7.

126. Cf. Bultmann, *Theology* I p. 351. It is one of the weaknesses of Güttgemanns' study that he fails to take adequate account of Paul's emphasis on suffering as a *shared* experience of all Christians.

127. Σῶμα for Paul means 'man in his outwardness, his relatedness to others and the world'; cf. Käsemann, *ENTT* p. 133; Robinson, *Body* pp. 15, 27ff.; Jewett, *Anthropological Terms* pp. 284ff.

128. However much one wishes to press the equation 'body' and 'flesh' in vv. 10–11, and to argue that v. 10b refers primarily to the *resurrected* body (so particularly Barrett, *II Cor.* pp. 140f.), it cannot be denied that by 'our *mortal* flesh' Paul is thinking primarily of the mortal body, the body of death.

129. Note the use of ὁ ἔσω ἄνθρωπος in Rom. 7.22 and II Cor. 4.16; Eph. 3.16 is the only other occurrence of the phrase in the Pauline corpus.

130. Paul's train of thought between chs. 4 and 5 is not as clear as it might be; but there is certainly a definite continuity between 'the inner man' and the 'resurrected body', however much of an event the putting on of the 'heavenly dwelling' (5.2) will be in the future. The Spirit after all is already present as the 'first instalment' (5.5). See further particularly C. F. D. Moule, 'St Paul and Dualism: The Pauline Conception of Resurrection', *NTS* 12, 1965–66, pp. 106–23. For bibliography and other treatments of the passage, see Bruce, *Cor.* p. 201; F. C. Lang, *II Korinther 5.1–10 in der neueren Forschung*, 1973.

131. On the positive sense of 'endurance' (ὑπομονή) see particularly Barrett, *Romans* pp. 46, 104.

132. See Dunn, *Baptism* p. 148; also Käsemann, *Römer* p. 219.

133. Cf. Schniewind, 'Seufzen des Geistes' pp. 88ff.

134. Paul may intend the birth metaphor as an allusion to the 'messianic woes'. 'Birth pains' certainly have this sense elsewhere (Mark 13.8 par.; Strack-Billerbeck I p. 950); for the use of the verb cf. Rev. 12.2; *Sib.Or.* V.514. See also above ch. IV n. 96. That Paul thought of believers' sufferings in general as the outworking of the messianic woes is likely (Barrett, *Romans* pp. 104, 165). But quite certainly this was how he thought of his own sufferings – the unavoidable corollary of seeing himself in terms both of eschatological apostleship and of the suffering servant (§20.2 above).

135. For the meaning of 'thorn in the flesh' and the wide variety of interpretations see the commentators – e.g. Windisch, *II Kor.* pp. 285–8; P. E. Hughes, *Paul's Second Epistle to the Corinthians*, Marshall, Morgan & Scott 1961, pp. 442–6; Güttgemanns pp. 162–5; Barrett, *II Cor.* pp. 314ff. In view of the thematic importance of

'weakness' in this section it most probably included some form of physical affliction. See also n. 125 above.

136. Bultmann, *Faith and Understanding*, 1933, ET SCM Press 1969, pp. 274f.; Grundmann, *Kraft* pp. 102–2; Stählin, *TDNT* I p. 491; Käsemann, *Legitimität* p. 39 (*ZNW* pp. 53f.); Kümmel in Lietzmann-Kümmel, *Kor.* p. 212; Güttgemanns pp. 168f.; Bornkamm, *Paul* pp. 169f., 181, 187f.; G. O'Collins, 'Power Made Perfect in Weakness (II Cor. 12.9–10)', *CBQ* 33, 1971, pp. 535f.; also J. Cambier, 'Le critère paulinièn de l'apostolat en II Cor. 12.6s', *Biblica* 43, 1962, pp. 481–518.

137. Cf. Wilckens, *Weisheit* pp. 48ff.; and see above §41.1.

138. See also Wengst, 'Zusammenkommen' p. 558; E. E. Ellis, ' "Christ crucified" ' *Reconciliation and Hope*, Morris Festschrift, pp. 69–75.

139. Some modern Pentecostalists maintain that all illness is contrary to the will of God; so e.g. T. L. Osborn, *Healing the Sick*, Tulsa 1959; see also Hollenweger, *Pentecostals* pp. 357f. In so doing they make the same dangerous mistake as Paul's Corinthian opponents.

140. Ἐπισκηνώσῃ is probably an allusion to the Shekinah (Windisch, *II Kor.* p. 392; Kümmel in Lietzmann-Kümmel, *Kor.* p. 212).

141. H. Saake, 'Paulus als Ekstatiker', *NovTest* XV, 1973, pp. 153–60, ignores the polemical context of II Cor. 12.2ff. and thus overestimates the value Paul placed on his 'visions and revelations'.

142. Philo, *Vit.Mos.* I.69.

143. Pliny, *Letters* VII.26.1. Both passages are cited by Windisch, *II Kor.* p. 394.

144. *Paulus und die sokratische Tradition* pp. 53f. He refers to Lucian, *Philopseudes* 34; *Alexander* 54, 55, 56, 59; and *Peregr.* 33, 43f.

145. The emphasis on Christ crucified is consistent throughout both (or all) of the Corinthian letters (see particularly I Cor. 1.17–25; 2.2; II Cor. 1.5; 5.14f.).

146. Deissmann, *Paul*: 'He is, and remains, the crucified' (p. 143; see also pp. 197f.). Paul is probably responding here to particular Corinthian charges and beliefs; cf. Schmithals, *Gnosticism* pp. 193ff.; Güttgemanns pp. 145–51.

147. See R. C. Tannehill, *Dying and Rising with Christ*, Berlin 1967, pp. 101–4. The point of comparison is not the event of receiving the gospel, but the experience of joy in suffering.

148. Wikenhauser, *Mysticism* p. 37 and B. A. Ahern, 'The Fellowship of his Sufferings (Phil. 3.10)', *CBQ* 22, 1960, pp. 4f., refer also to II Thess. 3.5 – 'the patience of Christ'. More generally on the so-called 'mystical genitive' (Deissmann, *Paul* pp. 162ff.) see O. Schmitz, *Die Christus-Gemeinschaft des Paulus im Lichte seines Genetivgebrauchs*, Gütersloh 1924, and with greater circumspection, M. Bouttier, *En Christ*, Paris 1962, pp. 69–79.

149. We could probably include Gal. 6.17 here. It is most unlikely that 'the marks of Jesus' signify the stigmata (against Fenner, *Krankheit* p. 40; for manifestation of the wounds of Jesus in the history of Christianity, including St Francis and Padre Pio, see Thurston ch. II). Paul may simply be describing the physical effects of his suffering metaphorically as Christ's brand marks, denoting Christ's ownership and perhaps also protection (cf. Deissmann, *Bible Studies* pp. 349–60; Schneider, *Passionsmystik* pp. 51f.; Schlier, *Galater* pp. 284f.). But it is possible that we have here the same theme as in II Cor. – in Paul's abused body the earthly Jesus manifests himself as Lord (see Güttgemanns pp. 133ff.). Güttgemanns draws Gal. 4.14b into his net as well (pp. 180ff.); but this depends on the assumption that Paul faces the same situation in Gal. as in II Cor. 10–13; can one make a straight equation between Gal. 1.6 and II Cor. 11.4? See also p. 270 above.

150. For particular points of exegesis see Dunn, *Baptism* pp. 142f.

151. The 'with Christ', 'with him' is implied by the συν of the verbs and the sense of the sentence.

152. Barrett, *Romans* pp. 80, 122. See also above ch. IV n. 96.

153. The gentive 'sufferings of Christ' must refer to the sufferings which Christ endured; Paul thinks of Jesus as a fellow sufferer rather than as the author of the sufferings. See e.g. Schlier, *TDNT* III pp. 143f.; Tannehill p. 91, who also discusses II Cor. 7.3 (pp. 93ff.). Windisch suggests that the genitive is intended ambiguously – including in its sense both the idea of Christ's own sufferings (a mystical 'suffering with') and the idea of sufferings endured at Christ's will (*II Kor.* p. 40). See also n. 148 above.

154. Cf. Windisch, *II Kor.* p. 41; Barrett, *II Cor.* pp. 61f. As Windisch points out, the idea of suffering the Messianic woes *with* the Messiah is foreign to Judaism.

155. See above n. 153; against Wikenhauser, *Mysticism* pp. 160ff.

156. See particularly Lohse, *Colossians* pp. 70ff.; also Moule, *Colossians* pp. 76ff.; both of whom rightly note that Paul is not thinking of Jesus' death as atonement here. For the history of interpretation see J. Kremer, *Was an den Leiden Christi noch mangelt*, Bonn 1956, pp. 5–154.

157. See Dunn, *Baptism* pp. 154ff. Paul refers only to his own sufferings, so that he may be thinking specifically of his role as eschatological apostle (cf. n. 134 above). But in view of Rom. 8.17; II Cor. 1.5f., it is unlikely that he linked Christ's sufferings *exclusively* to his own (see above §55.1). Schneider however, presses the text too far in postulating a church-mysticism as well as a Christ-mysticism: 'The mystical union with Christ leads to the mystical union with the ἐκκλησία . . .' (*Passionsmystik* p. 58).

158. Particularly pertinent is Lohmeyer's comment (*Kolosser* p. 77). Michaelis's attempt to take the phrases 'sufferings of Christ' in both II Cor. 1.5 and Col. 1.24 as sufferings predicted for his disciples by Christ (cf. Acts 9.16) is an unnatural interpretation of the genitive and fails to appreciate the profundity of this motif in Paul (*TDNT* V pp. 931ff.).

159. Bultmann, *TDNT* IV p. 895: 'the reference is to dying with Christ . . . as continually actualized in the concrete life of the apostle'. For νέκρωσις as a process rather than an act, see also Plummer, *II Cor.* p. 130; Windisch, *II Kor.* p. 145; Barrett, *II Cor.* pp. 139f.; against Güttgemanns pp. 114ff.; Collange pp. 154f.

160. Georgi, *Gegner* pp. 287f.

161. Cf. also Tannehill pp. 85f., who rightly refuses to confine the death-life talk to Paul's own experience (see above n. 157); against Güttegmanns pp. 95f., who however justifiably emphasizes the polemical thrust of the passage – pp. 112–24.

162. Καὶ τὴν δύναμιν κτλ. is best taken as epexegetic of γνῶναι αὐτόν (Tannehill p. 120).

163. For 'know' in the sense of 'experience' (that is, know in existential relationship, rather than know as possessing information) see Lightfoot, *Philippians* p. 148; Bultmann, *TDNT* I pp. 697f., 709f. 'To know . . . this power is to experience its effects in one's own life' (F. W. Beare, *Epistle to the Philippians*, A. &. C. Black 1959, p. 122).

164. The thrust of Paul's remarks suggests that one of the threats to the Philippian church had similarities to that posed by the false apostles of II Cor. 10–13; see particularly J. Gnilka, 'Die antipaulinische Mission in Philippi', *BZ* 9, 1965, pp. 258–76; and above ch. IX n. 57.

165. Cf. Gnilka, *Philipperbrief* pp. 196f. The unity of the experience of 'the power of

his resurrection' and 'participation in his sufferings' is indicated by the fact that both phrases are governed by the one definite article.

166. It is not necessary to restrict the thought to the suffering of martyrdom (against Lohmeyer, *Philipper* pp. 139f.).

167. Tannehill's study achieves a better balance than most between the different tenses (past and present) of dying and rising with Christ in Paul's theology.

168. Cf. e.g. Deissmann, *Paul* p. 145; Büchsel, *Geist* pp. 296f.; Schneider, *Passionsmystik* pp. 33f.; Dunn, *Baptism* pp. 139–42. The constant harking back to baptism such as we find in Wikenhauser, *Mysticism* ch. III and Ahern, *CBQ* 22, 1960, pp. 1–32, presupposes a theology of grace as peculiarly and (in effect) exclusively sacramental grace which can hardly be read out of either Paul's talk of grace (see above §43.8) or his talk of suffering and death.

169. Cf. Bouttier, *Paul* pp. 27f. In fact, however, the 'with Christ' formula which belongs so firmly to the suffering-death motif, does not carry with it the same corporate overtones which adhere to the 'in Christ' formula; ' "with Christ" . . . emphasizes the relationship of each believer to Christ rather than the relationship of each to the others' (Best, *Body* p. 59).

170. See especially A. Sand, *Der Begriff 'Fleisch' in den paulinischen Hauptbriefen*, Regensburg 1967, ch. 6 and pp. 298f.; also above p. 312.

171. Consequently the too bold antitheses e.g. of Schweitzer, *Mysticism* p. 129 ('a man can only be either in Christ or in the flesh, not both at once') have to be qualified, otherwise they lead inevitably to some form of gnostic soteriology or perfectionism (as was the case with Schweitzer – see above n. 74; cf. §58.4 below); his suggestion that 'Fellowship with Christ in suffering and death is the solution of the problem of post-baptismal sin' (p. 146) does not adequately redress the balance and is itself an inadequate exposition of our present theme.

172. See Deissmann, *Paul* pp. 147–57: he gives 'the name *Mystik* to every religious tendency that discovers the way to God direct through inner experience without the mediation of reasoning. The constitutive element in mysticism is immediacy of contact with the deity' (p. 149); Wikenhauser, *Mysticism* pp. 13f., 95–108, 164ff.; Lindblom, *Gesichte* pp. 122f.

173. Güttgemanns' criticism of the mystical interpretation is valuable at many points (pp. 102–12); although it is too heavily dependent on a somewhat strained interpretation of I Cor. 15.1–11, which does not give enough weight to other passages – including I Cor. 15.45! The weight of German scholarship in the first decades of this century which nevertheless found it necessary to speak in terms of 'Christ mysticism' or 'passion mysticism' in their interpretation of Paul is impressive – including Bousset, Deissmann, Dibelius, Lietzmann, Schweitzer, Weiss and Windisch.

174. See also Deissmann, *Paul* p. 182; Büchsel, *Geist* pp. 300ff.; Dibelius, 'Paulus und die Mystik' pp. 134–59.

175. See more fully Dunn, 'Paul's Understanding of the Death of Jesus', *Reconciliation and Hope*, Morris Festschrift pp. 126–31.

176. Bultmann, *Theology* I pp. 267f. Contrast Qumran (n. 80 above).

177. Cf. Dodd, *Romans* pp. 20–9; but with better balance (on the question of whether 'God's wrath' is personal or impersonal) achieved by Whiteley, *Paul* pp. 64–9.

178. Cf. Vos, 'Eschatology and the Spirit' pp. 234f.

179. Cf. E. Kamlah, 'Wie beurteilt Paulus sein Leiden?' *ZNW* 54, 1963, p. 232.

180. Against Bousset, *Kyrios Christos* p. 181.

181. From one aspect the history of Christianity is a history of such attempts – through *gnōsis*, through asceticism, through mysticism, through 'sanctification', through 'second blessing', through 'baptism in the Spirit' (cf. Dunn, 'Spirit-baptism and Pentecostalism' pp. 397–407). See also above §34.

182. Berkhof, *Spirit* p. 78.

183. Cf. Dunn, *CSNT* p. 141. See further Kennedy, *Paul* pp. 146, 214f., 220–8; Schneider, *Passionsmystik* pp. 107–17; Schrenk, 'Geist' p. 117; Wikenhauser, *Mysticism* ch. IV. On the particular question of influence from the mysteries on Paul's understanding of baptism, see R. Schnackenburg, *Baptism in the Thought of St Paul*, ET Blackwell 1964, particularly pp. 139–45; G. Wagner, *Pauline Baptism and the Pagan Mysteries*, ET Oliver & Boyd 1967. On the importance of the eschatological as marking off Pauline 'spirituality' from oriental-Hellenistic mysticism see also Vos, 'Eschatology' pp. 246ff. (with n. 55 against Reitzenstein); Schweitzer, *Mysticism* p. 74.

184. Cf. Percy, *Leib* pp. 35ff.

185. *Paulus und Christus* pp. 140, 236, 248f.

Chapter XI

1. See further E. Schweizer, 'Christus und Geist im Kolosserbrief', *CSNT* pp. 297–313.

2. Schweizer, *Church Order* 8c.

3. Cf. Schnackenburg, *CSNT* p. 295.

4. For discussion see G. W. Knight, *The Faithful Sayings in the Pastoral Letters*, Kampen 1968, chs. V and VI.

5. Cf. von Campenhausen, *Authority* pp. 77f.; J. Knox, 'The Ministry in the Primitive Church', *The Ministry in Historical Perspectives*, ed. R. R. Niebuhr & D. D. Williams, Harper & Row 1956, pp. 21f. J. P. Meier, '*Presbyteros* in the Pastoral Epistles', *CBQ* 35, 1973, pp. 323–45, however does not think that 'the "advanced state" of the hierarchy' (!) invalidates the case for the Pauline authorship of the Pastorals. I Peter probably reflects an earlier situation where Pauline influence is still vital, but presbyterial order is already established; cf. 4.1of. with 5.1ff. (cf. Schweizer, *Church Order* 9b).

6. The singular ἐπίσκοπος in both cases is probably to be taken generically, as the overlap with 'presbyters' implies. We are not yet at the situation of monarchical episcopacy.

7. So firmly, Kelly, *Pastorals* p. 13.

8. Ignatius, *Smyrn.* 13.1; *Polyc.*4.1; Polycarp, *Phil.*4.3; Hermas, *Vis.*II.4.3; Tertullian, *de Virg.Vel.*9; *de Pud.*9; see also Lucian, *Peregr.*12.

9. Cf. N. Brox, 'Amt, Kirche und Theologie in der nachapostolischen Epoche – Die Pastoralbriefe', *Gestalt und Anspruch des Neuen Testament*, hrsg. J. Schreiner, Würzburg 1969, pp. 120ff.

10. For fuller discussion see particularly Roloff, *Apostolat* ch. V; H. Maehlum, *Die Vollmacht des Timotheus nach den Pastoralbriefen*, Basel 1969.

11. Grau pp. 80–9.

12. Cf. Bultmann, *Theology* II pp. 105, 108. The teaching of I Tim. 2.12 is probably

envisaged as an official function: '. . . to teach, or to have authority over men' (cf.
I Tim. 3.2; Titus 1.9). Only prayer seems to be a general congregational activity (I
Tim. 2.8).
13. Cf. Goguel, *Church* pp. 71, 118; Friedrich, 'Geist' p. 85; Käsemann, *ENTT* pp.
86ff. Wobbe's treatment of charisma as grace of office (Amtsgnade) is based exclusively on the Pastorals (pp. 67–70).
14. In the only specific references to prophecy (I Tim. 1.18; 4.14) it too belongs to
the past and was part of Timothy's ordination service (though προαγούσας, 1.18,
could denote a prophetic word spoken some time before Timothy's ordination).
Has prophecy also become a formalized part of good order? 4.1, 'The Spirit ex-
pressly says . . .', could imply continuing prophetic activity; but probably it is an
appeal to a prophetic word from the past, that is, *before* the 'later times' which are
present to the author (Schweizer, *Church Order* 6c; cf. C. Spicq, *Les Épitres Pastorales*,
EB 1947, p. 136); indeed the phrase may already be an established formula to introduce a word from tradition, like the regular rabbinic formula, 'The Holy Spirit
cries and says . . .' (see above ch. VIII n. 218); cf. (*d*) below.
15. For this rendering see Daube, *Rabbinic Judaism* pp. 224–46; J. Jeremias,
ΠΡΕΣΒΥΤΕΡΙΟΝ ausserchristlich bezeugt', *ZNW* 48, 1957, pp. 127–32; followed
by Kelly, *Pastorals* pp. 107f.; C. K. Barrett, *The Pastoral Epistles*, Oxford 1963, p. 72;
G. Holtz, *Die Pastoralbriefe*, THNT 1965, p. 111. See also the discussion in Hasenhüttl pp. 247ff.
16. Von Campenhausen, *Authority* p. 116; Bultmann, *Theology* II pp. 104, 106f.
Käsemann suggests that in I Tim. 6.11–16 we have one of the earliest preserved
forms of a charge given at ordination – 'Das Formular einer neutestamentlichen
Ordinationsparänese', *Neutestamentliche Studien für Rudolf Bultmann*, Berlin [2]1957,
pp. 261–8.
17. Cf. Schweizer, *Church Order* 6c.
18. Sound teaching/doctrine – I Tim. 1.10; II Tim. 4.3; Titus 1.9; 2.1; cf. I Tim.
4.6, 16; 6.1, 3; II Tim. 2.2; Titus 2.10.
faithful saying – I Tim. 1.15; 3.1; 4.9; II Tim. 2.11; Titus 1.9; 3.8.
sound words – I Tim. 6.3; II Tim. 1.13; cf. II Tim. 2.15.
the faith – I Tim. 3.9; 4.1, 6; 5.8; 6.10, 12, 21; II Tim. 3.8; 4.7; Titus 1.13; 2.2.
that which has been entrusted – I Tim. 6.20; II Tim. 1.12, 14.
19. Cf. Schweizer, *Church Order* 6d; Hasenhüttl pp. 254ff. This is the only passage
in the Pastorals which speaks of the Spirit's 'indwelling'.
20. Roloff, *Apostolat* pp. 248f.
21. Käsemann, *ENTT* p. 93.
22. J. M. Ford, 'A Note on Proto-Montanism in the Pastoral Epistles', *NTS* 17,
1970–71, pp. 338–46.
23. See more fully Dunn, *Baptism* chs. XV and XVI.
24. H. Schlier, 'Zum Begriff des Geistes nach dem Johannesevangelium', *Neutestamentliche Aufsätze: Festschrift für J. Schmid*, hrsg. J. Blinzler, O. Kuss, F. Mussner,
Regensburg 1963, p. 233.
25. Dunn, 'John 6 – A Eucharistic Discourse?', *NTS* 17, 1970–71, pp. 336ff.; also
Baptism pp. 179f., 184ff.
26. See further G. Bornkamm, 'Der Paraklet im Johannes-evangelium', *Geschichte
und Glaube* I, München 1968, p. 69; R. E. Brown, 'The Paraclete in the Fourth
Gospel', *NTS* 13, 1966–67, pp. 126ff.
27. Cf. Dunn, *Baptism* pp. 177, 180.
28. For background and meaning of παράκλητος see particularly Brown, 'Paraclete'

pp. 113–32; G. Johnston, *The Spirit-Paraclete in the Gospel of John*, Cambridge 1970, ch. 7.

29. Bultmann, *Theology* II p.90; Schlier, 'Begriff' pp.235f.; Brown, *John* pp.644f.

30. Brown, 'Paraclete' p.128.

31. Johnston objects that 'it would have been preposterous for John to have presented any spirit as the Successor to the Logos incarnate in Jesus' (*Spirit-Paraclete* p.114; see also p.95). But it is precisely *not* just 'any spirit'.

32. Cf. Brown, 'Paraclete' pp.128ff.; Dunn, *Baptism* p.194.

33. Cf. S. Schulz, *Das Evangelium nach Johannes*, NTD 1972, p.192.

34. There is textual confusion as to whether εἰς or ἐν should be read. See the discussion e.g. in Brown, *John* p.707.

35. Cf. C. K. Barrett, *The Gospel according to St John*, SPCK 1955, p.408; R. H. Lightfoot, *St John's Gospel*, Oxford 1956, pp.287; Conzelmann, *Outline* pp.357f. John 16.13, τὰ ἐρχόμενα ἀναγγελεῖ ὑμῖν, perhaps contains an allusion to Isa.44.7 – τὰ ἐρχόμενα πρὸ τοῦ ἐλθεῖν ἀναγγειλάτωσαν ὑμῖν.

36. See particularly F. Mussner, 'Die johanneischen Parakletsprüche und die apostolischen Tradition', *BZ* 5, 1961, pp.59–64; also *The Historical Jesus in the Gospel of St John*, ET Herder 1967, ch. V; Brown, *John* pp.708, 714ff.; cf. Bultmann, *John* pp.573ff.; Johnston, *Spirit-Paraclete* p.91; Schulz, *Johannes* pp.204f.; E. Bammel, 'Jesus und der Paraklet in Johannes 16', *CSNT* pp.199–216.

37. Cf. H. Sasse, 'Der Paraklet im Johannesevangelium', *ZNW* 24, 1925, pp.273f.; H. Windsich, *The Spirit-Paraclete in the Fourth Gospel*, ET Fortress 1968, pp.12, 21; Mussner, 'Parakletsprüche' pp.65f., 68f.; Brown, 'Paraclete' pp.129f.; also *John* p.1142.

38. See Dunn, *Baptism* pp.195–8.

39. The contrast with second-century Catholicism is striking. Where Ignatius and Irenaeus point to the bishop(s) as the guarantor and determiner of what is right (Ignatius, *Smyrn*.8.1–9.1; Irenaeus, *Adv.Haer.* IV.26.2), John looks to no teaching or ruling office but only to the Spirit as the living interpreter of the original gospel (cf. J. Michl, 'Der Geist als Garant des rechten Glaubens', *Vom Wort des Lebens: Festschrift für Max Meinertz*, hrsg. N. Adler, Münster 1951, pp.147f.

40. Cf. Dunn, *Baptism* pp.203f. On the close conjunction between Spirit and word in John and I John see further Büchsel, *Geist* pp.485f.; C. K. Barrett, 'The Holy Spirit in the Fourth Gospel', *JTS NS* 1, 1950, pp.12–5; Schweizer, *TDNT* VI pp.442ff.; also 'Spirit of Power' pp.277f.; Schlier, 'Begriff' p.238; Käsemann, *RGG*³ II 1278; J. M. Boice, *Witness and Revelation in the Gospel of John*, Paternoster 1970, pp.151ff. E. Käsemann, *The Testament of Jesus*, ET SCM Press 1968, pp.45f., tends to subordinate the Spirit to the *present* word of preaching without stressing sufficiently the continuity between the present word and the word proclaimed 'from the beginning'; whereas K. Haacker, *Jesus and the Church in John*, Institute for the Study of Christian Origins, Tübingen 1971, pp.16ff., locates 'the Spirit in tradition', without stressing sufficiently the Spirit's present revelatory role in reinterpreting the original tradition.

41. See e.g. Brown, *John* p.180; R. Schnackenburg, *The Gospel according to St John* I, ET Herder 1968, p.437; against Johnston, *Spirit-Paraclete* p.45.

42. Cf. I John 4.8, 16 – 'God is love'; I John 1.5 – 'God is light'.

43. Though of course χάρισμα does not occur in the Johannine writings.

44. Schulz, *Johannes* pp.179ff.

45. Haacker rightly points out that John never uses the term 'children of God' in the singular (p.4); though he goes on to characterize John's view of the church by

Zinzendorf's word, '"the personal connection with the Saviour" as the summary and basis of spiritual fellowship' (p. 10).

46. Schweizer, 'The Concept of the Church in the Gospel and Epistles of St John', *New Testament Essays: Studies in Memory of T. W. Manson*, Manchester 1959, p. 235.

47. C. F. D. Moule, 'The Individualism of the Fourth Gospel', *NovTest* 5, 1962, p. 184.

48. Barrett, *John* pp. 472f. (quoting Hort, *Ecclesia* p. 33); Schweizer, *Church Order* 11i; Käsemann, *Testament* pp. 29ff.; Johnston, *Spirit-Paraclete* p. 51; Haacker pp. 16f.; Schulz, *Johannes* p. 187; other references in Dunn, *Baptism* p. 180 n. 13; against Mussner, 'Parakletsprüche' pp. 66f. 'From the beginning' (John 15.27) refers more to the original witness than to the original witnesses (cf. I John 2.7, 24; 3.11; II John 5f.); and in 17.20 the distinction is not between apostles and all other (future) believers, but between the first missionary generation and successive generations (cf. 10.16).

49. Hasenhüttl reminds us how prominently the witness of women to Christ features in the Fourth Gospel (p. 264); see particularly John 4; 11; 20.

50. Cf. A. Kragerud, *Der Lieblingsjünger im Johannesevangelium*, Oslo 1959; Schweizer, *Church Order* 11i; Brown, *John* pp. xcivf.

51. Schweizer, *Church Order* 11, 12c; also 'Concept of Church' p. 237; 'This is the Gospel, par excellence, of the approach of the single soul to God' (Moule, 'Individualism' p. 185); cf. Käsemann, *Testament* p. 40. John 21.15ff. and III John 9f. do not overthrow this conclusion, since the former is an appendix to the gospel and is probably from a different hand (see Kümmel, *Introduction* pp. 148f.), and in the latter the author clearly takes exception to Diotrephes's attempt to assert authority over the rest of the community. The attack of 'the elder' on Diotrephes in fact is best seen as the response of anti-ecclesiastical and individual pietism to the increasing influence of early Catholicism; cf. particularly E. Käsemann, 'Ketzer und Zeuge', *ZTK* 48, 1951, pp. 309ff., even though his further speculations are much more questionable. There is next to nothing to commend the suggestion that 'fathers' and 'young men' (I John 2.12ff.) are formal titles perhaps even equivalent to 'elders' and 'deacons' (against J. L. Houlden, *The Johannine Epistles*, A. & C. Black 1973, pp. 4, 70f.).

52. The test of I John 4.1ff. is perhaps best not conceived as an internal church test to be applied by some members to the inspired utterance of others. It seems rather to be a test which the individual believer can apply when he is out in the world (4.1, 4f.), a test whereby he can recognize a brother. In 4.1–6 there are in fact two tests – the stranger will reveal himself as a brother if he (*a*) makes a right confession (4.1–3), and (*b*) accepts the believer's message (4.4–6).

53. For the discussion of 'the Christian and sin' in I John see R. Schnackenburg, *Die Johannesbriefe*, Herder 1963, pp. 281–8. Nauck maintains that the same basic situation of conflict for the believer in the world (cf. above §53.3) is to be found in I John (*Tradition* pp. 107ff., 119ff.), but ignores the counter evidence, never once mentioning 3.9.

54. R. Law, *The Tests of Life*, T. & T. Clark [3]1914.

55. Perhaps the clearest historical expression of Johannine Christianity is the Holiness Movement of the nineteenth century – non-ecclesiastical, laying emphasis on the spiritual experience of the individual, and perfectionist in tendency.

56. Cf. Käsemann, 'Ketzer' pp. 309ff.; also *Testament* p. 39; Schweizer, *Church Order* 12e; also 'Concept of Church' pp. 239, 242; Conzelmann, *Outline* pp. 355f.

57. Käsemann, 'Ketzer' p. 306.

58. Against Goppelt, *Apostolic Times* p. 187.

59. Cf. Goguel, *Birth* pp. 13f., who rightly recognizes the primacy of religious experience in creating religious community and the consequences which follow when doctrine and rites become detached from and take precedence over religious experience. 'Religions usually degenerate in the end into a rationalistic theology, a formal morality, and a ritualistic cult. When in this way rites and practices are detached from religious experience, they can only survive as a form of restraint which the religious society exercises on its members. . . . Sometimes a religion which is nothing more has ceased to live. To take religion in this state of existence and define it as religion is almost the same as taking a decomposing corpse and defining it as life and a living being' (pp. 13f.).

BIBLIOGRAPHY

Restricted to about 500 titles, and omitting commentaries and dictionary articles.

Abelson, J., *The Immanence of God in Rabbinical Literature*, Macmillan 1912.
Achtemeier, P. J., 'Gospel Miracle Tradition and the Divine Man', *Interpretation* 26, 1972, pp. 174–97.
Adler, A., *Das erste christliche Pfingstfest*, Münster 1938.
Ahern, B. A., 'The Fellowship of his Sufferings (Phil. 3.10)', *CBQ* 22, 1960, pp. 1–32.
Anderson, A. A., 'The Use of "Ruah" in IQS, IQH, and IQM', *JSS* 7, 1962, pp. 293–303.
Arai, S., 'Die Gegner des Paulus im I Korintherbrief und das Problem der Gnosis', *NTS* 19, 1972–73, pp. 430–7.

Baer, H. von, *Der heilige Geist in den Lukasschriften*, Stuttgart 1926.
Baëta, C. G., *Prophetism in Ghana: A Study of Some 'Spiritual' Churches*, SCM Press 1962.
Baillie, J., *Our Knowledge of God*, Oxford 1939.
— *The Sense of the Presence of God*, Oxford 1962.
Baltensweiler, H., 'Wunder und Glaube im Neuen Testament', *TZ* 23, 1967, pp. 241–56.
Bammel, E., 'Jesus und der Paraklet in Johannes 16', *CSNT* pp. 199–216.
Barbour, R. S., 'Gethsemane in the Tradition of the Passion', *NTS* 16, 1969–70, pp. 231–51.
Barclay, W., *Flesh and Spirit*, SCM Press 1962.
Barrett, C. K., *The Holy Spirit and the Gospel Tradition*, SPCK 1947.
— 'The Holy Spirit in the Fourth Gospel', *JTS* 1, 1950, pp. 1–15.
— 'Christianity at Corinth', *BJRL* 46, 1964, pp. 269–97.
— *Jesus and the Gospel Tradition*, SPCK 1967.
— 'ΨΕΥΔΑΠΟΣΤΟΛΟΙ (II Cor. 11.13)', *Mélanges Bibliques en hommage au R. P. Béda Rigaux*, ed. A. Descamps and A. de Halleux, Gembloux 1970, pp. 377–96.
— *The Signs of an Apostle*, Epworth 1970.
— 'Paul's Opponents in II Corinthians', *NTS* 17, 1970–71, pp. 233–54.
— *New Testament Essays*, SPCK 1972.
M. Barth, 'A Chapter on the Church – The Body of Christ', *Interpretation* 12, 1958, pp. 131–56.

Bartsch, H. W., 'Die Empfänger des Römerbriefes', *St Th* 25, 1971, pp. 81–9.

Beare, F. W., 'Sayings of the Risen Jesus in the Synoptic Tradition', *Christian History and Interpretation: Studies Presented to John Knox,* ed. W. R. Farmer, C. F. D. Moule and R. R. Niebuhr, Cambridge 1967, pp. 161–81.

Beasley-Murray, G. R., 'Jesus and the Spirit', *Mélanges Bibliques en hommage au R. P. Béda Rigaux,* ed. A. Descamps and A. de Halleux, Gembloux 1970, pp. 463–78.

Bennett, D. and R., *The Holy Spirit and You,* Logos 1971.

Benz, E., *Paulus als Visionär,* Wiesbaden 1952.

— *Die Vision: Erfahrungsformen und Bilderwelten,* Stuttgart 1969.

Berger, K., 'Zu den sogennanten Sätzen heiligen Rechts', *NTS* 17, 1970–71, pp. 10–40.

— 'Die sog. "Sätze heiligen Rechts" im Neuen Testament', *TZ* 28, 1972, pp. 305–30.

Berkhof, H., *The Doctrine of the Holy Spirit,* Epworth 1965.

Bertrams, H., *Das Wesen des Geistes nach der Anschauung des Apostels Paulus,* Münster 1913.

Best, E., *One Body in Christ,* SPCK 1955.

— 'Bishops and Deacons: Philippians 1.1', *Studia Evangelica* IV, ed. F. L. Cross, 1968, pp. 371–6.

Betz, H. D., *Lukian von Samosata und das Neue Testament,* Berlin 1961.

— 'Jesus as Divine Man', *Jesus and the Historian: In Honour of E. C. Colwell,* ed. F. T. Trotter, Westminster 1968, pp. 114–33.

— *Der Apostel Paulus und die sokratische Tradition: Eine exegetische Untersuchung zu seiner 'Apologie' II Korinther 10–13,* Tübingen 1972.

— 'Geist, Freiheit und Gesetz', *ZTK* 71, 1974, pp. 78–93.

Betz, O., 'Zungenreden und süsser Wein', *Bibel und Qumran,* Festschrift für H. Bardtke, Berlin 1968, pp. 20-36.

— 'The Concept of the So-called "Divine Man" in Mark's Christology', *Studies in New Testament and Early Christian Literature: Essays in Honour of A. P. Wikgren,* ed. D. E. Aune, Leiden 1972, pp. 229–40.

Bickermann, E., 'Das leere Grab', *ZNW* 23, 1924, pp. 281–92.

Bieder, W., 'Gebetswirklichkeit und Gebetsmöglichkeit bei Paulus', *TZ* 4, 1948, pp. 22–40.

Bittlinger, A., *Gifts and Graces,* ET Hodder & Stoughton 1967.

— *Gifts and Ministries,* ET Eerdmans 1973.

Black, M., 'The Interpretation of Romans 8.28', *Neotestamentica et Patristica: Freundesgabe O. Cullmann,* NovTestSuppl VI, 1962, pp. 166–72.

Bloch, M., *Les Rois Thaumaturges,* Paris 1924.

Bloch-Hoell, N., *The Pentecostal Movement,* ET Allen & Unwin 1964.

Böcher, O., *Dämonenfurcht und Dämonenabwehr,* Kohlhammer 1970.

Bode, E. L., *The First Easter Morning: the Gospel Accounts of the Women's Visit to the Tomb of Jesus,* Rome 1970.

Boer, H. R., *Pentecost and Missions,* Lutterworth 1961.

Bonwetsch, N., *Die Geschichte des Montanismus,* Erlangen 1881.

Boring, M. E., 'How May We Identify Oracles of Christian Prophets in the Synoptic Tradition? Mark 3.28–29 as a Test Case', *JBL* 91, 1972, pp. 501–21.

Bornkamm, G., *Jesus of Nazareth*, ET Hodder & Stoughton 1960.

— *Paul*, ET Hodder & Stoughton 1969.

— 'Faith and Reason in Paul', 'Sin, Law and Death (Romans 7)', 'On the Understanding of Worship', 'The More Excellent Way', *Early Christian Experience*, ET SCM Press 1969.

— 'Der Paraklet im Johannes-Evangelium', *Geschichte und Glaube* I, München 1968, pp. 68–89.

Bourke, M. M., 'Reflections on Church Order in the New Testament', *CBQ* 30, 1968, pp. 493–511.

Bousset, W., *Die Himmelreise der Seele*, 1901, reprinted Darmstadt 1971.

— Rezension zu H. Weinel, *Wirkungen*, in *Göttingsche gelehrte Anziegen* 163, 1901, pp. 753–76.

— *Kyrios Christos* ²1921, ET Abingdon 1970.

Bousset, W. and Gressmann, H., *Die Religion des Judentums im späthellenistischen Zeitalter*, Tübingen ⁴1966.

Bouttier, M., *En Christ*, Paris 1962.

Bowker, J., '"Merkabah" Visions and the Visions of Paul', *JSS* 16, 1971, pp. 157–73.

— *The Sense of God*, Oxford 1973.

Brandt, W., *Dienst und Dienen im Neuen Testament*, Gütersloh 1931.

Braun, H., 'Römer 7.7–25 und das Selbstverständnis des Qumran-Frommen', *ZTK* 56, 1959, pp. 1–18.

Brosch, J., *Charismen und Ämter in der Urkirche*, Bonn 1951.

Brown, R. E., 'The Paraclete in the Fourth Gospel', *NTS* 13, 1966–67, pp. 113–32.

— 'How Much did Jesus Know?', *CBQ* 29, 1967, pp. 315–45.

Brox, N., '*ANAΘEMA IHΣOYΣ* (I Kor. 12.3)', *BZ*, 12, 1968, pp. 103–11.

— 'Amt, Kirche und Theologie in der nachapostolischen Epoche – Die Pastoralbriefe', in *Gestalt und Anspruch des Neuen Testament*, hrsg. J. Schreiner, Würzburg 1969.

Brumback, C., *What Meaneth This?*, Springfield 1947.

— *Suddenly . . . From Heaven*, Springfield 1961.

Bruner, F. D., *A Theology of the Holy Spirit*, Eerdmans 1970.

Brunner, E., *The Misunderstanding of the Church*, ET Lutterworth 1952.

Büchsel, F., *Der Geist Gottes im Neuen Testament*, Gütersloh 1926.

Bultmann, R., *The History of the Synoptic Tradition*, ET Blackwell 1963.

— *Jesus and the Word*, ET Scribner 1934, Fontana 1958.

— 'The Concept of Revelation in the New Testament', 'Romans 7 and the Anthropology of Paul', in *Existence and Faith*, ET Fontana 1964.

— *Theology of the New Testament*, ET SCM Press 1952, 1955.

Cambier, J., 'Le critère paulinièn de l'apostolat en II Cor. 12.6s', *Biblica* 43, 1962, pp. 481–518.

Campbell, J. Y., '*KOINΩNIA* and its Cognates in the New Testament', *JBL* 51, 1932, reprinted in *Three New Testament Studies*, Leiden 1965, pp. 1–28.

Campenhausen, H. Von, 'Der urchristliche Apostelbegriff', *StTh* I, 1947, pp. 96–130.

— *Ecclesiastical Authority and Spiritual Power in the Church of the First Three Centuries*, ET A. & C. Black 1969.

Cerfaux, L., *Christ in the Theology of St Paul*, ET Herder 1959.

— *The Church in the Theology of St Paul*, ET Herder 1959.

— *The Christian in the Theology of St Paul*, ET Chapman 1967.

Christenson, L., *Speaking in Tongues and its Significance for the Church*, Fountain Trust 1968.

Clemens, C., 'The "Speaking with Tongues" of the Early Christians', *ExpT* 10, 1898–99, pp. 344–52.

Cohn, N., *The Pursuit of the Millennium*, Secker & Warburg 1957.

Collins, J. N., 'Georgi's "Envoys" in II Cor. 11.23', *JBL* 93, 1974, pp. 88–96.

Colpe, C., 'Der Spruch von der Lästerung des Geistes', *Der Ruf Jesu und die Antwort der Gemeinde: Festschrift für J. Jeremias*, Göttingen 1970, pp. 63–79.

Conzelmann, H., 'Paulus und die Weisheit', *NTS* 14, 1965–66, pp. 231–44.

— *An Outline of the Theology of the New Testament*, ET SCM Press 1969.

Cranfield, C. E. B., '*Μέτρου πίστεως* in Romans 12.3', *NTS* 8, 1961–62, pp. 345–51.

— *A Commentary on Romans 12–13*, *SJT* Occasional Papers No. 12, 1965.

Crenshaw, J. L., *Prophetic Conflict*, Berlin 1971.

Cullmann, O., *Early Christian Worship*, ET SCM Press 1953.

— *The Christology of the New Testament*, ET SCM Press 1959.

— *Christ and Time*, ET SCM Press ³1962.

— *Salvation in History*, ET SCM Press 1967.

Currie, S. D., '"Speaking in Tongues"; Early Evidence outside the New Testament Bearing on "Glossais Lalein"', *Interpretation* 19, 1965, pp. 274–94.

Cutten, G. B., *Speaking with Tongues: Historically and Psychologically Considered*, Yale 1927.

Dahl, N. A., *Das Volk Gottes*, Darmstadt ²1963.

Dalman, G., *The Words of Jesus*, ET T. & T. Clark 1902.

Dautzenberg, G., 'Zum religionsgeschichtlichen Hintergrund der διάχρισις πνευμάτων (I Kor. 12.10)', *BZ* 15, 1971, pp. 93–104.

Davenport, F. M., *Primitive Traits in Religious Revivals*, Macmillan 1905.

Davies, J. G., 'The Genesis of Belief in an Imminent Parousia', *JTS* 14, 1963, pp. 104–7.

Davies, W. D., '"Knowledge" in the Dead Sea Scrolls and Matt. 11.25–30', *HTR* 46, 1953, reprinted in *Christian Origins and Judaism*, Darton, Longman & Todd 1962, pp. 119–44.

— *Paul and Rabbinic Judaism*, SPCK 1948.

Deissmann, A., *Die neutestamentliche Formel 'in Christo Jesu'*, Marburg 1892.

— *The Religion of Jesus and the Faith of Paul*, Hodder & Stoughton 1923.

— *Paul: A Study in Social and Religious History*, ²1925, ET 1927, Harper 1957.

Delling, G., *Worship in the New Testament*, ET Darton, Longman & Todd 1962.

— *Antike Wundertexte*, Berlin 1960.

— 'Zur Beurteilung des Wunders durch die Antike', *Studien zum Neuen Testament und zum hellenistischen Judentum*, Göttingen 1970, pp. 53–71.

Denis, A. M., 'L'investiture de la fonction apostolique par "apocalypse": Étude thématique de Gal. 1.16', *RB* 64, 1957, pp. 335–62, 492–515.

Dewar, L., *The Holy Spirit and Modern Thought*, Harper 1959.

Dibelius, M., *Die Geisterwelt im Glauben des Paulus*, Göttingen 1909.

— *Jesus*, 1939, ET 1949, SCM Press 1963.

— 'Gethsemane', *Botschaft und Geschichte* I, Tübingen 1953, pp. 258–71.

— 'Paulus und die Mystik', *Botschaft und Geschichte* II, Tübingen 1956, pp. 134–59.

Dietzel, A., 'Beten im Geist', *TZ* 13, 1957, pp. 12–32.

Dobschütz, E. von, *Ostern und Pfingsten*, Leipzig 1903.

Dodd, C. H., 'Jesus as Teacher and Prophet', *Mysterium Christi*, ed. G. K. A. Bell and A. Deissmann, Longmans 1930, pp. 53–66.

— 'The Appearances of the Risen Christ: an Essay in Form-Criticism of the Gospels', *Studies in the Gospels: Essays in Memory of R. H. Lightfoot*, ed. D. E. Nineham, Blackwell 1955, pp. 9–35.

— *The Founder of Christianity*, Collins 1971.

Dodds, E. R., *The Greeks and the Irrational*, California 1951.

— 'Supernatural Phenomena in Classical Antiquity', *The Ancient Concept of Progress*, Oxford 1973.

Doughty, D. J., 'The Priority of ΧΑΡΙΣ', *NTS* 19, 1972–73, pp. 163–80.

Dumermuth, F., 'Moses strahlendes Gesicht', *TZ* 17, 1961, pp. 241–8.

Dunn, J. D. G., *Baptism in the Holy Spirit*, SCM Press, 1970.

— 'II Corinthians 3.17 – "The Lord is the Spirit"', *JTS NS* 21, 1970, pp. 309–20.

— 'Spirit-baptism and Pentecostalism', *SJT* 23, 1970, pp. 397–407.

— 'Spirit and Kingdom', *ExpT* 82, 1970–71, pp. 36–40.

— 'Jesus – Flesh and Spirit: an Exposition of Romans 1.3–4', *JTS NS* 24, 1973, pp. 40–68.

— 'I Corinthians 15.45 – Last Adam, Life-giving Spirit', *CSNT* pp. 127–41.

— 'Prophetic "I"-sayings and the Jesus-tradition: the Importance of Testing Prophetic Utterances within Early Christianity', forthcoming in *TZ* 31, 1975.

— 'Romans 7.14–25 in the Theology of Paul', forthcoming in *NTS*.

Dupont, J., 'Le Chrétien, Miroir de la Gloire Divine d'après II Cor. 3.18', *RB* 56, 1949, pp. 392–411.

Dupont, J.—*contd.*
— *Gnosis: La Connaissance Religieuse dans les Épitres de Saint Paul*, Paris ²1960.
Durasoff, S., *Bright Wind of the Spirit*, Hodder & Stoughton 1973.
Dusen, H. P. Van, *Spirit, Son and Father*, A. &. C. Black 1960.

Ebeling, G., *The Nature of Faith*, ET Collins 1961.
Edwards, J., *A Treatise concerning Religious Affections*, Boston 1746, in *The Works of Jonathan Edwards*, Vol. II, ed. J. E. Smith, Yale 1959.
Eichholz, G., *Was heisst charismatische Gemeinde?*, Theol Ex 77, München 1960.
Eliade, M., *Shamanism: Archaic Techniques of Ecstasy*, Princeton 1970.
Ellis, E. E., 'Luke 11.49–51: An Oracle of a Christian Prophet?', *ExpT* 74, 1962–63, pp. 157f.
— 'The Role of the Christian Prophet in Acts', *Apostolic History and the Gospel*, F. F. Bruce Festschrift, ed. W. W. Gasque and R. P. Martin, Paternoster 1970, pp. 55–67.
— 'Paul and his Co-workers', *NTS* 17, 1970–71, pp. 437–52.
— 'Christ and Spirit in I Corinthians', *CSNT* pp. 269–77.
— '"Spiritual" Gifts in the Pauline Community', *NTS* 20, 1973–74, pp. 128–44.
Evans, C. F., *Resurrection and the New Testament*, SCM Press 1970.

Farrer, A. M., 'The Ministry in the New Testament', *The Apostolic Ministry*, ed. K. E. Kirk, Hodder & Stoughton 1946, pp. 113–82.
Fascher, E., ΠΡΟΦΗΤΗΣ: *Eine sprach- und religionsgeschichtliche Untersuchung*, Giessen 1927.
Fenner, F., *Die Krankheit im Neuen Testament*, Leipzig 1930.
Fiebig, P., *Antike Wundergeschichten zum Studium der Wunder des Neuen Testaments*, Bonn 1921.
— *Rabbinische Wundergeschichten des neutestamentlichen Zeitalters*, Berlin ²1933.
Filson, F. V., 'The Significance of the Early House Churches', *JBL* 58, 1939, pp. 105–12.
Flusser, D., *Jesus*, New York 1969.
Ford, J. M. 'Towards a Theology of "Speaking in Tongues"', *ThStud* 32, 1971, pp. 3–29.
— 'A Note on Proto-Montanism in the Pastoral Epistles', *NTS* 17, 1970–71, pp. 338–46.
Fridrichsen, A., 'Le péché contre le St. Esprit', *RHPR* 3, 1923, pp. 367–72.
— *The Problem of Miracle in Primitive Christianity*, 1925, ET Augsburg 1972.
— *The Apostle and his Message*, Uppsala 1947.
Friedrich, G., 'Geist und Amt', *Wort und Dienst* NF3, 1952, pp. 61–85.
Frodsham, S. H., *With Signs Following*, Springfield 1947.
Frövig, D. A., *Das Sendungsbewusstsein Jesu und der Geist*, Gütersloh 1924.
Fuchs, E., *Christus und der Geist bei Paulus*, Leipzig 1932.
Fuller, R. H., *The Mission and Achievement of Jesus*, SCM Press 1954.

— *The Foundations of New Testament Christology*, Lutterworth 1965.
— *The Formation of the Resurrection Narratives*, SPCK 1972.
Furnish, V. P., *Theology and Ethics in Paul*, Abingdon 1968.

Gardner, P., *The Religious Experience of St Paul*, Williams & Norgate, 1911.
Gee, D., *The Pentecostal Movement*, Elim revised 1949.
— *Concerning Spiritual Gifts*, Springfield revised, no date.
— *Spiritual Gifts in the Work of the Ministry Today*, Los Angeles 1963.
Gelpi, D. L., *Pentecostalism: A Theological Viewpoint*, Paulist Press 1971.
George, A. R., *Communion with God in the New Testament*, Epworth 1953.
Georgi, D., *Die Gegner des Paulus im 2. Korintherbrief*, Neukirchen 1964.
Gerhardsson, B., 'Die Boten Gottes und der Apostel Christi', *SEA* 27, 1962, pp. 89–131.
Giannini, A., *Paradoxographorum Graecorum Reliquiae*, Milano 1967.
Gilmour, S. M., 'Easter and Pentecost', *JBL* 81, 1962, pp. 62–6.
Gnilka, J., 'Die antipaulinische Mission in Philippi', *BZ* 9, 1965, pp. 258–76.
— 'Geistliches Amt und Gemeinde nach Paulus', *Foi et Salut selon S. Paul*, Rome 1970, pp. 233–45.
— 'Das Kirchenmodell des Epheserbriefes', *BZ* 15, 1971, pp. 161–84.
Goguel, M., *La foi à la résurrection de Jésus dans le christianisme primitif*, Paris 1933.
— *The Birth of Christianity*, ET Allen & Unwin 1953.
— *The Primitive Church*, ET Allen & Unwin 1964.
Goodman, F. D., *Speaking in Tongues: a cross cultural study of glossolalia*, Chicago 1972.
Goppelt, L., 'Tradition nach Paulus', *KuD* 4, 1958, pp. 213–33.
— *Apostolic and Post-Apostolic Times*, ET A. & C. Black 1970.
Grant, R. M., *Miracle and Natural Law in Graeco-Roman and Early Christian Thought*, Amsterdam 1952.
Grass, H., *Ostergeschehen und Osterberichte*, Göttingen ²1962.
Grau, F., *Der neutestamentliche Begriff χάρισμα*, Tübingen dissertation 1946.
Green, C., *Out-of-the-Body Experiences*, Hamilton 1968.
Greeven, H., 'Propheten, Lehrer, Vorsteher bei Paulus', *ZNW* 44, 1952, pp. 1–43.
— 'Die Geistesgaben bei Paulus', *Wort und Dienst* 6, 1959, pp. 111–20.
Grundmann, W., *Der Begriff der Kraft in der neutestamentlicher Gedankenwelt*, Stuttgart 1932.
Guillaume, A., *Prophecy and Divination*, Hodder & Stoughton 1938.
Gundry, R. H., '"Ecstatic Utterance" (NEB)', *JTS NS* 17, 1966, pp. 299–307.
Gunkel, H., *Die Wirkungen des heiligen Geistes nach der populären Anschauung der apostolischen Zeit und nach der Lehre des Apostels Paulus*, Göttingen 1888.
Gutierrez, P., *La Paternité Spirituelle selon Saint Paul*, EB 1968.
Güttgemanns, E., *Der leidende Apostel und sein Herr*, Göttingen 1966.

Guy, H. A., *New Testament Prophecy: its Origin and Significance*, Epworth 1947.

Haacker, K., 'Das Pfingstwunder als exegetisches Problem', *Verborum Veritas: Festschrift für G. Stählin*, hrsg. O. Böcher & K. Haacker, Wuppertal 1970, pp. 125–31.
— *Jesus and the Church in John*, Tübingen 1971.
Hahn, F., *Mission in the New Testament*, ET SCM Press 1965.
— *The Titles of Jesus in Christology*, ET Lutterworth 1969.
— *The Worship of the Early Church*, ET Fortress 1973.
— 'Der Apostolät im Urchristentum. Eine Eigenart und seine Voraussetzung', *KuD* 20, 1974, pp. 54–77.
Hainz, J., *Ekklesia: Strukturen paulinischer Gemeinde-Theologie und Gemeinde-Ordnung*, Regensburg 1972.
Hamilton, N. Q., *The Holy Spirit and Eschatology in Paul*, *SJT* Occasional Papers No. 6, 1957.
— 'Resurrection Tradition and the Composition of Mark', *JBL* 84, 1965, pp. 415–21.
Harnack, A., *What is Christianity*, ET Putnam 1901.
— *The Expansion of Christianity in the First Three Centuries*, ET Williams & Norgate 1904.
— *The Constitution and Law of the Church*, ET Williams & Norgate 1910.
Harper, M. C., *Power for the Body of Christ*, Fountain Trust 1964.
Harrington, D. J., 'Ernst Käsemann on the Church in the New Testament', *The Heythrop Journal* 12, 1971, pp. 246–57, 365–76.
Hasenhüttl, G., *Charisma: Ordnungsprinzip der Kirche*, Herder 1969.
Hatch, E., *The Organization of the Early Christian Churches*, Rivingtons ³1888.
Heitmann, C., and Mühlen, H., hrsg., *Erfahrung und Theologie des Heiligen Geistes*, München 1974.
Heitmüller, W., *'Im Namen Jesu'*, Göttingen 1903.
Hengel, M., 'Maria Magdalena und die Frauen als Zeugen', *Abraham unser Vater: Festschrift für O. Michel*, hrsg. O. Betz, M. Hengel, P. Schmidt, Leiden 1963, pp. 243–56.
— *Nachfolge und Charisma*, Berlin 1968.
Hendry, G. S., *The Holy Spirit in Christian Theology*, SCM Press ²1965.
Henneken, B., *Verkündigung und Prophetie im I. Thessalonicherbrief*, Stuttgarter Bibelstudien 29, 1969.
Hermann, I., *Kyrios und Pneuma*, München 1961.
Hester, J. D., *Paul's Concept of Inheritance*, *SJT* Occasional Papers No. 14, 1968.
Hill, D., *Greek Words and Hebrew Meanings*, Cambridge 1967.
— 'Prophecy and Prophets in the Revelation of St. John', *NTS* 18, 1971–72, pp. 401–18.
— 'On the Evidence for the Creative Role of Christian Prophets', *NTS* 20, 1973–74, pp. 262–74.
Hoekema, A. A., *What about Tongue-speaking?*, Paternoster 1966.

Hoffmann, P., *Studien zur Theologie der Logienquelle*, Münster 1972.

Holl, K., 'Der Kirchenbegriff des Paulus in seinem Verhältnis zu dem der Urgemeinde', *Gesammelte Aufsätze zur Kirchengeschichte* II, Tübingen 1928, pp. 44–67.

Hollenweger, W., *The Pentecostals*, SCM Press 1972.

Holtz, T., 'Das Kennzeichen des Geistes (I Kor. 12.1–3)', *NTS* 18, 1971–72, pp. 365–76.

Holtzmann, O., *War Jesus Ekstatiker?*, Tübingen 1903.

Hopwood, P. G. S., *The Religious Experience of the Primitive Church*, T. & T. Clark 1936.

Hort, F. J. A., *The Christian Ecclesia*, Macmillan 1897.

Horton, H., *The Gifts of the Spirit*, Assemblies of God [7]1962.

Hoyle, R. B., *The Holy Spirit in St Paul*, Hodder & Stoughton 1927.

Hull, J. H. E. *The Holy Spirit in the Acts of the Apostles*, Lutterworth 1967.

Hull, J. M., *Hellenistic Magic and the Synoptic Tradition*, SCM Press 1974.

Humphries, A. L., *The Holy Spirit in Faith and Experience*, SCM Press 1917.

Hurd, J. C., *The Origin of I Corinthians*, SPCK 1965.

Iber, G., 'Zum Verständnis von I Kor. 12.31', *ZNW* 54, 1963, pp. 43–52.

Iersel, B. M. F., *'Der Sohn' in den synoptischen Jesusworten*, NovTestSuppl III [2]1964.

James, W., *The Varieties of Religious Experience*, 1903, Fontana 1960.

Jeremias, J., *The Prayers of Jesus*, ET SCM Press 1967.

— *New Testament Theology I: The Proclamation of Jesus*, ET SCM Press 1971.

Jewett, R., 'Conflicting Movements in the Early Church as Reflected in Philippians', *NovTest* 12, 1970, pp. 362–90.

— 'Enthusiastic Radicalism and the Thessalonian Correspondence', *Proceedings of the Society of Biblical Literature 1972*, Vol. I pp. 181–232.

Johnston, G., *The Spirit-Paraclete in the Gospel of John*, Cambridge 1970.

Jones, R. M., *Studies in Mystical Religion*, Macmillan 1909.

Kamlah, E. 'Wie beurteilt Paulus sein Leiden?' *ZNW* 54, 1963, pp. 217–32.

Karris, R. J. 'Rom. 14.1–15.13 and the Occasion of Romans', *CBQ* 35, 1973, pp. 155–78.

Käsemann, E., *Leib und Leib Christi*, Tübingen 1933.

— *Die Legitimität des Apostels*, Darmstadt 1956, reprint of *ZNW* 41, 1942, pp. 33–71.

— 'Ketzer und Zeuge', *ZTK* 48, 1951, pp. 292–311.

— 'The Problem of the Historical Jesus', 'Ministry and Community in the New Testament', in *ENTT*.

— 'Sentences of Holy Law in the New Testament', 'The Beginnings of Christian Theology', 'On the Subject of Primitive Christian Apocalyptic', '"The Righteousness of God" in Paul', 'Worship in Everyday Life: a note on Romans 13', in *NTQT*.

Käsemann, E.—contd.
— The Testament of Jesus, ET SCM Press 1968.
— Perspectives on Paul, ET SCM Press 1971.
Kee, H. C., 'The Terminology of Mark's Exorcism Stories', NTS 14, 1967–68, pp. 232–46.
Kelsey, M. T., Speaking with Tongues, Epworth 1965.
— Dreams: the Dark Speech of the Spirit, Doubleday 1968.
— Healing and Christianity, SCM Press 1973.
— Encounter with God, Hodder & Stoughton 1974.
Kennedy, H. A. A., St Paul and the Mystery Religions, Hodder & Stoughton 1913.
Kertelge, K., 'Das Apostelamt des Paulus, sein Ursprung und seine Bedeutung', BZ 14, 1970, pp. 161–81.
— Gemeinde und Amt im Neuen Testament, München 1972.
— 'Apokalypsis Jesou Christou (Gal. 1.12)', in Neues Testament und Kirche: Für R. Schnackenburg, hrsg. J. Gnilka, Herder 1974.
Kildahl, J. P., The Psychology of Speaking in Tongues, Hodder & Stoughton 1972.
Kirk, K. E., The Vision of God, Longmans 1931.
Knox, J., Chapters in a Life of Paul, A. & C. Black 1954.
— 'The Ministry in the Primitive Church', The Ministry in Historical Perspective, ed. R. R. Niebuhr and D. D. Williams, Harper & Row 1956, pp. 1–26.
— 'Romans 15.14–33 and Paul's Conception of his Apostolic Mission', JBL 83, 1964, pp. 1–11.
Knox, R. A. Enthusiasm: A Chapter in the History of Religion, Clarendon Press 1950.
Koch, R., 'L'Aspect Eschatologique de l'Esprit du Seigneur d'après Saint Paul', Studiorum Paulinorum Congressus Internationalis Catholicus 1961, Rome 1963, pp. 131–41.
Kraft, H., 'Die altkirchliche Prophetie und die Entstehung des Montanismus', TZ 11, 1955, pp. 249–71.
Kragerud, A., Der Lieblingsjünger im Johannesevangelium, Oslo 1959.
Kramer, W., Christ, Lord, Son of God, ET SCM Press 1966.
Kremer, J., Was an den Leiden Christi noch mangelt, Bonn 1956.
— Das älteste Zeugnis von der Auferstehung Christi, Stuttgarter Bibel Studien 17, ³1969.
— Pfingstbericht und Pfingstgeschehen, Stuttgarter Bibelstudien 63/64, 1973.
Kretschmar, G., 'Himmelfahrt und Pfingsten', Zeitschrift für Kirchengeschichte LXVI, 1954–55, pp. 209–53.
Kuhn, H. W., Enderwartung und gegenwärtiges Heil: Untersuchungen zu den Gemeindeliedern von Qumran, Göttingen 1966.
Kuhn, K. G., 'Jesus in Gethsemane', EvTh 12, 1952–53, pp. 260–85.
Kümmel, W. G., Römer 7 und die Bekehrung des Paulus, Leipzig 1929.
— Kirchenbegriff und Geschichtsbewusstsein in der Urgemeinde und bei Jesus, Göttingen ²1968.

— *Promise and Fulfilment*, ET SCM Press 1957.
— *The Theology of the New Testament*, ET SCM Press 1974.
Küng, H., 'The Charismatic Structure of the Church', *Concilium* I.4, 1965, pp. 23–33.
— *The Church*, ET Burns & Oates 1968.
— *Why Priests?* ET Fontana 1972.
Kuss, O., 'Enthusiasmus und Realismus bei Paulus', *Auslegung und Verkündigung* I, Regensburg 1963, pp. 260–70.

Ladd, G. E., *Jesus and the Kingdom*, SPCK 1964.
Lake, K., *The Historical Evidence for the Resurrection of Jesus Christ*, Williams & Norgate 1907.
— *The Earlier Epistles of St Paul*, Rivingtons 1911.
Lampe, G. W. H., 'The Holy Spirit in the Writings of St Luke', *Studies in the Gospels*, ed. D. E. Nineham, Blackwell 1955, pp. 159–200.
— 'The Holy Spirit and the person of Christ', *Christ, Faith and History: Cambridge Studies in Christology*, ed. S. W. Sykes and J. P. Clayton, Cambridge 1972, pp. 111–30.
Laski, M., *Ecstasy*, Cresset 1965.
Lauterburg, M., *Der Begriff des Charismas und seine Bedeutung für die praktische Theologie*, Gütersloh 1898.
Leisegang, H., *Pneuma Hagion*, Leipzig 1922.
Leivestad, R., *Christ the Conqueror*, SPCK 1954.
Leuba, J. L., *L'institution et l'evénement*, Neuchâtel 1950.
Lewis, H. D., *Our Experience of God*, Allen & Unwin 1959.
Lewis, I. M., *Ecstatic Religion*, Penguin 1971.
Lightfoot, J. B., 'The Christian Ministry', *St Paul's Epistle to the Philippians*, Macmillan 1868, pp. 179–267.
Lindblom, J., *Prophecy in Ancient Israel*, Blackwell 1962.
— *Geschichte und Offenbarungen*, Lund 1968.
Lindsay, G., *William Branham, A Man Sent from God*, Jeffersonville 1950.
Lindsay, T. M., *The Church and the Ministry in the Early Centuries*, Hodder & Stoughton 1902.
Linton, O., *Das Problem der Urkirche in der neueren Forschung*, Uppsala 1932.
Lohfink, G., *Die Himmelfahrt Jesu*, München 1971.
Lohse, E., 'Ursprung und Prägung des christlichen Apostolates', *TZ* 9, 1953, pp. 259–75.
— 'Die Bedeutung des Pfingstberichtes im Rahmen des lukanischen Geschichtswerkes', *EvTh* 13, 1953, pp. 422–36.
Lombard, E., *De la glossolalie chez les premiers chrétiens et des phénomènes similaires*, Lausanne 1910.
Longenecker, R. N., *Paul, Apostle of Liberty*, Harper & Row 1964.
Loos, H. van der, *The Miracles of Jesus*, NovTestSuppl IX, 1965.
Lövestam, E., *Spiritus Blasphemia: Eine Studie zu Mk. 3.28f. par. Mt. 12.31f., Lk. 12.10*, Lund 1968.

Lührmann, D., *Das Offenbarungsverständnis bei Paulus und in paulinischen Gemeinden*, Neukirchen 1965.

Lütgert, W., *Die Vollkommenen im Philipperbrief und die Enthusiasten im Thessalonisch*, Gütersloh 1909.

— *Gesetz und Geist*, Gütersloh 1919.

Lyonnet, S., 'De glossolalia Pentecostes eiusque significatione', *Verbum Domini* 24, 1944, pp. 65–75.

Macdonald, A. B., *Christian Worship in the Primitive Church*, T. & T. Clark 1934.

Mackenzie, J. L., 'Authority and Power in the New Testament', *CBQ* 26, 1964, pp. 13–22.

MacNutt, F., *Healing*, Notre Dame 1974.

Maly, K., 'I Kor. 12.1–3, eine Regel zur Unterscheidung der Geister?' *BZ* 10, 1966, pp. 82–95.

Manson, T. W., *The Teaching of Jesus*, Cambridge 1931.

— *The Church's Ministry*, Hodder & Stoughton 1948.

Manson, W., *Jesus the Messiah*, Hodder & Stoughton 1943.

Marshall, I. H., 'The Divine Sonship of Jesus', *Interpretation* 21, 1967, pp. 87–103.

— 'Son of God or Servant of Yahweh – A Reconsideration of Mark 1.11', *NTS* 15, 1968–69, pp. 326–36.

Martin, I. J., 'I Corinthians 13 Interpreted in its Context', *Journal of Bible and Religion*, 18, 1950, pp. 101–5.

Marxsen, W., *The Resurrection of Jesus of Nazareth*, ET SCM Press 1970.

Menoud, P. H., *L'Église et les ministères selon le Nouveau Testament*, Neuchâtel 1949.

Meuzelaar, J. J., *Der Leib des Messias*, Assen 1961.

Meyer, R., *Der Prophet aus Galiläa*, Darmstadt ²1970.

Michaelis, W., *Reich Gottes und Geist Gottes nach dem Neuen Testament*, Basel 1931.

— *Die Erscheinungen des Auferstandenen*, Basel 1944.

Michel, O., 'Gnadengabe und Amt', *Deutsche Theologie* 9, 1942.

Michl, J., 'Der Geist als Garant des rechten Glaubens', in *Vom Wort des Lebens: Festschrift für Max Meinertz*, hrsg. N. Adler, Münster 1951.

Minear, P. S., *The Obedience of Faith*, SCM Press 1971.

Moberly, R. C., *Ministerial Priesthood*, ²1910, reprinted SPCK 1969.

Moffatt, J., *Grace in the New Testament*, Hodder & Stoughton 1931.

Montefiore, H. W., 'God as Father in the Synoptic Gospels', *NTS* 3, 1956–57, pp. 31–46.

Mosiman, E., *Das Zungenreden geschichtlich und psychologisch untersucht*, Tübingen 1911.

Moule, C. F. D., *Worship in the New Testament*, Lutterworth 1961.

— 'The Individualism of the Fourth Gospel', *NovTest* 5, 1962, pp. 171–90.

— ed., *Miracles*, Mowbray 1965.

— 'St Paul and Dualism: the Pauline Conception of Resurrection', *NTS* 12, 1965–66, pp. 106–23.
— *The Phenomenon of the New Testament*, SCM Press 1967.
— ed., *The Significance of the Message of the Resurrection for Faith in Jesus Christ*, SCM Press 1968.
— 'II Cor. 3.18b: "καθάπερ ἀπὸ κυρίου πνεύματος"', *Neues Testament und Geschichte: historisches Geschehen und Deutung im Neuen Testament*, Festschrift für O. Cullmann, hrsg. H. Baltensweiler and B. Reicke, Zürich 1972, pp. 231–7.
Müller, U. B., 'Die Parakletenvorstellung im Johannesevangelium', *ZTK* 71, 1974, pp. 31–77.
Munck, J., 'Paul, the Apostles and the Twelve', *StTh* 3, 1949, pp. 96–110.
— *Paul and the Salvation of Mankind*, ET SCM Press 1959.
Mundle, W., 'Das Kirchenbewusstsein der ältesten Christenheit', *ZNW* 22, 1923, pp. 20–42.
Murphy, G., *Charisma and Church Renewal*, Rome 1965.
Mussner, F., 'Die johanneischen Parakletsprüche und die apostolischen Tradition', *BZ* 5, 1961, pp. 56–70.
— *The Historical Jesus in the Gospel of St John*, ET Herder 1967.
— 'Wege zum Selbstbewusstsein Jesu. Ein Versuch', *BZ* 12, 1968, pp. 161–72.
— *The Miracles of Jesus*, ET Ecclesia 1970.

Neugebauer, F., *In Christo*, Göttingen 1961.
— 'Geistsprüche und Jesuslogien', *ZNW* 53, 1962, pp. 218–28.
Newbigin, L., *The Household of God*, SCM Press 1953.
Niederwimmer, K., 'Das Gebet des Geistes, Röm. 8.26f.', *TZ* 20, 1964, pp. 252–265.
Nilsson, M. P., *Geschichte der griechischen Religion*, München 1950.
Nock, A. D., *Essays on Religion and the Ancient World*, Oxford 1972.

O'Collins, G., 'Power Made Perfect in Weakness (II Cor. 12.9–10)', *CBQ* 33, 1971, pp. 528–37.
— *The Easter Jesus*, Darton, Longman & Todd 1973.
Oman, J., *Grace and Personality*, Cambridge 1917.
Osborn, T. L., *Healing the Sick*, Tulsa 1959.
Otto, R., *The Idea of the Holy*, ET Oxford 1923.
— *The Kingdom of God and the Son of Man*, ET Lutterworth 1938.

Packer, J. I., 'The "Wretched Man" of Romans 7', *Studia Evangelica* II, ed. F. L. Cross, 1964, pp. 621–7.
Pannenberg, W., *Jesus – God and Man*, ET SCM Press 1968.
Parke, H. W. and Wormell, D. E. W., *The Delphic Oracle*, Blackwell 1956.
Paulsen, H., *Überlieferung und Auslegung in Röm. 8*, Inaugural Dissertation, Mainz 1972.

Pearce-Higgins, J. D. and Whitby, G. S., *Life, Death and Physical Research*, Rider 1973.

Pearson, B. A., *The Pneumatikos-psychikos Terminology in I Corinthians*, SBL Dissertation 12, 1973.

Peddie, J. C., *The Forgotten Talent*, Oldbourne 1961.

Percy, E., *Der Leib Christi*, Lund 1942.

— *Die Botschaft Jesu*, Lund 1953.

Perrin, N., *The Kingdom of God in the Teaching of Jesus*, SCM Press 1963.

— *Rediscovering the Teaching of Jesus*, SCM Press 1967.

Petzke, G., *Die Traditionen über Apollonius von Tyana und das Neue Testament*, Leiden 1970.

Pfister, W., *Das Leben im Geist nach Paulus*, Freiburg 1963.

Plessis, P. J. Du, *Teleios: the Idea of Perfection in the New Testament*, Kampen 1959.

Potterie, I. de la and Lyonnet, S., *La vie selon l'Esprit*, Paris 1965.

Pratt, J. B., *The Religious Consciousness*, New York 1921.

Rahner, K., *Visions and Prophecies*, ET New York 1963.

— *The Dynamic Element in the Church*, ET New York 1964.

Rawlinson, A. E. J., *The New Testament Doctrine of the Christ*, Longmans 1926.

Reicke, B., 'Some Reflections on Worship in the New Testament', *New Testament Essays: Studies in Memory of T. W. Manson* Manchester 1959, pp. 194–209.

Reiling, J., *Hermas and Christian Prophecy: A Study of the Eleventh Mandate*, NovTestSuppl XXXVII, 1973.

Reitzenstein, R., *Poimandres*, Leipzig 1904.

— *Die hellenistischen Mysterienreligionen*, Leipzig ³1927.

Rengstorf, K. H., *Apostelamt und Predigtamt*, Stuttgart ²1954.

— *Die Auferstehung Jesu*, Witten/Ruhr ⁴1960.

Richstaetter, K., 'Die Glossolalie im Licht der Mystik', *Scholastik* 11, 1936, pp. 321–45.

Richter, W., 'Traum und Traumdeutung im AT', *BZ* 7, 1963, pp. 202–20.

Rigaux, B., 'L'anticipation du salut eschatologique par l'Esprit', *Foi et Salut selon S.Paul*, Rome 1970, pp. 101–30.

Riggs, R. M., *The Spirit Himself*, Springfield 1949.

Robinson, H. W., *The Christian Experience of the Holy Spirit*, Nisbet 1928.

Robinson, J. A. T., *The Body*, SCM Press 1952.

Rohde, E., *Psyche*, ET Kegan Paul 1925.

Rohde, J., 'Häresie und Schisma bei Clemens und Ignatius', *NovTest* 10, 1968, pp. 217–33.

Roloff, J., *Apostolat-Verkündigung-Kirche*, Gütersloh 1965.

— *Das Kerygma und der irdische Jesus*, Göttingen 1970.

Ropes, J. H., *The Singular Problem of the Epistle to the Galatians*, Harvard Theological Studies 14, 1929.

Rose, L., *Faith Healing*, Penguin 1971.

Saake, H., 'Paulus als Ekstatiker', *Nov Test* 15, 1973, pp. 153–60.

Samarin, W. J., *Tongues of Men and Angels*, Macmillan 1972.

Sand, A., *Der Begriff 'Fleisch' in den paulinischen Hauptbriefen*, Regensburg 1967.

Sanders, J. T., 'First Corinthians 13: its Interpretation since the First World War', *Interpretation* 20, 1966, pp. 159–87.

Sargent, W., *Battle for the Mind*, Pan Books 1959.

Sasse, H., 'Der Paraklet im Johannesevangelium', *ZNW* 24, 1925, pp. 260–77.

Satake, A., 'Apostolat und Gnade bei Paulus', *NTS* 15, 1968–69, pp. 96–107.

Schäfer, P., *Die Vorstellung vom heiligen Geist in der rabbinischen Literatur*, München 1972.

Schenke, L., *Auferstehungsverkündigung und leeres Grab*, Stuttgart 1968.

Schippers, R., 'The Son of Man in Matt. 12.32 = Luke 12.10 compared with Mark 3.28', *Studia Evangelica* IV, ed. F. L. Cross, 1968, pp. 231–5.

Schlatter, A., *Der Glaube im Neuen Testament*, Stuttgart ⁵1963.

Schleiermacher, F. D. E., *On Religion: Speeches to its Cultured Despisers*, ET Harper Torchback 1958.

Schlier, H., 'Zum Begriff des Geistes nach dem Johannesevangelium', *Neutestamentliche Aufsätze: Festschrift für J. Schmid*, hrsg. J. Blinzler, O. Kuss, F. Mussner, Regensburg 1963, pp. 233–39.

Schmidt, K. L., *Die Pfingsterzählung und das Pfingstereignis*, Leipzig 1919.

— 'Das Pneuma Hagion als Person und als Charisma', *Eranos Jahrbuch* 13, 1945.

— 'Le Ministère et les ministères dans l'église du Nouveau Testament', *RHPR* 17, 1937, pp. 313–36.

— 'Amt und Ämter im Neuen Testament', *TZ* 1, 1945, pp. 309–11.

Schmithals, W., *Gnosticism in Corinth*, ET Abingdon 1971.

— *Paul and the Gnostics*, ET Abingdon 1972.

— *The Office of Apostle in the Early Church*, ET SPCK 1971.

Schmitz, O., *Die Christus-gemeinschaft des Paulus im Lichte seines Genetivgebrauchs*, Gütersloh 1924.

Schnackenburg, R., *God's Rule and Kingdom*, ET Herder 1963.

— 'Christian Adulthood according to the Apostle Paul', *CBQ* 25, 1963, pp. 354–70.

— *The Church in the New Testament*, ET Burns & Oates 1965.

— 'Apostles Before and During Paul's Time', *Apostolic History and the Gospel*, Festschrift for F. F. Bruce, ed. W. W. Gasque and R. P. Martin, Paternoster 1970, pp. 287–303.

— 'Christus, Geist und Gemeinde (Eph. 4.1–16)', *CSNT* pp. 279–95.

Schneider, J., *Die Passionsmystik des Paulus*, Leipzig 1929.

Schniewind, J., 'Das Seufzen des Geistes', in *Nachgelassene Reden und Aufsätze*, Berlin 1952.

Schrage, W., *Die konkreten Einzelgeboten in der paulinischen Paränese*, Gütersloh 1961.

Schrenk, G., 'Geist und Enthusiasmus', *Studien zu Paulus*, Zürich 1954, pp. 107–27.

Schubert, K., 'Die Entwicklung der Auferstehungslehre von der nachexilischen bis zur frührabbinischen Zeit', *BZ* 6, 1962, pp. 177–214.

Schulz, S., *Q: Die Spruchquelle der Evangelisten*, Zürich 1972.

Schürmann, H., 'Die geistlichen Gnadengaben in den paulinischen Gemeinden', *Ursprung und Gestalt*, Patmos 1970, pp. 236–67.

— '"Das Gesetz des Christus" (Gal. 6.2)', *Neues Testament und Kirche: Für R. Schnackenburg*, hrsg J. Gnilka, Herder 1974, pp. 282–94.

Schutz, J. H., 'Charisma and Social Reality in Primitive Christianity', *Journal of Religion* 54, 1974, pp. 51–70.

Schweitzer, A., *The Quest of the Historical Jesus*, ET A. & C. Black 1910.

— *The Psychiatric Study of Jesus*, 1913, ET Boston 1948.

— *The Mysticism of St Paul*, ET A. & C. Black 1931.

Schweizer, E., *Das Leben des Herrn in der Gemeinde und ihren Diensten*, Zürich, 1946.

— 'The Concept of the Church in the Gospel and Epistles of St John', *New Testament Essays: Studies in Memory of T. W. Manson*, Manchester 1959, pp. 230–45.

— 'The Service of Worship', *Interpretation* 13, 1959, pp. 400–8.

— *Church Order in the New Testament*, ET SCM Press 1961.

— *Erniedrigung und Erhöhung bei Jesus und seinen Nachfolgern*, Zürich ²1962.

— *The Church as the Body of Christ*, ET SPCK 1965.

— 'Observance of the Law and Charismatic Activity in Matthew', *NTS* 16, 1969–70, pp. 213–30.

— *Beiträge zur Theologie des Neuen Testaments*, Zürich 1970.

— 'Christus und Geist im Kolosserbrief', *CSNT* pp. 297–313.

Scott, C. A. A., *Christianity according to St Paul*, Cambridge 1927.

Scott, E. F., *The Spirit in the New Testament*, Hodder & Stoughton 1923.

Scroggs, R., 'The Exaltation of the Spirit by Some Early Christians', *JBL* 84, 1965, pp. 359–73.

— 'Paul: Σοφός and πνευματικός', *NTS* 14, 1967–68, pp. 33–55.

Seitz, O. J. F., 'Two Spirits in Man: An Essay in Biblical Exegesis', *NTS* 6, 1959–60, pp. 82–95.

Sherrill, J. L., *They Speak with Other Tongues*, Hodder & Stoughton 1965.

Smalley, S. S., 'Spiritual Gifts and I Corinthians 12.16', *JBL* 87, 1968, pp. 427–33.

Smart, N., *The Religious Experience of Mankind*, 1969, Fontana 1971.

— *The Phenomenon of Religion*, Macmillan 1973.

Smith, M., 'Prolegomena to a Discussion of Aretologies, Divine Men, the Gospels and Jesus', *JBL* 90, 1971, pp. 174–99.

— *Clement of Alexandria and a Secret Gospel of Mark*, Harvard 1973.

Sohm, R., *Kirchenrecht*, Leipzig 1892.

Sparks, H. F. D., 'The Doctrine of Divine Fatherhood in the Gospels', *Studies in the Gospels*, ed. D. E. Nineham, Blackwell 1955, pp. 241–66.

Stahlin, G., 'Τὸ πνεῦμα 'Ιησοῦ (Apostelgeschichte 16.7)', *CSNT* pp. 229–51.

Stalder, K., *Das Werk des Geistes in der Heiligung bei Paulus*, Zürich 1962.

Stemberger, G., *Der Leib der Auferstehung*, Rome 1972.

Stendahl, K., ed., *The Scrolls and the New Testament*, SCM Press 1958.

Strauss, D. F., *The Life of Jesus Critically Examined*, ET 1846, reprinted 1892, SCM Press 1973.

Streeter, B. H., ed., *The Spirit*, Macmillan 1919.

Stuhlmacher, P., *Gerechtigkeit Gottes bei Paulus*, Göttingen 1966.

— *Das paulinische Evangelium I Vorgeschichte*, Göttingen 1968.

— 'Evangelium-Apostolat-Gemeinde', *KuD* 17, 1971, pp. 28–45.

Suggs, M. J., *Wisdom, Christology and Law in Matthew's Gospel*, Harvard 1970.

Sundkler, B. G. M., *Bantu Prophets in South Africa*, Oxford ²1961.

Sweet, J. P. M., 'A Sign for Unbelievers: Paul's Attitude to Glossolalia', *NTS* 13, 1966–67, pp. 240–57.

Swete, H. B., *The Holy Spirit in the New Testament*, Macmillan 1910.

Tannehill, R. C., *Dying and Rising with Christ*, Berlin 1967.

Taylor, J. V., *The Go-Between God*, SCM Press 1972.

Taylor, V., *The Person of Christ in New Testament Teaching*, Macmillan 1958.

Teeple, H. M., 'The Historical Beginnings of the Resurrection Faith', *Studies in New Testament and Early Christian Literature: Essays in Honour of A. P. Wikgren*, ed. D. E. Aune, Leiden 1972, pp. 107–20.

Therrien, G., *Le Discernement dans les Ecrits Pauliniens*, EB 1973.

Thurston, H., *The Physical Phenomenon of Mysticism*, Burns & Oates 1952.

Tiede, D. L., *The Charismatic Figure as Miracle Worker*, SBL Dissertation Series 1, 1972.

Torrance, T. F., *Royal Priesthood*, *SJT* Occasional Papers No. 3, 1955.

Travis, S. H., 'Paul's Boasting in II Corinthians 10–12', *Studia Evangelica VI*, ed. E. A. Livingstone, 1973, pp. 527–32.

Trocmé, E., *Jesus and his Contemporaries*, ET SCM Press 1973.

Tugwell, S., *Did You Receive the Spirit?*, Darton, Longman & Todd 1972.

Underhill, E., *Mysticism*, Methuen, reprinted 1960.

Unnik, W. C. Van, '"Den Geist Löschet nicht aus" (I Thess. 5.19)', *NovTest* 10, 1968, pp. 255–69.

— 'Jesus: Anathema or Kyrios (I Cor. 12.3)', *CSNT* pp. 113–26.

Vermes, G., *Jesus the Jew*, Collins 1973.

Vielhauer, P., *Oikodome*, Heidelberg 1939.

Vivier, L. M., *Glossolalia*, University of Witwatersrand M.D. Thesis, Johannesburg 1960.

Volz, P., *Der Geist Gottes*, Tübingen 1910.

Vos, G., 'The Eschatological Aspect of the Pauline Concept of the Spirit', *Biblical and Theological Studies*, Princeton Theological Seminary, Scribner 1912, pp. 211–59.

Vos, J. S., *Traditionsgeschichtliche Untersuchungen zur paulinischen Pneumatologie*, Assen 1973.

Walvoord, J. F., *The Holy Spirit*, Durham reprinted 1965.
Warfield, B. B., *Counterfeit Miracles*, Scribner 1918.
Warren, M., *Revival: An Enquiry*, SCM Press 1954.
Wegenast, K., *Das Verständnis der Tradition bei Paulus und in den Deuteropaulinen*, Neukirchen 1962.
Weinel, H., *Die Wirkungen des Geistes und der Geister im nachapostolischen Zeitalter bis auf Irenäus*, Tübingen 1899.
— *Biblische Theologie des Neuen Testaments*, Tübingen ⁴1928.
Weinreich, O., *Antike Heilungswunder*, Giessen 1909.
Weiss, J., *Earliest Christianity*, ET 1937, Harper 1959.
Wendland, H. D., 'Das Wirken des Heiligen Geistes in den Gläubigen nach Paulus', *TLZ* 77, 1952, 457–70.
Wengst, K., 'Der Apostel und die Tradition', *ZTK* 69, 1972, pp. 145–62.
— 'Das Zusammenkommen der Gemeinde und ihr "Gottesdienst" nach Paulus', *EvTh* 33, 1973, pp. 547–59.
Wennemer, K., 'Die charismatische Begabung der Kirche nach dem hl. Paulus', *Scholastik* 34, 1959, pp. 503–25.
Wetter, G. P., *Charis*, Leipzig 1913.
Wikenhauser, A., *Die Kirche als der mystische Leib Christi nach dem Apostel Paulus*, Münster ²1940.
— *Pauline Mysticism*, ET Herder/Nelson 1960.
Wilckens, U., *Weisheit und Torheit*, Tübingen 1959.
— 'Die Bekehrung des Paulus als religionsgeschichtliche Problem', *ZTK* 56, 1959, pp. 273–93.
— 'Die Ursprung der Überlieferung der Erscheinungen des Auferstandenen', *Dogma und Denkstrukturen*, E. Schlink Festschrift, hrsg. W. Joest and W. Pannenberg, Göttingen 1963, pp. 56–95.
— *Auferstehung: das biblische Auferstehungszeugnis historisch untersucht und erklärt*, Stuttgart 1970.
Williams, J. R., *The Era of the Spirit*, Logos 1971.
Wilson, C., *The Occult*, Hodder & Stoughton 1971.
Wilson, R. McL., 'Gnostics in Galatia?', *Studia Evangelica* IV, ed. F. L. Cross, 1968, pp. 358–67.
— 'How Gnostic were the Corinthians?' *NTS* 19, 1972–73, pp. 65–74.
Windisch, H., 'Das Problem des paulinischen Imperativs', *ZNW* 23, 1924, pp. 265–81.
— 'Jesus und der Geist nach synoptischer Überlieferung', *Studies in Early Christianity*, ed. S. J. Case, New York 1928, pp. 209–36.
— *Paulus und Christus*, Leipzig 1934.
— *The Spirit-Paraclete in the Fourth Gospel*, ET Fortress 1968.
Wobbe, J., *Der Charis-Gedanke bei Paulus*, Münster 1932.
Wolfson, H. A., *Philo: Foundations of Religious Philosophy in Judaism, Christianity and Islam*, Harvard 1947.

Wrede, W., *The Messianic Secret*, 1901, ET James Clarke 1971.
— *Paul*, ET London 1907.

Yamauchi, E., *Pre-Christian Gnosticism*, Tyndale 1973.
Yates, J. E., 'Luke's Pneumatology and Luke 11.20', *Studia Evangelica* II Part I, ed. F. L. Cross, Berlin 1964, pp. 295–9.

Zeller, E., *The Contents and Origin of the Acts of the Apostles Critically Investigated*, 1854, ET Williams and Norgate 1875.
Zuntz, G., *The Text of the Epistles*, Schweich Lectures 1946, London 1953.

ADDENDA

Müller, U. B., *Prophetie und Predigt im Neuen Testament*, Gütersloh 1975.
Sacken, P. von der Osten, *Römer 8 als Beispiel paulinischer Soteriologie*, Göttingen 1975.
Schütz, J. H., *Paul and the Anatomy of Apostolic Authority*, Cambridge 1974.

INDEXES

Throughout the indexes references to the text are cited by page number and are given first. References to notes are cited by chapter and note number.

INDEX OF BIBLICAL REFERENCES

I OLD TESTAMENT

Genesis
2.7	X.98
2.24	323
9.13	VIII.157
12.7	282
15.6	282
15.12	304
16.7–13	V.137
16.13	V.34
18.8	V.120
21.17–19	V.137
22.11–18	V.137
26.24	V.34
40f., 40.8	VIII.173

Exodus
3.2ff.	V.137, VI.56
3.2	V.34
3.20	46
4.22f.	II.158
7.4f.	46
8.15, 19	45, 46
9.3, 15	46
13.21f.	V.137
13.21	VI.56
14.24	VI.56
16.10	V.34
19.16	V.137
19.18	V.137, VI.56
24.11	V.34
24.16f.	V.137
24.17	VI.56
33.10f.	V.137
34.29–35	320; X.87
34.34	X.88, 103
40.34f.	V.137

Leviticus
9.6, 23	V.34
16.2	V.34
23.9–14	X.47
24.11ff.	53

Numbers
9.15f.	V.137
11.16–25	180
11.29	170
14.10	V.34
14.14	VI.56
16.37, 17.10	VIII.157

Deuteronomy
1.31	22
6.8	VIII.157
8.5	22
11.18	VIII.157
14.1	22; X.84
18.21f.	IX.184
32.5f.	II.158

Joshua
7	166

Judges
6.11ff.	V.137
6.12	V.34
6.21	VI.56
13.19–22	V.137

I Samuel
10.5f.	174
19.20–4	68, 174

II Samuel
3.12	165

I Kings
3.5	V.34
5–7	VI.50
8.10f.	V.137
17.17–24	165
18.12	46; VII.28
18.38	VI.56
19.11	VI.56

II Kings
2.6	46
4.32–7, 34	165

I Chronicles
28.12, 19	46

II Chronicles
1.7, 7.12	V.34

Job
28.1–27	29
42.18 (17b)	247

Psalms
2.7	27, 38, 65; III.120
8.3	46
16.8–11	119
16.8	V.103
16.9	119
22.2	21
30.22	VIII.23
31.5	II.59
33.6	46
42.5, 11, 43.5	19
45.6	II.151
74.9	82
77.20, 78.52	III.23
91.13	78
102.16	V.34

Proverbs
8.1–36	II.95
22.8	250

Isaiah
1.2	22; II.158
1.4	II.158

II OLD TESTAMENT APOCRYPHA AND PSEUDEPIGRAPHA

III DEAD SEA SCROLLS, PHILO, JOSEPHUS AND RABBINIC TEXTS

IV NEW TESTAMENT

Bold type indicates that some exegesis of the text is offered in these
pages/notes

V EARLY CHRISTIAN AND GNOSTIC WRITINGS

VI OTHER ANCIENT WRITERS

INDEX OF MODERN AUTHORS

(*Italics* indicate that a new title appears for the first time)

INDEX OF SUBJECTS

resurrection appearances in, *see*
Resurrection appearance
Glory, 107, 112, 320, 332; V.64,
X.93
Glossolalia, 86, 145, 148–52, 216f.,
231, 242–6, 266; VI.71,
VIII.235, 252, 254
definition, 148
ecstatic, 148–52, 191f., 234, 242f.,
VIII.232
as experience of Spirit, 152, 245,
247
interpretation of, 246–8, 299,
306; VIII.255
and language, 148f., 241, 243f.;
X.19
and foreign language, 149, 244;
VI.82ff.
Luke's understanding of, 149, 152
Paul's understanding of, 230f.,
243, 244
and prayer, 239–42, 245
psychological understanding, 148,
150f., 245
a sign?, 189–93
value of, VIII.254
how widespread, 245f.
Gnosticism, Corinthian, 207, 217–
21, 234f., 287, 307, 316f., 330;
VIII.95, 99
Gospel, 13, 55, 61, 108, 125, 129,
133, 276, 280, 282, 293f., 319,
351ff., 354; IX.119, 205, *see*
also Preaching, Tradition
Grace, 4, 200f., 201–5, 279, 326,
357f.; VIII.3, 9
as power, 202ff.
of Christ, 202, 300, 340ff., 358
Guidance, 172, 176–9, 222–5

Hand of God, 46, 165, *see* also
Laying on of Hands
Healings, 60, 71f., 163–6, 210f.;
IV.20f., VII.36, *see* also Mira-
cles
Hellenists, 140, 143, 153, 181, 185f.
History of religions, 5, 30f., 149ff.,
154, 161f., 164, 166, 173, 178,
192, 228f., 232, 302–7, 316f.,
330, 340f.; V.147

Holiness Movement, IX.41, X.181,
XI.55

Individualism of John, 354f., 356,
359f.; XI.45, 51
Inspiration,
in early community, 50f., 154
of Jesus, *see* Jesus
in John, 351–4
in Paul, 211f., 221f., 223ff., 225–
48, 252, 255f.
Interpretation of tongues, *see* Glossolalia

James, 130, 138f., 143f., 181f., 273;
VII.107
Jerusalem, 136–9
eschatological significance, 141f.,
146f., 154, 158, 160
and Luke, 137
and Paul, 138, 274f.; IX.19
Jesus,
bar nasa, 40, 50ff., 78
charismatic, Ch. IV, IV.56
distinctiveness of, 24ff., 32f., 75f.,
81f., 87, 90–2, 357
divinity of, 11f., 87, 91f., 325f.,
351; VII.144
and ecstasy, 84–7
eschatological consciousness, 43,
60f., 81f.
Evangelists' view of, 26f., 54f.,
56f., 62f., 72, 75; II.77
as example, *see* Continuity-discontinuity
exorcisms, 43–53
experience of God, Chs. II and
III
in Gethsemane, 17–20
healings, 60, 71f.
inspiration of, 11, 59, 61f., 78, 86,
88
at Jordan, 27, 62–7
Messiah, 15, 33, 39, 56, 139, 154
miracles, 69–76
mission, sense of, *see* Mission
power, consciousness of, 47f., 53,
61, 65, 88f., 91
prayers, 12, 15–26, 37, 67
preaching, 55, 60f.

DATE DUE

OCT 27 1988		
JUN 24 '91		
MAR 02 1992		
MAR 02 1992		
DEC 14 '93		
JUN 3 1992		
MAY 21 1996		
JUL 01 1996		

HIGHSMITH   #LO-45220